Schools & Scholars

IN FOURTEENTH-CENTURY ENGLAND

WILLIAM J. COURTENAY

PRINCETON, NEW JERSEY

PRINCETON UNIVERSITY PRESS

1987

COPYRIGHT © 1987 BY PRINCETON UNIVERSITY PRESS
PUBLISHED BY PRINCETON UNIVERSITY PRESS, 41 WILLIAM STREET
PRINCETON, NEW JERSEY 08540
IN THE UNITED KINGDOM:
PRINCETON UNIVERSITY PRESS, GUILDFORD, SURREY

LIBRARY OF CONGRESS CATALOGING IN PUBLICATION DATA WILL
BE FOUND ON THE LAST PRINTED PAGE OF THIS BOOK

ISBN 0-691-05500-9

PUBLICATION OF THIS BOOK
HAS BEEN AIDED BY A GRANT FROM THE
WHITNEY DARROW FUND OF PRINCETON
UNIVERSITY PRESS. THIS BOOK HAS BEEN
COMPOSED IN LINOTRON BASKERVILLE.
CLOTHBOUND EDITIONS OF PRINCETON
UNIVERSITY PRESS BOOKS ARE PRINTED
ON ACID-FREE PAPER, AND BINDING MA-
TERIALS ARE CHOSEN FOR STRENGTH AND
DURABILITY. PAPERBACKS, ALTHOUGH
SATISFACTORY FOR PERSONAL COLLEC-
TIONS, ARE NOT USUALLY SUITABLE
FOR LIBRARY REBINDING

PRINTED IN THE UNITED STATES OF
AMERICA BY PRINCETON UNIVERSITY PRESS
PRINCETON, NEW JERSEY

CONTENTS

(v)

PART II

THE GOLDEN AGE OF ENGLISH SCHOLASTICISM

(1315–40)

MAPS

PREFACE

THE CULTURAL life of fourteenth-century England was nourished and structured by two institutional settings. One of these was the school, the setting of formal education from elementary instruction in Latin reading, writing, and grammar, to the advanced and technical debates of the lecture halls of the university. The other was the court, where the tastes of far more visible patrons shaped the products of literary, artistic, and musical skills.

These worlds in retrospect appear geographically and chronologically distinct, with their own individual character, their own rules of intellectual and artistic creation, of thought and convention. The world of the schools culminated at Oxford, whose philosophical and scientific achievements crown the first half of the century. The world of royal and aristocratic courts centered on London, and the flowering of vernacular literature and late Gothic architecture mark the second half of the century, particularly the reign of Richard II.

In neither period, however, were these worlds entirely separate. More than for earlier generations, the schools and courts of the fourteenth century impinged on one another, sometimes shaping the content of thought and letters. There is more here than just the fact that the court poet had been to school, or that the needs of a future career led students while in school to think beyond their scholastic training. These two worlds intersected at the professional, post-educational level. Indeed, both scholar and poet needed a patron, and it was not uncommon for them to find one in the same person or agency.

Scholastic and court worlds blended in other ways than through patronage and careers. Training in theology and law, particularly the analytic skills and flexibility of mind engendered by scholastic methods and exercises, were useful in the service of both church and state. Nor was medieval Oxford isolated from the active and practical aspects of public life, as the influential political and ecclesiastical treatises of Fitzralph and Wyclif, and the later career of Ockham on the Continent amply attest.

The transition from the world of Ockham to the world of Chaucer, so important for our understanding of late medieval English thought as

well as Middle English literature, has eluded our attempts to understand and describe it adequately. Part of the problem has been that the
vast majority of sources for fourteenth-century English philosophy and
theology remain unpublished and largely unstudied, both because of
the difficulty of the manuscripts and the complexity of their content.
Only in the last decade or so have the works of such a major figure as
Ockham become available in critical edition. We now have some texts
and studies on Walter Burley, Richard of Campsall, Walter Chatton,
Richard Fitzralph, Robert Holcot, Adam Wodeham, Thomas Bradwardine, and William Heytesbury, but others, especially in the generation
between Ockham and Chaucer, are little more than names: John of Rodington, Richard Kilvington, Roger Roseth, Robert of Halifax, Thomas
Buckingham, Nicholas Aston, Osbert Pickingham, and Chaucer's contemporaries, Ralph Strode and Stephen Patrington. Still others are
hardly even names: Alexander Langeley, John Stuckley, Richard
Brinkley, John Hunter, whose writings would have been accessible to
Chaucer and whose opinions perhaps known to him. Similarly little attention has been given to humanism in fourteenth-century scholastic
circles, nor to the means by which or the degree to which the issues and
personalities of scholasticism became known to the authors of Middle
English literature. Thus, despite the growing interest in the relation of
late medieval nominalism to English literature, English scholasticism in
the generation before Chaucer, not to mention university life in the
generation of Chaucer himself, remains a terra incognita.

Research in the area of fourteenth-century thought has not yet progressed far enough to permit anything like a reasonably complete picture of the development of university teaching in that age. Within the˙
limitations of what we now know, however, the following work attempts
to meet several needs. It is, first of all, an overview of the intellectual
currents and developments in England in the fourteenth century.
Much new research has been done on particular problems and individuals, but that knowledge has not yet been brought together into a general picture. It is hoped that what has been done here will prove useful
as a companion to Chaucer studies and to Middle English literature by
providing a more accurate and detailed account of the philosophical
and theological milieu.

Secondly, the work is grounded in the assumption that one cannot understand the intellectual developments of the period without some understanding of and appreciation for the institutional setting—not only the universities but the entire educational system. Scholasticism was a product of schools and, at times, perhaps their victim. It was the changing educational environment of fourteenth-century England that explains some of the intellectual shifts, and it was in the institutional setting that the worlds of philosopher and poet first touched.

A generation ago W. A. Pantin suggested that the fourteenth century should be viewed "frontwards," as an extension of, or gradual development out of, the thirteenth century, not as a radical break with the past.[1] All too frequently the late Middle Ages have been viewed retrospectively from the standpoint of the issues and questions, the assumptions and judgments, of Renaissance and Reformation historians who have sometimes shared with those working on the thirteenth century a distaste for the intervening period. Pantin's advice still merits repeating today, and it applies to Ockham and the intellectual developments as much as to ecclesiastical structures and social history. Despite the differences between Ockham's nominalism and thirteenth-century realism, one can only understand early fourteenth-century thought by seeing it as a direct outgrowth of the interests and approaches of thirteenth-century thought, albeit some of its less well-known aspects.

On the other hand, important changes did take place. If one gives proper recognition to the logical, mathematical, and empirical interests of the thirteenth century, as the late E. A. Moody urged,[2] the beginnings of intellectual change came not with Ockham in the 1320s nor with Wyclif in the 1370s, but at mid-century in the decade before and after the Black Death. The generation of 1340–70 marks a significant watershed that gives to the latter half of the century a different character from that of the first half, a character that at times makes the educational, intellectual, and religious climate of late fourteenth-century England more akin to that of the fifteenth and sixteenth centuries than to the early fourteenth. This is true in part because of the declining role of the papacy in English affairs, the presence of "pre-reformers" such

[1] Pantin, ECFC, 2.

[2] E. A. Moody, "Empiricism and Metaphysics in Medieval Philosophy," *Philosophical Review* 67 (1958): 145–63.

as Wyclif, and the beginnings of religious dissent in the Lollard crisis. But it is also reflected in the fact that the intellectual values and writing styles of the early fourteenth century are far less apparent among England's learned after 1350. Indeed, some characteristics of sixteenth-century England sometimes attributed to Renaissance learning, Tudor policy, or the English Reformation, such as the centrality of the Bible, the shift from logic to moral philosophy, the concerns of practical over speculative theology, and the substitution of polemical, dogmatic writings for scholastic treatises and commentaries, had their roots in the mid-fourteenth century. Admittedly, many aspects of Wyclif as reformer have more to do with medieval church politics than with the Protestant Reformation. Yet in other ways Wyclif reflects a new set of interests, values, and approaches. He and others of his generation were early products of broader cultural changes that were already taking place in England when they were attending school.

The earliest portions of this book were conceived in Tübingen in the spring of 1976, and the final chapters were written at Madison in 1985. Across that decade many scholars, friends, libraries, and foundations provided the support, critique, and encouragement that made it possible. I am particularly grateful for the financial support provided by the Alexander von Humboldt Stiftung, the Guggenheim Foundation, the National Endowment for the Humanities, and the Vilas Trust, as well as the congenial working environments created for me at the Institut für Spätmittelalter und Reformation, Tübingen, through its then director, Professor Dr. Heiko Oberman, and the Newberry Library in Chicago and its Director of Research Services, Dr. Richard Brown. Among the many scholars whose advice proved helpful were Gedeon Gál, Guy Fitch Lytle, Stephen McGrade, Faye Getz, David Lindberg, Jo Ann Moran, Alastair Minnis, Russell Peck, Katherine Tachau, Jan Pinborg, and James Weisheipl, the last two of whom did not live to see its completion. I am also indebted to Darleen Pryds for preparing the bibliography. Finally, I would like to thank Paul Clogan, editor of *Medievalia et Humanistica*, and the editors of *Augustiniana* for permission to use material that appeared in an earlier version in those publications.

This book is dedicated to the memory of several scholars whose work has been the foundation for much contained here and without whom a study of this type could not have been written: Constantine Michalski and W. A. Pantin, whom I unfortunately never had the privilege of knowing; E. A. Moody and A. B. Emden whose kind and informative letters in their last years were of immense help; and Jan Pinborg, Beryl Smalley, and James Weisheipl—immediately responsive, always generous, friends of those years.

January 1987

ABBREVIATIONS

AFH	*Archivum Franciscanum Historicum*
AFP	*Archivum Fratrum Praedicatorum*
AHDL	*Archives d'histoire doctrinale et littéraire du moyen âge*
AM	*Antiqui und Moderni*, Miscellanea Mediaevalia 9, ed. A. Zimmermann. Berlin, 1974.
AUP	*Auctarium Chartularii Universitatis Parisiensis*, vol. 1, *Liber Procuratorum Nationis Anglicanae (Alemanniae)*. Paris, 1894.
BJRL	*Bulletin of The John Rylands University Library of Manchester*
CHLMP	*The Cambridge History of Later Medieval Philosophy*, ed. N. Kretzmann, A. Kenny, and J. Pinborg. Cambridge, 1982.
CIMGL	*Cahiers de l'Institut du moyen-âge grec et latin*
CUP	*Chartularium Universitatis Parisiensis*, ed. H. Denifle and E. Chatelain. 4 vols. Paris, 1891–94.
DNB	*The Dictionary of National Biography*
EHR	*English Historical Review*
ELI	*English Logic in Italy in the 14th and 15th Centuries*, ed. A. Maierù. Naples, 1982.
Emden, *BRUC*	A. B. Emden, *A Biographical Register of the University of Cambridge to 1500*. Cambridge, 1963.
Emden, *BRUO*	A. B. Emden, *A Biographical Register of the University of Oxford to 1500*. 3 vols. Oxford, 1957–59.
FcS	*Franciscan Studies*
FzS	*Franziskanische Studien*
Gilson, *HCP*	*History of Christian Philosophy in the Middle Ages*. New York, 1955.
HU	*History of Universities*
HUO	*The History of the University of Oxford*, vol. 1, *The Early Oxford Schools*, ed. J. I. Catto. Oxford, 1984.
JEH	*The Journal of Ecclesiastical History*

MedStud	*Mediaeval Studies*
MunAcad	*Munimenta Academica or Documents Illustrative of Academical Life and Studies at Oxford*, ed. H. Anstey. 2 vols. Rolls Series. London, 1868.
NS	*New Scholasticism*
Ockham, *Quodl.*	William of Ockham, *Quodlibeta septem*, Opera Philosophica, vol. 9, ed. J. C. Wey. St. Bonaventure, N.Y., 1980.
Ockham, *Sent.*	William of Ockham, *Scriptum in libros Sententiarum*, Opera Theologica, vols. 1–7, ed. G. Gál, S. Brown, G. Etzkorn, F. Kelley, R. Wood, and R. Green. St. Bonaventure, N.Y., 1967–84.
Ockham, *SL*	William of Ockham, *Summa logicae*, Opera Philosophica, vol. 1, ed. Ph. Boehner, G. Gál, and S. Brown. St. Bonaventure, N.Y., 1974.
O.H.S.	Oxford Historical Society
Pantin, *ECFC*	W. A. Pantin, *The English Church in the Fourteenth Century*. Cambridge, 1955; Notre Dame, 1963.
PhilHum	*Philosophy and Humanism. Renaissance Essays in Honor of Paul Oskar Kristeller*, ed. E. P. Mahoney. New York, 1976.
PhilJahr	*Philosophisches Jahrbuch*
PRUP	*Preuve et raisons à l'Université de Paris. Logique, ontologie et théologie au XIVe siècle*, ed. Z. Kaluza and P. Vignaux. Paris, 1984.
Rashdall, *Univ.*	H. Rashdall, *The Universities of Europe in the Middle Ages*, ed. F. M. Powicke and A. B. Emden. 3 vols. Oxford, 1936.
RCSF	*Rivista critica di storia della filosofia*
RepBib	F. Stegmüller, *Repertorium biblicum Medii Aevi*. 11 vols. Madrid, 1949–80.
RepSent	F. Stegmüller, *Repertorium Commentariorum in Sententias Petri Lombardi*. 2 vols. Würzburg, 1947.
RHE	*Revue d'histoire ecclésiastique*
Robson, *Wyclif*	J. A. Robson, *Wyclif and the Oxford Schools*. Cambridge, 1961.
Roensch, *ETS*	F. J. Roensch, *Early Thomistic School*. Dubuque, Iowa, 1964.

Roth, *EAF*   F. Roth, *The English Austin Friars, 1249–1538*. 2 vols. New York, 1966, 1961.

RTAM   *Recherches de Théologie ancienne et médiévale*

Smalley, *EFA*   B. Smalley, *English Friars and Antiquity in the Early Fourteenth Century*. Oxford, 1960.

Statuta Oxon   S. Gibson, *Statuta Antiqua Universitatis Oxoniensis*. Oxford, 1931.

TRHS   *Transactions of the Royal Historical Society*

VCH   *The Victoria History of the Counties of England*

Walsh, *RF*   K. Walsh, *A Fourteenth-Century Scholar and Primate: Richard FitzRalph in Oxford, Avignon and Armagh*. Oxford, 1981.

Xiberta, *SOC*   B. M. Xiberta, *De scriptoribus scholasticis saeculi XIV ex ordine Carmelitarum*. Louvain, 1931.

I

SCHOOLS AND ENGLISH SOCIETY

ONE

THE EDUCATIONAL FRAMEWORK OF
ENGLISH LEARNING

～❧～

FORMAL EDUCATION in the fourteenth century was a four-tiered system. It was somewhat similar to our categories of elementary, secondary, undergraduate, and graduate education into which it grew, but it also differed in a number of important respects. The similarities become readily apparent as we examine aspects of the medieval system, for recognition is triggered by memories of early schooling or by familiarity with the modern university. What is often more difficult to grasp are the differences between the two systems or intellectual worlds and the degree to which those differences made the acquisition of knowledge in the fourteenth century a peculiarly medieval experience.

THE SETTING

Academic Time

At the opening of the fourteenth century students shared with their nonacademic contemporaries the same sense of time: solar time.[1]

---

[1] The literature on medieval concepts of time, both before and during the gradual introduction of the mechanical clock in the fourteenth and fifteenth centuries, is vast. The pioneering work of Gustav Bilfinger, *Die mittelalterlichen Horen und die modernen Stunden: Ein Beitrag zur Kulturgeschichte* (Stuttgart, 1892), still remains one of the best introductions, and many of the recent studies are only glosses on his evidence and conclusions. The frequent treatments of the transition from "medieval" to mechanical time prove both the enduring fascination of the topic and our ability to forget that it has all been said before. Among the more influential publications on this topic are Lewis Mumford, *Technics and Civilization* (New York, 1934), 12–18; Lynn White, *Medieval Technology and Social Change* (Oxford, 1962); Carlo Cipolla, *Clocks and Culture, 1300–1700* (London, 1967); Jacques Le Goff, *Time, Work, and Culture in the Middle Ages* (Chicago, 1980), 29–52; and Jean Gimpel, *The Medieval Machine* (New York, 1976); and most recently David S. Landes, *Revolution in Time: Clocks and the Making of the Modern World* (Cambridge, Mass., 1983). On the earlier medieval concept of time in particular, see: Bilfinger, 1–105; Marc Bloch, *Feudal Society*, transl. L. A.

(3)

Whether in the fields outside a peasant village or in the urban work-rooms of a trade or craft, the "hours" of a medieval workday were not of equal duration but varied considerably in length as the amount of daylight increased or diminished throughout the year. The daylight period was divided into twelve units, or hours, as was the period of darkness, regardless of the time of year. In the summer of northern Europe the day could last up to sixteen of our hours and in winter be as short as eight. Work was conducted during the daylight hours, and recompense was based on the completed task or on a day's labor, not the hourly unit.[2]

The first hour was reckoned at dawn and the twelfth hour shortly before sunset. These times were approximate, since the ability to make precise calculations lay beyond the technology of everyday life for most of the medieval period. Moreover, the day was measured or divided not by these hourly units but by the larger periods of the day (the three-hour blocks, known as the canonical hours, namely the distance from prime to tierce, from tierce to sext, from sext to none, from none to vespers, and from vespers to compline) and the activities associated with them.[3]

Early morning was a time for intensive labor, in the classroom as everywhere else. Before the fifteenth century it was usually accomplished without a previous meal or, at most, some moistened bread.

Manyon (Chicago, 1961), 73–74; Le Goff; and in connection with mealtimes, B. A. Henisch, *Fast and Feast* (University Park, Pa., 1976), 20–21.

[2] Medieval exegesis on the parable of the laborers in the vineyard (Matt. 20:1–16) never interpreted the difference in the amount of time worked in terms of labor-hours. The proper unit of pay was the full-day's labor. Lesser efforts might be paid as divisions of that amount, but a day's pay was never calculated by multiplying smaller units. Michael de Massa, an Austin Friar at Paris writing around 1330, remarked in his commentary on Matthew (Vienna, Nationalbibl., ms. lat. 1512, fol. 180ᵛᵇ) that "generally speaking, it is better to pay workers according to the job (*ad mensuram operis*) than according to time (*ad mensuram temporis*), because those who are paid according to the measure of time work more deceitfully, and moreover are paid at the end of the day as if they had worked conscientiously. But those who are paid according to the job receive only what they earn and no more."

[3] The traditional names for the canonical hours had shifted meaning by the early fourteenth century. In England, prime meant early morning, well after dawn; tierce midmorning or slightly later; sext had dropped out of common use; none had moved to the meridian, giving us our noon; and vespers had moved from late afternoon to mid-afternoon. On the dating, reasons, and effects of these developments in the various parts of Europe, see Bilfinger, *Die mittelalterlichen Horen*, 1–170.

Dinner (*prandium*) in secular society was taken in late morning in winter and mid-morning in summer, although on fast days it was delayed until early afternoon. Town children would return home from school for the main midday meal, while older students would take it at their lodgings or in taverns.[4] University scholars, originally tied to ecclesiastical practice, took their meal just after midday, although the increasing presence of secular students in the fourteenth and fifteenth centuries brought that meal to the morning side of midday. After lunch was a time for rest, followed by the afternoon's labor. Supper (*cena*) occurred in late afternoon, around vespers. For those students who had no further obligations, the last bit of daylight could be spent in relaxation.[5]

The imprecision of medieval time ran deeper than the flexible length of the hour or the inability to record the passage of time accurately. The divisions of time themselves varied in the early fourteenth century. Prime could as easily be thought of as nearer mid-morning than dawn; none, which was originally rung two-thirds through the daylight period, moved to midday; vespers could still be late afternoon or, as was becoming common, mid-afternoon.[6] This meant that the first half of

---

[4] The death of a schoolboy on July 19, 1301, described in the Calendar of the Coroners Rolls, reveals the custom of a midday dinner between the morning and afternoon sessions of school. "On Tuesday, Richard, Son of John le Mazon, who was eight years old, was walking immediately after dinner across London Bridge to school. For fun, he tried to hang by his hands from a beam on the side of the bridge, but his hands giving way, he fell into the water and was drowned." Quoted from Edith Rickert, *Chaucer's World* (New York, 1948), 100.

[5] The fourteenth-century Oxford Dominican, Robert Holcot, illustrates some of these activities. The custom of exercising and sports outside the walls of the town is mentioned by Holcot, when he speaks of "currere in Bellomonte"; Robert Holcot, *In quatuor libros Sententiarum quaestiones*, 4, q. 7 (London, Brit. Lib. MS. Royal 10.C.6, fol. 122va; Cambridge, Pembroke MS. 236, fol. 102vb); the after-supper stroll ("ut dicimus deambulare post cenam est bonum"), an example taken from Aristotle, *Posterior Analytics* 94b and *Metaphysics* 994a, is mentioned in the same passage. See also Rashdall, *Univ.* 3: 403, where he cites Islip's statutes for Canterbury College (1361) that speak of "post vesperas communiter scholares spatiari et aerem capere paulisper consueverant." Walks should be taken with others, never alone. From numerous texts Rashdall concluded that "Walking alone was not merely unmonastic; it was considered undignified or 'bad form.' "

[6] The shift in the time of none from mid-afternoon (about 2:00 P.M.) to midday appeared in the late thirteenth century. The reasons for the shift remain uncertain. Most scholars have assumed that the change was brought about by the impatient appetites of the monks who, during the period from mid-September to Easter, were bound by the *Rule* to

the day was punctuated by the bells for prime, tierce, sext, and none, while the afternoon passed without as many audible reminders of the passage of time.

The expansion and contraction of the twelve-hour medieval day according to the amount of daylight at different times of year had an effect on academic life. Roman schoolchildren had been able to begin the winter day before dawn, awakened by a household water clock and escorted by a lantern-bearing slave (*paedagogus*).[7] Not so medieval children, who were spared pre-dawn labors made possible by time-measuring devices. Ninth-century Europe possessed the water clock, whether inherited from Roman civilization or reintroduced through the Arabs, but its tendency to freeze in the winters of northern Europe

take their main and only meal at none or, in Lent, at the tenth hour. Thus, without violating the letter of the *Rule*, the main meal could be taken at midday, as it was during the long days of summer, simply by ringing none earlier. Yet the question remains, why would such a clever innovation appear only at the beginning of the fourteenth century, since the *Rule* had been bent and restored many times during previous centuries?

Although the ringing of the canonical hours in medieval towns and countryside was in the hands of religious communities and, despite the declining importance of monasticism in the thirteenth and fourteenth centuries, was still ecclesiastically controlled, the bells that divided the thirteenth-century day for townspeople were those of neighborhood churches or houses of Austin Canons, such as St. Frideswide's at Oxford or St. Peter's at Bologna. Secular medieval society continued to follow the Roman practice of the main meal in late morning, and the crucial questions are the mealtimes and religious practices of urban religious communities, not those of rural monasteries. Jacques Le Goff (*Time, Work, and Culture*, 44–45) hypothesized that the urban worker's pause, which was taken at none, was gradually moved earlier by labor pressure, creating the half-day. Yet it is unlikely that that would have influenced the ringing of none, which was in the hands of ecclesiastical communities that would only have been influenced, if at all, by management, not by labor.

The answer probably has more to do with the transition from the medieval to modern sense of time. When days throughout the year are of equal duration and begin around 7:00 A.M., then the postponement of the main meal for monastic communities until mid-afternoon would be experienced as an unnecessary hardship. Moreover, as the urban workers' day by the end of the thirteenth century was set from mid-morning to mid-afternoon (tierce to none) without break (in place of the earlier practice of dawn to dusk, with midday pause), their complaint would have paralleled that of the monks. Allowing none to be rung near midday solved that problem and, as a by-product, created the half-day (before none and after none).

[7] H. I. Marrou, *A History of Education in Antiquity*, transl. George Lamb (New York, 1956), 362. The image of the schoolchild being led through the still-dark streets of early morning appears often in Latin literature. For references to the water clock see Seneca, *Epist.* 24, 20; Vegetius Renatus, *De re militari*, 3, 8.

prevented its having any significant impact on conceptions of time or on daily life. From the ninth to the thirteenth century the water clock was considered a remarkable and curious toy of kings and princes.[8]

The medieval school day, therefore, was not of equal duration, and classroom activities varied considerably in length. As the academic year moved from its beginning in October, the time in school became gradually shorter, while in spring the periods of study became longer and longer. The early fourteenth-century statutes of the university of Bologna requiring masters to begin and end lectures "on the bell" must be understood in terms of unequal, imprecise hours, continually changing in length, determined by the bells for prime and tierce.[9] In northern Europe the seasonal variation was greater. A lecture in early June in England might be almost twice as long as one given in mid-December. The first lecture of the day in December would begin around 9:00 A.M. (our time), while those in June might begin as early as 5:00 A.M.

The length of the working day (and of the lecture "hour") probably had its effect on the amount of "goods produced" in school and university, just as it did in village and industry, unless efficiency changed to meet the growth or diminution of time. It would be interesting to find in the diminishing and expanding length of the medieval hour the reason for the frequently encountered imbalance among the four parts of fourteenth-century commentaries on the *Sentences* of Peter Lombard (the main textbook in theology), which were at that time usually given during one academic year and in which the first and fourth books generally received far greater attention than the second and third. In actual fact, however, the most extensive treatment was given to the first book of the *Sentences*, which would have been delivered to the students dur-

---

[8] Einhard (*Annales* for 807) mentioned with wonder the water clock given by Haroun al Rashid to Charlemagne (*arte mechanica mirifice compositum*); cited from Cipolla, *Clocks and Culture*, 25. The thirteenth-century clock of the French monarchy was equally fascinating, although clockmaking by then was a well-established craft. See White, *Medieval Technology*, 119–21.

[9] Carlo Malagola, *Statuti delle università e dei collegi dello studio Bolognese* (Bologna, 1888), 42: "nullus doctor, in iure canonico vel civili legens, possit incipere legere lectionem suam in mane, nisi finita pulsacione campane S. Petri, que pulsatur ad primam. . . . Nec possit vel debeat lectionem suam ultra completam pulsacionem campane S. Petri ad terciam legere, continuare seu complere, aut aliquam vel aliquas glosas in legendo servare. . . . Extraordinarii vero legentes in nonis non incipiant, nisi finita pulsacione none ad S. Petrum, et usque ad carnisprivium pulsatis vesperis exeant."

ing the October to December period, when the day was shrinking to its smallest span. The amount of time devoted to book 1, therefore, does not correspond to the time available but underscores the importance those topics held for the scholars of that age. It would appear that medieval lecturers, as often happens with their modern counterparts, did not divide their material evenly according to the available amount of time. The lecturer probably slipped behind and lingered on the early portions of his text, which subsequently required him to jump ahead and curtail his treatment of later portions or, as did Robert Holcot, add questions later on those parts that did not get treatment at the appropriate time.[10]

Academic time understood as solar time changed in fourteenth-century England, although the stages in that transition from the medieval to modern sense of time are only partially revealed in educational documents. The earliest extant Oxford statutes prescribing times for disputations or lectures come from the opening years of the fifteenth century, when, as in the Bolognese statutes from the same period, the new time system of the modern clock was in place.[11] Precisely measured, equal units of time thus gradually replaced solar time for daily academic exercises in the fourteenth century. The change probably began to occur by the second quarter of the century, perhaps earlier in Eng-

[10] Holcot's only question on book 3 refers the reader to discussions that occur toward the end of book 4. That, and the fact that the question that becomes book 3 appears in various places in the manuscript tradition, suggest that it circulated as a separate question or quire and was probably written after his lectures on the *Sentences*.

[11] The change can be seen in the statutes (*c.* 1408) governing the Lenten disputations of those determining in arts. *MunAcad* 1: 240: "ita quod intrent scholas suis diebus ante prandium, ad pulsationem parvae campanae in ecclesia Beatae Mariae immediate post horam nonam, et exeant ad pulsationem ejusdem campanae immediate post horam duodecimam: ac etiam intrantes post prandium statim post horam primam, ad pulsationem praedictae campanae, exire teneantur immediate post horam quintam, ad pulsationem ejusdem campanae." A similar statute of the same date is given on p. 245. The first certain date for the new calculation at Paris occurs in 1376 (*AUP* 1: 483). A mixture of the old and new time systems can be seen in the Bolognese statutes of 1432; Malagola, *Statuti delle università*, 105. In Italy, morning lectures were calculated according to the canonical hours. The afternoon lectures were set according to the Italian twenty-four-hour day, which began at or shortly after sunset. The older system was still in operation at Avignon in 1503, when the temporal inequality between winter and summer days was offset by making pre-lenten lectures last one and a half (short) hours and post-lenten lectures one (longer) hour; see M. Fournier, *Les statuts et privilèges des universités françaises*, vol. 2 (Paris, 1891), 532.

land than in France, as the appearance of the mechanical clock and its development was closely associated with the Benedictine monastery of St. Albans, which had close ties with Oxford. Richard of Wallingford, who had studied at Oxford before becoming abbot of St. Albans and who continued to send his best monks there for training, spent much of his abbacy and the financial resources of his monastery on the construction of a large mechanical, astronomical clock, which rapidly became one of the wonders of that age.[12] Whatever the direction of influence, the development of the mechanical clock in England is contemporary with a growing fascination at Oxford with units of time and with measurement, which by 1340 had produced a mathematical physics as well as a quantitative theology. The problem of the divisibility of temporal and spatial *continua*, which was a fundamental issue within the philosophy, science, and theology of fourteenth-century Oxford, may have caught the interest of so many because it corresponded to changes in their daily experience. By 1345 the ability to divide units of time into minutes and seconds had been achieved.[13]

Southern England and the Benedictine monasteries that had university connections were also the places in the early fourteenth century where the newer developments in polyphony, the *ars nova*, first made an appearance in England.[14] The *ars nova*, which contemporaries con-

[12] In addition to the studies cited in n. 1, the dating and cultural influence of the introduction of the mechanical clock are explored in Lynn Thorndike, "Invention of the Mechanical Clock about A.D. 1271," *Speculum* 16 (1941): 242–43; H. A. Lloyd, *Some Outstanding Clocks over Seven Hundred Years, 1250–1950* (London, 1958); E. P. Thompson, "Time, Work-Discipline, and Industrial Capitalism," *Past and Present* 3 (1967): 56–97; On Wallingford see J. D. Bond, "Richard Wallingford," *Isis* 4 (1922): 459–65; J. D. North, *Richard of Wallingford: An Edition of his Writings* (Oxford, 1976).

[13] Lynn Thorndike, *A History of Magic and Experimental Science*, vol. 3 (New York, 1934), 290. The difference between equal and unequal hours was discussed by Robertus Anglicus toward the end of the thirteenth century. Yet on the eve of the invention of the mechanical clock and thus the possibility of marking precisely equal hours, Robert's interest still lay with unequal hours: "And we speak of the other hours, namely the unequal, in the reckoning of hours by astronomical instruments and also by astronomical clocks." L. Thorndike, *The "Sphere" of Sacrobosco and Its Commentators* (Chicago, 1949), 230.

[14] Frank Harrison, *Music in Medieval Britain* (London, 1958); Gilbert Reaney, "Ars Nova," in *Pelican History of Music*, vol. 1, ed. A. Robertson and D. Stevens (London, 1960), 261–319, esp. 309–14; see also J. Wolf, *Geschichte der Mensural-Notation von 1250–1460*, vol. 1 (Leipzig, 1904); *Oxford History of Music* (Oxford, 1929); Jacques Chailley, *Histoire musicale du Moyen Age* (Paris, 1950). The treatises of Philippe de Vitry and James of Liège, describ-

trasted with (and therefore labeled) *ars vetus*, presumably early polyphony, is particularly distinguished by the breves, semibreves, and minims—fractions of musical time that produced a new sense of rhythm
and structure. The *ars nova* was not a product of, nor the cause of, new
conceptions of time in English schools and universities. But its attraction and adoption may well have been facilitated by the quantitative,
"measuring" interests of contemporary university philosophy and by
the precise mathematical conception of time entering into the academic
and monastic culture of southern England in the early fourteenth century. The leading theoretician of the *ars nova* in England was Simon of
Tunstede, author of the *Quatuor principalia musicae* and regent master
of the Franciscan convent at Oxford in 1351.

Academic Seasons: Student Labor and the Summer Vacation

Beyond the changing pattern of daily academic life produced by the
older, solar notion of time, the seasons of the year presented some striking contrasts for student life in the Middle Ages. In winter the length of
classroom time, of lectures and debates, decreased markedly, while leisure time between sunset and sleep increased accordingly. It could be
spent in private study and reading. It could also be spent before a fire
or around the gaming tables of local taverns. At the other extreme, the
number of actual hours spent in academic activity in late spring left little
time for other pursuits, save on ecclesiastical holidays.

More significant (but unremarked by us because it is accepted practice) is the fact that students were not required to be in school during
several of the months of long daylight hours. Between the sixth and
thirteenth centuries one rarely encounters references to a vacation period in the educational experience of children and young adults, although the Roman practice of a school vacation from August to mid-

---

ing the *ars nova* from two different sides, both use language reminiscent of university scholastic discourse, although apparently neither was a university master. One of the major defenders of the *ars nova* in Italy, Francesco Landini, was also a devoted defender of
Ockham's logic; see Cesare Vasoli, "Polemiche occamiste," *Rinascimento* 3 (1952): 119–41;
Eugenio Garin, "La cultura fiorentina nella seconda metà del 300 e i 'barbari Britanni,' " in
La Rassegna della letteratura italiana 64 (1960): 181–95. For a discussion of the role of Simon
of Tunstede see A. G. Little, *The Grey Friars in Oxford* (Oxford, 1892), 60; Chailley, *Histoire
musicale*, 238.

October may have continued or have been revived for urban schools in the twelfth and thirteenth centuries. The university of Bologna in the early thirteenth century observed a two-month break in lectures from mid-August to early October,[15] perhaps following earlier Italian custom. Yet the pedagogical need for so extended a break was not apparent to everyone. In his *Parens Scientiarum* of 1231, Pope Gregory IX limited the summer recess for the University of Paris to one month, which may already have been normal for Paris and other schools of higher learning in northern Europe.[16] How effective that particular provision was is uncertain. By the early fourteenth century the trend was clearly in the opposite direction: toward a longer and earlier summer vacation. For the Norman nation (and probably the entire arts faculty) at Paris in 1337 vacation ran from the end of June to early October, but this was subsequently reduced (to conclude on August 26 for undergraduates and September 15 for students in theology and canon law).[17] At Oxford by the late fourteenth century lectures of regent masters ceased on July 5 or 6, to be resumed on October 10, although Trinity term technically ran from the Wednesday after Trinity (the eve of Corpus Christi) to September 14, with a full cessation from September 14 to October 10.[18]

[15] Marrou, *Education in Antiquity*, 362, basing his view largely on the lines in Martial's poem on the schoolmaster, *Epigrammaton* 10, 62, "cessent et Idus dormiant in Octobres: aestate pueri si valent, satis discunt," the last line implying physical activity in place of schoolwork. Augustine also refers to an early autumn break at the time of the grape harvest (*vindemiales ferias*), *Confessions* 9, 2.

[16] For Bologna see F. C. von Savigny, *Geschichte des römischen Rechts im Mittelalter*, c. xxi, sect. 92; the theological faculty in 1364 observed their "great vacation" from June 29 to September 29; F. Ehrle, *I più antichi statuti della Facoltà theologica dell'università di Bologna* (Bologna, 1932), 23–25. For Paris: C. E. Du Boulay, *Historia Universitatis Parisiensis*, vol. 3 (Paris, 1666), 141: "Porro vacationes aestivae non extendantur decetero ultra mensem; sed vacationum tempore bachalarii, si voluerint, suas continuent lectiones"; *CUP* 1: 138; Rashdall, *Univ.* 1: 489.

[17] *CUP* 2: 472, for January, 1337, where the academic year ran from early October to the end of June "a festo beati Dionisii usque ad festum beatorum Petri et Pauli apostolorum." Contemporary Montpellier had an even shorter school year for regents in medicine, late October to Easter; *Cartulaire de l'Université de Montpellier*, ed. A. Germain, vol. 1 (Montpellier, 1890), 345. The earliest full calendar for Paris (*CUP* 2: 709–16), marking the resumption of lectures in late August and dated by Rashdall to the end of the fourteenth century, is probably earlier, since canon lawyers are referred to as doctors and theologians as masters, a distinction that was rare by mid-century.

[18] C. Wordsworth, *The Ancient Kalendar of the University of Oxford* (O.H.S., 45) (Oxford,

The long vacation at Oxford, running usually from late June to early October, was probably not a result of masters seeking a shorter lecturing year. There was, as we shall see, no sizable semipermanent core of professional teachers at the university level who might have wanted to expand their vacation time at the expense of instruction. On the contrary, most teaching was done by bachelors and beginning masters fulfilling university requirements, and they often demanded the right to lecture during vacation in order to fulfill their responsibilities sooner and reach the stage whereby education would cease to be a financial burden and begin to open the path to financial opportunity.

The extension of summer vacation in northern Europe from one to over three months (particularly the inclusion of July) was more likely a result of nonacademic demands on student time that made them less available during the months of July, August, and September. What little evidence we have for fourteenth-century Oxford suggests that the majority of students came from rural middle-class background, "sons of yeomen, husbandmen, tenants of great lords or ecclesiastical institutions,"[19] whose need for additional agricultural labor during the harvest months may well have required the presence of their teen-age children. Long summer vacations in the fourteenth century parallel a rapid expansion of educational opportunity at all levels. As long as the recipients of education, be they in monasteries or cathedral schools of the early Middle Ages, were not involved in agricultural labor, no long vacation was necessary. Its appearance in the fourteenth century, therefore, suggests that a sufficient portion of students at one or more levels of education were expected to help with the harvest of the winter crop in late June and July and the summer crop in August and September. But it is unclear whether the summer vacation at the university level was simply an accommodation for students whose permission to attend school was contingent on the fulfilment of labor services to family or manor during the harvest months, or whether the agricultural cycle primarily affected town and village schools and, in so doing, established

---

1904), includes, xiii–xxv, the calendar for 1337, and on pp. 24–26 discusses and dates to the end of the fourteenth century the calendar reproduced in *MunAcad* 1: x–xi; 2: 447. See also Rashdall, *Univ.* 1: 489, 219–20. In early fourteenth-century London children were still in school in mid-July; see above, n. 4.

[19] Guy Lytle, *Oxford Students and English Society: c. 1300–c. 1510*, Ph.D. diss., Princeton University, 1976, 139.

a pattern for the "academic year" to which universities gradually but eventually conformed. Whatever the cause, the summer break is one indication that by the late thirteenth century education no longer exempted students from secular life, preparing them for ecclesiastical careers far removed from the responsibilities of agricultural labor or duties ancillary to military service. Education had expanded to include an increasing share of those who had obligations in the nonacademic world that could not be totally neglected or abandoned.

Educational Opportunity

Another important difference between medieval and modern education lies in the area of educational opportunity. On the one hand, although primary education remained limited to a relatively small portion of society, it was far more accessible than was once thought. By the fourteenth century schools were numerous, and an elementary education could be obtained near home or within a day's ride. Many towns in England possessed a school that was public in the sense that it was open to any young boy who was acceptable to the schoolmaster. In addition, cathedrals, monasteries, and mendicant convents offered instruction to their own clergy or members, and some monasteries also ran almonry schools for children who were not planning to enter the religious life. On a less formal but no less rigorous basis, private instruction for one or two pupils might be arranged with a priest or clerk. As with the beginning levels, access to the university was based on acquired skills and the ability to learn, not on social background. Thus the schools did not serve a small aristocratic or mercantilistic elite, two groups who rarely sent their children on to the highest university degrees until the late fourteenth century, but served a much broader and less socially prominent sector of English society.

But the schools were not open to everyone. Women were excluded and could receive learning only through a nunnery or, more frequently, through private tutorial arranged by the family. This is in contrast to attitudes in France or Italy, where provision was made in the larger cities for the formal education of girls up through the level of the liberal arts. Those of unfree status were also largely excluded. Villeins had to receive permission of the lord, who seldom gave it and usually attached limitations of time and level. Even among those of free status, educational opportunity was available only to those with both the interest and means. Despite a sharp increase in literacy in the fourteenth century, English society was still predominantly illiterate and learning appealed only to those families that were already literate or had the means and vision to forego the labor of a child. This point is an important one. Before the fifteenth century there were very few schools without tuition. Instead, the schoolmaster charged fees that increased with the level of instruction. And if the school were not in walking distance of one's home, the additional expenses of room and board had to be considered. Thus, the educational system in fourteenth-century England favored young boys from the lower-middle to upper-middle social-economic level of society. For one reason or another, primary education (and thus everything that lay beyond it) was outside the reach of most English families.

Another difference lies in the structuring of the medieval system. No set number of years was required to attain a specific level or degree, save in certain aspects of university studies. The emphasis, even at the universities, was on proficiency in oral performance, the reading of a set list of books, the fulfillment of the minimum residence requirements, and participation in certain formal academic acts. There were often minimum ages set for entry into a course of study or for a degree, but the length of study depended on how quickly one attained sufficient competence. So, while speaking of an average period of time spent at a particular level, one must keep in mind that for some it was much shorter and for others perhaps twice as long.

The Role of Government and Church

Learning was not required or enforced by the state or society but was incumbent only upon those who desired a career for which it was a prerequisite or an advantage.[20] By the fourteenth century most occupations apart from agriculture benefited from literacy, but few required advanced degrees. Education in the late Middle Ages was still, therefore, an opportunity, not an obligation.

[20] On learning as a career advantage see A. Murray, *Reason and Society in the Middle Ages* (Oxford, 1978), 110–37, 213–33, 292–314; J. Dunbabin, "Careers and Vocations," in *HUO* 1: 573.

The role of the church represents a further difference. Apart from parochial schools and theological seminaries, modern education is secular in purpose, staff, and students. By contrast, the schools of the fourteenth century were intimately related to the ecclesiastical structure. That does not mean that the curriculum was set by religious authorities, for what was taught was the traditional curriculum augmented by the newer sources and interests of the thirteenth and fourteenth centuries. Nor were most schools under the direct or continual scrutiny of the bishop or some other religious authority, and students in the grammar schools and universities were not necessarily expected to (nor did they always) enter the religious life, either as secular priests or as monks or members of a religious order. But the church as the mother of medieval education still retained her influence. Schoolmasters were usually secular priests (that is, those not in a monastic or mendicant order); students were tonsured, and those who continued beyond the level of the grammar school would be expected to take at least minor orders; the government of most schools was in ecclesiastical hands; the most respected higher degrees were theology and canon law; and the largest employer of educated talent was the church.

Our principal interest will be in higher education, for that is where the philosophical and theological ideas were expounded that influenced the other intellectual currents of that age. It would be narrow and misleading, however, to equate education, even higher education, with the university. The educational system was far broader, and only a small fraction of literate society would have been familiar with the lecture halls of Oxford or Cambridge. Each stage, therefore, should be studied separately in order to understand what was taught, who was taught, and how teaching was conducted.

ELEMENTARY AND SECONDARY EDUCATION

Fourteenth-century education at the beginning level would seem strange and ill-conceived to the modern observer.[21] The beginning stu-

---

[21] For the educational structure of this period, especially at the elementary and secondary level, see: Nicholas Orme, *English Schools in the Middle Ages* (London, 1973), which replaces A. F. Leach, *The Schools of Medieval England* (London, 1915), J. W. Adamson, "Education," in *The Legacy of the Middle Ages*, ed. C. G. Crump and E. F. Jacob (Oxford, 1926,

dent, usually about the age of seven, would first be taught the alphabet and then would be immediately introduced to the recognition and proper pronunciation of a useful but foreign language, Latin. It would have been a rare child who heard Latin spoken in the home. The child's language would have been French or English, depending on the social and cultural background of the family. For well into the second half of the century French was still spoken at home among the upper levels of society, and as a result Latin was taught by means of French until, in the second half of the century, it was gradually replaced by English.[22] But while French had commercial, administrative, and legal uses and, if not learned as a child, was taught at a later stage by way of Latin as part of a "business" curriculum, there was no reason to teach English at all in the first half of the fourteenth century. Latin was the language of church and state, the language in which one wrote and in which there was something to be read.

Little attention at the beginning stage was given to meaning or gram-

---

1932, 1969), 255–85, and Lynn Thorndike, "Elementary and Secondary Education in the Middle Ages," *Speculum* 15 (1940): 400–408. Further information and bibliography can be found in Nicholas Orme, *Education in the West of England, 1066–1548* (Exeter, 1976), Orme, "Schoolmasters, 1307–1509," in *Profession, Vocation, and Culture in Later Medieval England*, ed. C. H. Clough (Liverpool, 1982), 218–41, and Jo Ann Hoeppner Moran, *The Growth of English Schooling, 1340–1548: Learning, Literacy, and Laicization in Pre-Reformation York Diocese* (Princeton, 1985), who takes exception to Orme on a number of points, particularly as regards the character, purpose, and extensiveness of elementary education; J. T. Rosenthal, "English Medieval Education Since 1970—So Near and Yet So Far," *History of Education Quarterly* 22 (1982): 499–511; Orme, "Chaucer and Education," *The Chaucer Review* 16 (1981): 38–59; Orme, "Langland and Education," *History of Education* 11 (1982): 251–66. On cathedral grammar schools, see Kathleen Edwards, *The English Secular Cathedrals in the Middle Ages*, 2nd ed. (Manchester, 1967), 194: "Certainly every English secular cathedral of the later middle ages maintained a grammar school, which was meant to serve the educational needs of the whole city, not only of the choristers and other young clerks attached to the cathedral. For this reason it was normally in the city, not, like the theology schools, in the cathedral close."

    [22] On Latin as a foreign language see James J. Murphy, "The Teaching of Latin as a Second Language in the 12th Century," *Historiographia Linguistica* 7 (1980): 159–75.

    Historians have dated this transition from French to English as early as the 1340s and as late as the last decades of the century. It no doubt varied by region, type of school, and social class. In particular, see: W. H. Stevenson, "The Introduction of English as the vehicle of instruction in English Schools," *An English Miscellany Presented to F. J. Furnivall* (Oxford, 1901); Orme, *English Schools*, 96–101; Rickert, *Chaucer's World*, 119; John Gardner, *The Life and Times of Chaucer* (New York, 1977), 70; Moran, *Growth of English Schooling*, 34–39.

mar. Word recognition and pronunciation were sufficient and were taught in two ways. One way was through plainchant, by which the student learned the pronunciation of the words that occurred in the liturgical texts of the church, the hymns, and the Psalter. The other way was through reading a primer containing religious and devotional texts, such as the Creed, the Lord's Prayer, the *Ave Maria*, and simple prayers. Learning to pronounce the basic vocabulary of liturgical and doctrinal Latin had a dual pedagogical purpose that went back at least as far as the Carolingian reorganization of education in the late eighth century. For those who intended to continue their education beyond this elementary level, it was a good preparation for the study of Latin grammar. For those who aspired only to a career at the level of parish priest or some lesser ecclesiastical position, this preparation would enable them to fulfill the formal, verbal duties of their office. The care of souls required a higher level of education, which did not begin until the students were more mature.

In the society of the eighth to twelfth centuries, where education was almost exclusively for future ecclesiastics and Latin was the principal language, this educational foundation gave to all students an expertise they would use on a daily basis. This was less true in the fourteenth century. Many who sought and obtained an elementary education had no interest in the priesthood or any ecclesiastical career. Latin, however, was still a prerequisite for almost any public or professional career one might undertake, and liturgical Latin was as good a starting place as any.

Those who pursued their formal education beyond the primary level entered upon a more elaborate and thorough study of Latin at age eight or nine. This secondary level of education was concerned with Latin grammar, and it was almost exclusively linguistic and literary. Lasting anywhere from six to ten years, the course included correct spelling, syntax, inflections and standard constructions, reading and writing at an advanced level, speaking and comprehension, and the student might even be introduced to the rudiments of logic and speculative grammar, although these subjects were properly the domain of the arts faculty at a university. Instruction was in Latin or, at the early stages, in French. Only in the second half of the century was a student permitted to construe in English. There is little evidence that grammar schools provided instruction in the other liberal arts beyond a modicum of rhetoric necessary for style. Logic (dialectic) and the mathematical skills of the quadrivium (arithmetic, astronomy, geometry, and music) were left to the arts program of the university.

Elementary and secondary education, therefore, were identified in the fourteenth century primarily by their curricula and educational goals: reading, song, and grammar. But were these levels within the same school, separate programs, or even separate schools? In particular, were "reading" and "song" two names for the same educational experience, two subjects learned simultaneously by the same group, or two different institutions? The evidence we have does not produce clear and unambiguous answers to these questions.[23]

On the one hand we know that grammar assumed previous training in reading and pronunciation. At the beginning of the fourteenth century the elementary stage, for those who were to continue their education, would normally have been acquired in the same place from the same schoolmaster who taught the older students grammar. One rarely attended a reading or song school and then transferred or "graduated" into a grammar school. In the course of the fourteenth century, however, some grammar schools expected their students to have acquired the basic skills elsewhere before entering, and the age of entry was set at eight or nine years. Probably throughout the fourteenth century the practice of two levels within one school remained the more common experience for students who went on to the university.

On the other hand, we know of schools that gave instruction only in song, or in reading, or in both. Moreover, not everyone who did "reading" also did "song," or vice versa. Separate schools for reading and song existed by the late fourteenth century, and within the same school there might be two classes serving the needs of two different groups of students. This much is suggested by Chaucer's example of the young

[23] On this point see especially Moran, *Growth of English Schooling*, 92–122. Some evidence from the ancient period now suggests that the type and setting of elementary education were not identical for all levels of society. Ultimate career considerations, as determined by the *paterfamilias*, dictated the type of beginning school and program, and those destined for careers in rhetoric, law, and civil service might not have begun their studies in a *ludus litterarius*; see Alan D. Booth, "The Schooling of Slaves in First-Century Rome," *Transactions of the American Philological Society* 109 (1979): 11–19; Robert Kaster, "Notes on Primary and Secondary Schools in Late Antiquity," *Transactions of the American Philological Society* 113 (1983): 323–46.

"clergeon," who is helped in memorizing a Latin hymn by an older companion whose knowledge extended only to pronunciation: "I lerne song, I kan but smal grammeere."[24]

The subsequent training in grammar without the addition of higher studies equipped a young man with only a few marketable skills beyond those acquired at the elementary level. A modicum of Latin letters gave one sufficient learning to pass examination for minor orders or even the priesthood in some dioceses. Thus a university education was probably a more frequent goal of a grammar student than a grammar education was for a student at the primary level. Those who sought only a reading or song education had different economic and social aspirations and perhaps even different social backgrounds from those who advanced to the study of grammar. Reading and song schools separate from those of grammar, however, were probably rare before the end of the fourteenth century; their rapid growth appears to be a phenomenon of the fifteenth and sixteenth centuries, in response to a need for choristers, parish clergy, and chantry priests.

By the early fourteenth century primary and grammar education were available throughout the cities and larger towns of England for those of even modest means and, in certain circumstances, for those with no financial means at all. Evidence for this comes from contemporary references to public schools (some of which are mentioned as early as the twelfth century, although they need not have had a continuous existence), from the increasing numbers entering the universities for which the lower education was a prerequisite, and from the growing number of examples of literacy within lay society.[25] Education at this

---

[24] Geoffrey Chaucer, "The Prioress's Tale," *The Canterbury Tales*, ll. 1693–1726. The passage has sometimes been translated to suggest that the older child was simply a weak student whose understanding of Latin was minimal. It is more likely that Chaucer's older student was being instructed in song rather than reading.

[25] For the more recent literature on lay literacy in the fourteenth century see: J. N. Miner, "Schools and Literacy in Later Medieval England," *British Journal of Educational Studies* 11 (1962–63): 16–27; Raymond Irwin, *The English Library: Sources and History* (London, 1966); K. B. McFarlane, *The Nobility of Later Medieval England* (Oxford, 1973); M. B. Parkes, "The Literacy of the Laity," in *Literature and Western Civilization: The Medieval World*, ed. D. Daiches and A. Thorlby (London, 1973), 555–77; M.G.A. Vale, *Piety, Charity and Literacy among the Yorkshire Gentry, 1370–1480* (York, 1976); M. Aston, "Lollardy and Literacy," *History* 62 (1977): 347–71; J. K. Hyde, "Some Uses of Literacy in Venice and Florence in the 13th and 14th Centuries," *TRHS*, 5th ser., 29 (1979): 109–28; Jo Ann

level could be acquired from several different institutions. The most common was the public school. Teaching was done by one person, a secular master who, as has been noted, was a clerk and often a priest. He might on occasion be assisted by an usher or an advanced student. The schoolmaster would be responsible for the students, who might range in number anywhere from ten to fifty or more. The students themselves were secular clerks or lay, and might or might not be interested in an ecclesiastical career. In addition to these public schools, the cathedrals, houses of regular canons, and larger monasteries in England continued to offer instruction to those preparing for the priesthood or religious life, and there were almonry schools, where secular students were taught. Teaching in the almonry school was not done by the canons or monks but by a secular master identical in most respects to his counterpart in the public school. University colleges sometimes ran grammar schools, and the teaching of grammar in Oxford was under the supervision of the chancellor.[26] Finally, reading, song, and grammar instruction could be obtained privately from an ordinary chaplain, parish clerk, or parish priest. This informal education, however, was generally limited to the primary level.

THE UNIVERSITY

At the point at which the modern student would enter high school or move to an advanced stage in the lycée or Gymnasium, his medieval

Hoeppner Moran, "Literacy and Education in Northern England, 1350–1550: A Methodological Inquiry," *Northern History* 17 (1981): 1–23; Moran, *Growth of English Schooling*, 150–84; S. H. Cavanaugh, *A Study of Books Privately owned in England, 1300–1450*, Ph.D. diss., University of Pennsylvania, 1980; J. T. Rosenthal, "Aristocratic Cultural Patronage and Book Bequests, 1350–1500," *BJRL* 64 (1982): 522–48. Although chronologically earlier, relevant points are presented in Ralph V. Turner, "The *Miles Literatus* in Twelfth- and Thirteenth-Century England: How Rare a Phenomenon?" *American Historical Review* 83 (1978): 928–45; M. T. Clancy, *From Memory to Written Record, England: 1066–1307* (Cambridge, Mass. and London, 1979); and Brian Stock, *The Implications of Literacy: Written Language and Models of Interpretation in the Eleventh and Twelfth Centuries* (Princeton, 1983).

[26] Rashdall, *Univ.* 3: 346–48; R. W. Hunt, "Oxford Grammar Masters in the Middle Ages," in *Oxford Studies Presented to Daniel Callus* (Oxford, 1964), 163–93, reprinted in Hunt, *The History of Grammar in the Middle Ages*, ed. G. L. Bursill-Hall, Amsterdam Studies in the History of Linguistics, vol. 5 (Amsterdam, 1980), 167–97; A. L. Gabriel, "Preparatory Teaching in the Parisian Colleges during the Fourteenth Century," in his *Garlandia. Studies in the History of the Medieval University* (Frankfurt, 1969), 97–124.

counterpart entered the university. Medieval higher education consisted in the study of the seven liberal arts, natural and moral philosophy, theology, law, or medicine. These studies, which could take twenty
or more years to complete, were divided into two stages. The arts and
philosophical training were usually obtained between the ages of fourteen and twenty-one. The second stage, at which the on-going student
specialized in one of the three "higher faculties," namely theology, law,
or medicine, might take another fourteen years, with the completion of
the master's degree at age thirty-five or later. The early stage, as in our
own system, was usually a prerequisite for the later one and contained
fewer students as one moved to a higher level. Some of the weeding-out
was based on the degree of native intelligence, quickness, and self-dis-
cipline. Most of the attrition, however, was probably a result of financial, career, or personal considerations, and the decision to leave school
lay with the family and/or the individual student who could not afford
or would not spend the money and time necessary to go beyond a particular level, or whose career goals led him in a different direction. It
would be wrong to consider the attainment of an advanced degree to be
the goal of most medieval students. A few years of study was sufficient
purpose and reward. The degree was a goal only for those few whose
career plans were advanced by membership in the corporation of masters, who were more professionally committed, and who met the requirements and probably quota limitations of the corporation.[27]

The leading place for all forms of education in fourteenth-century
England was Oxford. It possessed the most respected schools for grammar.[28] It could for a time boast of the most famous teacher of skills use-

[27] The modern assumption by both students and teachers that education is only successful if one finishes a degree would have been a foreign notion in the high and late Middle
Ages. On quota restrictions for the magisterium and on the market economy of teaching,
see my forthcoming study *Teaching Careers at the University of Paris in the Thirteenth and Fourteenth Centuries*, Texts and Studies in the History of Mediaeval Education, ed. A. L. Gabriel
(Notre Dame, 1988).

[28] J. N. Miner, "The Teaching of Latin in Later Medieval England," *MedStud* 23 (1961):
1–20; Hunt, "Oxford Grammar Masters," 163–93; D. R. Leader, "Grammar in Late-Medieval Oxford and Cambridge" *History of Education* 12 (1983): 9–14. Especially important
during the critical decade of 1330–40 was the teaching of the grammar master, John of
Cornwall. See also J. J. Murphy, "Rhetoric in Fourteenth-Century Oxford," *Medium Aevum*
34 (1965): 1–20.

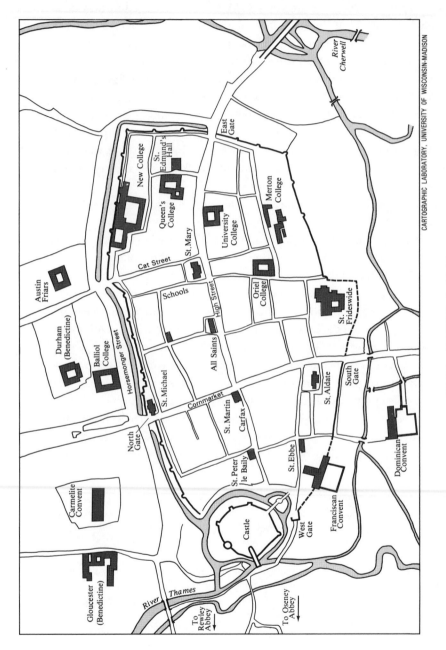

MAP 1. OXFORD, C. 1340

ful in a business or simple administrative career, Thomas Sampson.[29]
But Oxford was most famous as a center for higher studies, for the
study of philosophy, theology, and canon law. It was the leading university (*studium generale*) in England and well respected on the Continent.

Cambridge was much smaller than Oxford in the fourteenth century,
less prestigious, and less well known on the Continent, although it was
recognized in the early fourteenth century as having one of the few faculties in theology that conferred the right to teach anywhere (*ius ubique
docendi*). Apart from a few procedures and offices that were of local origin or imported directly from Paris, its organization, faculties, curricula, and courses of study, were based on those of Oxford. Perhaps the
only major difference, apart from size, was that the mendicant orders
were proportionally and constitutionally more influential at Cambridge
than at Oxford. In describing the fourteenth-century English university, most of the evidence will be derived from Oxford, which has more
complete sources for this period. It can be assumed, however, that what
is said of Oxford will, with few exceptions, apply to Cambridge as well.
Important features peculiar to Cambridge will be discussed at the end
of this chapter.

A number of prominent aspects of the modern university are of medieval origin, for example, the classroom lecture system, the core curriculum of liberal arts, the two-level division between undergraduate studies (the arts and sciences) and graduate studies (law, medicine, theology,
and the others we have since added), academic gowns, and the names
of many degrees. In most respects, however, the medieval university
was fundamentally different from its modern counterpart, especially
the American university.

The medieval university had no full-time administrators and no bu-
reaucratic staff. With the exception of the university bedel and the servants and assistants aiding masters and advanced scholars in their work,
the record keeping, decision making, judicial procedures, and repre-

[29] I.D.O. Arnold, "Thomas Sampson and the 'Orthographia Gallica,' " *Medium Aevum* 6
(1937): 193–209; H. G. Richardson, "Business Training in Medieval Oxford," *American
Historical Review* 46 (1940–41): 259–80; "Letters of the Oxford Dictatores," in *Formularies
which bear on the History of Oxford, c. 1204–1420*, ed. H. E. Salter, W. A. Pantin, and H. G.
Richardson, vol. 2 (Oxford, 1942), 331–41.

sentation of the university before outside authority were all fulfilled in universities north of the Alps by masters who were actively involved in teaching (and often publication) and who were elected to office for terms ranging from a few months to a few years, but, with the exception of the Parisian chancellor, there were no permanent or even semiper-manent positions.

Furthermore, the age structure of the university was different. The range in age of most university students today is from eighteen to twenty-five, while that for teachers is from thirty to sixty-five or seventy. By contrast, the medieval university community was young, incredibly young by modern standards. Undergraduates were as young as four-teen (the normal age for entrance into arts). Twenty-one was the mini-mum age for becoming master of arts. By nineteen a student might ac-tually be lecturing as a bachelor of arts, and many of the regent masters in arts were in their early twenties. Masters in any of the faculties were rarely over fifty, and the average age for masters in the higher faculties was probably closer to forty.

Universities became even younger in the fourteenth century, when the residence requirements, the length of degree programs, the mini-mum age for degree holding, and the length of mandatory teaching were all reduced. In theology at Oxford, for example, the reading of the *Sentences* was reduced from two years to one, the bachelor lectures on the Bible from one year to one term, regency from two years to one, and the minimum age for regency from thirty-five to thirty. Similar re-ductions in requirements took place in the other higher faculties as well.

By the second quarter of the fourteenth century in England it would have been rare in any faculty to find a master beyond the age of forty.[30] Furthermore, those teaching as masters of arts were often, as at Paris, simultaneously students in one of the higher faculties. It is in this light that we must look cautiously at the oft-mentioned distinction between

[30] William Heytesbury may have remained at Oxford for a long period of time and John Baconthorp returned to teaching late in life, but these are exceptions to the general rule. At Paris, where a number of teaching chairs were attached to cathedral canonries and where university teaching brought greater distinction, there were more long-term regen-cies among its secular masters. The effects of long-term stability or rapid turnover among teachers needs further study. On the growing youthfulness of some professional groups in the fourteenth century, see D. Herlihy, "The Generation in Medieval History, *Viator* 5 (1974): 347–64.

the teacher-run universities of northern Europe (where power was vested in the corporation of masters of arts) and the student-run universities of southern Europe, principally Bologna (where power was vested in the corporations or "universities" of students of law). The constitutional difference is important, as well as the size of the respective voting groups. But the average age of those in authority at Paris or Bologna did not differ greatly. They were approximately in their mid-twenties.

What accounts for this youthful university, especially youthful in early fourteenth-century England? These changes were not a response to the sudden availability of positions created by plague at mid-century, for they appear a generation or two earlier, particularly among the mendicants. One reason is that medieval universities usually required regency in order to become master and, in the higher faculties, limited the number of regent masters at any one time. Thus the completion of a degree program in one of the higher faculties was not based solely on ability but was subject to a low quota restriction: usually one candidate for each teaching chair or regent in any one year. For the religious orders at Oxford or Paris this meant that in order to allow a junior colleague to incept and fulfill his required period of regency, it was necessary for a master to give up his own active regency.[31] A second factor lies in the limited financial rewards of regency, especially in England. University teaching before the mid-fifteenth century was rarely seen as a long-term career, or even as a career. Teaching was part of a degree program, a degree requirement, and if it was continued over a period of years it was usually to finance one's further education or to provide income and visibility while one waited for something better in that real world outside the university. Thirdly, on a more positive note, the growth in teaching staff at cathedral and mendicant *studia* in the early fourteenth century provided more nonuniversity teaching employment, positions to which mendicants were assigned and which seculars sought. Finally, it is possible that demographic decline in the early fourteenth century was already placing career opportunities within the

---

[31] This rule apparently did not apply to secular masters at Paris, but an uncontrolled multiplication of regents with voice and vote in congregation and competing for students was not allowed. For further discussion see my *Teaching Careers*. The absence of records on Oxford promotions prevents our knowing about restrictions on the number of teaching chairs or the relationship of inception and termination of regency.

reach of younger persons, and that the reduced length of degree programs was a response.

One crucial and highly significant result of the newer university pattern was a continual and sometimes rapid turnover among the professors and the lack of teaching continuity for anything longer than a five-
year period. Even at Bologna, which had endowed professorships in
law, or at Paris, which had established chairs of theology and where a
few professors maintained an active regency for twenty-five years or
more, most promotions led almost immediately to careers outside the
university, and the average turnover in regent masters was one year for
religious and seven years for secular scholars.[32] Much of the teaching in
any of the faculties was done by the bachelors who, having completed
their years of study, were performing the duties of teaching and debating that could ultimately lead to becoming master. One remained a
teaching bachelor only for two or three years, although one might wait
much longer for an opportunity to incept as master. Thus, at the point
at which a person in the modern university would have completed his
training and early service and would stand at the beginning of a career
in teaching and writing, his medieval counterpart would have left the
university for an entirely different career. This may be why the best
productions of fourteenth-century Oxford are in those areas, such as
logic, linguistic philosophy, mathematics and mathematical physics,
where even in the modern world much of the best work is achieved
early in life. Disciplines where skills, experience, and maturity are acquired more slowly are, perhaps not surprisingly, those areas in which
the medieval university made a smaller contribution. The loss of interest in more abstruse, metaphysical questions in the fourteenth century
resulted from many factors, one of which may have been the decline in
the length of professorial regency. At the age at which Anselm produced his *Proslogium* or his *Cur Deus homo*, the age at which Aquinas produced his *Summa theologiae* or his *Summa contra Gentiles*, their fourteenth-century counterparts would no longer be teaching or writing in
an academic environment.[33]

[32] At Bologna chairs were endowed with a public stipend; at Paris income in the form of
a benefice was given to the person, not the position; for a more detailed discussion see
Courtenay, *Teaching Careers.*

[33] Some Oxford masters, such as Bradwardine, Fitzralph, and Wyclif, continued to write

The relation of age and vision was probably not a significant factor. Before the invention of eyeglasses in the late thirteenth century, the intensive study of manuscript texts expected of scholars and teachers must have been difficult past forty-five, as age changed the ability of the eye to focus. The gradual introduction of eyeglasses into England in the fourteenth century removed that limitation, but the older method of relying on memory and the talents of a younger research assistant (*socius*) with whom one communicated orally lived on.[34]

The continually changing composition of both students and teachers in the university community had other important consequences for medieval intellectual history. Few scholastic writers were professional philosophers and theologians in our sense of those terms. For them the university career was only one stage in life, albeit a very important one, that led to opportunities for service or achievement elsewhere. It was as much the needs of the Dominicans as anything else that kept Thomas Aquinas teaching and writing in the fifteen years between his university regency and his death. For others—and this became a frequent pattern in the fourteenth century—academic pursuits ended in one's mid-thirties to be followed by another type of career, often one of ecclesiastical administration. Who is to say whether John Duns Scotus, who died at the height of his academic career, would have remained an active writer or would have been diverted to administrative tasks according to the needs of order, pope, or king? For the majority of medieval scholastics, it is fair to say that they did not expect (and may not even have desired) to make a home and career for themselves in the world of ideas.

Motives among seculars differed in this regard from those in religious orders. The career of seculars rested on individual achievement, academic distinction, visibility, and patronage. Depending on one's connections and personal gifts, the quest for a secure and rewarding position in church or state came solely from the individual himself. For those in religious orders, career expectations were largely confined to the order, although higher positions in church or royal service were not out of the question. Whatever the course of a career, it was never a choice solely of the individual. Personal desires and aspirations from

---

in later years, but only Wyclif remained at the university, and the later works of each author have a character different from their earlier production.

[34] See J. Gimpel, *The Medieval Machine* (New York, 1976), 149, 185–86.

below were always blended with (and often gave way to) the needs of the order as interpreted from above by religious superiors. Similar differences in career aims may have guided the motives behind scholarly writing and the visibility it produced.

University Enrollments

The number of students known to have studied at Oxford and Cambridge rose steadily throughout the fourteenth century save in the years immediately following the Black Death.[35] Even allowing for increases in documentation during the century, which would in itself produce more names, the size of the student bodies seem to have grown even as the size of the population from which they were drawn declined. We have no way of determining the exact percentage of increase nor, for that matter, even the approximate number of students in residence at Oxford or Cambridge at any one time. The best estimates would place the number at Oxford somewhere around 1,000 at the beginning of the century to something over 1,500 by the end of the century. Of that number no more than fifteen percent belonged to the mendicant orders, while the number of students holding fellowships in colleges probably represented an even smaller percentage in 1300 but grew to a larger percentage by 1400.[36] Throughout the century Cambridge remained less than half the size of Oxford, which meant among other things that students in religious orders, most of which had houses of study at Cambridge, represented a higher percentage of the total student body than at Oxford.

[35] W. J. Courtenay, "The Effect of the Black Death on English Education," *Speculum* 55 (1980): 696–714. The size of a medieval university population at any one time is a matter of conjecture, and only approximate figures are possible. For the evidence and reasoning on the Oxford university population in the fourteenth century see: H. E. Salter, *Medieval Oxford* (Oxford, 1936), 107–10; E. F. Jacob, "English University Clerks in the Later Middle Ages: The Problem of Maintenance," *BJRL* 29 (1945–46): 304–25, esp. 313–14; T. H. Aston, "Oxford's Medieval Alumni," *Past and Present* 74 (Feb. 1977): 3–40, esp. 6–7; Courtenay, "Effect of the Black Death," 700.

[36] Salter, *Medieval Oxford*, 90–112, especially 97: "I estimate that in 1360 the six colleges which then existed would contain about 10 undergraduates, 23 bachelors, and 40 masters. The founding of New College nearly doubled these figures, but if all the colleges had been dissolved in 1400, it would not have been a crushing blow to the University."

The Classroom Experience

Regardless of the faculty in which a student matriculated, his daily experience in the opening years of study would be reminiscent of his earlier education. He had to acquire a reading and writing knowledge of a new form of scholastic Latin composed almost entirely of abbreviations. He would attend lectures of masters and bachelors, copying on his own unbound quires of paper or low-quality parchment in abbreviated Latin the official exposition of an authoritative text. He would also attend debates, often taking notes on the positions held, the forms of argumentation, and the magisterial solution. He would be expected to read a specified list of books: most of them required, some optional. If he intended to become a master himself, he would gradually obtain a few of the basic texts in his field, either by employing a scribe to prepare a copy from the *peciae* or quires that constituted an official exemplar at a university bookseller, or by copying the works himself.

Outside the classroom the student attended and eventually participated in debates. There was, at least in the fourteenth century, some of the atmosphere of a tournament about scholastic debate in which, along lines similar to the "round table" with capped lances, young scholastics would enter the lists to prove their skill, their *subtilitas*, against an appointed foe without intending to damage him in any serious way. Students "entered" upon the reading of the *Sentences*, one after the other, and "engaged" their fellow bachelors in debate.[37] They might attack directly (*impugnatio*), feign (*adumbratio*), or parry (*evasio*) a counterthrust. Proof of mental dexterity was crucial, and style was often as important as a tightly worded argument. Thus the opinions expressed and defended were not always products of free and open inquiry. A certain amount of aggressive attack on one's contemporaries and predecessors was expected, but it was also assumed that one would remain within the broad outlines of accepted teaching.

[37] For example in the fourteenth-century English *Sentences* commentary of an otherwise unidentified Frater Petrus, found on fols. 46ʳ–73ᵛ of MS. Vat. lat. 13002, the author cited his fellow bachelors according to the order of reading; fol. 53ʳ: "arguebat socius meus qui secundo intravit et fecit argumenta"; fol. 54ʳ: "unus alius dominus, qui quartus intravit, fecit contra istam conclusionem meam primam"; fol. 54ᵛ: "arguebat socius qui secundo intravit"; "arguebat socius reverendus qui secundus post me intravit"; similarly at Paris, Pierre Ceffons, *Lectura*, Troyes MS. 62, fol. 5ᵛ: "Magister Johannes qui 6° loco incepit."

This element of gamesmanship in fourteenth-century scholastic thought has made it difficult to determine the seriousness and significance of university lectures and debates, and the works that derive from them. Some historians, following in the footsteps of their humanist ancestors, have seen late scholasticism as logic-chopping, meaningless distinctions, in which the actual ideas were seldom taken seriously. Other historians, possibly because they view their own work to be of cosmic significance, see late scholastic debates as life-and-death struggles between radically opposed positions, with intense feeling and commitment on both sides. But the analogy of the knightly tournament suggests the answer. Those who championed certain ideas, who entered the field in behalf of a certain position, did not do so by chance. They did so because they were intellectually persuaded or because they belonged to a particular group or order that was aligned with a certain position. In every case they attempted to defend the chosen position to the best of their ability and in so doing bring glory on themselves and the group to which they belonged. But scholastic debate was an individual sport and an individual effort, as was the joust. Each author knew he would be associated with his positions throughout his life. He was careful to believe what he was expected to defend, and careful to defend what he in fact already believed. If we keep the tournament imagery in mind we will not be led into dismissing late scholasticism as amusement or pastime, for both the personal glory and the espoused cause could be, and were, taken seriously. It will also keep us, however, from seeing the conflicts of scholastic thought in too cosmic or absolute terms. After the tournament opponents could and did associate and may even have been close friends. It may be one of the distinguishing features of a Jan Hus or a Martin Luther that they carried the seriousness of the academic debate out of the classroom and into the streets.[38]

The Arts Curriculum

The course of studies in arts at the university, if followed through to the end, lasted for a period of approximately nine years.[39] One entered

[38] Even Bradwardine's pugnacious and provocative *Summa de causa Dei* circulated within university circles in England and on the Continent; and Wyclif may not have been directly responsible for the dissemination of his ideas among nonscholarly groups.

[39] J. A. Weisheipl, "Curriculum of the Faculty of Arts at Oxford in the early Fourteenth

around the age of fourteen or fifteen and, for the next four or five years, studied under the supervision of a particular master. The student heard his master lecture and debate, attended other lectures and debates, and studied a designated list of books connected with each course of lectures.

Books were divided into two categories. First of all there were the authoritative, required texts, officially designated as the proper readings for knowledge of a given subject. They formed the texts that were commented on in lectures. Not all books on the list needed to be read, but some had to have been heard in lecture and some read privately. In this category were the works of the grammarians, Aristotle, and some other treatises, comparable in the higher faculties to the Bible and Lombard's *Sentences* for theology, Justinian's *Digest* for civil law, or Gratian's *Decretum* in canon law. Some substitutions within the list were possible. A second category of books consisted of commentaries and works by contemporary and previous masters. One was expected to read these works, be able to cite them in scholastic debate, and determine the differences or unanimity in the teaching of the doctors. These books were not officially designated, and there was considerable latitude in their choice and use. Books of recent origin that were controversial and had not received recognition by consensus of the faculty might be prohibited from lectures, either public or private, and yet be permissible reading for an individual in private. Some of Aristotle's works were in that category in the early thirteenth century, as were Ockham's works at Paris in the late 1330s.

The content of the arts curriculum in the fourteenth century centered on the study of Aristotle. One was expected to know the seven liberal arts, and some instruction in these had been obtained in grammar school before coming to the university. For the quadrivium one studied the treatises of Boethius on arithmetic and music, the *Algorismus* ascribed to Sacrobosco and the works of Euclid and Alhazen or Witelo on geometry, and Ptolemy's *Almagest* and Sacrobosco's *De sphera* on astronomy. For the trivium one studied Priscian and Donatus on grammar,

---

Century," *MedStud* 26 (1964): 143–85; "Developments in the Arts Curriculum at Oxford in the Early Fourteenth Century," *MedStud* 28 (1966): 151–75; "The Nature, Scope, and Classification of the Sciences," *Studia Mediewistyczne* 18 (1977): 85–101. See also Rashdall, *Univ.* 3: 153–56; J. M. Fletcher's chapter in *HUO* 369–99; and on the Aristotelian corpus, B. G. Dodd, "Aristoteles latinus," in *CHLMP*: 45–79.

Aristotle, Cicero, Ovid, Boethius, or Virgil on rhetoric, and Aristotle and Boethius on logic.

Of these subjects, logic was by far the most important. The *libri logicales* were divided into the "old logic" (that which was known before the twelfth century) and the "new logic" (that which was recovered by the mid-twelfth century). Under the "old logic" (*logica vetus* or *ars vetus*) one read Porphyry's *Isagoge* (his introduction to Aristotle's *Categories*), Aristotle's *Categories* (*Praedicamenta*) and *On Interpretation* (*Perihermeneias*), Boethius' work on analysis (*Liber de divisione*, or *Liber divisionum*), his *Topics* (*De topicis differentiis*, or *Liber topicorum*), and the *Liber sex principiorum* attributed to Gilbert de la Porrée. The "new logic" (*logica nova* or *ars nova*) consisted of Aristotle's *Topics*, *Prior analytics*, *Posterior analytics*, and the *Sophistical Refutations* (*Sophistici elenchi*). In the thirteenth century the *logica vetus* and the *logica nova* together became known as the *logica antiqua* or *logica antiquorum* (ancient logic, or logic of the ancients).

The study of logic (*studia artium*) was followed by instruction in the three philosophies: natural, moral, and metaphysical. In *Studia naturalia* one studied Aristotle's scientific works (*libri naturales*), specifically the *Physics, On the Soul* (*De anima*), *On Generation and Corruption, On the Heavens* (*De caelo*), *Meteors* (*Metheora*), the works on animals, and the lesser treatises on psychology (*Parva naturalia*). Under *studia moralia* one applied oneself to Aristotle's *Ethics* and *Politics*. *Studia metaphysicae* required a thorough examination of Aristotle's *Metaphysics*. Ideally the student should have progressed from logic to natural science, then ethics, and finally metaphysics. Availability of instruction and the pressures of time, however, meant that these courses of study were usually acquired simultaneously, or as lectures on particular texts were available during a year. Required academic exercises filled both mornings and afternoons. Evenings and summers could also be times of study.

The lecture was the principal form of instruction. The morning hours were reserved for the lectures of the regent masters, which were also known as "ordinary" lectures. These magisterial lectures traditionally had two parts. In the first part each master made a division of the text and gave a line-by-line exposition (*expositio literalis*) of its meaning. In the second part he explored and solved a question that emerged from the interpretation of the text. Lectures were also held in the afternoon. They were known as "extraordinary" lectures, since they occurred outside the normal or ordinary time for lectures. Afternoon lectures were generally "cursory," confined for the most part to a literal exposition or paraphrase of the text. Cursory lectures were generally given by bachelors, under the direction of a master, but masters also might, on occasion, give cursory lectures. The student was expected to hear all the official books on which the curriculum was based expounded at least once but preferably twice: *ordinarie* (by a master) and *cursorie* (by a bachelor). In the end the student should know the texts almost by heart and be able to recall relevant passages to support arguments in debate.

In addition to lectures, the arts student was expected to attend the weekly disputation of his master (*disputatio solemnis*) and the weekly review sessions (*repetitiones*), usually under a bachelor. In his third and fourth years of study the student was expected to take part in public disputations. At first he participated as opponent (*opponens*) and attacked the chosen thesis by raising objections.[40] He then advanced to the principal role (*respondens*) in which he answered objections. The final solution, or determination, of the question was left to a master or a senior ("formed") bachelor. Before advancing to the stage of bachelor, the student had to respond at least one year in "sophistical" disputations (*de sophismatibus*), during which time he was known as a *sophista*. These public disputations concerned particularly difficult or enigmatic problems arising from propositions in grammar or logic, including the paradoxes (*insolubilia*). The student was also expected to respond in disputations *de quaestione*, which concerned problems in *scientia realis*, such as mathematics, physics, ethics, or metaphysics.

Lectures and disputations in arts were generally held in rented halls or in the halls of the few colleges that existed in the fourteenth century. Disputations *de sophismatibus* took place near the church, adjoining halls, or courtyard of St. Frideswide's[41] (a collegiate community of Austin Canons that eventually was transformed into a college by Cardinal Woolsey in 1525 and is today Christ Church College) or (in the case of the debates before determination) the convent of the Austin Friars on the north edge of Oxford.

---

[40] There was no statutory requirement for opponency in the arts faculty. In public disputations objections could be raised by students, bachelors, or even masters.

[41] These disputations took place *in parviso*, which has been interpreted as referring to the parvis, or courtyard, of St. Frideswide's. Weisheipl, "Curriculum of the Faculty of Arts," 154.

During the fifth year of study, if the requirements had satisfactorily been met, the undergraduate could be presented for examination and "determination." Shortly before Lent the candidate and the master under whom he was then working appeared before the elected board of four examining masters and swore oaths that the student had fulfilled the statutory requirements regarding age, moral character, and knowledge obtained through the reading of the required books, attendance at lectures, and participation in disputations. If all was in order, the candidate would be admitted to lecture (*admissio ad lecturam*) on one of the texts of the arts faculty. Normally he also applied for and was granted the right to "determine." If the licence to determine (*licentia determinandi*) was granted by the examiners, the candidate proceeded during that Lent to lecture on one of the official books in logic. Lecturing in arts, whether as part of determination or not, made one a bachelor (*baccalaureus artium*).

During the baccalaureate it was required that the bachelor have some place, or school, in which to lecture. This was usually in the "school" of his master. Moreover, during that Lent the determining bachelor held disputations under the direction of his master and was expected to "determine" questions, that is, give a solution to a disputed question in anticipation of, and preparation for, his future role as master. Both the disputation and the lecture of the determining bachelor were held in late morning or afternoon.[42] The determination would often last until late in the day, and the cursory lecture following it might carry over into dusk.

The period of the baccalaureate normally lasted three years, counting the year in which the candidate determined. In addition to his own disputations and lectures, he continued to attend lectures and disputations of the masters, particularly on those subjects he had not yet mastered. He was obliged to oppose and respond in the public disputations of the masters as well as the general disputation of bachelors held annually at the convent of the Austin Friars.

At the end of the seventh year of university study, the student in arts who had determined could be put forward for inception as a new master of arts. But "determining" was not required for inception. One could, with one additional year of study (eight years in all) proceed

[42] See above, n. 11.

from a B.A. to the M.A. without having determined. To obtain the academic honor of master of arts the candidate had to be at least twenty years of age, considered of good moral character, and sufficiently learned by reason of having met all academic requirements. The candidate's worthiness was first established by a group of regent masters in closed meeting. If their judgment was favorable, the candidate was then presented by his master to the chancellor of the University for the licence to teach (*licentia docendi*). Within one year from the granting of the licence the *licentiatus* incepted as a new master. Inception entailed two separate acts. The first ceremony was a disputation ("vesperies") held in the afternoon in the church of St. Mildred. The one incepting took the role of opponent, a recent inceptor the role of respondent, and a presiding master (usually the one promoting the new master) concluded the proceedings with a short address (*commendatio*). The second ceremony was investiture in which the *inceptor* received from his master the symbols of office (the book and the cap), gave a brief lecture (*principium*), and determined two disputed questions. These acts were followed by an obligation to hold public disputations regularly during forty days (*dies disputabiles*) after inception and to lecture as a regent master for two years.

The arts curriculum was the foundation for all higher studies at the university. It was the largest faculty, and arts scholars were younger than those in medicine, law, or theology. Entrance to the higher faculties of medicine, civil law, canon law, or theology did not require determination or regency in arts, but it was expected that the basic content of the arts curriculum should already have been acquired. Only theology specified that those who had not "reigned in arts" (that is, those who lacked the M.A.) must have studied arts for at least eight years. This requirement, drafted by the secular theologians who had taken the M.A., ensured that the regular theologians (monks and mendicants), who were not permitted by their orders to take the arts degree at the university, spent an equivalent amount of time in the study of philosophy. Law and medicine were probably less rigorous in this regard, since apparently most of those studying civil law and medicine had not been regents in arts. But some arts training was normal, and it may have been the practice for those going into these two lucrative professions to begin their higher studies at or shortly after the time of determination.

Regents in arts had an advantage over their noncredentialed fellow
students in theology, law, or medicine. Those who did not take the M.A.
were required to take an additional two years of study before being allowed entrance to the baccalaureate or the doctorate. This may have
been a penalty clause, or may have been based on the assumption that
those without the arts degree needed to do remedial work in the philosophical background to the higher discipline, but it was probably to offset the inequity that would otherwise have existed between those who
skipped inception and regency in arts and those who had spent two
years as regents.

Medicine

Medicine was not a large faculty in the fourteenth century.[43] Of the
known graduates of Oxford it accounts for no more than three percent.
But since doctors rarely left writings or held positions that would be recorded in documents, their actual numerical strength at Oxford was
undoubtedly higher than that percentage would reflect.

Six years of study was required for licencing and inception in medicine. Those who had completed their study in arts would be well versed
in Aristotle's *De anima, Physics,* the *Parva naturalia,* and his works on bi-
ology—all of which contained material then considered important for
understanding the human body and health. If one did not already possess the M.A., the length of study was two years longer, or eight years in
full.

During the last two or three years of that training, the candidate
would lecture cursorily on medical theory, using the text of Galen's
Liber tegni or Hippocrates' *Aphorismi,* and on medical practice, using the
text of Hippocrates' *Regimen acutorum,* the *Liber febrium* of Isaac Israel,
or the *Antidotarium* of Nicholas. In addition, he would have responded

[43] C. H. Talbot, *Medicine in Medieval England* (London, 1967); Rashdall, *Univ.* 3: 156;
C. H. Talbot, "Medicine," in *Science in the Middle Ages,* ed. D. C. Lindberg (Chicago, 1978),
391–428; C. H. Talbot, "Simon Bredon (*c.* 1300–1372), Physician, Mathematician and Astronomer," *British Journal for the History of Science* 1 (1962–63): 19–30; V. L. Bullough,
"Medical Study at Mediaeval Oxford," *Speculum* 36 (1961): 600–12; Bullough, "The Mediaeval Medical School at Cambridge," *MedStud* 24 (1962): 161–68; and forthcoming chapter by Faye Getz in *HUO* 2.

in the schools of the regent masters in medicine for a period of two years.

There were some noted professors of medicine at Oxford in the fourteenth century, such as John Gaddesden in the opening decades. Most, however, remain unknown. Among the colleges, Oriel, Balliol, Exeter, and Merton supported medical studies among their fellowships, and of the recipients the medical scholars at Merton were the most distinguished. Moreover, Merton provided an excellent atmosphere for a close interconnection between medicine and philosophy, such as existed at Padua, Bologna, and elsewhere. The compatibility of medicine and philosophy had a long history in Islamic and Jewish culture in the ninth to thirteenth centuries, and the continuing alliance of those disciplines among the Italian universities in the fourteenth and fifteenth centuries may have been influenced by the earlier non-Christian tradition as well as the practical need at Bologna to offset the power of the law faculties. In any event, the alliance is visible at Oxford in the fourteenth century. The medical faculty usually sided with the arts faculty in voting, and scholars would often pursue training in both medicine and the mathematical sciences, and on occasion in theology or law as well. Of these the most prominent example was Simon Bredon, doctor of medicine and theology as well as a mathematician and astronomer, who for a time was a fellow of Merton College and a colleague of Thomas Bradwardine, Thomas Buckingham, and others.

Civil and Canon Law

There is a temptation when viewing Oxford from the standpoint of intellectual history to regard the law faculties as the domain of career-oriented opportunists whose zeal for future wealth was matched by their neglect of the things of the mind. That view obscures a much closer relation between law and theology and attributes a purity of motive to theologians that is unrealistic for that age. The lure of career advancement was probably as strong a motive in theological education as it was in legal education, and the diatribes against self-serving, profit-seeking lawyers that became common among theologians in the late Middle Ages were probably motivated in part by jealousy that the best opportunities were going to lawyers.

On the one hand, it is true that law, like medicine, did not stress writing and publication as heavily as did the theological faculty. Commentaries and treatises in the fields of civil and canon law were almost invariably composed by professors of law, and the lectures of the bachelor were taken less seriously than in theology. Thus, from the standpoint of publication, law and medicine were closer to arts, in which the writings in the discipline were produced by the masters.

On the other hand, law and theology had much in common. First, they shared with arts certain teaching devices and debate techniques that were used at the higher stages of each degree program: the hypothetical case and the rules of obligations. In arts the candidate was given a proposition, perhaps a false proposition that was seemingly true or a true proposition that was seemingly false, and asked to explore its validity according to grammar and the rules of logic. How was the proposition to be taken, and in what sense was it true and in what sense false? Moreover, within an obligation, the candidate was forced to accept as given certain assumptions or aspects of the problem that continued to hold as long as the obligation lasted. In law the candidate was given cases or problems that seemingly brought certain aspects of the law into conflict. It was his task, within the structure of the case, to resolve the difficulty and prove that he both knew and understood the legal principles involved. In theology the techniques of *sophismata* and *obligationes* also prevailed. The candidate was given a theological proposition, which he was forced to accept as true, false, or uncertain for purposes of the disputation, and he was to resolve the question according to the logical and theological principles involved. In all three faculties we thus find the use of hypothetical cases and/or difficult propositions, and the debate conducted within the confines of a certain obligatory structure.

Secondly, theology and canon law overlapped to a surprising degree. The areas of human volition, moral theology, sin and merit, and the sacraments were common concerns to the two disciplines. Practically speaking, this meant that canon lawyers had to have some sensitivity to the theological issues involved, just as theologians needed some background in canon law. In a few cases (mostly toward the end of the fourteenth century) students incepted in both disciplines. The *Sentences* commentaries of the fourteenth century reflect an extensive knowledge of canon law, both texts and the commentary tradition.[44] Either

---

[44] Theologians knew and used some canon law at the beginning of the century. Doctrinal

through private reading or by attending lectures in the schools of law, bachelors in theology were expected to know the decretals as well as the Bible and Aristotle. How many lawyers were as conversant in theology is another question. Although interest and uses might differ, both theology and canon law rested on the common foundation of biblical and patristic teaching, just as similar problems were confronted in the confessional and the judicial chamber. The interrelation of theology and canon law should caution us against imagining too wide a separation or division between those faculties.

Both Oxford and Cambridge were important centers for the study of law.[45] In contrast to Paris, where the study of Roman law was proscribed by Pope Honorius III, thus handicapping for a time the study of canon law for which civil law was a prerequisite,[46] the study of civil and canon law was not prohibited in England. Oxford and Cambridge thus offered the only opportunities among leading *studia generalia* for the open

---

pronouncements were cited from the canon law source, but there was less interest in what canon lawyers had to say about those texts. Such areas of common concern, e.g. penance, would be extensively treated by each, but in separate ways. Toward the end of the century discussions of penance among theologians relied far more heavily on canon law and the tradition of the *summae confessorum*. If one looks at William Woodford or William Jordan one finds that the speculative/philosophical element has been sharply reduced and in its place the literature of practical theology, where canon law had made important contributions, has taken over. One could view this as a result of acquiescence on the part of theologians, or the abandonment of traditional theology, or its juridicalization in terms of sources, selection of themes and questions, or manner of treatment. But one could also see it as a recognition on the part of theologians that law had made a contribution that could no longer be ignored. What may be more to the point: if law was attracting more students and theology was losing its privileged place, it is natural that theological teaching (and the written results) would become more practical, to keep pace with student interests. At present we can only surmise. The changes that we see may reflect changing interests on the part of theologians; but they may also be a response by theologians to changing student interests and a recognition of where the burning questions of the day lay.

[45] Rashdall, *Univ.* 3: 156–57; L. Boyle, "The Curriculum of the Faculty of Canon Law at Oxford in the First Half of the Fourteenth Century," in *Oxford Studies presented to Daniel Callus* (Oxford, 1964), 135–62, and reprinted in L. Boyle, *Pastoral Care, Clerical Education and Canon Law, 1200–1400* (London, 1981); C. T. Allmand, "The Civil Lawyers," in *Profession, Vocation, and Culture*, 155–80; and most notably the essays by R. W. Southern, J. L. Barton, and L. E. Boyle in *HUO* 1: 1–36, 519–64.

[46] The 1219 prohibition on civil law at Paris was relaxed somewhat in the opening years of the fourteenth century; *CUP* 2: 121–22. Instruction in civil law was also available nearby at Orléans and Angers.

and complete study of law north of the Alps. Increasingly in the fourteenth century English students remained in England for their university education, leading to a proportional decline in English students at
Bologna and a corresponding increase at Oxford and Cambridge.

Among the higher faculties, law was second only to theology, although by the end of the fourteenth century it began to contest, at least
in numerical strength, the privileged position of the "queen of the sciences."[47] Law had always had a reputation as a lucrative profession.
This is not to say that theological students were unconcerned about
their post-university careers, but simply that law students followed a
more certain path to future financial security, even if that were not their
primary motivation. Whatever role monetary reward played, by the
end of the century law was appearing to be a more certain route as well
to prestige and high office in church and state.

Civil law and canon law were separate but closely associated faculties.
One could become a doctor in civil law without any study in canon law,
or one could become a doctor in both laws (*iuris utriusque doctor*). One
could not, however, study canon law without at least three years of
study in civil law. Civil law, inasmuch as it was a prerequisite for canon
law, was the foundation for the law faculty.

As with all higher faculties, it was expected that the entering student
in civil law would be in his early twenties and have studied arts. Those
who had actually been regents in arts would attend lectures for four
years; those who had not reigned in arts would be expected to remain
at this level for six years. The ordinary, morning lectures of the regent
doctors in civil law were on Justinian's *Digest*, which contained the juris-
prudence of Roman law. The extraordinary, or afternoon lectures, of
the bachelors were on the *Volumina*, that is the *New Digest* and the *Infor-
tiatum*. Before inception as a doctor in civil law one also had to give an
ordinary lecture for each regent master in civil law, and to have opposed and responded.

---

[47] But a statute dated around 1370 (*MunAcad* 1: 233) still affirms that bachelors and opponents in theology and masters of arts shall have precedence in processions and other occasions over the bachelors of canon law. The statutes in the Junior Proctor's Book of 1407
again acknowledge the preeminence of the faculty of theology; p. 238: ". . . et incipitur in
hoc libro ab illa scientiarum regina sacratissima theologica facultate, quae prima fuit in in-
tentione condentis, et inter caeteras facultates praerogativa praeeminet ampliori; cujus
quidem excellentiae famulatrix et ancilla, veneranda decretorum facultas. . . ."

The doctorate in civil law or at least three-years' study was required for entry into the faculty of canon law. For those who had been doctors of civil law, two years of study on the *Decretum* of Gratian and the *Decretales* were required. For others, three years of study on those works were required. During the baccalaureate the candidate was required to give extraordinary lectures for a year or more on the *Decretals*. He was also expected to oppose on treatises from the *Decretum*.

By 1333 the influx of new canonical collections forced a revision in the curriculum in canon law. Bachelors in canon law who had been regents in civil law were expected to provide some of the ordinary lectures in canon law, so that all the important texts could be covered. Regency was also reduced from two years to one. At the same time the *Decretales Gregorii IX* and the more significant parts of the *Liber Sextus* and the *Clementinae* began to displace the *Decretum* as the central text of professorial lectures. In addition to supplementing ordinary lectures, bachelors in canon law were expected to provide lectures on other portions of the *Decretales*. After a year or two of lecturing as a bachelor and having opposed and responded in the school of each regent, the candidate might proceed to the license and inception as a doctor of canon law.

Theology

The theological course of study at Oxford was the longest and hardest of all the faculties, as it was at Paris.[48] It required a thorough background in arts, interpreted as the possession of the university M.A. degree, or equivalent study elsewhere plus two years additional study in theology. In practice, this meant that one would enter the theological faculty as a student at around age twenty-one, rarely younger.

For students who had reigned in arts (all theological students except monks and mendicants, whose orders did not permit them to take the arts degree), four years of study and attendance at lectures on the Bible and the *Sentences* of Peter Lombard were required. In the fifth year one was permitted to "oppose" in debates (that is, take the position of the opponent), and in the seventh year "respond" (that is, take the position

---

[48] *MunAcad* 2: 388–97; Rashdall, *Univ.* 3: 158–60; A. G. Little, "Theological Schools in Medieval England," *EHR* 55 (1940): 624–30; Gordon Leff, *Paris and Oxford Universities in the Thirteenth and Fourteenth Centuries* (New York, 1968), 160–77; J. I. Catto's chapter in *HUO* 1: 471–517.

of the respondent).[49] Having completed seven years of study, the candidate could be admitted to "read" (that is, lecture on) the *Sentences*, which made him a bachelor of theology. These lectures were followed a year or two later with lectures on the Bible, the completion of which made him a "formed bachelor" (*baccalaureus formatus*). The candidate remained in residence at Oxford in this capacity for a year or more of disputations before becoming eligible for licencing and inception as a master, or doctor, of theology. As a regent master the theologian was obliged to lecture on the Bible for a period of two years, oversee the work of students under his direction, and sit in congregation.

At the beginning of the fourteenth century this course of study for those who possessed the M.A. lasted fourteen or fifteen years, counting the regency in theology. It was, however, gradually reduced in length. By the second quarter of the century lectures on the *Sentences* were usually completed in one year (a change that took place at Paris as well), and the bachelor lectures on the Bible were given in one term or during the long vacation in the summer after reading the *Sentences*. There is also evidence that regency could be completed in one year. This meant that by about 1350 the doctorate in theology, including the required regency, might be completed in less than ten years. Laxity was probably not the reason for easing the academic requirements, for the quality of the scholastic work produced in the first half of the fourteenth century remained high. Whatever the long-term results may have been, it was initially a response to increasing enrollment, the need to accommodate more students at each stage of the program, an attempt to reduce the inequity in years between the degrees in law and theology, and probably a recognition of career possibilities for younger men.

The Oxford theological curriculum resembled that of the theological faculty at Paris, but with some important differences. One difference was the place of the Bible within the theological baccalaureate.[50] Both

---

[49] *MunAcad* 2: 389; *Statuta Oxon.* 48: "opponere voluerint, si prius in artibus rexerint, ante quintum annum audicionis theologie opponere non presumant, aut ante septimum respondere. Qui vero in artibus magistralem non sunt honorem adepti, ante septimum annum opponere, aut ante nonum respondere aliqualiter non attemptent."

[50] For further discussion see B. Smalley, "Problems of Exegesis in the Fourteenth Century," in *Antike und Orient im Mittelalter*, Miscellanea Mediaevalia 1, ed. Paul Wilpert (Berlin, 1962), 266–74; W. J. Courtenay, "The Bible in the Fourteenth Century: Some Observations," *Church History* 54 (1985): 176–87.

universities required students to attend lectures on the Bible during their first four years, and both universities required regent masters to lecture on the Bible. Thus the student's knowledge of the Bible at each university was probably comparable, and Oxford produced its share of magisterial biblical commentaries in the fourteenth century, of which Holcot's are outstanding examples. At the level of the baccalaureate, however, the biblical lectures at Oxford and Paris differed both in length and character. Paris required its advanced students to lecture on the Bible before lecturing on the *Sentences*, a practice that went back to the early years of the university. Moreover, Paris required two years of biblical lectures. Since those were the lectures of a "junior" bachelor and were not expected to substitute for those of the regent masters, they were not innovative but remained simple expositions of biblical texts. Few of these student "exercises" have remained from the thirteenth or fourteenth centuries, probably because their content was similar and unimaginative and was, in any case, superseded by the biblical lectures of the regents.

At Oxford bachelors lectured on the Bible after lecturing on the *Sentences*. This may explain why, by the fourteenth century, the Oxford commentaries of biblical bachelors differed from those at Paris. They were shorter inasmuch as they were products of lectures presented in less than a year, usually during one term or even during the long summer vacation. But these lectures could contain important ideas and statements by their authors. Since the bachelor had already lectured on the *Sentences*, his biblical lectures often continued the theological and philosophical debates initiated in the *Sentences* commentaries. Little attention seems to have been directed to the exposition of the text and far more attention to theological questions occasioned by the text or for which the text may only have been a pretext. Few Oxford biblical commentaries of bachelors have survived, but the fragments we have reveal the excitement of intellectual debate and controversy that places them in character far closer to *Sentences* commentaries than to the subsequent magisterial lectures on the Bible.[51]

---

[51] A *socius* or *socii* of Holcot and Wodeham began lectures on the Bible around 1332 with issues of speculative philosophy and theology. Osbert Pickingham's *Introitus ad Bibliam* is speculative. For further discussion see H. Schepers, "Holkot contra dicta Crathorn," PhilJahr 77 (1970): 320–54, 79 (1972): 106–36; W. J. Courtenay, *Adam Wodeham* (Leiden,

There are further differences between the Paris and Oxford programs in theology. At Paris the number of chairs in theology was fixed,
but the oath of regency required in order to become master of theology
at the university was not strictly enforced; at Oxford there is no evidence of fixed chairs except among the religious orders, but there seem
to have been few if any exceptions to the requirement of regency.[52] Finally, the Parisian degree of master of theology in the fourteenth century required fourteen to sixteen years of study and could not be obtained before the age of thirty-five.

Various stages in the university programs produced scholastic works,
but there is no simple rule that automatically associates one genre of
writing with one stage in an academic career. For instance, commentaries on the works of Aristotle, one of the principal genres important for
our knowledge of medieval philosophy and science, were written by
bachelors and masters of arts, who would have been in the seventeen to
twenty-five age group. Yet those circulated in manuscripts were magisterial commentaries, and some were written much later in life. Those

---

1978), 95–109; Courtenay, "The Lost Matthew Commentary of Robert Holcot O.P.," *AFP*
50 (1980): 103–12.

[52] How many chairs of theology were there in the fourteenth century at Oxford? In this
regard, as in some others, the parallelism that seems to exist between Oxford and Paris may
be deceptive. At Paris the fixed number of chairs grew from eight (at the beginning of the
thirteenth century) to twelve (by mid-century) to twenty (at the end of the thirteenth century). In the fourteenth century the number of teaching chairs seems to have continued to
increase until there may have been thirty or forty. Moreover, at Paris the statutory requirement of a two-year regency after inception does not appear to have been enforced for all
masters; P. Glorieux, *Répertoire des maîtres en théologie de Paris au XIIIᵉ siècle* (Paris, 1933), 23.
At Oxford, which did not originate out of a cathedral school with a fixed number of teaching canons, there was not initially a set number of teaching chairs. In the course of the thirteenth century the religious houses were limited to one regent master per convent, but
there is no evidence to suggest that that restriction was applied to the seculars who might
live in halls or in colleges. There may have been an approximate number that was felt to be
sufficient, but this probably varied from decade to decade. It is unlikely that the colleges,
even after they began to play a more important role at Oxford, followed the pattern of the
religious houses, with one regent master or lector per unit. None of the religious convents
had semipermanent fellows who might stay on for a period of time. Nor were the colleges
limited to scholars preparing for degrees in theology or canon law. A college like Merton
could have several masters in arts and possibly several masters in theology, some of whom
may have been actively teaching simultaneously. Whether they could all vote in solemn
congregation or could "field" more than one bachelor to read the *Sentences* in any one year
is another matter.

produced by mendicants were usually written after they had completed a higher degree in theology or canon law and had returned to a mendicant school to teach philosophy. The age group of the latter type would fall between thirty and forty.

Collections of disputed questions and, particularly, the questions arising from quodlibetic debates (debates on any topic whatsoever proposed by masters or students and held during Advent and Lent), were, for the theological faculty, products of the years in which one was a master or, in nonuniversity *studia*, a formed bachelor; that is, approximately between the ages of thirty and thirty-seven. Originally in the thirteenth century the right to determine, or sum up, a quodlibetic dispute belonged to a master, and bachelors could only participate by opposing or responding. In the fourteenth century, at least in England, it became possible for formed bachelors to determine quodlibetal questions, certainly outside Oxford and Cambridge, and perhaps inside as well. Among Ockham's most important works are a long series of quodlibetal questions, probably disputed at London and Avignon, although he was never master of theology. Similarly, some of the quodlibetal questions of Holcot may date to a time in which he was not yet a master of theology.[53] *Questiones quodlibetales* were subsequently collected and sometimes revised, but the form in which they have come down to us is, at most, only a few years distant from the form in which they were presented orally. This type of theological publication became very rare at Oxford after 1335. John of Rodington, John Grafton, Robert Holcot, Geoffrey Herdeby, and Thomas Claxton are among the last examples.[54]

[53] Joseph Wey, however, in private correspondence, has suggested that the quodlibetal question of Holcot that can be dated to 1332 (when Holcot had completed his reading of the *Sentences* and before he was regent master) may not be a quodlibetal question at all but rather the opening lecture (*principium*) for book 2 of the *Sentences*. If so, then Holcot's years as *sententiarius* would be 1331–33, and the *Quodlibeta* of Holcot could all be placed a few years later, during his regency.

[54] The *Quodlibeta* of Claxton, O.P. (*c.* 1413) are preserved in Florence, Bibl. Naz., MS. conv. soppr. B.6.340. On the *Quodlibeta* of Herdeby, which date around 1358, see P. Glorieux, *La littérature quodlibétique*, vol. 2 (Paris, 1935), 318; A. Zumkeller, "Die Augustinerschule des Mittelalters: Vertreter und philosophisch-theologische Lehre," *Analecta Augustiniana* 27 (1964): 228; Roth, *EAF* 1: 549–50. On the development of quodlibetic disputations, in addition to Glorieux, see J. F. Wippel, "The Quodlibetal Question as a Distinctive Literary Genre," in *Les genres littéraires dans les sources théologiques et philosophiques mé-*

Biblical commentaries could be written by theological bachelors, but almost all commentaries that have survived were written during or after the years in which one was regent master in theology. They are thus mature works of scholarship whose content was not dictated by university regulations or the tastes of academic superiors. Similarly, sermons were products of mature years, although much of the structure and content of that genre was formulaic.

The richest source for late scholasticism, apart from treatises written on a specific topic, are the *Sentences* commentaries. They contain material of philosophic, political, mathematical, and scientific interest, as well as the theology one would expect to find there. Moreover, with a few exceptions, they can be placed at a precise time in the life of an author, for they were written during or just prior to reading the *Sentences* as a bachelor at a university and, if revised for publication, achieved their final form within a few years of their original conception.

One cannot, unfortunately, read these sources at face value, as if they were the products solely of the mind of the author at the moment of writing. The structure and content of all of them, to some degree, were conditioned by the rules established for the composition of such works. As the art of letter writing in the Middle Ages followed the rules of the *ars dictaminis*, so sermons, or commentaries, or disputations followed the rules of their genres. One must be careful, therefore, to separate the required structure and formulas from the individual character of the work.[55]

A further factor complicates the use of a *Sentences* commentary. In origin the work was a product of the writer's student years. The requirements of the university and the expectations of one's superiors conditioned to some degree the form and even the content of these works.

---

diévales, Publications de l'Institut d'études médiévales, 2nd ser., vol. 5 (Louvain-la-neuve, 1982), 67–84.

[55] Fortunately, in assessing the originality of English scholastic works, one need not be concerned with the practice of borrowing long passages from earlier commentaries (as did John of Mirecourt at Paris) or rereading the commentary of an earlier author under one's own name (as did Henry of Langenstein and many others). The latter practice, labeled *lecturae secundum alium*, became common on the Continent in the second half of the fourteenth century. Although it should not be equated with outright plagiarism (it was usually an act of respect for the original author and support for his opinions), it does complicate the assessment of originality. On *lecturae secundum alium* see D. Trapp, "Augustinian Theology of the 14th Century," *Augustiniana* 6 (1956): 146–274.

The *Sentences* commentary was an academic exercise in which controversy was stylistically required but excessive innovation discouraged. Officially the commentary was supposed to stay within the bounds of accepted opinion and simply gloss previous authorities. Originality was officially discouraged; one was supposed to engage one's fellow bachelors in debate only in the opening lecture (*principium*) on each book of the *Sentences*, never in the main body of the commentary; one should never cite contemporary opinion, and certainly not by name; and one had to swear before beginning one's lectures that one would adhere to authority and say nothing contrary to the faith or accepted opinion. In practice, the student knew full well that his work would never receive high praise nor come to the attention of others unless it did attack accepted opinion, engage in controversy, and produce some new insights and conclusions. The desired aim was to be as creative and innovative as possible without incurring suspicions of heresy and possible condemnation. At times the use of oratorical or conceptual techniques to shock one's audience into close attention was permitted, although university authorities disapproved of excessive "grandstanding" that seriously entertained, however briefly, sacrilegious or heretical ideas. For every scholar who lost that gamble—like Nicholas of Autrecourt, who was forced to recant and burn his writings—there were many more, like Durand of St. Pourçain or Peter Aureoli, who turned notoriety into a bishopric. Even some whose work was condemned advanced in career, as proven by the abbacy of John of Mirecourt. Free speculation not only had its delights, it had its rewards.

Composing and perfecting a *Sentences* commentary usually took several years. By the second decade of the fourteenth century it was not uncommon for a draft to be made a year or two prior to reading at a university, and those in religious orders might present an early version in lectures at a nonuniversity convent or monastery before reading at Oxford or Cambridge.[56] After the university reading, further revisions

---

[56] The earliest evidence for this practice in England is the contemporary statement on the fly leaf of the *Sentences* commentary of Richard Bromwich, who read at Oxford between 1307 and 1313. Worcester, Cath. MS. F.139: "Lectura quam fecit Frater Richardus de Bromwich et scripsit manu sua super quattuor libros sententiarum antequam legit librum sententiarum Oxon." Father Gedeon Gál is of the opinion (expressed in 1985) that Ockham's *Reportatio* on books 2–4 may represent a pre-Oxford reading, *c.* 1316–17, and that Ockham may only have read on book 1 (his *Ordinatio*) at Oxford.

would be made as the author prepared his work for publication. He might also incorporate into his *Sentences* commentary disputed or quodlibetal questions that were composed after his time as *sententiarius*. In a few instances further, post-*ordinatio* redactions were made. The more frequent pattern, however, was to leave behind versions that were only partially revised and, in that form, began to circulate and appear in the book collections of others.[57]

Oxford Colleges and Libraries

The landscape of Oxford or Cambridge today is dominated by the colleges that make up the early modern and modern universities. In the thirteenth and fourteenth centuries, however, those foundations, as was mentioned earlier, served the needs of only a small fraction of the secular students at either university: a negligible percentage in the thirteenth century and probably less than ten percent throughout most of the fourteenth.[58] Of the 800 to 1,500 secular students simultaneously in residence at Oxford in the period between the end of the thirteenth and the end of the fourteenth centuries, only some thirty to fifty students were served by Balliol, Merton, and University colleges in the thirteenth century, to which were added another forty to sixty students served by Exeter, Oriel, and Queens in the first half of the fourteenth. Throughout the century, particularly at Oxford, the majority of stu-

[57] It would appear that Chatton incorporated disputed questions in his *Reportatio* of 1321–23; see S. Brown, "Walter Chatton's *Lectura* and William of Ockham's *Quaestiones in Libros Physicorum Aristotelis*," in *Essays Honoring Allan B. Wolter*, ed. W. A. Frank and G. J. Etzkorn, Franciscan Institute Publications, Theol. ser. vol. 10 (St. Bonaventure, N.Y., 1985), 81–115. The incorporation into Holcot's *Sentences* commentary of questions that appear to have been written later, and the appearance among his quodlibets of questions that probably belong to the *Sentences* commentary is another case in point. For an example of a post-*ordinatio* redaction of a *Sentences* commentary see my *Adam Wodeham*. Among the many *Sentences* commentaries that show signs of incomplete revision, arrangement, and polishing are those of Graystanes, Fitzralph, and Holcot. On the multiple redaction process see C. Michalski, "Die vielfachen Redaktionen einiger Kommentare zu Petrus Lombardus," in *Miscellanea Fr. Ehrle*, vol. 1 (Rome, 1924), 219–64; D. Trapp, "Dreistufiger Editionsprozess und dreiartige Zitationsweise bei den Augustinertheologen des 14. Jahrhunderts?" *Augustiniana* 25 (1975): 283–92.

[58] See above, n. 29.

dents lived in halls and rented rooms, largely untouched by the life of the colleges or religious houses of study.

Yet, when one considers the intellectual life of the university, the role of colleges and convents looms much larger. The overwhelming majority of known Oxford authors in the fourteenth century belonged to colleges and convents: some seventy percent in the opening decades of the century to almost ninety percent by the end of the century. In almost all cases our knowledge of their writings is not derived from sources produced by the colleges and religious orders, so we may take those percentages as a reasonably accurate reflection of scholarly productivity at Oxford. Some of the incentive toward scholarship no doubt came from the expectations of patrons and religious superiors. Most of it, however, resulted from other factors, such as the premium placed on intellectual aptitude and achievement in the selection procedures of colleges and convents, the encouragement and direction provided by the communal environment itself, which stimulated learning through the exchange of ideas and through peer expectations, and affordable access to scribes. Perhaps even more crucial for college-affiliated scholars was their direct access to the major resource for learning: an extensive collection of books.

Manuscripts in the late thirteenth and early fourteenth centuries were expensive treasures that only the wealthier students could purchase for themselves. Other students had to rely on their own notes taken in lecture. In the battle for access to the texts and commentaries, fellows of a college had a distinct advantage over the unaffiliated secular student. By the end of the thirteenth century the three colleges in existence had already begun to accumulate a treasure of books, some purchased, some acquired as forfeited security for a loan, most donated to the college. These books were kept in chests and loaned out to the fellows on an annual basis (the *electiones*). In the total possession of the college, Balliol probably had close to 100 volumes by the middle of the fourteenth century, Oriel had almost 100, while Merton probably had close to 150.[59] By century's end, when Merton had built a library to

---

[59] On the libraries of Balliol and Merton colleges, see: R.A.B. Mynors, *Catalogue of the Manuscripts of Balliol College Oxford* (Oxford, 1963); F. M. Powicke, *The Medieval Books of Merton College* (Oxford, 1931); N. Ker, "The Books of Philosophy Distributed at Merton College in 1372 and 1375," in *Medieval Studies for J.A.W. Bennett* (Oxford, 1981), 347–94; N. Ker, "Oxford College Libraries before 1500," in *The Universities in the Late Middle Ages*,

house the noncirculating, or chained, portion of its collection, they probably possessed some 300 volumes, with a third or more of those in circulation among the fellows. Balliol's collection by the end of the fourteenth century would have numbered between 180 and 200 volumes. In an age that only belatedly began to assemble a general university library to serve the needs of the mass of students and masters, those who did have access to one of these college libraries had a distinct advantage within the academic community.[60] Only University College allowed members of the university outside the college to use its books.[61]

In contrast to the religious orders, colleges had two disadvantages in assembling a working library. First, colleges were new foundations, unaffiliated with preexisting, book-rich institutions. There was no core of books, such as monastic communities possessed, around which to build a collection. This meant that all texts and commentaries in logic, natural philosophy, theology, and other disciplines, as well as patristic literature and biblical commentaries, had to be slowly and expensively acquired from the ground up. Second, since the fellows were not themselves scribes, there was no intra-collegial system of book production. Thus, apart from the books received as donations, forfeiture, or spoils (in case of the death of a fellow), in the selection of which the colleges had no

---

ed. J. Ijsewijn and J. Paquet (Louvain, 1978), 293–311. The book list for Oriel College, dated to 1375 by C. L. Shadwell, "The Catalogue of the Library of Oriel College in the 14th Century," *Collectanea*, 1st ser., ed. C.R.L. Fletcher, o.h.s. 5 (Oxford, 1885), 57–70, can better be dated to 1349. None of these college libraries, however, compared with that of the Sorbonne, which contained 1,017 volumes by 1290 and 1,722 volumes by 1338; see K. W. Humphreys, *The Book Provisions of the Medieval Friars*, 1215–1400 (Amsterdam, 1964), 86–87, and R. H. Rouse, "The Early Library of the Sorbonne," *Scriptorium* 21 (1967), 42–71, 227–51.

[60] The construction of Congregation House, the upper floor of which was to house a library for the university, was begun in 1320 through the financial support of Thomas Cobham, bishop of Worcester, who willed his library to the university at his death in 1327. Those books, however, were sold to pay for his debts and funeral, and after they were redeemed by Oriel College, they were seized and put into the library in 1337 (Rashdall, *Univ.* 3: 64–65, 164–65). The collection was added to gradually, and the university set rules for the care of the collection and the hours of use, (*MunAcad* 1: 261). The collection and facilities were greatly enhanced through the bequest of Humphrey, duke of Gloucester, in 1447.

[61] Humphreys, *Book Provisions*, 88: "[University] College [Oxford] books were available to members of the university outside the college." "Most colleges forbade the lending of books to anyone but their own members."

voice, books had to be purchased or commissioned, and the acquisition of the most basic philosophical and theological texts was no easy task.

In the acquisition of books and in the ultimate construction of libraries, the mendicant orders outdistanced any other groups within the universities. By the middle of the thirteenth century the mendicant orders had begun to accumulate collections of manuscripts, some through purchase, some through the policy of confiscating libraries of deceased friars, some through donation (such as Robert Grosseteste's extensive gift to Oxford Greyfriars), but most through the efforts of scribes within the orders. To help the colleges compete and build their libraries, the Dominican, Robert Kilwardby, as archbishop of Canterbury, decreed in 1276 that all books of fellows of Merton College upon death would belong to the college library.[62] But throughout our period the mendicant libraries were far richer than those of the secular colleges. It was with some sense of justice that Richard Fitzralph accused the mendicants, especially the Franciscans, of having cornered the book market in Oxford by the middle of the fourteenth century.[63]

Cambridge

Cambridge in the fourteenth century was not only small in comparison to Oxford (about one-third the size), it was regional.[64] It drew its stu-

---

[62] Humphreys, *Book Provisions*, 85.

[63] *Defensio Curatorum*, in Brown's *Appendix ad Fasciculum Rerum Expetendarum* (London, 1690), 474, quoted by Rashdall, *Univ.* 1: 517, n. 1: "quod non reperitur in studiis communibus de Facultate Arcium, sacre Theologie et Juris Canonici aut etiam, ut fertur a pluribus, de Facultate Medicine atque Juris Civilis, nisi raro, aliquis utilis multum liber venalis, set omnes emuntur a fratribus, ita ut in singulis conventibus sit una grandis ac nobilis libraria et ut singuli fratres habentes statum in studiis . . . notabilem etiam habeant librarium." For other discussions, see Humphreys, *Book Provisions*, 84; Walsh, *RF*, 426. A less polemical acknowledgment of the size and richness of the mendicant libraries was given by Richard de Bury, *Philobiblion*, ed. E. C. Thomas (London, 1888), 203. In addition see Richard H. and Mary A. Rouse, "The *Registrum Anglie*: the Franciscan 'union catalogue' of British libraries," in *Manuscripts at Oxford: an exhibition in memory of Richard William Hunt*, ed. A. C. de la Mare and B. C. Barker-Benfield (Oxford, 1980), 55–56; the forthcoming edition and study of the *Registrum Anglie*, and "The Franciscans and Books: Lollard Accusations and the Franciscan Response," in *From Ockham to Wyclif*, ed. A. Hudson and M. Wilks (Oxford, 1987), 369–84.

[64] Thomas Fuller, *The History of the University of Cambridge* (Cambridge, 1840); C. H. Cooper, *Annals of Cambridge* (Cambridge, 1842–53); *Documents relating to the University and*

dents largely from East Anglia and the northeastern counties. As it was not as prominent as Oxford, it was slow in attracting the attention of patrons and the endowments that created the productive environments of the Oxford colleges. The bishop of Ely long remained the principal patron and, until the 1340s, Peterhouse, Michaelhouse, King's Hall, and University Hall (Clare) its only colleges. That must be viewed in contrast to the numerous religious houses already there by the 1320s: the convents of the four major mendicant orders, the priory of the Austin Canons at Barnwell, the Gilbertine house of studies (St. Edmund's), and the hostels that provided for Benedictine students. The physical center of the university was the district around the schools and St. Mary's.

Some caution must be used in assessing the two features of medieval Cambridge usually mentioned—namely, the importance of law and of the mendicant orders. In the thirteenth and early fourteenth centuries, theology was the most popular and prominent of the higher faculties, as it was at Oxford. By the end of the century law had displaced it, a shift that takes place earlier at Cambridge than at Oxford. Some of that shift was no doubt stimulated by the preference for law evidenced among the founders or endowers of some of the fourteenth-century colleges, most notably Gonville and Trinity halls. But that in itself was only a reflection of the changing pattern of patronage and preferment in fourteenth-century England, and it was that larger picture that conditioned student interests.

The mendicant presence at Cambridge also needs clarification. Since the mendicant convents at Cambridge were almost as densely populated as those at Oxford, their profile in the smaller university was larger. Yet the orders did not treat their Cambridge convents in the same way. Despite proximity to the center of the university community,

Colleges of Cambridge (London, 1852); J. Heywood, *Early Cambridge University and College Statutes in the English Language* (London, 1855); J. B. Mullinger, *University of Cambridge from the earliest times to the Royal Injunctions of 1535* (Cambridge, 1873); Rashdall, *Univ.* 3: 274–324; *VHC Cambridge and the Isle of Ely*, ed. L. F. Salzman, vol. 2 (London, 1948); J.R.H. Moorman, *The Grey Friars in Cambridge, 1225–1538* (Cambridge, 1952); Alan B. Cobban, *The King's Hall within the University of Cambridge in the Later Middle Ages* (Cambridge, 1969); V. L. Bullough, "The Mediaeval Medical School at Cambridge," *MedStud* 24 (1962): 161–68; M. B. Hackett, *The Original Statutes of Cambridge University* (Cambridge, 1970); T. H. Aston, G. D. Duncan, and T.A.R. Evans, "The Medieval Alumni of the University of Cambridge," *Past and Present* 86 (1980): 9–86.

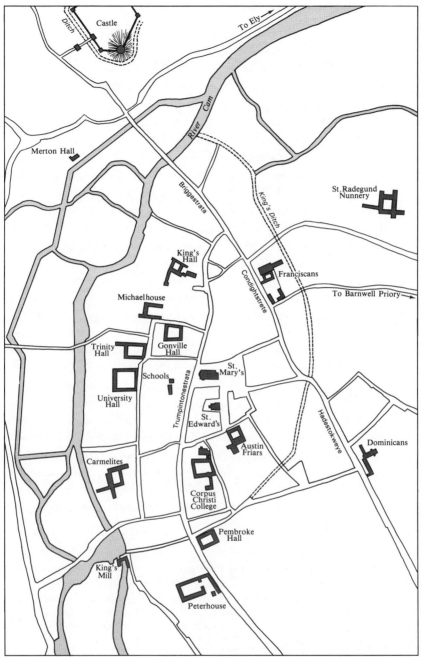

Castle
Ditch
To Ely
River Cam
Merton Hall
Briggestrata
King's Ditch
St. Radegund
Nunnery
King's
Hall
Michaelhouse
Condightstrete
Franciscans
To Barnwell Priory
Trinity
Hall
Gonville
Hall
Schools
St.
Mary's
University
Hall
Trumpintonestrata
St.
Edward's
Haddestokweye
Dominicans
Austin
Friars
Carmelites
Corpus
Christi
College
Pembroke
Hall
King's
Mill
Peterhouse

MAP 2. CAMBRIDGE, *c.* 1340

the Austin Friars made little contribution and do not appear to have sent any of their talented students there. The Carmelites considered their houses in London and Oxford to be far more important, although John Baconthorp apparently taught at Cambridge.[65] The Dominicans treated their Cambridge convent more seriously. Its library was well stocked.[66] Its graduates included Thomas Hopeman, William d'Eyncourt, and Thomas Ringstede. Robert Holcot may have lectured there as regent master.[67] Only the Franciscans, however, made an effort to use their Cambridge convent as a major center of study, probably because they had far more talented young scholars than could be accommodated at the Oxford convent. In the thirteenth and opening years of the fourteenth centuries, the Franciscans placed some of their best Oxford masters in the position of regents at Cambridge—for example, Richard Conington. After 1315 lectors (regent masters) at the Cambridge convent were drawn from various sources: from among those who had taken the baccalaureate at Cambridge (as would appear to be the case with Walter Beaufon, Henry Costesey, Ralph Pigaz, Bartholomew of Reppes, and John Walsham); those who had been bachelors, and perhaps masters, at Oxford (William Chitterne, Robert of Halifax, Adam of Ely, and William Folville); and foreign Franciscans (such as the Italian, John of Casale).[68] The Cambridge Franciscans in the 1320s and 1330s form an impressive group, albeit less distinguished than their Oxford counterparts. If the careers of Halifax, Rosetus, and Ely ever come to be more closely associated with Cambridge, the balance of reputation for the two university convents in the years after 1334 will shift. Yet the fact remains that it was largely through the university peregrinations of mendicant scholars that the channels of communication between Oxford and Cambridge remained most alive. Seculars rarely studied at both universities.[69]

---

[65] Xiberta, SOC, 172.

[66] On Blackfriars library see VCH: Cambridge, 269–76; N. Ker, Medieval Libraries of Great Britain, 2nd ed. (London, 1964), 24; on Greyfriars library see VCH: Cambridge, 276–82; Ker, Medieval Libraries, 23–24. Several of the manuscripts in the Ottoboni collection at the Vatican Library came from these two libraries; the Greyfriars manuscripts include MS. Ottob. lat. 2088 (Ockham, Ordinatio) and MS. Ottob. lat. 2071 (Ockham, Summa logicae).

[67] Smalley, EFA, 203–20.

[68] Moorman, The Grey Friars in Cambridge.

[69] A notable exception was Thomas Cobham, bishop of Worcester (1317–27), who

As the case of Cambridge illustrates, it is hard to discuss the fourteenth-century English universities without treating the religious orders, particularly the mendicants, who had their own tightly organized educational systems, of which the universities were only a part. It is to the schools of the religious orders that we now must turn.

---

earned his M.A. at Paris, his D.Cn.L. at Oxford in 1291, and his D.Th. at Cambridge by 1314, after having begun the study of theology at Oxford. Emden, *BRUO* 1: 450–51.

TWO

THE SCHOOLS OF THE RELIGIOUS ORDERS

⁓⚜⁓

THE EDUCATION of those in religious and monastic orders differed in several respects from that of secular clerics. First, students in orders might study philosophy at their university convents (as well as at their own schools), but they did not determine or reign in arts. Secondly, the Oxford statutes required a longer period of theological study for those who had not taken the arts degree and become *magistri artium*, and this applied primarily to mendicants and monks who, as a rule, took university degrees only in theology and canon law. As was noted in the previous chapter, the requirement of two extra years of graduate study for those who had not reigned in arts was not specifically antimendicant legislation, as is often suggested, since it applied as well to students in civil law and music, faculties in which mendicants normally did not study. It was probably, in origin, a way of establishing parity between M.A.s and non-M.A.s within the higher faculties. Yet, in reality, this burden fell on the mendicants and monks, since they were the vast majority of non-M.A.s. Thirdly, mendicant and monastic students, in contrast to secular clerics, were not individuals whose rate of academic progress was simply a matter of personal choice within the limits imposed by intellectual ability, financial resources, and the requirements and restrictions of the university. The needs of the order and its educational program had to be met and took precedence over personal choice. The mendicant student could, of course, make his desires known, but how he progressed, where he studied, and what he did depended not only on his academic skills but also on the needs and desires of his superiors. For a mendicant even more than a monk, the university functioned as part of the order's program of education; it existed for them, not they for it.[1]

¹ In reconstructing the educational experience of students in religious and monastic or-

The houses of the religious and monastic orders at Oxford and Cambridge, as at Paris, were fully recognized teaching units within the university corporation and theological faculty, once they had achieved a master of their own, either through conversion or inception. Their lectures were primarily for their own members, but outsiders could fulfill degree requirements by attending those lectures and disputations. The success of these religious houses of study is attested to both by the succession of distinguished mendicant bachelors and masters at Paris, Oxford, and Cambridge throughout the thirteenth and fourteenth centuries, and by their influence, as models, on the development of colleges for secular students, particularly in theology. The corporate structure and resources of the mendicant convents held some distinct advantages for their members over the life of the unaffiliated student: material needs were supplied (room and board); there was adequate space for study away from the noise and distractions of daily life on the streets; easy access to textbooks and a reference library; in-house instruction and tutorial; and influence in dealing with the power structures inside and outside the university.

The needs of each order led to the development of a variety of educational programs. The order needed Mass priests, who could chant and recite Latin properly. They needed educated preachers and confessors. They needed teachers of philosophy and theology at several levels of schools, from regional and provincial *studia* up to the universities of Paris, Oxford, and Cambridge. Instead of staffing each level with those who could not or would not progress higher, each order set specific educational requirements for the various religious or instructional tasks. Mass priests needed proper singing and pronunciation of Latin. Those who would preach and hear confession needed training in

---

ders, one must, in addition to university statutes, utilize the legislation of the order and whatever biographical information exists. For all types of evidence one must keep in mind that practices and requirements did not remain static. What the university and order required in the thirteenth century might be (and often was) considerably modified by the fifteenth. The fourteenth century was, in this regard as in so many others, a period of transition. On the religious orders at Oxford see M. W. Sheehan's chapter in *HUO* 1: 193–223. On the educational system of the mendicants outside England (in addition to items in subsequent notes) see: *Le scuole degli ordini mendicanti* (Todi, 1978); F. Lickteig, *The German Carmelites at the Medieval Universities*, Ph.D. diss., Catholic University of America, Washington, D.C., 1977.

grammar, philosophy, and moral theology. Those who would teach philosophy or theology needed a minimum number of years of instruction in those disciplines.

In addition to fitting education to job requirements, the teaching needs within an order often took precedence over the university program. This meant that the order often could not wait until those seeking a doctorate had attained it before becoming teachers. Both those who sought the highest university degrees as well as those who would teach at the provincial level were generally "borrowed" for a year or more between the end of their time as auditors in theology and the beginning of their baccalaureates in order to teach in the schools of the order. Among the Franciscans this lasted only a year or two; among the Austin Friars it might last for three or four years, or even longer.

The following descriptions apply only to those students in orders who received their education on English soil, but these were the vast majority of English students in the fourteenth century. The programs at Paris or in Italy were not identical with those at Oxford or Cambridge. Since most mendicants studied theology rather than canon law and took their highest degrees at Oxford, only the course of studies in theology at Oxford will be examined.

THE COURSE OF STUDY

The regulations and customs of the Oxford theological faculty governing students without M.A.s applied equally to all students in religious and monastic orders, regardless of individual differences among the academic programs of various orders.[2] Since these students (with a few exceptions) had not taken the arts degree at a university, they were required to do a longer period of theological study before being admitted to opponency. This period as auditors lasted six years, during which time they heard lectures on the Bible and the *Sentences*. Not all of that

---

[2] For the statutes on which this description is based, see: *Statuta Oxon*, cix, n. 1, 48–49, 78, and 178; Rashdall, *Univ.* 3: 158–59; A. G. Little, *The Grey Friars in Oxford* (Oxford, 1892), 44–45; Little, "The Franciscan School at Oxford in the Thirteenth Century," *AFH* 19 (1926): 825. It is interesting to note that the Oxford requirements favored secular scholars, while requirements at Paris favored those in religious orders. The latter group had a longer course of study at Oxford than did the seculars, while at Paris they could complete requirements in a shorter period of time.

time, however, need be spent in residence at Oxford. As long as these studies were under the direction of a master of theology, they could be done at a provincial school of theology as well as at a university. Only one year of Oxford residence was required before opponency.

With *admissio ad opponendum et respondendum* the academic career of a regular (i.e., in orders) probably differed little from that of his secular counterpart. At the beginning of the fourteenth century he spent three years in further studies and took part in disputations. The first two years he "opposed," and in the third he "responded."[3] After completing nine years of theological study he could be admitted to read the *Sentences* (*admissio ad lecturam libri Sententiarum*), which, as we have seen, usually took one year. Before being permitted to read the *Sentences*, a candidate had to petition the congregation of regent masters for a grace, dispensing him from the 1253 statute requiring the arts degree of anyone intending to become a bachelor of theology. After the settlement in 1314 of a dispute between the Dominicans and the university, granting these exemptions became automatic as long as the candidate had spent eight full years in the study of philosophy, either at a university or in one of the schools of his order, and nine years of theological study.

In the opening lecture (*principium*) to each book of the *Sentences*, the bachelor engaged his fellow *baccalaurei* in debate, challenging their arguments and conclusions. References to these bachelor colleagues (*socii*) in fourteenth-century manuscripts show that those in orders were primarily concerned with the opinions of their religious *socii*, although the occasional mention of a secular bachelor by a religious or a religious bachelor by a secular reveals that these principial confrontations were not restricted to one group or the other.[4] Moreover, despite university legislation, the religious *sententiarii* by the 1320s were challenging the views of their contemporaries, by name, throughout their commentar-

---

[3] *MunAcad* 2: 389. For text, see ch. 1, n. 49.

[4] Among his *socii* at Oxford Adam Wodeham, O.F.M., mentioned William Skelton of Merton College and Richard Radford, probably of University College. Richard Kilvington of Oriel College mentioned his Benedictine *socius*. See Courtenay, *Adam Wodeham* (Leiden, 1978), 86–111. Similar exchanges among mendicants and seculars at Paris can be seen in the commentaries of the Augustinians Gregory of Rimini, Alphonsus Vargas of Toledo, and Hugolino of Orvieto; see D. Trapp, "Augustinian Theology of the 14th Century," *Augustiniana* 6 (1956): 266–67.

ies, and even challenging the opinions of regent masters.[5] The topic of
the principial debates seems to have been set by the faculty of theology,
and the order in which the candidates read, debated, and responded
was established by custom.

Reading the *Sentences* was followed by biblical lectures as *baccalaureus
biblicus*, usually for one academic term, and then a year or two as *baccalaureus formatus*. Finally, after opposing in the school of each regent
master of theology, holding his "vespers," and receiving his license, the
candidate could incept as a *magister theologiae*. Two years of regency
(*magister in actu regens*) were required, but that office might run longer
or possibly shorter. For orders that had few candidates for the doctorate, each regent master had to remain at the university until a new
master was promoted. For orders, such as the Franciscans, that in the
fourteenth century promoted a candidate for inception almost annually, a regent master would sit in congregation only in the first year
of regency. In such cases it is unclear whether in the second year he remained regent, overlapping with the new regent master, or whether he
became *magister non regens*.

The course of theological studies for "regulars," therefore, took a
minimum of ten years (to become a formed bachelor) or twelve years (to
become a master of theology). In many cases, because of additional requirements of the orders, the theological curriculum leading to a doctorate took several years longer. Leadership within the university convents was based on seniority and rank. The top administrative official
who would represent the convent in civil and legal matters was the prior
or guardian. Second in command was the lector or regent master in theology, followed by the *magister studentium* (for those orders that had that
office), appointed from among the formed bachelors.

University requirements applied only to those "regulars" who sought
university degrees. Not all students sent by the orders to the university
convents for education were expected to take degrees; in fact the majority were there simply for instruction, not credentials. On the other
hand, those chosen by their orders for promotion to the baccalaureate
and doctorate not only had to conform to university requirements but

[5] A Benedictine bachelor, Robert Graystanes, was one of the first to do this at Oxford
(Westminster Abbey, MS. 13). It is also clear in the *Sentences* commentaries of Holcot,
Wodeham, and Kilvington.

to those of the order as well. Despite many similarities, each order had its own educational system that differed from the others in geographical organization, nomenclature, and even requirements and practices. It is these differences that gave to education in each order a special character all its own.

DOMINICANS

Of all the mendicant orders, only the Dominicans began with a solid commitment to education.[6] Every priory was required to have a lector who could provide instruction in theology for those preparing for preaching, hearing confessions, pastoral care, and evangelism. The common life was relaxed to allow every student a cell for study, and a library, meager at first but larger by the fourteenth century, was usually located at the end of the dormitory. It was out of this foundation of education at a local priory that the educational system of the order developed.

That system was a multitiered, pyramidal structure ascending from local priories, through provincial schools of logic, natural science, and theology, to the universities. The English province of the Dominicans was divided into subdivisions known as "visitations" or "nations." In the fourteenth century these were four: Oxford, Cambridge, London, and York. Visitations, in turn, were further subdivided into vicariates composed of a number of priories. Only at the highest and lowest levels of Dominican schools, that is, at the *studium generale theologiae* and the priory, was the same type of teaching done in the same place. In between, education was diversified, spread out among convents that

---

[6] This account is based on C.F.A. Palmer, "The Friar Preachers, or Black Friars, of King's Langley," *The Reliquary* 19 (1878): 37–218; Little, "Educational Organisation of the Mendicant Friars in England (Dominicans and Franciscans)," *TRHS* N.S. 8 (1894): 49–70; Little in *VCH: Oxfordshire*, vol. 2 (London, 1907), 107–22; Bede Jarrett, *The English Dominicans* (London, 1921); William A. Hinnebusch, *The History of the Dominican Order*, vol. 2 (New York, 1973), 1–98; M. O'Carroll, "The Educational Organisation of the Dominicans in England and Wales 1221–1348: A Multidisciplinary Approach," *AFP* 50 (1980): 23–62. For the basic education of the majority of Dominicans who did not go to the *studia particularia et generalia*, see L. Boyle, "Notes on the Education of the *Fratres communes* in the Dominican Order in the Thirteenth Century," *Xenia Medii Aevi Historiam Illustrantia oblata Thomae Kaeppeli O.P.* (Rome, 1978), 249–67, reprinted in Boyle, *Pastoral Care, Clerical Education and Canon Law, 1200–1400* (London, 1981).

taught different disciplines on a rotating basis. The system was complex. A group of priories that pooled their resources to maintain a school of logic (*studium artium*) held in a different priory of the group every year or two need not be the same group that pooled their resources to maintain a school of science, or natural philosophy (*studium naturalium*). Even the lesser schools of theology were probably operated on such a rotating basis.[7] None of these schools was a separate institution but operated within an existing priory, which took its turn with the expense and responsibility of educating students from other priories. The geographical location of Dominican schools, therefore, poses some problems for the historian.

Within this fluid educational system in which the levels between priory and university had no fixed geographical location from year to year, the Dominican student progressed from one subject to the next. His first studies were in the old and new logic, which he acquired in a *studium artium* of the order. Here he remained from two to three years, acquiring a training similar to that gained at the university. He attended lectures, disputations, and repetitions. At the larger schools he would have been under the direction of a lector (who at the very least had studied natural philosophy as well as logic) and a master of students, who was in charge of *repetitiones*. From the *studium artium* he moved on to a *studium naturalium*, where he studied the scientific works of Aristotle and probably received an introduction to the *Metaphysics* and *Ethics* as well. There were probably fewer schools of natural philosophy than of logic in each province, perhaps one or two for each visitation. The young friar would remain at a *studium naturalium* for two or three years.

The order selected the most promising students from the *studia naturalium* for advancement to the study of theology. Few Dominicans

---

[7] By the fourteenth century some of the Dominican provinces designated two of the larger priories as permanent *studia particularia theologiae*. If such was the practice in the English province, these convents would have been London and probably Norwich. However, there is evidence that the *studia theologiae* were not geographically fixed but rotated, as did the *studia artium* and the *studia naturalium*. In the Cambridge visitation there seems to have been a *studium particulare theologiae* at Thetford in 1395, at Ipswich in 1397, and at Norwich in 1398. Similarly for the York visitation, there was one at Lincoln in 1390 and Newcastle-on-Tyne in 1397; and for the London visitation at Guildford and London, both in the same year: 1397. See Little, "Educational Organisation," 54, 60. O'Carroll, "Educational Organisation," 29–31, is of the opinion that the schools of theology rotated far less than those of arts.

went directly to the university convents of Oxford and Cambridge for their theological training. By 1305 it was the practice to require a minimum of two years attending lectures on the Bible and the *Sentences* at a *studium particulare theologiae* (also known as a *studium solemne*). These provincial theological schools were probably not geographically fixed but rotated among the larger convents. The London convent, however, regularly offered theological training in the fourteenth century. Because of the number of foreign Dominicans who came to London for theological study, the London convent was an unofficial *studium generale*. The lectors at the *studia particularia* often were masters who had completed their regency at a university. But a doctorate was not a requirement. As early as 1257 the master general received from the papacy the right to appoint qualified friars as lectors in the *studia particularia theologiae*. It was expected that such lectors would at least have studied theology for a number of years at a university.

Each visitation had the privilege of sending annually one student to Oxford and one to Cambridge. Moreover, after 1326 all provinces had the right to send two friars to any *studium generale* outside the province. This policy brought far more foreign Dominicans to England than it exported English friars to the Continent. The English province occasionally sent Dominicans to Paris, Cologne, or Bologna, but they rarely if ever completed their studies there.[8] No English Dominican ever occupied the Dominican non-French chair of theology at Paris, although some studied at Paris, as did William Macclesfield.[9] Nicholas Trevet lectured at St. Jacques (1307–14) after having been regent in theology at Oxford.

Of the two English universities, Oxford was the more prestigious. In fact, until the second decade of the fourteenth century, it was the only "official" *studium generale* for the Dominicans in England. Some ninety friars were resident in the Oxford convent in 1317, while that number

---

[8] English masters of theology were often appointed lectors at the Dominican house of studies at Bologna in the early fourteenth century; see B. Smalley, *EFA*, 76, whose information was derived from T. Kaeppeli; W. J. Courtenay, "The Early Stages in the Introduction of Oxford Logic into Italy," in *ELI*, 13–32. To the English Dominicans at Bologna given in that article, the name of Richard Winkley, lector at Bologna in 1331 should be added.

[9] Emden, *BRUO* 2: 1200–01; Roensch, *ETS*, 51–57, 218–23.

had dropped to seventy in 1377.[10] The actual selection of students sent to Oxford or Cambridge was made by the provincial and the provincial chapter, probably at the recommendation of the lector and master of students at the provincial schools of theology, and with the approval of the master general of the order. In addition to good moral character, those selected had to have completed their training in logic and philosophy and to have spent two years in a provincial school of theology attending lectures on the *Sentences*, the Bible, and various treatises of Thomas Aquinas.

Blackfriars at Oxford was located outside the southwestern edge of the city, near the Franciscan convent, between the Trill Mill stream and the River Thames at Folly Bridge (see map 1). Dominicans coming from the convent to the schools would have crossed Preacher's Bridge and passed the entrance to Greyfriars on Littlegate Street.

Most students sent to the university were not expected to take degrees but only to study for a year or two before returning to teach in one of the provincial schools of natural philosophy or theology. A smaller elite group was chosen to advance to the baccalaureate and the doctorate. After 1320 the appointment to read the *Sentences* or incept as master at Paris, Oxford, or Cambridge was made by the general chapter upon the recommendation of the masters and bachelors actually in residence at the university convents. Candidates for these honors were chosen from among the students at the university, from those teaching in *studia particularia*, or, in the case of the doctorate, from among formed bachelors. No one was promoted to bachelor of theology unless, in addition to the requirements for entry to the university convent, he had already completed at least one year of study at a *studium generale*. Even for those who were slated to attain the highest degree, university studies were interrupted by a year or two as *sententiarius* and *magister studentium* at a *studium particulare*.

The various offices at the university convent paralleled the structure of the *studium particulare*. Lectures on the *Sentences* were given by a bachelor, known as *Cursor sententiarum*. It may have been usual for English Dominicans, at least in the first half of the fourteenth century, to complete the reading of the *Sentences* over a two-year period, as did Robert Holcot. When qualified candidates were available, one bachelor began

[10] Little, "The Franciscan School," 820.

reading each year, overlapping with the previous bachelor, who would be undertaking his second year. Ideally one bachelor from each visitation was put forward in turn over a four-year period. It was a point of irritation to Holcot (from the Oxford visitation), reading between 1329 and 1333, that Crathorn (from the York visitation) was permitted to complete his reading of the *Sentences* in one year (1330–31).[11] The biblical lectures required of the bachelor were often fulfilled in summer term, after the completion of the *Sentences*. From *sententiarius* and *biblicus* the friar advanced to the rank of master of students (*magister studentium*), a position found in the mendicant *studia generalia* and *particularia*, with the apparent exception of the Franciscans. The principal tasks of the *magister studentium* were to oversee the work of junior colleagues and to give lectures on logical, natural, and moral philosophy, which in the case of the Dominicans often meant lectures on the philosophical works of Thomas Aquinas.

After a dispute in the opening years of the fourteenth century between the order and the university, Dominicans were allowed to hold the vesper disputation of an incepting master at Blackfriars. As regent master, the *lector principalis* lectured on the Bible, officiated at various debates, and represented the convent at academic functions. Unlike his junior colleagues at the convent, the lector was permitted to work behind closed doors and to be assisted in his work by a fellow friar. In this respect the Dominican system was less lenient than the Franciscan, which permitted the bachelor as well to have the help of a *socius* in the preparation of his lectures.

Because of the Dominican system of diversification and rotation, they had few centers that possessed continuity of education. One convent that did was Oxford, which was simultaneously a *studium artium*, a *studium naturalium*, and a *studium theologiae*. It was followed in importance by Cambridge, London, and York. King's Langley (Langley Regis) near

---

[11] The currently accepted dates for the terms as *sententiarius* of Holcot and Crathorn are given in H. Schepers, "Holkot contra dicta Crathorn," *PhilJahr* 77 (1970): 320–54; Courtenay, *Adam Wodeham*, 95–109. The recent discoveries of Joseph Wey and Hester Gelber may, however, revise that dating by placing Holcot's reading in 1331–33 and identifying a second Dominican opponent, John Grafton, who attacked Holcot (and Wodeham?) in his opening lecture on the Bible and who may have read in 1332–33. The one-year readings of Crathorn and Grafton suggests that Holcot's two-year reading may not have been normal practice.

St. Albans was a regular *studium artium* and *studium naturalium* for all visitations in preparation for Oxford. Founded on royal lands by Edward II in 1307, the Dominican priory at Langley was a steady recipient of royal gifts, and by the end of Edward's reign had over one hundred friars. Similarly, Northampton was a semipermanent *studium*. In 1258 Henry III made a gift of timber for the construction of study cells, and Robert Holcot, who was from a village near Northampton, returned there to teach toward the end of his life, probably as prior of the convent. Finally, the convents at Norwich, Exeter, Lincoln, and Newcastle functioned as important *studia* from time to time.

Throughout the thirteenth century English Dominicans were as intellectually active as the Franciscans, but that comparability was lost by the second decade of the fourteenth century. After Nicholas Trevet, the Dominicans were to be distinguished only by a handful of writers: Robert Holcot, William Crathorn, William Jordan, and John Acton. That small number has to be viewed over against the impressive number of English Franciscans who, in the first half of the fourteenth century, constituted the single most active intellectual unit at either Oxford or Cambridge.

FRANCISCANS

The early association of the Dominican order with education and the emerging universities should not blind us to the fact that as far as England is concerned the Franciscans rivaled the Dominicans in establishing convents in towns that were or soon became places of study. The Franciscans settled at Oxford and York only three years after the Dominicans. They arrived almost simultaneously in London, Norwich, and Bristol. And they preceded the Dominicans in establishing convents at Canterbury (1224), Northampton (1225), Cambridge (1226; twelve years before the arrival of the Dominicans), Worcester (1227), Hereford (1228), Stamford (1230), Lincoln (1230), Salisbury (1230), and Newcastle (1237).

The Franciscan educational system in England was established by the fourth provincial minister, Friar William of Nottingham, in the 1240s.[12]

---

[12] On Franciscan education see: Little, "Educational Organisation"; Little in *VCH: Oxfordshire* 2: 122–37; M. Brlek, *De Evolutione Iuridica Studiorum in Ordine Minorum* (Dubrov-

In structure it resembled the Dominican system, but it had a number of individual characteristics and differences. By mid-thirteenth century the Franciscans had established schools at Oxford, Cambridge, London, Canterbury (for the Benedictines at the cathedral), Hereford, Leicester, Bristol, Norwich, and Northampton. Eight years of philosophical training in logic, natural philosophy, moral philosophy, and metaphysics were acquired at a local convent or, more commonly, at one of the provincial schools. The number and location of these schools of arts and philosophy is not known. As a rule the Franciscans did not separate these lower *studia* from the provincial schools of theology. London, for example, provided training in the arts, philosophy, and theology. This may have been true of the other *studia particularia* as well.

By the second quarter of the fourteenth century the Franciscans had a *studium secundae speciei* for each of their seven custodies, as the subdivisions of the province were known. These schools were London (for the London custody), Norwich (for the Cambridge custody), Stamford (for the Oxford custody), Exeter (for the Bristol custody), Coventry (for the Worcester custody), York (for the York custody), and Newcastle (for the Newcastle custody). The custodial schools of the Franciscans held a place of importance only slightly less than that of the university convents. The full range of scholastic exercises were offered, and some of the most talented Franciscans in the first half of the fourteenth century wrote major works in that environment. The custodial school of London could claim the most impressive list of names: William of Ockham, Walter Chatton, Adam Wodeham, but Norwich at various times had Wodeham, Ralph Pigaz, and Haverel. If the *studia particularia* of the other mendicant orders had their share of comparable talent, the surviving evidence does not reveal it, save for the Augustinians at York. Perhaps the continuity of tradition created by geographically fixed schools, in combination with the Franciscan practice of placing their best scholars in those schools before, after, and sometimes during their university teaching, gave the custodial schools a prominence the *studia particularia* of the Dominicans do not appear to have had.

Upon completion of his philosophical studies, usually around age twenty-three, a friar might be chosen for theological studies. The early

---

nik, 1942); Little, *Grey Friars*; Little, "Franciscan School," 803–74; Courtenay, *Adam Wodeham*, 45–53.

stages of this training were often continued at the provincial school for the custody in which the friar's convent was located. Or he might be placed directly in a university convent. Unlike the Dominicans, who had their English students promoted to the *magisterium* in England (the converted secular theologian, John of St. Giles, was the first and last English Dominican to be regent at Paris), the Franciscan order until the early fourteenth century sent several of its best students to Paris for the baccalaureate and regency in theology. As shall be examined in more detail in chapter 5, that practice changed by the second decade of the century, and Oxford and Cambridge became the appropriate destination of English Franciscan scholars.

By the second quarter of the fourteenth century those who aspired to advanced degrees in theology had to deliver lectures on the *Sentences* at a custodial school before being permitted to read the *Sentences* at a *studium generale*. Most Franciscan *Sentences* commentaries after 1310 were delivered in a first-draft form before they were read at Paris or Oxford. This ensured that university lectures and the published work that grew out of them would be of superior quality.

The Franciscan convent at Oxford occupied two sites by the middle of the thirteenth century (see map, page 22). Both properties were on the southwest side of the town, near Blackfriars. The older property was situated just inside the walls, in the parish of St. Ebbe. It housed the schools, where lectures and disputations were held, perhaps a *scriptorium*, which prepared copies of the works of bachelors and masters,[13] and probably the library of the Franciscans, the richest in Oxford. The other and larger property lay outside the walls, near the Thames. Most of the student friars lived at this second site, which, in addition to the larger dormitory facilities, had cloisters, chapel, and refectory. The two dates for which we can calculate the number of Franciscans in residence at Oxford, namely 1317 and 1377, show the convent population to be 84 and 103, respectively.[14] The presence in the early 1230s of Robert Grosseteste, a secular cleric and the most renowned Oxford scholar of that day, as principal lector at Greyfriars, and the eventual gift of much

---

[13] Little was of the opinion (*Grey Friars*, 56) that there was probably not a room set aside as a *scriptorium*. Considering the size of Franciscan book production and Wodeham's reference to his consultations with his *scriptor* within the walls of Oxford (*Adam Wodeham*, 179–80), there must have been some such facility.

[14] Little, "Franciscan School," 820.

of his library to the Oxford convent, gave the Franciscans a competitive edge over the other mendicant orders which they maintained until the third quarter of the fourteenth century.

The last three or four years of theological training were spent lecturing and disputing at the university. By the fourteenth century it was the practice among Franciscans at Oxford to limit the reading of the *Sentences* to one academic year, although a biennial reading was possible. After the *Sentences* the candidate remained at the university for two more years, lecturing on the Bible and taking part in disputations. After completing twelve or thirteen years of theological study in this way, the friar had fulfilled the requirements for licensing and inception. Promotion to the doctorate was not automatic. Appointment to the Oxford or Cambridge convents as *lector principalis* was made by the provincial chapter or the *curia* of the minister general, usually at the request of those at the Oxford and Cambridge convents. In the fourteenth century Franciscan masters held the post of regent master only for a year or two.

In the first half of the fourteenth century the Franciscans were the single most productive and visible group within the theological faculty at Oxford. They had twice the number of known authors as the Dominicans and three or four times the number of distinguished theologians. Yet if the number of Franciscans in residence at Oxford had increased by 1377 (as suggested by the distribution of the king's pittance in that year), the quality of scholarship after 1350 had declined disastrously. In contrast to the Dominicans, whose numbers appear relatively stable throughout the fourteenth century, the number of *known* Greyfriars at Oxford, as reflected in Emden's register, dropped 55 percent in the second half of the century, and the number of known authors was also cut in half. The results of this sharp contrast will be discussed in subsequent chapters.

CARMELITES

The Carmelites, or Whitefriars, came into existence as a mendicant order in the mid-thirteenth century and arrived in England about two decades after the Dominicans and Franciscans. Within a few years of their arrival (1242), their rule was revised at Aylesford in Kent, and a number of foundations were made almost immediately afterward.[15]

The location of Carmelite convents in England was dictated not only by the previous presence of the Dominicans and Franciscans; they specifically chose places where the *educational* efforts of the other mendicants were already well established. Thus they founded houses at London (1247), Cambridge (1247), York (1253), Oxford (1256), Bristol (1256), and Norwich (1256). They did not, however, immediately create an educational system. Some teaching probably went on in these convents, especially through contact with the other mendicant orders, but there was no attempt to take a direct part in the universities of Oxford or Cambridge.

At the general chapter in London in 1281 a plan of studies was created for the order. Schools for instruction in grammar, logic, natural philosophy, and theology were to be available in the four "distinctions" (the Carmelite subdivisions of the province): London, Oxford, Norwich, and York. Although the Oxford convent formed one of the most important parts of the educational program, it was never a *studium generale* for the Carmelites because it was not generally open to Carmelites from other provinces. Instead, London was designated in 1294 as the *studium generale* for the English Carmelites.

Although we know little about the *studia artium* and *studia naturalium* among the Carmelites, their system by the early fourteenth century probably resembled that of the Dominicans and Franciscans. The highest places in the system belonged to the convents of Oxford, Cambridge, and London. There were probably also *studia particularia* at Norwich, York, Winchester, Coventry, and possibly Northampton. Both the London and Oxford convents were *studia philosophiae* as well as *studia theologiae*.

The London convent was located outside the walls of the city, in the western suburb that housed a number of large palaces and episcopal residences. It was a large piece of property between the river and Fleet Street. As was true of the Oxford convent, located on the west side of

---

[15] Little in *VCH: Oxfordshire* 2: 137–43; Lickteig, *The German Carmelites*; Margaret E. Poskitt, "The English Carmelite province: 15th Century," *The Aylesford Review* 1 (1956): 98–102; "The English Carmelites: Houses of Study and Educational Methods," *The Aylesford Review* 5 (1963): 226–37. I am grateful to Bruce Flood for calling Poskitt's work to my attention. On the Carmelite scholastic authors in general, see Xiberta, *SOC*.

Oxford in the Beaumont palace, given to the order by the king, the London property housed secular students and occasionally wealthy donors as well as friars. The London convent was probably the larger of the two. The figures for 1317 and 1377 suggest that Oxford White Friars was little more than half the size of the Dominican or Franciscan Oxford convents.[16] Though smaller, those numbers appear to have remained stable across the century, and they include many more known authors than do the figures for the Dominicans.

Carmelite convents that had *studia* were under the direction of a prior, but those in charge of instruction had a certain degree of independence. In order of authority these were the regent master or, in the case of the *studia particularia*, the principal lector, the master of students, and the bachelors who gave lectures on the *Sentences* and the Bible. The prior appointed a *socius* to care for the needs of the master and bachelors.

The course of studies for those proceeding to the highest university degrees was the same as for the other orders: eight years of arts, eight years as a student of theology before reading the *Sentences* at a *studium* (*particulare?*), followed by one or two years as *Sententiarius* (*lector principalis*) at a *studium generale*.[17] A minimum of one year at the level of formed bachelor was required before inception.

Lecturers (bachelors) on the Bible and *Sentences* at Oxford, Cambridge, and London were appointed by the English provincial chapter. Since only one candidate could be put forward each year in any of these *studia*, the opportunity to lecture rotated among the four "distinctions." A formal, opening lecture (*principium*) was required annually of the regent master (for his lectures on the Bible) and the master of students (for his lectures on natural and moral philosophy) as well as the bachelors, who were to engage their fellow *socii* in debate.

In contrast to Dominicans and Franciscans, the Carmelites came late to education and to the universities. They produced their first masters of theology only at the end of the thirteenth century, and their best students in the early fourteenth century were sent to the Paris *studium generale*, despite the fact that the English province played a role of leader-

---

[16] Little, "Franciscan School," 820.

[17] At the General Chapter of 1336 a two-year reading was required of all Carmelite bachelors; see Little, "Franciscan School," 826.

ship in the order. Gerard of Bologna, Guy of Terrena, John Baconthorp, Paul of Perugia, Michael Aiguani, and John Brammart were all primarily associated with the University of Paris. The English *studia*, however, did become prominent in the fourteenth century. The London convent attracted a large group of foreign students throughout the century, as it was one of the few *studia generalia* of the order, although Oxford was intellectually more important. John Baconthorp taught there as well as at Paris. Robert Walsingham, in the years from 1310 to 1320 was widely influential on such thinkers as Henry of Harclay, John Baconthorp, Robert Graystanes, Luke of Ely, and others. And in the middle years of the fourteenth century the *Sentences* commentary of Osbert Pickingham attracted attention both in England and on the Continent.

AUSTIN FRIARS

The Hermits Friars of the order of St. Augustine, known in England as the Austin Friars, developed an educational system similar to the other mendicant orders.[18] Unlike the Franciscans, the Austin Friars were not overly disturbed or split by the issue of corporate poverty, but their later founding and their adherence to a monastic, eremitical ideal delayed their growth and their adoption of what came to be the two cardinal features of thirteenth-century mendicancy: an active life of preaching, teaching, and pastoral care in urban centers; and intellectual preeminence in the growing universities. This latter goal was achieved at Paris earlier than at Oxford, but by the early fourteenth century the educational system of the Austin Friars in England had taken form.

The English province, which included England, Scotland, and Ireland, was subdivided into five districts, known among the Austin Friars as "limits." These were Cambridge (primarily East Anglia), Oxford (which included London and the whole south and west country of Eng-

---

[18] The following account is derived from Little in *VCH: Oxfordshire* 2: 143–48; Roth, *EAF* 1: 18–95, 136–77; it has been supplemented and in some cases corrected through Eelcko Ypma, *La formation des professeurs chez les Ermites de Saint-Augustine de 1256 à 1354* (Paris, 1956); Ypma, "Les 'Cursores' chez les Augustins," *RTAM* 26 (1959): 137–44; Ypma, "La promotion au lectorat chez les Augustins et le 'De lectorie gradu' d'Ambroise de Cora," *Augustiniana* 13 (1963): 391–417.

land), Lincoln (for the Midlands and Wales), York (for northern England), and Ireland. There were no houses in Scotland until the sixteenth century.

As with the other mendicant orders who espoused the ideal of enlisting only from among those who had attained the age of fourteen, young friars were expected to have already completed their primary and secondary education. Where younger or deficient candidates were recruited, remedial education in grammar was probably administered in the local convent. Separate grammar schools for grammar and logic may have existed among the Augustinians on the Continent but apparently not in England. As a rule, each recruit entered the convent nearest his place of birth and there undertook a year's novitiate, during which time other studies were discouraged.

Those who were being prepared for preaching, hearing confessions, teaching, and/or high administrative office would, after the novitiate, continue their studies at a higher school within the order. It would appear that each limit maintained a *studium particulare* for the study of philosophy, which was to parallel or substitute for the training in the arts faculty at the university. The convent at Leicester housed the *studium particulare* for the limit of Lincoln, Bristol for the limit of Oxford, and Norwich for the limit of Cambridge. No mention is made of one for the York limit, but considering the quality and nature of the York library, the York convent was probably both a *studium particulare* in philosophy and a *studium concursorium* in theology. By the end of the fourteenth century and probably earlier, it was also possible to study philosophy at the *studia generalia* and even at the Oxford and Cambridge convents. The young Austin Friars who studied philosophy at one of the *studia particularia* seldom came in contact with fellow students in the other mendicant orders. Although the Franciscans had some teaching in their convents in Leicester and Bristol in the thirteenth century (and perhaps in the fourteenth century as well), only in Norwich and possibly in York did a *studium particulare* of the Austin Friars exist side by side with a custodial school of the Franciscans.

The time spent in the study of philosophy probably varied with each student. Three years was the minimum time for the study of philosophy at a *studium particulare*, although it could last five or six years. For those whose philosophical training had to be equivalent to the university arts program, a total of eight years of study was required. Philosophy entailed two separate courses, one in the old and new logic and one in natural philosophy. If both courses were not available in one *studium particulare*, the student might have to study in two separate schools or complete his philosophical training at a *studium generale*. In order to teach philosophy it was necessary to have studied it for five years.

The content of the philosophical training for the Austin Friars probably differed from the other mendicant orders only in the commentaries that were used to interpret the basic textbooks. The interpretive guides among the Austins were the commentaries of Giles of Rome and, later, of Gerard of Siena, Thomas of Strasbourg, and Paul of Venice.

After the philosophical training, those who were being prepared for preaching, confession, or higher study would undertake the study of theology for a period of a year or more, depending on their goal. One or more years of theological training were necessary in order to teach philosophy or undertake the type of pastoral care that entailed preaching and hearing confession. Generally speaking, only those intending to complete their theological training in order to teach theology or to improve their eligibility for high office would be sent to the university theological program.

In fourteenth-century England the Austin Friars could study theology in three different types of *studia generalia*. The principal schools were the two *studia generalia ordinis*: Oxford and Cambridge. These were under the direction of the prior general of the order and open to students from all provinces. In the course of the fourteenth century the Augustinians sent a number of Italian, German, and east European students to England for theological study. In addition to the university programs in theology there were for a time *studia generalia concursoria* at York and Lincoln that prepared students in theology who did not necessarily aspire to the highest university degrees. Finally, there were at least three *studia generalia provinciae*, under the direction of the prior provincial, that provided work in theology. The provincial theological school in the Cambridge limit was located at Lynn, in the Lincoln limit at Stamford, and in the Oxford limit at London. Here proximity to other mendicant theological schools was greater.

The theological program of the Austin Friars was lengthy and complex. It began with five years of study on the Bible and the *Sentences*, one or more years of which were done in a *studium generale provinciae* or *con-*

cursorium before the student was admitted to a university convent. Moreover, students were expected to remain at a university three years (with extensions up to five). These early years of theological study culminated in the lectorate (*lectoratus*), a "degree" administered by the order qualifying one to teach philosophy or theology in any school of the order to which one might be appointed, with the exception of the universities (*studia generalia ordinis*), which had their own separate requirements. It was not a university degree and did not necessarily lead directly to the baccalaureate. But for an Austin Friar it was a high point in his academic career, and the examination for lector was rigorous and lengthy.

In the thirteenth century admission to the lectorate was based only on the necessary years of study, a thorough examination of the knowledge acquired, and a demonstration of that knowledge by disputation. In the fourteenth, however, a period of teaching was introduced to ensure that the candidate had mastered the skills of textual analysis and communication as well as debate technique. Perhaps unfortunate experiences had encouraged them to test book knowledge in the classroom before accrediting candidates. This period of student teaching, known as the *cursoratus*, was probably done in the lesser schools of the order, not at the universities. The candidate remained a *cursor* for a year, lecturing on the "old logic" and natural philosophy, awaiting his promotion to the lectorate. Gradually this period of student teaching was extended. By 1497 one was expected to have studied theology four years before promotion to the *cursoratus* and to remain cursor for an additional three years before promotion to the lectorate, making the latter contingent upon seven years of study. All of this probably had little to do with the university program. The five years of study originally necessary to become a lector in the order could be counted toward the six years necessary before being admitted to opponency in the university.[19]

[19] It is well to keep in mind that the terms *cursor* and *lector* have different meanings in different contexts. The title *cursor* as used among the Austins should not be confused with the rank or function of the secular *baccalaureus biblicus* at Paris, who was also known as *cursor* because he read (lectured on) the Bible *cursorie* rather than *ordinarie* (the form of magisterial lectures on the Bible). Among the mendicants at Paris those with a baccalaureate in the Bible were known as *biblici*, and the *cursores* among the Austins were students *cum* philosophy lecturers who had not yet attained the lectorate or the baccalaureate. Similarly, *lector* (lecturer) could apply to anyone who lectured. Used in the strict sense among the Aus-

The Augustinian student had some advantages over his counterpart in the other mendicant orders at Oxford. Upon entering the university convent as a student he was assigned a private cell in the dormitory, with bed, table, and chair—an advantage that other mendicants achieved only on entering upon the baccalaureate. Secondly, although the convent was located outside the wall and moat of Oxford, on the present site of Wadham College, east of Balliol and north of New College, the Augustinian student found himself near the center of university teaching. The faculties of both arts and theology used the Austin Friars' facilities. The arts faculty used the refectory, situated in the north range of the cloister of the friary, as a principal lecture hall and eventually required all bachelors of arts each year to dispute once and respond once at the friary, a task that was known as "doing the Austins." The faculty of theology used the church (along the south walk of the cloister) and the chapter room as its "school" until the erection of the Divinity School (now part of the Bodleian library) in 1479–80, a short distance away. The Austin Friar had easy access to philosophical and theological lectures and disputes by seculars and could associate freely with students from the other religious and monastic orders.

The Austin Friar seldom advanced immediately from the lectorate to the baccalaureate. There were two reasons for this. First, to meet their teaching needs the order might and often did require even those who were destined for the doctorate to lecture in nonuniversity *studia*. Secondly, while promotion to the lectorate was possible for many, dependent as it was only upon the ability of the student and recognition by his superiors, the university program for the baccalaureate and doctorate permitted only one student per order to begin his baccalaureate and only one candidate for the doctorate to incept in any one year. This meant that out of the many who had obtained the lectorate, those destined for the doctorate had to wait their turn, and the final ordering lay with the general chapter and the prior general. At Paris, where the demand was greatest and where Austin lectors from all parts of Europe waited for their chance at the one annual appointment, the years as lector could drag on. Gregory of Rimini, certainly no inferior mind nor persona non grata among the Augustinians, taught in the schools of his

---

tins, however, it referred to a specific office between the levels of student and bachelor, while among the Franciscans it was identical with the *magister regens* (regent master).

order for twelve years after his Paris studies before returning to Paris for the baccalaureate. English Austins were more fortunate, for their province practically controlled the openings at the university convents of Oxford and Cambridge, and in the late fourteenth century English students could be sent to the newer Italian universities for the baccalaureate and doctorate. The years of teaching between the lectorate and baccalaureate were probably far shorter among English Austins, perhaps only a year or two for those who intended to go on for the doctorate.

The Austin Friars at Oxford numbered about the same as the Carmelites in the fourteenth century, save in the last two decades when, during the papal schism, Italian and German students migrated in part to Oxford and probably doubled the resident friars at the Austin convent. In marked contrast to the Franciscans, there are very few known Augustinian authors before mid-century, at which time the Austin Friars at Oxford seem to have come into their own, already stimulated, perhaps, by continental influences.

BENEDICTINES

The monastic orders were the last "regulars" to succumb to the appeal of the university and to reorganize their educational system accordingly. Until the twelfth century the monasteries of western Europe had been the centers of intellectual life, and in the twelfth and thirteenth centuries they continued to provide a life of spirituality and letters, of study on the Bible and patristic literature, producing sermons and spiritual treatises that nourished the life of the soul and prepared the monk to seek his individual perfection. The monastery had always been a school, but a school of the Lord's service (*dominici schola servitii*), not a school of philosophy or speculative theology.

Although the Cistercians were, technically speaking, the first monks to establish a house of study at Oxford (at Rewley Abbey in 1281), the Benedictines, or black monks as they were known, contributed far more to the intellectual life of Oxford in the fourteenth century.[20] Plans for a

[20] The Benedictines at Oxford are among the most underresearched groups within the university community. See H. E. Salter in *VCH: Oxfordshire* 2: 68–71; D. Knowles, *The Religious Orders in England*, vol. 2 (Cambridge, 1961), 14–24; Rashdall, *Univ.* 3: 184–91. The latter must be read with caution. Rashdall, 190: "These monastic colleges possess very little

Benedictine house of studies had been proposed in 1277 and 1279, but it was not until a wealthy benefactor created a hall for young student monks from St. Peter's Abbey in Gloucester in 1283 that monk-students had any "home" at Oxford. The property was at the west end of Oxford (in Stockwell Street on land now occupied by Worcester College), adjacent to the Carmelite convent. The ownership of the land and a small portion of the buildings was transferred to Malmesbury in 1298–99. But the general chapter of the Canterbury province gradually gained control of the property.

Gloucester College, as it came to be known, was neither a priory nor a college in the proper sense. The *prior loci*, appointed by the abbot of Malmesbury, oversaw the physical setting; the *prior studentium* and the regent master (when finally acquired), appointed by the chapter, oversaw the students and studies. The common buildings, such as the refectory, chapel, and library, were held and supported by the chapter, while the individual houses, or entries, were owned by individual monasteries for the use of their own monks. Individualism was far more prominent than collegiality.

Gloucester College did not house all black monks at Oxford. Many lived in other accommodations. But in the course of the fourteenth century it did come to be the principal location and focus for the monks from southern England, and it retained its predominantly southern character even after 1336, when the provinces of Canterbury and York

---

importance in the history either of learning or of education. Monks never applied themselves cordially to the scholastic philosophy or theology. The older monastic Orders never produced a single great theologian from the days of S. Bernard till the reign of the scholastic theology was over and was superseded by an age of learned [!] theology. The aim of these monastic colleges was probably very simple and practical. It was only a select few of the younger monks who were sent to them. What the monastic houses wanted was not to produce great theologians or to contribute to the advancement of learning, but simply to have a few instructed theologians capable of preaching an occasional sermon to their brethren and of imparting an elementary theological education to the novices. Another purpose which probably interested the average abbot more than the educational needs of his house was the supply of canonists competent to transact its legal business and to represent it in the ecclesiastical courts." This statement might with some justification be applied to the black monks at the University of Paris (but not their Cistercian colleagues); see T. Sullivan, *Benedictines at the University of Paris in the Late Middle Ages*, Ph.D. diss., University of Wisconsin, Madison, 1982. As for Oxford, the ill-informed gratuitousness of this description will become clear in subsequent chapters.

were merged into one chapter and northern students were allowed access to Gloucester College. The need for more space in the early fourteenth century was solved in 1320 when, at the urging of the bishop of Norwich, the monks acquired the property of the Carmelites, since the latter moved across the street into a new and larger convent. Among the many abbeys that maintained lodgings at Gloucester College and sent students were Bury St. Edmunds, Worcester Cathedral, Glastonbury, Malmesbury, St. Peter's at Gloucester, St. Albans, Westminster, Norwich, and St. Augustine's Canterbury.

Christ Church Canterbury, the largest and most prominent of the Benedictine houses, did not take part in Gloucester College but housed its monks separately. In 1331 they established their own hall (on the site of the present St. Edmund's Hall), which they sold to the monks of Westminster around 1360, when they established a new Canterbury Hall. Northern monks, originally excluded from Gloucester College, lived apart or associated with the monks of Durham, which maintained students in Oxford from 1289 on. Eventually, in the mid-fourteenth century, the bishop of Durham established Durham College at the north edge of Oxford, on what is now the site of Trinity College.

Gloucester, Canterbury, and eventually Durham were the highest stage in the Benedictine educational system that had gradually been taking shape at the end of the thirteenth century and the beginning of the fourteenth. Instruction in grammar and the equivalent of the university training in logic and natural philosophy had to be acquired by the monks before they could progress to degrees in theology or canon law. By the mid-thirteenth century there were attempts to introduce instruction in arts and scholastic theology into the larger monasteries and monastic cathedral chapters. Since the monks lacked university training and thus the technical knowledge required of these disciplines, mendicant preachers were assigned to the monastic community to provide instruction. Throughout the latter half of the thirteenth century, instruction in philosophy and theology at Christ Church Canterbury was in the hands of the Franciscans, and the same was probably true for Worcester and Norwich. In the early years of the fourteenth century that changed, and Benedictine houses became academically self-sufficient. The major houses—certainly Canterbury, Durham, Glastonbury, Gloucester, Worcester, Westminster, Bury St. Edmunds, and Norwich—maintained instruction in grammar, logic, philosophy, and some theology by the

second quarter of the fourteenth century. Moreover, Gloucester College provided remedial work in grammar and the basic courses in philosophy alongside the lectures on the Bible and the *Sentences*. The stages
in the philosophical and theological curricula closely resembled those of
the mendicant orders. Students progressed from auditors to bachelors,
and, for the chosen few, to masters. Bachelors and masters took part in
disputations, and bachelors engaged their fellow *socii* in debate. In the
process, several abbeys in the fourteenth century achieved a high level
of scholastic intellectual life, most notably Worcester, Glastonbury, St.
Albans, and Durham.

Far more than either the Austin Friars or the Cistercians, the Benedictines made a significant contribution not only to the intellectual life
of their abbeys but to the scholastic quality of the universities. In the two
decades from 1320 to 1340, major works of scholastic theology were
produced by Robert Graystanes, John Stuckley, the notorius Monachus
Niger, and Roger Swineshead (who became a Benedictine), while both
Adam Wodeham and Richard Kilvington took seriously the opinions of
their Benedictine *socii*. It would also be hard to imagine the intellectual
history of the second half of the fourteenth century in England without
the existence of the Durham theologian, Uthred of Boldon.

CISTERCIANS

The Cistercian system of education in England resembled the Benedictine in that no specific *studia particularia* were set up to provide secondary education or the equivalent of the university arts training.[21] As
monks from Benedictine priories or smaller abbeys received their

---

[21] On the origin and development of Cistercian university education see: G. Müller,
"Gründung des Bernhardkollegiums zu Paris," *Cisterzienzer Chronik* 20 (1908): 1–14, 38–
50; E. Kwanten, "Le Collège Saint-Bernard à Paris," *RHE* 43 (1948): 443–72; C. H. Law-
rence, "Stephen of Lexington and Cistercian University Studies in the Thirteenth Century," *JEH* 11 (1960): 164–78; B. W. O'Dwyer, "The Problem of Education in the Cistercian Order," *Journal of Religious History* 3 (1965): 238–45; L. Lekai, *The Cistercians* (Kent,
Ohio, 1977), 77–90, 236–43. For the Cistercians at Oxford see: A. G. Little, "Cistercian students at Oxford in the Thirteenth Century," *EHR* 8 (1893): 83–85; R. C. Fowler, "Cistercian Scholars at Oxford," *EHR* 23 (1908): 84–85; C. H. Talbot, "The English Cistercians
and the Universities" in *Los Monjes y los Estudios*, 4 Semana de Estudios Monasticos (Poblet,
1963), 209–34; D. Thomson, "Cistercians and Schools in Late Medieval Wales," *Cambridge
Medieval Celtic Studies* 3 (1982): 76–80.

grammar training in the local house and their arts training in a larger abbey or monastic cathedral with which their house was affiliated, so too Cistercian monks received their pre-university training in their monastery, except for those who belonged to an abbey too small to support a school. Generally speaking, only monks from the larger monasteries were interested in or encouraged toward a university education. The pattern, therefore, was to go directly from their own abbey to Rewley Abbey, Oxford, for training in theology. Cistercians were prohibited from studying canon law.

There were, however, some important differences between the Benedictine and Cistercian practice with regard to higher education. The Cistercian order, as a reform movement within Benedictine monasticism, did not initially favor (or see much spiritual benefit in) formal education beyond reading, writing, and the study of Scripture and the Fathers. Since their members came into the order in their teens, they had in most cases (by the fourteenth century) received their elementary and secondary education before becoming monks. No formal schools, such as the Cluniacs operated for oblates, were needed in Cistercian monasteries. Moreover, many of the early Cisterican writers, following the spiritual lead of St. Bernard, saw the urban university as another Babylon where religious fervor and biblical truth were leached out in a rational, scholastic, analytic process that concentrated on problems of natural theology and philosophy and tended at times, in their view, in the direction of heresy. The movement in the mid-thirteenth century through which the Cistercians joined the university community and added a "scholastic" style of writing and thinking to their traditional "patristic" or scriptural approach was not greeted with enthusiasm by all Cistercian communities, and an ambivalent or half-hearted attitude toward scholasticism and university education remained within the Cistercian order throughout its history.

This ambivalent attitude toward the monastic uses of higher education seems to have been greater in England than on the Continent. Despite the fact that the College of St. Bernard at Paris was founded by and perhaps forced upon the Cisterican order by an Englishman and onetime student at Oxford, Stephen of Lexington, abbot of Clairvaux, French Cistercians, especially the abbots of Clairvaux and her daughter houses, played the leading role in staffing and utilizing that college and the University of Paris. In the course of the fourteenth century the Cistercians played a major role in scholastic theology, but these were either French Cistercians, like John of Mirecourt or Pierre Ceffons, or German and East European Cistercians, like James of Eltville, Conrad of Ebrach, or Gottschalk of Nepomuk. There are no comparable English theologians of a scholastic bent among the Cistercians, despite the fact that they had equal access to education. Thus, while English Benedictines in the fourteenth century not only entered actively into university life and scholastic thinking but also produced theologians of international reputation, the English Cistercians seem to have used the Parisian and Oxford educational experience as a status achievement and a way of accrediting those who would become administrative leaders within the order.

A second difference between the Benedictines and Cistercians is that English Benedictines made Oxford their principal university for higher education and maintained two, and then three colleges near the center of the town—colleges that were in some cases mixed communities in which secular students lived side by side with monastic students. Rewley Abbey, by contrast, lay outside Oxford, and the cloistered, separate existence and strong monastic discipline was probably retained. Moreover, the Paris house of studies always remained the principal college for Cistercians. The better English Cistercian students in the late thirteenth and early fourteenth centuries went to Paris for their university education, and the commitment to Oxford was marginal. The outbreak of the Hundred Years War did not alter this situation. It was not until mid-century that the English Cistercian presence at Paris declined, but the Oxford house did not grow or improve as a result, perhaps because of the effects of the Black Death. In the late fourteenth century, when Benedictines poured into Oxford in increasing numbers, the body of Cistercian students at Oxford remained small.

Not much is known of the living arrangements and curriculum at Rewley Abbey. It is likely that some remedial training in grammar and the subsequent training in logic and natural philosophy were provided, in addition to the lectures in theology. This is suggested by the fact that in the first half of the fourteenth century a high percentage of those Cistercians known to have been at Oxford appear to have been there for longer than the period necessary for theological training alone.

The number of students and lecturers at Rewley Abbey was never very large. If we compare the number of known Cistercians to the number of known Austin Friars or Franciscans (where we do have some information on the average total number), we can assume that Rewley maintained a level of twenty to twenty-five Cistercians during the first half of the fourteenth century. That number appears to have dropped in the third quarter of the fourteenth century and, unlike the Augustinians or Benedictines, did not increase or even recover in the last quarter. Where the higher faculty of study is known, all Cistercians were in theology and none in canon law. Again, since there is a high percentage for which we do not know the higher faculty, we can assume that some, perhaps many, of those at Rewley were studying logic and natural philosophy in preparation for theology. The number of authors among the Cistercians remained small, despite fluctuations in enrollment: only two or three per generation. A higher percentage became abbots, but the proportion of future abbots among Oxford Cistercians drops off in the second half of the fourteenth century. A high percentage of those who were authors also became abbots of Cistercian monasteries.

AUSTIN CANONS

The religious order best situated to take advantage of the intellectual opportunities of Oxford was the Austin Canons, a religious movement of the early twelfth century particularly dedicated to the care of souls among the transient merchant, pilgrim, and student population of Europe in that century.[22] The Austin foundations of St. Frideswide's, located at the main gate into Oxford from the south, and Oseney Abbey, across the fields to the southwest, were the two principal religious institutions of twelfth-century Oxford, and the order favored learning among its members. In a role similar to St. Geneviève at Paris, St. Frideswide's appears to have employed teachers of renown, such as Theobald of Etampes and Robert Pullen, to provide lectures in arts and theology, and it may have been the school of St. Frideswide's that attracted Alexander Nequam to Oxford in the last decade of the twelfth

[22] Rashdall, *Univ.* 3: 9–10, 17–23, 37–39; Salter in *VCH: Oxfordshire* 2: 90–93; J. C. Dickinson, *The Origins of the Austin Canons and their Introduction into England* (London, 1950), 79–83, 113–23, 186–90; Karl Bosl, *Regularkanoniker (Augustinerchorherren) und Seelsorge in Kirche und Gesellschaft des europäischen 12. Jahrhunderts*, Bayerische Akademie der Wissenschaften, phil.-hist. Klasse, n.F. 86 (Munich, 1979).

century to study theology before he himself became an Austin Canon at Cirencester Abbey.

Yet Oseney and St. Frideswide's played little part in the origin and development of Oxford beyond that of beneficent host. Oseney owned many of the halls that were rented by students and masters for lodging and teaching. St. Frideswide's guarded the university treasury chest placed there for safekeeping, its church and other buildings were occasionally used for meetings and disputations, and its bells helped mark the stages in the academic day. But neither monastery developed an intellectual tradition that even mildly approached that of St. Victor at Paris, and neither employed masters nor attempted to conduct a school after the early thirteenth century. The mendicant orders attracted those interested in learning. Even the abbot of Oseney, John of Reading, resigned his position to join the Franciscan order at Oxford in 1235. Apart from the occasional younger member who may have attended lectures in the schools outside his monastery, the teaching connection between the university and these monasteries was minimal.

The crucial difference between the Austin Canons and the Cistercians and Benedictines regarding Oxford education is that neither Oseney nor St. Frideswide, to the best of our knowledge, ever became houses of study for the order. Austin Canons attending Oxford—few in the thirteenth and early fourteenth centuries, more after 1360—lived in private lodgings or rented rooms in one of the colleges, most often University College. Not until the creation of St. Mary's College in 1435 did the Austin canons have their own house of study at Oxford. Parallel to the role of the Cistercians at Oxford, the Austin graduates went on to positions of authority within the order and some into higher ecclesiastical office through royal or papal service. Similarly, in terms of scholarship, they were almost as undistinguished as their Cistercian colleagues.

LIBRARIES OF THE RELIGIOUS ORDERS

The mendicant orders were the first scholarly communities at Oxford to possess books in number.[23] Their vow of poverty initially limited

---

[23] J. Leland, *De rebus britannicis collectanea*, vol. 4 (London, 1770), 59–60; N. R. Ker, *Medieval Libraries of Great Britain*, 2nd ed. (London, 1964), 141–44; K. W. Humphreys, *The Book Provisions of the Medieval Friars, 1215–1400* (Amsterdam, 1964).

their ability to buy manuscripts, but that vow also made them appropriate recipients for donated books. Moreover, following the model of monastic communities, the friars trained scribes within their orders to copy needed works and those produced by their own members. They also employed professional scribes. By the third quarter of the thirteenth century several of their collections had reached significant proportions.

The largest and most diverse library belonged to the Franciscans.[24] Within its sizable and rich collection it housed the books given by Robert Grosseteste (mostly original copies of his own writings or books with his annotations), some works of Roger Bacon, the holograph copy of John Duns Scotus's Oxford lectures on the *Sentences* and probably other works from Scotus's library, and copies (often unique copies) of scholastic works of numerous Oxford theologians, particularly Franciscan authors. Unlike many Franciscan libraries that were single units, the Oxford Greyfriars library was divided between the chained (noncirculating) collection, which contained among other major and valuable works the personal copies of Grosseteste and Scotus, and the secret library, which was distributed on loan to the brothers. Already large, the Franciscan library appears to have grown at a faster rate than others in the fourteenth century. It was principally the Franciscan library at Oxford that Richard Fitzralph had in mind when he criticized the mendicants for absorbing the entire book market.[25]

The library of the Dominican Oxford convent was large, probably second only to that of the Franciscans. Considering the proximity of Merton College, this was the book-rich quarter of Oxford. By the second quarter of the fourteenth century the Dominican library would have had a small but sufficient biblical and patristic collection, some texts in canon law, and extensive holdings in logic, natural philosophy,

[24] Leland, *Collectanea* 4: 60; Little, *Grey Friars*, 55–62; W. Pronger, "Thomas Gascoigne," *EHR* 53 (1938): 622 of 606–26; R. W. Hunt, "The Library of Robert Grosseteste," in *Robert Grosseteste, Scholar and Bishop*, ed. D. A. Callus (Oxford, 1955), 121–45; Ker, *Medieval Libraries*, 141–42; Humphreys, *Book Provisions*, 46–66, 99–118; Servus Gieben, "Thomas Gascoigne and Robert Grosseteste: Historical and Critical Notes," *Vivarium* 8 (1970): 56–67; W. J. Courtenay, "Alexander Langeley, O.F.M.," *Manuscripta* 18 (1974): 96–104. Also see articles by Rouse, cited above in ch. 1, n. 63.

[25] ". . . scarcely a useful book is to be found in the market, but all are bought up by the friars, so that in every convent is a great and noble library, and every one of them who has a recognised position in the Universities (and such are now innumerable) has also a noble library." Cited from Little, *Grey Friars*, 61, where the date of 1357 is misprinted as 1257.

and scholastic theology. In addition to the major Parisian authors, such as Thomas Aquinas, Albert the Great, and Peter of Tarantaise, they held copies of works by Robert Kilwardby, Richard Fishacre, Nicholas Trevet, and many other Dominican writers from the late thirteenth and early fourteenth centuries.[26]

Libraries of the other mendicant orders were also large by the end of the thirteenth century and, by the early fourteenth, were housed in a separate room or building.[27] All these collections had multiple copies of the *Biblia sacra*, of Aristotle's works, of the *Decretum* and the *Decretales*, as well as the *Sentences*. They had the major biblical commentaries, a wide selection of patristic texts, works of the ninth to twelfth centuries, and the principal works of the leading scholastic doctors of Paris and Oxford. The individual character of each library lay in the large number of works by authors of each order, many of them little more than names to us today. They would also preserve works of little-known but favored authors not of their order, as the Carmelites did of the Benedictine, Robert Graystanes.

The libraries of the monastic orders differed in some respects from those of the mendicants.[28] On the one hand, they had some distinct advantages not possessed by either the mendicants or the secular colleges. They could and did draw books from the constituent monastic libraries, which were already large collections. They also had a long tradition in the copying of manuscripts, which gave them an initial advantage in book production. On the other hand, they came to the university late: only toward the end of the thirteenth century, and the monastery libraries, while rich in biblical and patristic texts, were poor in the philosophical and theological scholastic texts used at the university. Visitation records contain ample evidence of books being siphoned from the monasteries into the libraries of the monastic colleges in the fourteenth and early fifteenth centuries, many of them no doubt sent with students

[26] Leland, *Collectanea* 4: 59; Pronger, "Thomas Gascoigne," 622; Ker, *Medieval Libraries*, 142.

[27] Ker, *Medieval Libraries*, 142–44; Humphreys, *Book Provisions*.

[28] Ker, *Medieval Libraries*, 145–46; H.E.D. Blakiston, *Oxford Historical Society Collectanea*, vol. 3 (Oxford, 1896), 36–41; M. R. James, *Ancient Libraries of Canterbury and Dover* (Cambridge, 1903), 165–72; W. A. Pantin, *Canterbury College, Oxford* (Oxford, 1947); D. Knowles, *The Religious Orders in England*, vol. 2 (Cambridge, 1961), 14–28, 331–53.

going to a university with the abbot's or prior's blessing.[29] Having no need to purchase or acquire the biblical and patristic foundation to which they had such easy access, the monastic book funds could be diverted toward acquiring more strictly scholastic texts.

Higher education among the religious orders was as much outside the universities as within. The *studia particularia*, especially those of the mendicant orders, formed in a sense the iceberg beneath the visible tip of university education, and the interaction of those *studia* in the non-university towns and cities formed a crucial part of the educational structure of fourteenth-century England and, indeed, of Europe as a whole.

[29] For example, books were sent from Durham to Durham College at Oxford in 1315, 1400, and 1409. Episcopal visitations frequently discovered deplenished libraries in cases of houses supporting students at Oxford. For evidence from the Newark house of Austin Canons see C. K. Brampton, "The Probable Order of Ockham's Non-polemical Works," *Traditio* 19 (1963): 483; F. G. Cowley, *The Monastic Order in South Wales, 1066–1349* (Cardiff, 1977), 146: "When Bishop Guy de Mone visited Carmarthen priory [again Austin Canons] in 1401 . . . the decrees, decretals and books of Clement VI and the *casus* of Bernard, 'which deserve to be called the treasures of the house,' were at Oxford."

THREE

HIGHER EDUCATION OUTSIDE
UNIVERSITIES

༻✧༺

UNIVERSITIES were, in the fourteenth century, the principal purveyors of higher education, but they did not hold a monopoly in that market. For those who desired or needed a recognized degree that conferred the *ius ubique docendi*, the *studium generale* was the only means to that end. For others, the content of higher education could be obtained elsewhere, perhaps nearer home, within an atmosphere that somewhat resembled the university.

Certain disciplines could be acquired through apprenticeship, bypassing the university altogether. Many of those practicing medicine in fourteenth-century England held no medical degree from a university, although throughout the late Middle Ages there was a concerted effort both in England and on the Continent to prevent nongraduates from practicing medicine.[1] A knowledge of common law was also acquired through apprenticeship and was not studied at a university. Apprentices in both disciplines received the training necessary for practice, although the type of knowledge imparted at the university was not gained. The theory and practice in the *ars vetus* and *ars nova* were apparently provided in cathedrals.

For students of theology the case was somewhat different. The actual content of a university education in England could be acquired outside Oxford or Cambridge. The mendicant orders, as we have seen, ran their own *studia particularia* with a curriculum that paralleled that of the university. For parish clergy (numerically a more significant group), cathedrals offered the requisite theological education, often by a university master of theology.[2] Theological education under the authority and

---

[1] Rashdall, *Univ.* 3: 156.

[2] Information on the organization and personnel of English cathedral schools in the thirteenth and fourteenth centuries has been drawn from A. G. Little, "Theological Schools in

supervision of a bishop was one of the oldest forms of Christian education, and it rose to its greatest prominence in the early twelfth century and was eventually required by canon law. At secular cathedrals the maintenance of instruction was one of the responsibilities of the chancellor, although already in the twelfth century the actual teaching was frequently done by others appointed under his direction. The cathedral schools of Salisbury, Lincoln, London, and York were particularly prominent, and they probably maintained a modest program of theological and pastoral instruction in the thirteenth century even as the universities of Paris and Oxford shouldered more of the burden of higher education in theology and canon law. In many dioceses, however, the commitment to clerical education was less strong, and the chancellorship, like other cathedral dignities, tended to become a reward or living for someone whose training and duties were far removed from teaching.

In the closing years of the thirteenth century several scholar-bishops encouraged the renewal of their cathedral schools by placing more emphasis on the availability of instruction and appointing as chancellors university theologians (preferably masters) capable and interested in giving lectures. Richard of Gravesend, who became bishop of London in 1280, required the cathedral chancellor to be a doctor or bachelor of theology and to lecture or find an adequate replacement—requirements reiterated by his successor, Ralph Baldock in 1308. The incumbent chancellor in 1280, Ralph of Ivingho, may not have been up to the task, for about 1285–92 the then archdeacon of Essex, Robert Winchelsey, former chancellor of Oxford, a noted theologian and future archbishop of Canterbury, gave theological lectures at London. In 1308 Bishop Ralph Baldock initiated a policy (continued by Bishop Stephen Gravesend) of appointing Mertonian theologians, some of them among the most distinguished graduates of Paris and Oxford: Robert de Clothale, Thomas Wilton, William Reynham, Thomas Duraunt, and Thomas Bradwardine.

Medieval England," *EHR* 55 (1940): 624–30; Pantin, *ECFC*, 110–19; John Le Neve, *Fasti Ecclesiae Anglicanae, 1300–1541*, rev. ed., 11 vols. (London, 1962–65), in combination with Emden, *BRUO*; Kathleen Edwards, "Bishops and learning in the reign of Edward II," *Church Quarterly Review* 138 (1944): 57–86; Edwards, *The English Secular Cathedrals in the Middle Ages*, 2nd ed. (Manchester, 1967), 197–201; N. Orme, "Education and Learning at a Medieval English Cathedral: Exeter 1380–1548," *JEH* 32 (1981): 265–83.

At Salisbury Bishop Simon of Ghent (1297–1315) inherited as chancellor Master Ralph of York, whose commitment to lecturing was apparently weak. In 1300 Ghent ordered the chancellor to give lectures on theology, and in 1309 he was able to replace him with William de Boys (Bosco), a Mertonian scholar who had just completed his regency in theology and his term as chancellor of Oxford. After the death of Boys, Ghent appointed another Mertonian doctor of theology, Henry de la Wyle, who had been senior proctor of the university in 1285 and who remained chancellor at Salisbury until his death in 1329. Portions of his large personal library were left to Merton and Balliol colleges as well as Salisbury cathedral. Oxford theologians at Lincoln were equally prominent: John Dalderby, appointed chancellor by 1291; Ralph Barry in 1300; Anthony Bec in 1316. Similar appointments of well-known Oxford theologians as cathedral chancellors were made elsewhere: Thomas of Corbrigge at York in 1280; Luke of Ely at Lichfield before 1304 (under Bishop Langton, a nonuniversity civil service appointment); and Walter Giffard at Exeter in 1314 under Bishop Stapeldon, D.Cn.L. Several cathedrals tended to recruit chancellors from Merton College, specifically London, Salisbury, and York. Once attained, the post seems to have been distinguished and challenging enough such that, unless raised to the episcopate or cathedral deanship, one usually remained chancellor until death.

Some of this revival in cathedral education may have been stimulated by increased local demand, but the vision and patronage of scholar-bishops played an important part. By the first quarter of the fourteenth century it was almost impossible for a cathedral not to offer instruction. The ideal of a university master of theology either as chancellor or as *scholasticus* was not always realized and perhaps not even desired by many bishops. Cathedrals such as Chichester, Hereford, and Wells appointed nontheologians, often lawyers, to the office of chancellor in the first half of the fourteenth century, as on occasion did Exeter, Lichfield, and even Salisbury. The monastic cathedrals, whose monks had come late to university education, originally drew upon the talents of mendicant masters, especially Franciscans, to teach the monks. By the early fourteenth century, however, there were sufficient monastic graduates of the university to permit cathedrals like Canterbury and Worcester to replace Franciscan masters with their own Benedictine masters.

Cathedrals, especially those in towns with several mendicant convents that also offered instruction, could provide much of the curriculum and some of the scholastic atmosphere of Oxford or Cambridge. We have *quaestiones disputatae, Lecturae in Sententias, Quodlibeta,* and Aristotelian commentaries from such centers as London, York, Norwich, and Worcester.[3] These centers deserve our attention in order to gain a full understanding of the educational structure of fourteenth-century England. Since their histories are similar, they can be illustrated with three examples, specifically those for which we have the best documentation. We cannot assume, however, that other such places played a less significant role, for these schools by their very nature, produced little documentation, and those active there usually did not see their activities or productions worthy of remembrance.

LONDON

In retrospect London was initially a good candidate for university status. By the twelfth century it already possessed many characteristics that elsewhere (e.g., Paris) contributed ultimately to the emergence of a university. It had a sizable and enthusiastic body of students engaged in sophistical disputations, as Fitz-Stephen reveals.[4] It had a cathedral school in which theology was taught, with a chancellor in charge of instruction and licensing. It had vigorous monastic and regular-canon schools near the city (Westminster Abbey and St. Saviour in Southwark, paralleling the resources of St. Denis and St. Geneviève at Paris) and grammar schools within its walls (St. Paul's, St. Martin's-le-Grand, and St. Mary-le-Bow, the latter two independent of the authority of the cathedral chancellor).[5] Again parallel to Paris, London was a major center of population, a commercial center, and a seat of royal government. And London cannot have been totally immune to town-gown clashes

[3] Continental examples include Cologne and Erfurt, before they became universities, and Amiens. Theological lecturers at Constance, Arras, Beauvais, Reims, and Rouen are also indicated in the Parisian *rotulus* of 1349; *CUP* 2: 624–25.

[4] William Fitz-Stephen, *Description of the Most Noble City of London*, in E. K. Kendall, *Source Book of English History* (New York, 1900), 65–71.

[5] On the schools of London see John Stow, *A Survey of London* (1603), with introduction and notes by C. L. Kingsford, vol. 1 (Oxford, 1908; 1971), 71–73; Nicholas Orme, *English Schools of the Middle Ages* (London, 1973), 168–70, 210–11.

that played such an important role in the legal recognition of the University of Paris.

London's early promise did not mature in the thirteenth century. Paris retained and increased its lead as the desired destination, the appropriate setting for English students of arts and theology. When an insular alternative or supplement to a continental education was developed, students flocked to Oxford and, in smaller numbers, Cambridge. London became a crossroads, a stopping place for men of learning en route from one university to the other. The London grammar schools remained active in the thirteenth century and probably expanded in size. But there is no evidence to suggest that higher education experienced any comparable growth. In fact, it probably diminished as the new *studia generalia* assumed the major burden of instruction and certification in philosophy, theology, and canon law. We should not assume, however, that arts and sciences atrophied even further in the fourteenth century. On the contrary, London in that period experienced a revival of higher learning that altered the intellectual face of the city.

The Topography of Learning

The center of what might be thought of as London's "Latin Quarter" was the district around the three oldest grammar schools of St. Paul's, St. Martin's-le-Grand to the north, and St. Mary-le-Bow a little to the east, all at the western end of the city. To that traditional student base (a young population between the ages of seven and fourteen) there were added in the fourteenth century an increasing number of students of university age (fourteen to thirty) engaged in the study of logic, natural philosophy, and theology. If not in one of the religious orders, these older students would be found at the cathedral school of St. Paul's.

As with most cathedral chapters in the late thirteenth century, there was a movement to upgrade the quality and frequency of theological lectures. In 1281 at St. Paul's the burden of these lectures was shifted from canons appointed to that task, whose willingness and abilities varied, to outside and distinguished theologians specifically chosen for that office.[6] The chancellor of the cathedral was expected to be a master of theology, and it was his responsibility to head the school, to ensure that lectures and disputations were held, and to lecture himself. The first occupant of the upgraded office was Richard de Swinfield, archdeacon of London, who was succeeded by Robert Winchelsey, previously rector at Paris and chancellor at Oxford, whose career led ultimately to the archbishopric of Canterbury. The distinguished series of chancellors at St. Paul's in the first half of the fourteenth century will be examined later in this chapter.

Numerous canon lawyers could also be found in the neighborhood of St. Paul's and St. Mary-le-Bow. They were attached to or attracted by the business of the episcopal and archidiaconal courts of the London diocese or the court of appeal for the Canterbury province, known as the Court of Arches, since it was held at St. Mary-le-Bow. Many of these men had received their training in canon law at a university, although some may have studied law at St. Paul's or through apprenticeship. Their presence provided an opportunity for contact and exchange between those practicing law and those studying law and theology in this part of the city.[7]

The district around St. Paul's was, moreover, the center of book production in fourteenth-century London. Over half of the scribes, limners, parchmeners, bookbinders, and stationers (booksellers) of known address lived within the shadow of St. Paul's Cathedral.[8] That density suggests a center for the book market, one that coincides remarkably well with the location of the major schools.

West of St. Paul's, in the same neighborhood, were a number of mendicant convents that offered instruction in philosophy and theology to students within and occasionally outside the order. The Franciscan convent, Greyfriars, was located to the northwest of St. Paul's, between St. Martin's-le-Grand and Newgate, in the less desirable quarter of the

---

[6] Edwards, *English Secular Cathedrals*, 199–200.

[7] A. T. Carter, *A History of the English Courts*, 5th ed. (London, 1927), 143–49; B. L. Woodcock, *Medieval Ecclesiastical Courts in the Diocese of Canterbury* (London, 1952), 6–8.

[8] Paul Christianson, "Books and their Makers in Medieval London," *Wooster* 96, no. 3 (Spring, 1982): 10–15. Although the evidence assembled by Christianson begins in the late fourteenth century, the development of craft neighborhoods in London, such as the one connected with book production, is earlier.

butchers, in Stinking Lane.[9] Blackfriars lay to the southwest, along the
wall between Ludgate and the Thames.[10] The Carmelite convent,
Whitefriars, was situated farther to the west, on the other side of the
Fleet ditch between the townhouse of the bishop of Salisbury and the
Temple.[11] All three convents were within a short distance of one another and the other schools. Only the Augustinian Hermits were outside this immediate district.[12] Their convent lay at the northeastern
edge of the city. Whether because of location or not, the Austin Friars
played a minor role in the intellectual life of fourteenth-century London.

As we have noted, the London convents of the Carmelites, Franciscans, and Dominicans had, by the early fourteenth century, begun to
shoulder a large share of the burden of mendicant education in southern England. For example, the London Carmelite convent was a *studium
generale* for the entire order, while the Oxford convent was a *studium*
only for the English province. This meant that London Whitefriars offered the full program of studies in logic, natural philosophy, and theology, and probably maintained a student population equal to or larger
than the Oxford convent. Moreover, non-English Carmelites who were
sent to England for advanced study went to the London convent, not
Oxford.[13]

Greyfriars, London, had a similarly active and rich intellectual life. It
was the principal school for the London custody, and it drew students
from Franciscan convents south of London, from Salisbury to Canterbury. There young friars received their advanced training in philosophy and theology before a smaller number were selected to study at a
university, usually Oxford. Since the Oxford and Cambridge convents

[9] *VCH: London*, vol. 1 (London, 1909), 502–7; C. L. Kingsford, *The Grey Friars of London*
(Aberdeen, 1915).

[10] *VCH: London*, 498–502.

[11] Ibid., 507–10.

[12] For ground plan and historical sketch see L. W. Cowie, "The London Austin Friars,"
History Today 29 (1979): 38–45.

[13] Margaret Poskitt, "The English Carmelites," *The Aylesford Review* 5 (1963): 226–37;
"The English Carmelite Province," *The Aylesford Review* 1 (1956): 98–102; Franz-Bernard
Lickteig, *The German Carmelites at the Medieval Universities*, Ph.D. diss., Catholic University
of America, Washington, D.C., 1977. John Baconthorp as prior provincial would have re-
sided at the London convent, and Osbert Pickingham taught there as well as at Oxford;
Xiberta, *SOC*, 175–76, 242.

had to serve Franciscans from all the custodies and from other provinces, space in the university convents was limited, and most Franciscans probably received the bulk of their education at a custodial school, such as London. Yet Greyfriars, London, was more than just a custodial school for the southern region, since outstanding scholars from other parts of England, such as Walter Chatton, taught there.[14]

Although the Dominican order did not designate a set number of convents to be perpetual schools, a few houses were specifically equipped with study cells for students and provided instruction in philosophy and theology on a nearly regular basis. The London convent was one of these and, in the fourteenth century, was a *studium solemne* or *studium particulare theologiae* for the London visitation. As with Oxford, it accepted students from outside the visitation and province, and in some cases had the same quota as Oxford.[15]

At the western end of the "Latin Quarter" of London lay a district of abbatial, episcopal, and aristocratic palaces that had been established between the twelfth and fourteenth centuries to be near the seat of government.[16] The choicest sites lay in that stretch of land between the Thames and the principal thoroughfare from the city to the royal palace of Westminster, namely Fleet Street and the Strand. Beginning at the eastern end near Ludgate, the Thames embankment displayed the gardens and residences of the bishop of Salisbury, the Carmelites, the Temple, the bishops of Exeter, Bath and Wells, Llandaff, Coventry, Worcester, the Savoy Palace of the duke of Lancaster, and the "inns" of the bishops of Carlisle, Durham, Norwich and York.

In several of these London episcopal residences in the early fourteenth century one could find distinguished masters within the *familia* of a bishop, especially if the latter was himself a man of learning.

---

[14] Chatton's presence as lecturer in London is argued by G. Gál in his introduction to Ockham *SL*, 47*–56*.

[15] At the Chapter of 1314 it was affirmed that the Irish convents were permitted to send the same quota of students to London and Oxford, namely two. *VCH: London*, 500, n. 44.

[16] On the abbatial and episcopal residences on the West End of London see: Marjorie B. Honeybourne, "The Fleet and its Neighbourhood in early and Medieval Times," *London Topographical Record* 19 (1947), esp. 68–73; M. B. Honeybourne, *A Sketch Map of London Under Richard II* (London: London Topographical Society, 1960); C. L. Kingsford, "Historical Notes on Medieval London Houses," *London Topographical Record* 10 (1916): 44–144; Timothy Baker, *Medieval London* (London, 1970). Help in locating some of this material was provided by John Clark of the London Museum.

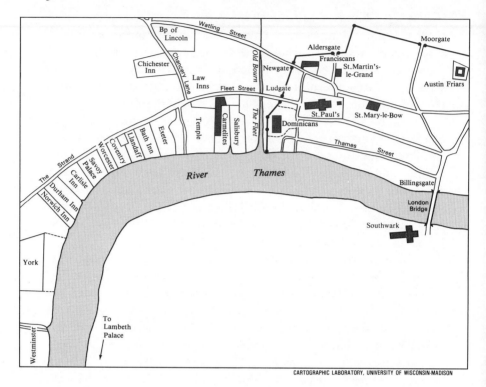

MAP 3. FOURTEENTH-CENTURY LONDON

Scholar-patrons who held high office in royal service and/or church and who consequently were often resident in London already formed an important group in the late thirteenth and early fourteenth centuries: archbishops Kilwardby, Pecham, and Winchelsey at Lambeth Palace, Simon of Ghent and Roger Martival at Salisbury Inn, John Dalderby at Lincoln Inn, and Ralph Baldock, Gilbert Segrave, and Stephen Gravesend at St. Paul's. That situation prevailed into the mid-fourteenth century, despite the appointment of several lawyers and nonuniversity civil servants to episcopal office. In fact, in the period from 1318 to 1345 there were a number of theologian-bishops who favored Oxford graduates in arts and theology and brought them into households that were frequently in London. These scholar-clients were not part of the teaching resources of London, since as far as we know they never gave lectures, and we should not confuse them with those who provided instruction at the cathedral school and the mendicant convents. But they were an intellectual resource whose presence should not be ignored. They did engage in disputations and were expected to enrich the intellectual life of the episcopal households to which they were attached, even as they pursued careers in court and church. To the degree that they maintained an interest in ideas, as many of them did, we can assume they had some contact with the scholarly world to the east of Fleet Street as well as the political world to the west.

The scholarly community west of the Fleet coincided with the principal legal community of London, centered in the neighborhood of the Temple and the Chancery.[17] Much of the lawyer's work was conducted in Westminster hall, but their residences, places of study, and places of consultation were in Fleet Street near Temple Bar, where Serjeants' Inn came to be located, or in Chancery Lane, where one found the Inns of Court and Inns of Chancery. This was a district not only for the practice of law but for legal education as well. In the fourteenth century the structure of the legal community and probably of legal training were becoming set. When the system becomes visible to us in the fifteenth century, we find that those seeking training in common law studied as apprentices in the Inns of Chancery, attending lectures on common law, participating in disputations or moot courts, and observing court cases. The best students were brought into the Inns of Court (Lincoln's Inn, Gray's Inn, Middle Temple, and the Inner Temple), voluntary associations whose names derive from the properties leased by the association for residence and instruction. These inns were governed by a small body of senior lawyers, known as benchers, whose status and du-

[17] T.F.T. Plucknett, *A Concise History of the Common Law*, 3rd ed. (London, 1940), 195–202; S. E. Thorne, "The Early History of the Inns of Court, with Special Reference to Gray's Inn," *Graya* 50 (1959): 79–98, A.E.B. Simpson, "The Early Constitution of the Inns of the Court," *Cambridge Law Journal* 28 (1970): 241–56, and E. W. Ives, "The Common Lawyers," in *Profession, Vocation, and Culture in Later Medieval England*, ed. C. H. Clough (Liverpool, 1982), 181–217, discount the educational role of the Inns in the fourteenth century, although they recognize that legal knowledge was acquired at the law courts. A more structured and developed educational system is portrayed in Ronald Roxburgh, *The Origins of Lincoln's Inn* (Cambridge, 1963) and P. Classen, *Studium und Gesellschaft im Mittelalter*, ed. J. Fried (Stuttgart, 1983), 197–237. E. W. Ives, "The Common Lawyers," in *Profession, Vocation, and Culture in Later Medieval England*, ed. C. H. Clough (Liverpool, 1982), 181–217, while recognizing the courts as places for gaining legal knowledge, discounts the educational role of the Inns in the fourteenth century.

ties somewhat resembled fellows of colleges at Oxford and Cambridge. In the absence of endowment and permanent property the inns resembled halls of medieval universities. But the internal organization of seniority and teaching more closely resembled the colleges. Above the level of student apprentices (inner and utter barristers) were the lecturers, or readers, from whose ranks the serjeants-at-law were chosen.

This system of legal education more closely resembled the fourteenth-century university than is generally recognized, particularly one primarily devoted to law, such as Bologna. Students were enrolled in corporations that rented property and that were under the control of advanced students. Instruction took the form of lectures and disputations (the arguing of an assigned position in a case). The better students advanced through a series of academic stages, across a minimum or standard number of years, that eventually included the giving of two or more courses of lectures.[18] The ceremonies surrounding the creation of a new serjeant-at-law were comparable to and generally exceeded those connected with the inception of a new regent master. Advancement to the level of serjeant-at-law required resignation from the "student-run" inns, or corporations, and entrance into Serjeants' Inn.[19] Differences certainly did exist. Yet Plucknett's observation that Fortescue was wrong when (c. 1470) he "likened the serjeants to the doctors in the universities," since apprentices rather than serjeants taught in the Inns of Court, is less valid for the fourteenth century than for the thirteenth.[20] Much of the teaching at a late medieval university, as we have seen, was done by the bachelors, and regent masters were occupied as much with administration as with teaching. It is worth noting that while the elementary to graduate levels of education in London were centered at the west end of the city, the postgraduate theologians congregated in Fleet Street and the Strand, to the west of the city, in close association with the students, attorneys, barristers, and serjeants-at-law.

If London's academic landscape did not include colleges, we should also remember that the role of colleges in early fourteenth-century Oxford and Cambridge was also minor in comparison to halls and rented rooms. And to the extent that intellectual life in contemporary Oxford

[18] John Fortescue, *De Laudibus Legum Anglie*, ed. and transl. S. B. Chrimes (Cambridge, 1942), 116–25.

[19] Plucknett, *Concise History*, 201, n. 4.

[20] Plucknett, *Concise History*, 201–2; Fortescue, *De Laudibus*, 120–21.

or Paris depended on mendicant houses of study or on brilliant secular scholars, London possessed very active and notable equivalents.

Libraries and Curriculum

Overall, the student community of London was much smaller than that of Oxford or even Cambridge. The number of grammar students may have been comparable and the number of mendicants may even have been larger, but against the bulk of Oxford undergraduates and non-mendicant students in the higher faculties, London only had its cathedral school. Thus the total scholarly population of London was probably not more than four hundred, one-quarter the size of Oxford. Yet the London academic community did operate as a consortium of autonomous but interrelated units, and it did maintain a high level of instruction. One could obtain at London the content of an Oxford education, and at least on the level of logic, natural philosophy, and theology the schools of London provided training equivalent to that acquired at a university.

We know least about the content of the curriculum at St. Paul's. The interests of those appointed to the office of chancellor and the size and character of the library suggest, however, that it should have been strong in logic (both the *logica antiqua* and the *logica moderna*) and mathematical physics, and somewhat conservative in theology. In the early fourteenth century considerable care was taken to appoint to the office of chancellor theologians of distinguished reputation, most of them from Merton College, Oxford, thanks to the patronage of Stephen Gravesend, bishop of London from 1318 to 1338. The list of chancellors appointed by Gravesend included Thomas Wilton (1320–27, but in Paris the first two years), William Reynham (1327–33), Thomas Duraunt (1334–37), and Thomas Bradwardine (1337–49), who was elevated to the see of Canterbury in 1349, but whose tenure in that office was almost immediately terminated by the plague.[21] Gravesend may not

[21] For the biographies of Gravesend, Wilton, Reynham, Duraunt, and Bradwardine see Emden, *BRUO*. For mention of the appointment or tenure of Reynham, Duraunt, and Bradwardine as chancellors at St. Paul's, see the *Register* of Stephen Gravesend in *Registrum Radulphi Baldock, Gilberti Segrave, Ricardi Newport, et Stephani Gravesend, episcoporum Londoniensium*, ed. R. C. Fowler, Canterbury and York Series, 7 (London, 1911), 253, 280, 302, 309, 312, 313.

himself have been a fellow of Merton College, although it is possible he could have been affiliated before going to Paris *c.* 1306, presumably to study theology. His ties with Merton, however, are reflected in the patronage he provided to Mertonians and in his bequest of the largest portion of his library to Merton College.

In the fourteenth century the cathedral chancellor was obliged to give lectures himself or find a qualified substitute if illness, the other duties of his office, or absence prevented his presence in the classroom.[22] If the lectures Robert Winchelsey gave at London while chancellor at St. Paul's are any indication, the chancellor was expected to provide advanced lectures in theology equivalent to what would be taught at a similar level in a university.[23] We may assume, therefore, that others were teaching in addition to the chancellor and that the intellectual views of the chancellor set the quality and tone for the theological program.

Unfortunately, with the exception of Bradwardine, we are not as well informed on the ideas and intellectual ties of the chancellors in the second quarter of the century as we would wish. Wilton was a doctor of Paris and widely cited on the Continent in the fourteenth century. His famous debate with Walter Burley over the intention and remission of forms probably took place on the eve of his return to England to assume the duties of his office.[24] Although Burley at one point linked the views of Wilton and John of Jandun, and all three figures have been associated with Averroism in the literature, that label is too vague to provide much insight into Wilton's ideas. His association with Scotus seems more firmly grounded.[25] In all probability he continued his strong interests in natural philosophy while at London.

Less is known of the interests of Reynham, apart from his possession of a copy of the last book of Thomas Aquinas's commentary on the *Sentences*.[26] Duraunt borrowed the Psalms commentary of the Dominican Nicholas Gorham during his tenure in office, which he may have used

[22] Pantin, *ECFC*, 111.

[23] Ibid. Winchelsey's *Quaestiones disputatae apud London* are found in Oxford, Magdalen College, MS. 217.

[24] Emden, *BRUO* 3: 2054–55; J. Weisheipl, "Ockham and some Mertonians," *MedStud* 30 (1968): 184–87; "Repertorium Mertonense," *MedStud* 31 (1969): 222–24.

[25] P. Glorieux, "Duns Scot et les 'Notabilia Cancellarii,'" *AFH* 24 (1931): 3–14.

[26] Emden, *BRUO* 3: 1571.

in his biblical lectures or simply had copied.[27] Bradwardine is our best indication of the continuing scholarly interests of the chancellors of St. Paul's, since we know he wrote as well as taught while in London, completing there his monumental *Summa de causa Dei*.[28] Bradwardine's campaign against the Pelagians among his contemporaries certainly influenced his teaching at London and gave a strong Augustinian and biblical character to theology at St. Paul's.

The library of St. Paul's was already rich by the mid-thirteenth century and was greatly expanded in theology and canon law through the bequest of Bishop Ralph Baldock, who died in 1313.[29] Baldock's will left 126 volumes of works written before 1290, more than adequately covering Oxford and Parisian texts and commentaries in arts and theology of the thirteenth century. More recent works entered in the course of the fourteenth century. We know only a portion of the acquisitions, since inventories have not survived and the list of donations is incomplete. A number of books in canon law from Gravesend's library were given to St. Paul's.[30] Bradwardine's library, which was probably rich in quality if not in size, may well have been divided between Merton, St. Paul's, and Canterbury.[31]

The library of the almonry school, separate from that of the cathedral, also grew in the fourteenth century through the bequests of its schoolmasters. William de Tolleshunt in 1328 left various books on grammar, logic, and natural history that were appropriate for the elementary and secondary level.[32] But he also left books in natural philos-

[27] Emden, *BRUO* 1: 611–12.

[28] Emden, *BRUO* 1: 244–46; G. Leff, *Bradwardine and the Pelagians* (Cambridge, 1957), 2, 266; H. A. Oberman, *Archbishop Thomas Bradwardine. A Fourteenth Century Augustinian* (Utrecht, 1958), 17–18; Weisheipl, "Repertorium," 177–83; Weisheipl, "Ockham," 189–93.

[29] On the library of St. Paul's see W. Dugdale, *History of St. Paul's* (London edition of 1818), 313, 324–28, 392–401; J. W. Clark, "The Libraries at Lincoln, Westminster and St. Paul's," *Cambridge Antiquarian Society, Proceedings* 9 (1896–98): 37; Emden, *BRUO* 3: 2147–48; N. R. Ker, *Medieval Libraries of Great Britain*, 2nd ed. (London, 1964), 120–21.

[30] Emden, *BRUO* 2: 805–7. Among his bequests Gravesend left a *Liber concordantiarum* to Duraunt.

[31] Nothing is known of the content or fate of Bradwardine's personal library, but he certainly would have had a number of books in contemporary logic, natural philosophy, and theology in addition to copies of his own works.

[32] E. Rickert, *Chaucer's World* (New York, 1948), 121–22.

ophy and logic that were more appropriate for the "undergraduate" level, along with works on medicine, civil law, canon law, and sermons that could only have served the needs of more advanced students in the "graduate" disciplines. That is less true of the extensive bequest of another schoolmaster at St. Paul's, William Ravenstone, in 1358.[33] The majority of his 84 manuscripts were on grammar, Roman literature, mathematics, logic, music, and liturgy that would have served the needs of the boys in the grammar school. Yet we also find there some works on physics, canon law, and theology.

We are better informed on the content of teaching among the mendicant convents. As has already been noted, *studia* of the type we encounter at London were required to provide the basic curriculum of the arts and theological programs of the universities. This meant that there would be one or more masters or bachelors lecturing on the logical and scientific works of Aristotle, along with lectures in mathematics. For example, it is now reasonably certain that the Aristotelian commentaries of William of Ockham were the product of lectures given to students at London Greyfriars between the years 1320 and 1324.[34] There would also be one or more lecturers in theology so that students could be instructed in the Bible and the *Sentences*. During those same years, Walter Chatton lectured on the *Sentences*, probably in the same London convent.[35] At the end of that decade another Franciscan, Adam Wodeham, lectured on the *Sentences* at London before beginning or completing his time as *Sententiarius* at Oxford.[36]

Various types of disputations were also held in the London convents. Students received training in opposing and responding. Formed bachelors might also engage in quodlibetal disputations. Most of the *Quodlibeta* of Ockham were composed and delivered at a nonuniversity *studium* in England before 1324, almost certainly at London.[37] The quality of teaching was quite high. Generally speaking, the same mendicants who displayed their knowledge in the lecture halls of Oxford had already lectured or would soon lecture at a nonuniversity *studium* of the order. In this system London was probably assigned the largest share of

33 Rickert, 122–26.

34 See introductions to Ockham, *SL*, 47*–56*, and *Quodl.*, 26*–41*.

35 See introduction to Ockham, *SL*, 47*–56*.

36 Courtenay, *Adam Wodeham* (Leiden, 1978), 31–32, 123–31, 166–71.

37 Ockham, *Quodl.*, 26–41.

talent, as the above illustrations of Ockham, Chatton, and Wodeham would suggest.

Some of the educational character and administration of the London convents was in the hands of the provincial minister or prior, who was often resident in the London convent of the order. The orders usually elected men of distinguished learning, most of whom had already held the office of regent master at a university. John Baconthorp, perhaps the most noted Carmelite theologian in the first half of the fourteenth century, was their provincial from 1326 to 1333.[38] At roughly the same time Simon Boraston was the Dominican prior provincial (1327–36), followed soon after by Richard Winkley (1336–39).[39] Both men were noted theologians, had been regent masters at Oxford, and continued a life of active scholarship after their regencies. In 1339, toward the end of his term in office, Winkley prepared an inventory of the Dominican library at London, which probably contained several hundred volumes by then.[40] Unfortunately, that document has not survived. The list of Franciscan provincial ministers is even more distinguished.[41] During a particularly productive period for the Franciscan school that list included Richard Conington (c. 1310–16), William of Nottingham (1316–30), John of Rodington (c. 1336–40), and John Went (c. 1340–48). All had been lectors at Oxford and their opinions were frequently cited by other masters.

We know only a fraction of the books in the mendicant libraries of London, which were among the richest in England. All were dispersed at the time of the Reformation and very little remains today. Moreover, the items mentioned by Leland and Bale are only those that attracted their interest, and some of those items certainly entered the religious orders' collections in the fifteenth century.[42] But what evidence we have

---

[38] Emden, *BRUO* 1: 88–89; Xiberta, *SOC*, 167–240, 499.

[39] W. Gumbley, "Provincial Priors and Vicars of the English Dominicans," *EHR* 33 (1918): 243–51; A. G. Little, "Provincial Priors and Vicars of the English Dominicans," *EHR* 33 (1918): 496–97; Emden, *BRUO* 1: 221; 3: 2060.

[40] J. Bale, *Index Britanniae Scriptorum*, ed. R. L. Poole and M. Bateson (Oxford, 1902), 513, noted that he derived his information "ex inventario Bibliothece Fratrum Praedicatorum Londini per provincialem eorum Ricardum de Winkele, A.D. 1339."

[41] A. G. Little, *Franciscan Papers, Lists, and Documents* (Manchester, 1943), 189–207.

[42] Many of the manuscripts in the libraries of the religious orders had probably already been dispersed through loan or theft by 1536, when John Leland began his inventory tour of English antiquities on behalf of Henry VIII. The subject groupings in Leland's lists sug-

is worth a reexamination. The libraries were shelved according to subject categories: scriptural commentaries, sermons, patristic literature,
logic, natural philosophy, and theological works such as *Sentences* commentaries, quodlibets and disputed questions, and various theological
treatises. The Dominican library possessed most of the works of Fishacre and Kilwardby, some writings of Grosseteste, and numerous commentaries of English Dominican authors.[43] They must also have had all
or most of the works of Thomas Aquinas, although none was noted by
either Leland or Bale. The Carmelite library held, in addition to the
basic collection, works of Carmelite authors, such as Baconthorp,
Brome, Beston, Barningham, and Walsingham. Perhaps more unusual, they also had several works of Fitzralph and Ockham's commentary on the *Physics*.[44] It is less surprising that the Franciscan library had
almost all of the philosophical and theological works of Ockham as well
as scriptural commentaries and theological works of more recent Franciscan authors: Adam Wodeham on the Song of Songs, Henry Costesey
on Psalms, Robert Cowton on the *Sentences*.[45] The remarkable thing is
that there is no mention of the obvious: works by Bonaventure or Scotus, and the surprising inclusion of several works of Holcot, Fishacre,
and Bradwardine.[46]

   The picture of London's intellectual life should include the non-
teaching but active scholars resident for a time in London, specifically
those masters attached to the household of a bishop whose governmental responsibilities required his presence in London as much as in his
own diocese. John Grandisson, bishop of Exeter (1327–69) and a con-
scientious churchman, was resident from time to time at Exeter Inn.
His door and table would have been open to the scholars who benefited
from his patronage, among them Richard Fitzralph, the Dominican

---

gest that he went through the libraries section by section, noting what remained or at least
what had value to him and possibly the king. John Leland, *De rebus Britannicis collectanea*,
vol. 4 (London, 1770), 49–54.

   [43] On the contents of the Dominican library in London see: Leland, *Collectanea* 4: 51–52;
Bale, *Index*, 513; Ker, *Medieval Libraries*, 124.

   [44] On the Carmelite library see: Leland, *Collectanea* 4: 52–54; Ker, *Medieval Libraries*,
124–25. Barningham was regent in theology at Paris in the early fifteenth century.

   [45] On the Franciscan library see: Leland, 49–51; Ker, 123.

   [46] Specifically, Fishacre's commentary on the *Sentences*, Holcot's Sapiential commentary
and his commentary on the *Sentences*, and Bradwardine's *De causa Dei*.

Richard Winkley, and Thomas Buckingham.[47] The same holds true for the important and oft-mentioned circle of scholars that surrounded Richard de Bury, bishop of Durham.[48] Before his appointment to the see of Durham, Bury was already attended by a large household staff that included a number of clerks and masters, and his patronage of Oxford bachelors and doctors of theology increased after his consecration as bishop. Between 1334 and his death in 1345 Bury's household included at various times such distinguished Oxford masters as Thomas Bradwardine, Walter Burley, Richard Bentworth, Richard Fitzralph, Robert Holcot, Richard Kilvington, Walter Segrave, John Maudith, and John Acton. While they were part of the episcopal *familia*, these scholar-clients were expected to travel and reside with the bishop. Before 1340 (i.e., when at one time or another most of the above-mentioned scholars were attached to his household), Bury's principal residence was Durham Inn in London, not in the north of England, as is sometimes imagined.

Workshops of Learning

A third aspect of the intellectual life of London in the early fourteenth century is the surprisingly large number of scholastic works that were written or revised there. It was probably in London that Ockham wrote his commentaries on Aristotle's logic and physics, revised the first book of his *Sentences* commentary (the *Ordinatio*), wrote his monumental *Summa logicae*, and engaged in the majority of his quodlibetic disputes.[49] It was also in London that Walter Chatton apparently gave his *Reportatio*, the only full commentary on the *Sentences* left by that important Franciscan author.[50] Adam Wodeham lectured on the *Sentences* at Lon-

[47] Emden, *BRUO* 2: 800–801 (on Grandisson), 2: 692–94 (on Fitzralph), 3: 2060 (on Winkley), and 1: 298–99 (on Buckingham); Walsh, *RF*, 47–50.

[48] On the Bury circle see J. de Ghellinck, "Une bibliophile au XIV siècle: Richard d'Aungerville," *RHE* 18 (1920): 271–312, 482–502; 19 (1923): 157–200; N. Denholm Young, "Richard de Bury (1287–1345)," *TRHS* 4th ser., 20 (1937): 135–68; Neal Ward Gilbert, "Richard de Bury and the 'Quires of Yesterday's Sophisms,' " in *Philosophy and Humanism: Renaissance Essays in Honor of Paul Oskar Kristeller*, ed. E. P. Mahoney (New York, 1976), 229–57. Katherine Walsh has also noted that the Bury circle was primarily in London; Walsh, *RF*, 20.

[49] See above, n. 34.

[50] See above, n. 35.

don and later incorporated portions of these lectures into his *Lectura secunda*.[51] It was in his London lectures that Wodeham gave his most extensive and perceptive treatment to problems of epistemology.[52] All copies of Robert Holcot's *Sentences* commentary are products of a later revision, which, in view of the number of times London is used in the text as an example, may have been completed in that setting.[53] Walter Burley remained active during the period in which he was associated with Bury in London. The works composed, revised, or completed during that period are his commentary on the *Liber de sex principiis*, the *Expositio super artem veterem*, the last section of his commentary on Aristotle's *Physics*, his commentary on the *Ethics*, and his commentary on Aristotle's *Politics*.[54] Finally, as has been noted, one of the most widely read and influential works of the period, Thomas Bradwardine's *Summa de causa Dei*, was completed in London in the years before 1344.[55]

NORWICH

Our second example is more typical of a nonuniversity center of study. Although Norwich was perhaps the second largest city in fourteenth-century England and an important commercial center, it was not the

[51] See above, n. 36.

[52] Courtenay, *Adam Wodeham*, 210–14; G. Gál, "Adam Wodeham's Question on the 'Complexe Significabile' as the Immediate Object of Scientific Knowledge," *FcS* 37 (1977): 66–102; K. Tachau, "The Problem of the *Species in medio* at Oxford in the Generation after Ockham," *MedStud* 44 (1982): 394–443; "The Response to Ockham's and Aureol's Epistemology: 1320–1340," in *ELI*, 185–217.

[53] R. Holcot, *In quatuor libros sententiarum quaestiones*, 4, q. 3: "Similiter tu qui es Londonie, haberes dubitare an aliquis homo sit Rome conversus in te." Most manuscripts have London, e.g. London, Brit. Lib., MS. Royal 10.c.6, fol. 115[vb]; Oxford, Oriel College, MS. 15, fol. 196[rb]; Cambridge, Pembroke College, MS. 236, fol. 95(93)[rb]; Oxford, Corpus Christi College, MS. 138, fol. 88[r]; Oxford, Balliol College, MS. 71, fol. 127[vb]; Oxford, Merton College, MS. 113, fol. 63[ra]; Troyes, Bibl. de la Ville, MS. 634, fol. 59[vb]; Paris, Bibl. Nat., MS. lat. 14576, fol. 95ra; Paris, Bibl. Nat., MS. lat. 15884, fol. 59va; while Florence, Bibl. Naz., MS.J. 6.20, fol. 58va, and Heiligenkreutz, MS. 185, fol. 70vb have Paris as the example.

[54] Weisheipl, "Ockham and some Mertonians," 174–88; "Repertorium Mertonense," 185–208; A. Uña Juarez, *La filosofía del siglo XIV. Contexto cultural de Walter Burley* (El Escorial, 1978).

[55] Courtenay, *Adam Wodeham*, 117–18; "Augustinianism at Oxford in the Fourteenth Century," *Augustiniana* 30 (1980): 58–70.

seat of government and law and did not attract scholars for those reasons. Those who went there did so for study or local preferment.

The area bounded by the cathedral enclosure and the convents of the Franciscans and Dominicans was, among other things, the educational district of Norwich.[56] There was a vigorous and famous grammar school.[57] The cathedral priory gave instruction in grammar, philosophy, and theology both to monks and to future diocesan clergy. Each of the four major mendicant orders had convents in the city that were *studia particularia* both for philosophy and theology, and they used the multiplicity of teaching convents to create an environment of interchange and debate that would prepare their top candidates for the challenges and confrontations of the university program.

How rigorous the program and how talented the scholars at the convents of the Blackfriars, Whitefriars, or Austin Friars were is hard to say. Norwich was a frequent but not continuous house of study for the Dominicans. Perhaps for that reason we are unable to connect with it any Dominicans of known scholarly reputation. This is also true, by and large, for the Benedectines at the cathedral priory, and for the Carmelite and Austin houses, which did not produce men of recognized learning until the second half of the fourteenth century and yet were the major *studia* of those orders in the region. Each of these institutions prepared candidates for Oxford and Cambridge and, considering the results later in the century, must have been doing a more than adequate job. But no scholarly evidence has survived. In the first half of the fourteenth century, the intellectual reputation of Norwich was carried almost entirely by the Franciscan convent, whose distinction attracted students from outside the province and as far away as Italy.

The intellectual world of Norwich Greyfriars first becomes visible to us in the late 1320s, when Adam Wodeham was lecturing there as *sententiarius* in preparation for performing the same task at Oxford, and Ralph Pigaz was resident at the convent, perhaps as lecturer in philosophy or acting in a capacity similar to the office of *magister studentium*.[58] Pigaz had already read the *Sentences* at a university, probably Cam-

[56] *VCH County of Norfolk*, ed. W. Page, vol. 2 (London, 1906), 428–33; Ker, *Medieval Libraries*, 135–40.

[57] H. W. Saunders, *A History of the Norwich Grammar School* (Norwich, 1932); Orme, *English Schools*, 144–45, 179, 245–46, 312.

[58] Courtenay, *Adam Wodeham*, 30–31, 61, 65–66, 85, 164–67.

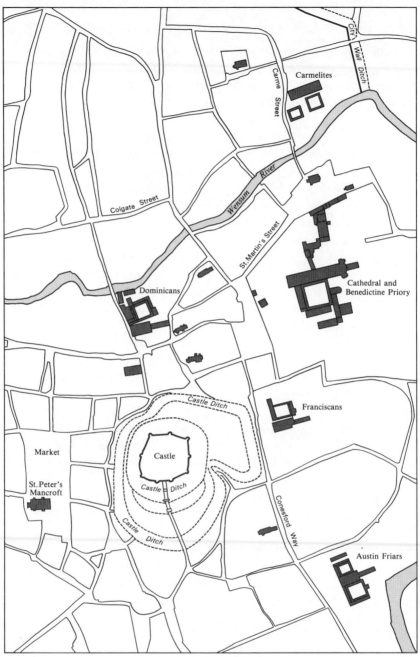

Carme Street

Carmelites

City Wall Ditch

Wensum River

Colgate Street

St.Martin's Street

Dominicans

Cathedral and
Benedictine Priory

Castle Ditch

Franciscans

Market

Castle

Castle Ditch

St.Peter's
Mancroft

Castle Ditch

Conesford Way

Austin Friars

MAP 4. FOURTEENTH-CENTURY NORWICH

bridge, around 1326 or 1327 and was on the verge of becoming regent master (lector) at the Cambridge convent, *c.* 1329.[59] While Pigaz's works are not known to have survived, his opinions were cited frequently by Wodeham in his Oxford commentary and, in all probability, in his Norwich lectures, which at present remain undiscovered. While at Norwich the topic that received the most attention from Wodeham and Pigaz (or so it remained in the memory of Wodeham) was the Trinity and the problems it presented in the area of logic.[60]

Shortly after the mid-1330s the scribal activities of an Italian Franciscan, Nicholas Comparini of Assisi, reveal again the scholarly activity of the Norwich convent.[61] In or before 1337 an otherwise unknown Franciscan by the name of Haverel (Avenel?) lectured on the *Sentences* for two years, no doubt preparing himself for similar duties at one of the university convents.[62] Nicholas also recorded the questions (possibly quodlibetal, since they include a *determinatio*) disputed at Norwich by Bartholomew of Reppes (Rippes, Reps), presumably in or before 1337–38.[63] Reppes had long since incepted at Cambridge as lector and regent master for the Franciscans (*c.* 1332) and may have been regent master at Norwich in 1337.

It is unknown whether the works of Roger Roseth (Rosetus) and Adam of Ely (two more significant Franciscans included or cited in the Norwich manuscript of Nicholas) were at that time, or ever, connected with the Norwich convent. Roseth commented on the *Sentences* between 1332 and 1337, perhaps at Norwich, but more likely at Oxford or Cambridge.[64] He may, like Nicholas, have been an Italian, since he is later described as having read in an English *studium*.[65] If so, a Cambridge set-

[59] J.R.H. Moorman, *The Grey Friars in Cambridge, 1225–1538* (Cambridge, 1952), 145, 201.

[60] H. G. Gelber, *Logic and the Trinity: A Clash of Values in Scholastic Thought, 1300–1335*, Ph.D. diss., University of Wisconsin, Madison, 1974.

[61] V. Doucet, "Le Studium Franciscain de Norwich en 1337 d'après le MS. Chigi B.V.66 de la Bibliothèque Vaticane," *AFH* 46 (1953): 85–98; W. J. Courtenay, "Nicholas of Assisi and Vatican MS. Chigi B.V.66," *Scriptorium* 36 (1982): 260–63.

[62] Vatican Library, MS. Chigi B.V.66, fols. 87ʳ–125ᵛ.

[63] Ibid., fols. 126ʳ–128ᵛ; on Bartholomew of Reppes see Moorman, *Grey Friars*, 145, 204.

[64] Courtenay, *Adam Wodeham*, 120–21, 137, 142–43, 157–58.

[65] Oxford, Bodl., MS. Canon. Misc. 177, "Rugerio Suiscepto sive Roseto in studio Anglicano." Some manuscripts do identify him as an English Franciscan: Bruxelles, MS. 1551, and the 1381 inventory of the Franciscan library at Assisi.

ting becomes more likely, as the pressure to accept foreign friars, particularly Italians, into the English *studia generalia* appears to have made
the positions of *sententiarius* and *magister regens* more accessible at Cambridge than at Oxford.[66]

Adam of Ely, whose name is cited in the Norwich manuscript and
who may have been there in 1337, is presumably identical with Adam
Junior, who has left us a commentary on the *Sentences* that can be dated
around 1337.[67] It may have been given at Oxford, since scholars from
East Anglia went there on occasion (as the career of Luke of Ely reveals)
and Adam of Ely had as one of his *socii* an innovative and somewhat
nonconformist Benedictine bachelor, known simply as the *Monachus Niger*, whose work circulated on the Continent and received the antago-
nistic attention of Gregory of Rimini.[68] The principal place of higher
studies for the Benedictines, as we have seen, was Oxford. But the lectures of Adam of Ely and the *Monachus Niger* may have taken place at
Cambridge, where Adam was eventually regent master (*c.* 1346).[69] But
apart from the name of Adam of Ely appearing in the 1337 manuscript
of Nicholas Comparini, there is nothing that connects either of these
men with the Norwich convent; unfortunately, since it would integrate
an important Benedictine cathedral school with the scholarly activity of
the mendicant convents.

The reputation of Norwich among the continental *studia* lasted well
into the third quarter of the century. When Peter of Candia, the future
Pope Alexander V, came from Italy and Paris to study in England, Norwich was one of the two *studia* he attended.[70] It was there as much as at

[66] This shift in policy brought in as regent masters at Greyfriars, Cambridge, John de
Casale (*c.* 1340–41), James de Pennis (*c.* 1345–46), Peter de Aragonia (*c.* 1348–49), Roger
de Sicilia (*c.* 1351–52), Leonardo Rossi de Giffono (*c.* 1360), and Thomas of Portugal (*c.*
1371). See Moorman, *Grey Friars.*

[67] J.-F. Genest, *Le "De futuris contingentibus" de Thomas Bradwardine*, Mémoire pour le Di-
plome de l'Ecole pratique des hautes études, 5ᵉ section, Paris, 1975, lxviii–lxxiv, 116–26,
189–92; Genest, "Le *De futuris contingentibus* de Thomas Bradwardine," *Recherches Augustiniennes* 14 (1979): 268–71.

[68] D. Trapp, "Augustinian Theology of the Fourteenth Century," *Augustiniana* 6 (1956):
201–13, 235–39; "Moderns and Modernists in Fribourg Cordeliers 26," *Augustinianum* 5
(1965): 241–70.

[69] Moorman, *Grey Friars*, 100, 145, 174.

[70] F. Ehrle, *Der Sentenzenkommentar Peters von Candia*, Franziskanische Studien, 9 (Münster i.W., 1925).

Oxford that he came into firsthand contact with the type of English philosophy and theology that had captivated Paris in the 1340s.[71] It is remarkable that Norwich's reputation survived as well as it did, considering the devastating effect the plague of 1348–49 had on that city, particularly on the members of the religious houses, some of which were all but emptied of life within a year.[72]

For several of the mendicant orders Norwich and Cambridge were closely connected, the former acting as a "feeder" institution for the latter and receiving back its higher academic and administrative officials. The careers of Ralph Pigaz, Bartholomew of Reppes, and Adam of Ely illustrate that connection well. But Norwich could and did act as an independent center within the Franciscan system, with ties to London and Oxford almost as remarkable as its ties with Cambridge. One need only reflect on the academic migrations of Wodeham, Nicholas Comparini, and Peter of Candia.

YORK

York was the most important center of learning in the northern half of England.[73] It possessed several elementary and grammar schools in the fourteenth century. It had one of the most distinguished cathedral schools. Moreover, in contrast to Norwich, York possessed convents of all four major mendicant orders, which were *studia particularia* for the

[71] W. J. Courtenay, "The Role of English Thought in the Transformation of University Education in the Late Middle Ages," in *Rebirth, Reform and Resilience: Universities in Transition, 1300–1700*, ed. J. A. Kittelson (Columbus, Ohio, 1984), 103–62; "The Reception of Ockham's Thought at the University of Paris," in *PRUP*, 43–64; and with Katherine Tachau, "Ockham, Ockhamism, and the English-German Nation at Paris, 1339–1341," *History of Universities* 2 (1982): 53–96; N. W. Gilbert, "Ockham, Wyclif, and the 'Via Moderna,'" in *AM*, 85–125; Gilbert, "Richard de Bury," 229–57.

[72] For example, all members of the Friars of Our Lady in Norwich died in 1349.

[73] Information for the following account has been drawn from: *VCH: City of York* (London, 1961); Ker, *Medieval Libraries*; M. R. James, "The Catalogue of the Library of the Augustinian Friars at York," in *Fasciculus Ioanni Willis Clark dicatus* (Cambridge, 1909), 2–96; Roth, *EAF* 1; Le Neve, *Fasti Ecclesiae Anglicanae*, vol. 6 (London, 1963); Emden, *BRUO*; Jo Ann Moran, *Education and Learning in the City of York, 1300–1560*, University of York, Borthwick Institute Papers No. 55 (York, 1979); *The Growth of English Schooling, 1340–1548* (Princeton, 1985); Barrie Dobson, "The Later Middle Ages," in *A History of York Minster*, ed. G. E. Aylmer and R. Cant (Oxford, 1977), 44–109.

region around York or, in the case of the Dominicans, for most of northern England. Yorkshire was also the point of origin for two of the leading scholastic figures of the first and second halves of the century, respectively the secular theologian, logician, and physicist, Richard Kilvington, and the Carmelite Stephen Patrington.

Among the many song, reading, and grammar schools of the city, St. Peter's at York Minster was the largest and most respected, educating children from families of means from the city and diocese as well as a large number of poor scholars. Average enrollment in the cathedral grammar school has been estimated between 100 and 150 students. Those not living at home or with relatives found lodging in St. Mary's Abbey near the cathedral or in Holy Trinity Hospital, located farther away in the undercroft of the Merchant Adventurers' Hall along the Foss. The school had its own building, having been moved in 1289 from a room off the cathedral nave to a vacant prebendal house. Grammar masters before the Black Death were usually M.A.s hired for a three- to five-year term, although the level of required education dropped and the period of tenure lengthened in the third quarter of the century.

In addition to the schools for song and grammar at the cathedral, the large Benedictine abbey of St. Mary's housed a school, and there was a grammar and song school at St. Leonard's Hospital. Surviving manuscripts that can be traced to St. Mary's library suggest that it may have provided lectures in theology or that among its monks there were those (perhaps university graduates) who had an interest in scholastic theology. Such would explain the proportion of works in scholastic philosophy and theology. Instruction at the level of reading and grammar could apparently also be obtained in the households of various cathedral canons.

At the level of higher education, the single most important school was that of the cathedral, whose high towers marked the northern corner of the medieval city. In its succession of chancellors and not infrequently in its archbishops York possessed men of learning who maintained the reputation of the cathedral school throughout most of the fourteenth century. William Wickwane, as chancellor of York and head of the theological school, showed his support of the grammar school in 1271 by complaining to the archbishop for withholding the funds normally des-

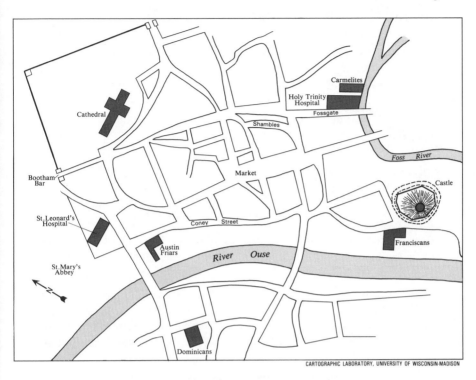

MAP 5. FOURTEENTH-CENTURY YORK

ignated for the grammar school (to pay the schoolmaster and maintain the building).[74] Wickwane, a university graduate, succeeded Walter Giffard as archbishop in 1279 and appointed to the vacant chancellorship Thomas Corbrigge, a doctor of theology from Oxford. During Corbrigge's tenure as chancellor, Wickwane died and was succeeded as archbishop by John le Romeyn, D.Th. from Paris and long regent there, who had been chancellor of Lincoln cathedral from around 1272 to 1279, before becoming archbishop of York in 1285. Corbrigge continued to serve as the York chancellor for a decade, and in 1299 he became archbishop of York (1299–1304), continuing the tradition of learned men in that office.

The record of chancellors at York in the fourteenth century is im-

[74] *The Register of Walter Giffard*, ed. W. Brown, Surtees Society, no. 109 (Durham, 1904), 42, cited from Moran, *Education and Learning*, 5.

pressive. Robert de Ripplingham, a Mertonian, D.Th. from Oxford, and noted theologian, was chancellor at York from 1297 until his death in 1332. His activity as a teacher at York is commemorated in the Minster by a stained glass representation of Ripplingham lecturing to his class. William de Alberwick, similarly a Mertonian and doctor of theology at Oxford, but who had been chancellor of the university as well, succeeded Ripplingham as chancellor at York from 1332 until his death in 1349.

The second half of the century was not too different, except for the appointment of a canon lawyer immediately after the Black Death. Simon de Bekingham, who was papal Auditor of Causes at York in 1346 as well as a licentiate in civil and canon law from Oxford, gained the office through papal provision and held it until his death in 1369. Thereafter the chancellorship reverted to theologians. Thomas de Farnelawe, a Mertonian and Oxford doctor of theology, was chancellor from 1369 until his death in 1379. John de Shirburne, another Oxford doctor of theology, succeeded him as chancellor at York from 1380 until his death in 1410.

The office of chancellor was rarely abandoned except by a move upward into the episcopate, and unless a person were fortunate enough to be so recognized and rewarded, he remained as cathedral chancellor until death. Moreover, the chancellorship was an active position that entailed lecturing in theology and overseeing the schools of the cathedral from the level of the song and grammar schools up to the level of theological instruction, in which the chancellor was personally engaged unless he appointed a substitute. The students were drawn not only from among the younger clergy of the cathedral but included as well clergy from the diocese who, from the time of Archbishop Romeyn, could obtain a temporary licence of nonresidence in order to attend lectures in the cathedral school. On occasion one finds the presence of students from other parts of England as well.

What is particularly remarkable at York is not only the dominance of theology over law in the office of chancellor, but the succession of Mertonians—a phenomenon also observed at London but not so consistently maintained there throughout the century. This practice probably reflects, in part, the continuing reputation of Merton as the Oxford unit most likely to house the most gifted theological scholars among the seculars. But it may also have derived from a close tie between the college and the cathedral chapter whereby the cathedral expected to derive its chancellors from that source, and the college, for its part, expected to have access to that office in time of vacancy.

Each of the major mendicant orders had a convent in York, spread out through the older part of the city rather than grouped near the cathedral. The Franciscan convent was located on the southern edge of the castle moat and bordering on the Ouse, and was the third most important custodial school in England, after London and Norwich. As we saw in the previous chapter, the York convent provided training in philosophy and theology for friars in the York custody, and several of the early English Franciscan masters came from there, such as Adam of York and Thomas of York.

The Austin convent in York, located in the northwestern quarter of the city near St. Leonard's Hospital and the river, was probably a *studium particulare* in philosophy and a *studium concursorium* in theology for the York limit. The Austin friary in the second half of the century (and probably in the first as well) had two masters, probably one for philosophy and one for theology, as was the case with the Franciscans at London and Norwich. The Austin library by the late fourteenth century housed one of the finest collections of manuscripts of any mendicant library. The richness of the collection, which comprised some 656 volumes containing over 2,100 treatises, is revealed by the fortunate survival of the library catalogue, compiled in 1372 by Brother John Erghom, who himself had endowed the library with more than a third of its holdings. One cannot assume that the size and composition of the other mendicant libraries was similar, since the building of any collection depended largely on donations. But biblical and scholastic manuscripts were important for any teaching convent, and the patristic, philosophical, and theological core was probably similar, after making allowances for partiality to authors of a particular order. Jo Ann Moran has rightly noted that the Austin catalogue has not received the scrutiny it deserves, particularly "its extensive range," which included apocalyptic and prophetic literature, such as the works of Joachim of Fiore and Simon Hinton; Latin, Arabic, and Jewish treatises on astrology and magic; an extensive cross-section of ancient Greek and Latin authors; and scholastic treatises and *questiones* of university scholars from Yorkshire.[75]

Within the cycle of Dominican education, York probably functioned frequently as a school and was certainly among the most important convents in northern England, the principal one for the York visitation, which included Lincoln, Newcastle, Lancaster, Scarborough, Yarm, Carlisle, Beverly, Pontefract, Bamburg, and Berwick. The convent was located on the southwest side of the Ouse (across the river from the Augustinian convent), on the edge of the city ditch and "had thirty-four cells, each with a study."[76]

The Carmelite convent in York, about which we know academically the least, was located along the Foss at Fossgate, near the Merchant Adventurers' Hall. It was among their earliest foundations and was a *studium particulare* for the York distinction, offering instruction in grammar, philosophy, and theology.

As with any of the centers that possessed a number of mendicant schools, the pre- and extra-university program of studies among the York convents would have required interaction in the form of disputations and perhaps lectures as well. In this academic activity the cathedral school was included. The 1355 disputation on the Immaculate Conception between the Franciscan master, john Mardislay, and the Dominican master, William Jordan, took place at the cathedral. Moreover, the preaching of the Augustinian master, John Waldeby, in the 1360s was influential throughout the city and was not confined to a mendicant audience at the Austin friary.

The cases of London, Norwich, and York, better documented but probably not too different from other cities and towns in which the *studia particularia* of the mendicant orders coincided with a vigorous cathedral school, underscore the importance of nonuniversity centers of higher education for the intellectual life of fourteenth-century England. They were not isolated but were fully integrated with the universities in a

---

[75] Moran, *Education and Learning*, 27.
[76] Moran, *Education and Learning*, 26.

broad educational system. They also acted as the avenues through which the influence of universities was conveyed to a larger society and through which university scholars made that transition from the world of learning to learning about the world—the world of post-university careers.

FOUR

BEYOND THE SCHOOLS: THE
PATRONAGE OF IDEAS

꙼꙼꙼

THE TOWN of Oxford lies in the upper reaches of the Thames Valley, which was in the fourteenth century a major governmental and commercial route. To the north lay the royal estate of Woodstock, visited frequently by king and court, and far to the southeast, down river, were Westminster and London, the centers of government and trade. The scholastic debates of that age may appear worlds apart from the realities of everyday life, but the careers of Oxford scholars do not seem so isolated. For many (and probably as an ideal for most) the university led to a career that moved toward London as surely and unalterably as the water that flowed under the bridges outside Oxford.

As was noted earlier, medieval universities, to which Oxford was no exception, did not provide a permanent home for a learned *intelligentia*. Much of the actual teaching was done by bachelors as part of their preparation to become masters in a particular faculty, and by the fourteenth century in England one usually remained regent at a university for only a few years. Thus, while inception into the guild of masters at a *studium generale* conferred the theoretical right to teach anywhere (*ius ubique docendi*) for as long as one wished, it did not in practice mean that the recipient taught for long anywhere. At Oxford, inception and regency were expenses to be borne and did not, in themselves, confer any lucrative stipend. University teaching in England, unlike the position of grammar master, was seldom viewed as a serious career option.

PATRONS OF SCHOLARS AND SCHOLAR-PATRONS

The Patronage System

The importance of patronage in art, literature, and music in the fourteenth century has long been acknowledged. Chaucer was for a time Clerk of the King's Works and, like Boccaccio, was involved in diplomatic service, probably in a secretarial capacity. Similarly, Eustache Deschampes, Guillaume Dufay, Roger van der Weyden, and Jan van Eyck all acted as envoys while attached to the courts of their respective patrons. The role of patronage in learning apart from literature, however, has been less well explored.[1] How did the graduate find a patron, and what effects did this practice have on the careers of scholastics and on the intellectual life of the fourteenth century?

Finding a patron to support one's education and subsequent career was among the highest priorities of the secular university student. For those whose families lacked the financial resources or inclination to pay for a university education, the need for extrafamilial support began early, but at one stage or another almost all students sought the help of others better placed, whether through a network of friends and contacts often from the region of origin, or by application to those who had positions to offer. Patron-client relationships ran deep through every sphere of late medieval society. As Guy Lytle expressed it, "it was the working out in practice of the principle and rewards of hierarchy; on the other hand, it was the only counterbalance to hierarchical privilege for those whose ambition exceeded their birth."[2]

[1] An exciting introduction to the interrelation of literature, patronage, and court life in fourteenth-century England can be found in Gervase Mathew, *The Court of Richard II* (London, 1968), but it should be read alongside *English Court Culture in the Later Middle Ages*, ed. V. J. Scattergood and J. W. Sherborne (London, 1983); see also Richard Green, *Poets and Princepleasers: Literature and the English Court in the Late Middle Ages* (Toronto, 1980). For the patronage of scholars and ideas see Pantin, *ECFC*, especially chs. 2, 3, and 6; Guy F. Lytle, "Patronage Patterns and Oxford Colleges, c. 1300–c. 1540," in L. Stone, ed., *The University in Society*, vol. 1 (Princeton, 1974), 111–49; *Oxford Students and English Society: c. 1300–c. 1510*, Ph.D. diss., Princeton University, 1976; "A University Mentality in the Later Middle Ages: The pragmatism, humanism, and orthodoxy of New College, Oxford," in *Genèse et débuts du grand schisme d'occident* (Paris, 1980), 201–30; " 'Wykehamist Culture' in pre-Reformation England" and "Patronage and the Election of Winchester Scholars during the late Middle Ages and Renaissance" in R. Custance, *Winchester College* (Oxford, 1982), 129–66, 167–88; "The Careers of Oxford Students in the Later Middle Ages" in *Rebirth, Reform and Resilience: Universities in Transition, 1300–1700*, ed. J. M. Kittelson and P. J. Transue (Columbus, Ohio, 1984), 213–53, and his forthcoming chapter in *HUO* 2; Jean Dunbabin's chapter in *HUO* 1, 565–605. For the literature on the continental parallels of this topic see Jürgen Miethke, "Die Kirche und die Universitäten im 13. Jahrhundert," in *Schulen und Studium im sozialen Wandel des hohen und späteren Mittelalters*, ed. J. Fried, Vorträge und Forschungen, 30 (Sigmaringen, 1986), 285–320.

[2] Lytle, "Patronage Patterns," 115.

Most Oxford graduates looked to church, state, or religious order for their long-range career goals, and these institutions were interrelated administratively and sometimes scholastically. A university education, no matter how extensive or distinguished, only partially prepared or qualified one for a prestigious position in the "outside" world. For those who did not inherit their social contacts by being born into a prominent, aristocratic family (and those who did were few in early fourteenth-century Oxford), the link between the university and public society had to be forged, first by finding a patron before or while still at the university, and, secondly and more importantly, by becoming part of the patron's extended *familia* soon after graduation. The mendicants perhaps had an initial advantage in that the order provided financial support during and beyond the university years and could provide administrative experience and contacts through the "international" structure of their orders. But the fact that mendicants sometimes sought support from bishops, cardinals, and papal legates suggests that the benefits of extramural patronage were not unknown or closed to any group. Probably if one had not come to the attention of some person of standing within five or ten years of leaving Oxford, or come to the attention of the leadership of one's order within that same period of time, there would be little hope for a distinguished career in subsequent years.

The student would choose a patron from among one or more of those who controlled positions with income or, at first, from those who could provide access to those who did. Throughout the early stages of one's career these less tangible favors remained important: the favor of an introduction to those who held power, the ability to place a client at the right place at the right time. But ultimately (the sooner the better), it was the tangible " reward that mattered, and the student needed someone who could offer financial support or, better, someone who controlled positions with income: king, pope, bishops, nobility, monasteries, colleges, confraternities, lay possessors of rights of appointment to church livings; in short, anyone who had something tangible to give. The patron need not be an Oxford or Cambridge graduate nor even university trained, but only one who considered higher education, among other qualifications, to be important and desirable. Patrons who were themselves scholars took a particularly active and personal role in this process.

The type of patron chosen often varied with the stage of career. In coming to a university and during the undergraduate years, patronage came in the form of financial aid from friends of the family, from persons in the student's home town or region, or from a college, if he were fortunate enough to be selected. The population of particular halls and colleges was often determined by geographical and patron/client ties, somewhat parallel to patterns of migration from rural districts to particular quarters of towns. During the years of graduate training students in theology and canon law cultivated university masters and officials, episcopal contacts, perhaps distinguished alumni of their college, or others through whom they might receive a benefice or be brought to the attention of the papacy or royal administration. In postgraduate years the principal patrons were the king, the pope, bishops, and, for lesser church offices, colleges, the aristocracy, and other lay possessors of advowsons.

Although the categories of patrons were numerous, the source from which they acquired positions to offer was generally the same. Ecclesiastical livings were by far the largest source of income that could be distributed through patronage. Most positions had specific qualification requirements that had to be observed, at least in appearance if not in reality: for example, literacy and some theological training for ordination; ordination as subdeacon, deacon, or priest for certain church livings; a licentiate or masters degree in theology or law for certain positions within a cathedral hierarchy. Moreover, positions differed with regard to residence requirements. Many appointments included care of souls and required the holder to be in residence and to fulfill the duties of his charge, unless he gained a temporary exemption and could appoint a vicar in his place. So much attention has been focused on absenteeism and plurality of benefices that we tend to forget the large number of clerics who sought a single but sufficiently rewarding parish church, and who saw it as a full-time commitment. Other positions required only part-time residence, and some, no residence at all. These latter benefices did not represent employment but were means to some other end and were often given as partial income or reward to those who were fulfilling other services and whose financial, social, and political aspirations lay higher than the parish ministry.

Patrons often used a different mixture of criteria in filling vacancies over which they held advowson. In the best of circumstances, from among those who had the required educational qualifications and were willing to fulfill the duties of the office as understood by the patron, they chose candidates on the basis of family, region, academic discipline, academic distinction, or on recommendation of a friend or superior. In less ideal circumstances, such as after the Black Death, when vacancies exceeded qualified candidates, or at any time when the need to do a favor for a friend exceeded the need to appoint someone fully qualified, personal considerations dominated.

The actual operation of patronage in late medieval society is complex and only partially revealed by the documents. Given the social and political need to hide or disguise patronage and favoritism in many circumstances, it is often difficult from this remove to identify exactly who was the patron of a particular client. The person who held the right of appointment and conferred it is not necessarily the primary patron of the client. In addition to rewarding one's own followers, relatives, or friends, one often needed to do a favor for someone else, to repay a past service, to gain credit toward some future service, or simply to bow to external pressure. When Bishop Grandisson or Edward III asked the pope to provide for one of their own, the collation to benefice was more a result of episcopal or royal patronage than of papal. Probably more often than not, certainly more often than we realize and can ever document, the patron of record was only the channel through which someone else's client was rewarded.

This system of indirect and multiple patronage was not simply a result of conflicting jurisdictions or the hierarchical fact that higher-placed patrons could pressure those of lower status. For every patron the amount and timing of demand rarely coincided with the supply of available openings. Vacancies might occur at a time when a patron had no candidate of his or her own to put forward and would thus be in a position to do a favor for someone else. At other times a patron might have many needy clients or many debts to repay, and yet have no suitable available position over which he or she could exercise direct control, *pleno iure*. Within this disequilibrium of supply and demand the circumstances of the time were all important, and it was those with the most mouths to feed, those most in need of patronage to offer (a constant condition of king and pope) who absorbed the largest share of supply. For those choosing patrons, it was important to know not just how many livings potential patrons could control, but whether they were strong and independent enough to reward their own, or whether they needed to do favors for others or buy friends for themselves, and thus might save their patronage for someone else's clients.

Scholars whose career aims were directed toward high office in church and government (for we should not automatically assume that this desire was universal among students) rarely cultivated only one patron. In fact, the entire system seemed to encourage multiple patrons, both successively and simultaneously. Walter Burley at various times found himself in the service of John XXII, Edward III, and Richard de Bury. While in Avignon Richard Fitzralph was working on behalf of Edward III as well as John XXII and, later, Clement VI. Where there was no conflict of interest visible to the patrons, multiple patrons were permitted and desirable.

The Papacy

Various currents, independent and sometimes conflicting, conditioned relations between the papacy and English scholars in the fourteenth century.[3] First and foremost, the papacy was and continued to be a major supporter of universities through protection, encouragement, and patronage. English scholars at Paris in the thirteenth century felt this more directly, where they enjoyed the status of the *ius ubique docendi* and had access to the executive and judicial power of the Conservator of Apostolic Privileges of the University.[4] Cambridge and Oxford looked more to the king for protection, but even in England the papacy influenced royal policy in the reign of Edward I to appoint men of learning to high office in the church, all other things being equal. Moreover, the papal constitution *Cum ex eo* of Boniface VIII, which attracted young and often talented scholars into the ranks of the parish clergy by allowing them to pay for their advanced education out of the revenues of the church they would eventually serve (at least for a time), had a remarkable effect on improving the supply of educated clerks among the lower clergy in England and creating a sudden infusion of financial support for English universities.[5]

---

[3] Pantin, *ECFC*, chs. 3–5.

[4] Pearl Kibre, *Scholarly Privileges in the Middle Ages* (Cambridge, Mass., 1962), chs. 4, 5, 7, and 9.

[5] In addition to Pantin, see L. Boyle, "The Constitution 'Cum ex eo' of Boniface VIII," *MedStud* 24 (1962): 263–302, and "Aspects of Clerical Education in Fourteenth-Century

The most useful form of papal favor, however, was the ability to provide a benefice or influence the appointment to a church living. The
policy of papal provision, which for long in canon law and ecclesiastical
tradition covered certain types of appointments under certain conditions, was expanded in 1265 to cover theoretically all benefices that
would become vacant in England.[6] In fact, however, papal provision
was implemented slowly, and did not become common until the fourteenth century. It was an attempt by the Avignon papacy to centralize
the process of appointment to church offices and livings and, ideally, to
promote better qualified candidates than those that might be selected
by lay patrons. Education in the early fourteenth century was considered one of those desirable qualities, and the expansion of papal provision increased the patronage capacity of one of the university's principal supporters, to whom scholars increasingly looked for financial
support and career opportunities. In practice, papal provision was usually done in cooperation with the king and through negotiations with
those who had rights of advowson. Furthermore, the new system was
far from automatic. Papal provision was essentially the ability to grant
an expectative and initiate a process that could result in collation to a
benefice, often within one to three years. For high office it was independently effective only in those times when a strong pope coincided
with a weak or young monarch.

Most English scholars seeking papal support and patronage did so by

---

England," in *The Fourteenth Century*, Acta 4. Center for Medieval and Early Renaissance
Studies, SUNY (Binghamton, N.Y., 1977), 19–32, both essays now found in L. Boyle, *Pastoral Care, Clerical Education and Canon Law, 1200–1400* (London, 1981); R. M. Haines,
"The Education of the English Clergy during the Later Middle Ages: Some Observations
on the Operation of Pope Boniface VIII's Constitution Cum Ex Eo (1298)," *Canadian Journal of History* 4–5 (1969–70): 1–22; "Education in English Ecclesiastical Legislation of the
Later Middle Ages," in *Councils and Assemblies*, Studies in Church History 7, ed. G. J. Cuming and D. Baker (Cambridge, 1978), 161–75. On Haines' interpretation see the warnings
of R. N. Swanson, "Universities, Graduates and Benefices in Later Medieval England," *Past
and Present* no. 106 (Feb. 1985): 28–61, esp. 32–33.

[6] G. Barraclough, *Papal Provisions* (Oxford, 1935); G. Mollat, *La Collation des bénéfices ec-
clésiasiques sous les Papes d'Avignon, 1305–78* (Paris, 1921); A. Deeley, "Papal Provision and
Rights of Royal Patronage in the Early Fourteenth Century," *EHR* 43 (1928): 497–527;
Pantin, *ECFC*, 47–102; E. F. Jacob, "On the Promotion of English University Clerks during
the Later Middle Ages," *JEH* 1 (1950): 172–86; Kibre, *Scholarly Privileges*, 227–50.

indirect means. These took the form of petitions to the pope as one attained some advanced level of achievement within the university. The approach could be made by the scholar himself, but the chances of success were far higher if he was brought to the attention of the Roman *curia* through someone already well known there: a friend at the papal court, a bishop, some powerful layman, or the king. By the second quarter of the fourteenth century universities began to submit rolls of names of university scholars, acting as a prescreening deliberative body and as a corporate or collective person whose standing could match that of many lay or episcopal patrons. These lists, which often (but need not) coincide with the accession of a new pope, might be submitted by the whole university, but they could as well come from an individual faculty, a particular academic level within a faculty, a college, or at Paris, a nation, either separately or as part of a general roll. Depending on the nature of the list, masters and graduates, regents and nonregents down to the level of bachelors of arts might be included. Having one's name on a rotulus allowed one to seek the patronage of the pope without ever crossing the channel to Avignon and at far less personal cost.[7]

Other scholars created a more direct and personal tie with the papacy by residing for a time in Avignon.[8] This was made possible by the fact that the papacy was more than a means of securing positions in one's own region or country. The Roman *curia* was also an employer. Papal offices were within the direct gift of the pope and provided both financial support and a nonuniversity career post. Some of these were in England and only occasionally required visits to Avignon. In this category were the positions of papal tax collector and papal mandatory. Other positions resulted from presence, or required presence, at the

---

[7] E. F. Jacob, "Petitions for Benefices from English Universities during the Great Schism," *TRHS*, 4th ser., 27 (1945): 41–59; Pantin, *ECFC*, 49–51, 64–65. For the operation of the *rotuli* at the continental universities, see P. Kibre, *The Nations in the Mediaeval Universities* (Cambridge, Mass., 1948), 10, 18–20, 148; *Scholarly Privileges*, 230–34. Rashdall's account, *Univ.* 1: 555–58; 2: 88–89, and passim, still contains useful information, although his views on the beginning and frequency of the *rotuli* have been revised.

[8] In addition to Pantin, see G. Mollat, *The Popes at Avignon*, transl. from the ninth French edition (London, 1963); E. F. Jacob, *Essays in Later Medieval History* (Manchester, 1968), 58–78; Bernard Guillemain, *La cour pontificale d'Avignon (1309–1376): Etude d'une société* (Paris, 1962).

papal court in Avignon. For English clerks at Avignon, this category included the positions of papal chaplain (given both to lawyers and theologians), penitentiary, positions in the chancery and the judicial branches of the *curia*, such as scribe, abbreviator, advocate, or as auditor of the Sacred Palace, all of which employed lawyers. There were also judicial and teaching positions that depended on theological knowledge and academic distinction.

This last category is particularly important for the issue of the papacy as patron of scholastic theology. From the middle of the thirteenth century the *curia romana* had sheltered and nourished a *studium generale* with a limited student body but a distinguished group of lectors drawn from Bologna, Paris, Oxford, Toulouse, and other *studia*.[9] Avignon in the fourteenth century became an important place for teaching in southern France, alongside Toulouse and Montpellier. A distinguished master of Paris or Oxford might exercise his *ius ubique docendi* where he would be most visible to and in contact with those in charge of papal patronage. William of Gainsborough, before becoming bishop of Worcester (1302), was lector at the papal court in Rome. In addition to acting as lector, English masters were sometimes appointed to investigative commissions on points of doctrine or ones that were charged with the responsibility of determining the orthodoxy of the writings of a fellow theologian. The doctrinal opinions that emanated from the *curia romana* or these papal commissions were formulated by university masters, mostly from Paris but some from Oxford.

Thus, after completion of the theological degree, whether at Paris or Oxford, many sought advancement at the papal court. Some, like Walter Burley, gravitated there by way of Paris. Others, like John Lutterell, Walter Chatton, or John of Reading, went there directly from Oxford. The principal attraction of Avignon was the possibility of patronage. The route, midway through the pontificate of John XXII, was well described by Stephen of Kettelbergh in advising Lutterell to join him at Avignon.

Any master, expert in theology in name and deed, who comes here to the Apostolic See, does not leave the Court [empty-handed]. In the first place the lord pope freely provides them with great dignities and prebends, and according to the various conditions of the persons, transfers some to the pinnacle of episco-

9 Rashdall, *Univ.* 2: 28–31, 173–81.

pal dignity and others to archiepiscopal sees, granting to each, as is becoming, that which his merits demand.[10]

The period from 1315 to 1345 provided numerous opportunities for distinguished scholars, particularly theologians, to find employment at Avignon that might be rewarded with advancement in the church hierarchy. Papal concern over doctrinal orthodoxy took the form of bringing the person and works of suspect theologians to Avignon for examination and, if necessary, trial. Increased litigation of this sort required expanding the number of distinguished doctors of theology resident in Avignon. Then, in the 1320s, as the crisis with the Franciscans deepened, theologians were needed to advise on the issue of apostolic poverty and, in the early 1330s, the issue of the beatific vision, on which John XXII held some fascinating but nontraditional views. Particularly in the years 1322 to 1334, English masters went to Avignon seeking employment and patronage with a good chance of finding both.

It is difficult to get a precise idea of the number of English scholars resident at Avignon at any one time. What evidence we do have suggests that the number was higher in the first half of the century than in the second. There was always a need for lawyers within the papal bureaucracy, and the prominence of the English *studia* in that discipline meant a constant supply of English canon lawyers to Avignon. The number of English theologians resident at the *curia* increased, as we have seen, in the period from 1320 to 1340, thus swelling the ranks of the English colony in Avignon. But the percentage of theologians declined after 1345, except for those called there in some official capacity or sent as envoys of university, bishop, lay magnate, or king.

This last practice reminds us that the papacy was not the sole or even principal source of patronage in the high and late Middle Ages. As the system of papal provision gradually grew and expanded in the fourteenth century, it became at the same time a less self-contained, direct, or certain route toward securing a benefice, largely because it came into direct conflict with two other currents in fourteenth-century England: royal power and antipapal sentiment within the upper levels of lay society. So, while the papacy had more to offer and was therefore a more likely and useful patron, it also became less useful as an independent source of patronage and eventually one that could be bypassed or ap-

[10] Pantin, *ECFC*, 16–17; from *Snappe's Formulary*, ed. H. E. Salter (Oxford, 1924), 304.

proached through another patron. Papal service became increasingly replaced by royal service.

The tie with Avignon began to weaken well before mid-century and the promulgation of the statutes of Provisors (1351) and Praemunire (1353), which ostensibly excluded papal provision and related foreign litigation. During the pontificates of Benedict XII (1334–42) and Clement VI (1342–52), royal patronage within the English church was extended under the guise of papal provision. Clement was particularly eager to appoint royal nominees, thus making residence at the *curia romana* an unnecessary step en route to a high ecclesiastical career. Until 1335 we still find English theologians, for example, Richard Fitzralph, traveling to Avignon for their own advancement; after 1340 those who went were there on diplomatic service, part of the retinue of someone who was, or were lawyers who continued to find employment as auditors of causes in the Sacred Palace.

Royal Patronage

The power of the king in the area of patronage far outweighed that of the papacy, and it grew in the fourteenth century at the expense of both pope and ecclesiastical institutions in England.[11] Church livings represented the largest source of income for rewarding the efforts of those in royal service, and the king, or more precisely the royal administration, had the most to offer because of what lay directly in its power (the large number of crown livings and appointments to the well endowed royal chapels), what it had access to from time to time by reason of feudal or regalian rights, what could be negotiated with the papacy under the guise of papal provision, and what it could shake loose from other patrons by pressure or for a price.

Just as papal patronage was distributed among those in church careers, so royal patronage was reserved primarily for those in royal service, for the extended network of family and friends (or friends of friends), for important petitioners and their clients, and as payments or

[11] See Pantin, *ECFC*, 30–46; J. H. Tillotson, "Pensions, Corrodies and Religious Houses: An Aspect of the Relations of Crown and Church in Early Fourteenth-Century England," *The Journal of Religious History* 8 (1974): 127–43; J. R. Wright, *The Church and the English Crown, 1305–1334: A Study Based on the Register of Archbishop Walter Reynolds* (Toronto, 1980).

rewards that facilitated the operation of government. The king was the single largest patron for ecclesiastical positions in England, and royal service (after the church) the second largest employer of Oxford graduates in the fourteenth century. Royal clerks and officials rarely needed other patrons, and when we find them in the service of pope, prince, or bishop, it is often as an extension of royal service. Four times as many known graduates were connected with royal service as were associated either with the episcopate or the nobility. On the average thirty percent of the known civil lawyers were absorbed into royal service, some twenty percent of canon law graduates, and thirteen to fifteen percent of the theologians. As those figures reflect, even allowing for the larger number of theological graduates in the first half of the century, royal service attracted or employed far more lawyers than theologians, and for the latter, ecclesiastical patrons were a more likely potential source of appointments. Yet ambitious theologians left little to chance and sought multiple patrons—a task made easier by the closer interdependence of royal and ecclesiastical administrations.

Among the English resident at the papal court in Avignon, therefore, one could find a significant number who were there on royal business, just as some were proctors for English prelates or religious houses. Even among papal officers, both English and non-English, one could find men who had, to one degree or another, been retained by the king as well as other patrons.

Many university scholars entered royal service indirectly. They were brought to the attention of the royal administration through ecclesiastical or judicial channels. Academic distinction, at least in the late thirteenth or early fourteenth century, was useful if one wished to get the attention of someone in high office, but ultimately fidelity and the ability to perform assigned tasks well were the qualities that advanced one.

The Episcopal Familia

For those who had made a significant scholastic contribution while at Oxford or were in the process of establishing such a reputation, the patron most useful in bridging the gap between university and society was the scholar-bishop.[12] Episcopal patronage of Oxford scholars was part

[12] On scholar-bishops as patrons see above, n. 1, esp. Pantin, *ECFC*; Lytle, *Oxford Students* and "Patronage and the Election of Winchester Scholars."

of a system that had its roots in the thirteenth and earlier centuries. The rise of the universities had not completely eclipsed the cathedral school, where theology and related disciplines were taught to the younger clergy or to those who had not had an opportunity to attend a university. As was mentioned in the last chapter, it was expected in the thirteenth and fourteenth centuries that every cathedral should have a master of theology as chancellor or chaplain. From the standpoint of the bishop this practice not only provided a way of distributing personal favors in what was recognized as a worthy cause, but it could bring talent and prestige to the cathedral and town (if the master was well known), provide an able instructor for younger members of the bishop's *familia*, improve the quality of diocesan education, and create future influential supporters if the scholar's career led to high office. The bishop could in this way support his alma mater; but he could also locate the best talent early and place a future Fitzralph or Bradwardine in his debt. From the standpoint of the candidate, the possibility of attracting an episcopal patron and establishing a career that might itself lead to the episcopate, as it had for several Oxford scholars in the thirteenth and early fourteenth centuries, was a strong incentive to distinguish oneself in the schools. Having your writings copied and your opinions and arguments cited by colleagues created the kind of visibility that might attract an important and influential patron. Despite the fact that the number of distinguished scholars achieving episcopal office was declining in the fourteenth century, there were sufficient examples to make scholarship—more than its own reward—a viable avenue for career advancement.

Many of the university men in royal service had come to the attention of royal officials through support of a bishop or by already being part of an episcopal household. In the early decades of the fourteenth century, qualified assistants to university-trained bishops were enlisted from the higher ranks of the graduate faculties of canon law and theology, and sometimes found support for the last stages of their education. After regency they might be absorbed into the bishop's retinue as clerks and, inasmuch as the bishop was himself a royal official to some degree, scholars attached to an episcopal household were automatically within the outer fringe of royal service.

*   *   *

There were two ways to extend episcopal patronage. One was through those cathedral positions in the gift of the bishop or ones in which he had an influential voice. Lincoln during the episcopate of John Dalderby (1300–1320) strongly favored Oxford theologians. In addition to the appointments of Barry and Bek to the chancellorship already noted, Gilbert Segrave was made archdeacon of Oxford in 1303, Roger Martival (former Oxford chancellor and future bishop of Lincoln) dean in 1310, and Henry Mansfield (also an Oxford chancellor and almost bishop of Lincoln) dean in 1315. The other way involved the appointment of chaplains and clerks in the household of the bishop. The *familiae* of Roger Martival and John Grandisson included several distinguished theologians, yet diocesan and cathedral appointments during their episcopates were not particularly favorable to Oxford graduates. Nor were they during the episcopate of Richard de Bury, but with more reason. Offices in monastic cathedrals, such as Durham, were under the control of the community and, in any event, the administrative organization within monastic cathedrals was different from the secular cathedrals.

In the previous chapter, in the context of the episcopal households in London, the patronage networks of the bishops of London, Exeter, and Durham were briefly examined. But since this form of patronage was one of the most important postgraduate types as well as the avenue through which many graduates came into royal service, it needs to be examined in more detail.

1. *John Grandisson, Bishop of Exeter* (1327–69).   Grandisson was an Oxford and Paris graduate whose rise to the episcopate was aided by family and educational background, but was primarily achieved through service to John XXII.[13] Grandisson's close association with the papacy continued throughout most of his tenure as bishop and became a means through which he provided for and advanced a number of Oxford graduates. John Lutterell, William of Ockham's principal opponent, was in the service of Grandisson while resident at the papal court in Avignon. Lutterell's friend, Stephen of Kettelbergh, was later provided

---

[13] Emden, *BRUO* 2, 800–801; *DNB*, vol. 8 (Oxford, 1917), 371–72.

by Grandisson with the canonry and prebend of Crediton in Devon. William of Polmorva, while regent in theology at Oxford and before his election as chancellor of the university, was made subdean of Exeter cathedral. Grandisson was also the first significant patron of Richard Fitzralph, one of the two or three most distinguished theologians at Oxford in the decade or more that separated Ockham and Adam Wodeham. When he came under the protection and into the service of Grandisson in 1327, Fitzralph was a master of arts, well advanced in the theological program, and would soon become bachelor of the *Sentences* (probably 1328–29). Recognizing his talents and future potential, Grandisson chose Fitzralph to accompany his nephew, John of Northwode, to Paris for a year of study and to act as his tutor. Fitzralph probably continued that service upon his return to Oxford to complete his residence for inception, for upon receiving his doctorate (1331) Grandisson put Fitzralph's name forward for papal provision and called him Northwode's master. It was probably Grandisson's intention to promote Fitzralph within his episcopal *familia*, since he would have been an excellent candidate when next the chancellorship of Exeter became vacant. In 1331 he granted Fitzralph a retaining fee as the surety for a promised benefice. Fitzralph, however, who was just then becoming chancellor of Oxford, was looking beyond Exeter and would soon be attracting other patrons by way of Grandisson. Even in later years his friendship for Grandisson remained, and after his consecration as bishop of Armagh, he stayed with Grandisson at Exeter and there spent the winter of 1347–48.

An equally noted theologian, Thomas Buckingham, found a patron in Grandisson. After completing his doctorate at Oxford (before 1342) Buckingham became chancellor of Exeter cathedral, a position he held from around 1345 to 1349. By that time he was already an established name in theological discussions at Oxford and Paris and may well have been one of those against whom Bradwardine wrote his *Summa de causa Dei*. While at Exeter, Buckingham engaged in theological disputations out of which many of his *Quaestiones* (*c.* 1350) arose. Whether the other theologians involved in these disputations were part of the episcopal *familia* at Exeter (possibly teaching in the cathedral school?) or doctors of theology teaching at the mendicant convents, is unknown. Both the Dominicans and Franciscans maintained convents in Exeter.

When Buckingham died in 1349, presumably a victim of the plague, the office of chancellor at Exeter may have been left vacant until the appointment of John Wyliot, probably in the autumn of 1350. Wyliot, a member of Merton College, had just completed his regency in theology at Oxford and had been chancellor of the university the previous year. How active Wyliot was either at Oxford or Exeter is unknown as no works of his survive, nor was he cited in the works of others. He did succeed in outliving his patron. He remained cathedral chancellor until his death in 1383.

2. *The Circle of Richard de Bury.*   Bury was a man whose fortunes were advanced by his education and the social contacts it created for him.[14] Born into a knightly family near Bury St. Edmunds in East Anglia, he was orphaned at an early age and was raised and educated by his uncle. He attended Oxford (1302–12), where he studied arts and some theology. His academic career was not distinguished, for he was never cited by contemporaries, and no works of his survive from that period in his life. It was sufficient, however, in addition to his family contacts, to secure for him a position in 1322 as tutor of Edward of Windsor, the future Edward III.

When his former pupil came into his majority in 1330, Bury began to receive a series of benefices and offices within the gift of the king. He became Edward III's secretary, was named archdeacon of Northampton, and received prebends at Lincoln, London, Hereford, Chichester, Lichfield, and Salisbury. The year 1333 was particularly fortuitous for Bury. While on a diplomatic mission in Avignon from February to November, where he conversed with the Franciscan theologian Walter Chatton, met the Italian humanist Petrarch, and may have met the Mertonian and Parisian theologian Walter Burley, he was appointed dean of the cathedral at Wells and (October 14) selected by Edward III as the royal nominee to the vacant see of Durham, the wealthiest bishopric in England. After a period of negotiation, in which Bury edged out the candidate elected by the cathedral chapter (the subprior and Oxford

[14] The following account depends heavily on J. de Ghellinck, "Un bibliophile au XIV siècle: Richard d'Aungerville," *RHE* 18 (1922): 271–312, 482–508; 19 (1923): 157–200; and N. Denholm Young, "Richard de Bury (1287–1345)," *TRHS*, 4th ser., 20 (1937): 135–68.

theologian Robert Graystanes, who had already been consecrated by
William Melton, archbishop of York), Bury was installed as bishop of
Durham on June 15, 1334.

Before his appointment to the see of Durham, Bury was already attended by a large household staff, dressed in his livery. When he went
to Avignon this consisted of twenty clerks and thirty-six esquires. It is
possible that Chatton, who left England at the end of 1332 and was in
Avignon by January 1333, may have been numbered among those
clerks. Upon Bury's return to England and after his consecration as
bishop of Durham, we find Oxford bachelors and doctors of theology
among the clerks of his *familia*. At one time or another between 1334
and 1345 Bury's household included Thomas Bradwardine, Walter
Burley, Richard Bentworth, Richard Fitzralph, Robert Holcot, Richard
Kilvington, Walter Segrave, John Maudith, and John Acton.[15]

Although Bury enjoyed the custom, associated with Thomas à Becket
at Canterbury, of having learned clerks at table who would read and debate controversial points of theology late into the evening,[16] it is unlikely that the above mentioned names were all present at one time, that
they operated as a colloquium or seminar, or that such discussions at
Bury's table were limited to clerks of his own household. The burdens
of royal service probably did not allow Bury the leisure for regular
"table-talk" until after 1340, when he retired from public service to attend to his diocese in the north of England. Among those who belonged
to his *clerici familiares*, Bradwardine probably had the longest tenure.

[15] The list of learned clerks associated with Bury is principally derived from William de
Chambre's *Continuatio Historiae Dunelmensis*, ed. J. Raine, Surtees Soc. Publ., 9 (Newcastle,
1839), 128: "Multum [enim] delectabatur de [comitiva] clericorum; et plures semper
clericos habuit in sua familia. De quibus fuit Thomas Bradwardyn, postea Cantuariensis
Archiepiscopus, et Ricardus Fyzt Rauf, postmodum Archiepiscopus Armachanae, Walterus Burley, Johannes Maudit, Robertus Holcot, Ricardus de Kylwyngton, omnes doctores
in theologia; Ricardus Benworth, postea Episcopus Londoniensis et Walterus Segraffe,
postea Episcopus Cicestrensis." In addition to Ghellinck and Young, the "Bury Circle" is
discussed by Neal W. Gilbert, "Richard de Bury and the 'Quires of Yesterday's Sophisms,' "
in *Philosophy and Humanism. Renaissance Essays in Honor of Paul Oskar Kristeller*, ed. E. P. Mahoney (New York, 1976), 229–57.

[16] Chambre, *Historia Dunelmensis*, 128: "Et quolibet die in mensa solitus erat habere lectionem, nisi forte per adventum magnatum impediretur; et post prandium singulis diebus
disputationem cum clericis praenominatis, et aliis suae domus, nisi major causa impediret."

He cut short his Oxford regency to become Bury's chaplain around 1335, was with him on his mission to France in 1337, and acted as his proctor in London while Bury was on a mission for the king in the north of England in 1340.[17] Thus Bradwardine would have known those who came and went in Bury's service between 1335 and 1340, although they may not all have known each other, since their time in Bury's service was probably briefer. This latter group included Burley, who was with Bury on his missions to France in 1336 and 1337; Kilvington, who was with Bury in Flanders in 1339; Bentworth, who was with Bury in France in 1336, and probably Fitzralph and Holcot, who were for a time part of Bury's household during this period. It was only in 1339 and later, when Bradwardine remained in London and Bury retired to Durham, that Segrave and Acton are known to have joined the episcopal family. Burley, who is first known to have had contact with Bury in December of 1336, when the latter pardoned him for poaching,[18] may have been in service to Bury almost as long as Bradwardine. In all probability only three or four would have been together in the company of Bury at any one time. The most intellectually exciting combination of which we are certain was composed of Bradwardine, Burley, and Kilvington, all of whom took part in the French diplomatic mission in 1338.[19]

No doubt Bury's household provided a setting for post-Oxford intellectual stimulation and may even have functioned as a household school for Bury's younger relatives, but those were not its essential purposes, nor was that why his company and patronage were sought by those individual scholars. Bury's *familia* was for them primarily the most direct (possibly the only) doorway into royal service. What better route to the king's favor and patronage could there be than proving themselves conspicuously useful in the service of the king's former tutor and principal advisor. And in this they were not ill-guided. Edward III made Fitzralph archdeacon of Chester, dean of Lichfield (1337), and archbishop of Armagh (1347–60). Bradwardine became Edward's confessor, chancellor of St. Paul's in London, and archbishop of Canterbury, a post and career quickly terminated by the Plague. Walter Burley be-

[17] Young, "Richard de Bury," 160–65; *Reg. Pal. Dun.* (Rolls Series), 3: 490–92.

[18] A rather curious incident. Bury pardoned Burley of all trespass vert and venison in December, 1336; Young, "Richard de Bury," 161.

[19] Young, "Richard de Bury," 160–64.

came the tutor of the Black Prince and the almoner of Queen Philippa (1337). Richard Kilvington became dean of St. Paul's in London. Richard Bentworth became chancellor of England and bishop of London. Walter Segrave became dean and treasurer at Chichester. John Maudith became dean of Aukland. Of the clerks known to have been part of Bury's *familia*, only Acton, who came into Bury's service just as he was retiring from public life, and Holcot failed to obtain significant advancement. Holcot's problem may have been that he was a Dominican at a time when attitudes, later to be voiced so sharply by Fitzralph and Wyclif, were beginning to turn against the mendicant orders. It may also have been aided by the antagonism toward Holcot's theology expressed in Bradwadine's *De causa Dei* (1338–44). If association with Bury did not advance Holcot's career, either within or outside his order, it was probably not for lack of trying. His motivations in joining Bury's household were probably no more nor less scholarly or worldly than those of Bradwardine, Burley, and Fitzralph.

Career ambitions did not eclipse but may actually have stimulated continued scholarly activity. A significant portion of the works of Bradwardine, Burley, Fitzralph, and Buckingham date from the post-Oxford period and may have been stimulated by the atmosphere of intellectual exchange in episcopal households. In turn, scholarly clerks served Bury as experts in the acquisition of the impressive library he collected, and thus indirectly helped father Bury's own work, the *Philobiblon*.

We should not assume (as is usually done) that these scholars retired to the north of England to reside for a period of years at Durham. As part of the bishop's household they were expected to reside and travel with him. Specific tasks were probably no more than simply fulfilling the needs of the bishop at the moment. One function was certainly to enhance Bury's public image by swelling the retinue that travelled with the bishop—part of his display of wealth, power, and learning. The scholar-client would be expected to be present with the bishop at public occasions and to accompany him on diplomatic missions abroad, to act as a messenger or envoy, possibly to aid in the work of the episcopal chancery, and to provide the bishop with stimulating company and conversation. In return the university master would gain experience, visibility, make political and social contacts, and be "on hand" at the center of power and patronage when new opportunities and appointments were to be distributed. In the early years of Bury's episcopacy that center was, as we have seen, London and the court at Westminster. Early in 1334 Bury was made Lord Treasurer of England, and from September 1334 until June of 1335 he was Lord High Chancellor and guardian of the Privy Seal, a position he gave up to undertake duties as ambassador. He was in France in 1336, Scotland in 1337, Germany in 1338, France and Flanders in 1338–39, and at Durham with various missions to Scotland between 1340 and his death. Before 1340 Bury's principal residence, to the degree he had one, was in London. When Bury went north around 1340 on what came to be a semipermanent basis, Bradwardine remained in London as his proctor. Only Maudith, Acton, and Kilvington (a northerner) were definitely among his clerks at that time, and we may well assume that the others, when in England and still in the bishop's service, made Durham House in London their residence. Although Bury's needs inclined him to employ more lawyer-clerks toward the end of his life, his strong attachment to scholastic theology and to Oxford theologians remains evident in his *Philobiblon*.

THE MARKET VALUE OF LEARNING

The major question of concern, of course, is how university graduates fared in this patronage system. From the middle of the thirteenth century into the early years of the fourteenth there was a concerted effort on the part of church leaders, particularly the papacy, to improve the quality of learning throughout all levels within the church. In that endeavor universities benefited greatly, receiving a large share of talented younger men seeking positions in the church, particularly after Boniface VIII's innovative *Cum ex eo* decree. And appointments to the episcopate in England in the second half of the thirteenth century show a degree of respect for learning matched only by the closing years of the eleventh century and the opening of the twelfth. It has been suggested, however, that in the course of the fourteenth century, particularly in the second half, there was a shift away from university graduates both for high office in the church and for parish positions, thus producing a crisis in education that hindered the university's ability to attract qualified students and reduced the scholar's share of financial resources available through patronage. These are issues that need to be examined. To what degree can we identify shifting patterns of patronage in fourteenth-century England? Were university graduates being passed over, neglected in the distribution of church livings and church offices? And, whether correctly or not, did university scholars perceive this to be the case and shape their field of study and the course of their careers accordingly?

Parish Churches and Cathedral Livings

Guy Lytle, in a brilliant thesis and subsequent articles, argued for a decline in the percentage of parish livings and cathedral canonries and prebends awarded to university scholars between 1340 and 1430.[20] In the case of the parish positions he placed the drop at around fifty percent, and in the case of resident and nonresident canonries and prebends about thirty percent. Others have argued that the acquisition of benefices and prebends by university graduates was abnormally high in the second quarter of the fourteenth century, and that if one considers the entire period from 1300 to 1450, the dip after 1350 was slight and the recovery earlier and stronger.[21] Although statistical precision on

[20] Lytle, "Patronage Patterns"; *Oxford Students*, 223–73; "The Careers of Oxford Students." Lytle's evidence was drawn from the diocesan records of Bath and Wells, Durham, Exeter, Hereford, London, Winchester, and York, and the cathedrals of Salisbury, London, Coventry-Lichfield, and Bath-Wells. For subsequent modifications and additional evidence see Lytle's forthcoming chapter in *HUO* 2 and his revised thesis to appear under the title *Universities, Church, and Society in Late Medieval England*.

[21] Lytle's thesis has been sharply criticized by British historians, and the debate is far from over. In particular see: T. H. Aston, "Oxford's Medieval Alumni," *Past and Present* no. 74 (Feb. 1977): 3–40, esp. 31–32; B. Dobson, "Oxford Graduates and the So-Called Patronage Crisis of the Late Middle Ages," in *The Church in a Changing Society* (Uppsala, 1978), 211–16; Aston, G. D. Duncan, and T.A.R. Evans, "The Medieval Alumni of the University of Cambridge," *Past and Present*, no. 86 (Feb. 1980): 9–86, esp. 70–84; M. J. Bennett, *Community, Class and Careerism: Cheshire and Lancashire Society in the Age of 'Sir Gawain and the Green Knight'* (Cambridge, 1983); Dunbabin in *HUO* 1: 565–605. Less adversarial modifications have been suggested by Courtenay, "The Effect of the Black Death on English Higher Education," *Speculum* 55 (1980): 696–714, and Swanson, "Universities, Graduates and Benefices." Swanson has wisely noted the confusions introduced by different definitions of university-trained personnel (some study, degree-holding, before or after appointment), differences among various ways of counting benefice holders (all appointments, actual possession, nonexchange appointments, man-years of occupancy), and the impossibility of knowing the degree to which university education was actually a significant factor in appointment. Swanson's preference for "man-years of graduate occupancy,"

this question can probably never be attained due to the nature of the records, some decline in support for scholars in the second half of the fourteenth century is generally acknowledged.

If some form of a "crisis of patronage" took place, the reasons for this temporary shift away from university-trained clerics as well as the results of that shift upon university recruitment and fields of study is more conjectural. Lytle tended to ground the reasons for change in the attitudes of the patrons who controlled advowsons and a new political and social atmosphere in which the need to retain supporters and their clients within a growing network of royal and aristocratic alliances favored family and friend over both educational level and religious commitment. The purported decline in university enrollments in the second half of the fourteenth century, the endowment campaigns and the attempt to attract wealthy students who might later become patrons, and the decline in halls and corresponding growth in colleges are all seen as stages in the university's response to this crisis. Swanson, who limits the crisis to the years 1380–1430, sees the causes more in terms of a declining number of available benefices because of appropriation, and the dislocations of the Great Schism that produced changes in the mechanisms of patronage.[22]

I have argued elsewhere that the evidence for a sharp decline among university students in the second half of the fourteenth century appears weak.[23] Unlike many other groups in society, universities were able to, and apparently did, replenish their ranks after the Black Death from among survivors. Nevertheless, the quality of students may not have been as high and may even have declined as the drop in qualified teachers at the elementary and secondary levels began to have its effect dur-

---

however, is the least helpful method in determining patronage motivations. Man-years concern effects. They reflect the quantitative influence exercised in cathedral or parish by occupants with a particular background, and in cases of nonresidence, it does not even reflect that. Longevity has nothing to do with the factors that determine a patron's choice of a candidate. If the question is patronage, that is revealed by the type of candidates patrons attempt to appoint, the perceived success rate of university men actually appointed, the rate of turnover, and the degree and distribution of financial support provided for study and subsequent career.

[22] In addition to Swanson, "Universities, Graduates and Benefices," see K. Wood-Legh, *Church Life in England under Edward III* (Cambridge, 1934); Swanson, *Universities, Academics and the Great Schism* (Cambridge, 1979).

[23] Courtenay, "The Effect of the Black Death."

ing the next decade or two. Immediately after the first and most severe outbreak of plague the sudden and unusually large number of vacancies in teaching positions and church livings coincided with a diminished number of graduates from which to choose potential appointees, and it is natural to suspect that in that situation the percentage of ecclesiastical livings presented to scholars would have dropped. Yet the fact that the decline in percentage of church livings awarded to scholars was already evident in some dioceses by the second quarter of the fourteenth century, well before any temporary drop in available graduates at mid-century, and the fact that the percentage of university appointees did not rise with the growth in university enrollment and the production of graduates in the last quarter of the century, supports Lytle's conclusion that university training became a less important factor for ecclesiastical patronage in the course of the century. The decline in university graduates among appointments in the diocese of Exeter in the decade before the Plague under a bishop-patron as strong and as favorably disposed to education as Grandisson is chilling testimony to the changing evaluation of scholarship. The data from York present a similar picture.

Prospective students, however, were probably less aware of these shifts in patronage or viewed them differently. Enrollment levels at Oxford appear to have dipped only slightly at mid-century and gradually climbed in the second half of the century. The declining availability of church positions for university scholars does not appear to have deterred very many from seeking some university education, but other changes at Oxford can to some degree be attributed to it. The more aggressive way scholars sought to exploit the traditional sources of support or create new ones must, as Lytle has rightly noted, be placed in this broader social and patronage context. In particular, the growth of colleges in the late fourteenth and early fifteenth centuries was an important response to the need for alternate forms of support while in school and provided closer geographical and personal ties with particular regions and patrons. Further, the shift away from theology in the direction of law, to be discussed in more detail in the last chapters of this book, may well have been a response to the observed preference for law over theology among those appointments that did go to university graduates.

Cathedral Dignities

The situation with offices in cathedrals is more complex and does not exactly parallel the changes in appointments to parish and cathedral livings.[24] University graduates occupied a far higher percentage of the offices of archdeacon, chancellor, precentor, and dean at the opening of the fourteenth century, and the drop in the appointment of scholars to these dignities, while evident, varies from office to office, diocese to diocese, with sharp declines in one area being offset by moderate gains elsewhere. Moreover, the smaller number of positions in this category means that incomplete or missing documentation during certain episcopates has a far greater impact on the statistical profile, thus making the percentages of change less reliable.[25]

The percentage of university graduates among cathedral deans appears to have declined at Lichfield and Lincoln but held steady or increased slightly, as in the case of Salisbury, London, and York. University graduates among chancellors (initially very high), precentors, treasurers, and archdeacons, however, declined markedly in the second half of the fourteenth century. The fact that the office of cathedral chancellor follows the general trend suggests that in some dioceses it was becoming a sinecure used for reward rather than a post with teaching and educational administrative responsibilities. Exeter, Lincoln, Salisbury, and York apparently continued to appoint university graduates as chancellors, but Bath/Wells and Chichester all but gave up the

[24] For a description of the structure (positions and duties) of cathedral and diocesan administrations, see A. Hamilton Thompson, *The English Clergy and their Organization in the Later Middle Ages* (Oxford, 1947); Kathleen Edwards, *The English Secular Cathedrals in the Middle Ages*, 2nd ed. (Manchester, 1967); Robert E. Rodes, *Ecclesiastical Administration in Medieval England: The Anglo-Saxons to the Reformation* (Notre Dame, 1977).

[25] Based on the *magistri* among the list of officeholders provided in John Le Neve, *Fasti Ecclesiae Anglicanae, 1300–1541*, 10 vols., compiled and revised by J. M. Horn and B. Jones (London, 1962–64), and modified by additional information from the Bodleian copy of Emden's *BRUO*, the percentage of university graduates (not necessarily Oxford) appointed to cathedral offices changed between the first and second halves of the fourteenth century as follows: deans, from 62 to 67 percent; precentors, from 62 to 33 percent; treasurers, from 52 to 34 percent; archdeacons, from 61 to 47 percent; chancellors, from 81 to 56 percent. This method, and consequently these percentages, are far from precise for reasons mentioned in n. 21. But the number of times *magister* is used as an honorary title for someone with no university connection is probably less than the number of university graduates not so designated.

attempt. Moreover, in the second half of the fourteenth century an increasing number of cathedral chancellorships went to lawyers, even at places that traditionally had stressed theology, such as Salisbury and London. Only Lincoln appears to have considered it a post appropriate only for a theologian. On occasion the chancellorship was given to a bachelor or licentiate, ignoring the traditional expectation of inception and university regency. The drop in university graduates among cathedral chancellors may have had some effect on cathedral schools. The marked shift in the direction of law, however, is clear in almost all the cathedral offices that went to university graduates and no doubt gave a strong signal to undergraduates as to which higher faculty to choose.

The Episcopate

This picture of declining opportunities for university graduates does not hold true for appointments to the episcopate in the course of the fourteenth century, as has often been argued.[26] Nevertheless, there were changes in this category that need to be viewed against the background of the type and extent of appointments in the late thirteenth century.

After strong papal encouragement for a university-trained episcopate, a mutually beneficial relationship was worked out between university and royal government. The king, who drew many of his principal advisors, diplomats, and career administrators from the higher ranks of the clergy, found at universities a source of able and learned personnel to fill offices in government and, not infrequently, vacancies in the episcopate. A distinguished academic career attracted notice outside university circles, particularly among scholar-bishops who provided an avenue for advancement in church and state. The university, on the other hand, could attract much of the best talent of the age (at least from among those whose birth did not automatically ensure high office), since it was a means by which personal talent and a skillful intellect could be transformed into a comfortable living or a position of responsibility, perhaps even into wealth and power. From the third quarter of

[26] Pantin, *ECFC*, 14–18, saw the proportion of scholars within the episcopate declining in the fourteenth century. A contrasting view, one that I share, is presented by J. Rosenthal, *The Training of an Elite Group: English Bishops in the Fifteenth Century*, Transactions of the American Philosophical Society, N.S., vol. 60, pt. 5 (1970), 12–19.

the thirteenth century Oxford began to capture a significant percentage of the higher cathedral and diocesan positions, with the possibility of making the episcopate and the bench preserves of Oxford alumni.

That pattern was still in evidence in the opening decades of the fourteenth century. A high proportion of early fourteenth-century English bishops were university trained, some in canon law, many in theology. But an important shift was also occurring—one that may not have been clearly visible to aspiring graduates at the time. Pantin noted the attempt under Edward II to appoint to the episcopate men whose almost sole qualification was royal service, men without university background. Pantin's sample of the educational level of bishops at several points in the fourteenth century suggested a pattern by which scholarship counted for less, and men of distinguished university service were either fewer within the episcopate or were given only the less important, more distant sees. This shift might be seen as a movement away from education as a major criterion for high office within the church.

The picture suggested by Pantin needs some qualification. First, among those who became masters of theology, one must distinguish between those who only attained the degree and those who established reputations through debates and writings, who were cited by their contemporaries and later generations, and who thus became recognized names within late scholasticism. Those who became chancellor of the university were drawn from both groups. With a few exceptions, only recently incepted secular theologians were elected to that office, and although scholastic distinction at the time of election helped make one a popular candidate, political and social factors could be as important as intellectual achievement. Consequently, some university chancellors were men of distinguished learning, but others were not, and Pantin tended to define scholarly distinction by the office of chancellor rather than the reputation of the theologian as revealed in the writings of his contemporaries. Secondly, it is important to look at all the bishops of the fourteenth century, not just at those who were in office every twenty-five years. When these two observations are taken into account, a somewhat different picture emerges.

Already within the reign of Edward I there was a movement away from mendicant theologians whose intellectual gifts were widely recognized, men like Robert Kilwardby and John Pecham whose appointment to Canterbury followed in the tradition of Robert Grosseteste at

Lincoln. Those university men appointed to the episcopate after 1280 (over sixty percent of the bishops) were, in addition to the earlier and almost universal requirement of royal service, almost invariably secular theologians whose achievements at Oxford were as much if not more administrative than intellectual: Robert Winchelsey at Canterbury, John Monmouth at Llandaff, Simon of Ghent at Salisbury, Thomas Corbrigge at York, John Dalderby at Lincoln, and William of Gainsborough, O.F.M. (the only mendicant) at Worcester. In the last five years of Edward's reign, of the last seven appointments, there were only two university men, one of them a lawyer. This trend continued under Edward II who, had he been given free reign, would surely, to borrow Pantin's label, have appointed more "mere administrators" to the episcopate. Even so, the percentage of university men declined to about 50 percent of the appointments, and most of those were lawyers.

This policy shifted dramatically under Edward III. Of those promoted to the episcopate some 75 to 85 percent had university credentials among their other qualifications. Moreover, within that number were men of recognized scholastic achievement: Antony Bek and Richard Fitzralph (by papal provision), Thomas Bradwardine, Thomas Ringstede, and William Rede, as well as those who had a high respect for scholarship and education, particularly Richard de Bury and William of Wykeham. Oxford chancellors continued to find the route to the episcopate open, although not with the same frequency or with as choice positions as happened in the late thirteenth century.[27] Henry of Harclay might well have achieved high office had he not died early while still chancellor of Oxford. And an early death almost certainly prevented John of Northwode, nephew of John Grandisson and friend of Richard Fitzralph, from rising to high ecclesiastical office.

Throughout the reign of Edward III the proportion of university-trained men among the episcopate does not decline but actually increases. Nor is it accurate to say that the number of distinguished scholars declines appreciably. It is true that the most famous mendicant

---

[27] The university chancellors who became bishops under Edward III were Henry of Gower, bishop of St. Davids in 1328; Ralph of Shrewsbury, bishop of Bath and Wells in 1329; Richard Fitzralph, archbishop of Armagh in 1346; Robert of Stratford, bishop of Chichester in 1337; William Courtenay, bishop of Hereford, London, and Canterbury. In almost all these cases family and political connection were far more important than university connection.

scholars did not enter episcopal ranks, but that is because mendicants in general were rarely appointed in late medieval England. A number of secular theologians distinguished in scholarship or university service were also not so rewarded, such as Walter Burley, Thomas Wilton, William of Alberwick, Nigel of Wavere, William Skelton, Richard Kilvington, William Heytesbury, Thomas Buckingham, Simon Bredon, John Dumbleton, Richard Swineshead, and Nicholas Aston. But several of those died during or soon after their academic careers, and the others usually found responsible and rewarding posts within cathedrals. Walter Burley served long in royal and episcopal service, and his close connection with Bury, Queen Philippa, and the Black Prince might well have gained him a bishopric had a suitable appointment and his own desires coincided during his lifetime. But one has to keep in mind that scholastic achievement only made one visible and recognized; it did not by itself prepare one for high office, which depended more on the quality of service rendered to those in power, personal character, family, the number and importance of supporters, and a certain degree of luck. The ratio between scholastic talent and high ecclesiastical office in the fourteenth century was probably not too far below what it had been in the late thirteenth or early fourteenth centuries.

The promotion of Bradwardine to Canterbury or, later, of William Rede to Chichester, demonstrate that a sizable scholarly reputation was not a hindrance, all other things being equal. Perhaps more to the point, the pool of distinguished Oxford scholars after 1345 shrank considerably, and thus we should not expect the same percentage within the episcopate as in earlier years. The most productive scholar of the third quarter of the century, John Wyclif, made too many enemies within the church by his writings and personality ever to be considered for high office, but his chief enemy, William Courtenay, former chancellor of Oxford, was promoted to the see of Canterbury. In fact, the proportion of Oxford chancellors promoted to the episcopate remained roughly the same in the second half of the century.

Changes, however, did take place. One finds among the episcopate a higher proportion of aristocrats as well as of lawyers. But these changes seem to parallel rather than anticipate or precede changes that took place at English universities after mid-century. The most influential bishops of the fourteenth century remained men of university training or those who respected its traditions and potential but who were not in their own right gifted thinkers: Robert Winchelsey at Canterbury, Simon of Ghent at Salisbury, Thomas Cobham at Worcester, John Grandisson at Exeter, Richard de Bury at Durham, William Wykeham at Winchester, and William Courtenay at Canterbury.

Although a brilliant university career did not ensure a distinguished ecclesiastical career, no one viewed it as a handicap. More important was the means of transition from university to society. The most useful royal servant (and the one most likely to receive a significant ecclesiastical appointment and income) was one who was of good family and bearing, sufficiently good at accounts, skilled in negotiation and diplomacy, and willing always to obey royal commands; one, perhaps, whose love of king and country, or at least king and other patrons, exceeded his love of books and ideas. It is surprising that thought and letters survived as well as they did in fourteenth-century England, since most of what was produced by university men was produced only within their ten to twenty-year university period. Had higher education and a life of learning been a viable career in itself, the intellectual creativity and possibly the history of philosophy and science in the late Middle Ages might well have been different. As it was, those who did not make the transition from university to a public career in church, state, or religious order rarely produced any writings after leaving the schools. This is true of Campsall, Holcot, Wodeham, Costesey, Halifax, Heytesbury, and others. By contrast, the burdens of high office did not prevent and may even have stimulated further scholarship, as is evidenced by Bradwardine's *Summa de causa Dei* (while chancellor of St. Paul's, London), Fitzralph's *De quaestionibus Armenorum* and *De pauperie salvatoris* (while archbishop of Armagh), Buckingham's *Quaestiones* (while chancellor at Exeter), and Bury's *Philobiblon* (while bishop of Durham). Even the long writing career of Walter Burley occurred in the context of an active ecclesiastical and diplomatic life at Paris, Avignon, and in England. Those who were rusticated to the solitude of a small-town cloister or a parish church either lacked the incentive to continue their university interests or had their energies consumed in activities that are simply less visible to us.

FIVE

ENGLISH TIES WITH CONTINENTAL LEARNING

To one familiar with the intellectual history of the second half of the thirteenth century the symbiotic relationship of Paris and Oxford is accepted as fundamental. The organization of the two universities was similar, and they had almost a monopoly on degrees in the most prestigious of the higher faculties, theology. Paris profited from a series of impressive English masters: Roger Bacon and Robert Kilwardby in arts; Alexander of Hales, John of Wales, John Pecham, William of Ware, and John Duns Scotus in theology. Many of these had experience in both universities, and some careers, like those of Bacon, Richard Rufus of Cornwall, Duns Scotus, and John Baconthorp, show a pattern of cross-fertilization. One finds in works produced at Oxford, both in theology and in arts, a continuing awareness of (and often dependence on) the thought of Parisian masters. The rapidity with which the Parisian Articles of 1277 were echoed at Oxford through a similar condemnation is only one instance of the close interrelation of the two universities. The intellectual life of the two centers around 1300 was in fact so interdependent that it would be imprudent to treat the history of one university separate from the other.

The universities were among the last havens for Europe's cosmopolitan, pre-national, common culture, where one was "at home" in many lands and spoke the supranational language of Latin. Whatever shifts had begun to take place in political allegiances in the thirteenth century through the emerging national monarchies, the sense of regional self-interest was less apparent among university scholars, especially theologians. Anti-papal royal policy under Philip the Fair was developed and implemented by nonuniversity lawyers.[1] The theological faculties of Paris and Oxford continued to seek support for their graduates at both

---

[1] F. J. Pegues, *The Lawyers of the Last Capetians* (Princeton, 1962).

royal and papal courts, and the long-range political implications of the papal humiliation at Anagni (1303) and the shift of the papal residence to Avignon (1305) were initially ignored by English as well as French theologians. The supranational status of the university and the time-honored presence of foreign scholars posed problems for both France and England during the Hundred Years' War. They were certainly not the last governments to grapple with the question of where legitimate study ends and espionage begins.

If Paris and Oxford belonged to the same intellectual world in the opening years of the fourteenth century, they were not on equal foot-ing. Paris had long been the premier university of northern Europe, and it continued to dominate English theological education. The reli-gious orders reflected that bias in their appointments. The Dominican order often sent its best English students to St. Jacques in Paris for the baccalaureate, although English Dominicans were never appointed re-gent masters at Paris.[2] The Franciscans in the period from 1260 to about 1310 selectively sent their best English students to Paris to read the *Sentences* and become masters of theology: John Pecham, William de la Mare, William of Ware, John Duns Scotus, William of Alnwick, Robert Cowton, and others. The leading English Carmelite in the first quarter of the fourteenth century, John Baconthorp, was a Paris grad-uate. Secular theologians could choose their own place of learning, pro-vided they had the resources. For those who sought the highest and best, a few years in Paris rounded out a perfect course of study, some-times crowned with the aureola of the Parisian doctorate. Until 1310 Paris was as excellent a route for an ecclesiastical career in England as on the Continent and opened the doors to both papal and royal patron-age. Such men as Stephen Gravesend, Henry Burghersh, Thomas Wil-ton, Walter Burley, and John Grandisson are just a few of those who crossed the Channel in the first quarter century to complete their stud-ies. Paris was the center of theological education; Oxford largely a sat-ellite.

---

[2] John of St. Giles, who became a Dominican (1230) while regent in theology at Paris, was the last English regent at St. Jacques. John Gilbert, O.P., petitioned the pope in 1366 to be allowed to complete his theological studies at Paris. He obtained his doctorate, but it is not certain whether he held the Dominican non-French chair. His case is in sharp contrast to Dominican policy and English practice at that time.

The relative status of the two universities as well as the unity of intellectual life, based to a large degree on the existence of a Paris-based, supranational educated elite, changed radically in the fourteenth century. In 1300 Paris was an international university in which the French element among the masters was strong but hardly dominant. By 1400 Paris had become a northern French university in which the presence of foreign scholars was minimal.[3] In 1300 Oxford philosophy and theology resembled and often duplicated Parisian works. By 1330 Oxford had few remaining ties with Paris and was producing works in philosophy and theology that were independent of and often superior to equivalent work at Paris.

These transformations in the student bodies of the two universities, their differing geographical and intellectual horizons, and their declining contact with each other make it difficult and hazardous to speak of pan-European intellectual currents in the fourteenth century, as is so often done. Moreover, the development of intellectual maturity and the end of dependence on Paris represent a fundamental shift in English education that had ramifications far outside the university world. The political and cultural implications of this shift, its relation to the Hundred Years' War and the papal policy of the crown, can only be understood against the background and effects of the earlier period of Parisian domination.

THE LAST YEARS OF PARISIAN HEGEMONY
(1290–1320)

The English presence at the University of Paris was almost entirely confined to two faculties: arts and theology. The lack of records for the

---

[3] That change was largely a result of the papal schism, which added the departure of Italian, Dutch, German, and east European students to the earlier departure of the English. The Foreign element between 1385 and 1415 was composed largely of Scottish and Spanish students. The growing provincialness of the University of Paris was not effectively reversed in the fifteenth century, despite the return of German and Dutch students. As with the English departure, which was more a result of the academic sufficiency of Oxford than tensions between France and England, the growth in the status of *studia* all across Europe in the fifteenth century provided regional alternatives and limited the influx back into Paris. On foreign students at Paris in the fifteenth century see A. Gabriel, "Les étudiants

English Nation in the Paris arts faculty in the thirteenth century prevents our knowing the proportion of English students in arts at Paris as well as the numbers and types of students who chose Paris over Oxford for their philosophical training. By the time we have documentation (1333) the proportion of English students in that nation is still over 26 percent.[4] One can presume the proportion in the late thirteenth century and early years of the fourteenth was higher. Throughout these years there was also a steady stream of regular and secular theological students who were either assigned to or chose Paris for all or part of their higher education. Some remained on the Continent for their subsequent careers, but most returned to England to seek preferment in church or state.

There were two major consequences for Oxford and England that derived from the presence of English students at Paris and the close intercommunication between the two universities. Both stemmed from an unintentional but nevertheless effective Parisian educational colonialism. The most visible was the unity of intellectual traditions in the areas of arts and theology. One finds at Oxford (just as at Cologne, Naples, Bologna, and elsewhere) the same methods, terminology, and topics that one finds in the theological writings from Paris. This was not due so much to the international character of thirteenth-century education as to the central role of Parisian theology. Much of English theology in the last decades of the thirteenth century and the opening years of the fourteenth was centered around Parisian controversies. The English Dominicans echoed the Parisian defense of Thomas Aquinas and attacked the *correctorii*. Many of the English Franciscans were Paris graduates and introduced or continued Parisian theological concerns at the Oxford convent. The Austin Friars were Aegidians and glossed the thought of their Parisian leader, Giles of Rome.

A second and perhaps more important consequence of Parisian educational colonialism was the formation of cultural and political hori-

---

étrangers a l'Université de Paris au xvᵉ siécle," *Annales de l'Université de Paris* 29 (1959): 377–400; "The English-German Nation at the University of Paris from 1425–1494," in *Garlandia. Studies in the History of the Medieval University* (Frankfurt, 1969), 167–200; " 'Via antiqua' and 'via moderna' and the Migration of Paris Students and Masters to the German Universities in the Fifteenth Century," in *AM*, 439–83; J. Favier, *Nouvelle Histoire de Paris. Paris au XVᵉ siècle, 1380–1500* (Paris, 1974), 68–79.

[4] *AUP* 1: 14–18.

zons and attitudes of an important segment of England's ecclesiastical elite. Among those English bishops in the late thirteenth and early fourteenth centuries whose rise to positions of wealth and influence in church and state was aided by educational preparation, prominence, and contacts, those with Parisian experience outranked those whose education was gained solely at Oxford. Between 1272 and 1313 all three occupants of the see of Canterbury were graduates of Paris as well as Oxford. Thomas de Cantelupe, the influential bishop of Hereford (1275–82), had studied arts, theology, and law at Paris, was a doctor of civil law from Orléans, and held doctorates in canon law and theology from Oxford. In 1290 the archbishopric of Canterbury was held by John Pecham and the archbishopric of York by John le Romeyn, both with doctorates of theology earned at Paris. In 1310 those same sees were held respectively by Robert Winchelsey and William Greenfield, both of whom had studied arts at Paris.

The Parisian dimension in English education helped sustain the prominent role played by the Ile de France during the reigns of Henry III and Edward I. Years as a student at the French capital instilled far more than the methods and academic content of the university. One acquired friends, some fluency in the local dialect, aesthetic tastes, and an appreciation for certain architectural styles. In fact, Parisian educational experience may even have helped delay the development of a peculiarly English culture among bishops, whose patronage was crucial for art, architecture, literature, and music. In contrast to the Norman-French or Angevin-French influences in the twelfth century, English culture in the thirteenth and early fourteenth centuries was heavily dependent on Paris. From architectural styles to court manners, to the content and structure of scholastic debates, Paris was the model for the intellectual and ecclesiastical elite of England. The importance of the Parisian experience for some of those helping to shape royal policy may have been one of the stabilizing influences on Anglo-French relations during the reigns of Henry III and Edward I.

THE ANGLICIZING OF ENGLISH EDUCATION
(1315–40)

The intellectual predominance of Paris began to fade in the second decade of the fourteenth century, and the relationship of Paris and Oxford reversed itself in the two decades between William of Ockham and Gregory of Rimini. Oxford had never been simply derivative. It had made its own contributions in the thirteenth century to scholastic learning and to Parisian thought, particularly in the areas of mathematics and science. But the period of Robert Grosseteste and Richard Fishacre was followed by almost two generations in which the leaders of Oxford's intellectual life, such figures as Roger Bacon, Robert Kilwardby, John Pecham, and John Duns Scotus, belonged to the Parisian world as well. In 1320 Oxford theologians were still concerned primarily with theological issues of Parisian origin, and the contemporaries cited and debated were most often Parisian theologians. At the same time the fourteenth-century English authors cited at Paris were almost exclusively Paris graduates. The decade 1330–40 marks a fundamental change. By 1340 English theologians hardly mention any *modernus* (that is, any fourteenth-century scholastic) who was not English, while Parisian theologians, such as Gregory of Rimini, John of Mirecourt, or Alphonsus Vargas, concentrated much of their attention on recent English authors.

The gradual transformation of the intellectual horizons of Oxford can be appreciated by comparing the citations to contemporaries in the *Sentences* commentaries of three English Franciscans: William of Ockham (writing or revising *c.* 1317–22), Adam Wodeham (*c.* 1330–32), and Alexander Langeley (*c.* 1338). Those with whom Ockham felt himself in debate, although he was never a student at Paris, were Parisian masters: Thomas Aquinas, Duns Scotus, Henry of Ghent, Giles of Rome, Godfrey of Fontaines, and, to a lesser degree, Peter Aureoli. He knew the Oxford commentary of John of Reading, but it was the fact that Reading was an important disciple of Scotus that made him of interest to Ockham. Even the opinions of Durand of St. Pourçain found a place in Ockham's work. With Wodeham that balance is strikingly reversed. Wodeham still cited Thomas, Henry, Giles, and Godfrey, and the opinions of Scotus form a major focus of his commentary. He also took a keen interest in Peter Aureoli. But the only subsequent Parisian theologians he mentioned are Francis Mayronis and Gerard Odonis, both Franciscan authors. There is no mention of Durand, Peter Palude, Francis of Marchia, Landulf of Caracciolo, Michael de Massa, or any of a number of Parisian theologians writing in the decade that separates Wodeham's and Ockham's commentaries. Instead, Wodeham was most interested in the opinions of Ockham, Walter Chatton, and Richard Fitzralph, along with a large number of other English theologians who had written in the previous two decades. By the time we reach the commentary of Langeley the only theologians cited after 1310 are English.

The principal reason for this shift lay in the quality of Oxford thought. During that period, particularly from 1330 to 1340, Oxford entered its most productive period and far outdistanced Paris in the development of logic, mathematics, science, philosophy, and theology. Paris did not recognize that achievement until after 1340, but the change at Oxford was well under way by 1315. Oxford entered its golden age with Ockham, Reading, Chatton, Fitzralph and John of Rodington, and continued with Robert Holcot, Adam Wodeham, Thomas Bradwardine, Richard Kilvington, Robert of Halifax, Thomas of Buckingham, and William Heytesbury, to name only the most prominent. The results were so exciting that there was little need to look elsewhere.

It is difficult to determine what caused this period of high creativity at Oxford. It seems unlikely that it could ever have come about without the changes in educational patterns that occurred in the years before and after 1320. The first to change were the Franciscans. They matched their astounding ability to recruit talent in the first two decades of the fourteenth century with a decision to send their best English students to Oxford rather than Paris for the completion of their theological education. William of Alnwick and Robert Cowton were among the last English Franciscans to take their theological degree at Paris. After 1315 the Oxford convent received the best English friars.

Secular theologians began to follow a similar pattern in greater numbers. There had always been many talented clerics in the thirteenth century who took their university work at Oxford. But in the last decades of the thirteenth century and the opening decades of the fourteenth many completed their education at Paris. For example, scholars such as Stephen Gravesend, Thomas Wilton, and Walter Burley crossed the Channel to read and incept in theology. By 1325 the example of Richard of Campsall, who remained at Oxford for his education in the first two decades of the century, had become the norm, and by 1330 there seem to have been few exceptions. Thomas Bradwardine, Thomas of Buckingham, John Maudith, John Ashenden, Simon Bredon, Richard Billingham, John Dumbleton, William Heytesbury, Richard Swineshead, William Rede, and Ralph Strode all took their degrees at Oxford.[5]

That shift was reflected in the English episcopate as well. Edward II, as we have seen, preferred to appoint candidates from his own household staff, many of whom lacked university training although some had studied law. Civil servants would have received a larger share of vacancies had Edward been allowed a free hand in appointments. The conflict between king and church over appointments is most tellingly illustrated by the crisis over Canterbury in 1313, after the death of Archbishop Winchelsey. The chapter elected Thomas Cobham, master of arts from Paris, doctor of theology from Cambridge, and a doctor of canon law from Oxford. Edward, however, succeeded in securing the appointment of Walter Reynolds, one of his own household officials and a man without any university education. English scholars with French educational experience, such as Thomas Cobham, Stephen Gravesend, or Henry Burghersh secured appointment with difficulty either through the support of the church or political elements opposed to Edward II.

The promotion of civil servants and lawyers during the reign of Edward II gradually eclipsed those with any Parisian background, which was usually in arts or theology. Theologians of any university obtained only the less important bishoprics: Roger Martival at Salisbury (1315), Thomas Cobham (also a lawyer) at Worcester (1317), and Stephen Gravesend at London (1319). From 1319 until the end of Edward's reign, no other theologians were appointed. When the Council of Regency (1327–30) restored the practice of appointing university graduates to episcopal office, the only appointee with some Paris training was John Grandisson, invested as bishop of Exeter in the first year of Edward III's reign. Grandisson was also the last Parisian appointee.

The decline in Parisian influence over English education thus began to take place almost two decades before the outbreak of war between France and England made study abroad difficult and sometimes impossible. Already toward the end of the thirteenth century Oxford reacted against the Parisian reluctance to accord full parity between the two arts

---

[5] The only English secular masters after 1330 known to have spent part of their theological study at Paris were John Dumbleton and an otherwise unknown Master Clay, probably in 1345–46, the year before Crécy. See Z. Kaluza, *Thomas de Cracovie* (Wroclaw, 1978–79), 136–37.

degrees.[6] But it took somewhat longer for English students to see Oxford as a fully comparable institution. By 1325 Oxford was no longer losing talent to Paris but retained its best minds for the full course of study within its walls.

That shift in patterns of education was paralleled in other areas of English culture. The same period saw the development of the English Perpendicular style in design and architecture and a departure from the Parisian models of the previous generation. Thus by the time Edward III decided to adopt a military solution to his diplomatic and territorial problems with Philip of Valois, the educated among the leaders of English society and government, especially the scholar-bishops (an important element for shaping public opinion), had few ties with Parisian culture. They were Oxford graduates. From this perspective the educational shift from Paris to Oxford, accidental as it may have been, may have facilitated the break with France.

Hostilities between France and England had a chilling effect on educational exchange. A few French students continued to go to Oxford, mostly for the study of law, but between 1333 and 1337 English students and masters in arts in the English Nation at Paris practically disappear. They did not return until the Truce of Malestroit made Parisian study possible during the academic years 1343–44 and 1344–45. After the battle of Crécy (1346) names of certain English origin do not appear in the documents of the English Nation.[7] The English presence also declined in the theological faculty. Only the Cistercians are known to have continued to send English students to Paris.[8]

---

[6] *CUP* 2: 182–84; M. B. Hackett, "The University as a Corporate Body," in *HUO* 1: 54.

[7] The "on- and off-again" policy governing foreign students continued in the third quarter of the fourteenth century, but it does not appear to have brought English students to Paris or French students to Oxford. It was more for political effect than as a serious penalty when Edward III ordered the expulsion of all French scholars in 1369; see Rashdall, *Univ.* 3: 57. Included in the terms of the Treaty of Brétigny in 1360 was the following provision (Rashdall, *Univ.* 3: 236): "Subjects of each king should be free to study and enjoy the privileges of each other's universities, 'comme ils povoient faire avant ces présentes guerres et comme ils font au présent.' "

[8] In 1340 Henry, a Cistercian bachelor of theology, was called to Avignon along with Nicholas of Autrecourt for possible false and erroneous teaching. Henry must have been in residence at Paris at least the previous two or three years. Richard of Lincoln, also a Cistercian at Paris, was accused of "fantastic" opinions in 1342, but was eventually cleared of that charge and permitted to read the *Sentences* at Paris (1346–47). It seems probable that

What Oxford received from Paris after 1325 was slight and usually came by way of the foreign students in the theological faculty who, like John Klenkok (1354), were acquainted with Parisian scholasticism before coming to England. None of the few English students known to have studied arts at Paris after 1335 are known to have attended Oxford or Cambridge subsequently, although Hugh of Stamford O.P. did return to Oxford to complete his degree in theology after a period of study at Paris in the 1350s.[9] Occasionally secular scholars also took a year or two of their theological training at Paris, as in the case of Fitzralph and John Trillek (1329–30), or John Dumbleton and Master Clay, fellows of the Sorbonne for a time in the 1340s.[10] The French students who attended English *studia* in the fourteenth century had little if any prior Parisian experience. The channel of communication from Paris to Oxford, long the nourishment of Oxford's intellectual life, all but ceased by 1330. Part of that declining contact was voluntary, and for the decade 1330–40 Oxford did not suffer but thrived on its insularity.

Paris had always had less interest in Oxford and acquired Oxford material less directly or systematically. The approved list of books available for copying in Parisian bookstores in 1304 almost totally ignores any English contributions to scholastic learning.[11] What Paris received from Oxford came through English scholars who studied or taught at Paris, primarily those in the theological faculty. In this area the English students and masters in the arts faculty at Paris always played a less significant role, since they did not in most cases have any prior Oxford experience. What they brought to Paris was not Oxford logic and certainly not Oxford theology, but the grammar traditions of their pre-university education.

---

some of these suspect opinions were the result of the contemporary English practice of applying sophistical methods of argumentation to theological problems, a practice that was being introduced at Paris in the period 1338–42 and was still viewed with suspicion in 1348 by many in positions of authority inside and outside the university.

[9] *Calendar of Entries in the Papal Registers relating to Great Britain and Ireland. Petitions to the Pope*, vol. 1, ed. W. H. Bliss (London, 1896), 398.

[10] On Fitzralph and John of Northwode in Paris in 1329–30 see *CUP* 2: 670. John Trillek, later bishop of Hereford, was there in the same year with four (English?) *socii*, but may have arrived earlier and stayed longer; *CUP* 2: 662. He would have been around nineteen and thus either completing his arts degree or beginning his study of theology. On Dumbleton and Master Clay see Kaluza, *Thomas de Cracovie*, 136–37.

[11] *CUP* 2: 107–12.

The absence of Oxford-trained logicians in the Parisian theological faculty after 1330, and more especially the absence of theological students who had already begun their theological studies in an English *studium*, goes far to explain the lack of English influence on the Parisian theology of the 1330s. It was unfortunate for Paris that its direct contact with English education, particularly Oxford, all but ceased at the very time Oxford philosophy, science, and theology entered their most expansive and productive period.

FOREIGN SCHOLARS AND SCHOLARS ABROAD

In reviewing intellectual and cultural contacts between England and the Continent it is well to keep in mind that Paris formed only one of the important continental destinations for English students and masters in the early fourteenth century. And the almost negligible presence of French scholars at Oxford or Cambridge did not mean the absence of other foreign scholars. As long as those contacts remained, either through Englishmen abroad or foreign students and masters at English *studia*, England had direct access to developments and influences from the Continent and, insofar as those centers had contact with Paris, indirect access to Parisian thought as well.

English scholars might, on occasion, be found in various cities in continental Europe on royal or ecclesiastical business, at a general chapter meeting of a religious order, or as fugitives from royal or papal displeasure, as in the case of William of Ockham and his English *socius* at Munich. Yet the places where one would frequently encounter English scholars abroad would be far fewer, primarily the papal court at Avignon and the University of Bologna.

In the preceding chapter we examined the strong appeal of Avignon in the first half of the century and the residence there of a number of distinguished English lawyers and theologians, among them Anthony Bek, John Lutterell, Ockham, Walter Chatton, Walter Burley, and Richard Fitzralph. These and other English scholars would have mixed and shared ideas with scholars from Paris, Toulouse, Bologna, and elsewhere. They might also have had access to some of the early humanists who visited the papal court.

How much of this reached back and enriched the English *studia* is another matter. Avignon was probably, even at best, a weak source for the introduction of continental ideas into England. Many of those after 1330 who left England for the papal court never returned home. Those who did (principally those on diplomatic or legal business) rarely if ever returned to Oxford or Cambridge during their post-university careers. Although they did not abandon their scholarly interests, what ideas they brought back from abroad were probably communicated within a royal, episcopal, and London setting. Thus the contact between the English universities and the papal court, as far as it concerns the flow of ideas, worked primarily in one direction: from Oxford to Avignon, not from Avignon to Oxford.

Another popular center for English scholars abroad was Bologna. The university there was the principal place for the study of both civil and canon law, and as such it had attracted English students throughout the twelfth, thirteenth, and early fourteenth centuries. John of Ponteys, bishop of Winchester (1282–1304), was a doctor in civil law from Bologna and had lectured at Modena in 1270. Bologna's reputation in England as a major school of law did not diminish. Two generations later Ralph Stratford, bishop of London (1340–54), was a doctor in both laws from Bologna. Bologna was similarly attractive to theologians. In the fourteenth century the convents of the mendicant orders at Bologna, which offered training in theology to their members, began to form the nucleus of an unofficial faculty of theology. Well before the establishment in 1364 of a consortium of theological *collegia* affiliated with the university, English theologians had ventured or were sent to Bologna to give theological lectures and hold disputations. William of Alnwick (in 1323), Thomas Waleys (in 1326–27), and Walter Burley (in 1341) are just a few of those active at Bologna in the first half of the fourteenth century. England also supplied many of the lectors for the Dominican convent in Bologna.[12] None of these scholars were at Bologna on royal or episcopal service, but were fully engaged in lectures and disputations. Those who returned to England were absorbed back into the academic life of their order.

The decline of the English presence at Paris in the second and third decades of the fourteenth century was eventually matched by a similar drop in the number of university-trained Englishmen at other *studia*

---

[12] For example, Thomas Waleys, lector in 1326–27, and Richard Winkley, lector in 1331. See Smalley, *EFA*, 76.

outside England. There is no evidence of English scholars at Bologna or other *studia* in Italy after mid-century, although study at Toulouse in the late 1360s brought Robert Waldeby O.E.S.A. his doctorate and appointment as tutor for the future Richard II.[13] Similarly, the number of English theologians in Avignon drops in the 1340s, and the Anglo-Irishman Fitzralph was among the last. Yet even if the final result was the same as at Paris, it is significant that English scholars continued to go abroad to centers other than Paris *during* Oxford's most active period in the fourteenth century.

Offsetting the declining presence of English scholars abroad was an increase in the number of foreign scholars studying in England. In the two decades before the Black Death, at a time when Oxford was moving toward isolation from Paris, the largest group among the known foreign scholars was Italian, and most of them were Franciscan. Italian students were increasingly attracted to Oxford in the course of the fourteenth century, never representing less than twenty percent of the known foreign students there. At the beginning of the century these Italian students were not in religious orders, and they came to Oxford to pursue or supplement their study of law. Soon the mendicants, faced with more students than the Paris convents could accommodate and promote, exercised their right to send students from outside the English province to Oxford, inasmuch as it was a *studium generale*. They came to Oxford for theology, after initial training in philosophy and theology in the *studia particularia* of Tuscany and Lombardy. The Franciscans sent students from Assisi, Florence, Perugia, Milan, and Bologna. By mid-century almost all the Italian students known to be at Oxford were in religious orders, most of them Franciscan but some Augustinians and Dominicans as well. The concentration was from northern and central Italy. Through them the mendicant convents at Oxford had access, at least after 1320, to whatever intellectual currents were prevalent in the mendicant convents of Tuscany. And since almost all these Italians returned to Italy, the latter received a steady flow of information and works of Oxford theology, logic, and natural philosophy. Oxford gave them much, but in return there was little new in the Italian *studia* at that time that they could give to Oxford.

[13] Roth, *EAF* 1: 86–87.

By mid-century the number of known students from Germany and eastern Europe increased and by 1370 approximately equalled the Italian presence. Again, it was largely the mendicant *studia* that provided the avenue of communication. And much of the intellectual exchange was still in the direction from England to the Continent. Friedrich von Regensburg, a Franciscan, took back with him to Germany a copy of the *Sentences* commentary of the English Benedictine known simply as Monachus Niger.[14] Beginning in the 1360s Bohemian students came to Oxford, where they were introduced to English scholasticism, including the writings of John Wyclif.

The German, east European, and Italian mendicants also acted as a means through which Oxford and Paris each kept abreast of recent developments at the other university. For example, John Klenkok, who went to Oxford from Prague in the early 1350s but who was already aware of some Augustinian Parisian theologians, introduced the writings of Gregory of Rimini into the Austin convent. When he and others like him returned to the Continent, they brought back a knowledge of the recent Oxford theology of the 1350s. While at Paris John Hiltalingen of Basel knew the Oxford commentary of Klenkok as well as the writings of Osbert Pickingham, O.Carm., Nicholas Aston, Richard Brinkley, O.F.M., John Dumbleton, Richard Billingham, Geoffrey Herdeby, O.E.S.A, William Jordan, O.P., Uthred of Boldon, O.S.B., and Richard Feribrigge. Peter of Candia, a Greek Franciscan (and later Pope Alexander V) was sent from Italy to Norwich and Oxford around 1370 and subsequently carried with him to Paris his familiarity with English writers.

In the last two decades of the century, largely because of the papal schism, Oxford received a large influx of foreign students, most of them from Italy and Germany. After 1382 Paris was, for all practical purposes, closed to German and Italian students. What had been for them the leading university for the study of theology was, for more than a generation, not a serious possibility. Many Italians returned to Italy and the *studia* of Bologna, Padua, and Florence. Germans met the crisis through the foundation of a series of new universities. Some Italians and Germans, however, chose Oxford as a place to complete their the-

[14] D. Trapp, " 'Moderns' and 'Modernists' in MS Fribourg Cordeliers 26," *Augustinianum* 5 (1965): 241–70.

ological education. The anonymous author of a *Lectura Oxoniensis* around 1380 was probably German, and the prominent Queen's College logician John Scharpe was from Münster.[15]

Initially the increase in foreign students at Oxford came from among those who had left Paris to find an educational setting more compatible with their papal affiliation, one that protected their chances of acquiring church livings in their own countries. Soon foreign mendicants were being sent directly from Germany and Italy to oppose, to read the *Sentences*, and to incept in theology. The Austin Friars were the most vigorous mendicant order in channeling their best students to Oxford. Long before the General Chapter of 1391, which forbade Augustinians to study at Paris, the order was pouring foreign candidates into Oxford at an alarming rate, making it difficult for English Austins to be promoted.[16]

Most of the German students came from Saxony, although there were some from Bavaria. The ties between Oxford and Erfurt, already in evidence in the previous generation, became stronger. The Italians were invariably from Lombardy and Tuscany. The largest single group after 1385 came from Padua and the surrounding cities of Venice, Udine, Rimini, and Ferrara. Their number included Dominicans such as Ardicione Pizzegoti, who became prior of the Padua convent in the first two decades of the fifteenth century, and Thomaso de Udine, who was prior at Bologna and Padua. There were Venetian patricians, such as Giovanni Contarini. The Augustinians included Giovanni Becchetti, who became dean of the theological faculty at Padua, Angelo of Viterbo, who subsequently was rewarded with several bishoprics, and Paolo Veneto, the most renown dialectician in Italy in the early fifteenth century.[17] The second largest group came from Florence and included Franciscans as well as Dominicans and Augustinians.

[15] D. Trapp, "Clm 27034. Unchristened Nominalism and Wycliffite Realism at Prague in 1381," *RTAM* 24 (1957): 320–60; Emden, *BRUO* 3: 1680.

[16] Roth, *EAF* 1: 68–69.

[17] There has been some confusion over which of the two Pauls of Venice active in the closing years of the fourteenth century is the author of the *Logica parva* and the sometime resident at Oxford. Moreover, the authenticity of the *Logica magna* has also come into question. On both of these issues see Paulus Venetus, *Logica Parva*, transl. and introd. by Alan R. Perreiah (Munich, 1984) and Perreiah, *Paul of Venice. A Bibliographical Guide* (Bowling Green, Ohio, 1986).

Students who came directly from Paris would have brought with them a familiarity with the ideas, works, and disputations taking place in the theological faculty at Paris. Through them Oxford theologians had access to the works and debates that had occurred in the two generations between Gregory of Rimini and Pierre d'Ailly, specifically the thought of John Buridan, Hugolino of Orvieto, Nicole Oresme, John of Ripa, Henry Totting of Oyta, Marsilius of Inghen, and many others. Moreover, there can be little doubt that Oxford at the end of the fourteenth century had some contact with the circles of early Italian humanism. The mendicant *studia* in Italy had been open to lay scholars at least since the time of Dante, and their libraries gradually acquired humanist writings at the same time that the friars, in turn, influenced lay piety.[18] The Augustinians at Padua had been closely associated with Petrarch.[19] Contarini belonged to the group of those who became patrons of arts and letters in Venice, and he had already absorbed some of those interests before going to Oxford, as his correspondence reflects.[20] The mendicant convents of Florence, although still wedded to scholastic theology, were also not strangers to humanist studies. The students who came to Oxford had studied for some years in their local *studia*, and in the case of those from Padua and Florence they brought with them an interest in the classics that had already begun to penetrate the schools.[21]

The fact that neither Parisian philosophy and theology nor early Italian humanism sparked any particular interest at Oxford until late in the fifteenth century cannot be explained on the grounds of isolation from

[18] R. Arbesmann, *Der Augustiner-Eremitenorden und der Beginn der humanistischen Bewegung* (Würzburg, 1965); P. O. Kristeller, *Medieval Aspects of Renaissance Learning* (Durham, N.C., 1974), 93–114; R. Manselli, "Due biblioteche di *Studia* Minoritici: Santa Croce di Firenze e il Santo di Padova," in *Le scuole degli ordini mendicanti (secoli XIII–XIV)*, Centro di studi sulla spiritualità medievale, 17 (Todi, 1978), 353–71.

[19] Arbesmann, *Augustiner-Eremitenorden*, 19–23, 52–69, 83–93, 113–15.

[20] A. Luttrell, "Giovanni Contarini, A Venetian at Oxford: 1392–1399," *Journal of the Warburg and Courtauld Institutes* 29 (1966): 424–36.

[21] C. T. Allmand's remark, that lawyers and their patrons in both government and church were a means of contact with Italian humanists and thus a channel for humanist influence in fifteenth-century England, applies also to theologians and to the second half of the fourteenth century; see Allmand, "The Civil Lawyers," in *Profession, Vocation, and Culture*, 163. Arguing for the late appearance of humanist learning in England is R. Weiss, *Humanism in England during the 15th Century* (Oxford, 1967). But for earlier evidence on classicizing tendencies among English mendicants see Smalley, *EFA*.

continental influences. Avenues of academic communication still existed. And if English scholars rarely studied abroad in the second half of the century, Englishmen (scholars and nonscholars) did visit the Continent for reasons of commerce or diplomacy as well as governmental administration and military service. Chaucer, for instance, visited Spain (1366), France (1369), and Italy (1372). It is likely that he knew Petrarch, and the indirect influence of Dante and Boccaccio are evident in his works. Chaucer was not unique. But he was also not typical of most educated, well-travelled Englishmen of his day, whose awareness of Italian or continental learning did not go beyond a common interest in moral philosophy and practical theology. For most, all that was necessary for religion or life was provided within the boundaries of England. In place of Compostela or Rome, a pilgrimage to Canterbury was quite sufficient. And the learning needed for the mind's enrichment or the body's career could as easily and as well be obtained at the Inns of Court in London or up the Thames at the University of Oxford.

THE EXPORTATION OF ENGLISH LEARNING
(1340–50)

If Oxford continued to have access to but showed little interest either in Italian humanism or Parisian scholasticism after 1330, continental centers of learning showed considerable interest and enthusiasm for Oxford thought. Indeed, England had almost as great an intellectual impact in the fourteenth century as did northern France in the twelfth or Italy in the fifteenth.

The evidence now available reveals the flow of newer works of English logic, physics, and theology into Italy and Germany as early as 1337.[22] In Italy the earliest centers for the reception of English thought were Bologna and Assisi, and in Germany, Cologne and Erfurt. No doubt the channels of communication were English scholars abroad and Italian and German students at Oxford. The remarkable thing is that this predates by some five years any comparable evidence of post-1325 English works available at Paris.

[22] W. J. Courtenay, "The Early Stages in the Introduction of Oxford Logic into Italy," in *ELI*, 13–32; "The Role of English Thought in the Transformation of University Education in the Late Middle Ages," in *Rebirth, Reform and Resilience: Universities in Transition, 1300–1700*, ed. J. A. Kittelson and P. J. Transue (Columbus, 1984), 103–62.

Despite the closing of the traditional avenues of communication between Paris and Oxford, philosophical and theological works produced
in England in the period 1320–40 did eventually make their way to
Paris and command the attention of students and masters in the arts
and theological faculties. Ockham's writings in natural philosophy and
in logic had attracted a sufficient following in the arts faculty by 1338
for opposing masters (the majority) to prohibit their use between 1339
and 1342.[23] By the fall semester of 1343, in the *Sentences* commentary of
Gregory of Rimini, one finds a wealth of new English sources, particularly those of Oxford. Not only is Ockham cited frequently, but citations
from Chatton, Fitzralph, Wodeham, Bradwardine, Kilvington, Heytesbury, Buckingham, Halifax, and Monachus Niger also abound. Almost
no *Sentences* commentary at Paris in the next few generations was un-
influenced by those English writings.[24] Already by 1345 Paris was captivated by English thought as if little else existed. Richard de Bury's famous remark, although often discounted as too pro-English, is not far
from the truth, as the events after 1340 bear out.[25] After a period of in-
activity Paris scholars had become obsessed with the "English subtleties," although they denounced them in public—an awkward stance created perhaps by the need to acquire, in the charged anti-English
atmosphere of the 1340s, the most intellectually challenging learning of
the day.

Through what avenues did this newer English thought enter Paris?
The interest in Ockham among the *artistae* may have developed naturally out of the presence at Paris of the works of Ockham in logic and

[23] W. J. Courtenay and Katherine H. Tachau, "Ockham, Ockhamism, and the English-
German Nation at Paris, 1339–1341," *History of Universities* 2 (1982): 53–96.

[24] G. Ouy, *Un commentateur des "Sentences" au XIVe siècle, Jean de Mirecourt,* doc. thesis,
Ecole des Chartes, Paris, 1946; W. J. Courtenay, "John of Mirecourt and Gregory of Rimini
on Whether God Can Undo the Past," *RTAM* 39 (1972): 224–56; 40 (1973): 147–74; Kaluza, *Thomas de Cracovie.*

[25] "They [Parisian scholars] wrap up their doctrines in unskilled discourse, and are losing
propriety of all logic, except that our English subtleties, which they denounce in public, are
the subject of their furtive vigils." N. W. Gilbert, "Richard de Bury and the 'Quires of Yesterday's Sophisms' " in *Philosophy and Humanism. Renaissance Essays in Honor of Paul Oskar
Kristeller,* ed. E. P. Mahoney (New York, 1976), 229–57; J. E. Murdoch, "*Subtilitates Anglicanae* in Fourteenth-Century Paris: John of Mirecourt and Peter Ceffons," in *Machaut's
World. Science and Art in the Fourteenth Century,* ed. M. P. Cosman and B. Chandler, Annals
of the New York Academy of Sciences, 314 (New York, 1978), 51–86.

natural philosophy, which were known there as early as 1324. By 1325 Ockham's natural philosophy had found sufficient support to cause Michael de Massa to attack those he called *Occanistae*.[26] That attack was renewed by the masters in arts in 1339. It resulted in a prohibition of both public and private lectures on the works of Ockham (September 1339), renewed in the following year (December 1340), and a statute against the *secta Occanica* (*c*. February 1341).[27]

It is probable that supporters of Ockham's natural philosophy were to be found among the Scottish students in the arts faculty, who represented a constant channel of communication between Paris and the British Isles. John Rathe, who shared Ockham's rejection of species, was regent in arts from 1334 until the summer of 1340, during which time he was also a student in theology.[28] He entered upon his opponency in theology in the fall of 1340, only a few months before the statute of the arts faculty was promulgated. His pupil, Walter of Wardlaw, was one of the few regents in arts who did not sign the anti-Ockhamist statute in September of 1341 and was also the regent under whom all the English students present in 1343–44 were studying.

A second channel of communication from Oxford to Paris after 1335 was the continued flow of English Cistercians to the Collège St. Bernard at Paris. Since their philosophical training and early theological study would probably have been obtained in England under Cistercian masters who had studied at Oxford, it is possible that some of the works of English philosophy and theology would have been brought by English students to the library of the Parisian Cistercian house of study. One of the earliest Paris *Sentences* commentaries to reflect the interest in the newer English thought is that of John of Mirecourt (1344–45), who had access to those writings independent of the commentary of Gregory of Rimini (1343–44).[29]

A third channel was by way of Italian students from the mendicant

[26] Vatican Library, MS. Vat. lat. 1087, fol. 88ᵛ.

[27] The arts faculty statute of December 29, 1340, often cited as the principal anti-Ockhamist document from Paris, concerned other matters entirely. See Courtenay and Tachau, "Ockham, Ockhamism"; Courtenay, "The Reception of Ockham's Thought at the University of Paris," in *PRUP*, 43–64.

[28] Courtenay and Tachau, "Ockham, Ockhamism," 64–70.

[29] Courtenay, "John of Mirecourt"; J.-F. Genest's discovery of additional English sources in Mirecourt will soon be published.

studia in Italy, where the works of English philosophy and theology had been brought by those who had studied at London, Norwich, Cambridge, and Oxford.[30] Throughout the 1330s, in contrast to the small number of French students studying in England, one encounters Italian students in the English *studia*. Most of them belonged to the mendicant orders and, like the Franciscan, Nicholas of Assisi, returned eventually to Italy to teach in one or more of the provincial *studia*. Slowly the libraries of the Italian convents, particularly those of the Franciscans at Assisi, Perugia, and elsewhere, acquired manuscripts of the newer English works,[31] and their use in the classroom would have stimulated interest in those works among the other mendicant orders in centers, like Perugia and Bologna, where the mendicants operated what were for them *studia generalia*, where lectures on philosophy were given, and where the *Sentences* were read.[32] In some respects these mendicant *studia generalia*, especially where they coincided with cathedral and collegiate schools, were more important for intellectual formation than the universities, which for the thirteenth and fourteenth centuries have received almost all our attention.

Thus the channels of communication between the Continent and England, which had diminished for Paris in the 1330s, were active for Italy in that same period. Maierù speaks of the later effects as an intellectual invasion of Italy by English thought,[33] and the date of many of the manuscripts and the biographies of individuals such as Nicholas of Assisi indicate that this "invasion" took place at least as early as its Parisian counterpart, possibly earlier. Boccaccio, in writing to Petrarch in 1339, used Ockham as the leading example of a logician, revealing that his reputation and probably his works as well were known and respected in Italy in the 1330s.[34] It was in the Italian *studia* that the first

[30] Courtenay, "English Logic in Italy"; "Nicholas of Assisi and Vatican MS. Chigi B.V.66," *Scriptorium* 36 (1982): 260–63.

[31] Courtenay, "English Logic in Italy."

[32] Ibid.; *Le scuole degli ordini mendicanti.*

[33] A. Maierù, "Lo *Speculum puerorum sive Terminus est in quem* di Riccardo Billingham," in *A Giuseppe Ermini* (Spoleto, 1970), 297–397.

[34] Giovanni Boccaccio, *Opera latine minori*, ed. A. Massèra (Bari, 1928), 113, cited from Neal W. Gilbert, "The Early Italian Humanists and Disputation," in *Renaissance Studies in Honor of Hans Baron*, ed. A. Molho and J. Tedeschi (Florence, Italy, and Dekalb, Ill., 1971), 215.

Parisian theologian to reflect the newer English thought, Gregory of Rimini, received his theological perspectives and training, and many of his English sources would have been acquired in Italy, specifically at Bologna, Padua, and Perugia, before coming to Paris.

The exportation of Oxford thought to the schools and universities of the Continent in the middle years of the fourteenth century was one of the most important developments in the intellectual history of that period. It radically altered the techniques and content of Parisian theology in ways that lasted well into the fifteenth and sixteenth centuries. It revolutionized the study of logic in Italy, captivated the attention of Italian *studia*, and antagonized humanist grammarians and rhetoricians, largely because of its success on Italian soil. In the form of John Wyclif's writings it inspired elements in Hussite theology and helped provoke a religious reform that swept Bohemia and became a concern of orthodox theologians all across Europe in the early fifteenth century. The dissemination of English thought on the Continent was a movement that depended not only on English students abroad but, even more, on the presence of foreign scholars at Oxford, particularly from Germany and Italy, who took English works and ideas back with them to their homelands. The content of the newer English thought is the principal subject toward which the following chapters lead.

II

THE GOLDEN AGE OF ENGLISH
SCHOLASTICISM
1315–40

OXFORD SCHOOLS IN THE EARLY
FOURTEENTH CENTURY

✦

BETWEEN the classroom and the scholastic treatise lay many social experiences. The student sat with others at the feet of a master. In disputations, whether as opponent, respondent, or eventually determiner, he debated others. His lectures as bachelor and later as master were delivered before an audience of his contemporaries, some junior, some senior. But the most important social experience conditioning his thought was his encounter with earlier writers, the way in which he shaped his own original contribution in the face of past opinion.

The lecture halls and libraries were not mere physical settings for study, reflection, and writing. They were alive with memories, traditions, the ongoing presence of the personalities who had taught there and whose works were still read. Fourteenth-century scholars had a sense of time and history, but temporal distance was less meaningful than it would be for later centuries. Aristotle, Augustine, and Aquinas were as near as the library shelf, and their voices had to be heard. The school experience, when it gave birth to a written product, meant a responsibility to authority and past tradition as well as the challenge of creativity.

The fourteenth-century scholar was thus aware of "schools" and "schools of thought," and he did not confuse the concepts. The term "school" (*schola*) meant a place of study and implied a group only by association with a place.[1] Its basic meaning remained what it had been throughout the medieval period: the classrooms where teaching went on, the physical setting of learning. Every educational institution was a "school," from the simplest song school up to the *aulae* of magisterial

---

[1] C. D. Du Cange, *Glossarium mediae et infimae latinitatis*, vol. 6 (Paris, 1846), 109–11; although the *Mittellateinisches Würterbuch* is not complete, the card file in their Munich office was consulted for *schola* and *sequax*.

disputations in the theological faculty of a university. At the university level *schola* could include all lecture halls commonly used for academic exercises. But it might also designate specific areas within a university community where one could find the halls most frequently used for arts, law, medicine, and theology. At Paris this meant the areas around the rue de Fouarre for arts, the clos Brunel for law, and the monastic, mendicant, and secular houses of study for theology, particularly the area surrounding St. Jacques and the Collège de Sorbonne. At Oxford it meant the house of the Austin Canons at St. Frideswide's priory, school street, and the Augustinian friary (see map 1).

A second meaning of *schola* in the fourteenth century was derived from the first and never far removed from it. The teaching of "the schools" or "school" meant whatever was commonly taught in the lecture halls and convents of a particular university, what any master, regardless of order or philosophical persuasion, would accept and maintain. It did not, in the fourteenth century, refer to a consensus among various rival "schools of thought" but rather to the standard teaching of the university classroom, "sicut ponit tota schola Oxoniensis."[2] Similarly, the phrase *in scholis* could refer to the physical setting or to the common teaching produced in that setting, but never the teaching of separate philosophical or theological currents.

The term *schola* could also be used in a third sense to refer to all doctors (*magistri*), present and past, who belonged to a particular religious order. Thus John Hiltalingen of Basel, an Austin Friar lecturing at Paris in 1365, occasionally used phrases like "a certain ancient doctor of this school" or "our school" (*schola nostra*).[3] In keeping with that usage modern historians speak of a Victorine school, a Franciscan school, an Augustinian school (specifically theologians belonging to the Austin Friars), or Mertonians. But these were not "schools of thought," nor did they necessarily imply any specific philosophical or doctrinal commit-

---

[2] The anonymous *Tractatus de sex inconvenientibus*; C. Wilson, *William Heytesbury. Medieval Logic and the Rise of Mathematical Physics* (Madison, 1956), 8, 170. Similar expressions are found in Osbert Pickingham, "et communis schola huius universitatis"; Xiberta, *SOC*, 261; Wodeham, *Lectura Oxon.* 1, d. 33, q. 2, a. 3, dub. 4 (Oyta abbrev., Paris, 1512, fol. 80rb): "nec in aliquo sensu admittitur a sanctis vel a schola"; Ibid., q. 3, a. 3, (fol. 82va): "nullus sanctus aut doctor negat talem aliquam, nec etiam omnis schola"; Wodeham, *Lect. secunda*, d. 1, q. 4, a. 2 (Cambridge, Gonville and Caius College, MS. 281, fol. 141rb): "praesens scola."

[3] D. Trapp, "Augustinian Theology of the 14th Century," *Augustiniana* 6 (1956): 248.

ment. Hiltalingen was referring to theologians of his order who had lectured at the Augustinian convent in Paris, as he was then doing. They formed a "school" because they were all doctors of the Austin Friars and had lectured in the same halls, not because they necessarily maintained certain set opinions in philosophy and theology. In this sense of *schola* Durand of St. Pourçain belonged to the Dominican school just as much as Hervaeus Natalis or Peter Palude; Gregory of Rimini to the Augustinian school just as much as Giles of Rome; and Ockham to the Franciscan school just as much as Scotus or Bonaventure.

Finally, fourteenth-century scholars were also aware of "schools of thought," although the term "school" was rarely used in that sense. From reading Aristotle they were aware of Pythagoreans, the Eleatic school, and the Platonists. From Albert the Great or Thomas Aquinas they knew of a Stoic school (*Stoicorum tota schola*), an Epicurean school (*Epicureorum secta*), of Nominalists (*Nominales*), and disciples of Gilbert de la Porrée (*Porretani*). They could, by the second quarter of the fourteenth century, refer to the opinion of the Thomists (*Thomistae*), Scotists (*Scotistae*), or Ockhamists (*Occanistae*). The "-ism" ending beloved by modern authors in describing ideologies and movements was not used in this way in the fourteenth century, although it was a linguistic possibility as applied to heresies or other religious groups (*Pelagianismus, paganismus, Iudaismus*).[4] For the most part, fourteenth-century scholars never thought in terms of abstract ideologies; they personified ideas as groups of people, some real, some only hypothetical constructs.[5]

Most of these terms were labels of convenience, used to group and simplify opinions against which an author would place his own ideas.

[4] N. W. Gilbert, "Ockham, Wyclif, and the 'Via Moderna,'" in *AM*, 119.

[5] To a fourteenth-century scholastic the label "Augustinian" would have meant an Austin Friar, and the label "Nominalist" may have meant a twelfth-century disciple of Peter Abelard. Secondly, the labels used in the fourteenth century describe opinions of others, never of oneself. There are no fourteenth-century analogues to Gabriel Biel's or Luther's self-designation as an Ockhamist; see Biel's introduction to the *Collectorium*, his commentary on the *Sentences*; for Luther see O. Scheel, *Dokumente zu Luthers Entwicklung*, nr. 33 (Responsio ad condemnationem doctrinalem per Lovanienses et Colonienses factam. 1520); nr. 37: (Adversus execrabilem Antichristi bullam. 1520). And we cannot assume that when Adam Wodeham called John of Reading "a faithful disciple of Scotus" that Reading would necessarily have acknowledged that label with enthusiasm, although Reading's Scotism can be derived from his own works; Courtenay, *Adam Wodeham* (Leiden, 1978), 62.

Some were pejorative, such as "Averroist," and not really descriptive of anyone's thought.[6] Other terms were evaluatively neutral, but their use did not imply that the author necessarily had any one thinker or group of thinkers in mind. Often the terms applied only to the issue under discussion and reveal, for example, what one, following Scotus or Thomas on this particular question, would hold. That is usually the case with such expressions as "via Thomae" or "via Gregorii." They describe the solutions of Thomas Aquinas or Gregory of Rimini on a particular question and do not refer to a school of thought. *Via* acquired this other meaning only in the fifteenth century.[7]

Thus when fourteenth-century scholars thought of schools, they principally had in mind the physical setting of teaching. Yet there were periods in the late Middle Ages when the concept of "schools of thought" had some meaning. Many of the labels used in the fourteenth century to describe contemporary ideas derived from the late thirteenth and early fourteenth centuries when intellectual currents grouped themselves around certain personalities and philosophical commitments. The prominence of schools of thought then and in the fifteenth century has led some historians to make school affiliation and school mentality one of the distinguishing features of late scholasticism.[8] In their view the creativity of the individual minds that erected the monuments of thirteenth-century scholasticism supposedly gave way in the fourteenth century to arid school traditions, where the ideas

---

[6] The appropriateness of the Averroist label has received considerable discussion. J. H. Randall, "Paduan Aristotelianism: an Appraisal," in *Aristotelismo padovano e filosofia aristotelica*, Atti del XII Congresso internazionale di filosofia, 9 (Florence, 1960), 199–206; Randall, *The School of Padua and the Emergence of Modern Science* (Padua, 1961); P. O. Kristeller, "Paduan Averroism and Alexandrism in the Light of Recent Studies," in *Renaissance Thought*, vol. 2: *Papers on Humanism and the Arts* (New York, 1965), 111–18; C. B. Schmitt, *A Critical Survey and Bibliography of Studies on Renaissance Aristotelianism, 1958–1969* (Padua, 1971); Randall, "Paduan Aristotelianism Reconsidered," in *Philosophy and Humanism. Renaissance Essays in Honor of Paul Oskar Kristeller*, ed. E. P. Mahoney (New York, 1976), 275–82; F. van Steenberghen, *Maître Siger de Brabant* (Louvain, 1977).

[7] For further discussion see my *"Antiqui and Moderni in Late Medieval Thought," Journal of the History of Ideas* 48 (1987): 1–8.

[8] D. Hay, *Europe in the Fourteenth and Fifteenth Centuries* (New York, 1966), 338–44; C. Michalski, "Les courants philosophiques à Oxford et à Paris pendant le XIVᶜ siècle," *Bulletin internat. de l'Académie Polonaise des Sciences et des Lettres*, classe hist/phil. (Cracow, 1922), 63.

of former geniuses were repeated, glossed, watered down, or misinterpreted, and where energies were diverted into school rivalry rather than positive achievement. That view of the late medieval universities as arid and unproductive ignores the remarkable developments in logic, mathematics, physics, and theology in the fourteenth century. Moreover, it is founded on the misconception that the scholasticism of the fourteenth and fifteenth centuries is essentially the same and that school traditions continued largely uninterrupted from the late thirteenth to the early sixteenth century. That is emphatically not the case. Throughout most of the fourteenth century school traditions in the usual sense were absent. It was, particularly in England, a century of individual achievement, unfettered by slavish obedience to the thought of earlier masters. One might, therefore, better view the emergence of schools of thought at the end of the thirteenth century as a brief interlude in the predominant pattern of individuality in thirteenth-century thought.[9]

THE EMERGENCE OF SCHOOLS OF THOUGHT

In the period from 1280 to 1320 strong centripetal, cohesive forces were at work to bring some uniformity of teaching into the mendicant orders. The Dominican order at Paris in 1286 bound itself to teach and

[9] A number of intellectual movements commonly attributed to the fourteenth century are not discussed in this chapter. For example, Averroist was a pejorative label rarely used in the period, and the label "Latin Averroist," created in the nineteenth century, does not accurately characterize any fourteenth-century group or individual, even in Italy; see above, n. 6. It certainly had no place in England. The Mertonians were not a school of thought but fellows of a college. Their contributions to the development of logic, mathematics, and physics will be considered in chapter 8. Augustinianism in the sense of a revival of interest in the writings and thought of Augustine was an important intellectual current, even though it never resulted in any group consciousness. It will be examined in chapter 10. Augustinianism in the sense of the thought of the Augustinian Hermits was not, in England, a defined body of beliefs, nor did it contribute in any discernible way to the Augustinian revival. The philosophy and theology of the Austin Friars in the first half of the century is treated in this chapter. Finally, Nominalism was never a school of thought in the fourteenth century and did not even become a label for contemporary opinion until the fifteenth century. Certain individuals, such as Ockham, may have expressed philosophical opinions that can be labeled nominalist, but it is doubtful whether that label can be used to characterize all their thought, nor was it ever used that way in the period.

defend the thought of Thomas Aquinas.[10] In the following year at Florence the Augustinian Hermits similarly bound themselves to teach the doctrine and opinions of Giles of Rome, both those he had written and those he might later write.[11] These actions were part of a larger campaign to defend the thought of Thomas and Giles in the two decades after the promulgation of the Parisian and Oxford Articles of 1277, since some of their opinions were contrary to the views of those who drafted the articles.[12] Interestingly, the Franciscans did not single out one of their own theologians for intellectual reverence and emulation, although they had two good candidates in Bonaventure and Alexander of Hales. Having supported the condemnations of 1277 and having achieved official recognition for such anti-Thomist and anti-Aegidian views as the plurality of substantial forms, the Franciscans had little need to restrict the diversity of their intellectual heritage by tying themselves to the thought of one of their doctors. Eventually, however, John Duns Scotus attracted the kind of following that made him, *de facto*, the leading doctor of the Franciscans.

Coincident with the selecting of an eminent doctor as a norm or doctrinal focus for the younger theologians of an order, distinct schools began to emerge toward the end of the thirteenth century. Among the Dominicans, both at Oxford and Paris, we find a series of bachelors and

[10] *Acta capitulorum generalium ordinis Praedicatorum*, ed. B. M. Reichert, Monumenta ordinis fratrum Praedicatorum historica, 1 (Rome, 1896), 235: "Districtius iniungimus et mandamus, ut fratres omnes et singuli, prout sciunt et possunt, efficacem dent operam ad doctrinam venerabilis magistri Fratris Thome de Aquino recolende memorie promovendam et saltem ut est opinio defendendam. . . ." See also A. Walz, "Ordinationes capitulorum generalium de Sancto Thoma eiusque cultu et doctrina," *Analecta ordinis Praedicatorum*, 16 (1923–24): 169–170.

[11] *Analecta Augustiniana*, 2 (1907–08): 275: "Quia venerabilis magistri nostri fratris Aegidii doctrina mundum universum illustrat, definimus et mandamus inviolabiliter observari, ut opiniones, positiones et sententias scriptas et scribendas praedicti magistri nostri omnes ordinis nostri lectores et studentes recipiant eisdem praebentes assensum, et eius doctrinae omni qua poterunt sollicitudine, ut et ipsi illuminati alios illuminare possint, sint seduli defensores."

[12] See the discussion and extensive bibliographical notes on the question in Gilson, *HCP*, 410–27; J. A. Weisheipl, *Friar Thomas d'Aquino* (New York, 1974), 333–50; *Les premières polémiques thomistes: Robert d'Orford, Reprobationes dictorum a fratre Egidio in primum sententiarum*, ed. A. P. Vella (Paris, 1968); R. Hissette, *Enquête sur les 219 articles condamnes à Paris le 7 mars 1277* (Louvain, 1977).

masters committed to the thought of Thomas.[13] Few of them had the purity of Thomism that their modern counterparts find desirable. This is due partly to their being open to other influences, partly to misinterpretations of Thomas's thought, and partly to their use of the *Scriptum* (Thomas's *Sentences* commentary) as the principal text for Thomism. In 1308 and again in 1313 the *Scriptum* was made the text to be read and commented on by bachelors and lectors in the Dominican order.[14] Unlike the *Summa theologiae*, the *Scriptum* was from beginning to end a work of Thomas (albeit the young Thomas), had less to do with positions called into question in 1277 and hotly debated in subsequent years, and, as a *Sentences* commentary, paralleled in genre the principal works of Bonaventure and Scotus. It had a more natural, time-honored place in the university curriculum.

In the early fourteenth century, most of the theologians among the Austin Friars whose works have survived show a similar dependence on Giles of Rome.[15] Giles's political thought was not universally adopted among his coreligious, but the influence of his philosophy and theology is marked. By 1310 one finds the beginning of a Scotist school, which within a decade became one of the strongest intellectual currents among the Franciscans at Paris.[16]

What explains this move toward conformity in doctrine? Initially, as has been noted, the enhancement of Thomas and Giles was part of a defense by their respective orders of men whose views had indirectly come under attack at Paris in the condemnation of 1277. The legislation was a means of concentrating the energies of Dominicans and Augustinians in defense of the orthodoxy of their leading theologians, particularly against their Franciscan critics. The "celebrification" of Thomas and Giles, and eventually Scotus, served other aims as well. It

[13] Roensch, *ETS*.

[14] *Acta cap. gen. ord. Praed.*, 2: 38, 64; A. Maierù, "Tecniche di insegnamento," in *Le scuole degli ordini mendicanti* (Todi, 1978), 336–38. On the other hand, both Peter of Aquila (*c.* 1334) and Gregory of Rimini (*c.* 1343) relied primarily on the *Summa theologiae* for their knowledge of Thomas. Capreolus, who used Gregory extensively, was not the first to make the *Summa* the principal text for Thomas's thought.

[15] D. Trapp, "Augustinian Theology of the 14th Century," *Augustiniana* 6 (1956): 146–274; A. Zumkeller, "Die Augustinerschule des Mittelalters: Vertreter und philosophisch-theologische Lehre," *Analecta Augustiniana* 27 (1964): 167–262.

[16] Gilson, *HCP*, 465–71.

was part of a rivalry, a means of competing with the other orders for academic and theological superiority and preferment—a motive that also underlay the canonization of Thomas in 1323. The desire for more uniformity in teaching may also have been viewed as a safeguard against suspect or heretical teaching. The issues addressed at the Council of Vienne (1311–12) and the investigations into the orthodoxy of John Quidort of Paris, Peter John Olivi, Meister Eckhart, Durand of St. Pourçain, William of Ockham, and John of Pouilly show the concern of some church authorities for greater doctrinal and theological unity.[17] By 1315, particularly at Paris, the emergence of fixed school traditions appeared well under way.

The movement to establish a one-to-one correspondence between a religious order and a particular teaching tradition began to collapse by the third decade of the century. Thomism was the first victim, followed by Aegidianism, and, eventually, even Scotism. Only toward the end of the century does one find a return of school consciousness, the emergence of Thomism, Albertism, Scotism, and the *Nominales*. The fifteenth century, at least on the surface, appears to be a century of school consciousness and school rivalry. What blocked or suspended this development throughout most of the fourteenth century?

DOMINICAN THEOLOGY AND THE
FATE OF THOMISM

A young friar studying at the Oxford Dominican convent in the second decade of the fourteenth century could have drawn upon two intellectual traditions in addition to those present in other halls and convents of the university town. The most immediate would have been the strong current of Thomism, to which a number of Dominican regent masters had adhered in the last two decades of the thirteenth century and which continued to dominate the atmosphere of the convent in the first decade of the fourteenth. English friars such as Richard Knapwell (Clapwell), Robert Orford, Thomas Sutton, and William Macclesfield had

[17] J. Koch, *Kleine Schriften*, vol. 2 (Rome, 1973), 191–450; J. Miethke, "Die Kirche und die Universitäten im 13. Jahrhundert," in *Schulen und Studium im sozialen Wandel des hohen und späteren Mittelalters*, ed. J. Fried, Vorträge und Forschungen, 30 (Sigmaringen, 1986), 285–320.

been among the strongest supporters of the unicity of substantial form in man, the pure potentiality of primary matter, the spirituality of separated substances (that angels were not composed of form and matter), the real distinction of essence and existence, and matter as the principle of individuation—the major philosophical tenets of Thomism as it was known in the late thirteenth century.[18] Their opponents had been largely English Franciscans, such as John Pecham, archbishop of Canterbury, Roger Marston, and William de la Mare, whose *Correctorium Fratris Thomae* had been one of the most fundamental and far-reaching attacks on Thomas.[19]

However, the non-Thomist tradition was not external to Blackfriars. The Oxford version of the Parisian Articles of 1277 had been drawn up by the Dominican Robert Kilwardby, as archbishop of Canterbury, almost immediately after the Parisian list of 219 propositions, some of them Thomist, had been condemned.[20] Kilwardby's reduced list of thirty "errors" was, in balance, more anti-Thomist, although such was not its primary intent. Kilwardby, by reason of office, was even more of an outside, nonuniversity figure than was Etienne Tempier, the bishop of Paris under whose authority the Parisian Articles of 1277 were issued. But Kilwardby was also an Oxford doctor with considerable theological prestige. His articles met with acceptance by the majority of the theological faculty at Oxford, who may have played some role in their formation.

Kilwardby was representative of a pre-Thomistic intellectual tradi-

---

[18] Roensch, *ETS*.

[19] M. Grabmann, "Le 'Correctorium Corruptorii' du dominicain Jean Quidort de Paris," *Revue Néo-Scolastique de philosophie* 19 (1912): 404–18; P. Glorieux, *Les premières polémiques thomistes*, vol. 1, *Le Correctorium Corruptorii "Quare"* (Kain, Belgium, 1927); R. Creytens, "Autour de la littérature des correctoires," *AFP* 12 (1942): 313–30; Glorieux, "Les correctoires. Essai de mise au point," *RTAM* 14 (1947): 287–304; Gilson, *HCP*, 410–27; Roensch, *ETS*.

[20] *CUP* 1: 558–59; D. E. Sharp, "The 1277 Condemnation by Kilwardby," *NS* 8 (1934): 306–18; D. A. Callus, *The Condemnation of St. Thomas at Oxford* (Oxford, 1946); J. Isaac, *Le Peri hermeneias en occident de Boèce à Saint Thomas*, Bibl. thomiste, 29 (Paris, 1953); O. Lewry, "The Oxford condemnations of 1277 in grammar and logic," in *English Logic and Semantics from the End of the Twelfth Century to the Time of Ockham and Burleigh*, ed. H.A.G. Braakhuis et al., 4th European Symposium on Medieval Logic and Semantics (Nijmegen, 1981), 235–78.

tion among English Dominicans, of which Richard Fishacre was an earlier example.[21] In contrast to the philosophical positions that came to be
associated with Thomas, Fishacre and Kilwardby shared beliefs that
were firmly grounded in the Augustinian tradition and incompatible
with Aristotelianism, either in its Averroistic or Christian forms. Both
Fishacre and Kilwardby maintained the plurality of substantial forms in
man; the Augustinian belief in seminal reasons, which attributed active
potency to matter; the hylomorphic composition (form and matter) of
all created things, including angels and souls; an epistemology of divine
illumination; a latent, a priori knowledge of God in man; and a simple,
rational distinction between the soul and its functions.

The theology of Fishacre and Kilwardby also contrasted markedly
with the Parisian Dominican tradition of Albert, Peter of Tarentaise
(Tarantasia), and Thomas. The former did not subscribe to the belief
that theology was a science in the Aristotelian sense, and its subject matter for them was Christological rather than theocentric. In a way compatible with many of their Franciscan contemporaries, they did not allow a primacy of the intellect over the will, either in God or man. God's
will was not bound by the orders of nature and salvation that had been
created, nor was the sequence of cause and effect an automatic, natural
process in which the will of God played no part. The conferring of
grace or the efficaciousness of the sacraments operated on the basis of
a covenant or contract between God and his church, a decision of the
divine will.

Thomism, therefore, was not the only alternative for Dominicans at
Oxford. It was an innovation that emerged in 1277 in opposition to the
attacks on Thomas and to the Parisian and Oxford articles. In favor of

---

[21] F. Pelster, "Das Leben und die Schriften des Oxforder Dominikanerlehrers Richard
Fishacre," *Zeitschrift für katholische Theologie* 54 (1930): 515–53; D. E. Sharp, "The Philosophy of Richard Fishacre (d. 1248)," *NS* 7 (1933): 281–97; M. D. Chenu, "Les réponses de
saint Thomas et de Kilwardby à la consultation de Jean de Verceil, 1271," in *Mélanges Mandonnet*, 2 vols. (Paris, 1930), 1, 191–222; F. Stegmüller, "Les questions du Commentaire des
Sentences de Robert Kilwardby," *RTAM* 6 (1934): 55–79, 215–28; Sharp, "Further Philosophical Doctrines of Kilwardby," *NS* 9 (1935): 39–65; E.M.F. Sommer-Seckendorff, *Studies in the Life of Robert Kilwardby O.P.* (Rome, 1937); Gilson, *HCP*, 354–59; W. J. Courtenay,
"The King and the Leaden Coin," *Traditio* 28 (1972): 185–209, repr. in Courtenay, *Covenant and Causality in Medieval Thought*, ch. 6 (London, 1984); B. Hamm, *Promissio, Pactum,
Ordinatio, Freiheit und Selbstbindung Gottes in der scholastischen Gnadenlehre* (Tübingen, 1977),
180, 251, 339, 483, 487.

Thomism stood the leadership of the order and an impressive series of Dominican masters at Paris. Against it were the tradition of Fishacre and Kilwardby, the theological consensus outside the Dominican order at Oxford, and ultimately a change in interests that made many of the philosophical and theological tenets of Thomism irrelevant. Thomism at Oxford, although it reigned unchallenged at Blackfriars from 1280 to 1305, was imported from Paris. It did not produce theologians of the stature of Hervaeus Natalis or Peter of Palude. Nor was it shaken by the internal critique that Durand of St. Pourçain posed for Parisian Thomism. Oxford Dominicans did not cite Durand, positively or negatively, a disinterest reflected in the paucity of English manuscripts of any redaction of Durand's *Sentences* commentary.[22] By the time Durand wrote, the interests of the English Dominicans had shifted to commentaries on Scripture, on classical authors, on the works of Augustine, political treatises, and sermons.[23] Thomism, whether in the philosophical or theological sense, was not central to the writing careers of Nicholas Trevet (between 1303 and 1325), Thomas Waleys (between 1318 and 1340), Simon Boraston (between 1320 and 1338), John Bromyard (between 1326 and 1340), or William d'Eyncourt (between 1330 and 1340).[24] Thus, well before Ockham entered the scholastic scene, Oxford Dominicans had begun to find nourishment elsewhere than in the thought of Thomas. The only Oxford theologian between 1310 and 1380 for whom Thomas was the principal authority was John Lutterell, a secular theologian, chancellor of Oxford, and a leading opponent of Ockham.[25]

The decline of Thomism was not limited to Oxford. By the time Thomas was canonized in 1323 his thought had ceased to attract the better minds within the Dominican order even at Paris. Meister Eck-

---

[22] J. Koch, *Durandus de S. Porciano O.P.*, Beiträge zur Geschichte der Philosophie des Mittelalters, 26 (Münster i.W., 1927).

[23] Smalley, *EFA*; J. B. Allen, "The Library of a Classicizer: The Sources of Robert Holkot's Mythographic Learning," in *Arts libéraux et philosophie au moyen âge* (Paris and Montréal, 1969), 721–29.

[24] Emden, *BRUO* 3: 1902–3 (for Trevet); 3: 1961–62 (for Waleys); 1: 221 (for Boraston); 1: 278 (for Bromyard); and 1: 577 (for d'Eyncourt); Smalley, *EFA*.

[25] F. Hoffmann, *Die Schriften des Oxforder Kanzlers Johannes Lutterell*, Erfurter Theologische Studien, 6 (Leipzig, 1959); J. Koch, "Neue Aktenstücke zu dem gegen Wilhelm Ockham in Avignon geführten Prozess," in *Kleine Schriften*, 2 vols. (Rome, 1973), 2: 275–365.

hart, the Dominican theologian and mystic who lectured at Paris from 1311 to 1313, went his own way. On the Continent, Durand of St. Pourçain, roundly attacked by his fellow Dominicans for his un-Thomistic positions advanced in various redactions of his *Sentences* commentary between 1310 and 1327, became one of the most frequently cited Dominicans of the century. His influence was marked on many later Parisian Dominicans, even Bernard Lombardi (1327–28).[26] Thomas remained an authority for Dominicans, both at Oxford and Paris, but few followed him to the exclusion of other sources—a decline in Dominican interest paralleled by a drop in the number of manuscripts of Thomas's works that date from the first half of the fourteenth century.[27] The repromulgation of the order's decision to teach and defend Thomas, such as at Saragossa in 1309 or Metz in 1313, reveals that the legislation of 1286 was not being universally observed and that younger Dominicans were pulling away from strict conformity to Thomas's writings.[28]

AEGIDIANISM AND THE AUSTIN FRIARS

Although the Augustinian convent in Oxford hosted many of the academic activities of the university, it was not itself a great center of philosophical or theological production. Of the 145 known masters and bachelors at Oxford in the fourteenth century, indeed from the entire Augustinian school at Oxford from the thirteenth century to the Reformation, only sermons, chronicles, political tracts, and a few scholastic fragments have survived.[29] The only entire *Sentences* commentary that has survived from the Oxford friary is by John Klenkok, a German.[30]

[26] M. Grabmann viewed Lombardi as a faithful disciple of Thomas; for a revised evaluation see J. Koch, *Durandus de S. Porciano O.P.*, 314–40.

[27] This information was privately communicated by L. J. Bataillon of the Leonine Commission.

[28] *Acta cap. gen. ord. Praed.*, 2: 38, 64. Some Dominican adherents to Thomas can be found in the period between 1320 and 1400, for example, Henry de Cervo at Cologne or possibly James of St. Andrea at Siena. On Cervo see M. Grabmann, *Mittelalterliches Geistesleben*, vol. 3 (Munich, 1956), 352–69. At the major *studia generalia*, however, the philosophical and theological commitments of the leading Dominicans were far from Thomistic; for example, William Crathorn and Robert Holcot at Oxford, or Francis of Tarvisio at Paris.

[29] Emden, *BRUO*; Roth, *EAF*.

[30] D. Trapp, "Augustinian Theology," 223–39; "Notes on John Klenkok, OSA, (d. 1374)," *Augustinianum* 4 (1964): 358–404.

Known writers, such as John Waldeby or William Flete were mystics and have left no scholastic works.[31] Since there is no particular reason to assume the manuscript survival rate among Augustinian houses should differ greatly from the other mendicant orders, one can only conclude that the Oxford (and Cambridge) Austins were either unproductive in publishing their lectures and disputations or wrote works that failed to attract any significant readership even among the Augustinians. Of the Austin masters in the early fourteenth century, William of Hecham, William of Lincoln, Richard Wetwang, and William of Markely, only some questions and sermons of Hecham have survived, although Wetwang was known to have published quodlibets and theological questions.[32] In the entire next generation, out of twenty-nine known Austins at Oxford, there was not a single author.

From what can be discerned on the philosophical and theological opinions of the Oxford Augustinians, the mandate of the order to teach the thought of Giles of Rome seems to have been observed. An abbreviated version of five theological questions of William of Hecham has survived, and although Giles is not cited directly, many of his positions are adopted.[33] The dependence on Giles is more clearly visible in two anonymous and fragmentary commentaries on the *Sentences* by English Austins, which probably date from the third decade of the fourteenth century.[34] Giles is referred to frequently as "our doctor," and his positions on the nature of theology are defended against Scotus and Peter Aureoli.

The hegemony of Giles of Rome over the theology of the Augustinian Hermits at Oxford lasted longer than that of Thomas over the Dominicans. Its demise came from internal apathy and the arrival of a new type of Augustinianism, that of Gregory of Rimini, imported into Oxford at mid-century.[35] But Aegidianism was an easier burden than Thomism because it was not a fixed set of doctrines but took different forms. Giles himself in the years from 1275 to 1300 had moved from dependence on Thomas, his master, to a more independent Augustin-

---

[31] Roth, *EAF* 1: 69–72, 400–407, 538–40, 581–88.

[32] Roth, *EAF* 1: 547–48, 591–92.

[33] Worcester Cath., MS. Q.99, fols. l^r, 4^v, 9^r, 12^r; Roth, *EAF* 1: 379–82, 547–48; A. G. Little and F. Pelster, *Oxford Theology and Theologians* (Oxford, 1934), 265–66, 287–90, 335–37.

[34] Oxford, Balliol College, MS. 63, fols. 60^r-66^v, 67^r-85^v; Roth, *EAF* 1: 598–99.

[35] Trapp, "Augustinian Theology," 182–207; Zumkeller, "Augustinerschule," 216–23.

ianism.[36] Thus those who followed the teaching of Giles had much to choose from. At one extreme Aegidianism could be interpreted as a variation on Thomism. Henry of Friemar the elder, writing around 1300, relied on both Thomas and Giles but preferred Thomas's version where they differed.[37] Dionysius of Borgo San Sepolcro, writing at Paris in 1317, attempted to harmonize the thought of Thomas and Giles, erasing their differences.[38] The thought of the later, more Augustinian Giles, is best represented in Augustinus of Ancona (c. 1303), John de Lana of Bologna (c. 1316), Gerard of Siena (c. 1325), and Thomas of Strasbourg (1335–37).[39] Their willingness to expound and adhere to the mature thought of Giles of Rome has led historians to label the latter two "orthodox Aegidians." At the other extreme were those Austin Friars who developed the thought of Giles further, sometimes in directions that were not in keeping with much of Giles's writings. To this group of so-called "ultra-Aegidians" belonged James of Viterbo (c. 1288), Alexander of S. Elpidio (1299–1300), and one whose interests in problems of natural philosophy carried him further from Giles's metaphysical concerns, Michael de Massa (c. 1325).[40]

Aegidianism in either of these senses was never a doctrinal program in competition with Thomism and Scotism. Few Augustinians forgot the early connection of Thomas and Giles, and the differences between these two authorities were never brought into confrontation within this early period, certainly not at Oxford. Moreover, neither Scotism nor Franciscan theology was attacked as a unit. The opponents of the Augustinians (some of whom could also be used favorably) remained individual theologians, such as Henry of Ghent, John Duns Scotus, or Peter Aureoli. Only Aureoli (who was neither a Thomist nor a Scotist)

---

[36] E. Hocedez, "Gilles de Rome et S. Thomas," in *Mélanges Mandonnet* 1: 358–409, noticed a number of significant differences between Thomas and Giles. Since then the list has grown. See P. W. Nash, "Giles of Rome, auditor and critic of St. Thomas," *The Modern Schoolman* 28 (1950/51): 1–20; "Giles of Rome and the Subject of Theology," *MedStud* 18 (1956): 61–92; "Giles of Rome: a pupil but not a disciple of Thomas Aquinas," in *Readings in Ancient and Medieval Philosophy*, ed. J. Collins (Westminster, Maryland, 1960), 251–57.

[37] Zumkeller, "Augustinerschule," 200–201.

[38] Zumkeller, "Augustinerschule," 207.

[39] Zumkeller, "Augustinerschule," 201–2, 205–6, 208–9, 212–14.

[40] Zumkeller, "Augustinerschule," 196–99, 209–10; D. Trapp, "Augustinian Theology," 181–82.

stands out as a consistent target, but that development did not take place until after 1320.[41]

GREYFRIARS AND SCOTISM

In contrast to the eclipse of Thomism and the declining importance of Dominican theologians at Oxford and Paris, the first half of the fourteenth century was dominated by the Franciscans. They represented, alongside the secular theologians at Oxford and the Augustinian Hermits at Paris, the single most active and talented group of scholastic writers. Franciscan thought was so important after 1277 that the early Thomist school might well be viewed as a reaction to Franciscan thought and to potential defectors within their own ranks. The Franciscans, by contrast, were not particularly concerned with the Thomists. Academic debates among Franciscans centered more on personalities within their own order and on such secular theologians as Henry of Ghent.

Within Franciscan theology John Duns Scotus was the most influential figure in shaping fourteenth-century thought.[42] No other writer of the order was as frequently cited or discussed, and even those Franciscans who were most critical of his approach and solutions, such as William of Ockham, held Scotus in great esteem and followed his lead in many areas, especially in theology. Throughout the early fourteenth century the autograph copies of several of Scotus's works, with his own extensive marginalia, stood in the library of the Franciscan convent at Oxford, thence to influence a generation or more of English and foreign (especially Italian) Franciscans who studied at Oxford. Scotus never became simply an intellectual alternative to Aureoli or Ockham in fourteenth-century Franciscan thought. Scotus was its foundation. However critical of Scotus later Franciscans were on particular points, they invariably remained in his debt and under his influence.

In assessing Scotus's influence one must distinguish between his metaphysics and his theology. Only his closest followers, for whom the term

---

[41] Roth, *EAF* 1: 598–99.

[42] For the details of Scotus's life, see: F. Pelster, "Zur Scotus-Forschung," *Theologische Revue* 28 (1929): 145–52; C. Balic, *Les commentaires de Jean Duns Scot sur les quatre livres de sentences* (Louvain, 1927); Emden, *BRUO* 1: 607–10; and Allan Wolter's introduction to Scotus's *Philosophical Writings* (New York, 1962).

"Scotist" is most appropriate, adopted the two principal tenets of his metaphysics: the univocity of being and the formal distinction. On the other hand, the shape Scotus gave to the dialectic of the powers of God, his view of omnipotence, his theory of divine acceptation (*acceptatio divina*) and covenantal theology (*pactum*), his view of justification and the sacraments struck subsequent Franciscans (and even many seculars, Dominicans, and others) as so convincing that what is often called Nominalist theology in the late Middle Ages is only a variation on Scotus.[43] But Scotus's metaphysics and the areas of his theology influenced by his metaphysical assumptions and terminology were not as widely accepted and proved to be major points of contention within the scholastic development of the fourteenth century.[44] Moreover, his doctrine of predestination before foreseen merits or demerits (*praedestinatio ante praevisa merita*) was in sharp contrast not only to Thomas but to the entire tradition of Franciscan theology.[45]

Like Thomas, Scotus quickly attracted a following. His strongest support was at Paris, where Scotus had lectured from 1302 until 1307, except for a brief exile. Within a decade of his departure from Paris there was already an impressive list of Franciscan disciples lecturing there: Antonius Andreas, James of Aesculo, William of Alnwick, John of Bassolis, and Hugh of Novo Castro.[46] Moreover, a long line of Scotists can be traced throughout the subsequent two decades at Paris. By contrast, Scotus did not have the same success at Oxford, despite the fact that his lectures there from 1300 to 1302 resulted in his Opus Oxoniense. Sco-

[43] H. Schwamm, *Das göttliche Vorherwissen bei Duns Scotus und seinen ersten Anhängern* (Innsbruck, 1934); W. Pannenberg, *Die Prädestinationslehre des Duns Skotus* (Göttingen, 1954); W. Dettloff, *Die Lehre von der Acceptatio divina bei Johannes Duns Scotus* (Werl i.W., 1954); Dettloff, *Die Entwicklung der Akzeptations- und Verdienstlehre von Duns Scotus bis Luther* (Münster i.W., 1963); H. A. Oberman, *The Harvest of Medieval Theology* (Cambridge, Mass., 1963); Hamm, *Promissio, Pactum*; Courtenay, *Covenant and Causality*; A. Wolter, "Native Freedom of the Will as a Key to the Ethics of Scotus," in *Deus et Homo ad mentem I. Duns Scoti*, Acta Tertii Congr. Scotistici Internat. (Rome, 1972), 359–70. The works of Schwamm and Dettloff are particularly useful in tracing the development of a Scotist school.

[44] Much of Ockham's critique of Scotus lies in this area.

[45] P. Vignaux, *Justification et prédestination au XIVᵉ siècle* (Paris, 1934); Pannenberg, *Prädestinationslehre*; Oberman, *Harvest of Medieval Theology*, 185–217.

[46] C. Bérubé, "La première école scotiste," in *PRUP*, 9–24; see also Schwamm, *Das göttliche Vorherwissen*; Dettloff, *Entwicklung der Akzeptations*.

tus's immediate Franciscan contemporaries at Oxford, such as William
of Nottingham, Richard Conington, and Robert Cowton, opposed Scotus on several major points, in part because they remained under the
influence of Henry of Ghent.[47] Dominicans, such as Thomas Sutton,
were also critical of Scotus's thought.[48] Remarkably, the only known audience at Oxford favorably disposed toward his views was among the
secular theologians. Peter Bradlay, around 1303, defended the univocity of being.[49] Henry of Harclay, who lectured on the *Sentences* at Oxford between 1300 and 1308, closely followed Scotus's teaching on a
number of philosophical and theological points.[50] This moderate support withered by 1310. Harclay became critical of Scotus and, as regent
master and chancellor of the university, moved to positions that anticipated the direction in which Ockham was to go, except for Harclay's atomism.[51] For almost a decade (1308–16) one cannot find Scotistic theses

[47] Dettloff, *Entwicklung der Akzeptations*, 10–22; H. Theissing, *Glaube und Theologie bei Robert Cowton OFM* (Münster i.W., 1969).

[48] Roensh, *ETS*, 44–51, 237–46.

[49] Emden, *BRUO* 1: 242; E. Synan, *The Works of Richard of Campsall*, vol. 1 (Toronto,
1968), 18–20.

[50] C. Balic, "Henricus de Harclay et Ioannes Duns Scotus," in *Mélanges offerts à Etienne
Gilson* (Toronto, 1959), 93–121; A. Maurer, "Henry of Harclay's Question on the Univocity of Being," *MedStud* 16 (1954): 1–18; Maurer, "Henry of Harclay's Questions on Immortality," *MedStud* 19 (1957): 79–107; Maurer, "Henry of Harclay's Questions on the Divine Ideas," *MedStud* 23 (1961): 163–93; Maurer, "Henry of Harclay: disciple or critic of
Duns Scotus?" in *Die Metaphysik im Mittelalter*, Miscellanea Mediaevalia 2 (Berlin, 1963):
563–71; Maurer, "St. Thomas and Henry of Harclay on Created Nature," in *III Congresso
internazionale di filosofia medioevale* (Milan, 1966), 542–49; Maurer, "Henry of Harclay's Disputed Question on the Plurality of Forms," in *Essays in Honor of Anton Charles Pegis* (Toronto, 1974), 125–59; on the development of Harclay's thought and a more detailed survey of the literature, see G. Gál, "Henricus de Harclay: Quaestio de significato conceptus
universalis," *FcS* 31 (1971): 178–234.

[51] Fr. Pelster, "Heinrich von Harclay, Kanzler von Oxford, und seine Quästionen," in
Miscellanea Fr. Ehrle, vol. 1 (Rome, 1924), 307–56; J. Kraus, "Die Universalien lehre des
Oxforder Kanzlers Heinrich von Harclay in ihrer Mittelstellung zwischen skotistischem
Realismus und ockhamistischem Nominalismus," *Divus Thomas* (Fribourg) 10 (1932): 36–
58, 475–508; 11 (1933): 76–96, 288–314; Gál, "Henricus de Harclay"; M. Henninger,
"Henry of Harclay's Questions on Divine Prescience and Predestination," *FcS* 40 (1980):
167–223; Henninger, "Henry of Harclay on the Formal Distinction in the Trinity," *FcS* 41
(1981): 250–335; R. C. Dales, "Henry of Harclay on the Infinite," *Journal of the History of
Ideas* 45 (1984): 295–301. On Harclay's atomism see J. Murdoch and E. Synan, "Two Ques-

being presented and defended at Oxford. When they reappeared, it was among the Franciscans, such as William of Alnwick, who returned to Oxford as regent master in 1316, and John of Reading, who lectured on the *Sentences* at Oxford at about that time.

William of Alnwick came from the same region as Scotus, and he probably attended the custodial school at Newcastle on Tyne.[52] Between 1303 and 1308 he studied with Scotus at Paris, where he acted as Scotus's secretary. After reading the *Sentences* himself, probably at Paris, he returned to Oxford, where he was appointed regent master in theology. He may have brought with him the autograph copies of Scotus's works as well as the revised edition of the *Opus Oxoniense*. Sometime after 1317 he returned to the Continent and lectured as master at Paris, Montpellier, Bologna, and Naples before becoming bishop of Giuvenazzo near Bari in 1330.[53]

John of Reading read the *Sentences* during Alnwick's regency, although Reading's Scotism may have been acquired independently.[54] Although Wodeham called Reading Scotus's "most faithful disciple," there is no evidence that Reading studied under Scotus.[55] In any event,

---

tions on the Continuum," *FcS* 26 (1966): 212–25; Murdoch, "Henry of Harclay and the Infinite," in *Studi sul XIV secolo in memoria di Anneliese Maier*, ed. A.Maierù (Rome, 1981), 219–61.

[52] Emden, *BRUO* 1: 27. Alnwick's adherence to Scotus's thought is reflected not only in his theological works, such as his *Sentences* commentary, his disputed questions, and his *Quodlibeta*, but by the fact that he edited Scotus's work and even wrote an abbreviated version on Scotus's commentary.

[53] Alnwick's connection with Italy may be important for the reception of Scotus's thought south of the Alps. The only remaining copy of the Scotus autograph (including the marginalia) is located at Assisi, and the Franciscan libraries of Italy attest to a close contact with the early editing process on the Scotus corpus. C. Piana, "Gli inizi e lo sviluppo dello Scotismo a Bologna e nella regione Romagnolo-Flaminia," *AFH* 40 (1949): 49–80, esp. 52–53; A. Maier, "Wilhelm von Alnwicks Bologneser Quaestionen gegen den Averroismus," in Maier, *Ausgehendes Mittelalter*, vol. 1 (Rome, 1964), 1–40.

[54] E. Emden, *BRUO* 3: 1554; E. Longpré, "Jean de Reading et le Bx. Jean Duns Scot," *La France Franciscaine* 7 (1924): 99–109; G. Gál, "Quaestio Ioannis de Reading De necessitate specierum intelligibilium. Defensio doctrinae Scoti," *FcS* 29 (1969): 66–156; S. F. Brown, "Sources for Ockham's Prologue to the *Sentences*," *FcS* 26 (1966): 36–65; Brown and Gál in introduction to Ockham, *Sent.* 2: 18*–34*; G. J. Etzkorn, "John Reading on the Existence and Unicity of God, Efficient and Final Causality," *FcS* 41 (1981): 110–221.

[55] Wodeham, *Lectura Oxon.* 1, dist. 1, q. 12 H (Vatican Library, MS. Vat. lat. 955, fol. 70ᵛ;

the presence of Alnwick and Reading at Oxford Greyfriars meant that Scotism was well represented during the years Ockham was in residence awaiting his turn as *sententiarius*. And there is no question but that Scotus was the single most important philosopher and theologian on Ockham's horizon.

Scotism never effectively took root at Oxford, and the combined voices of Alnwick and Reading were not sufficient to establish a school of thought. The writings of Nottingham, Conington, and Cowton stood in opposition, and Cowton was an influential figure outside as well as within Franciscan circles. Moreover, by 1323 three other Franciscan non-Scotists, each different but no less challenging, were being studied in England. One was the Parisian theologian, Peter Aureoli, whose writings gradually became known in England after 1318.[56] The second was Walter Chatton, who lectured at a Franciscan *studium particulare* during the years 1321–23, probably at London.[57] Chatton was in sympathy with certain aspects of Aureoli's thought, although he did not cite him directly and went his own way on many issues. The third theologian was Ockham, who posed the most sweeping alternative to the metaphysics of Scotus.

The intellectual climate at Oxford in the decade before 1320 was also not favorable to Scotism. The philosophical realism to which Scotus subscribed was coming into question, particularly in the thought of Richard of Campsall, Henry of Harclay, and eventually Ockham. A strong interest in theological problems that centered on logic, mathematics, and physics (for which Scotus was only partially useful) gradually replaced the more traditional metaphysics. And in contrast to Paris, uniform and competing intellectual traditions lagged far behind the

---

Paris, Univ., MS. 193, fol. 65[ra]): "discipulus et sequax valentissimus frater Johannes de Radingia, magister."

[56] Aureoli has long been considered a major figure, but the forms and extent of his influence are increasing as more work is done on the period 1315–35. Especially helpful among recent items are K. H. Tachau, "The Response to Ockham's and Aureol's Epistemology (1320–1340)," in *ELI*, 185–217; "Peter Aureol on Intentions and the Intuitive Cognition of Non-Existents," *CIMGL*, n. 44 (1983): 122–50.

[57] Chatton will be treated in more detail in chapter 9. His relationship to Aureoli is best illustrated in G. J. Etzkorn, "Walter Chatton and the Controversy on the Absolute Necessity of Grace," *FcS* 37 (1977): 32–65.

practice of individual creativity. Changing interests and Franciscan alternatives to Scotus arrested the growth of Scotism at Oxford almost at
its inception, although Scotus himself remained one of the most influential authorities of that century.[58]

THE DISAPPEARANCE OF SCHOOLS OF THOUGHT

What factors brought an end to the schools of thought, first at Oxford
and then at Paris? What produced the marked individualism, the independence of mind, the freedom from school restraints that are so apparent by the second quarter of the fourteenth century? Alongside the
centripetal forces noted earlier that worked toward doctrinal uniformity imposed from above within the orders, there were a number of centrifugal forces that pulled the schools apart.

One of these elements was built into the medieval academic system
itself, namely the role of the regent master and his relation to the students under his charge. Regency, at least among the mendicant orders,
came to be limited to one or two years, and it is rare to find a mendicant
master remaining at the same university or even in teaching after his
required regency was fulfilled. If the mendicant convents were the natural, perhaps only, university environments for a school of thought
based on the teaching of a mendicant master, the absence of teaching
continuity or long-term master-pupil relationships at those convents

---

[58] In contrast to Oxford, Scotus continued to dominate Franciscan theology at Paris after
1322. His influence can be seen in the work of Petrus Thomae, Francis of Marchia, Landulf
of Caracciolo, and William of Rubione. In Francis Mayronis, Anfredus Gonteri, and Peter
of Aquila (Scotellus) he found close and enthusiastic devotees. At Paris, if not at Oxford,
Scotus became *de facto* the leading doctor of the Franciscan order, and Scotism its leading
approach. But even there it did not survive intact past 1340. Its demise coincided with the
importation of the newer Oxford thought and with the collapse of the Franciscan hegemony over Parisian theology. Only a few Franciscans, none of them true Scotists, established
reputations for themselves after 1340: Richard Brinkley at Oxford, John of Ripa and Peter
of Candia at Paris. The shrinking of the Franciscan profile, which may have played no
small part in the decline of Scotism at Paris, was probably due to the internal problems of
the order, particularly the difficulties of recruiting talented young minds—a problem that
plagued the Franciscans in the wake of the splintering of the order in the 1320s. As with
Thomism, although somewhat later, one finds a revival of Scotism in the fifteenth century
with William of Vaurouillon and Nicholas of Orbellis. By the end of the fifteenth century
it was again one of the leading schools of thought.

made its preservation almost impossible. Nor was it effectively imposed from above. There is no evidence of any attempt by a religious order to appoint regents of some particular philosophical or theological persuasion. *Lehrrichtung* and *Lehrstuhl* were never joined in the fourteenth century. There was no academic parallel to the master-apprentice relationship of the craft guilds or an artistic atelier. Nor were students and bachelors "clients" of regent masters. When in the manuscripts we encounter the phrase *magister meus*, it is almost invariably a courtesy title, even as one might today refer to an academic opponent as "my friend and esteemed colleague."[59]

A second centrifugal element was that innovation and individuality were rewarded by the university system, as was discussed in the opening chapter.[60] Whatever programmatic conformity might at times be desired by the general chapter of an order, a student could not fulfill academic expectations or distinguish himself by simply glossing the work of an earlier master or defending his theses.

These two factors, built into the educational system, suggest a third: schools of thought in the thirteenth and fourteenth centuries were not the normal state of affairs. Thomism and Aegidianism were innovations that emerged in 1277 in opposition to the attacks on Thomas and Giles. They represented policy dictated from above, which did not have a natural, widespread appeal within the respective orders. Moreover, the orders had other alternatives or models. For the Dominicans there were Richard Fishacre and Robert Kilwardby at Oxford; Meister Eckhart and Durand of St. Pourçain at Paris. For the Franciscans, among whom the influence of Henry of Ghent was great, there were the older authorities of Alexander of Hales and Bonaventure, and the recent views of Peter of John Olivi, Peter Aureoli, and William of Ockham.

---

[59] Taking *magister meus* and similar expressions to mean that one scholar was the pupil of another has caused numerous misunderstandings and dating problems for fourteenth-century research. See, for example, the confusion about the academic relationship of Uthred of Boldon, John Wyclif, and John Kenningham caused by this false assumption; W. R. Thomson, *The Latin Writings of John Wyclyf* (Toronto, 1983), 228–29. It does not imply any master-pupil relationship, nor that the person referred to holds a master's degree. This courtesy title of address appears toward the middle of the fourteenth century and was frequently used by a bachelor of theology when referring to his fellow bachelors. Less frequently it could be used in reference to a respected, senior colleague, even one no longer living.

[60] Ch. 1, 27, 29–30, 46–47.

Among the Augustinians there was, eventually, Gregory of Rimini and a reconstituted Augustine.

A fourth element—and probably the most significant of the group—was the change in interests that crystallized in the second quarter of the fourteenth century. On the negative side it was a declining interest in the type of metaphysical questions that so preoccupied Bonaventure, Thomas, Scotus, Henry of Ghent, and others in the second half of the thirteenth century. On the positive side it was a fascination with problems of language, logic, mathematics, time, and motion and their applications in theology—issues that did not lend themselves as easily to a school-of-thought approach. This revolution, which occurred at Oxford in the 1320s and was exported to Paris in the early 1340s, was probably the single most important dimension of fourteenth-century thought, a revolution to which Ockham contributed but did not create.

SEVEN

OCKHAM AND ENGLISH
NOMINALISM

❧

IN OUR current picture of the intellectual development of the fourteenth century it is the thought of the Venerable Inceptor that, more
than any other factor, is credited with the eclipse of competing schools
in the decade from 1330 to 1340 and the subsequent establishment of
nominalism as the leading "school" at Oxford and Paris. Nominalism
has traditionally been seen as the most vigorous force in the universities
in the late Middle Ages, embracing many of the leading philosophers
and theologians. And when the Parisian nominalists of 1474 defended
their approach and history, they traced their ancestry back to Ockham
and his confrontation with the papacy that began in the 1320s.[1]

Apart from the question of whether there was among certain late medieval thinkers a common body of thought that can be appropriately
described as or labeled "nominalist," there is the more immediate question of the degree to which Ockham's thought dominated intellectual
life in England in the generation or more between Ockham and Wyclif.
Was there in England an Ockhamist and/or a nominalist school in the
fourteenth century and, if so, who should be associated with it and for
what reasons?

Before answering those questions we need to look first at Ockham
himself. Some attention must be given to those characteristic features of
his thought, those axiomatic principles and approaches that help us understand the close integration of his philosophy and theology. Our primary concern, however, will be with those elements that were discussed
by contemporaries and that influenced subsequent English thought,
either by their acceptance or rejection.

---

[1] *University Records and Life in the Middle Ages*, ed. by L. Thorndike (New York, 1944),
356–57; Latin text in Du Plessis d'Argentré, *Collectio judiciorum de novis erroribus* (Paris,
1755), 1: ii, 286–88.

* * *

Ockham was born sometime around 1285 in the village of Ockham, less than a day's ride southwest of London.[2] His early education would have been received in the neighborhood of his village, perhaps through a priest or at some nearby religious house. He entered the Franciscan order before the age of fourteen,[3] and was probably sent to the custodial school in London for his philosophical training. There in 1306 at Southwark (a section of greater London belonging to the diocese of Winchester, from which he came) he was ordained subdeacon by Robert Winchelsey, archbishop of Canterbury.[4] He was subsequently sent on to Oxford to study theology, and around 1317–19 as Franciscan bachelor of theology he lectured on the *Sentences* of Peter Lombard.

After completing his residency at Oxford, he lectured for a time on philosophy, probably at the Franciscan convent in London, where he would have been in the company of Walter Chatton and Adam Wodeham.[5] This was the most active period in Ockham's academic life. During this time he revised his commentary on the first book of the *Sentences* (which became known as his *Ordinatio*), lectured on Aristotle's logic and physics, wrote most (perhaps all) of his textbook in logic (*Summa logicae*), and most of his quodlibetal questions (*Quodlibeta septem*). Attacks on his teaching probably led to a summons to Avignon to answer charges of heretical teaching.[6] Ockham's departure from England, which came

---

[2] Earlier literature on Ockham is surveyed in V. Heynck, "Ockham-Literatur 1919–1949," *FzS* 32 (1950): 164–83; J. P. Reilly, "Ockham Bibliography: 1950–1967," *FcS* 28 (1968): 197–214. For references to the documentation from which Ockham's biography is reconstructed, see: Emden, *BRUO*, 2: 1384–87; L. Baudry, *Guillaume d'Occam. Sa vie, ses œuvres, ses idées sociales et politiques*, vol. 1 (Paris, 1950); J. Miethke, *Ockhams Weg zur Sozialphilosophie* (Berlin, 1969); Ph. Boehner, *Collected Articles on Ockham* (St. Bonaventure, N.Y., 1958); C. K. Brampton, "Guillaume d'Ockham fut-il maître en Theologie?" *Etudes Franciscaines* 13 (1963): 53–59; Brampton, "The Probable Order of Ockham's non-polemical Works," *Traditio* 19 (1963): 469–83; Brampton, "Traditions relating to the Death of William of Ockham," *AFH* 53 (1960): 442–49; the introductions to the volumes of the critical edition of Ockham, *Opera Philosophica et Theologica* (St. Bonaventure, N.Y., 1967 ff.).

[3] Ockham was one of several Franciscans mentioned by William Woodford, *Defensorium*, c. 62, who entered the order as *pueri* (i.e., before the age of fourteen).

[4] *Registrum Roberti Winchelsey Cant. Archiepiscopi*, ed. R. Graham, Cant. & York Soc. 52 (Oxford, 1956), 981.

[5] G. Gál and J. Wey, respective introductions to Ockham, *SL* and *Quodl.*

[6] George D. Knysh, in a paper given at the Ockham conference, St. Bonaventure, N.Y.,

only a few months before he was possibly to have become regent master at Oxford, brought to an end his academic career.

In July of 1324 Ockham crossed the Channel and traveled south to Avignon. There, in the Franciscan convent, he remained for four years while his case was investigated and his orthodoxy judged. It was in Avignon that he came to know Michael of Cesena, the Minister General of the Franciscans, and was eventually made aware of John XXII's stand on the issue of apostolic poverty. Possibly because of his growing conviction that the pope had fallen into heresy and was therefore not in a position to judge any theologian's orthodoxy, Ockham accompanied Michael of Cesena and Bonagratia of Bergamo on their flight from Avignon on the night of May 26, 1328, taking a boat from Aigues Mortes to Genoa, and thence on into Tuscany, where he received the protection of Louis of Bavaria. Upon Louis's return to Munich, Ockham traveled with him and remained at the Franciscan convent in Munich, writing a prodigious and influential series of treatises and books against John XXII and his successors for the last twenty years of his life.[7] He

Oct. 10–12, 1985, under the title "Biographical Rectifications Concerning Ockham's Avignon Period," has argued that Ockham was not summoned before the Roman curia in 1324 while in England but in May 1327, while he was in Avignon on other business. The papal document to which he has called attention makes it clear that in the view of John XXII an important stage of the formal inquisition began in the spring of 1327. But this need not call into question the earlier stages of judicial investigation nor the assumption that Ockham went to Avignon to take part in those proceedings. It is highly unlikely that he would have been sent to the Avignon convent to teach before completing his doctorate and regency at Oxford.

[7] Although Ockham's political writings were composed in Germany, after he left England, and had a less direct effect on intellectual and political developments in his homeland, they do represent a fundamentally important part of his contribution. In particular see B. Tierney, "Ockham, the conciliar theory and the canonists," *Journal of the History of Ideas* 15 (1954): 40–70; Tierney, *Foundations of the conciliar theory* (Cambridge, 1955); Miethke, *Ockhams Weg zur Sozialphilosophie*; A. S. McGrade, *The Political Thought of William of Ockham* (Cambridge, 1974); J. J. Ryan, *The Nature, Structure and Function of the Church in William of Ockham* (Missoula, 1979); Miethke, "Zur Bedeutung der Ekklesiologie für die politische Theorie im späteren Mittelalter," in *Soziale Ordnungen im Selbstverständnis des Mittelalters*, Miscellanea Mediaevalia 12/2 (Berlin, 1980), 369–88; Miethke, "Marsilius und Ockham. Publikum und Leser ihrer politischen Schriften im späteren Mittelalter," *Medioevo* 6 (1980): 543–67; Miethke, "Wilhelm von Ockham," in *Gestalten der Kirchengeschichte*, ed. M. Greschat, vol. 4 (Stuttgart, 1983), 155–75.

died on April 10, 1347, unchanged in his opposition to the papacy and two years before the Plague reached southern Germany.[8]

Ockham contributed extensively to philosophy, theology, and political thought, and his writings are almost as numerous as those of Thomas Aquinas or Duns Scotus.[9] As with Scotus, many of Ockham's works were composed within a relatively short period of time. His academic writings, as we have seen, were written between 1317 and 1324 or 1326. These include his *Ordinatio* on book 1 on the *Sentences* and his *Reportatio* on books 2–4, his *Summa logicae* and *Quodlibeta septem*, his commentaries on Aristotle's logic and *Physics*, and his treatises on the eucharist (*De corpore Christi* and *De sacramento altaris*) and on God's knowledge of future contingents (*De praedestinatione et de praescientia Dei et de futuris contingentibus*). Of his many political or polemical writings, which occupied his life after 1328, the most important are his *Opus nonaginta dierum, Contra Ioannem, Contra Benedictum, Dialogus, Quaestiones de potestate papae*, and the *Breviloquium*. But it was not the extensiveness and range of his writings that made him a leading figure of late medieval thought in England and on the Continent. Rather, it was their quality and the controversial nature of some of his formulations and conclusions.

The most important factor to keep in mind in understanding the thought of Ockham is that he was a Franciscan theologian. All his writings, from his *Summa logicae* and his commentary on Aristotle's *Physics*, through his *Sentences* commentary and treatises on the eucharist, to his political treatises, were produced during or after his theological studies had brought him to the edge of the *magisterium*. Even the most philosophical of his writings were for those who would eventually be studying theology. This does not mean that Ockham's philosophy and scientific thought were theologized, or that his arguments in those areas

---

[8] The controversy over the year of Ockham's death has now been resolved by G. Gál, "William of Ockham died 'impenitent' in April 1347," *FcS* 42 (1982): 90–95.

[9] All the non-polemical writings of Ockham (*Opera philosophica et theologica*) are now available in critical edition through the Franciscan Institute, St. Bonaventure, N.Y., 1967–85. The critical edition of his political writings (*Opera politica*, ed. H. S. Offler) is only half complete, and the important *Dialogus*, early editions of which are notoriously defective, still awaits a modern edition.

were any less rigorous; only that he often had the aim of theological applicability in mind and wrote for an audience similarly disposed.

Moreover, the principal form of theology within which he lived and thought was Franciscan. Although he would perforce have studied the important theologians of the late thirteenth century, particularly Thomas Aquinas, Giles of Rome, Henry of Ghent, and Godfrey of Fontaines, would have been thoroughly conversant with the Bible and with large portions of Patristic theology, and would have read much of Anselm, Bernard, and Hugh of St. Victor, he would have been primarily educated in the tradition of Franciscan theology: the *Summa Halensis*, Bonaventure, and, above all, John Duns Scotus. To deal with fourteenth-century thought as a contrast between Aquinas and Ockham is to put the emphasis in the wrong place. The principal influence on Ockham was Scotus, who was as well the theologian with whom Ockham most frequently disagreed.

Much of Ockham's concern with Henry of Ghent, Godfrey of Fontaines, or Giles of Rome was filtered through the writings of Scotus, although Ockham does not always disagree with them for the same reasons as did Scotus. More importantly, large sections of Ockham's theology, as we shall see, particularly his understanding of divine omnipotence, grace and justification, sacramental theology, and ethics, were heavily influenced by the thought of Scotus. Even Ockham's epistemology, which was grounded in the immediate intuition of singular objects (*cognitio intuitiva*), must be seen as a development out of Scotus's epistemology.

On the other hand, much of Ockham's thought, both in philosophy and theology, was directed specifically against Scotus and his disciples. For Ockham, Scotus had confused numerous philosophical and theological questions by postulating distinctions that could not be maintained and by his reification of abstract terms and quiddities, transforming connotative terms into ontological realities. Ockham adopted and used the anti-necessaritarian aspects of Scotus's thought (the latter's stress on divine omnipotence, covenantal theology, and the dialectic of the *potentia absoluta / potentia ordinata* distinction) to attack other areas of Scotus's thought, to simplify and deontologize, and in many cases to introduce a greater consistency. In so doing Ockham made some original departures in medieval thought, but for the most part he adopted and revised elements taken from others, not only from Scotus but from other Franciscans, such as Peter Olivi, Peter Trabibus, Adam Wodeham (his own pupil), and Walter Chatton, as well as secular theologians such as Henry of Harclay and Walter Burley.[10]

LANGUAGE AND UNIVERSALS: THE ISSUE OF
OCKHAM'S NOMINALISM

One of the features of language that simplifies our thinking and expression is the ability to reduce longer, more complicated linguistic and conceptual structures into a single word or short expression. For Ockham, however, problems arise when those simplified linguistic forms are given ontological status. The term "whiteness," for instance, is a mental concept abstracted from multiple individual propositions, such as "object 'a' is white," "object 'b' is white," "object 'c' is white," etc., and does not refer to any "real thing" apart from white objects. Similarly, a universal proposition, such as "man is a rational animal" is simply a shortened form of all the individual propositions, such as "person 'a' is rational," "person 'b' is rational," etc.[11] Every general proposition composed of universal terms, whether positively or negatively expressed, is equivalent to the totality or conjunction of all the individual propositions or instances that prove the general rule and from which the general proposition is ultimately derived. Reality and logical statements made about it concern individual substances and qualities. Yet singular propositions composed of individual terms can be converted into an equivalent universal proposition composed of general terms.

Thus for Ockham general terms as well as abstract terms, be they nominative or predicate, are linguistic shorthand for equivalent singu-

---

[10] On Ockham's modifications of his opinions in light of other's views, see G. Gál, "Gualteri de Chatton et Guillelmi de Ockham Controversia de Natura Conceptus Universalis," *FcS* 27 (1967): 191–212; S. Brown, "Walter Burleigh's Treatise *De suppositionibus* and its Influence on William of Ockham," *FcS* 32 (1972): 15–64; Courtenay, *Adam Wodeham* (Leiden, 1978).

[11] Ockham, *SL*, pts. 1 and 2. For translation see M. J. Loux, *Ockham's Theory of Terms* (Notre Dame, 1974); A. J. Freddoso and H. Schuurman, *Ockham's Theory of Propositions* (Notre Dame, 1980). An excellent discussion of this particular point, using the example "all crows are black," can be found in A. S. McGrade, "Ockham and the Birth of Individual Rights," in *Authority and Power: Studies on Medieval Law and Government*, ed. B. Tierney and P. Linehan (Cambridge, 1980), 149–65.

lar or concrete terms. Despite the fact that logic is concerned with general terms and general propositions, we should not forget their origins nor be misled into believing that general or abstract terms correspond to objects in external reality.

Ockham's position on the origin and ontological status of universal concepts can best be described as modified nominalism or realistic conceptualism.[12] On the one hand, Ockham believed that individuals of the same species are similar, in contrast to individuals of another species.[13] Although we only encounter particular individuals in external reality and never any entity equivalent to species, category, or archetype, our judgment that a rose bears a greater resemblance to a tulip than to a horse is not a misperception created solely by and in the mind but is grounded in our experience and is true apart from our knowing it.[14] In answer to the epistemological formulation of the problem of universals, i.e., how do we recognize or arrive at the general concept, Ockham's answer is that of any good Aristotelian. We do not begin with a universal in the mind through which we recognize individual examples in external reality; we begin with our experience of individuals and slowly build up our idea of similarity.

It is on the issue of similarity or its ontological status that Ockham separated himself from most of his contemporaries and according to which his position can be called nominalistic. Ockham rejected what until his generation had been a common medieval understanding, namely that similarity among things, no matter how we come to know it, is grounded in a common nature that inheres in all things of the same species or all things that possess some quality. Ockham rejected that idea of common nature. Socrates is a rational animal, as is Plato. But they do

[12] Ph. Boehner, "The Realistic Conceptualism of William Ockham," in Boehner, *Collected Articles*, 156–74.

[13] One of the best discussions of this point is S. Brown, "A Modern Prologue to Ockham's Natural Philosophy," in *Sprache und Erkenntnis im Mittelalter*, ed. A. Zimmermann, Miscellanea Mediaevalia 13.1 (Berlin, 1981), 107–29.

[14] Ockham, *SL*, pt. 1, ch. 18, as transl. by Loux, *Ockham's Theory of Terms*, 88: "*Animal* is predicated of both *man* and *donkey*, but the similarity in substance between two men is greater than that obtaining between a man and a donkey. The same is true in the case of *color*. This term is predicable of both whiteness and blackness, but neither this blackness nor one of its parts agrees as much with this whiteness or one of its parts as one bit of whiteness agrees with another."

not "share" rationality as a common nature or possession that inheres in them and makes them rational. Socrates and Plato are similar in ways that Socrates and a chimera are not; but the former do not share similarity.

In keeping with his view of universal concepts, Ockham redefined simple supposition. Supposition is a theory of reference. It does not concern the meaning of words as words, but rather what words "stand for" when used in a proposition or sentence. The term "man," for instance, stands for different things in different propositional contexts. In "man is a rational animal" the term "man" stands for any and all humans (simple supposition), i.e., a universal concept. In "man is a three-letter word" it stands for the word itself (material supposition). In "that man is John" it stands for a particular person (personal supposition). Since for Ockham the universal concept as used in a proposition could not stand for a real entity that was itself individual and yet inhered in many individuals, a term functioning in simple supposition stood for an intention in the mind. Universal terms as used in propositions about extra-mental reality continued to have reference for Ockham, but that reference was entirely to sets of concrete individuals and did not refer to entities existing apart from things, outside the soul.

It is impossible to know whether this perception of the interrelation of language and external reality led Ockham to a number of related positions in logic and natural philosophy, or whether his reinterpretation of supposition and the Aristotelian categories led him to a nominalistic view of general concepts. At the point at which we meet these issues in his writings, they are fully integrated with other aspects of his thought. Ockham was opposed to any logic that assigned ontological status to parts of speech and particular linguistic expressions, for example, those expressing relationships. In fact, he was of the opinion that many theological and philosophical problems were created or made difficult by the presence of just such false notions. The only concrete realities or entities for Ockham were *res permanentes*: substances and qualities, and the other categories of quantity and motion, relation, place, time, etc., are simply descriptions or ways of speaking about substances and qualities. There is a remarkably high degree of consistency in Ockham's philosophy, particularly between his logic and his natural philosophy, whether one considers it valid or not. He at least was convinced it represented a truer picture of what Aristotle said or meant to say.[15] And if, from the standpoint or perspective of the history of philosophy, *sub specie aeternitatis*, we choose to describe his position as nominalist, that would seem a valid description.

OCKHAM'S NATURAL PHILOSOPHY

Ockham's understanding of motion, time, place, causality, and relation are, as has been said, of a piece with his logic and his nominalism.[16] This area of Ockham's thought, however, produced such important discussions in subsequent generations that it deserves a more extended treatment.

External reality for Ockham was composed of individually existing substances and their qualities. The other Aristotelian categories were not independent, objective "things" (*res permenentes*) existing separately

[15] Cf. Ockham's remarks in *SL*, pt. 1, ch. 7, and his second preface to his commentary on Aristotle's *Physics*, as discussed by Brampton, "Personalities at the process against Ockham at Avignon, 1324–26," *FcS* 26 (1966): 4–25, esp. 12–13; G. E. Mohan, "The Prologue to Ockham's Exposition of the Physics of Aristotle," *FcS* 5 (1945): 235–46; V. Richter, "Zum Incipit des Physikkommentars von Ockham," *PhilJahr* 81 (1974): 197–201. It is misleading to imagine that a thoroughly realistic interpretation of the categories had long been accepted by Ockham's day. It would appear rather that Aristotle's highly grammatical approach, already modified in an ontological direction under the influence of Averroes and others, underwent further and heated discussion in the last two decades of the thirteenth century, in which a more realistic interpretation, as found in Giles of Rome, vied with the reduced ontology of Peter Olivi; cf. E. A. Moody, "Ockham and Aegidius of Rome," *FcS* 9 (1949): 417–42; D. Burr, "Petrus Ioannis Olivi and the Philosophers," *FcS* 31 (1971): 41–71; Burr, "Quantity and Eucharistic Presence: The Debate from Olivi through Ockham," *Collectanea Franciscana* 44 (1974): 5–44; Burr, "The Persecution of Peter Olivi," *Transactions of the American Philosophical Society*, N.S. 66.5 (1976).

[16] H. Shapiro, *Motion, Time and Place according to William Ockham* (St. Bonaventure, N.Y., 1957); J. A. Weisheipl, "Developments in the Arts Curriculum at Oxford in the Early Fourteenth Century," *MedStud* 28 (1966): 151–75; Weisheipl, "Ockham and some Mertonians," *MedStud* 30 (1968): 163–213; Weisheipl, "Ockham and the Mertonians," in *HUO* 1, 607–58; Weisheipl, "The Interpretation of Aristotle's Physics and the Science of Motion," in *CHLMP*, 521–39; J. E. Murdoch, "William of Ockham and the Logic of Infinity and Continuity," in *Infinity and Continuity in Ancient and Medieval Thought*, ed. N. Kretzmann (Ithaca, 1982), 165–206; E. Stump, "Theology and Physics in *De sacramento altaris*: Ockham's Theory of Indivisibles," in *Infinity and Continuity*, 207–30; S. Brown, "Modern Prologue," 107–29; A. Goddu, *The Physics of William of Ockham* (Leiden, 1984).

from and external to the mind or soul (*res extra animam*), but described aspects or modifications on substances and qualities. For example, motion was not a *res extra* separate or distinct from things in motion but a way of describing that something present at point "a" is subsequently at point "b," point "c," and so forth. Motion is a description of successive states.[17] That did not mean for Ockham that motion was broken down into atoms of time, for *continua* were infinitely divisible.[18] Similarly, time was not an entity separate from things in time. Without existing things, time, in our sense, would also not exist. Relations, such as paternity, filiation, and even causal relationships were not entities separate from the things related or causes of their being related.

Ockham granted the reality of secondary causality in the natural order with two limiting observations. One was that the nexus of cause and effect was a valid inference from experience but not something directly experienced itself or fully demonstrable. What we know from experience is that where (or when) "a" is present, under certain conditions, "b" will occur. This phenomenon is not a result of God's direct action, nor does it occur outside of or apart from God's will and general supporting and conserving causality. It is a result of a system, the laws of nature, that God has ordained for the physical universe. The second limiting observation is that this causal relationship is not a necessary one in the sense that things cannot ever happen or could not ever have happened otherwise, or that God is bound or limited absolutely by his ordination. God can and, for Ockham, has occasionally and miraculously suspended the normal causal relationships that pertain in nature, both for some specific good and to remind us that nature and its laws stand under, not over, the Creator. Thus for Ockham, as earlier for al-Ghazali, proofs for causality, or ones based on causality that derive their force from assuming the relationship to be necessary and eternal, are invalid.

[17] A. Maier, *Zwei Grundproblemen der scholastischen Naturphilosophie*, 3rd ed. (Rome, 1968); *On the Threshold of Exact Science: Selected Writings of Anneliese Maier on Late Medieval Natural Philosophy*, ed. and transl. S. D. Sargent (Philadelphia, 1982), 21–39; J. E. Murdoch and E. D. Sylla, "The Science of Motion," in *Science in the Middle Ages*, ed. D. C. Lindberg (Chicago, 1978), 206–64.

[18] Murdoch and Synan, "Two Questions on the Continuum: Walter Chatton (?), O.F.M. and Adam Wodeham, O.F.M.," *FcS* 26 (1966): 212–88; Murdoch, "William of Ockham and the Logic of Infinity and Continuity."

Causality operates, however dependably and predictably, within a contingent universe. Consequently our inferences about causal relationships or from causal relationships are contingently valid, not absolutely necessary.[19]

The aspect of Ockham's natural philosophy that caused the most immediate negative reaction was his teaching on quantity. This occurred in the context of Eucharistic theology where, in order to explain transubstantiation in a way that did not violate accepted premises of Aristotelian philosophy, some substance-like entity, separate from real substance, seemed required both philosophically and theologically. For Aristotle, substance and accidents always exist together, never apart. The accidental qualities of some substance, such as its color, shape, taste, smell, etc., inhered in that substance, and in external reality one never encountered a substance without its proper accidents, or accidents that did not inhere in some substance. Yet in the doctrine of transubstantiation the substance of bread was transformed into the body of Christ, so that after consecration the substance of the body of Christ was present without its proper accidents, and the accidents of bread and wine were present yet not inhering in the body of Christ (lest it be subject to change and corruption). In what, then, did the accidents inhere? For Thomas Aquinas and for many others, they inhered in the quantity (*quantum*) of the bread, which was a separate, existing structural accident, distinct from either the substance of bread or the substance of the body of Christ.[20]

For Ockham quantity was nothing other than saying that a substance was extended in space, part separate from part.[21] It was not a *res extra*, and consequently the accidents of bread and wine could not inhere in it. Although it violated the normal structure and operation of the laws

---

[19] E. Hochstetter, *Studien zur Metaphysik und Erkenntnislehre Wilhelms von Ockham* (Berlin, 1927), 144–73; Courtenay, "The Critique on Natural Causality in the Mutakallimun and Nominalism," in Courtenay, *Covenant and Causality*, ch. 5.

[20] Aquinas, *Summa theologiae*, pt. 3, q. 77, a. 2; *Summa contra Gentiles*, 50.4, ch. 65.

[21] G. N. Buescher, *The Eucharistic Teaching of William Ockham* (Washington, 1950); E. Iserloh, *Gnade und Eucharistie in der philosophischen Theologie des Wilhelm von Ockham* (Wiesbaden, 1956); Courtenay, *The Eucharistic Thought of Gabriel Biel*, Ph.D. diss., Harvard University, 1967; Courtenay, "Cranmer as a Nominalist: *Sed contra*" in Courtenay, *Covenant and Causality*, ch. 10.

of nature and went against the authority of Aristotle, it was Ockham's belief that after consecration the accidents of bread and wine inhered in nothing, but were upheld by the miraculous power of God. Ockham's solution not only reinterpreted the category of quantity and affirmed an exception to Aristotelian physics as then understood; it undercut a favored solution to a difficult theological problem, one that was receiving increased attention in the high and late Middle Ages through Eucharistic devotion, confraternal piety, and growing lay interest in the Mass.

Certain portions of Ockham's reinterpretation of the Aristotelian categories had already been anticipated by earlier writers, particularly Peter Olivi and Henry of Harclay, but it is Ockham's name that became linked with this approach, and it was among the principal issues that identified the *Ockhamistae* at Paris in the next generation.[22] The preface to Ockham's commentary on Aristotle's *Physics* alerts the reader to the fact that Ockham knew his interpretation was controversial and that he was bending Aristotle's meaning beyond the bounds of accepted interpretation, particularly against the interpretation of Averroes.[23] But the reinterpretation of Aristotle's categories was fundamental to Ockham's thought and one that affected his logic almost as much as his physics. Time, motion, place, and relation were not entities in themselves but features of existing substances and qualities. Just as universal propositions are equivalent to multiple singular propositions, so these other categories can be broken down into or expanded into statements about substances and qualities under certain conditions. While it is true, therefore, that there is no necessary connection between Ockham's nominalistic position on universals and his reduction of the ontological status of most of the Aristotelian categories (one can be a realist with a reduced number of categories, or a nominalist with the full Aristotelian set as traditionally understood), these issues were closely linked in Ockham's thought and vision.[24]

[22] Courtenay and Tachau, "Ockham and the Ockhamists in the English-German Nation at Paris," *History of Universities* 2 (1982): 53–96. For the literature on Olivi's treatment of the categories, which gave real status only to substance, quality, and action, see above, n. 9; on Harclay see G. Gál, "Henricus de Harclay: Quaestio de significato conceptus universalis," *FcS* 31 (1971): 178–234.

[23] See above, n. 15.

[24] Although these elements do go together in Ockham, they need not in principle, as was

Ockham's attack on the reification of universal concepts, abstract nouns, or categories other than substance and quality has led scholars to see Ockham as a thoroughgoing anti-Platonist, attempting to rid philosophy and theology of the last vestiges of Neoplatonism. To a large extent this is true, since the techniques of de-ontologization operate throughout Ockham's thought. But Ockham's motive for de-ontologizing philosophy and theology probably had more to do with his understanding of the relation of language and reality and the relation of God and the world than with the opposing force of strong contemporary Avicennians, Averroists, or Neoplatonists.[25]

Some major aspects of Ockham's thought can, therefore, be characterized as nominalist, but it is at least debatable whether those aspects are central or extensive enough to allow us to describe *all* of Ockham's thought under that label. Certainly the term "nominalist" would have been foreign to him and would have had meaning only as a pejorative description of the thought of Peter Abelard and his disciples in the twelfth century.[26] Nor did any of Ockham's contemporaries or subsequent thinkers for almost a century ever characterize Ockham's thought under that label. His own perception of his scholarly (or scholastic) activity would have come closer to seeing it as an attempt to purify Aristotle and philosophy from Platonic and Neoplatonic accretions (in logic, ontology, epistemology, and natural philosophy) and to purify theology from a similar body of unwarranted ontological assumptions, particularly those associated with inherent forms and necessary categories—systems which, whether natural or supernatural, required God to act, think, or will in necessary ways. To the degree that nominalism operated in Ockham's thought, it was a means of achieving those aims, not the result of his "system."

---

pointed out by Paul Spade, *Peter of Ailly: Concepts and Insolubles: An Annotated Translation* (Dordrecht, 1980), 96, n. 26.

[25] There is no question that Ockham attacked Averroes on a number of issues and may have felt concern over the lingering atmosphere of Greco-Arabian necessitarianism. But recent scholarship has been unable to find evidence for any significant Averroist school at Oxford or Paris in the early fourteenth century.

[26] On the use of the term "nominalist" in the thirteenth and fourteenth centuries, see F. Pelster, "Nominales und reales in 13. Jahrhundert," *Sophia* (1946): 154–61; P. Vignaux, "Nominalisme," in *Dictionnaire de théologie catholique*, vol. 11.1 (Paris, 1930), 717–84; Courtenay, "Nominalism and Late Medieval Religion," in Courtenay, *Covenant and Causality* (London, 1984), ch. 12.

EPISTEMOLOGY AND EMPIRICISM

Discussions of the revolutionary impact of Ockham's thought sometimes center on his "scientific" empiricism.[27] Several things are usually
implied by that phrase. First, Ockham's grounding human knowledge
in intuitive cognition: the existential, sensible, direct confrontation between the knowing mind and the existing object. Second, the primacy
of inductive reasoning on the basis of experience and observation.
Third, Ockham's insistence that a demonstration in the strict sense of
demonstratio was a proof whose conclusion is certain because its premises
are self-evident or derived from propositions that are self-evident. By
so restricting the definition of a demonstrable proof, theology in this
life (for *viatores*) could not be strictly demonstrable or "scientific," since
the articles of faith were not self-evident. But by reducing the claims for
a rational, natural theology and by reducing (but *not* eliminating) the
number of theological truths that could be established both by revelation and unaided reason, the rigor of logic and rational demonstration
could be restored, since they no longer had to be bent to the service of
natural theology.

In this as in so many areas Ockham was not inventing terminology or
new insights as much as he was sorting out views within contemporary
discussion, following the lead of Scotus. The movement away from
viewing theology as a science was well under way by the time Ockham

[27] E. Hochstetter, *Studien zur Metaphysik und Erkenntnislehre Wilhelms von Ockham* (Berlin,
1927); D. Webering, *Theory of Demonstration according to William Ockham* (St. Bonaventure,
N.Y., 1953); Ph. Boehner, *Collected Articles on Ockham*, ed. E. M. Buytaert (St. Bonaventure,
N.Y., 1958); H. Shapiro, *Motion, Time and Place according to William Ockham* (St. Bonaventure, N.Y., 1957); E. A. Moody, *Studies in Medieval Philosophy, Science, and Logic* (Berkeley
and Los Angeles, 1975); and Edward Grant, *Physical Science in the Middle Ages* (New York,
1971). Serious doubts about the "scientific" value of Ockham's teachings have been raised
on various issues by Anneliese Maier in the volumes of her *Studien zur Naturphilosophie der
Spätscholastik*; J. Weisheipl in *HUO* 1: 607–58; T. K. Scott, "Ockham on Evidence, Necessity
and Intuition," *Journal of the History of Philosophy* 7 (1969): 27–49; Scott, "Nicholas of Autrecourt, Buridan and Ockhamism," *Journal of the History of Philosophy*, 9 (1971): 15–41;
John Murdoch's comments on Heiko Oberman's paper in *The Cultural Context of Medieval
Learning*, ed. J. Murdoch and E. Sylla (Dordrecht, 1975), 429–35; and K. H. Tachau, "The
Problem of *Species in medio* at Oxford in the Generation after Ockham," *MedStud* 44 (1982):
394–443; Tachau, "The Response to Ockham's and Aureol's Epistemology (1320–40)," in
ELI, 186–217.

was in school.[28] In fact, the reaction against the universal applicability of the Aristotelian model of learning was already in evidence in the last quarter of the thirteenth century, expressed first in the Parisian Articles of 1270 and 1277, which condemned certain Aristotelian presuppositions, and further questioned by such disparate theologians as Giles of Rome and Duns Scotus. Ockham's denial that theology was a science in any strict sense placed him with the majority opinion of his day.

Ockham was also not the inventor of intuitive cognition, a term already in use in the late thirteenth century and given particular meaning in Scotus.[29] In Ockham's formulation intuitive cognition is the existential knowledge by which we judge an object to exist when it is present to our senses and not to be present or exist verifiably when it is not present to our senses.[30] Intuitive cognition served several purposes for Ockham. In contrast to the Aristotelian epistemology, according to which the agent intellect abstracts from the sensible species emanating from an object a composite of intelligible species that in turn is implanted upon the passive intellect, intuitive cognition stressed immediate, existential knowledge by which the mind comes into direct contact with the known object. More importantly, the hypothesis of intuitive cognition was also aimed at eradicating the distance, presented in thirteenth-century versions of Aristotelian epistemology, that separates the knower from the object and makes one dependent on mediating species.

The only aspects of Ockham's teaching on intuitive cognition that were new were his complete rejection of the epistemology of abstraction (in the older sense), instead of retaining both (as did Scotus); his complete rejection of species (anticipated by but not fully evident in Durand of St. Pourçain); his belief that intuitive cognition gave immediate

[28] On the movements to affirm and reject the "scientific" nature of theology see M.-D. Chenu, *Théologie comme science aux XIII* siècle* (Paris, 1957); P. De Vooght, *Les sources de la doctrine chrétienne* (Bruges, 1954); P. Nash, "Giles of Rome and the Subject of Theology," *MedStud* 18 (1956): 61–92.

[29] The early study by S. Day, *Intuitive Cognition. A Key to the Significance of the Later Scholastics* (St. Bonaventure, N.Y., 1947) has been supplemented and revised in the work of K. H. Tachau, *Vision and Certitude in the Age of Ockham*, Ph.D. diss., University of Wisconsin, Madison, 1981.

[30] Ockham, *Sent.* 1, prol. q. 1 (1: 70): "per notitiam intuitivam rei potest evidenter cognosci res non esse quando non est vel si non sit." Ockham, *Sent.* 2, qq. 12–13 (5. 256): "Intuitiva est illa mediante qua cognoscitur res esse quando est, et non esse quando non est." See discussion in Tachau, "Problem of *Species in medio*" and "Response to Ockham."

knowledge of non-presence (or in Ockham's wording "nonexistence": what was not existentially present to the knower) as well as what was present; and his belief that there could be intuitive cognition of a non-existent.[31] This last position grew out of Ockham's firm theological belief (shared by other theologians, including Thomas) that God, as the principal sustaining cause of all that happens, could cause directly what he normally causes through a secondary agent, i.e., could cause the effect without the mediation of the proper, secondary cause. Ockham attempted to protect the certainty of our knowledge by saying that while God could create intuitive knowledge of a nonexistent, he could not cause an evident assent to that experience (our judgment that what is experienced is also true). Ockham's desire to protect the certainty of empirical knowledge is clear; his success in doing so is and was open to question.

Ockham's teaching on intuitive cognition ran into considerable difficulty.[32] Not only did his contemporaries consider his way of handling an intuitive cognition of a nonexistent unsatisfactory, but his particular formulation of what was meant by intuitive cognition was questioned, even by his closest associates. In abolishing species it was felt that Ockham had sidestepped the problem rather than solved it, and the unresolved issues came to the surface almost immediately. If most scholastics in the subsequent decades of the fourteenth century continued to use the language of intuitive cognition, this was only partially due to Ockham's contribution to that discussion.

Ockham's epistemology and empiricism, particularly against the background of his natural philosophy, brings up one of the most important questions of fourteenth-century intellectual history, namely Ockham's contribution to the development of late medieval science.

---

[31] This particular aspect of Ockham's epistemology has generated a considerable literature. In addition to Day and Tachau, cited above: Ph. Boehner, "The *Notitia intuitiva* of Non-Existents According to William of Ockham," in *Collected Articles*, 268–300; R. C. Richards, "Ockham and Skepticism," *NS* 42 (1968): 345–63; T. K. Scott, "Ockham on Evidence"; M. M. Adams, "Intuitive Cognition, Certainty, and Skepticism in William of Ockham," *Traditio* 26 (1970): 389–98; Scott, "Nicholas of Autrecourt"; P. A. Streveler, "Ockham and his Critics on: Intuitive Cognition," *FcS* 13 (1975): 223–36; L. D. Davis, "The Intuitive Knowledge of Non-Existents and the problem of Late Medieval Skepticism," *NS* 49 (1975): 410–30.

[32] For reactions to Ockham's epistemology see Tachau, *Vision and Certitude*.

The answer one gives to this question depends very much on where one puts the emphasis in Ockham's thought. Certainly Ockham's stress on the certainty of existential knowledge, whether ultimately successful or not, alongside his de-Platonizing of Aristotle and the rigor of his *Summa logicae* can be seen as contributions to a more critical, empirical attitude in the fourteenth century, as can his stress on the primacy of the individual, our *cognitio rei particularis*. Ockham's logic is particularly suited to the investigation of the individual and the building up of a legitimate, scientific structure of universal knowledge. Similarly, Ockham opposed considering any aspect of creation (whether it be creatures, events, or the laws of nature) to be absolutely necessary, and he used arguments *de potentia absoluta* (arguments about what God could have done, possibilities outside of the given, *de facto*, ordained order) to distinguish the "absolutely necessary" from the "contingently necessary." Ockham's approach may well have encouraged the exploration of possibilities *secundum imaginationem* and opened the speculative frontiers beyond the limits of the Aristotelian universe. By exploring the boundary between the logically possible and the logically impossible, Ockham focused attention on the way things actually operate—not because they do so necessarily, but because it was the system chosen and established by God. Thus Ockham played a prominent role in the movement away from understanding change and motion in terms of "why" to stressing the more empirical question of "how" those processes take place.

At the same time, other scholars have noted some fundamental, "unscientific" aspects to Ockham's thought. Most visible, of course, are the resulting lack of certainty built into any assertion of an intuitive cognition of a nonexistent, as well as Ockham's stress on arguments *de potentia absoluta*, which seemingly deflect study away from what *is* to what *might have been* or theoretically *could be*. More important and fundamental, perhaps, would be the discrepancy between the development of mathematical physics—the single most important development in fourteenth-century science—and Ockham's separation of mathematics and physics.

This problem cannot be solved through the usual method, namely a simple, a priori comparison of what is considered essential to Ockham's thought and what is considered essential to fourteenth-century science. It can be more profitably pursued by examining the degree to which individual thinkers who contributed to the development of fourteenth-century science depended on Ockham, whether they "should have" or not.

OCKHAM'S THEOLOGY

Ockham's theology is often called nominalistic and even made part of the core definition of what nominalism really is.[33] Such an approach recognizes the importance of theology for Ockham, the centrality of the dialectic of divine power (the *potentia absoluta/ordinata* distinction), and a covenantal view of the structure and operation of the created universe. But to term these latter ideas "nominalistic" can be misleading. There is no question that there was a compatibility between Ockham's philosophical nominalism and particular positions that he held in theology. Essential in this regard is Ockham's understanding of the contingent, covenantal character of the physical universe as well as the theological order of salvation established by God; Ockham's tendency to replace innate or inherent virtue in things with assigned or ascribed value that can operate in nature as well as in the church; his stress on the functional, conventional nature of spoken and written languages; and his use of language analysis as a major tool for the decipherment of philosophical as well as theological problems.

At the same time it must be recognized that Ockham did not arrive at his theology simply by importing nominalist philosophical principles into it; nor did he formulate his view of the relation of language and reality on the basis of previously developed or overriding nominalistic insights in his theology, although the latter would make more chronological sense. At heart, Ockham's theology is not nominalistic but only comfortably compatible with nominalism. Its origin lies in pre-Thomistic Dominican theology: the creation of a covenantal theology that by Ockham's time had become favored among Franciscans, most notably Duns Scotus. It could well be said that Ockham took certain fundamental ideas of Scotus's theology and used them to attack other aspects of Scotus's thought, to streamline the latter by removing what he felt to be unneeded distinctions and concepts. The result was a theology and a

---

[33] H. A. Oberman, "Some Notes on the Theology of Nominalism with attention to its Relation to the Renaissance," *Harvard Theological Review* 53 (1960): 47–76; *The Harvest of Medieval Theology* (Cambridge, Mass., 1963).

philosophy that were not only theoretically compatible but fully integrated.[34]

Pactum *and Contingency*

The central idea that Ockham took from Scotus and from the larger body of thirteenth-century theology was the balance or interplay between the unlimited freedom of God and God's self-limitation to work within the physical and spiritual orders he established. On the one hand, Ockham affirmed the absolute omnipotence of God, the God of Abraham, Isaac, and Jacob, who stands above and outside the categories of our universe and is, in this life, ultimately hidden from our full knowledge. Both the natural laws of the physical universe and those of the sacramental system of salvation within the church are contingent on God's will, which is one with his reason. On the other hand, divine freedom should not be so stated as to undermine the regularity and reliability of the physical and spiritual worlds, limit unduly the integrity and freedom of man, or compromise the notion that God will reward human effort in attaining salvation.[35]

The apparent incompatibility of total divine omnipotence and the secure functioning of the created orders was resolved through the thirteenth-century distinction of the absolute and ordained power of God.[36] Outside of his ordination, or the plan that God has established for his creation, God was and is free and unlimited, save by the principle of noncontradiction (that he cannot make contradictories true at the same time). God could have arranged things differently; there is no necessity that stands over him, determining his actions from without. Yet *from* the area or sphere of absolute possibility (*de potentia Dei absoluta*) God has chosen to implement or realize a lesser number of possibilities,

---

[34] Unless one is prepared to label as nominalist or protonominalist all those who employ the distinction of absolute and ordained power, or the theory of ascribed value and covenantal causality, it would be best to restrict the term "nominalist" to its proper, philosophical meaning.

[35] One of the best introductions to this system of salvation is still Oberman, *Harvest of Medieval Theology.*

[36] In addition to Oberman, *Harvest of Medieval Theology*, 30–56, see Courtenay, "The Dialectic of Omnipotence in the High and Late Middle Ages," in *Divine Omniscience and Omnipotence in Medieval Philosophy*, ed. T. Rudavsky (Dordrecht, 1985), 243–69.

which he has put into operation, in time, through his ordination (*de potentia Dei ordinata*), and which he continues to uphold despite his freedom to do otherwise. If one considers divine power in and of itself (simply or absolutely), without regard for what God has in fact chosen to do, then it appears to be almost limitless. If one reflects on the orders God has established for nature and grace, then divine power appears *self-limited*. Occasional miraculous suspensions of the ordained laws of nature and grace are not *absolute* actions but foreordained reminders that those laws are *gifts*, not absolutely necessary relationships.

The distinction between viewing divine power simply (*absoluta*) or according to God's created and revealed systems (*ordinata*) was used in thirteenth-century theology, became more prevalent in Scotus's thought, and became a principal tool in Ockham's theology, testing the degree of necessity involved in laws that operate in nature and in the process of salvation. What is peculiar to Ockham here is not the meaning he gave to this distinction nor the use he made of it (for he defined and used it as had Thomas Aquinas: to demonstrate contingency and separate the absolutely necessary from the relatively necessary), but the degree to which he used it. As with the Aristotelian principle of economy or parsimony that eventually became known as Ockham's razor, Ockham used the distinction on divine power to cut through a long series of philosophical and theological problems as well as to cut away Platonic and, indeed, Scotistic accretions.

This distinction between what God could do and what he has in fact done, is doing, and will do, became in Ockham (as it had already begun to function in Scotus) a means of seemingly guaranteeing the omnipotence of God in the strongest Augustinian language while, at the same time, guaranteeing that human effort would be rewarded and that the universe would continue to function as God created it. The laws of nature, while not absolute or absolutely necessary in any sense, were established by God and would continue to function, apart from the occasional miracle by which God revealed his power and our contingency in a benevolent way. Only one who stepped outside God's covenant with mankind and nature, as did Noah's contemporaries or the Israelites at various times, need fear for the certainty of the physical order. Similarly, the laws regulating the process of salvation, the terms according to which God's grace and ultimately the reward of eternal life are given, were established by God's free will and obtain because of his benevolent, consistent will, not because they are absolutely necessary or inherent in the nature of things.

With this principle in mind, Ockham accepted a number of theological teachings of Scotus. He retained Scotus's distinction between a good act and a meritorious act, the latter being based not on the quality of the act itself or its conformity with divine commands, but on its being accepted by God (*acceptatio divina*) as sufficiently meritorious. An act was meritorious of grace and of eternal life because God accepted it as such; God did not accept it because it was already meritorious. Ockham also retained Scotus's belief, one that had a long history within Franciscan theology, that God had of his own free will committed himself to reward with the gift of grace those who, on the basis of what remained of their natural powers after the Fall (*ex puris naturalibus*), did their best to fulfill the commands of God (*facientibus quod in se est Deus non denegat gratiam*). If one continued to use that grace to the best of one's ability, God would ultimately reward that person with eternal life.

Ockham modified Scotus's teaching on grace and justification only in two respects. The first of these concerned the doctrine of predestination.[37] Scotus had maintained that God's predestination (or predetermination of those who would be saved) is based on God's inscrutable will alone, not on merits foreseen through divine foreknowledge of future contingents. For Scotus, in contrast to almost all of his contemporaries, predestination took place before foreseen merits (*ante praevisa merita*). Ockham, in keeping with the majority opinion of the thirteenth century, considered predestination to be based on foreseen merits (*post praevisa merita*). From the standpoint of Scotus's thought, this reintroduction of humanly conditioned predestination removed a principal protection against the Pelagian implications of a human-effort (*facere quod in se est*) approach to salvation. From the standpoint of Ockham's thought, however, it brought Scotus's teaching into greater conformity with the traditional view or common opinion, protected the freedom and integrity of human effort, and made the doctrine of justification more internally consistent. For Ockham, the dialectical approach to divine power was sufficient protection against Pelagianism. One did not

[37] On Scotus's doctrine of predestination see W. Pannenberg, *Die Prädestinationslehre des Duns Skotus* (Göttingen, 1954). For Ockham see *The Tractatus de praedestinatione et de praescientia Dei et de futuris contingentibus of William Ockham*, ed. Ph. Boehner (St. Bonaventure, N.Y., 1945); Oberman, *Harvest of Medieval Theology*, 185–248.

need to undercut human effort further by placing salvation solely within the inscrutable will of God.

A second example of where Ockham altered Scotus's view of the process of salvation was his teaching on penance. In order to initiate the return to God, according to Scotus, it was not necessary to have full contrition for one's sins (something that could only be achieved through the absolution of a priest in confession), nor even attrition (regret), but only *bare* attrition (*parum attritus*). Again, Ockham here sided with the common opinion that a higher level of sorrow and regret was required by God, and that Scotus had set too low a price on what was required of man.

Sacramental Theology

At the heart of Scotus's and Ockham's teaching on grace and justification lies the concept that the salvation value of a good act is not inherent in the act itself but is ascribed to it by God, both because the commands of God that define what is morally good originate in the will of God and because merit is based on acceptation, not acceptation on merit. The same idea was applied by Scotus and Ockham (as well as other Franciscan theologians and even some thirteenth-century Dominicans) to the sacraments.

In contrast to the realm of physical nature, in which God has implanted certain forces that cause their effects through their own agency as well as the sustaining power of God, the sacraments, *de facto*, do not operate by inherent virtue for Ockham but by an ascribed virtue or power.[38] It is not an inherent power in the water of baptism, the words of consecration, or the oil of ordination that causes the sacramental effect. Instead, God has established a system whereby the proper effect will occur when the sacrament is properly performed both in word and symbol. Thus it is not caused by a virtue that these symbols have in themselves but by a virtue ascribed to them by God, according to his covenant or pact (*pactum*). The only sacrament in which the signs or symbols receive their own inherent virtue is in the Eucharist where,

---

[38] Courtenay, *Covenant and Causality in Medieval Thought* (London, 1984); B. Hamm, *Promissio, Pactum, Ordinatio. Freiheit und Selbstbindung Gottes in der scholastischen Gnadenlehre* (Tübingen, 1977).

after consecration, the body and blood of Christ are really present. In this teaching of ascribed sacramental virtue Ockham and others before and after him moved away from a physical, mechanical view of sacramental causality. With the exception of the Eucharistic host, there is nothing in the sacramental elements that causes their effect. The dependable, *ex-opere-operato* operation of the sacraments has been retained, however, inasmuch as their efficacy does not rest on the moral or religious standing of the priest performing the sacrament but on the system established by the actions of Christ. The proper sacramental effect will take place when the sacrament is performed in the proper way.

As important as this teaching is within the total framework of Ockham's theology, it cannot be considered an identifying characteristic of Ockham's thought, in and of itself. One can find the teaching among the Scotists and, in England, among those influenced by such Dominicans as Fishacre and Kilwardby.[39]

The portion of Ockham's sacramental teaching that is more characteristic is his teaching on the Eucharist and, in particular, his view of quantity. As was mentioned before, quantity for Ockham was not a *res extra*, distinct from the quantified substance. It was only a way of saying something was extended in space, having part separate from part. This theory had already been proposed by Peter Olivi, although not in quite the language used by Ockham. Later writers associated this view of quantity with Ockham, so that historically one may accept it as one of the distinguishing features of his thought.

Ethics

The ethical system of Ockham has already been anticipated in the discussion of pact and contingency.[40] The ethical norms, the moral laws

---

[39] Courtenay, *Covenant and Causality*, ch. 6.

[40] Ethics and the importance of *recta ratio* are discussed frequently in the academic and political writings of Ockham; see in particular his *Sent.* 3, qq. 11–12; *Quodl.* 1, q. 20; 2, q. 14; 3, qq. 14–16. W. Kölmel, "Das Naturrecht bei Wilhelm von Ockham," *FzS* 35 (1953): 39–85; D. Clark, "Voluntarism and Rationalism in the Ethics of Ockham," *FcS* 31 (1971): 72–87; A. B. Wolter, "Native Freedom of the Will as a Key to the Ethics of Scotus," in *Deus et Homo ad mentem I. Duns Scoti*, Acts of the Third International Scotist Congress (Rome, 1972), 359–70; Linwood Urban, "William of Ockham's Theological Ethics," *FcS* 33 (1973): 310–50; McGrade, *Political Thought of William of Ockham*, 173–96.

ordained by God, are not absolute ethical norms such that God could
not, had he so chosen, have established some other system. God *could
have* arranged things so that murder, theft, and adultery would be good
actions (i.e., actions in conformity with the divine will as expressed in
revealed commandments). The biblical examples of God's command
that Abraham sacrifice Isaac, the Israelites despoiling Egypt, Abraham's child by Hagar were for Ockham sufficient evidence that the
presently ordained moral system was not absolutely necessary and co-
terminous with the total will of God. As with Scotus, the ethical system
is contingent and its content not absolutely necessary. Good acts are effectively good because God has so ordained things; God did not choose
the present moral system because it was the only one that was inherently
good. The system chosen and instituted by God, however, is not, for
Ockham, arbitrary. It is not only rationally consistent and rationally de-
fensible; it is a product of divine reason as well as will, since in God will
and reason are one. *De facto* the system God has chosen and ordained is
the one under which we live. God's will is not only revealed in Scripture;
it is written in our hearts in terms of natural law, which we know
through the dictates of right reason (*recta ratio*).

OCKHAMISM AND ENGLISH NOMINALISM

It was a standard assumption throughout the first half of this century
that many, perhaps most, Oxford scholars in the two generations after
Ockham were influenced by Ockham and that nominalism, initiated by
him, was the prevailing current of thought.[41] Despite the cautions
voiced by Moody and Boehner,[42] that view has lingered, giving the

---

[41] C. Michalski, "Les courants philosophiques à Oxford et à Paris pendant le xivᵉ siècle,"
Bulletin intern. de l'Académie Polonaise des sciences et des lettres, classe d'hist. et de phil.
(Cracow, 1922), 59–88; "Les sources du criticisme et du scepticisme dans la philosophie du
xivᵉ siècle," *Fifth International Congress of Historical Sciences* (Bruxelles, 1923–24), 241–68;
"Le criticisme et le scepticisme dans la philosophie du xivᵉ siècle," *BIAPSL*, cʜ/ᴘ (Cracow,
1927), 41–122; "Les courants critiques et sceptiques dans la philosophie du xivᵉ siècle,"
BIAPSL, cʜ/ᴘ (Cracow, 1927), 192–242; F. Ehrle, *Der Sentenzenkommentar Peters von Candia*
(Münster i.W., 1925); E. Gilson, *HCP*, 487, 498–520; G. Leff, *Medieval Thought from Saint
Augustine to Ockham* (St. Albans, 1958); A. Maurer, *Medieval Philosophy* (New York, 1962);
D. Knowles, *The Evolution of Medieval Thought* (London, 1962).

[42] E. A. Moody, "Ockham, Buridan, and Nicholas of Autrecourt," in *Studies in Medieval*

impression that the positions propounded by Ockham led in England and on the Continent to the formation of a school that triumphed over its immediate competitors, Thomism and Scotism.

As has been shown in the last chapter, Thomism was all but extinct at Oxford when Ockham was a student of theology and Scotism, although present, was hardly dominant even in Franciscan circles. The independence of thought that made "school" affiliation unworkable in the Oxford environment also made the establishment of Ockhamism or nominalism (as a school of thought) equally impossible, and in all probability no such "program" was ever envisaged. We do not find any significant Ockhamist following developing at Oxford.[43] What we find, in fact, is that most of Ockham's immediate academic contemporaries rejected one or more aspects of his thought, and that even his most sympathetic supporters, such as Adam Wodeham, show considerable independence of mind on a number of major issues.

The principal points of controversy were Ockham's reinterpretation of the categories, his position on universals and his definition of simple supposition, his definition of intuitive cognition and his rejection of sensible and intelligible species, and his (largely Scotistic) position on grace and justification. It is abundantly clear that Ockham quickly became a major figure, but also that he was controversial, and not always for the same reasons. John of Reading attacked Ockham on points where Ockham departed from Scotus; Walter Burley, on points where Ockham departed from realism; and the anonymous author of the *Logica contra Ockham*, on a mixture of the two. John Lutterell had the broadest critique, rejecting Ockham's nominalism as well as his Scotism. Ockham's closest disciple, Wodeham, supported Ockham's nominalism and reinterpretation of the categories (as did William Heytesbury and John Dumbleton), but criticized aspects of Ockham's epistemology and psychology. And the parallels between Ockham and Robert Holcot are too few to allow us to apply the label "Ockhamist" to Holcot. In short, the patterns in what was accepted or rejected are not consistent enough to group others into fixed camps. New evidence on this question will

---

Philosophy, 160; Ph. Boehner, "Introduction" in William of Ockham, *Philosophical Writings: A Selection* (New York, 1964), li.

[43] For a more extensive discussion see Courtenay, "The Reception of Ockham's Thought in fourteenth-Century England," in *From Ockham to Wyclif*, ed. Anne Hudson and Michael Wilks, Studies in Church History, Subsidia 5 (Oxford, 1987), 89–107.

certainly be uncovered in the coming years, but it is unlikely that a vigorous Ockhamist group in England will ever reemerge.

Although it is presently impossible to find any figures who accept all aspects of Ockham's thought, it is possible to find some who hold positions compatible with his views on universals, simple supposition, and the categories of quantity, motion, and time. Yet the prehistory of these views in the writings of Olivi, Campsall, and Harclay should make us cautious about their being derived directly from Ockham. If we choose, on the other hand, to apply the label "nominalist," we must acknowledge that it included rather than stemmed from Ockham, that it was hardly dominant in the second quarter of the fourteenth century, and that it lost out to realism after 1350, as will be shown in the last two chapters.

What is important in fourteenth-century English thought and what England contributed to academic and intellectual developments on the Continent was not so much Ockhamism or nominalism but rather the revolutionary innovations in philosophical and theological *methods* that occurred in arts and theology in that period in England, innovations to which Ockham contributed but for which he is not the sole or even primary source. It is to those developments that we now turn.

EIGHT

Logica Anglicana AND THE RISE OF
THE NEW PHYSICS

꩜

AMONG THE exports for which England was famous in the minds of continental scholars in the late Middle Ages, logic ranked high. It was a commodity as essential to the faculties of arts, theology, and law as wool was for European commerce, and just as closely associated with England. The intellectual economies of the continental universities in the period 1340–1450 were heavily, although by no means exclusively,[1] de-

---

[1] It is now apparent that the logic of John Buridan, which directly and by way of Albert of Saxony and Marsilius of Inghen influenced the teaching of logic in Germany and Italy, probably owed less to Ockham or Burley than to earlier Parisian sources, such as Peter of Spain. Many of the resemblances between Buridan and Ockham, such as their nominalism and semantics, seem to have been coincidental rather than directly related. The dependence of Buridan on Ockham has undergone numerous transformations. It was once considered axiomatic by Prantl, Ehrle and others, who relied on fifteenth-century accounts of the origin of nominalism and tended to identify late medieval terminist logic with Ockhamist logic. The misconception that Buridan signed the Parisian statute 1340, which purportedly was directed against Ockham, led Michalski and Gilson to discount Ockham as an immediate source of Buridan's logic. Hochstetter, Moody, and Boehner gave new life to the picture of the "Ockhamist" Buridan by disassociating Ockham from the 1340 statute. Moody's was the more sweeping formulation (E. A. Moody, *Studies in Medieval Philosophy, Science, and Logic* [Berkeley, 1975], 129–130): "The writings of John Buridan, by contrast [with those of Autrecourt] exhibit direct influence of Ockham's teachings on almost every page, and, despite the modifications and differences to be noted between the teachings of the two men, these writings substantially justify the long established tradition which links the names of Buridan and the other "nominalists of Paris" with that of Ockham." Ruprecht Paqué, while noting that Buridan was not rector at the time of the Parisian arts statute of December, 1340, returned to the notion that the statute was directed against Ockham and that Buridan and Ockham differed greatly, a view shared by T. K. Scott. Those presently involved in editing the logical works of Buridan acknowledge parallels between Ockham and Buridan, and occasionally direct influence. For recent discussions of this issue see E. A. Moody, *Truth and Consequence in Medieval Logic* (Amsterdam, 1953); T. K. Scott, *John Buridan: Sophisms on Meaning and Truth* (New York, 1966); R. Paqué, *Das Pariser Nominalistenstatut* (Berlin, 1970); T. K. Scott, "Nicholas of Autrecourt, Buridan, and Ockhamism,"

pendent upon English treatises, which explored the new elements in logic that went beyond the Aristotelian and Boethian foundation. The "sophisms of the English" entered the language of "national" types. For Italian humanists from Petrarch to Bruni and beyond, it was a characteristic to be despised and avoided; for the university scholars it was an achievement to be admired and emulated.[2] England's contribution to scholastic philosophy, particularly extensive and innovative during the two decades 1320–40, was probably the single most important development affecting the content of higher education in the late Middle Ages. It reshaped the arts curricula in France, Italy, Germany, and eastern Europe. It supplemented the types of argumentation available to the medieval lawyer. It transformed the style and content of late scholastic theology.

There were three interrelated aspects to the English intellectual contribution in the fourteenth century. One was the expansion of terminist logic itself. A second was the development of mathematical physics.

Journal of the History of Philosophy 9 (1971): 15–41; J. Pinborg, ed., *The Logic of John Buridan* (Copenhagen, 1976); W. J. Courtenay and K. H. Tachau, "Ockham, Ockhamists, and the English-German Nation at Paris, 1339–1341," *History of Universities* 2 (1982): 53–96.

[2] The pejorative and often condescending attitude of the Italian humanists toward English logic is best typified by the following statement of Leonardo Bruni in his *Dialogus ad Petrum Histrum*, as translated by Jan Pinborg in "The English Contribution to Logic before Ockham," *Synthese* 40 (1979): 20: "What about logic, which is the one art necessary for disputation. . . . The barbarians who live beyond the Ocean have made an assault upon it. But what people! Good God! Even their names make me shudder: Farabrich, Buser, Ockham, Suiset and many more of the same kind, who apparently have got their names from the courtiers of Rhadamanthys. To be serious: Dear Coluccio, can you show me anything in logic which has not been disturbed by the British sophisms?" On the humanist critique of English logic see P. O. Kristeller, "Florentine Platonism and its relations with Humanism and Scholasticism," *Church History* 8 (1939): 201–11; E. Garin, *La disputa delle arti nel Quattrocento* (Florence, 1947); E. Garin, *Prosatori latini del Quattrocento* (Milan, 1952); Q. Breen, "Giovanni Pico della Mirandola on the Conflict of Philosophy and Rhetoric," *Journal of the History of Ideas* 13 (1952): 384–426; C. Vasoli, "Polemiche occamiste," *Rinascimento* 3 (1952): 119–41; E. Garin, "La cultura fiorentina nella seconda metà del 300 e i 'barbari Britanni,' " *La Rassegna della litteratura italiana* 64 (1960): 181–95, and in *L'età nouva* (Naples, 1969), 139–66; P. O. Kristeller, *Renaissance Thought* (New York, 1961), 42–44, 100–103; P. O. Kristeller, *Medieval Aspects of Renaissance Learning* (Durham, N.C., 1974), 106–7. For a more positive assessment of the influence of English logic on Italian education see Alfonso Maierù, "Lo 'Speculum puerorum sive Terminus est in quem' di Riccardo Billingham," *Studi medievali* 10.3 (1970): 297–397; Maierù, *Terminologia logica della tarda scholastica* (Rome, 1972).

And the third was a new theology based on methods and insights achieved in the first two areas. These developments did not occur in chronological sequence, for some of the advances in logic and physics were achieved by theologians. The changes, however, are easier to grasp if they are taken in the order of the medieval curriculum.

"MODERN" LOGIC

Terminist logic was a twelfth-century innovation in the field of semantics that originated at Paris out of the interaction between dialectic and grammar.[3] On the one hand, the *logica moderna*, or *modernorum*, as it is called today, was an exploration of elements that were thought implicit in the *logica vetus* and the *logica nova* but insufficiently developed. It was never thought to be a system opposed to Aristotelian or Boethian logic but purely supplemental. Thus, after the traditional subjects contained in the *logica antiqua* (predicables, the categories, propositions, syllogisms, demonstration, inference, and fallacies), there were added the subjects of the *logica moderna*, which initially and primarily concerned

---

[3] The literature in this area is now abundant. For the major texts and interpretive studies (many of them containing texts) see: William of Sherwood, *Introduction in logicam*, ed. M. Grabmann, in *Sitzungsberichte der Bayerischen Akademie der Wissenschaften*, Phil.-hist. Abteil., 10 (Munich, 1937); Sherwood, *Syncategoremata*, ed. J. R. O'Donnell, in *MedStud* 3 (1941): 46–93; N. Kretzmann, *William of Sherwood's Introduction to Logic* (Minneapolis, 1966); Kretzmann, *William of Sherwood's Treatise on Syncategorematic Words* (Minneapolis, 1968); J. P. Mullally, *The Summulae Logicales of Peter of Spain* (Notre Dame, 1945); Peter of Spain, *Summulae Logicales*, ed. I. M. Bocheński (Turin, 1947); Peter of Spain, *Tractatus syncategorematum*, tr. J. P. Mullally (Milwaukee, 1964); Walter Burley, *De puritate artis logicae tractatus longior*, ed. Ph. Boehner in Franciscan Institute Publications, 9 (St. Bonaventure, N.Y., 1955); Ockham, *SL*; Martin Grabmann, "Bearbeitungen und Auslegungen der aristotelischen Logik aus der Zeit von Peter Abaelard bis Petrus Hispanus," *Abhandlungen der Preussischen Akademie der Wissenschaften*, Phil.-hist. Klasse, 5 (Berlin, 1937); Ph. Boehner, *Medieval Logic* (Manchester, 1952); E. Arnold, "Für Geschichte der Suppositionstheorie," *Symposion; Jahrbuch für Philosophie* 3 (1952): 1–134; Moody, *Truth and Consequence*; C. Wilson *William Heytesbury: Medieval Logic and the Rise of Mathematical Physics* (Madison, 1956); I. M. Bocheński, *A History of Formal Logic* (Notre Dame, 1961); W. and M. Kneale, *The Development of Logic* (Oxford, 1962); L. M. De Rijk, *Logica Modernorum*, 2 vols. (Assen, 1962, 1967); Kretzmann, "Semantics, History of," in *The Encyclopedia of Philosophy*, vol. 7 (New York, 1967), 358–406; J. Pinborg, *Die Entwicklung der Sprachtheorie im Mittelalter* (Münster, 1967); D. P. Henry, *Medieval Logic and Metaphysics* (London, 1972); P. V. Spade, *The Mediaeval Liar: a Catalogue of the 'Insolubilia'-Literature* (Toronto, 1975).

the properties of terms (hence terminist logic), such as signification, supposition, appellation (supposition for presently existing things), rules governing the operation of verbs, predicates, and relative terms, ampliation (extending the personal supposition of universal terms to cover past and future instances as well as the present), restriction (limiting the supposition of universal terms), and distribution.[4] By the early thirteenth century the *logica moderna* included treatises on the *syncategoremata* (the logical operators or structural terms of propositions, such as the adjectival and adverbial quantifiers 'some', 'every', 'insofar as', 'both', 'either', 'neither', 'no', 'only'; and the connectives 'if-then', 'and', 'but', 'besides', 'unless', 'or') and *sophismata* (ambiguous or obscure propositions, which formed the material in the disputations in the arts faculty known as '*de sophismatibus*'). Treatises on *insolubilia* (contradictory

[4] The *logica antiqua* usually followed the arrangement of Aristotle's *Organon* with the treatises of Porphyry, Boethius, and others added. Thus predicables, or concepts treated according to the mode of predication, such as genus, species, accident, property, or difference, derived from Porphyry's *Isagoge* (introduction to Aristotle's *Categories*). The categories were entities or predicates applicable to real things: substance, quality, quantity, relation, action, affection, position, time, place, and state. Propositions, discussed in Aristotle's *Perihermenias*, or *De interpretatione*, were statements or sentences considered as language expressions, not directly concerned with their objective content, existential import, or some actual "state of affairs." Propositions could be categorical (simple propositions composed of subject, verb, and predicate) or hypothetical (compound propositions composed of several categoricals), just as syllogisms could be categorical (composed of factual propositions or premises) or hypothetical (in which at least the major premise is a compound proposition). Discussions of syllogisms were based on Aristotle's *Prior Analytics*, discussions of demonstration and demonstrative syllogisms on Aristotle's *Posterior Analytics*, discussions of inference on Aristotle's *Topics*, and fallacies on Aristotle's *On Sophistical Refutation*.

The subjects of the *logica moderna* were not based on the arrangement of the Aristotelian corpus but on specific logical functions. Signification concerned the *meaning* or sense of a word, without regard for either its propositional use or its relation to extra-linguistic reality. Supposition concerned the *reference* of a word inasmuch as words, or terms, stand for, or "supposit" for, universal concepts or entities (simple supposition), individual things (personal supposition), or terms themselves (material supposition). Supposition applied only to terms used in propositions. Appellation could be considered a subcategory of supposition in which a term supposits only for some existing thing. Likewise, restriction limited or qualified the application or supposition of terms through some adjective, adverb, other part of speech, or verb tense, while ampliation expanded supposition of subject terms through the use of modal words. Distribution concerned the analysis of generalizing particles, such as 'every.'

propositions, such as the liar paradox), *obligationes* (rules for argumentation) and *consequentia* (rules of inference) were gradually added in the thirteenth and early fourteenth centuries.

On the other hand, the interest in the meaning and reference of terms, which lies at the heart of the *logica moderna*, was also an outgrowth of grammar, a concern for the philosophical implications of language developed by Anselm of Canterbury, Peter Abelard, and others on the basis of Priscian's grammar and the Stoic logic upon which it drew.[5] Terminist logic, therefore, in the form and to the extent that it developed in this period, owed much to the recovery of the full corpus of Aristotle's writings, particularly his *Sophistical Refutations* with its discussion of fallacies. But it was also an independent and direct outgrowth of the *logica vetus* and the study of grammar. It was simply the newer part of formal logic, and those who developed it never rejected the *logica antiqua*.[6] Its ancillary role in the twelfth and thirteenth centuries is underscored by the fact that in that period it never became a required part of the course of study in arts at Paris or Oxford. It was ad-

[5] Anselm's contribution to logic and grammar has only recently been recognized; see D. P. Henry, "The Scope of the Logic of Saint Anselm," in *L'Homme et son destin d'après les penseurs du moyen âge.* Actes du premier congrès international de philosophie médiévale (Louvain, 1960); Henry, "Remarks on Saint Anselm's Treatment of Possibility," in *Spicilegium Beccense*, vol. 1 (Paris, 1959), 19–22; Henry, *The 'De grammatico' of St. Anselm: The Theory of Paronymy* (Notre Dame, 1964); Henry, *The Logic of St. Anselm* (Oxford, 1967); W. J. Courtenay, "Necessity and Freedom in Anselm's Conception of God," *Analecta Anselmiana* 4.2 (1975): 39–64; M. Colish, "Eleventh-Century Grammar in the Thought of St. Anselm," in *Arts libéraux et philosophie au moyen âge*, Acts of the 4th International Congress of Medieval Philosophy (Montréal and Paris, 1969), 785–95; "St. Anselm's Philosophy of Language Reconsidered," *Anselm Studies: An Occasional Journal* 1 (1983): 113–23. On Abelard see Peter Abelard, *Dialectica*, ed. L. M. De Rijk (Assen, 1956); M. M. Tweedale, *Abailard on Universals* (Amsterdam, 1976). On Priscian: De Rijk's remark, "Neither Donatus (*c.* A.D. 400) nor Priscian (*c.* A.D. 500), who became the famous masters of grammar for the Early Middle Ages, rose above the level of mere compilers of their Greek and Latin predecessors, and they did not aim at originality or doctrinal improvements either" (*Logica Modernorum* 2: 97–98) leads one to overlook the importance of Stoic elements in Priscian; for that connection see E. A. Moody, *Truth and Consequence*, 2–3; Pinborg, *Entwicklung der Sprachtheorie*, 21–23, 45–56, 201–2.

[6] One can, therefore, speak of terminist logic in the twelfth and thirteenth centuries, but it can be misleading to speak of "terminists" or "terminism" as if there were a group that practiced a type of formal logic opposed to some other group of logicians. There was only one formal logic, which had its older and newer parts. A division between parties or approaches to logic was a later, fourteenth-century development.

vanced work on the frontiers of logic, engaged in by those who had already mastered the basics.

The early development of terminist logic, specifically in the period 1150 to 1250, was not particularly English but was a common achievement of the schools, primarily Paris. By 1250 it had been refined and consolidated into a body of treatises, of which those of William of Sherwood (Shyreswood), Peter of Spain, and Lambert of Auxerre are the best known. It was, it should be noted, a development that was contemporaneous with the full recovery and translation of Aristotle's works and the restructuring of the arts curriculum at Paris and Oxford around the logic and natural philosophy of Aristotle. The *Summulae logicales* and the *Tractatus syncategorematum* of Peter of Spain were, in a sense, the culmination of the first phase of terminist logic. The production of textbooks shortly before 1250 that united the *logica antiqua* with the *logica moderna* suggests that the latter was then about to become part of the curriculum in arts at Paris. Its failure to do so can be ascribed largely to the appearance of different approaches to logic that gradually dominated Paris in the period 1250 to 1325.

The new, nonterminist approaches to logic evolved from a growing interest in metaphysics and questions of ontology associated with Arabic philosophy and Christian Aristotelianism. Parisians did not seek to create a new logic consciously opposed to terminism. Instead, terminist logic fell into disuse at Paris because it concerned itself with mental and linguistic structures rather than the forms and principles that made up extra-mental reality, either in the physical or metaphysical sense. Although not incompatible, the two approaches were significantly different.

Terminist logic, with its foundation in grammar, assumed that the parts of speech did not stand for absolute linguistic or objective entities but acquired their meaning from the linguistic context, the way in which they were used in formulated propositions. The truth value of propositions depended on *how* terms were being used as well as the time and conditions under which the proposition was thought, spoken, or written. Terminist logic, therefore, concerned itself with supposition, reference, and particular linguistic problems arising from ambiguity, contradiction, modal propositions, tensed propositions, and the operation of syncategorematic terms. This contextual approach seemed ill-suited for a metaphysics that dealt with necessary and absolute truths, self-evident propositions, and demonstrative science, and for which ontological and epistemological realism were major presuppositions.

In place of terminism, a metaphysical approach to logic developed that focused on external reality and was far more realist.[7] It drew its inspiration and terminology from Avicenna, Averroes, Maimonides, and others, who seemingly spoke more directly to the psychological and criteriological problems with which Parisians were concerned in the second half of the thirteenth century. Both logic and theology became metaphysically oriented. Within the corpus of the *logica antiqua*, the works that related to Aristotle's *Physics* and *Metaphysics* were of special interest, such as the *Categories, On Interpretation, Posterior Analytics, On the Soul*, as well as the treatise on *Six Principles*, in which the categories of 'time', 'place', 'relation', and the like were assumed to refer to real entities. The language of formal logic was used to discuss metaphysical questions in such a way that the boundary between logic and metaphysics was blurred.[8] In this process the work of Peter of Spain was largely ignored at Paris, even though Peter was a realist on the question of universals. Those who continued to use supposition theory and other vestiges of terminist logic, as did Albertus Magnus or Thomas Aquinas, relied on a broader tradition that included Robert Kilwardby.[9]

[7] Apart from Albert the Great, the leading figures of Parisian scholasticism in the second half of the thirteenth century wrote few commentaries or treatises in logic. They did, however, introduce discussions of aspects of logic in other works of philosophy or theology. It is indicative that the contributions of Thomas Aquinas to medieval logic noted by Bocheński in his *History of Formal Logic* were drawn almost exclusively from Thomas's theological, metaphysical, and epistemological writings. The later implications of this metaphysical approach to logic can be seen in E. A. Moody, "Ockham and Aegidius of Rome," *FcS* 9 (1949): 417–42, reprinted in Moody, *Studies*, 161–88; Moody, *Truth and Consequences*, 5–6; Moody, "*Empiricism and Metaphysics in Medieval Philosophy,*" *The Philosophical Review* 67 (1958): 145–163, repr. in *Studies*, 287–304; De Rijk, *Logica Modernorum* 2.1: 597; for an important and related aspect of this development, see Pinborg, *Entwicklung der Sprachtheorie*, 19–135; Pinborg, "English Contribution," 19–42.

[8] Almost every Parisian scholar in the period of "high scholasticism" (1250–1310) bears traces of this metaphysical logic. It is less in evidence in Albert and Thomas than in the later scholastics, such as Henry of Ghent, Giles of Rome, and John Duns Scotus.

[9] Some of the points on which Albert and/or Thomas used terminist logic are supposition, appellation, and modal propositions. William of Sherwood (rather than Peter of Spain) has sometimes been suggested as one of the principal sources; see Bocheński, *History of Formal Logic*, 163–65; Kretzmann, *William of Sherwood's Introduction to Logic*, 5. The assumption Sherwood taught and/or wrote at Paris as well as his influence there has come

In conjunction with this metaphysical approach to logic and under the influence of the Arab commentaries on the epistemology and psychology of Aristotle which became influential at Paris after 1260, there appeared a group of "Modists" (*Modistae*) in the second half of the thirteenth century of whom Martin of Dacia, Boethius of Dacia, Radulphus Brito, Simon of Faversham, and Siger of Courtrai were the principal representatives.[10] From one perspective the logical and grammatical works of the Modists, which became known as "speculative grammar," had their roots in the same fertile mixture of logic and grammar that produced terminism. Thus the treatises *de modis significandi* can be seen as grammatical counterparts to the treatises *de proprietatibus terminorum* in logic.[11] Yet from another perspective the assumptions behind the

---

into question; see De Rijk, in his edition of Peter of Spain's *Tractatus* (Assen, 1972), and "Some Thirteenth Century Tracts on the Game of Obligation," *Vivarium* 14 (1976): 26–61, esp. 42; H.A.G. Braakhuis, *De 13de eeuwse tractaten over syncategorematische termen*, doctoral thesis, University of Leiden, 1979, 1: 309–16, 514; Pinborg and S. Ebbesen, "Thirteenth Century Notes on William of Sherwood's Treatise on Properties of Terms," *CIMGL* 47 (1984): 103–41, all of whom favored an English setting for Sherwood's scholarly activity, a view shared by Pinborg, at least in 1981. A Parisian setting has been reaffirmed by N. Kretzmann, J. Longeway, E. Stump, and J. van Dyk, "L. M. De Rijk on Peter of Spain," *Journal of the History of Philosophy* 16 (1978): 325–33; a view cautiously favored by Osmund Lewry, "Grammar, Logic and Rhetoric, 1220–1320," in *HUO* 1: 406–10.

[10] Pinborg, *Entwicklung der Sprachtheorie*; G. L. Bursill-Hall, *Speculative Grammars of the Middle Ages* (Hague, 1972); Pinborg, *Logik und Semantik im Mittelalter* (Stuttgart, 1972); T. Coleman, *Modistic Grammar*, Ph.D. diss., University of Toronto, 1976; R. W. Hunt, *The History of Grammar in the Middle Ages*, ed. G. L. Bursill-Hall (Amsterdam, 1980); F. P. Dineen, "Distinguo. Modi significandi and Covert Case Roles," *Historiographia Linguistica* 7 (1980): 39–52; A. De Libera, "The Oxford and Paris traditions in Logic," in *CHLMP*, 174–87; Pinborg, "Speculative Grammar," in *CHLMP*, 254–69. There are no direct connections between the modist grammar and logic of Boethius of Dacia and his philosophical positions under attack in the Parisian Articles of 1277 beyond the fact that Averroes was a source for both and that Boethius, like many modists, sought a "purer" Aristotle. The ability of modist logic to thrive at Paris in the post-1277 climate suggests that it was not an object of the condemnation. The Oxford condemnation in 1277, which included theses in grammar and logic, is another matter. Some of the propositions condemned at Oxford find echoes in modist treatises that were reaching Oxford at the time of the condemnation. See Osmund Lewry, "The Oxford Condemnations of 1277 in Grammar and Logic," in *English Logic and Semantics from the End of the Twelfth Century to the Time of Ockham and Burley*, ed. H.A.G. Braakhuis, C. H. Kneepkens, and L. M. de Rijk, Artistarium supplementa 1 (Nijmegen, 1981), 235–78, and "Grammar, Logic and Rhetoric: 1250–1320," in *HUO* 1: 401–33.

[11] Mullally offered an interesting series of parallels between the *Summulae logicales* of the

logic of the *Modistae* contrasted sharply with those of the terminists, and in the period 1270–1325 one finds at Paris only the faintest echo of the terminology and approach of the *logica moderna*.[12]

Modist logic was based on a theory of universal grammar and systematic syntax that emphasized the unchanging formal meaning of words (once imposition takes place) and the invariability and universality of the components of meaning, such as the parts of speech and the secondary grammatical categories of case, number, gender, tense, and voice. Each root word or stem has many modes of signifying (*modi significandi*) corresponding to these grammatical forms, and each linguistic form refers to a nonlinguistic reality or entity. Since in Aristotelian semantics (as traditionally interpreted) words signify objects by means of concepts, the *modi significandi* correspond to modes of understanding (*modi intelligendi*) and of being (*modi essendi*). Within each of the three realms there is a direct counterpart in the other two.

Although modist grammar was not necessarily or inherently opposed to terminist logic, its approach to language differed. Modist logic subordinated mental language to grammatical structure. The *Modistae* rejected the notion that words change meaning over time and that their actual meaning in a proposition depends on context. In their analysis of terms, they concentrated on formal meaning and sense rather than material meaning and reference. Propositions were analyzed on the basis of grammatical structure with little regard for context, and no use was made of the theory of supposition upon which much of terminist logic depended. Modist logic was essentially a theory of the relation of language and reality compatible with an epistemology of abstraction, certain lingering Neoplatonic presuppositions, and metaphysical realism.

There was no overt conflict between the two approaches in the late thirteenth century. As long as the *logica moderna* remained merely an appendix to the *logica antiqua*, the implications of its theory of language remained hidden, and it could be used or ignored as one chose. Paris essentially ignored terminism in the second half of the thirteenth century. Oxford logicians in the same period remained wedded to termin-

---

terminist Peter of Spain and the *Grammatica speculativa* of the modist Thomas of Erfurt in order to establish Thomas's dependence on Peter; see Mullally, *Summulae logicales*, lxxxii–xcvii.

[12] Pinborg, "Die Logik der Modistae," *Studia Mediewistyczne* 16 (1975): 39–97; Pinborg, "English Contribution."

ism, and the language of the *Modistae* had almost no echo in England save in those who taught in a Parisian context as well. In addition to commentaries on Peter of Spain's *Summulae logicales* by Robert Kilwardby[13] and Simon of Faversham and various treatises of Roger Bacon, there were some important additions to the sophistical literature, such as the *Abstractiones* of Magister Richardus Sophista.[14] Despite the fact that Oxford remained closely allied with Paris throughout the thirteenth century, Oxford was more conservative and provincial in nature. It was wary of excessive Aristotelianism and clung to the "traditional" logic that honored the grammatical, linguistic approach of the *logica moderna* as much as the philosophical approach of the *logica antiqua*.

In the early fourteenth century terminist logic underwent a period of growth and development in England that made it a formidable opponent to modist logic. The major early contributors were Richard of Campsall, Ockham, and Walter Burley.[15] It is difficult in retrospect to know whether the interests in natural philosophy, empiricism and epistemology led Oxford to develop its heritage of terminist logic, or

[13] Kilwardby's contributions in logic are only distantly related to the development of terminism and the *Modistae*. Kilwardby's logical works were written at Paris at a time when terminist logic was well developed and easily available, and yet there are few traces of it in his work. Only later, in his defense of the Oxford condemnation of 1277, does one have the impression that Kilwardby shared the terminist concern for the ways in which context affects meaning and reference. On the other side, while there are faint traces in Kilwardby's Priscian commentary (*c.* 1240) of positions that would a quarter-century later be present in modist treatises, Kilwardby had no connection with such modist forerunners as John Pagus or Nicholas of Paris. See S. Harrison Thomson, "Robert Kilwardby's commentaries in Priscianum and in Barbarismum Donati," *NS* 12 (1938): 55–65; R. W. Hunt, "Studies on Priscian in the Twelfth Century," *Medieval and Renaissance Studies* 1 (1941–43): 194–231; 2 (1950): 1–55; Pinborg, *Entwicklung der Sprachtheorie,* 28–30; Pinborg, Lewry, Fredborg, Green-Pedersen, and Nielsen, "The Commentary on 'Priscianus Maior' Ascribed to Robert Kilwardby," *CIMGL* 15 (1975); Lewry, "The Oxford Condemnations of 1277"; and Lewry, "Grammar, Logic and Rhetoric," 412–13, 419–26.

[14] On the Magister Abstractionum see De Rijk, *Logica modernorum,* 2.1: 62–72; G. Gál in his introduction to Ockham, *SL,* 50*–53*; Pinborg, "Magister abstractionum," *CIMGL* 18 (1976): 1–4; W. J. Courtenay, *Adam Wodeham* (Leiden, 1978), 54–56.

[15] The *Prior Analytics* commentary of the Pseudo-Scotus (John of Cornwall) dates slightly earlier (1300–10), C. H. Lohr, "Medieval Latin Aristotle Commentaries," *Traditio* 27 (1971): 278. His analysis of words for knowing (*scitum, notum*), believing (*creditum, opinatum*), doubting (*dubium*), and willing (*volitum, dilectum*) made important contributions to the development of modal logic. See Bocheński, *History of Formal Logic,* 225–27.

whether the dominant position that logic and physics already held at Oxford in the thirteenth century gave them a greater interest in those subjects or approaches. In any event, the development of terminist logic at Oxford in the fourteenth century went hand in hand with the development of empiricism, epistemology, and physics as surely as modist logic at Paris had contributed to the development of metaphysics and ontology.

Richard of Campsall was a secular theologian and a fellow successively of Balliol and Merton colleges at Oxford.[16] When he became a fellow of Merton College in 1305 he was already a bachelor in arts and, in 1308, he incepted and became regent master in arts. His works in logic, most of which have been lost, probably date to the years 1308–10. After his regency he entered the theological faculty, reading the *Sentences* around 1317–18, engaging the Franciscan Walter Chatton in debate, and by 1322 becoming regent master in theology.

Campsall's work was traditional in the sense that he confined his philosophical writings to commentaries on the *logica antiqua*. His approach, however, was formal and terminist. His method of verbal analysis centered on supposition, which he divided into simple, personal, and material. He was fascinated with the "liar paradox," which he attempted to solve by considering it a paralogism (a constructable but unreasonable argument) that could be solved through an analysis of supposition. At several points he distinguished between a false literal meaning, *de virtute sermonis*, and a true intended (colloquial or metaphoric) meaning, *ex usu loquendi*, as Kilwardby and Bacon had done earlier. And he had an overriding concern for modal propositions that involved necessity, contingency, and possibility, as well as temporal propositions. His formalism was demonstrated in his practice of determining rules in logic that could be applied to various problems.

Campsall is reflective of the continuing and vigorous interest in a ter-

---

[16] Emden, *BRUO* 1: 344–45; E. A. Synan, "Richard of Campsall, an English Theologian of the 14th Century," *MedStud* 14 (1952): 1–8; Synan, *The Works of Richard of Campsall*, 2 vols. (Toronto, 1968, 1982); J. A. Wiesheipl, "Repertorium Mertonense," *MedStud* 31 (1969): 208–9; C. H. Lohr, "Medieval Latin Aristotle Commentaries," *Traditio* 28 (1972): 391. H. Gelber, *Logic and the Trinity: a Clash of Values in Scholastic Thought, 1300–1335*, Ph.D. diss., University of Wisconsin, Madison, 1974, 203–4, 208–11, 229–30; Courtenay, *Adam Wodeham*, 60–61.

minist approach at Oxford, which gathered momentum in the fourteenth century. His writings do not appear to have been popular (the
few that have survived occur in unique manuscripts), but his name was
cited frequently by contemporaries and later scholastics, particularly
for the way in which he applied rules of logic to problems in theology.

Ockham's contribution to logic was far more revolutionary, and its impact, both through his writings and by word of mouth, was far greater.[17]
His *Summa logicae*, which was widely read but whose size and complexity
prevented it from becoming the textbook he intended, recast terminist
logic. In content most of the *Summa logicae* is a clear and straight-for-
ward presentation of terminist formal logic, as it had been developed in
the thirteenth century. He maintained a clear division between logical
order and reality, and he further refined terminism through his analysis of supposition, of connotative terms and relative terms, of condi-
tional propositions, of confusions between literal (*de virtute sermonis*) and

---

[17] The literature on Ockham's logic is vast. The principal texts and recent studies are:
Ockham, *SL*; Michael J. Loux, transl. with introduction, *Ockham's Theory of Terms: Part I of
the Summa logicae* (Notre Dame, 1974); A. J. Freddoso and H. Schuurman, *Ockham's Theory
of Propositions: Part II of the Summa logicae* (Notre Dame, 1980); E. A. Moody, *The Logic of
William of Ockham* (New York, 1935); Ph. Boehner, *Collected Articles on Ockham* (St. Bonaventure, N.Y., 1958); J. Salamucha, "Die Aussagenlogik bei Wilhelm Ockham," *FzS* 32
(1950): 97–134; G. Martin, "Ist Ockhams Relationstheorie Nominalismus?" *FzS* 32 (1950):
31–49; D. P. Henry, "Ockham and the Formal Distinction," *FcS* 25 (1965): 285–92;
H. Greive, "Zur Relationslehre Wilhelms von Ockham," *FzS* 49 (1967): 248–58; G. Gál,
"Gualteri de Chatton et Guillelmi de Ockham controversia de natura conceptus universalis," *FcS* 27 (1967): 191–212; R. Price, "William of Ockham and *Suppositio Personalis*," *FcS*
30 (1970): 131–40; J. Swiniarski, "A New Presentation of Ockham's Theory of Supposition
with an Evaluation of some Contemporary Criticisms," *FcS* 30 (1970): 181–217; G. Gál,
"Henricus de Harclay: Quaestio de Significato Conceptus Universalis (Fons doctrinae
Guillelmi de Ockham)," *FcS* (1971): 178–234; S. Brown, "Walter Burleigh's 'Treatise de
Suppositionibus' and its influence on William of Ockham," *FcS* 32 (1972): 15–64; P. Spade,
"Ockham on Self-reference," *Notre Dame Journal of Formal Logic* 15 (1974): 298–300;
Spade, "Ockham's Distinctions between Absolute and Connotative Terms," *Vivarium* 13
(1975): 55–76; Spade, "Some Epistemological Implications of the Burley-Ockham Dispute," *FcS* 35 (1975): 212–22; M. J. Loux, "*Significatio* and *Suppositio*: Reflections on Ockham's Semantics," *NS* 53 (1979): 407–27; A. A. Coxito, *Lógica, Semântica et Conhecimento na
Escolástica Peninsular Pré-Renascentista* (Coimbra, 1981); and the articles by J. Biard, G. Leibold, A. Maurer, C. Panaccio, V. Richter, and A. Siclari in *Sprache und Erkenntnis im Mittelalter*, Miscellanea Mediaevalia, 13 (Berlin, 1981).

intended meanings, of propositions *de 'incipit' et 'desinit', de praeterito et de futuro, de possibili, impossibili, et contingenti*. The area of modal logic was similarly expanded.[18] In two respects, however, Ockham's *Summa* represents an important turning point. It was the first full-scale exposition of formal logic to abandon the traditional medieval order, found in Sherwood, Peter of Spain, and others, that appended the *logica moderna* as a group of treatises after the *logica antiqua*. That arrangement had been largely an accident of the order in which the works were recovered or developed. Ockham reorganized the entire body of logical subjects into a simpler progression from terms, to propositions, to syllogisms and fallacies, using the principles of terminist logic throughout.[19] His second contribution, which had its forerunners in Olivi and Harclay, lay in his nominalism, his restricting significative use of a term to individuals, and his reinterpretation of the categories, allowing real existence to only two metaphysical entities: substance and quality.[20]

At first glance it would appear that the form terminism took in Ockham placed it in direct opposition to both metaphysical logic and to that of the *Modistae*, so that the fundamental differences in presuppositions and approaches were clear, perhaps for the first time. But the actual effect of Ockham's logic is difficult to assess. His effect on the structure of logical works in England was only partial. Although terminism received extensive development in England after Ockham, some aspects of which were directly dependent on his work, most treatises were short, dealing with particular aspects of the *logica moderna*: sophisms, insolubles, composite and divided senses, propositional proofs, conse-

---

[18] See the discussion of Ockham's modal logic in Bocheński, *History of Formal Logic*, 227–31.

[19] The need to reorganize the content of formal logic was felt by others as well. The organization of the earliest version of Burley's *De puritate artis logica* (before he was aware of Ockham's *Summae logicae*) reflects a different but nevertheless new order: general rules, sophisms, obligations and demonstration.

[20] Ockham's understanding of universals and his limiting of categories were comparable, but did not necessarily entail each other. As Paul Spade has expressed it, *Peter of Ailly: Concepts and Insolubles* (Dordrecht, 1980), 96, n. 26: "This feature of Ockham's doctrine [his limiting of entities to substance and quality] is sometimes confused with his rejection of real universals, as though the two claims went hand in hand. They do not; one can be a realist about universals and yet admit only two metaphysical categories, or alternatively, be a nominalist about universals but allow individual entities in any number of categories."

quences, or obligations. Some works, such as the *Logica* of Ralph Strode, reverted to the earlier organization. Ockham's structure had a more lasting effect on the Continent. At Paris, Buridan, basing his work on Peter of Spain, stayed with the traditional order. Buridan's disciples, however, Albert of Saxony and Marsilius of Inghen, adopted the new order, which was bequeathed to Germany and Italy at the end of the fourteenth century.

Ockham's role in the spread of terminism and nominalism is also unclear. Since modist logic was not a force in England and terminist traditions were strong, most aspects of Ockham's logic were readily acceptable to English contemporaries. Opposition to particular points did occur: from Thomists (John Lutterell), Scotists (*Logica contra Ockham*), and terminists of a realist persuasion (Walter Burley). Three aspects were particularly controversial. One of these was Ockham's belief that the object of knowledge was the proposition, not the external reality to which the conclusion referred. Another was his belief that only the categories of substance and quality were real, and that the other categories, such as duration, or motion, or quantity were simply ways of describing a substance or quality in time, in motion, or extended in space. A third aspect was Ockham's rejection of the traditional understanding of simple supposition, which Ockham thought referred not to some extra-mental entity but to a mental concept, an intention of the soul (*intentio animae*). On the Continent, Ockham's nominalism was only one of several grounds for opposition to modist logic. The eclipse of the *Modistae* at Paris had more to do with Buridan than Ockham. The attack on the *Modistae* at Erfurt by Aurifaber apparently owed more to John of Jandun than to Ockham.[21] Only toward the end of the century, with Pierre d'Ailly and Jean Gerson, do we encounter an opposition to modist logic that is grounded in Ockham's logic.

---

[21] For the clash of views at Erfurt in 1340 between the modist Thomas of Erfurt and Johannes Aurifaber, see Pinborg, *Entwicklung der Sprachtheorie*, 137–92; "A Note on Some Theoretical Concepts of Logic and Grammar," *Revue Internationale de Philosophie* 29 (1975): 286–96. The crises in the arts faculty at Paris in 1339 and 1340 were of a different nature. The first crisis was between supporters (*Occanistae*) and opponents of Ockham's nominalistic reinterpretation of Aristotle's categories and its implications for physics. The crisis of 1340 concerned masters, bachelors, and students who rejected certain propositions as false *de virtute sermonis* without acknowledging that they were true in the intended sense. See Courtenay and Tachau, "Ockham, Ockhamists," 53–96.

* * *

Walter Burley was older than Ockham and was, as we have seen, among his earliest and most vigorous opponents.[22] Yet Burley influenced Ockham in at least one respect,[23] and Ockham may even have influenced Burley. Burley's writings on logic date back to at least 1300, but all those that can with certainty be dated before the appearance of Ockham's *Summa logica* are commentaries on the *logica antiqua*. Burley's contribution to terminist logic, however, was substantial. In his revised and lengthened version of *De puritate artis logicae*, written after and against certain statements in Ockham's *Summa logicae*, he adopted Ockham's reorganization of logical subjects from terms to propositions, to syllogisms. In addition, Burley wrote treatises on supposition, *de relativis, de finito et infinito, de toto et parte, de exclusivis, de exceptivis*, on *syncategoremata, sophismata*, insolubles, obligations, and consequences. In contrast to the work of Campsall, Burley's treatises in logic were widely circulated in England and on the Continent. Their popularity did not derive simply from their clarity and method of exposition. They presented the *logica moderna* in a form that was grounded in realist presuppositions even more than was that of Peter of Spain.

In light of that, it is important that one not equate terminism and Ockhamism. There were varieties of terminism, just as many radically different approaches could and did bear the label "Ockhamist" in the fourteenth century. Burley, Ockham, and John Buridan were all terminists. Yet Burley was a realist and one of Ockham's most ardent opponents, and Buridan, who shared certain nominalist presuppositions with Ockham, derived his terminism from the tradition of Peter of Spain and rejected much of Ockham's natural philosophy as well as some of his logic.[24]

---

[22] Emden, *BRUO* 1: 312–14; J. A. Weisheipl, "Ockham and some Mertonians," *MedStud* 30 (1968): 174–88; "Repertorium Mertonense," *MedStud* 31 (1969): 185–208; A. Uña Juarez, *La Filosofía del Siglo XIV: Contexto cultural de Walter Burley* (Escorial, 1978).

[23] Brown, "Walter Burleigh's 'Treatise de Suppositionibus.' " Ockham also knew and used Burley's *De obligationibus* and *De insolubilibus*.

[24] For the sources of Buridan's terminism, in addition to those listed in n. 1, see: Mullally, *The 'Summulae logicales' of Peter of Spain*, xlvii, lxxviii, xcviii, xcix. The clearest statement of the Ockhamist and non-Ockhamist elements in Buridan's natural philosophy has been given by J. E. Murdoch and E. D. Sylla, "The Science of Motion," in *Science in the Middle Ages*, ed. by D. C. Lindberg (Chicago, 1978), 217: For Buridan ". . . the reality of alteration only involves the mobile and the *forma fluens*, or the forms successively acquired. In this

*   *   *

The contributions of Campsall, Ockham, and Burley were only a beginning. Until the end of the century there was an unbroken line of English scholars who contributed to logic—over twenty-five whose works
are extant, and most of them well-known to continental scholars in the
late fourteenth and fifteenth centuries. Most of the fourteenth-century
treatises concerned aspects of the *logica moderna*, taking the *logica antiqua* for granted or subsuming it under the approach of the *logica moderna*. There were many treatises on propositions and propositional
proofs, of which the most popular were the *De propositionibus, De veritate
et falsitate propositionis*, and *De probationibus conclusionum* of William
Heytesbury (written *c*. 1335–38), the *Speculum iuvenum* or *Speculum
puerorum* of Richard Billingham (written *c*. 1350), and the *Tractatus de
veritate propositionum sive logica* of Richard Feribrigge (*c*. 1360).[25] Closely
related were the treatises on supposition, such as those by William Sutton (*c*. 1335) and Thomas Maulvelt (Manlevelt) (before 1360).[26] There

---

(and in giving a like answer with respect to augmentation and diminution), he was at one
with Ockham; indeed, many of the considerations he employed in establishing these conclusions were themselves quite Ockhamist. In the case of local motion, however, he breaks
completely with his English predecessor. . . ." It was Anneliese Maier who noted Buridan's
rejection of Ockham's theory of local motion, *Zwischen Philosophie und Mechanik* (Rome,
1958), 121–31. Whether Buridan adopted his theory of alteration from Ockham is still under debate, since as Murdoch and Sylla recognized, that particular theory of alteration was
"by then quite standard."

[25] For these works of Heytesbury, see Weisheipl, "Repertorium Mertonense," 212–17.
Billingham's work has been edited by Maierù, "Lo 'Speculum puerorum sive Terminus.' "
See also De Rijk, "The Place of Billingham's 'Speculum puerorum' in 14th and 15th Cen-
tury Logical Tradition with the Edition of Some Alternative Tracts," *Studia Mediewistyczne*
16 (1975): 99–153; "Richard Billingham's Works on Logic," *Vivarium* 14 (1976): 121–38.
Portions of the *Logica* of Feribrigge have been transcribed from Padua, Bibl. Univ., MS.
1123 by Francesco del Punta; see his edition of Paul of Venice, *Logica Magna*, pt. 2, fasc. 6,
Classical and Medieval Logic Texts, 1 (Oxford, 1978), 215–36; Del Punta, "La 'Logica' di
R. Feribrigge nella tradizione manoscritta Italiana," in *ELI*, 53–85. Del Punta is in the proc-
ess of completing a full, critical edition. On Feribrigge, see also N. Kretzmann, "Medieval
Logicians on the Meaning of the *Propositio*," *Journal of Philosophy* 67 (1970): 767–87.

[26] On Sutton see Weisheipl, "Repertorium Mertonense," 219. On Maulvelt see Pin-
borg, *Entwicklung der Sprachtheorie*, 146, who mentions that the earliest copy of Maulvelt's
Tractatus de suppositionibus appears in a manuscript from Erfurt, copied in 1364, now at
Göttingen. Neither the form of Maulvelt's name nor his English origin can be established
with certainty. He is called Thomas Anglicus in several manuscripts (Erfurt, MS. CA.Q.255;
Erfurt, MS. CA.Q.288; Melk, MS. 1941), but this may reflect nothing more than, like John of

were also treatises on *Sophismata*, particularly those by Richard Kilvington (*c.* 1328) and Heytesbury;[27] *Insolubilia* by Thomas Bradwardine (1321–24), Walter Segrave (*c.* 1330), Roger Swineshead (*c.* 1332), Heytesbury, Roger Nottingham (1343), Henry Hopton (*c.* 1355), Richard Lavenham (*c.* 1365), and John Hunter (Venator) (mid- to late fourteenth century);[28] *Obligationes*, such as Roger Swineshead's *De obligatoriis*, Heytesbury's *Casus obligatorii*, or that by Robert Fland (*c.* 1355);[29] and *Consequentiae*, such as Heytesbury's *Tractatus consequentiarum*, Sut-

---

Holland, that he probably studied in England and was associated with English logicians in the minds of continental scholars. In any event, he probably taught at Louvain, and the variations of his name (Maulveldt, Mauleveld, Manlevel, Manloval) suggest a Low Countries origin. I am grateful to Jan Pinborg for the manuscript information on Maulvelt.

[27] There is, as yet, no catalogue surveying the *sophismata* literature, although Kretzmann's chapter, "Syncategoremata, exponibilia, sophismata," in *CHLMP*, 211–45 is a step in that direction. Kretzmann is also preparing an edition of Kilvington's *Sophismata*, with a biographical introduction by Barbara Ensign Kretzmann. For the present see F. Bottin, "Un testo fondamentale nell' ambito della 'nuova fisica' di Oxford: I Sophismata di Richard Kilmington," in *AM*, 201–205; Kretzmann, "Socrates is whiter than Plato begins to be white," *Nous* 11 (1977): 3–15; Kretzmann, "Richard Kilvington and the Logic of Instantaneous Speed," in *Studi sul XIV secolo in memoria di Anneliese Maier*, ed. A. Maierù and A. Paravicini Bagliani, Storia e Letteratura, 151 (Rome, 1981), 143–78. On Heytesbury's *Sophismata* and the related *Regulae solvendi sophismata*, see Wilson, *William Heytesbury*; Weisheipl, "Developments in the Arts Curriculum," 161; Weisheipl, "Ockham and some Mertonians," 195–99; Weisheipl, "Repertorium Mertonense," 212–17; E. Sylla, "William Heytesbury on the Sophism 'Infinita sunt finita,' " in *Sprache und Erkenntnis im Mittelalter*, 628–36; Kretzmann, "Sensus Compositus, Sensus Divisus, and Propositional Attitudes," *Medioevo* 7 (1981): 195–229. The opening chapter of the *Regulae* has been translated by Paul Spade, *William Heytesbury on "Insoluble" Sentences* (Toronto, 1979).

[28] See Weisheipl, "Developments in the Arts Curriculum," 165–67. The *insolubilia* has been admirably surveyed by Paul Spade, *The Mediaeval Liar: a Catalogue of the Insolubilia-Literature* (Toronto, 1975), who has also edited many of the treatises. See in particular: P. V. Spade, "The Origins of the Mediaeval *Insolubilia*-Literature," *FcS* 33 (1973): 292–309; "An Anonymous Tract on *Insolubilia* from Ms Vat. lat. 674: An Edition and Analysis of the Text," *Vivarium* 9 (1971): 1–18, "William Heytesbury's Position on 'Insolubles': One Possible Source," *Vivarium* 14 (1976): 114–20; "Robert Fland's Insolubilia: An Edition, with Comments on the Dating of Fland's Works," *MedStud* 39 (1978): 56–80; "Roger Swyneshed's Insolubilia: Edition and Comments," *AHDL* 46 (1979): 177–220; *William Heytesbury; Peter of Ailly.*

[29] See Weisheipl, "Developments in the Arts Curriculum," 163–65; P. V. Spade, "Roger Swyneshed's *Obligationes*: Edition and Comments," *AHDL* 44 (1977): 243–85; "Richard Lavenham's *Obligationes*: Edition and Comments," *RCSF* 33 (1978): 224–41; "Robert Fland's *Obligationes*: An Edition," *MedStud* 42 (1980): 41–60.

ton's *De Consequentiis*, Feribrigge's *Consequentiae*, and Robert Fland's *Consequentiae*.[30] Many of these subject areas of the *logica moderna* were also included in the textbooks written after 1330, which solidified the achievements of English logic and presented them in a form that would serve the needs of beginning scholars. One thinks in particular of Heytesbury's popular *Regulae solvendi sophismata* (1335), of the *Logica* of Richard Brinkley from the 1350s, the *Logica* of Ralph Strode (*c.* 1360), John Wyclif's *Tractatus de logica* (*c.* 1361), and the *Logica* of John Hunter.[31]

The treatises and textbooks produced in the second and third quarters of the fourteenth century at Oxford became popular on the Continent as well as in England. An early wave of diffusion took place in the 1330s and 1340s. Later works were often carried to the Continent by foreign students who had received a formative part of their education at Oxford, such as John of Holland, who became regent at Prague in 1369, or Paul of Venice, who returned to Padua to teach at the end of the century.[32]

The English treatises in logic provided more than introductions to the various areas of the *logica moderna*. They made continental students aware of different approaches and assumptions in late medieval logic. William Sutton, whose work became popular in German universities,

---

[30] See Weisheipl, "Developments in the Arts Curriculum," 161–63; P. V. Spade, "Five Logical Tracts by Richard Lavenham," in *Essays in Honor of Anton Charles Pegis* (Toronto, 1974), 70–124; "Robert Fland's *Consequentiae*: An Edition," *MedStud* 78 (1976): 54–84.

[31] For Heytesbury see above, n. 27. Brinkley's *Logica* is being edited by Zenon Kaluza with the fragment of Brinkley's *Sentences* commentary. Portions of Brinkley's *Logica* have been edited in G. Gál and R. Wood, "Richard Brinkley and his 'Summa Logicae,'" *FcS* 40 (1980): 59–101. The *Logica* of Ralph Strode is being edited by Alfonso Maierù. Wyclif's *Tractatus* can be found in *Tractatus de logica*, ed. M. H. Dziewicki, 3 vols. (London, 1893–99; repr. New York, London, and Frankfurt, 1966). John Hunter (Johannes Venator) may be identical with John Huntman; Emden, *BRUO* 2: 987–88. Sections of his *Logica* are provided by Francesco del Punta in his edition of Paul of Venice, *Logica Magna*, 237–51.

[32] On Holland see Emden, *BRUO* 2: 915; Spade, *Mediaeval Liar*, 66–68. An edition of his works by E. P. Bos is in progress. Paul of Venice has received considerably more attention. In addition to Emden, *BRUO*, 3: 1944–45, see Paul of Venice, *Logica magna*, pt. 1, fasc. 1, ed. and trans. by N. Kretzmann (Oxford, 1979); *Logica magna*, pt. 2, fasc. 6, ed. and trans. by F. del Punta and M. M. Adams (Oxford, 1978); *Logica magna (Tractatus de Suppositionibus)*, ed. and trans. by Alan R. Perreiah (St. Bonaventure, N.Y., 1971). The authenticity of the *Logica magna* has recently been questioned by Perreiah, *Paul of Venice. A Bibliographical Guide* (Bowling Green, Ohio, 1986).

compared the theories of Ockham and Burley on supposition, favoring the latter.[33] Heytesbury, Dumbleton, and Maulvelt identified themselves more closely with terminism and, within that, with Ockhamist presuppositions.[34] Feribrigge and Hunter, on the other hand, show no influence of nominalism.[35] Maulvelt's influence seems to have been confined to the German universities, while Heytesbury, Billingham, Strode, Feribrigge, and Hunter were also influential south of the Alps.

Perhaps the most significant change that occurred at Oxford in terminist logic in the early fourteenth century was the way in which the theory of supposition gradually absorbed other areas of terminist logic and entered linguistic areas for which it was not originally intended but for which it proved immensely useful. In the early thirteenth century supposition was simply one of the subdivisions of treatises dealing with the properties of terms, and it concerned only the subject term of the proposition. By the second quarter of the fourteenth century in England supposition theory and the illustrative examples of supposition problems found in the *sophismata* together comprised the largest portion of terminist logic.

The tendency for supposition theory to absorb other approaches to the meaning and reference of terms goes back to the mid-thirteenth century. *Copulatio*, the subdivision of the properties of terms concerned with the significative function of predicates, which was treated as a separate category well into the thirteenth century, was absorbed under the heading of supposition by Peter of Spain. The same fate eventually befell the other categories of treatises *de proprietatibus terminorum*, such as ampliation, restriction, appellation, and the supposition of relative terms, which did remain one of the most important sub-treatises of supposition. By the fourteenth century the *syncategoremata*, always of crucial importance for terminist logic, gradually ceased to be treated as a separate category and were given more individual attention within treatises on supposition or on sophisms.

The growth of supposition theory in the fourteenth century was made possible by recognizing that the principles applied not only to the subject term of a proposition but to the other parts of speech as well.

[33] Weisheipl, "Developments in the Arts Curriculum," 157–59.

[34] See Weisheipl, "Ockham and some Mertonians"; Pinborg, *Entwicklung der Sprachtheorie*, 146, 152n, 196.

[35] N. Kretzmann, "Medieval Logicians," 784–85.

Thus there were treatises *de relativis* (for the supposition of relative terms), treatises *de 'incipit' et 'desinit'* (for the supposition of predicate terms in propositions containing those verbs), treatises *de maximo et minimo* (for the supposition of comparative and superlative adverbs and adjectives), and treatises dealing with the supposition of modal infinitives and attitudinal terms such as *scire, credere, dubitare, intelligere, appeto, debeo, possum promittere, possibile, impossibile, contingens, necesse*, and the like. Some of these topics had a foundation in the *logica antiqua*, such as the discussion of 'more' and 'less' in *De sex principiis* or Aristotle's discussion of necessity, contingency, possibility, and impossibility.[36] They were also based on the early treatises on *sophismata* and *syncategoremata*. But the fourteenth-century treatment was far more extensive, and its implications far greater.

Behind most of the developments in fourteenth-century terminist logic lay the belief that many philosophical and even theological problems resulted from the ambiguity of terms used in propositions, from insufficient attention to modal constructions, tensed propositions, and hypothetical syllogisms, and from a failure to observe the rules of inference or those governing fallacies. Resolving ambiguity was the motive that lay behind the preoccupation with supposition and sophisms, just as it produced the expression *de virtute sermonis* to clarify the distinction between literal and intended meaning of terms or expressions.[37]

By mid-century it would appear that the *logica moderna* had become part of the regular arts curriculum at Oxford. The period of 1325 to 1340 was also remarkably creative, and much of the work in logic had a distinctive character. Treatises did not confine themselves to the *logica antiqua et moderna* but addressed problems of physics and mathematics, with a view toward their applicability to theology. This was true for

---

[36] In particular, *On Interpretation*, ch. 9; *Physics*, 2–4; *Metaphysics*, 5. Obligations and insolubles had their foundation in *Prior Analytics* 1, *Metaphysics* 9, and in *Topics*.

[37] Those who drafted the famous statute of the Parisian arts faculty in December 1340, which attacked those who rejected propositions on the basis of their strict verbal meaning without considering the intention of the author, were properly employing an important terminist distinction between literal meaning (*de virtute sermonis*) and intended meaning (*ex usu loquendi*, whether colloquial or metaphoric). Those attacked were neither terminists nor Ockhamists (in the proper sense of those labels). The phrase *de virtute sermonis* and the distinction within which it operated was nothing uniquely Ockhamist but was standard in terminist logic. It first appears in logic texts of the early thirteenth century and was used by Bacon, Burley, Campsall, Ockham, Buridan, and others.

Richard Kilvington's *Sophismata*, written shortly before 1330, William Heytesbury's *Sophismata* and his *Regulae solvendi sophismata* (1335), and John Dumbleton's *Summa logica et philosophiae naturalis* (*c.* 1338). Some of the interesting developments in logic in these years also took place in theological works: for example, Adam Wodeham's discussion of paralogisms, or Robert Holcot's discussions of modal propositions, tensed propositions, and the effect on supposition theory of mental, spoken, or written propositions in different languages. The hybrid nature of these works alerts us to the fact that for this period the traditional categories of logic, physics, metaphysics, and theology do not apply. Works ostensibly in one field were designed to make contributions in one or two other areas as well.[38]

Many of the newer treatises that began appearing in Oxford logic after 1320 concerned the supposition of terms in propositions about motion and change (*motus, mutatio, incipit, desinit*), growth and decay or expansion and contraction (*augmentatio, diminutio, intensio, remissio, con-*

---

[38] This unity of interests and approach has been extensively examined by John Murdoch, although he tends to see it as a characteristic of the fourteenth century in general. Admitting that these subject areas were never completely isolated in medieval thought, this particular fusion or interrelation was a more limited development that occurred at Oxford in the period 1325 to 1340 and at Paris from 1340 to 1380. In particular, see J. Murdoch, *"Rationes mathematice": Un aspect du rapport des mathématiques et de la philosophie au moyen âge* (Paris, 1962); *"Mathesis in Philosophiam scholasticam introducta*: The Rise and Development of the Application of Mathematics in Fourteenth Century Philosophy and Theology," in *Arts libéraux* 215–54; "Philosophy and the Enterprise of Science in the Later Middle Ages," in *The Interaction between Science and Philosophy*, ed. Y. Elkana (Atlantic Highlands, N.J., 1974), 51–74; "From Social into Intellectual Factors: An Aspect of the Unitary Character of Late Medieval Learning," in *The Cultural Context of Medieval Learning*, ed. J. Murdoch and E. Sylla (Dordrecht, 1975), 271–348; "A Central Method of Analysis in Fourteenth-Century Science," *XIVth International Congress of the History of Science. Proceedings*, 2 (Tokyo, 1975), 68–71; "The Development of a Critical Temper: New Approaches and Modes of Analysis in Fourteenth-Century Philosophy, Science, and Theology" in *Medieval and Renaissance Studies*, 7, ed. S. Wenzel (Chapel Hill, 1978), 51–79; *"Subtilitates Anglicanae* in Fourteenth-Century Paris: John of Mirecourt and Peter Ceffons," in *Machaut's World: Science and Art in the Fourteenth Century*, ed. M. P. Cosman and B. Chandler, Annals of the New York Academy of Sciences, 314 (New York, 1978), 51–86; "Propositional Analysis in Fourteenth-Century Natural Philosophy: A Case Study," *Synthese* 40 (1979): 117–46; "The Analytic Character of Late Medieval Learning: Natural Philosophy without Nature," in *Approaches to Nature in the Middle Ages*, ed. L. D. Roberts (Binghamton, N.Y., 1982), 171–213; *"Scientia mediantibus vocibus*: Metalinguistic Analysis in Late Medieval Natural Philosophy," in *Sprache und Erkenntnis*, 1: 73–106.

densatio, rarefactio), measurement (*maximum, minimum, latitudo, longitudo, continuum, finitum, infinitum, proportio*) and time (*tempus, duratio, instans, praeteritum, de futuris contingentibus*, and the whole area of tensed propositions). These interests were not totally absent in the logic of the thirteenth century, but they were systematically explored in the fourteenth century in an unprecedented manner. This new logic paralleled and in many cases blended with what has been called the new physics as reflected in a series of treatises (derived from the *libri naturales* of the arts curriculum, principally Aristotle's *Physics*) on motion, change, measurement, and time. These physical treatises were roughly contemporaneous with the logical treatises, and some of them were in fact a blend of the two worlds within the arts curriculum. It is difficult to say whether the exploration of these problems was a development of logic, as would be suggested by Kilvington's *Sophismata* and by the structure and content of Heytesbury's *Regulae solvendi sophismata* or whether the interests in the new physics determined the content and direction of logic. In any event, what we find by 1335 is a logic particularly suited to the analysis of problems in physics and mathematics, and a mathematical physics that depends heavily upon language analysis.

THE NEW PHYSICS

When Ockham tried shortly after 1320 to explain in the simplest form the nature of syncategorematic terms in formal logic, he chose a mathematical example. "Just as in arabic numeration a zero by itself signifies nothing, but attached to another figure makes that signify, so a syncategorema properly speaking signifies nothing, but when attached to something else makes that signify something or stand for some one or more things in a determinate way, or exercises some other function about a categorema."[39] When Thomas Bradwardine, more than two decades later, published his monumental attack on contemporary "Pelagian" theology, his *Summa de causa Dei*, he patterned its structure after Euclid's *Elements*, and its theological propositions were cast as axiomatic theorems, *in more geometrico*. These two glimpses into fourteenth-century thinking in England show a predilection for the mathematical

---

[39] Ockham, *SL* pt. 1, ch. 4; transl. from I. M. Bocheński, *History of Formal Logic*, 157.

model.[40] They not only reflect the close relationship of mathematics and logic on the one hand and mathematics and theology on the other; between the dates of 1324 and 1344 lay the development of a new quantitative, mathematical approach to physics that was closely related to changes in logic as well as in theology. The implications for theology are the subject of the next chapter, but some consideration needs to be given to the interrelation of logic, mathematics, and physics.

The discussion of mathematical problems in the context of logic was not, strictly speaking, a new development in the fourteenth century, for there were important precedents. In addition to Pythagorean, Stoic, and Boethian sources, English thinkers inherited an Oxford mathematical tradition from Robert Grosseteste in the early thirteenth century. Moreover, terminist logic throughout the thirteenth and fourteenth centuries had been intent on the formulation of *rules* for solving logical problems or rules that governed certain grammatical situations. This axiomatic approach to logic, which lies at the heart of formal logic, had its parallel as well as its model not only in Aristotle's *Topics* and *Sophistical Refutations* but in Euclid's *Elements*. Furthermore, the thrust of fourteenth-century terminist logic was to simplify a more elaborate procedure by reducing the necessary steps for arriving at solutions and by using symbols to represent longer phrases or procedures. Often this was done by substituting a letter for a phrase or proposition. The more extensive use of Latin abbreviations also served this purpose, for example ē (est), ⇥ (esse), ṅ (nisi), ã (aliqua), a^a (alia), a^{or} (maior), a^s (antecedens), ꝯ (contra) 9° (conclusio), 9⁹ (conceptus), 9ñs (consequens), ∅ (instans, i.e., a split zero). Syncategorematic terms were usually more highly abbreviated than categorematic terms. Again, the use of symbols and the shortening of steps in problem solving were aspects that logic shared with mathematics.

The subject of physics or, more broadly, the whole of natural philosophy was based on the works of Aristotle that formed the major portion of the *libri naturales* necessary for that part of the arts curriculum. Thirteenth-century inquiry sought the *causes* of motion, change, growth, and decay. The important question was *why*, and discussions centered

---

[40] On the interrelation of mathematics, logic, and theology, see Murdoch, *"Mathesis in Philosophiam"*; "The Interrelation between Science and Philosophy"; "From Social into Intellectual Factors"; *"Scientia mediantibus vocibus"*.

on first causes, final causes, or inherent virtues. By the third and fourth decades of the fourteenth century in England, however, the focus of discussion had shifted to the question of *how*, on the process of change itself, understood in a quantitative manner. A mathematical description of change was substituted for an ontological or teleological explanation. Perhaps some of the non-Aristotelian conclusions that were reached were encouraged by the atmosphere at Paris and Oxford in the wake of the 1277 condemnation of certain philosophical positions, particularly Aristotelian positions. In any event, the results were a strikingly new physics that combined mathematical precision with the possibility of exploring an entirely new set of problems.

A questioning atmosphere over against the approach to physics taken in the late thirteenth century can already be found in Ockham and Burley. Although not directly related to the mathematical approach, the *Tractatus de successivis*, culled from Ockham's commentary on Aristotle's *Physics*, and Burley's *De primo et ultimo instanti* had wide influence in the fourteenth century. The application of mathematics to physics, however, was essentially the work of five secular masters, most of them associated with Merton College, Oxford: Thomas Bradwardine, Richard Kilvington, William Heytesbury, John Dumbleton, and Richard Swineshead, sometimes known as "the Calculator."

Thomas Bradwardine was by far the most remarkable of the group.[41] He was one of the few figures in the century who made major contributions in physics as well as in theology, and no account of intellectual

---

[41] On Bradwardine's contribution to physics and what is often called the Mertonian School, see: A. Maier, *Die Vorläufer Galileis im 14. Jahrhundert*, 2nd ed. (Rome, 1966), 81–215; *An der Grenze von Scholastik und Naturwissenschaft*, 2nd ed. (Rome, 1952), 257–384; *Zwischen Philosophie und Mechanik*; M. Clagett, *The Science of Mechanics in the Middle Ages* (Madison, 1959); J. Murdoch, *Geometry and the Continuum in the Fourteenth Century: A Philosophical Analysis of Thomas Bradwardine's "Tractatus de continuo,"* Ph.D. diss., University of Wisconsin, Madison, 1957; E. Grant, *Physical Science in the Middle Ages* (New York, 1971), 55–57; R. Dales, *The Scientific Achievement of the Middle Ages*, (Philadelphia, 1973), 105–9; E. Sylla, *The Oxford Calculators and the Mathematics of Motion, 1320–50: Physics and Measurement by Latitudes*, Ph.D. diss., Harvard University, 1970; "Medieval Quantifications of Qualities: the 'Merton School,' " *Archive for History of Exact Sciences* 8 (1971): 9–39; "Medieval Concepts of the Latitude of Forms: The Oxford Calculators," *AHDL* 40 (1973): 223–83; J. Coleman, "Jean de Ripa O.F.M. and the Oxford Calculators," *MedStud* 37 (1975): 130–89; and the essays by W. A. Wallace, M. S. Mahoney, and J. Murdoch/E. Sylla in D. Lindberg, ed., *Science in the Middle Ages* (Chicago, 1978).

life in the fourteenth century would be complete without him. Brad-wardine was born around 1300 in the village of that name or in the nearby town of Chichester. Therefore, like Ockham, he belonged to the southerners in the university division. While in arts he was a fellow of Balliol College, becoming a fellow of Merton College when he began his theological studies. During his regency in arts, which probably occurred in 1321–23, he composed his treatise *De insolubilibus* as well as two other treatises: *Arithmetica speculativa* and *Geometria speculativa*, which were re-spectively summaries of Boethius and Euclid. His treatise on the contin-uum may also date from this period, but it was not as popular as the first three works.

Bradwardine was a student of theology and had twice served as proc-tor of the university when, in 1328, he published his *De proportionibus velocitatum motuum*. The work was remarkable in several respects. First, he provided an analysis of the relations between velocity, force, and re-sistance and in so doing set the pattern for discussions of physical laws at Oxford in the next generation. The adoption of quantitative meas-urement in understanding physical processes in the fourteenth century stemmed primarily from Bradwardine's treatise. Secondly, he sought and found theorems that would explain all cases of a given kind, thus providing self-consistent formulas in the physics of motion. Thirdly, he rejected the Aristotelian assumption that velocity was directly propor-tional to changes in force or resistance, arguing instead that velocity in-creases (or decreases) arithmetically as the proportion of force to resist-ance increases (or decreases) geometrically. Put another way, velocity does not increase at the same rate as force is increased, resistance re-maining constant; rather velocity is increased at the same rate as the in-crease in the ratio or proportion of force to resistance is squared, cubed, etc. Fourthly, Bradwardine distinguished a number of aspects with re-gard to motion that had not previously been examined. He distin-guished the quality from the quantity of velocity, instantaneous velocity as distinct from velocity over a period of time, and he initiated a sepa-rate discussion of the relation of force to distance, that is, of the dy-namic and kinematic functions.

His close contemporary, Richard Kilvington, was born around 1305 in the diocese of York.[42] The impediment of his illegitimate birth (he

---

[42] On Kilvington, see Emden, *BRUO* 2: 1050–51; Maier, *Die Vorläufer*, 174, 301–3; Wil-

was the son of a priest) had been removed under John XXII by 1332. In March of that year, already a master of arts, a student of theology, and a fellow of Oriel College, Oxford, he was ordained subdeacon. In September of the following year he was ordained priest. He read the *Sentences* around 1333 and subsequently became a doctor of theology at Oxford.[43] By 1339 he had left the university and was engaged abroad in the service of the king. He continued in that capacity as part of the household of Richard de Bury, bishop of Durham and one of the chief administrative figures under Edward III. In 1354 Kilvington became dean of St. Paul's in London, a position he held until his death in 1361. He was buried at St. Paul's.

Kilvington's principal work in logic, his *Sophismata*, was written before 1330, probably while a master of arts. It is thus roughly contemporary with another seminal work, Thomas Bradwardine's *Tractatus de proportionibus velocitatum* written in 1328. Kilvington was never connected with Merton College, nor was he a student of Bradwardine, as is sometimes maintained. Kilvington's importance for both modern logic and mathematical physics alerts us to the fact that the development of a "new physics" at Oxford was not confined to the Mertonians.

Kilvington's *Sophismata* follows earlier models in modern logic in that it treats ambiguous propositions whose difficulties stem usually from *syncategoremata* and the supposition of words such as *incipit, infinitum, tempus, desinit, instans, gradus, spacium, pars proportionalis, divisum, velocius, motus,* and similar terms concerned with problems of beginning, ceasing, time, motion, velocity, and proportion. From the standpoint of logic his work represented the fullest analysis to date of propositions containing those verbs, nouns, and adjectives, most of them considered syncategorematic in function by the time Kilvington was writing.

---

son, *William Heytesbury*, 163–68; Bottin, "Un testo fondamentale"; Kretzmann, "Socrates is whiter"; Courtenay, *Adam Wodeham*, 86–89.

[43] The date of Kilvington's *Sentences* commentary is still under discussion. Inasmuch as he cites an opinion in his commentary that seems to have originated with Adam Wodeham in 1330, and since he was, as of September 26, 1331, referred to only as a master of arts, the earliest date for his reading of the *Sentences* would be 1332–33. At the other end, since he is referred to as a bachelor of theology by August 28, 1335, the latest date for his reading would be 1334–35. Kilvington's familiarity with the early theological opinions of Bradwardine suggests a date around 1333 or 1334, as J.-F. Genest has already proposed; see Genest, "Le *De futuris contingentibus* de Thomas Bradwardine," *Recherches Augustiniennes* 14 (1979): 268.

Many of Kilvington's "difficult" propositions involved the words *incipit* and *desinit*. The analysis of these had a long history, going back to Aristotle's discussions in *Metaphysics* and *Physics*.[44] By the early thirteenth century they had become syncategorematic problems in modern logic and were so treated by Peter of Spain and by William of Sherwood.[45] Kilvington's treatment of these terms was novel in a number of ways. Until Kilvington, discussions of beginning and ending, even as late as Ockham and Burley in the early 1320s, had been limited to their operation in propositions and the effect they had upon supposition. The logic context was still there in Kilvington, but the implications were drawn out to cover problems in physics as well. While previous discussions were applied only to objects (*res permanentes*), Kilvington expanded their applicability to cover *res successivae*, such as motion and time. The result was an analysis of physical problems through logic and mathematics, contributing to the development of rules for uniform motion, proportional speeds, and the concept of limit.[46] In these respects his work paralleled the ideas discussed in Bradwardine's treatise on proportions and anticipated the work of Heytesbury.

William Heytesbury was born around 1312 in the county of Wiltshire and diocese of Salisbury.[47] He matriculated in the arts faculty at Oxford, and by 1330 had become a fellow of Merton College. He wrote his *Regulae solvendi sophismata* in 1335, probably during his regency in arts. His other works, notably his *Sophismata*, his treatises on propositions,

[44] *Metaphysics*, 5, chs. 1 and 17; *Physics*, 3, 5, and 6, esp. ch. 5.

[45] Peter of Spain's *Tractatus syncategorematum*, which may have been written before the work of the same title by Sherwood, has a long section on *incipit* and *desinit*. See Peter of Spain, *Tractatus syncategorematum*, 58–65; William of Sherwood, *Treatise on Syncategorematic Words*, 106–16.

[46] See discussions in Maier, *Die Vorläufer*, 301–3; Bottin, "Un testo fondamentale."

[47] The importance of Heytesbury has been recognized throughout this century, but he was only given detailed examination by Wilson, *William Heytesbury*. What Wilson, Clagett, and others saw as the important contributions of Heytesbury were based on the assumption that the *Regulae* predated a number of other works that contained similar discussions. That assumption is no longer valid, at least as it applies to natural philosophy. Heytesbury's chapter on *'incipit' et 'desinit'* postdates and is dependent upon Kilvington's *Sophismata*. Heytesbury's chapter on *maximum et minimum* is at least contemporary with the treatise of the Franciscan, Roger Rosetus, and it is difficult to tell which is the earlier work, if indeed they are anything more than two illustrations of contemporary discussion. Heytesbury's *De tribus predicamentis* postdates and is dependent on the work of Ockham and Bradwardine.

consequences, and obligations, and his *De sensu composito et diviso* would appear to have been written in the years immediately before or after 1335. Except for a brief period in 1340, when he became a founding fellow of Queen's College, his Oxford years seem to have been spent at Merton. After completing his regency in arts, he entered the theological faculty, becoming a doctor of theology before 1348. He was chancellor of the university in 1371 and possibly also in 1353–54. Those dates would suggest that he may have remained at Oxford after his required regency and, in that event, would have had an unusually long tenure as regent master, some twenty-five years! If that was the case, however, it is strange that he left no commentaries on the *Sentences* or on Scripture. His will was composed in December 1372, a month or two before his death.

Heytesbury's name was a familiar one in late medieval logic and natural philosophy. He authored many short treatises in logic, e.g., on insolubles, consequences, propositions, composite and divided senses, and sophisms, the longest of which were his *Sophismata* and *Regulae solvendi sophismata*.[48] His works were known on the Continent, especially in Italy, and his views were frequently cited.[49] His principal work, the *Regulae*, has been seen as an innovative and influential contribution to the development of mathematical physics, particularly in his definitions and analyses of local motion, velocity, acceleration, difform motion over time, and uniform acceleration. He maintained, for instance, that velocity is to be measured by the distance traversed, local motion by the distance traversed by the fastest moving point in a body, and acceleration by the latitudes of motion acquired. He has been credited with defining uniformly accelerated motion as that in which equal increments of velocity are acquired in equal units of time; and with stating the "mean-speed theorem" that a body undergoing uniformly accelerated motion traverses a distance equal to that which would be traversed in the same time by a body moving at a uniform speed equal to the mean speed of the accelerated body. Much of Heytesbury's work, however, is derivative from contemporary or earlier authors, especially Bradwardine and Kilvington. This seems true for Heytesbury's analysis of in-

---

[48] For the works and manuscripts of Heytesbury see Weisheipl, "Repertorium Mertonense," 212–17.

[49] See the essays by Courtenay, Braakhuis, and Federici Vescovini in *ELI*.

stantaneous velocity and the concepts of limit and infinite aggregate. Until more work has been done on Kilvington's mathematical physics and the relationship of Heytesbury's conclusions to those of Bradwardine and Kilvington, it might be better to speak of the achievements of the Oxford calculators (as is now generally done) rather than the achievements of individual contributors.

The same holds true for the last two major figures associated with Merton College: John Dumbleton and Richard Swineshead.[50] Dumbleton from Gloucestershire was an almost exact contemporary of Heytesbury and was a fellow of Merton by 1338. Except for the brief period (1340) during which he and Heytesbury were founding fellows of Queen's College and his time in Paris, Dumbleton remained at Merton until his death, presumably in 1349, at which time he was a bachelor of theology and had not yet incepted as a master. Richard Swineshead was probably younger, being first mentioned at Merton in 1344–45. His short treatises on local motion and the intension and remission of forms as well as his lengthy *Calculationes* were probably written between 1345 and 1355, at which time he was still at Merton.[51]

Dumbleton's *Summa logicae et philosophiae naturalis*, composed between 1335 and 1349, continued the interests of Bradwardine and Heytesbury in mathematical physics, combined in this instance with the adoption of Ockham's natural philosophy, as we have seen in the previous chapter. Swineshead, whose work is less dependent on Ockham's natural philosophy, applied Bradwardine's treatment of velocities to problems of proportion between force and resistance, transferring discussions of increase and decrease in resistance from a function of time to a function of space. His resistance equations connecting variations in time with variations in space permitted problems of velocity through nonuniform media to be solved as problems of time. Swineshead's work further extended the measuring of qualities and motions in terms of latitudes and degrees.

[50] On Dumbleton see Weisheipl, "Repertorium Mertonense," 210–11; "Ockham and some Mertonians," 199–207. On Swineshead (who must be distinguished from the logician Roger Swineshead), see Weisheipl, "Repertorium Mertonense," 219–21; "Ockham and some Mertonians," 207–13.

[51] Since a disputation by John of Casale in 1352 relies in part upon Swineshead's *Liber calculationum*, the latter can be dated before 1352. Anneliese Maier suggested a date of 1350. There is no reason, however, why it could not have been written as early as 1345.

At the heart of the new physics as pursued by these Oxford scholars was the overriding interest in measuring the interaction of motion, time, and distance, and rendering the conclusions in terms of mathematical formulae and, eventually, line segments that visually graph the ratios and proportions.[52] These approaches were derived, in part, through the exploration of problems in suppositional logic of beginning and ceasing, more and less, maximum and minimum, and the other questions of terminist logic that could be applied to alteration, augmentation, diminution, divisibility, continua, infinites, and a host of other problems that were the common property of logic and physics. Many of these approaches and solutions could, in turn, be applied to problems in theology which, from its side, offered equally fertile soil for the exploration of these problems in logic and physics.

Before turning to the new theology and its integration with logic and physics, however, we need to examine briefly the relation of Ockham's physics to the mathematical physics of the Oxford calculators. It has been argued that the mathematical approach to physics found in these scholars from Merton, Oriel, and Queens was diametrically opposed to the nominalistic physics of Ockham.[53] Such, however, is not the case, as the writings of Heytesbury and Dumbleton at Oxford and Gregory of Rimini at Paris reveal. There is nothing about the quantitative and mathematical approach to physics that requires time, motion, place, relation, and quantity to be real entities apart from individually existing substances and qualities. Although Ockham himself, writing well before Bradwardine and Kilvington, did not pursue either his analysis of syncategorematic supposition or his interest in the intension and remission of forms in the direction of quantification and mathematical for-

---

[52] Manuscripts for Kilvington, Rimini, and Ceffons contain line segment drawings; for example, see Kilvington, *Sophismata*, MS. Vat. lat. 3088, fol. 37[vb], and almost any manuscript of Rimini, *Super secundum sententiarum*, dist. 2, q. 2, a. 1. It is generally assumed that these drawings were introduced into manuscripts after the introduction of line segments by Nicole Oresme. But since the arguments in these authors seem, on occasion, to depend on the illustrations, it is possible that line segment graphs were employed before Oresme and may have been introduced into Paris from English sources in the 1340s.

[53] Maier, *Die Vorläufer Galileis*, 1–52, 132–215; *Zwei Grundprobleme der scholastischen Naturphilosophie*, 3rd ed. (Rome, 1968), 154–60; *Metaphysische Hintergründe der spätscholastischen Naturphilosophie* (Rome, 1955), 141–223; *Zwischen Philosophie und Mechanik*, 3–143; Weisheipl, "Developments in the Arts Curriculum"; "Ockham and Some Mertonians"; "Ockham and the Mertonians," in *HUO* 1: 607–58.

mulae, there was nothing in his outlook that would have prevented his doing so. One must not assume, therefore, that the opposition of Bradwardine and Ockham on the issue of grace and justification had its parallel in the sphere of natural philosophy. And one must also be careful not to misconstrue Ockham's reinterpretation of the category of quantity as a rejection of quantification, or his disallowing "real" status to time, motion, and space as a rejection of the importance of these categories as cardinal features of individually existing things. The fact that things move across space in time was, for Ockham, their most fascinating characteristic.

NINE

Theologica Anglicana

ᴀᴍᴏɴɢ ᴛʜᴇ many theological bachelors reading the *Sentences* at Oxford around 1330 were two mendicant friars whose commentaries quickly became major works in late medieval theology: Robert Holcot and Adam Wodeham. In Holcot's work one finds an extensive application of the new logic to theology, and in the context of theology some further refinements in the logic of tensed propositions and modals.[1] In Wodeham's work, particularly in distinctions one to eight of the first book, one finds an analysis of theological problems in terms of the language of the new physics: augmentation and diminution, rarefaction and condensation, intension and remission of forms, latitude and degree, greatest and least, movement and velocity, beginning and ceasing, instantaneous change, proportion, and infinites.[2]

These two authors reflect the degree to which English theology by 1330 differed from what it had been a generation earlier. Those changes were not due simply to the influence of logic and physics. Many were a result of broader changes in interests and structure that occurred within theology in the second quarter of the century. Some of those shifts were taking place on the Continent at roughly the same time, apparently independent of events in England, but others occurred first

[1] F. Hoffmann, "Robert Holcot: Die Logik in der Theologie," in *Die Metaphysik im Mittelalter*, 2nd International Congress of Medieval Philosophy (Berlin, 1963), 624–39; E. A. Moody, "A Quodlibetal Question of Robert Holkot O.P. on the problem of the Objects of Knowledge and Belief," *Speculum* 39 (1964): 53–74; H. Schepers, "Holkot contra dicta Crathorn," *PhilJahr* 77 (1970): 320–54; 79 (1972): 106–36; F. Hoffmann, *Die theologische Methode des Oxforder Dominikanerlehrers Robert Holcot* (Münster i.W., 1972); H. Gelber, *Logic and the Trinity: A Clash of Values in Scholastic Thought, 1300–1335*, Ph.D. diss., University of Wisconsin, Madison, 1974.

[2] This aspect of Wodeham has been touched on by J. Murdoch, "From Social into Intellectual Factors: An Aspect of the Unitary Character of Late Medieval Learning," in *The Cultural Context of Medieval Learning*, ed. J. Murdoch and E. Sylla (Dordrecht, 1975), 271–348, but it needs further investigation.

in England and only later influenced developments at Paris and elsewhere.

Of Sums and Conclusions: Changes Among and Within Genre

Pan-European shifts among the types of scholastic theological writing in the late thirteenth and early fourteenth centuries include the shrinking importance of *summae theologicae*. These works, composed during the magisterial and post-magisterial period of scholastic careers, had never been as popular in England as they were at Paris in the last half of the thirteenth century, but in all *studia* they ceased to be among the major forms of theological writing by the opening years of the fourteenth century. When works composed later circulated under that title, as in the case of Thomas Bradwardine's *Summa de causa Dei* (completed for circulation in 1344) or Richard Fitzralph's *Summa de quaestionibus Armenorum* (completed for circulation around 1350), they were no longer broad compendia of systematic theology but had become lengthy theological opinions, learned judgments on a limited group of issues and written against a particular position or group of persons.

A decade or so later another favored thirteenth-century genre was gradually abandoned, at least as a vehicle for the circulation of ideas in manuscript form. Quodlibetal debates may have retained their place in the theological faculties, but increasingly after 1320 we find their publication as *quaestiones de quolibet* rare. In England Ockham's *Quodlibeta septem* were among the last examples that circulated widely and were cited as known works. The evidence suggests that quodlibetal disputations continued as an academic exercise engaged in by masters at the universities and by formed bachelors (and perhaps masters) at the major teaching convents in nonuniversity centers. Geoffrey Herdeby's *Quodlibeta*, delivered at Oxford shortly after mid-century, survived for a time in at least one manuscript, but they did not apparently circulate on the Continent.[3] Robert Holcot's *Quodlibeta* have survived in three English manuscripts, yet important as they are for our understanding of Holcot's thought, they were not, to my knowledge, cited by any other

[3] Roth, *EAF*, 1: 548–50.

author.[4] In view of the incomplete state of editing found in the manuscripts of this work and of Holcot's *Sentences* commentary, especially the
high probability that questions original to Holcot's commentaries on the
Sentences and Matthew were included among his quodlibetal questions,
and questions written after he was *sententiarius* included in his *Sentences*
commentary, it is difficult to determine what the final form of either his
quodlibetal or sentential questions was to be and how they were to circulate.[5]

A number of factors probably led to the decline in the publication of
quodlibetal disputations as such. The reduced period of regency
among the mendicants allowed less time for participation in quodlibetal
debates and less time to prepare them for circulation. Unlike *Sentences*
commentaries, which were expected to go through at least one draft before being delivered at a university, which would attract attention as the
bachelor rose to master, and which could be revised during the years
between *sententiarius* and *magister regens*, quodlibetal disputations were
undertaken just before or after inception when the remaining university years were few. The fact that quodlibetal disputations were no
longer the preserve of masters but could be given by formed bachelors
at centers outside universities may have contributed to the declining
status of this genre. Or, as Stephen Brown has suggested with reference
to Walter Chatton,[6] questions originally given as quodlibetal disputations may have been incorporated into revised editions of *Sentences*
commentaries, thus presenting more of the authors speculative theological work within the covers of one manuscript.

As this last view suggests, *Sentences* commentaries themselves were
undergoing changes in the early fourteenth century, perhaps more in

---

[4] Cambridge, Pembroke College, MS. 236, fols. 117–221; London, Brit. Lib., MS. Royal
10.C.6, fols. 141–74; Oxford, Balliol College, MS. 246, fols. 182–264.

[5] Joseph Wey has conjectured that Holcot's *Determinatio* 11, which is included among his
Quodlibeta, is the principium for book 2 of the *Sentences*. For the inclusion in the *Quodlibeta*
of questions drawn from his commentary on Matthew, see Courtenay, "The Lost Matthew
Commentary of Robert Holcot, O.P.," *AFP* 50 (1980): 103–12; H Gelber, *Exploring the
Boundaries of Reason: Three Questions on the Nature of God by Robert Holcot, OP* (Toronto,
1983). On the other side, there are a number of indications that the single question of Book
III of Holcot's commentary on the *Sentences* was written after the completion of book 4.

[6] S. Brown, from a paper presented at the meeting of the American Society of Church
History, Chicago, Dec. 1984, under the title "The Changing Nature of Late Medieval Theology."

England than anywhere else. First of all, they become the single most important source for fourteenth-century theology, either in England or on the Continent. In the thirteenth century they shared prominence with and were sometimes overshadowed by sources from the later, more mature years of a theologian. Such was the case for Alexander of Hales, Albert the Great, Bonaventure, and Thomas Aquinas. With Duns Scotus and his generation *Sentences* commentaries become the principal genre of scholastic theology, sometimes the only source we have for an author. They also proved to be a particularly flexible and adaptive source, absorbing and reflecting the changing interests of that age.

Secondly, we find that *Sentences* commentaries gradually severed their dependence on the structure of Peter Lombard's work and concentrated on those questions that were of most interest to the author and his contemporaries. Wodeham was one of the last English scholastics to make an attempt at relating his questions to Lombard's distinctions. The artificiality of that attempt is clearly revealed by the structure of his Oxford lectures, where the first book ends with the Trinity and the third book begins with future contingents.[7] Despite the enormous length of Wodeham's commentary, the number of theological topics treated has been reduced in comparison to the earlier literature and has been structured around issues central to that age: beatitude and fruition, the Trinity, interrelation of divine will and human freedom, grace and divine acceptation, future contingents, the Eucharist, and questions of penance.

The *length* of Wodeham's commentary (70 questions in all) was, by 1330, also exceptional. Fitzralph and Holcot's commentaries were shorter and contained fewer questions (25 and 19 questions, respectively), and those of William Crathorn, Richard Kilvington, Robert of Halifax, Roger Rosetus, and Thomas Buckingham even shorter. Some of this reduction in size and scope probably resulted from a reduction in the time of "reading" from two years to one, but the length of individual questions, subquestions and *dubia* often increased, and the reduction in the range of topics was counterbalanced by an increased intensity of analysis in those questions chosen for treatment.[8]

[7] Courtenay, *Adam Wodeham* (Leiden, 1978).

[8] One might well wonder whether theologians were reducing the number of questions

A fourth change in the appearance of English *Sentences* commentaries in the second quarter of the century is in the identification of contemporaries within the texts and margins of the scholastic manuscripts. No longer are arguments attributed simply to *quidam* or *alii*. One now encounters the names of fellow masters and bachelors both in the early drafts of *Sentences* commentaries and in the editions finished for circulation. The *alii* had become public.

This shift, as with most changes in the scholastic literature, was not sudden. It was already apparent by the early 1320s. In the manuscripts of Ockham, the authors of the previous generation whose positions are attacked are named, but the names of close contemporaries are absent, as was the custom. University practice discouraged bachelors from attacking contemporary bachelors or masters by name, and throughout the thirteenth century this magisterial expectation was observed, contributing to an atmosphere of depersonalized debate. In the manuscript of Robert Graystanes's *Sentences* commentary, composed at Oxford around 1322, the margins bristle with contemporary names, many of which occur in the text as well.[9] While the same cannot be said for the commentaries of Richard Fitzralph and John of Rodington, the more candid and aggressive display of scholastic confrontation among contemporaries is found in Walter Chatton's *Reportatio* and even more in the Oxford *Lectura* of Adam Wodeham. Subsequent commentaries are not all so rich in references to contemporaries, but a new freedom in this regard was well established, and the numerous references to contemporary opinion found later at Paris in the commentaries of Gregory of Rimini and John Hiltalingen of Basel owe the opening of this possibility to the English authors of the 1320s.

What other changes did the naming of contemporaries reflect, and to

---

to those that already had a logical, physical, or mathematical dimension, which appears to be the case for some questions, or whether they were introducing those analytical tools into questions that were more strictly theological in the earlier period. The reduction in the number of questions has already been noted by P. Glorieux, "Sentences," *Dictionnaire de théologie catholique*, 14 (Paris 1941), 1860–84; and Murdoch, "From Social into Intellectual Factors," 275.

[9] Although a working copy of Graystanes's commentary on the *Sentences*, and thus in a state difficult to work with, this unique manuscript (London, Westminster Abbey MS. 13), is one of the richest and least examined sources for Oxford thought immediately after Ockham and Reading.

what did the practice lead? It probably means that bachelors of theology were permitted, perhaps even encouraged, to engage their university colleagues directly in debate. In the earlier literature an artificially contrived opposing argument was permitted, the position of some fictional opponent. Now the student had to show his familiarity with actual arguments of real opponents, and the growing requirement for more exact wording and location of citations from authorities was now paralleled by exact references to contemporary opinion. Thinly veiled anonymous arguments gave way to exact quotations from identified contemporaries. This could also lead to the surfacing of deeper conflicts in theological perception and approach.

Other changes that are not so apparent on the surface of the manuscripts are the preference for a certain range of topics as well as the adoption of new techniques of analysis and styles of writing in the classroom and *scriptorium*. Since these are even more fundamental to what is meant by fourteenth-century English theology, they deserve closer examination.

Content and Interests

E. A. Moody in an article in 1958 suggested that the strong metaphysical concerns of theologians in the second half of the thirteenth century was a minor current in comparison with the long-standing interests in epistemology and empiricism that were present throughout much of the thirteenth century and which, in the fourteenth century, dominated philosophy and theology.[10] Whether epistemology and empiricism were in fact the major concerns of the fourteenth century, it is certainly true that metaphysical questions and a number of other favored topics of thirteenth-century theology all but disappear from the folios of *Sentences* commentaries and disputed questions in the fourteenth century. Among the topics that disappear or are drastically reduced at Oxford are: theology as a science, its practical or speculative nature, and its subject; the eternity of the world; the Incarnation, Christology and the hypostatic union; providence and predestination (with the major exception of Bradwardine); virtues and vices; angelology; and numerous

---

[10] E. A. Moody, "Empiricism and Metaphysics in Medieval Philosophy," *Philosophical Review* 67 (1958): 145–63.

others. Even when these concerns are reflected in the titles of questions, the content has changed, as with Holcot's question on angels, or Wodeham's questions on Christology, which are actually concerned with future contingents.

The range of topics in English theology between 1325 and 1345 reveals many of the overriding interests of that age. At the beginning of that period, specifically in the commentaries of Robert Graystanes (*c.* 1322), Walter Chatton (*c.* 1322), and John of Rodington (*c.* 1325), there was still an attempt to cover the distinctions of Lombard, especially for book 1, and many of the traditional questions of late thirteenth-century theology were still being treated. Although the number of questions pursued (just under 100 for all three authors) was considerably fewer than for Ockham (171 questions), the practice of devoting more than half the commentary to book 1 was followed by most of these writers. Scotus's formulation of certain questions was copied by many of the Franciscans, and yet changes in the language and structure of some questions in Ockham's commentary was adopted by Chatton and Rodington in theirs. As was mentioned before, Wodeham was the last English theologian to attempt a commentary the size of Ockham's, although with only 70 questions, many of them substantially longer.

The growing role of logic and physics, to be considered in more detail below, is already evident in these commentaries. Ockham uses supposition theory to analyze propositions like "Deus generat Deum," "Deus est Pater, Filius, et Spiritus Sanctus," "Solus Pater est Deus," or "Deus factus est homo."[11] Subjecting these sentences to propositional analysis was already practiced in thirteenth-century commentaries, and a linguistic-grammatical approach to theological statements was at least as old as Anselm.[12] Yet in Ockham and later writers the applications of terminist logic have been refined, and the absence of so many other tradi-

---

[11] Cf. Ockham, *Sent.* 1, dist. 4; dist. 21; *Sent.* 3, q. 10.

[12] The close interrelation of logic, grammar, and theology found in Anselm and later twelfth-century theologians is less apparent in the second half of the thirteenth century. Yet most of the articles of faith that are treated and analyzed as theological propositions by Ockham can also be found in Thomas Aquinas's *Sentences* commentary, although not approached quite in the same way. Similarly, the Dominican Peter of Tarantasia frequently used logic, specifically theories of predication, signification, and supposition, in theological analysis. See, for example, Tarantasia (Innocent V), *Sent.* 1, dist. 4, qq. 3–4; dist. 9, q. 4; dist. 21, q. 1; dist. 24, q. 3; dist. 26, q. 2; dist. 28, q. 3; dist. 31, q. 1; etc.

tional questions makes this type of approach stand out all the more in Ockham and others. Moreover, Ockham's revisionary analyses of relation, motion, time, and quantity are well represented in his commentary.[13] Even the *maximum/minimum* issue receives attention in the third book.[14] Roughly the same amount of use of terminist logic and interest in physics appears in the authors of the 1320s. With Fitzralph in 1328 we have fewer and longer questions, but we also have more of the newer interests reflected: instantaneous change and speed, velocity and motion, intention and remission of forms, successive motion, and infinites.[15] By 1330 the new interests have become thoroughly integrated with theology.

One section of *Sentences* commentaries that reflects both changing interests and changing style are the opening questions of the commentary. Well into the second decade of the fourteenth century at Oxford, these commentaries began with a prologue that traditionally treated such questions as whether theology was a science, what its subject was, whether it was practical or speculative, and sometimes questions on our knowledge of God. The weakening notion of the scientific character of theology had already, by the opening of the fourteenth century, shifted the focus toward epistemological questions, or reformulations of the older ones in the direction of the type of religious knowledge and insight obtained by a simple believer or a student of theology.[16]

At the same time we find the number of questions in prologues being reduced. Ockham devoted twelve questions to his prologue, Chatton seven, Graystanes four, Rodington six, and Wodeham, attempting to preserve the traditional structure, devoted two in his Oxford lectures (as did Holcot and Halifax) and six in his *Lectura secunda*.[17] Fitzralph had no prologue, nor did most of those writing after 1325. Moreover,

---

[13] Ockham, *Sent.* 2, qq. 7–11.

[14] Ockham, *Sent.* 3, q. 8.

[15] Fitzralph, *Sent.* 1, qq. 9–10, 15–16; *Sent.* 2, q. 1.

[16] J. Leclercq, "La théologie comme science d'après la littérature quodlibétique," *RTAM* 11 (1939): 351–74; M. D. Chenu, *La théologie comme science au XIIIe siècle* (Paris, 1957). Note the educational and soteriological focus in the opening questions of Wodeham (Utrum studium theologiae sit meritorium vitae aeternae) and Holcot (Utrum quilibet viator existens in gratia assentiendo articulis fidei mereatur).

[17] A full list of questions in fourteenth-century English commentaries will be published separately.

questions of the scientific and speculative nature of theology disappear
in favor of more epistemological concerns.

New Methods: Tools of Analysis

The first element was a more extensive use of theological *sophismata* in
theological instruction, debate, and lecturing, parallel to the use of similar difficult cases in logic, natural philosophy, or in law.[18] Some of the
problems were drawn from those timeless concerns that had been part
of Christian theology at least since the fifth century: God as both three
and one, divine foreknowledge and human free will, or grace and justification. Others were presented not for their centrality as critical theological problems but because the difficulty of their wording gave ample opportunity to employ the techniques of analysis and solution
acquired from logic. They were good *training* questions for students.

As has been noted, Ockham's *Summa logicae* was written for students
who would be employing that knowledge in solving theological questions or in defending positions that they took or were obliged to take in
debates in the schools. Terminist logic called attention to the way words
were used in propositions, including theological propositions. In addition to the different ways a word stood or supposited for something
else, there were the various meanings the same word could have, depending on context, as well as the way in which an author used or intended a particular word or phrase. Authoritative statements (biblical
or patristic) as well as theological propositions could usefully be approached in this way, and for schoolmen of the fourteenth century
these techniques not only trained skillful debaters but opened the possibility for solving some of the most difficult problems of Christian theology.

The use of the techniques and rules of terminist logic, or the fruitful
parallels that could be drawn between solutions to problems of physics
or geometry and those of theology, was not a one-way street from arts
to theology. Many of the issues, as John Murdoch long ago noted, were
considered common to the fields of mathematics, logic, natural philos-

---

[18] The use of legal *sophismata* or difficult hypothetical cases as a way of testing both a
knowledge of the law and the techniques of "distinguishing" has not yet been adequately
explored. The same methodology and practices were used in the law faculty as in arts and
theology.

ophy, and theology, and the very borders between those disciplines were far less significant then than they are today.[19] Moreover, solutions to these common problems in the theological sphere could be applied to the logical and physical dimensions of the problem, and the theological context could be used to solve problems in logic and physics that had not yet been addressed or only partially covered in commentaries or treatises appropriate to those areas, especially such problems as the intension and remission of forms, latitude and degree, and, to a lesser extent, proportions. The tools of analysis were often the same: the measure or limit languages of beginning and ceasing (*incipit et desinit*), first and last instants (*de primo et ultimo instanti*), and greatest and least (*de maximo et minimo*).

Both at the level of the bachelor attempting to defend himself and his position against the objections of his opponents and at the level of the advanced bachelor and master seeking to solve or improve the understanding of a theological problem, a number of distinctions (many of them used in the other disciplines as well) were employed.[20] The question was always in what sense or senses was a proposition true, and in what sense or senses false, for most problems or propositions in scho-

[19] Murdoch was the first to spell out the close interrelation and mutual interdependence of logic, physics, mathematics, and theology in the fourteenth century. In particular, see his "*Mathesis in philosophiam scholasticam introducta*: The Rise and Development of the Application of Mathematics in Fourteenth Century Philosophy and Theology," in *Arts libéraux et philosophie au moyen âge* (Paris and Montréal, 1969), 215–54; "Philosophy and the Enterprise of Science in the Later Middle Ages," in *The Interaction between Science and Philosophy*, ed. Y. Elkana (Atlantic Highlands, N.J., 1974), 51–74; "From Social into Intellectual Factors"; "*Subtilitates Anglicanae* in Fourteenth Century Paris: John of Mirecourt and Peter Ceffons," in *Machaut's World*, ed. M. Cosman, Annals of the New York Academy of Sciences, 341 (New York, 1978), 51–86. While Murdoch sees these features as characteristic of fourteenth-century thought in general, I see them developing within the century. Although the interest in the application of logic and physics to theology appears at least as early as 1310 at both Oxford and Paris and is probably a more gradual process than our sources suggest, the particular languages and applications that Murdoch has highlighted develop first at Oxford and are only later imported into Paris.

[20] Insufficient attention has been given to the differences between solemn disputations given by masters or formed bachelors, which were often one-person disputations, and those training or examining disputations, often with an *obligatio* structure, between two bachelors or between a bachelor and a master, which were two-person events. The dynamics of the disputation as well as the purpose of "distinguishing" could be and probably often were quite different.

lastic discourse had this dual face. The distinctions did not provide ready-made answers but permitted the theologian or logician to cut through the ambiguities and hidden fallacies in order to "distinguish" the true and false senses of a proposition.

The most common distinction was between the broad (*large*) and narrow (*stricte*) senses of a word or phrase, which in turn could be divided into varying degrees of loose application or strict meaning. A related distinction was between the proper meaning of terms, *de virtute sermonis* (i.e., any form of proper supposition), and their meaning when used as a figure of speech, a colloquial expression, or as specially intended by the author, *ex usu loquendi*.[21] A third distinction, particularly useful in analyzing two-part propositions with confused supposition, relative pronouns of ambiguous reference, conjunctions and disjunctions, or those containing modal, epistemic or volitional terms, was the distinction between composite and divided sense, between whether one affirmed the parts separately (often recognizing a case of potentiality or different moments in time) or conjoined (often implying simultaneity).[22] The famous distinction between propositions considered according to logical possibility or unrestricted divine capacity, *de potentia absoluta*, and those considered according to actual possibility within an ordained system, *de potentia ordinata*, is another of these scholastic devices that functioned in exactly this way.[23]

[21] On the meaning and function of the phrase *de virtute sermonis* see Walter Burley, *De puritate artis logicae*, 1, ch. 6: "De suppositione impropria"; Ockham, *SL*, pt. 1, ch. 77: "De suppositione impropria"; Ph. Boehner, *Collected Articles on Ockham* (St. Bonaventure, N.Y., 1958), 248–53. Contrary to R. Paqué and others, the expression *de virtute sermonis* or *de virtute verborum* is a standard scholastic distinction by the early fourteenth century and is not something specifically Ockhamist. Moreover, Burley, Campsall, Ockham, and others use it as part of a distinction in which *ex usu loquendi* is the other half. The only group known to have limited true propositions only to those that are *de virtute sermonis* true are those attacked in the Parisian arts statute of December, 1340. For further discussion see my "Force of Words and Figures of Speech: The Crisis over *Virtus sermonis* in the Fourteenth Century," *FcS* 44 (1984).

[22] See N. Kretzmann, "*Sensus Compositus, Sensus Divisus*, and Propositional Attitudes" *Medioevo* 7 (1981): 195–229.

[23] See Courtenay, "The Dialectic of Divine Omnipotence," in Courtenay, *Covenant and Causality in Medieval Thought* (London, 1984), 4, 1–37. In exploring the meaning and application of the distinction between considering things *de potentia absoluta* and *de potentia or-*

With all of these distinctions both sides or approaches are implied, whether stated or not. Unless they are seen as a working pair, their function as a distinction will not be apparent. Although some propositions could be false or true in both senses of a distinction, the usual function of these pairs is to point out that viewed in one way a proposition is false, and viewed in the other way it is true.

As of 1330 the potentiality was there for using *sophismata*-solving techniques based on terminist logic to solve theological problems, not simply by creating and applying a "new logic" in theology but by analyzing biblical and patristic statements according to supposition and context. It was, in theory at least, a major exegetical tool. The techniques of the new theology offered a real breakthrough in theological problem solving, opening a new frontier in the discipline, but only if used in that broad and positive way, as was suggested in Ockham's *Summa logicae*. In a more limited context, such as in the defensive techniques of analysis and distinguishing employed by a respondent in a debate, the problem under discussion was not solved in any ultimate sense but only resolved in the context of a particular question. The difference here is in using theological *sophismata* as a way of solving textual problems among doctrinal authorities or as a means of training students to argue on their feet and adequately defend themselves in debate according to a set of accepted rules and procedures. The very techniques that could be used to solve the problems inherent in God's command for Abraham to sacrifice Isaac, or in how "this is my body" functions in the Eucharistic consecration, could be used defensively in a student debate to reject as false biblical statements that were not *de virtute sermonis* true.[24] Depending on how the techniques were used, they could develop or undermine theology.

Here, far more than in *pactum* theology, is where terminist logic and biblical theology interpenetrated and enlightened each other. Throughout the English *Sentences* commentaries of the 1330s and 1340s we find these techniques applied to theological problems and to

---

dinata one needs to examine not only how particular authors define those phrases but how they actually apply them in various discussions.

[24] This was the problem in the arts faculty at Paris in 1340. See *CUP* 2, 505–7. For the circumstances of this statute, see Courtenay and K. Tachau, "Ockham, Ockhamists, and the English-German Nation at Paris, 1339–1341," *History of Universities* 2 (1982): 53–96.

authoritative statements drawn from the Bible or the fathers. Surprisingly, they had far less of an effect on biblical commentaries, perhaps because of the restricting weight of traditional exegesis. There is no evidence to suggest, however, that the new techniques were ever employed in the classrooms of Oxford, Cambridge, or London as defense techniques in student debates in a way parallel to the problems that developed at Paris in 1340.[25] Limiting true propositions only to those that were *de virtute sermonis* true appears to have been a Parisian phenomenon, and even there a small minority position.

The New Style: The Mathematization of Theology

Structuring the teaching and exploration of theology around theological propositions or *sophismata* had its effect on the style of writing as well as the style of debate. Within the increasingly complex and elaborate structures of scholastic argumentation one finds the continual testing of propositions, subjecting them to linguistic analysis, and on occasion the use of *conclusiones* as propositions to be tested, not solutions to be simply adopted. The complex structures for exploring and resolving a scholastic question appear to be a development only partially connected with the influence of logic. Holcot, for example, retained the pivotal point of one main response but preceded it with some ten to twenty subquestions and arguments which, after the proposal, analysis, and discussion of some propositional conclusions, are finally responded to, often at length. That structure can be seen as a more elaborate form of the structure used by Thomas Aquinas in his commentary on the *Sentences*. Wodeham, on the other hand, usually placed his subquestions as *dubia* after the main question had been explored and answered. Wodeham's own position is only gradually revealed as the arguments and counterarguments are explored.

The altered nature of theological "conclusions" is only partially achieved in the English texts of the second quarter of the fourteenth century. At their beginning point in the early fourteenth century they were, as the name suggests, the points being affirmed by the author in response to the question. Later at Paris, for example in the *Sentences*

---

[25] See above, nn. 21 and 24.

commentary of John of Mirecourt, they were additional propositions to be tested as to their various possible meanings, on which their truth or falsity depended.[26] This later use already begins to appear in the Oxford writings of the 1330s, tentatively in Holcot and Wodeham, and far more in Thomas Buckingham, John Stuckley, or in the author of the *Centiloquium*. Appropriate scholastic treatment comes to mean that all propositions, even the tentative conclusions of the author himself, should be subjected to linguistic analysis.

The most revealing instance of the influence of the arts curriculum on theology (or, better, their close interpenetration) lies in the mathematization of theology in the second quarter of the century. On the one hand, this means the degree to which physico-mathematical problems are discussed, even initiated, in the context of theological argumentation.[27] One finds this to be the case with Holcot, Wodeham, Rosetus, Buckingham, Bradwardine, Langley, and others. On the other hand, it also meant that some scholastic works, most notably Bradwardine's *Summa de causa Dei*, were written in an Euclidian style, one proposition or theorem forming the ground for the proof of the next. As Damasus Trapp noted some years ago,[28] the phrase "in more geometrico" describes the theological enterprise at Oxford and Paris, and it was a conception that was born out of the fact that many Oxford theologians had been and still were mathematicians and natural philosophers as well.

[26] For the changing function of *conclusiones* see the introductory essays by Paul Vignaux and André Combes to the edition of John of Ripa, *Conclusiones* (Paris, 1957), 7, 14; Courtenay, "John of Mirecourt and Gregory of Rimini on Whether God Can Undo the Past," *RTAM* 39 (1972): 242–45.

[27] Murdoch, "*Mathesis in philosophiam scholasticam.*" Simo Knuuttila, "Remarks on the Background of the Fourteenth Century Limit Decision Controversies," in *The Editing of Theological and Philosophical Texts from the Middle Ages*, ed. M. Asztalos (Stockholm, 1986), 245–66.

[28] D. Trapp, "Augustinian Theology of the 14th Century," *Augustiniana* 6 (1956): 148, was the first to call attention to this phenomenon: "Maximum and Minimum are concepts in vogue. Algebraic symbols are applied to handle complex entities of the syllogism; pure algebraic reasoning replaces the long and flowing phrase. Is it only a time-saving device or is it a typical logico-critical, a quasi-mathematical manifestation? Geometry becomes an ideal for theology. The Commentaries are arranged *more geometrico*; among the quoted authors those are preferred who reason *more geometrico*. The 14th century introduces the arabic numbers into wide circulation. A new mathematical consciousness is all-pervading, al-

It is difficult at this remove to know the motivation that lay behind the choice of theological topics in England in the fourteenth century. Certainly, many of the topics chosen were ones that provided an opportunity for the application of measure and limit languages, for example the augmentation of grace, the capacity of the soul for infinite beatitude, the beginning moment for a movement toward sin or salvation, or the instant of transubstantiation. These topics also provided contexts for the exploration of other problems in physics, mathematics, or logic. And yet it could as well be argued that the questions chosen for examination were precisely those that were most theologically pressing or challenging for them, and that the measure languages were developed in order to solve problems of intrinsic theological worth. Many questions of interest to thirteenth-century theologians could also have been fruitfully explored through the measure languages but were ignored, as for example the eternity of the world or angelic motion. In examining the areas of fourteenth-century theological concern and the questions they pursued most frequently, therefore, one must give adequate recognition to the importance of the topics chosen, not simply their usefulness as pretexts for logical, physical, or mathematical reasoning. The new analytical tools were so fascinating precisely because they offered a means of solving some of the most important theological questions of that age. In fact, most of the achievements in Oxford logic, mathematics, and physics were accomplished by theologians, either in treatises while they were students of theology, or in their *Sentences* commentaries and other works after they became bachelors and masters of theology.

Personae et Fontes

The names of those who populated the lecture halls of Oxford, Cambridge, London, and Norwich in the period 1320 to 1350 and through whom we gain a picture of English theology in this period are not as yet well known. Therefore it is appropriate that some brief biographical details and comments be given about these authors. It should be kept in mind, however, that they represent only a portion of those who were active during these years, some of whose opinions, for example those of

---

though it does not rise beyond the level of algebra. The theologians accept a new shorthand symbol for *instans*, the zero of time, from the zero sign of India."

Richard Drayton, Nigel of Wavere, and William Skelton, are known only as cited by others.[29]

In the period from 1320 to 1328 we have four theologians who have surviving *Sentences* commentaries: Walter Chatton, Robert Graystanes, John of Rodington, and Richard Fitzralph.

The first of these, Walter CHATTON, was a Franciscan from northern England who was a slightly younger contemporary of John of Reading and William of Ockham, and who, like Ockham, entered the order before the age of fourteen.[30] At some time between 1318 and 1328 Chat-

[29] The chronological order of *Sentences* commentaries and thus their dating has, to a large degree, depended on an author's citations of contemporaries and earlier authors. This method, however, is not as secure as we have thought or would like it to be. The manuscript text of any *Sentences* commentary probably differs somewhat from that delivered in the year or years as *sententiarius*. It may include material from a year or two before the "official" reading, from the period as *sententiarius*, as well as later revisions. Even one of the least revised commentaries, that of Crathorn, can be dated (1330) by its reference to a full eclipse in the year of reading and yet refers to Fitzralph as "doctor," which would have been impossible before Fitzralph's inception in 1331. The number of contemporary authors who cite each other, because of the opportunity provided by the process of revision, has been growing: Ockham and Chatton, Ockham and Reading, Ockham and Marchia, Holcot and Wodeham. These problems do not make precise dating impossible, but they do require more caution than has been exercised.

[30] Only a small portion of Chatton's writings have been published so far: Maria Elena Reina, "La prima questione del prologo del 'commento alle sentenze' di Walter Catton," *RCSF* 25 (1970): 48–74, 290–314; Jeremiah O'Callaghan, "The Second Question of the Prologue to Walter Catton's Commentary on the Sentences. On Intuitive and Abstractive Knowledge," in J. R. O'Donnell, ed., *Nine Mediaeval Thinkers*, Studies and Texts, 1 (Toronto, 1955), 233–69; L. Cova, *Commento alle Sentenze. Prologo, questione terza* (Rome, 1973); L. Cova, "La quarta questione del Prologo del 'Commento alle Sentenze' di Walter Catton," *RCSF* 30 (1975): 303–30; *Reportatio*, 1, d. 3, q. 2: G. Gál, "Gualteri de Chatton et Guillelmi de Ockham controversia de natura conceptus universalis," *FcS* 27 (1967): 191–212; *Lectura*, 1, d. 3, q. 2: N. A. Fitzpatrick, "Walter Chatton on the Univocity of Being: A Reaction to Peter Aureoli and William Ockham," *FcS* 31 (1971): 88–177; *Reportatio*, 2, d. 4, qq. 1–4, and d. 13: K. H. Tachau, "Walter Chatton on Sensible and Intelligible Species," *Rivista di storia della filosofia* (formerly *RCSF*) 40 (1985): 711–48; J. E. Murdoch and E. A. Synan, "Two Questions on the Continuum: Walter Chatton (?), O.F.M. and Adam Wodeham, O.F.M.," *FcS* 26 (1966): 212–88. For biographical information see: Emden, *BRUO* 1: 395–96; C. K. Brampton, "Gauthier de Chatton et la provenance des mss. lat. Paris Bibl. Nat. 15886 et 15887," *Etudes Franciscaines* 14 (1964): 200–205; G. Gál, in the introduction to Ockham, *SL*, 47*–56*; Courtenay, *Adam Wodeham*, 66–74. For interpretive studies, in addition to what is included in the above articles, see L. Baudry, "Gauthier de Chatton et son commentaire des sentences," *AHDL* 14 (1943–45): 337–69; J. Auer, "Die 'skotistische'

ton read the *Sentences* at Oxford and there became regent master around 1330.

Chatton composed two *Sentences* commentaries: a *Reportatio* on all four books of the *Sentences*, which appears to have been delivered around 1321–22 probably at London; and his *Lectura*, an incomplete (it breaks off in book 1, dist. 7) but more thoroughgoing work, which may have been intended as an *ordinatio* and which shows signs of being composed or revised in close association with Ockham while the latter was composing his *Quodlibeta* and his commentary on Aristotle's *Physics*, again probably at London between 1322 and 1324.[31] Whether Chatton lectured as *sententiarius* at Oxford before 1321 and subsequently revised those lectures for circulation (presumably the incomplete *Lectura*), or whether the *Reportatio* and *Lectura* were early versions for an Oxford reading that came after 1324, has not yet been adequately determined. After completing his regency at Oxford, Chatton went to Avignon late in 1332, where he remained in papal service until his death in 1344.

Robert GRAYSTANES was a Benedictine monk from Durham.[32] The

---

Lehre von der Heilsgewissheit Walter von Chatton, der erste 'Skotist,' " *Wissenschaft und Weisheit* 15 (1952): 1–19; C. Knudsen, *Walter Chattons Kritik an Wilhelm von Ockhams Wissenschaftslehre* (Bonn, 1976); L. Cova, "Francesco di Meyronnes e Walter Catton nella controversia scolastica sulla 'notitia intuitiva de re nonexistente,' " *Medioevo* 2 (1976): 227–51.

[31] The dating of Chatton's *Reportatio*, established by Baudry, has stood up in light of subsequent discoveries. Theories as to where it was read, however, have varied. Baudry's assumption that the *Reportatio* was read at Oxford was overturned by Brampton (art. cit.), who argued that Chatton would never have said "Tertio opinio, quae currebat in villa tempore ille quo audivimus in villa (Paris, Bibl. Nat., MS. lat. 15887, fol. 73ra, and Florence, Bibl. Naz., MS. conv. soppr. C.5.357, fol. 171vb) if he were lecturing *in villa*, namely Oxford. Gál went on to establish that wherever Chatton gave his *Reportatio*, Wodeham and Ockham were there as well; see his introductions to Ockham, *Sent.*, 1, 30,* and Ockham, *SL*, 47*– 56*. The collective evidence points to London, but it should be noted that *villa* does not necessarily refer to Oxford. It was a common expression for a university town, and the full text reads: "currebat in villa tempore quo audivimus in villa prophetica Romanorum iam dictis," or in the Florence MS. "villa philosophica Romanorum."

The *Lectura*, which represents a more extensive and later redaction, has been shown by Stephen Brown to have been produced in close proximity to Ockham while the latter was writing his *Quodlibeta* and *Expositio physicorum*, thus probably also at London in the year or two before 1324. Brown has also suggested that some of the new questions in Chatton's *Lectura* may originally have been quodlibetal disputations. Brown, "Walter Chatton's *Lectura* and William of Ockham's *Quaestiones In Libros Physicorum Aristotelis*," in *Essays Honoring Allan B. Wolter*, ed. W. A. Frank and G. J. Etzkorn (St. Bonaventure, N.Y., 1985), 81–115.

[32] The manuscript of Graystanes's commentary (London, Westminster Abbey Library,

sole copy of his *Sentences* commentary suggests a date around 1322, since he is familiar with many authors active between 1310 and 1320, such as Walter Burley, Richard of Campsall, Richard Drayton, John of Reading, and William of Ockham, but does not cite any author after 1320 and refers to Aquinas as Frater Thomas, never Sanctus Thomas. His cautious attitude toward Ockham's views has already been examined. Graystanes was particularly influenced by the thought of the Carmelite theologian Robert Walsingham, and the secular theologian Luke of Ely. A copy of Graystanes's commentary, perhaps the one that survives, was in the Carmelite convent in Oxford around 1542, where it was noticed by Leland.[33] After Oxford Graystanes returned to Durham, where his administrative career culminated in his election by the Chapter as bishop of Durham in 1333, an appointment quashed by Edward III in favor of his former tutor, Richard de Bury.

John of RODINGTON, a Franciscan academically some three years junior to Chatton, lectured on the *Sentences* at Oxford around 1328–29.[34] His Oxford regency is placed around 1333–34, and he became Minister Provincial of England in 1336. The work that has been done so far on Rodington creates a picture of a Scotist who was influenced by Ockham, but further research may well modify that judgment.

MS. 13) is a working draft, probably in the hand of the author. There are numerous internal cross-references (based on an unusual pagination system) and directions for the proper location of blocks of material that make sense only on such a hypothesis. The fact that Graystanes, to my knowledge, is not cited by subsequent authors probably has little to do with his originality or importance but rather with the almost negligible circulation of his commentary, as was the case for Pierre Ceffons at Paris and Clairvaux. In fact, Graystanes's commentary may well be our richest source for Oxford theology in the early 1320s, although no work has been done on him as yet.

[33] John Leland, *De rebus britannicis collectanea*, 6 vols. (London, 1774), 4, 59.

[34] In addition to remarks made in the works of Grabmann, Michalski, and Lang, see J. Lechner, *Jo. v. Rodington, OFM und sein Quodlibet de conscientia*, Beiträge zur Geschichte der Philosophie des Mittelalters, supp. 3.2 (Münster, 1935), 1125–68; Lechner, "Die Quästionen des Sentenz-kommentars des Joh. v. Rodington O.F.M.," *FzS* 22 (1935): 232–48; Lechner, "Kleine Beiträge zur Geschichte des Englischen Franziskaner-Schrifttums im Mittelalter," *PhilJahr* 53 (1940): 75; J. Barbet, "Le Commentaire des Sentences de Jean de Rodington OFM (1348) d'après les mss. Reims 503 et Toulouse 192," *Bulletin d'information de l'Institut de recherche et d'histoire des textes* 3 (1954): 55–63; M. Tweedale, *John of Rodynton on Knowledge, Science, and Theology*, Ph.D. diss., U.C.L.A., 1965; Courtenay, *Adam Wodeham*, 82–83 The limits on the dating of Rodington's commentary are established by the fact that he cites Ockham and in turn is cited by Wodeham.

Finally, for the 1320s, Richard FITZRALPH, a secular theologian from the English settlement in Ireland, lectured on the *Sentences* at Oxford in 1328–29, just before going to Paris for a year of study as tutor of John of Northwode, nephew of John Grandisson, bishop of Exeter.[35] His commentary, in twenty-five questions without prologue, covers the major topics of books 1 and 2, as these would be understood in the late 1320s: fruition and beatitude, the Trinity, the powers of the soul, the augmentation and diminution of charity, future contingents, divine omnipotence, creation, motion, time, angelology, and the fall of man. By contrast, one question each was devoted to books 3 and 4: the operation of the human will, and transubstantiation. Fitzralph, a major figure in church life in Avignon, England, and Ireland throughout the middle years of the fourteenth century, was among the most cited scholastics of the period, both in England and later at Paris, despite the fact that modern historians have seen his thought as far less original and profound than that of many of his contemporaries.

The next decade, 1330 to 1340, marked the high point of English scholasticism, if we are to judge by the number and quality of authors who become well known in England and on the Continent and whose work has survived. The decade began with a trio of close contemporaries: two Dominicans, Robert Holcot and William Crathorn, and the Franciscan Adam Wodeham.

Robert HOLCOT was a Dominican friar from the area of Northampton, who became a bachelor of theology at Oxford in 1329 or 1330.[36] His earliest works are his commentary on the *Sentences*, given as lectures across the biennium 1329–31 or 1330–32 and subsequently (but incompletely) revised for publication, and his *Questiones de quolibet*, which were

---

[35] The literature on Fitzralph is abundant, but most of the earlier work on his career and significance has been superseded by Walsh, *RF*. See also Courtenay, *Adam Wodeham*, 75–81, where the date of Fitzralph's inception should be 1331; and G. Leff, *Richard Fitzralph* (Manchester, 1963).

[36] B. Smalley, "Robert Holcot, OP," *AFP*. 26 (1956): 5–97; Smalley, *EFA*, 133–202; H. A. Oberman, "Facientibus quod in se est Deus non denegat gratiam. Robert Holcot, O.P., and the Beginnings of Luther's Theology," *Harvard Theological Review* 55 (1962): 317–42; F. Hoffmann, "Robert Holcot: Die Logik in der Theologie"; Hoffmann, *Die theologische Methode*; Schepers, "Holkot contra dicta Crathorn"; Courtenay, *Adam Wodeham*, 95–106; Gelber, *Exploring the Boundaries*.

written around 1334.[37] His biblical commentaries, written while he was regent master of theology at Oxford and possibly Cambridge (approximately 1334–37), were exceedingly popular and, alongside the *Sentences* commentary, established him as a major figure in late medieval theology.

Holcot's interest in logic was strong, and one finds throughout his commentary on the *Sentences* and his *Quodlibeta* an interest in treating theological questions from the standpoint of logic. Holcot was particularly fascinated by problems emerging from tensed propositions and the form (thought, spoken, or written) in which propositions were given.

Reading simultaneously with Holcot, but across one year (1330–31) rather than two, was William CRATHORN, a Dominican from northern England, whose commentary has survived in three manuscripts.[38] Crathorn was critical of Ockham and Holcot (often for different reasons), and although Holcot depicted some of Crathorn's positions as absurd, he stands out as one of the more creative and interesting thinkers of the period, arriving at a position on the question of the object of propositional knowledge that paralleled that of Wodeham and was later to receive fame as the "complexe significabile" theory of Gregory of Rimini.[39]

---

[37] See above, n. 5.

[38] Basel, Universitätsbibl. B.V. 30, pp. 1–166 (from the Dominican convent at Basel before 1347); Erfurt, CC Q. 395, fols. 1ᵛ–53ʳ (MS. dated 1341); and Vienna, Nationalbibl., MS. Pal. lat. 5460, fols. 40ʳᵇ–54ʳᵇ. A fourth manuscript, Münster, Universitätsbibl. 175, fols. 1ʳ–25ʳ, 26ᵛ–28ʳ, was destroyed in 1945. On Crathorn see J. Kraus, "Die Stellung des Oxforder Dominikanerlehrers Crathorn zu Thomas von Aquin," *Zeitschrift für katholische Theologie* 57 (1933): 66–88; Kraus, *Quaestiones de universalibus magistrorum Crathorn, O.P., anonymi O.F.M., Io. Canonici, O.F.M.* (Münster i.W., 1937); K. A. Sprengard, *Systematisch-Historische Untersuchungen zur Philosophie des XIV. Jahrhunderts*, 2 vols. (Bonn, 1967–68); H. Schepers, "Holkot contra dicta Crathorn"; V. Richter, "Handschriftliches zu Crathorn," *Zeitschrift für kath. Theologie* 94 (1972): 445–49.

[39] H. Elie, *Le complexe significabile* (Paris, 1936); M. Dal Pra, "La teoria del 'significato totale' delle proposizione nel pensiero di Gregorio da Rimini," *RCSF* 11 (1956): 287–311; E. A. Moody, "A Quodlibetal Question of Robert Holkot, O.P. on the Problem of the Objects of Knowledge and of Belief," *Speculum* 39 (1964): 53–74; N. Kretzmann, "Medieval Logicians on the Meaning of the *Propositio*," *The Journal of Philosophy* 67 (1970): 767–87; F. Hoffmann, "Der Satz als Zeichen der theologischen Aussage bei Holcot, Crathorn, und Gregor von Rimini," in *Der Begriff der Repraesentatio im Mittelalter*, Miscellanea Mediaevalia, 8 (Berlin, 1971), 296–313; G. Nuchelmans, *Theories of the Proposition* (Amsterdam, 1973),

Adam WODEHAM, like Holcot, stands among the recognized intellectual leaders of the period after Ockham.[40] He was a Franciscan from the area around Southampton, and he studied theology at Oxford after studying in the early 1320s at London. His Oxford lectures on the *Sentences* (1330–32) have survived in multiple manuscripts and several redactions, including an abbreviation by Henry Totting of Oyta around 1375, probably composed at Paris. Fragments of Wodeham's London lectures on the *Sentences* have been preserved in a work known as his *Lectura secunda*. A third series of lectures given at Norwich before 1330 have not survived, or at least have not yet been discovered among remaining manuscripts.

Wodeham was a close disciple of Ockham and the editor of some of the works Ockham left behind in England when he went to Avignon in 1324. Yet despite the fact that Wodeham shared many of the presuppositions and conclusions of Ockham, he was also considerably independent in his thought and criticized Ockham on a number of major points, including Ockham's understanding of intuitive cognition and Ockham's rejection of sensible and intelligible species.[41]

One last figure who belongs to this academic generation is Thomas FELTHORP, who read the *Sentences* about the same time as Wodeham.[42]

177–242; W. Eckermann, *Wort und Wirklichkeit* (Würzburg, 1978). On Crathorn's contribution see H. Schepers, "Holkot contra dicta Crathorn," and on Wodeham see G. Gál, "Adam of Wodeham's Question on the 'Complexe Significabile' as the Immediate Object of Scientific Knowledge," *FcS* 37 (1977): 66–102.

[40] Wodeham maintained a formidable reputation for several centuries. John Major, writing in the early sixteenth century, placed Wodeham among the two or three greatest men of letters in England since the Venerable Bede; see Major's introduction to Henry Totting of Oyta's abbreviation of Wodeham's Oxford lectures on the *Sentences* (Paris, 1512). Since my *Adam Wodeham* (Leiden, 1978), which contains references to the literature as of that date, a number of shorter studies on Wodeham have appeared. In addition to the article by Gál, cited in the previous note, see R. Wood, "Adam Wodeham on Sensory Illusions with an Edition of 'Lectura Secunda,' Prologus, Quaestio 3," *Traditio* 38 (1982): 213–52; K. Tachau, "Adam Wodeham on First and Second Intentions," *CIMGL* 35 (1980): 29–55; Tachau, "The Problem of *Species in medio* at Oxford in the Generation after Ockham," *Med-Stud* 44 (1982): 394–443; Tachau, "The Response to Ockham's and Aureol's Epistemology (1320–1340)," in *ELI*, 185–217.

[41] Tachau, "Problem of *Species in medio*"; Tachau, *Vision and Certitude in the Age of Ockham*, Ph.D. diss., University of Wisconsin, Madison, 1981.

[42] Courtenay, *Adam Wodeham*, 85–86; Z. Kaluza, "Quelques traces du commentaire des

Fragments of his commentary have recently been recovered, but they have not yet been studied enough to place him within a context.

Shortly after 1332 two secular masters with considerable reputations in logic and mathematical physics read on the *Sentences* at Oxford. The earlier of the two was probably Thomas BRADWARDINE, who is first mentioned as a bachelor of theology in 1333 but whose commentary has not survived except to the degree it is contained in his subsequent and monumental work, his *Summa de causa Dei*.[43] His treatise on future contingents, which has now been recovered and edited in its full form, was written before 1335, probably around 1332–33.[44] By 1335 Bradwardine had already become notorious for his views on the necessity of events and was so criticized by Kilvington before 1335.[45] After his regency (perhaps 1334–35), Bradwardine left Merton College and Oxford, becoming part of the circle of Richard de Bury, then becoming chancellor of St. Paul's in London (1337), and finally archbishop of Canterbury in 1349, the year of his death.

Richard KILVINGTON, son of a priest from Yorkshire, was a fellow of Oriel College and academically a year or two younger than Bradwardine.[46] His impressive *Sophismata*, as we have seen, was written before

---

sentences de Thomas Felthorp," *Freiburger Zeitschrift für Philosophie und Theologie* 30 (1983): 189–99.

[43] G. Leff, *Bradwardine and the Pelagians* (Cambridge, 1957); H. A. Oberman, *Archbishop Thomas Bradwardine, A Fourteenth-Century Augustinian* (Utrecht, 1958).

[44] J.-F. Genest, "Le *De futuris contingentibus* de Thomas Bradwardine," *Recherches Augustiniennes* 14 (1979): 249–336.

[45] Kilvington, *Super Sent.*, q. 4 (Paris, Bibl. Nat., MS. lat. 14576, fol. 163ra), as cited by Genest, 268: "Ad tertium respondet Bradwardin, dicens omnia evenire de necessitate, et concedit quod Deus deserit prius hominem quam homo deserat Deum."

[46] Emden, *BRUO* 2: 1050; A. Maier, *Die Vorläufer Galileis im 14. Jahrhundert*, 2nd ed. (Rome, 1966), 174, 301–3; Maier, *Ausgehendes Mittelalter*, vol. 1 (Rome, 1964), 75; F. Bottin, "Analisi linguistica e fisica Aristotelica nei 'Sophysmata' de Richard Kilmington," in *Filosofia e Politica, e altri saggi* (Padua, 1973), 125–45; Bottin, "L'*Opinio de Insolubilibus* di Richard Kilmyngton," *RCSF* 28 (1973): 408–21; Bottin, "Un testo fondamentale nell'ambito della 'Nuova Fisica' di Oxford: I *Sophismata* di Richard Kilmington," in *AM*, Miscellanea Mediaevalia 9 (Berlin, 1974), 201–5; Courtenay, *Adam Wodeham*, 86–89; N. Kretzmann, "Socrates is Whiter than Plato Begins to be White," *Nous* 11 (1977): 3–15; Kretzmann, "Richard Kilvington and the Logic of Instantaneous Speed," in *Studi sul XIV secolo in memoria di Anneliese Maier*, ed. A. Maierù and A. Paravicini Bagliani (Rome, 1981), 143–78; Kretzmann, ed.,

1330, and he read the *Sentences* between 1331 and 1335, perhaps around 1333–34, since he is familiar with the theological opinions of both Wodeham and Bradwardine. Although not as widely read or as well known as Holcot or Wodeham, Kilvington's *Sentences* commentary has survived in many manuscripts and was cited frequently by continental authors. Unlike Bradwardine, whose *Sentences* commentary has not survived in its original state, Kilvington provides us with insight into the type of theological writing and thinking done by an Oxford author who was, at the same time, one of the major contributors to logic and physics and whose *Sophismata* was probably written within five or ten years before his *Sentences* commentary. From Oxford, Kilvington went on to join the household of Richard de Bury, and in 1354 he became dean of St. Paul's in London, a position he held until his death in 1361.

During the next few years there were a number of authors whose commentaries on the *Sentences* cannot be precisely dated beyond the fact that they read between 1334 and 1340. Since no one of these, to my knowledge, is cited by any other within that group, the choice of chronological arrangement must remain arbitrary until further research is done.

Robert of HALIFAX was a Franciscan who read the *Sentences*, probably at Oxford, during the second half of the 1330s.[47] His *Sentences* commentary has survived partially or completely in seventeen continental manuscripts, which suggests a popularity also revealed by the frequent citations to his thought. Unfortunately, there are no other known works of Halifax. As with so many others in the period between Wodeham and the Black Death, Halifax's commentary abounds in the use of the measure and limit languages to analyze the most favored theological problems of his decade. His subsequent career and date of death are unknown.

Roger ROSETH or ROSETUS, another Franciscan lecturing at Oxford or Cambridge between 1334 and 1337, shared with Halifax and

---

Infinity and Continuity in Ancient and Medieval Thought (Cornell, 1982), 248–57, 284–96, 331–40.

[47] Courtenay, "Some Notes on Robert of Halifax, O.F.M.," *FcS* 33 (1973): 135–42. Contrary to the information supplied by Michalski, Emden, and Murdoch, the date of Halifax's *Sentences* commentary must be placed in the mid- to late 1330s. He cited the opinions of Wodeham and Bradwardine, and he in turn was cited by Gregory of Rimini.

Wodeham the same strong interest in the new "languages" of logic and physics.[48] Rosetus's commentary begins with the question on which the principal debates around 1332 (i.e., Wodeham and his fellow bachelors) were focused: the infinite or finite capacity of the soul for grace and beatitude. The implications of this question, especially as treated by Rosetus, were so important for logic and physics that the question circulated separately as a treatise *de maximo et minimo*. Rosetus was familiar with the opinions of Wodeham and Bradwardine, which were cited in his commentary. Again, his subsequent career and date of death are unknown.

One of the last of the important Mertonian theologians, Thomas BUCKINGHAM, read the *Sentences* at Oxford between 1335 and 1340, probably around 1336.[49] Reduced to a small number of very extensive questions, Buckingham's *Sentences* commentary focused on the issues of fruition, human volition, and divine omnipotence. A close but critical colleague of his fellow Mertonian Thomas Bradwardine, Buckingham tried in a subsequent work entitled *Quaestiones theologicae*, probably written after 1344, to establish an acceptable middle ground between Bradwardine's position on divine omnipotence, future contingents, and human free will, and the position of the so-called "Pelagians" against whom Bradwardine was arguing.[50] The richness of analysis and argu-

---

[48] V. Doucet, "Le Studium franciscain de Norwich en 1337 d'après le MS. Chigi B.V.66 de la Bibliothèque Vaticane," *AFH* 46 (1953): 85–98; Courtenay, "Nicholas of Assisi and Vatican MS. Chigi B.V.66," *Scriptorium* 36 (1982): 260–63; P. Spade, *The Mediaeval Liar: A Catalogue of the 'Insolubilia'-Literature* (Toronto, 1975), 101–2; J. Murdoch, "From Social into Intellectual Factors."

[49] Emden *BRUO* 1: 298–99; M. D. Chenu, "Les Quaestiones de Thomas Buckingham," in *Studia medievalia in honorem . . . R. J. Martin* (Bruges, 1949), pp. 229–41; Pantin, *ECFC*, 113–15, 263–66; J. A. Robson, *Wyclif and the Oxford Schools* (Cambridge, 1961), esp. 40–69, 83–85, 247–52; Courtenay, *Covenant and Causality in Medieval Thought* (London, 1984), ch. 8; Z. Kaluza, "La pretendue discussion parisienne de Thomas Bradwardine avec Thomas de Buckingham: Temoignage de Thomas de Cracovie," *RTAM* 43 (1976): 219–36; A. R. Lee, *Thomas Buckingham. A critical edition with commentary of the first question of the 'Questiones super Sententias,'* B.Litt. thesis, Oxford, 1975; B. R. De la Torre, *Thomas Buckingham's 'Ostensio meriti liberae actionis,' Conclusiones 1 to 15: 'De contingentia futurorum et arbitrii libertate': An Edition and Study*, Ph.D. diss., University of Toronto, 1979.

[50] A summary of the contents of Buckingham's *Quaestiones theologicae*, written shortly after 1344, is given in Chenu, "Les 'Quaestiones' de Thomas Buckingham." Two manuscripts of this work remain: Oxford, Merton College, MS. 143, fols. 1–83; Oxford, New College, MS. 134, fols. 322–435.

ments found in Buckingham's *Sentences* commentary was emulated and, at times, directly borrowed by Parisian theologians of the 1340s, such as John of Mirecourt.[51] After leaving Oxford around 1340, Buckingham became chancellor of Exeter cathedral in 1346 and appears to have held that position until his death, probably in 1356.

Four other theologians with extant works read at Oxford, Cambridge, or Norwich by 1337. Adam of ELY, known as ADAM JUNIOR to distinguish him from Wodeham, and the anonymous Benedictine, cited always as MONACHUS or MONACHUS NIGER, read the *Sentences* in the same year either at Oxford or Cambridge. Ely was the less controversial and therefore, perhaps, the less cited of the two authors.[52] His theological concerns paralleled those of Buckingham, and Ely was among the earliest authors to cite Bradwardine. Monachus Niger, by contrast, was far more innovative and challenging in his conclusions, thus attracting considerable notoriety among theologians at Paris after 1340.[53]

The *Sentences* commentary of the Franciscan HAVEREL survives only in a *reportatio* version copied by an Italian scribe, Nicholas Comparini of Assisi, as given in lectures at the custodial school in Norwich.[54] The same scribe also preserved the Norwich *Determinatio* of Bartholomew of REPPES[55] and one of the few copies of the *Sentences* commentary of another Franciscan, John WENT,[56] delivered at Oxford around 1336–37.

Our final author from the period before 1340 is Alexander LANGELEY, a Franciscan who lectured on the *Sentences* at Oxford in the closing

---

[51] On Mirecourt's borrowing arguments and authorities from Buckingham see G. Ouy, "Un commentateur des 'Sentences' au xivᵉ siècle, Jean de Mirecourt," thèse de Ecole des Chartes, Paris, 1946; Courtenay, *Covenant and Causality*, ch. 8.

[52] V. Doucet, *Commentaires sur les Sentences* (Quaracchi, 1954), 7–8; Genest, "Le 'De futuris conting.,' " thèse de l'Ecole Pratique des Hautes Etudes (5ᵉ section) (Paris, 1975), xxi, 95–100, 116–26, 189–92.

[53] D. Trapp, "Augustinian Theology," 201–13, 235–39; Trapp, " 'Modern' and 'Modernists' in ms. Fribourg Cordeliers 26," *Augustinianum* 5 (1965): 241–70; Courtenay, *Adam Wodeham*, 90–95; P. Streveler, "Gregory of Rimini and the Black Monk on Sense and Reference. An Example of Fourteenth Century Philosophical Analysis," *Vivarium* 18 (1980): 67–78; L. Kennedy, "Theology the Handmaiden of Logic: A *Sentences* Commentary used by Gregory of Rimini and John Hiltalingen," *Augustiniana* 33 (1983): 142–64; Kennedy, "Philosophical Scepticism in England in the Mid-Fourteenth Century," *Vivarium* 21 (1983): 35–57; J.-F. Genest, "Le 'De futuris conting.,' " (thèse), xxi.

[54] V. Doucet, "Le Studium franciscain de Norwich."

[55] Doucet, "Le Studium franciscain de Norwich"; Courtenay, *Adam Wodeham*, 83–85.

[56] Doucet, "Le Studium franciscain de Norwich."

years of the decade.[57] His commentary has survived in only one manuscript, but he was cited on the Continent by Peter Ceffons around 1348 and by the first author contained in ms. Vat. lat. 986, writing around 1358.[58] His commentary concentrated on the favored questions of fruition, epistemology, augmentation of grace, future contingents, and problems of sin and penance.

After 1340 the number of English authors drops off sharply. In the decade from 1340 to 1350 we have only four theologians whose works have survived. The first is the Benedictine monk of Norwich, John STUCKLEY, whose commentary on the *Sentences* in abbreviated form has survived only in one Clairvaux manuscript, alongside a few other English authors.[59] Under the general problems of the nature of sin and the contingency of the future, Stuckley discussed the infinite capacity of the soul for beatitude, the latitude of forms, finite and infinite intensities, the augmentation and diminution of grace, *maxima* and *minima*, modal and tensed propositions, quantitative and qualitative infinites, the relation of grace and free will, predestination, divine responsibility for sin, and the possibility of the meritorious hatred of God.

Nicholas ASTON was a secular theologian and a fellow of Queen's College at Oxford.[60] His *Sentences* commentary, read at Oxford between 1352 and 1354, has sometimes been compared to that of the Monachus Niger. Despite the controversial character attributed to his commentary by modern scholars, Aston enjoyed a prominent subsequent career. He incepted in 1358 and was chancellor of Oxford from 1358 or 1359 until

---

[57] Courtenay, "Alexander Langeley, O.F.M.," *Manuscripta* 18 (1974): 96–104.

[58] K. H. Tachau, "French theology in the mid-fourteenth century," *AHDL* 51 (1984): 41–80.

[59] See in the first and longer version (thèse) of J.-F. Genest, "Le 'De futuris contingentibus,'" 194–204; Emden, *BRUO* 3: 1809; Courtenay, "The 'Sentences'-Commentary of Stukle: A New Source for Oxford Theology in the fourteenth Century," *Traditio* 34 (1978): 435–38.

[60] Emden, *BRUO* 1: 68; D. Trapp, "Augustinian Theology of the 14th Century," *Augustiniana* 6 (1956): 229–31; Z. Kaluza, "L'Oeuvre théologique de Nicolas Aston," *AHDL* 45 (1978): 45–82; "Le problème du 'Deum non esse' chez Etienne de Chaumont, Nicolas Aston et Thomas Bradwardine," *Mediaevalia Philosophica Polonorum* 24 (1979): 3–19; J. Bender, *Nicholas Aston: A Study in Oxford Thought after the Black Death*, Ph.D. diss., University of Wisconsin, Madison, 1979.

1361. He served as dean of Chichester from 1362 until his death, after 1366.

Osbert PICKINGHAM, a Carmelite, lectured on the *Sentences* at Oxford by 1354.[61] Several copies of his commentary have survived in manuscripts spread across Europe from Bohemia to Spain. In his *Lectura* and *Introitus ad Bibliam* Pickingham treated questions of fruition and cognition, the meritoriousness of actions *ex puris naturalibus*, grace and justification, sin and merit, the freedom of the human will, and transubstantiation. He also revealed his interests in geometry and proportions. As one might expect by this date, he was familiar with Bradwardine, Buckingham, Heytesbury, and Aston.

Finally, an abbreviated *Sentences* commentary by Richard BRINKLEY has recently been recovered.[62] Brinkley was a Franciscan who wrote around mid-century and was the author of an introductory *Logica*, portions of which have now been edited.

AREAS OF APPLICATION

Logic and Theology

We have already examined briefly three of the areas in which the new logic was applied in theology: the use of theological *sophismata* for both teaching and analysis; the application of linguistic analysis to theological propositions; and the use of distinctions common to logic and theology in the fourteenth century. No other area of theology shared so common a boundary with logic, however, as the topic of the divine nature and attributes. Questions on this topic occupy fully a third of Fitzralph's *Sentences* commentary, almost a quarter of Wodeham's and a similar amount in Holcot's. If one includes problems of future contingents within this framework, its importance for the period up to 1332 is even greater.

Foremost was the problem of the Trinity: God as three and one, which disconcertingly but intriguingly went directly counter to mathematics and Aristotelian logic. Their indisputable belief of the triune nature of the one God, however, meant that Aristotelian logic had to be

---

[61] Xiberta, *SOC*, 241–84.

[62] Emden, *BRUO* 1: 267–68; G. Gál and R. Wood, "Richard Brinkley and his 'Summa logicae,'" *FcS* 40 (1980): 59–101. An edition and study of the abbreviation of Brinkley's *Sentences* commentary is being prepared by its discoverer, Zenon Kaluza.

modified or supplemented in a way that would bring it into conformity with belief. From Campsall and Harclay in the second decade of the century to Holcot and Wodeham two decades later, new rules were developed to solve the paralogisms built into the doctrine of the Trinity.[63]

The close association of logic and trinitarian theology goes back to the earliest stage of the development of scholastic theology. The prominent Aristotelian character of Boethius's *De trinitate*, which was widely read and commented on in the early twelfth century, led theologians of that period to explore the parallels and interrelationships between the Trinity and the problem of universals. That approach was modified in the course of the twelfth century, and already in Lombard's *Liber sententiarum* many of the questions on the Trinity in book 1 were centered around reasons for the validity or inappropriateness of propositions about the Trinity. The developments of terminist logic in the first half of the thirteenth century, particularly the treatises on exponibles and *syncategoremata*, provided advanced means for analyzing trinitarian propositions. The results can be seen in book 1 of the *Sentences* commentaries of Bonaventure, Aquinas, and others.

The advances of the fourteenth century in this regard were not, therefore, in the use of logic or even terminist logic, but in the changing nature of proposed solutions to specific problems and a reliance upon the continuing developments in English logic in the early fourteenth century. It was particularly fertile ground for the investigation of fallacies and the development of "rules," such as the *regula Anselmi*, or the *ars Campsale*.[64] Various distinctions were developed to adjust or accom-

[63] On the *ars Campsale* and the developments in fourteenth-century logic applicable to paralogisms on the Trinity, see: F. Hoffmann, *Die theologische Methode*; H. Gelber, *Logic and the Trinity*; H. Gelber, *Exploring the Boundaries of Reason*; A. Maierù, "Logica aristotelica e teologia trinitaria. Enrico Totting da Oyta," in *Studi sul XIV secolo in memoria di Anneliese Maier*, ed. A. Maierù and A. Paravicini Bagliani (Rome, 1981) 281–512. "Logique et théologie trinitaire: Pierre d'Ailly," in *PRUP* 253–68; "A propos de la doctrine de la supposition en théologie trinitaire au xivᵉ siècle," in *Mediaeval Semantics and Metaphysics*, Studies dedicated to L. M. de Rijk, ed. E. P. Bos (Nijmegen, 1985), 221–38; "Logique et théologie trinitaire dans le moyen-âge tardif: deux solutions en présence," in *The Editing of Theological and Philosophical Texts*, 185–201.

[64] The "rule" of Anselm used by Richard of Campsall (*ars Campsale*) to reject formal nonidentity in the Godhead stated that "in God all properties as well as the divine essence are one where the opposition of relation does not stand in the way." See H. Gelber, *Logic and the Trinity*, ch. 6. The development of axiomatic rules that could be applied in theology par-

modate Aristotelian logic to trinitarian belief, such as a distinction of reason, or the Scotistic formal distinction of nonidentity. Even Ockham, who rejected the formal distinction on the level of creatures, accepted it as applied to the Godhead.[65]

The years 1330–34 mark a crisis for the applicability of logic to problems of trinitarian theology. Holcot in his *Sentences* commentary rejected the distinction of nonidentity and argued that in logic and nature there was only identity or real distinction.[66] In light of that, Holcot called for the development of a new logic of faith that would cover those theological issues that would not work within the confines of Aristotelian logic. Subsequently in his *Quodlibeta*, probably around 1334, Holcot modified his view, affirming that in order to be valid, the subject of the premises of an expository syllogism cannot be one and many.[67] The inapplicability of Aristotelian logic for many propositions and syllogisms about the Trinity was, therefore, not unique to those problems but applied to any syllogism in which a fallacy of accident occurred. This solution, worked out initially by Aureoli, Campsall, and Ockham, was also adopted by Wodeham.[68]

Discussions of the persons of the Trinity naturally opened up the whole range of appellation (meaning, appropriateness, and interchangeability of the divine names), supposition (what the names as used in propositions stand for, and the truth or falsity of propositions in which the names are exchanged or substituted), and relation (between persons of the Trinity, or between person and abstract noun, such as paternity or filiation). Some of the subtle shifts within what was otherwise a common approach can be illustrated by comparing treatments of book 1, dist. 21.

Lombard had provided numerous possible points of discussion in this distinction, but all of them centered on propositions that included the term "solus", as in "The Father alone is Father." The one that attracted the most attention, however, was that discussed in chapter 2:

---

allel to rules in logic was already apparent in Alain de Lille's *Regulae theologiae* (*PL* 210, 621–84).

[65] Ockham, *Ordinatio* 1, d. 2, q. 11 (2: 360–72); H. Gelber, *Logic and the Trinity*, 172–85.

[66] Holcot, *Sent.* 1, q. 4, ad 5 prin. arg.; text cited in H. Gelber, *Exploring the Boundaries of Reason*, 26–27, n. 72. See also F. Hoffmann, *Die theologische Methode*.

[67] Gelber, *Exploring the Boundaries of Reason*, 27–28.

[68] Gelber, *Logic and the Trinity*.

"*Solus Pater est Deus*," which was to be rejected as false unless, as Lombard added, it occurs within an authoritative statement.[69]

The distinction naturally lent itself to discussions of the ambiguity that occurs when terms that express relationships ('father,' 'son') are also proper names. But most of the attention was focused on the nature of exclusives. As Alexander of Hales noted in his brief comment on this distinction, statements such as "The Father alone is God" or "The Son alone is God" could not be simply rejected as heretical, since in the Gloria the church sings "Tu solus altissimus, Jesu Christe" without intending to say that the Father is not also "the Highest."[70]

Most thirteenth-century theologians treated the distinction at some length, including Bonaventure, Thomas, and Scotus.[71] In his *Sentences* commentary Thomas emphasized the propositional nature of his approach: "Whether this proposition, 'God alone is God,' be false"; "Whether this proposition: 'The Father alone is God,' be true"; "Whether this proposition: 'The Trinity is God alone,' be true"; "Whether the Father be God alone." Thomas approached the term "solus" according to whether it was being used categorematically or syncategorematically. In his *Summa theologiae*, while retaining his remarks on the categorematical and syncategorematical senses, Thomas focused more on the nature of exclusive words and propositions, discussing the particular trinitarian propositions within the body of the question. The corresponding titles now ran: "Whether an exclusive expression, which seems to exclude otherness, can be joined to an essential name in God"; and "Whether [an exclusive expression] can be joined to a personal term." For Thomas, if "The Father alone is God" is understood to mean that "Only the Father is God," thus excluding the Son and Holy Spirit, the proposition is false. But if it is understood in the sense that "He, who alone is the Father, is God," then the proposition is true. Ockham

---

[69] Peter Lombard, *Sententiae in IV libris distinctae*, vol. 1 (Grottaferrata, 1971), 175–76: "sed non videtur debere dici a nobis, verbis nostris utentibus, nisi ubi sermo auctoritatis occurrit: 'solus Pater est Deus' vel 'Pater est solus Deus.'"

[70] Alexander of Hales, *Glossa in quatuor libros sententiarum Petri Lombardi*, vol. 1 (Quaracchi, 1951), 213.

[71] Bonaventure, *Sent.* 1, d. 21, a. 1–2 in *Opera Omnia*, vol. 1 (Quaracchi, 1882), 379–86; Thomas, *Sent.* 1, d. 21, q. 1–2 in *Opera Omnia*, vol. 1 (Stuttgart, 1980), 58–60; Thomas, *Summa theol.* 1, q. 31 in *Opera Omnia* 2: 233–34; Scotus, *Ordinatio* 1, d. 21, q. un. in *Opera Omnia*, ed. C. Balić, vol. 5 (Vatican, 1959), 323–38.

adopted a similar position but stated the question in a more "terminist" way: "Whether this ought to be conceded *de virtute sermonis*: 'The Father alone is God.' "[72] Although the actual treatment of Thomas, Scotus, and Ockham did not differ greatly, those who dealt with the distinction or issue after 1320, such as Rodington and Wodeham, looked toward Scotus's formulation as the most satisfactory.[73]

Perhaps the most remarkable development in the scholastic treatment of trinitarian theology came around 1334. The long continuity of exploring trinitarian problems from the perspective of logic crumbled, and with it the dominant part trinitarian theology had in the *Sentences* commentaries of the early fourteenth century. As has been remarked, the attempt to cover adequately at least the first book of Lombard's *Sentences* was abandoned, and in the reduced scope and freer choice of the post-1334 period, problems of trinitarian theology lost their hold on English theologians in favor of a short list that included problems of the will, sin, law, grace, future contingents, and transubstantiation. And while these problems might not employ terminist logic to the same degree, they did employ the language and tools derived from the integration of logic and physics.

Three problems traditionally handled in book 1 of the *Sentences*, because they derived from discussions of the divine persons and attributes, were grace and justification (under gift of the Holy Spirit), divine foreknowledge (under divine omniscience), and divine omnipotence. All three issues retained their place on the reduced list of important topics, and the last two continued to provide a setting in which purely logical analysis was employed.

From the standpoint of logic, both these topics provided an avenue for the exploration of the character of tensed as well as modal propositions. Divine foreknowledge raised the problem of the necessity or contingency of future events and, with it, the question of whether propositions about the future functioned differently than propositions about the present or past. This was joined with questions about the nature of

[72] Ockham, *Sent.* 4: 38–44.

[73] Rodington, *Sent.* 1, d. 21, q. un. (Assisi MS. 133, fols. 64vb–65rb), and Wodeham, *Lectura secunda*, d. 21 (Cambridge, Gonville and Caius MS. 281, fol. 229^v).

time, the relation of time and eternity, and the contrast between future and past that associated contingency with the former and necessity with the latter.

Throughout the late thirteenth and early fourteenth centuries the view that God existed in eternity, outside the flow of time, allowed a number of solutions to the problem of future contingents to be worked out that did not permit the certainty of divine foreknowledge to erode the indeterminacy of the future, which most felt must remain open for human choice and potentially meritorious action. Aside from those future events revealed in scripture, such as "the Antichrist shall come," mental, spoken, or written propositions of those living in time were not directly linked to divine foreknowledge. From the late 1320s, however, discussion focused on *revealed* future contingents, either biblical examples (such as Christ's statements about the Antichrist, the general Resurrection, his Second Coming, or the Final Judgment) or conjectured new revelations (such as the possibility that God might reveal to someone his own salvation or damnation).[74]

Increasingly in the atmosphere of English theology in the 1320s and 1330s the issues of divine omniscience and omnipotence influenced one another. Did divine omniscience imply that events could never be otherwise and thereby restrict human freedom and the power of God? Could God know more than he knows, or other than he knows? Could God change events and thereby alter his knowledge of them? Here, as on the equally fascinating human level, cognition and will not only had the ability to inform one another but to operate at the expense of the other.

Thus there were developed a number of problems that brought into tension the issues of divine knowledge and volitional power. Bradwardine's emphasis on the certainty of divine foreknowledge and predestination seemed to contemporaries to argue for the necessity of all future events, while his emphasis on divine omnipotence seemed simultaneously to make all past events contingent, since for Bradwardine they should not be exempt from the will and power of God.[75]

---

[74] In the late 1320s a certain Master Walter argued that a future event, once revealed, is no longer contingent but happens of necessity. His opinion was cited by Wodeham (*c.* 1332) and by Holcot (*c.* 1334). For the texts see Courtenay, "Augustinianism at Oxford in the Fourteenth Century," *Augustiniana* 30 (1980): 67.

[75] The full text of Bradwardine's treatise on future contingents has been edited by J.-F.

These developments gave new life to the analysis of the proposition that "God can make the world (or any past event) not to have been."[76]

These questions were usually approached by analyzing the senses of a proposition, employing the various scholastic distinctions, and looking closely at the meaning and applicability of such terms as 'necessary,' 'contingent,' 'possible,' 'impossible,' 'able,' 'can,' 'could,' 'may,' 'might,' 'believe,' 'will,' 'know,' and other epistemic or modal words. From the standpoint of scholastic theology, there was the expectation that some of the most troublesome issues that plagued the understanding of the interaction of divine knowledge or power and human free will might, through propositional analysis, be solved.

Fruition and the Human Will

The enjoyment of the proper goal of human nature, namely the love of God and final beatitude, was the opening and concluding topic of Lombard's *Sentences* and as such invariably received some treatment in traditional commentaries that followed Lombard's arrangement. Discussions of these issues were prominent in the *Sentences* commentaries of Scotus, Durand, Aureoli, and Ockham, but they intensified in the 1320s and 1330s, in part because of the controversy over the Beatific Vision occasioned by the statements of John XXII to the effect that there was no Beatific Vision until the Final Judgment.[77] Not resolved until Benedict XII's constitution in 1336,[78] that controversy was particularly sensitive for English theologians. One of the major opponents to Pope John's position was the English Dominican theologian, Thomas of Waleys, who was hunted, arrested, and imprisoned at Avignon until the pontificate of Clement VI, despite outcries from the Dominicans and

---

Genest, "Le *De futuris contingentibus* de Thomas Bradwardine," *Recherches Augustiniennes* 14 (1979): 249–336; Bradwardine, *Summa de causa Dei*, ed. H. Saville (London, 1618). For further discussion see Courtenay, "John of Mirecourt and Gregory of Rimini on Whether God Can Undo the Past," *RTAM* 39 (1972): 224–56, 40 (1973): 147–74, repr. in *Covenant and Causality in Medieval Thought*, ch. 8; "Augustinianism at Oxford," 58–70.

[76] See Courtenay, "John of Mirecourt."

[77] *Enchiridion Symbolorum*, ed. H. Denzinger and A. Schönmetzer, 32nd ed. (Rome, 1963), 295.

[78] For the critical portions of the constitution "Benedictus Deus" of January 29, 1336, see *Enchiridion Symbolorum*, 296–97.

from numerous theologians at Paris and Oxford.[79] Moreover, Walter Chatton, one of the leading English theologians of the second quarter of the century, was on the commission to review the doctrine of the Beatific Vision and propose theologically acceptable wording. While it lasted, the controversy influenced discussions not only of volition and beatitude, but of epistemology, the operation of vision, soteriology, and eschatology.

Insufficient attention has been given to the extent to which scholastic writers of the first half of the fourteenth century developed a philosophy of human psychology. Gilson observed this dimension of Ockham's thought and labeled it "psychologism," "the first known case of a new intellectual disease" that attempts to solve philosophical problems by means of psychological analysis.[80] Stephen McGrade, by contrast, has forcefully argued that this aspect of fourteenth-century philosophy is as potentially rich for those working in the history of the behavioral sciences as fourteenth-century logic has proven for contemporary analytic philosophy.[81]

The setting for this examination of the meaning and interrelation of such mental operations as cognition and volition as well as such human emotions or states as hatred, sorrow, love, enjoyment, and pleasure was, again, the problem of fruition and beatitude. Ockham and the Franciscan majority within English theology in the early fourteenth century rejected Thomas's view that fruition or enjoyment (*fruitio*) was a cognitive act and the Beatific Vision an intellectual vision.[82] The actual beginning point for Ockham's treatment of the subject, however, was Peter Aureoli's provocative assertion that enjoyment, as a form of love, is identical with pleasure.[83]

Aureoli divided all volition into four types: two negative psychic

<hr/>

[79] Th. Kaeppeli, *Le procès contre Thomas Waleys O.P.* (Rome, 1936); B. Smalley, "Thomas Waleys O.P.," *AFP* 24 (1954): 50–57; Smalley, *EFA*, 75–79.

[80] Etienne Gilson, *The Unity of Philosophical Experience* (New York, 1937), 86–90.

[81] A. S. McGrade, "Ockham on Enjoyment—Towards an Understanding of Fourteenth-Century Philosophy and Psychology," *Review of Metaphysics* 34 (1981): 706–28.

[82] Ockham, *Ordinatio* 1, d. 1, q. 2. For some earlier background see P. Nash, "Giles of Rome and the Subject of Theology," *MedStud* 18 (1956): 61–92.

[83] Aureoli, *Scriptum* 1, d. 1, sect. 7, nn. 50–56, ed. E. Buytaert, vol. 1 (St. Bonaventure, N.Y., 1953), 397.

states: sadness (*tristitia*), caused by the absence of a desired object; and a desire to flee (*fuga*), caused by the presence of a repelling object; and two positive psychic states: desire (*desiderium*), caused by an object not yet possessed; and pleasure (*delectatio*), caused by gaining the object. The two negative volitions were considered forms of hate (*odium*) and the two positive volitions forms of love (*dilectio*). Total avoidance and total pleasure are the two extremes; sadness and desire stand in the middle and, although usually opposing states with different objects, could, when generated by the same object, describe the conflicting sensations of emotional love, corporeal or spiritual.

That structure provided the common framework for subsequent discussion. The disturbing feature of Aureoli's formulation, however, was his view that we desire and love an object because it is pleasurable. As McGrade has expressed it, Aureoli "made pleasure the beginning as well as the end of all volition and behavior."[84]

Ockham distinguished love (*dilectio*) and enjoyment (*fruitio*) from pleasure (*delectatio*), as had Scotus.[85] Enjoyment was a form or type of love and was, in fact, the cause of pleasure, not identical with it. But in contrast to Scotus's grounding of pleasure in the object, Ockham saw pleasure as immediately resulting from the act of the will. Things are pleasurable as a result of the intention to love, the volition of love. One must positively will something before pleasure is experienced. To put it another way, the degree of pleasure we derive from an act is a result of and in proportion to the degree of enjoyment we put into it. Enjoyment precedes and produces pleasure. One can also have enjoyment without pleasure. One could, out of love for God and a desire to fulfill the divine will, accept the fact that one is not predestined, if such should be revealed.[86] It is possible to derive enjoyment from an act of love that foregoes pleasure, both in life and religious experience.

[84] McGrade, "Ockham on Enjoyment," 712.

[85] Scotus, *Ordinatio* 1, d. 1, p. 2 q. 1; *Reportata Paris.*, 1, d. 1, q. 3; Ockham, *Sent.* 1, d. 1, q. 3 (1: 403–28).

[86] Willing one's own damnation out of a desire to conform to the will of God, and the related problem of the hatred of God, are discussed in detail later in this chapter. Ockham's approach to this issue is shaped by the principle of separability (his belief that certain emotional states and acts of the will normally found together can be separated) and the principle of the freedom of the will (both the right not to be compelled and to will the opposite, and the right to conform and yet choose a less appropriate or inappropriate form

McGrade has correctly noted that Ockham's exploration of love as distinct from pleasure is part of a "general account of human motivation."[87] And although Ockham was primarily interested in the love and enjoyment of God both in this life and in the Beatific Vision, he also acknowledged and validated lesser types of "non-referring volitions." Things other than God—the Aristotelian virtues, for example—could legitimately be loved for their own sake. So long as they are not cherished as the highest possible good, they could be enjoyed and not simply "used" in reference to a further volition directed at God. Such valuings or loves were not morally defective but were valid "middle acts" of the will in between enjoyment and use.[88]

As this last point reveals, this entire discussion of volition and motivation was conducted in a way that concentrated on the psychological act, and only secondarily on the object of that act. What was being worked out, both in England and on the Continent, was a total analysis of human motivation and behavior that would theoretically cover daily

---

of response). Ockham, *Sent.* 1, d. 1, q. 6 (1, esp. 504–5): "Tertia conclusio est quod aliquis potest nolle beatitudinem in particulari creditam esse possibilem, ita quod potest nolle habere beatitudinem. Haec conclusio persuadetur, quia quidquid potest esse dictatum a recta ratione potest cadere sub actu voluntatis; sed recta ratio potest dictare quod iste carebit semper beatitudine; ergo potest velle carere semper beatitudine, ergo potest nolle eam sibi. Confirmatur, quia damnatus, tam poena sensus quam poena damni, posset, si sibi relinqueretur, conformare se divinae voluntati, tam scitae quam creditae, in volito; sed voluntas divina vult istum semper carere beatitudine; ergo potest hoc esse volitum a voluntate tali, et per consequens eadem ratione a voluntate viatoris." (1: 505): "Quaelibet voluntas potest conformari voluntati divinae in volito; sed Deus potest velle ipsum pro semper carere fruitione beatifica; ergo etc." See also *Sent.* 1, d. 48 (4: 686–91); *Sent.* 2, q. 15 (5: 338–58); *Sent.* 4, q. 16 (7: 340–61). Indeed, if love and fruition are to be free acts of the will (and they must to be meritorious), then they cannot be necessarily compelled by the clear vision of God. One must be able to behold and know God without the response of love, and be able to love and enjoy without concomitant pleasure. Ockham, *Sent.* 1, d. 1, q. 3 (1: 420): "Ad istum respondeo quod si posset probari quod per potentiam [absolutam] divinam unum esset separabile ab alio et non e converso, posset forte probari causalitas in uno respectu alterius et non e converso. Et ita si non posset esse delectatio sine actu volendi,—cum sit probatum prius quod potest esse actus volendi sine delectatione—, sequetur quod actus sit causa. Tamen dico quod naturaliter sunt separabiles, ita quod actus volendi potest esse sine delectatione et non e converso."

[87] McGrade, "Ockham on Enjoyment," 715.

[88] Ockham, *Sent.* 1, d. 1, q. 1 (1: 376): "Ad primam dico quod est actus talis medius quo aliquid amatur nec tamquam finis simpliciter ultimus nec actualiter refertur in aliud." See also *Sent.* 1, d. 1, q. 4.

experience and interpersonal relations as well as religious experience. As for the religious experience, Ockham maintained that one could, in this life (*in via*), on the basis of one's own innate natural powers (*ex puris naturalibus*) enjoy God as the supreme object of love.[89]

It was exactly these issues that were explored in the intensive discussions on acts of the will in the *Sentences* commentaries of the next three decades. Gordon Leff observed that Fitzralph's questions concerning the nature of willing were the most systematically explored in his *Sentences* commentary.[90] In combination with discussions of the other acts of the soul, specifically cognition, memory, love, and enjoyment, this theme occupied a third of the questions in Fitzralph's work. And although much of Fitzralph's treatment was in the world of the late thirteenth century, dominated by the contributions of Thomas, Henry of Ghent, Scotus, and such questions as the priority of intellect or will, his contemporary awareness is reflected in his use of Aureoli's arguments, his opposition to Ockham's view that the faculties of cognition and volition are not distinct from the soul itself, and his exploration of the problem of initiating an act of the will as part of the larger problem of beginning and ceasing, first instants of action or change, and immediate or successive motion.[91]

Exploring problems of the will in terms of motion and change as well as causes and motivation was already apparent in Graystanes's treatment of fruition, which included discussions of motion, velocity, proportion, and the vacuum.[92] Graystanes also found much of Scotus's and Ockham's reasoning on these issues convincing. He shared the views that things other than God could, *inordinate*, be enjoyed, and that pleasure was really distinct from and a result of operations of willing and loving.[93] Similarly, Rodington, against Aureoli, distinguished enjoyment

---

[89] Ockham, *Sent.* 1, d. 1, q. 2 (1: 396–97): "Dico primo quod obiecto fruibili ostenso voluntati per intellectum sive clare sive obscure sive in particulari sive in universali, potest voluntas active elicere actum fruitionis, et hoc ex puris naturalibus, circa illud obiectum."

[90] Leff, *Richard Fitzralph*, 109.

[91] Fitzralph, *Lectura in sententias*, 1, qq. 5 and 9; Leff, *Richard Fitzralph*, 93–95, 110–37.

[92] Graystanes, *Sent.* 1, d. 1, q. 1 (Westminster Abbey, MS. 13, pp. 158, 165).

[93] Graystanes, *Sent.*, 1, d. 1, q. 1 (Westm. 13, p. 158): "Quod aliud a Deo potest esse obiectum fruitionis inordinate." "Dico quod aliud a Deo potest esse obiectum indebite fruitionis." (Westm. 13, p. 171), where he opposes the position of Aureoli.

from pleasure, viewing the former as the cause of the latter.[94] Curiously, while ostensibily attacking Scotus on the question of whether one can enjoy the divine essence and not the persons, or one person and not the others, Graystanes was not persuaded by Ockham's critique but developed a view close to that of Scotus. In the beautified state and not just *in via* one can enjoy the essence without the persons, or one person without the others, although this was viewed as within the capacity of the will taken by itself (*absoluta*), or an actual possibility (*ordinata*) if not contrary to divine command.[95]

Wodeham, in contrast to what one might expect, expanded on some aspects of Ockham's position, but rejected others. Although intellect and will, as powers of the soul, are identical with the essence of the soul for Wodeham, the acts of cognition and volition are separate (*res distinctae*) from the soul itself, and consequently love (both *amor* and *dilectio*) as well as enjoyment (*fruitio*) are *res distinctae*.[96] Neither in this life (*in via*) nor in the beatific state (*in patria*) is the soul identical with the fruition of God, because fruition is freely caused by the soul.[97] Similarly, cognition and fruition are really distinguished in the sense that the knowl-

[94] Rodington, *Sent.* 1, d. 1, q. 6, a. 1 (Bruxelles, Bibl. roy., MS. 1552, fol. 35ᵛ): "Quantum ad primum est una opinio [Ock.] quae ponit 4 conclusiones. Prima quod fruitio et delectatio distinguntur realiter." Ibid., a. 2 (Bruxelles 1552, fol. 36ʳ): "Et teneo istam conclusionem quod delectatio est qualitas distincta realiter a dilectione. . . . Secunda conclusio quod cognitio et dilectio sunt causae immediatae delectationis." Ibid., a. 4 (Bruxelles 1552, fol. 37ʳ): "Ad argumentum principale dico quod Deus potest facere de potentia absoluta fruitionem sine delectatione."

[95] Graystanes, *Sent.*, 1, d. 1, q. 1, a. 4 (Westm. 13, p. 161): "Dico quod viator ordinate potest frui una persona non simul fruendo omnibus." Ibid. (Westm. 13, p. 165): "Ergo teneo quod tam in via quam in patria potest voluntas frui una persona non fruendo alia, et essentia non fruendo persona, de potentia voluntatis absoluta. Et idem teneo de potentia voluntatis ordinata, nisi fuerit aliquod praeceptum in contrarium ordinatum."

[96] Wodeham, *Lectura Oxon.*, 1, d. 1, q. 2, a. 2 (Paris, Univ., MS. 193, fol. 16ᵛᵇ): "Sed istis non obstantibus, teneo partem oppositam, quod fruitio est res distincta ab anima." Cf. Ockham, *Sent.* 2, q. 20 (5: 435): "Dico . . . quod potentiae animae, de quibus loquimur in proposito, scilicet intellectus et voluntas . . . sunt idem realiter inter se et cum essentia animae." Ockham alludes to the same position in *Sent.* 1, d. 1, q. 2 (1: 396).

[97] Wodeham, *Lectura Oxon.*, 1, d. 1, q. 2 a. 1 (Paris, Univ. MS. 193, fol. 16ʳᵇ): "Nec in via nec in patria est anima fruitio Dei, quia fruitio libere causatur ab anima. Sed nihil libere causatum in anima est ipsa anima." Ibid.: "Non minus est amor res distincta ab anima quam ipsa cognitio. Sed cognitio est res distincta; ergo, etc."

edge of enjoyment really differs from the enjoyment itself, although every act of desire (as well as hate) is at the same time a type of cognition or apprehension since it, like all other experiences, is a certain kind of cognition.[98]

More surprisingly, Wodeham sided with Aureoli against Ockham by holding that beatific enjoyment is identical with pleasure.[99] Yet he favored Ockham's position (against Scotus) that the object is only a partial cause of pleasure, enjoyment, and love.[100] Throughout this discussion Wodeham was not choosing among established views but pointing out that "either-or" formulations did not reflect reality. Instead of asking whether enjoyment was identical or separate from pleasure, one had to speak about specific enjoyments and specific pleasures, since some were and some were not, as Aureoli had already noted.[101]

Both Holcot and Halifax were reluctant to apply the term "enjoyment" to anything other than the love of God and cautiously avoided positing a middle act between enjoyment and use.[102] Halifax, however, did make a distinction between enjoyment and pleasure, as had Scotus and Ockham.[103]

---

[98] Wodeham, *Lectura Oxon.*, 1, d. 1, q. 3.

[99] Wodeham, *Lectura Oxon.*, 1, d. 1, q. 4, a. 2 (Vatican Library, MS. Vat. lat. 955, fol. 27ʳ): "Istis non obstantibus, teneo quod fruitio beatifica est realiter delectatio."

[100] Wodeham, *Lectura Oxon.*, 1, d. 1, q. 4, dub. 3.

[101] Wodeham, *Lectura Oxon.*, 1, d. 1, q. 3, a. 2; q. 4, a. 3.; Aureoli, *Scriptum* 1, d. 1, sect. 7, n. 50 ff. (1: 394 ff.). Ockham noticed the problem this caused in attacking Aureoli's position. Ockham, *Sent.* 1, d. 1, q. 3 (1: 407): "Sic igitur ponit ista opinio [Aureoli] quod aliquis amor est realiter delectatio et aliquis non. Et ideo argumenta aliorum [Scoti] probantium quod dilectio et delectatio distinguuntur realiter non concludunt contra istam opinionem, nec etiam contra istam contra quam arguunt, sicut patebit."

[102] Holcot, *Sent.* 1, q. 3 (q. 4 in Lyons ed.), a. 2: "Utrum sit aliquis actus medius qui nec sit frui nec uti." "Omnis amor sit fruitio vel usus. . . . Et quando arguitur quod aliquid diligitur propter se et tamen non ut ultimus finis nec etiam refertur ad aliud actualiter, concedo, et dico quod talis dilectio est usus, quando res diligitur propter aliud habitualiter. Nam non requiritur ad usum actualis relatio in aliud magis dilectum, sicut superius dictum est. Et ideo quando dicitur: diligo hoc propter illud, ly 'propter' potest dicere causalitatem actus vel habitus, et sive sic sive sic. Dilectio talis est usus." Halifax, *Sent.* 1, d. 1, q. 1, a. 2 (Paris, Bibl. Nat., MS. lat. 15880, fol. 39ᵛᵇ): "Solum Deus est obiectum fruitionis ordinatae." Ibid.: "Omne aliud a Deo potest esse obiectum usus ordinati."

[103] Halifax, *Sent.* 1, dist. 1, q. 1, dub. 1 (Paris, Bibl. Nat. MS. lat. 15880, fols. 42ʳᵃ–44ᵛᵇ): "Nulla delectatio quae est passio consequens operationem virtutis sensitivae est fruitio. . . .

* * *

Other issues were raised by these discussions of willing, loving, and enjoying. Particularly absorbing during the years 1330–35 was the question of the infinite or finite capacity of the soul for grace and beatitude—a topic that lent itself to examinations of infinites, infinite augmentation, continua, and the limit languages that were used in these problems. The question of the potentially infinite capacity of the soul for beatitude became one of the principal contexts within which the problems of *maxima* and *minima* were pursued.

The analytical language employed in this problem was provided in the Latin translation of Averroes's discussion of Aristotle's assertion of a maximum limit of potency and capacity.[104] Every power had a range from least effective (*minimum quod sic*) up to maximum effect (*maximum quod sic*), beyond which lay the least amount of incapacity (*minimum quod non*). This approach focused attention on that point or moment between maximum potency and the impotency that lay beyond (in the case of an agent or active power), and the point or moment between the minimum power to affect or not affect an object or patient (*minimum quod sic* and *minimum quod non*). The subject fell within the broader problems of the intension and remission of forms and first and last instants, and as such it was closely connected with the augmentation of grace, treated in distinction 17 of book 1, or in the opening questions on book 4, where sacramental causality was discussed. But with beatific fruition and the love of God, the focus was not on *how* a form is augmented or diminished but *to what extent* a form could be intensified, namely, the problem of highest degree.

The first full-scale treatments of the capacity of the soul for grace and the comparative capacities of the *viatores* and *beati* for the highest pos-

---

Nulla fruitio est delectatio secundo modo accepta. . . . Nullus actus intellectus vel voluntatis est delectatio. . . . Omnis actus voluntatis vel intellectus creati posset esse sine delectatione, saltem per potentiam divinam. . . . Visio clara essentiae divinae et fruitio eiusdem possunt esse in creatura rationali sine delectatione, et hoc per divinam potentiam. . . . Beatitudo non potest esse sine delectatione. . . ."

[104] Averroes's discussion of a *maximum quod sic* (as used in Aristotle) and a *minimum quod non* focused attention on a point between capacity and incapacity that seemed to go against the Aristotelian principle that continua were not composed of indivisibles. See C. Wilson, *William Heytesbury* (Madison, 1956), 59–63.

sible degree began with Henry of Ghent.[105] If the joy of the blessed and
the degree of grace possessed by them is maximal (whether because of
the highest degree that can be given or the highest degree of which they
are capable), and if grace in this life can always be augmented, is it not
possible that a holy person in this life could attain a state equal to that
of the blessed? Henry with his contemporaries believed that the grace
possessed by the *contemplator* would always be greater than the grace
possessed by a *viator*. One of his fellow theologians had proposed a solution *in more geometrico*, comparing the augmentation of grace in this
life to the lengthening of a line which, no matter how long it became,
could never equal the quantity of a surface of which it was a part.[106] The
mathematical example, however, did not suit Henry because it implied
a difference in kind, and grace in this life had to be identical with the
grace of beatitude. And, lest the spiritual overachiever in this life over-
take the stationary condition of those in the next, Henry toyed with the
idea of an augmentation of grace for the blessed.

In a subsequent quodlibet Henry returned to the issue and began to
employ the language of limits.[107] Things have an *extremum quantitatis
speciei*, a maximum limit that controls the degree of perfection according to their essence. He establishes a range between a *primus gradus in-
tensionis* below which a certain form does not exist, and, at the other
end, a *gradum summum* beyond which a certain form cannot go. Despite
the infinite virtue of God, the infinity of uncreated grace, and the augmentation of human capacity that accompanies the augmentation of
grace, Henry maintained that grace cannot be augmented infinitely,
either in this life or the next. And the maximum augmentation of grace
in this life never attains the degree and kind of love by which God is
loved *intensive* by the least amount of love possessed by those *in patria*.

Through numerous geometrical analogies used in quodlibetal disputations at Paris between 1279 and 1293 over infinite augmentation,
first and last instants, and highest limit, Henry and his contemporaries,
principally Giles of Rome and Godfrey of Fontaines, set the mathematical tone for subsequent discussions both of the augmentation of grace

[105] Henry of Ghent, *Quodlibeta* 4, q. 25 (Paris, 1518; Louvain, 1961), fols. 143ᵛ–144ʳ; 5, q.
22, fols. 198ᵛ–201ʳ.

[106] Henry of Ghent, *Quodl.* 4, q. 25.

[107] Henry of Ghent, *Quodl.* 5, q. 22.

and the highest degree of charity.[108] Comparable theological problems were introduced, such as the first and last instants of Christ's incarnation, the augmentation of knowledge (again in the context of the Beatific Vision), and the maximum limits for the pains and sorrows of the damned.

The indivisibilist position on *continua* developed in the opening years of the fourteenth century offered a possible solution to the limit problem of the *maximum quod sic* and the *minimum quod non*. Ockham, in energetically supporting the view that *continua* are infinitely divisible and infinitely extendable, courageously rejected the notion of minimal and maximal limits.[109] The thesis that the infinite augmentation of grace in this life was possible seemed, however, to lend support to the mystics and religious fringe groups whose theories of complete perfectibility in this life had precipitated the condemnation of errors associated with the Beghards and Beguines at the Council of Vienne in 1312.[110] Thus for those who could not accept the idea of any limit to the augmentation of grace, some other limit had to be found.

Questions over the augmentation of grace and the problem of limits between the realms of the *viatores* and *beati* received particular attention in England during the years 1328–35, and in the 1330–32 period questions on the capacity of the soul, *visio clara*, and *lumen gloriae* were the topics chosen for the *principia* debates among the bachelors of theology. Fitzralph, although uncertain on a number of points, joined Ockham in

---

[108] In addition to the examples from Henry already cited, see Giles of Rome, *Quodlibet* 1, q. 18 on the infinite increase of charity; *Quodl.* 2, q. 14 on the intension and remission of forms; *Quodl.* 4, q. 5 on whether one can give an *ultimum instans* in which Christ was living; *Quodl.* 4, q. 13 on parts in an augmented thing; *Quodl.* 5, q. 19 on whether there be essential degrees in matter; *Quodl.* 5, q. 20 on whether time is a continuous quantity; *Quodl.* 6, q. 7 on *instans*; *Quodl.* 6, qq. 9–10 on intension and remission of forms; *Quodl.* 6, q. 17 on whether aenigmatic cognition is able to be infinitely augmented; *Quodl.* 7, qq. 11–13 on the augmentation of charity. Similarly Godfrey of Fontaines, *Quodlibet* 2, q. 10, *Quodl.* 6, q. 13; *Quodl.* 7, q. 12; *Quodl.* 9, q. 12; *Quodl.* 10, q. 7.

[109] Ockham, *Sent.* 1, d. 17, q. 8 (3: 563): "Ad istud dico quod primum assumptum est falsum, scilicet quod in quibuscumque permanentibus potest fieri minimum et etiam maximum unica factione. Immo dico quod veraciter loquendo, sicut in quibuscumque permanentibus divisibilibus in infinitum—cuiusmodi sunt omnia continua, et etiam omnes qualitates ad quas potest esse motus, secundum multos—non est dare minimum quin, quocumque dato, potest fieri minus per divinam potentiam, ita non est dare maximum quin, quocumque magno dato, potest fieri maius."

[110] See *Enchiridion Symbolorum*, 282.

rejecting the concept of a *summus gradus indivisibilis*.[111] But since the life span of anyone is limited, augmentation of grace equal to that of the blessed was impossible. Wodeham, however, felt that argument was flawed, since theoretically, *de potentia absoluta*, God could infinitely extend the life of anyone. Consequently, Wodeham argued for the finite capacity of the soul for grace, unless altered by miraculous action.[112] In anticipation of the doctrinal declaration on some of these matters that emerged in 1336, these questions received a great deal of attention in the *Sentences* commentaries of Holcot, Kilvington, Halifax, and Rosetus. In fact, the opening question of Rosetus's commentary circulated as a separate treatise on *maxima* and *minima*.[113]

[111] Fitzralph, *Sent.* 1, q. 11, a. 3 (Florence, Bibl. Naz., MS. conv. soppr. A.3.508, fol. 47vb; Oxford, Oriel College, MS. 15, fol. 53vb; Paris, Bibl. Nat., MS. lat. 15853, fol. 81va): "Dico quod nullus est summus gradus talis, et hoc dico gradus indivisibilis, sicut probat argumentum. Nec Augustinus loquitur de gradu indivisibili, sed de gradu divisibili, scilicet de caritate perfecta quae multam continet latitudinem."

[112] Wodeham, *Lectura Oxon.*, prol., q. 1 (MS. Vat. lat. 955, fol. 4^v; Paris, Univ., MS. 193, fol. 5rb): "Aliter igitur mihi videtur dicendum quod et capacitas animae est finita, quia ista non est nisi ipsa substantia animae, et quod ipsa de quavis forma in ea receptibili de cuius specie non est dare maximam possibilem repleri potest proportionaliter in spiritualibus secundum intensionem, sicut vas corporale repleri potest secundum extensionem aqua vel alio liquore, ita quod non potest simul sine speciali miraculo plus illius speciei recipi hic et ibi."

"Unus modus possibilis hoc salvandi bene gressus esset iste, quod sicut non obstante quod cyphus posset repleri aqua ita quod plus de aqua non sit in eo sine miraculo receptibile, tamen per illud miraculum quo Deus posset ponere plura corpora in eodem loco, posset Deus in eodem cypho aqua priori remanente aliam aequalem priori vel minorem simul ponere, et pari ratione si sibi placeret tertiam et quartam, et sic sine statu; ita in proposito non obstante quod aliqua anima, puta 'a,' possit repleri gratia ita quod plus de tali gratia secundum speciem non possit simul sine speciali miraculo naturaliter recipi in ea, tamen per miraculum similem proportionaliter priori poterit Deus ponere in ea, si ipsa homo meruerit, aequalem priori simul cum priori et tertiam et quartam et sic sine fine, et proportionaliter in alia vita de praemio. Et sic evadere utrumque inconveniens ante tactum.

"Alius modus possibilis sine tali miraculo et subtilior priori esset quod sicut vas corporale, puta cyphus, non possit plus naturaliter recipere una vice de aqua quam certam quantitatem, puta ciphatum, tamen ipse posset de meliori liquore, puta de vino, tamdem recipere aqua abiecta, et illo abiecto adhuc tamdem de meliori. Et sic non esset finis quin Deus ultra omnem liquorem possibilem posset facere liquorem in duplo meliorem vel melioris speciei, tunc totus liquor una vice in eo naturaliter receptibilis numquam posset esse ita bonus quin adhuc meliori posset repleri."

[113] Rosetus, *Sent.*, q. 1, also falsely attributed to Holcot and printed as his first *Determinatio*.

* * *

Problems of growth and limit were not the only issues stimulated by and explored within treatments of cognition and volition, which occupied fully a third of the questions in English *Sentences* commentaries in the period 1325–45. Equally important were the motivational and proportional issues involved in conflicting cognitions and conflicting volitions. Problems of choice, of the movement of the will away from one object and toward another, were particularly difficult when there were two equally desirable yet opposed objects or courses of action (approach-approach conflicts), or two equally undesirable yet opposed objects or courses of action (avoid-avoid conflicts). The most famous formulation of the positive version of this problem, namely the ass being attracted and immobilized between two equal and equally distant stacks of hay, is associated with the name of John Buridan at Paris.[114] But perhaps because it spoke more directly to human experience, the latter problem of "perplexity between two evils" (*perplexitas inter duo peccata*) was the usual way this motivational issue was raised and explored in English theology.

The question of perplexity was not initially one of theological concern but was examined in canon law commentaries in the thirteenth century and only came into theology in the fourteenth century in the context of the problem of the erroneous conscience.[115] The latter problem had taken on particular meaning when Ockham postulated that the actions of an erroneous conscience done in invincible ignorance were not only excusable but could, *de potentia absoluta*, be meritorious on the basis of right intention.[116] In the period between 1320 and 1330 only minor attention was given to this issue, but in 1330 Holcot introduced the problem of perplexity into theology, joined it to the problem of er-

---

[114] The story of the *asinus Buridani* was later attributed to Buridan, but on what authority is not known. For the arguments and literature, see E. J. Monahan, "Human Liberty and Free Will According to John Buridan," *MedStud* 16 (1954): 72–86.

[115] Gregory the Great, *Moralia in Job*, Lib. 35, cap. 14; Gratian, *Decretum*, pt. 1, d. 13, c. 2; Michael G. Baylor, *Action and Person: Conscience in Late Scholasticism and the Young Luther* (Leiden, 1977), 20–91. For additional material on the twelfth and thirteenth centuries see J. Gründel, *Die Lehre von den Umständen der menschlichen Handlung im Mittelalter* (Münster i.W., 1963); L.-B. Gillon, *La théorie des oppositions et la théologie du péché au XIIIᵉ siècle* (Paris, 1937).

[116] Ockham, *Sent.* 3, q. 13 (8: 424): "Et ideo voluntas eliciens actum conformiter tali rationi erroneae, virtuose et meritorie agit."; cf. Baylor, 87–90.

roneous conscience, and made it one of the recurring themes of his commentary.[117] From that point on it became a major question for theologians at Oxford throughout the next decade. Kilvington gave it extensive treatment, evaluating it in terms of degrees and proportions of volition, but despite his physico-mathematical approach to the question, it still remained for him largely a moral problem.[118] The less extensive treatment of Halifax was considered significant enough to circulate outside the proper structure of his commentary.[119] Rosetus and Monachus Niger made the topic the opening question of their *Sentences* commentaries, and Langeley devoted a significant portion of his commentary to the problem, as did the author of one of the anonymous commentaries in Vat. lat. 13002.[120] Rosetus's treatment was the most interesting, since although he did not discuss perplexity directly, he gave one of the longest examinations of the problem of the erroneous conscience and tied it to the question of *maxima-minima*.

Human Freedom and Divine Action

Beyond yet closely related to problems of conflicting cognitions and volitions within human psychology lay questions about the interaction and potential conflicts between human and divine will. Some of these were already entailed in the uneasy marriage of divine foreknowledge with an open future, contingent on human actions freely willed. Others were inherent in the age-old problem of compatibility between divine predestination and human control over one's own religious destiny. As will be seen in the next chapter, the question of the augmentation of grace was being pursued in the charged atmosphere of a renewed debate over Pelagianism, particularly between advocates for the efficaciousness of sincerely wanting and doing one's best (*facere quod in se est*), such as Ockham, Holcot, and Wodeham, and their Augustinian opponents, who took a stronger view of grace and predestination, such as Bradwardine and the English Austin Friars influenced by Gregory of Rimini.

[117] Holcot, *Sent.* 3, q. un., QQ, and *De imputabilitate peccati*, prin. arg. 6 and solution.

[118] Kilvington, *Sent.*, q. 6.

[119] Halifax, *Sent.*, q. 9, a. 3. It receives separate treatment in MS. Vat. lat. 4353, fols. 58ᵛ–59ʳ.

[120] Rosetus, *Sent.*, q. 1; Monachus Niger, *Sent.*, q. 1, a. 2–3; Langeley, *Sent.* 2, q. 3; and the anonymous commentary on *Sent.* in MS. Vat. lat. 13002, fols. 81ᵛᵇ–85ᵛᵇ.

So much attention in recent literature and in the previous pages has been focused on the analytic tools of the measure languages and the degree to which theological problems provided an occasion for pursuing problems of mathematics and physics that one tends to overlook the fact that these means of analysis helped open up and solve theological problems, which for the users of these techniques was ultimately a more important task. The double service these problems performed should not be ignored. The topic of the augmentation of grace was one of many happy chances where one of the burning questions of the day, namely justification and salvation, coincided with interest in mathematically quantifiable issues of change, alteration, growth, augmentation, diminution, instantaneous change, motion, all within a temporal framework. It was also a question that was particularly appropriate for treatment according to the latitude of forms, and issues of proportion and degree. Yet if the physical side of augmentation focused more on *how* it took place than on *why* (as in questions of causality that predominated in the thirteenth century), so too the theological side focused on *how* human effort and divine gift operated together, and in what proportions. The controversial nature of Scotus's theory of divine acceptation, the necessity of the habit of grace only *de potentia ordinata*, and the attack on inherent virtue in the processes of nature and grace—all issues raised in the list of suspect propositions on which Ockham was examined at Avignon—reveal the degree to which the doctrines of justification, sanctification, and the sacraments stood out as among the foremost issues of the day, well before Bradwardine's attack on his "Pelagian" contemporaries.

The fourteenth-century crisis over Pelagianism was only one episode in a recurring struggle between an optimistic assessment of human nature, strengthened by the interest and confidence in nature and the natural in the twelfth century, and the traditional Augustinian emphasis on human limitations and, correspondingly, divine activity through grace.[121] The supporters of the view that man had the power to do the good and that his best efforts would be rewarded by God (the approach epitomized in the formula *facere quod in se est*) was as strong in the early

---

[121] The issues of the fifth- to sixth-century crisis over Pelagianism were most heatedly debated during the ninth, twelfth, and fourteenth centuries. On aspects of the twelfth-century phase, see G. Bullet, *Vertus morales infuses et vertus morales acquises selon Saint Thomas d'Aquin* (Fribourg, 1958); Courtenay, *Covenant and Causality* (London, 1984), ch. 3.

fourteenth century as in any other period of high and late medieval theology.[122] The augmentation of grace was only one of several avenues
through which the interrelation and interaction of God and man in the
process of salvation was explored. Hidden within discussions of fruition, human nature, volition, penance, and the virtues were numerous
questions that were essentially on grace and justification, to which these
theologians return time and time again.

For example, among the questions on fruition was whether someone,
in the present state (as *viator*) and on the basis of natural powers apart
from grace, could love God above all else. Ockham had argued that
when fruition is understood in the broad sense, not limiting it to the
beatific act, the will is able in this life (*in via*) actively to elicit an act of
fruition, *ex puris naturalibus*, when the object of enjoyment is presented
to the will through the intellect, whether clearly (that is, through a vision miraculously revealed) or obscurely (knowledge of God as revealed
through nature and Scripture), as particular object or as universal concept.[123] The same view was shared by Holcot and Wodeham, the latter
being attacked by Halifax for wording that seemed Pelagian and was, in
fact, almost identical with the wording used by Ockham, whom Halifax
did not mention in this context.[124] Anticipating opposition, Wodeham
argued that he was speaking only about the natural ability to love and
enjoy God and to perform good acts; the meritorious quality of these
acts depended on divine acceptation. Yet the thrust of his position is in
keeping with the view, encountered often in Franciscan theology, that
man can initiate the return to God, and that God will reward with grace

---

[122] A. M. Landgraf, *Dogmengeschichte der Frühscholastik*, vol. 1.1 (Regensburg, 1952), 249–
64. On the historical development of *facere quod in se est* see H. A. Oberman, *The Harvest of
Medieval Theology* (Cambridge, Mass., 1963), 132–41.

[123] Ockham, *Sent.* 1, d. 1, q. 2 (1: 397): "Dico primo quod obiecto fruibili ostenso voluntati
per intellectum sive clare sive obscure sive in particulari sive in universali, potest voluntas
active elicere actum fruitionis, et hoc ex puris naturalibus, circa illud obiectum."

[124] Wodeham, *Lectura Oxon.*, 1, d. 1, q. 10, a. 1, concl. 1 (Vat. lat. 955, fol. 66ᵛ; Paris, Univ.
193, fol. 49ʳᵇ; Paris, Maz. 915, fol. 41ʳᵃ): "Quod in via, stante cognitione viatoris aenigma-
tica in universali vel in particulari, voluntas potest causare in se active dilectionem Dei
super omnia et propter se sive fruitionem Dei, quia voluntas potest se conformare recto
dictamini intellectus." And later (Vat. lat. 955, fol. 67ᵛ; Paris, Univ. 193, fol. 49ᵛᵇ): "Mihi
videtur quod etiam sine infusione doni supernaturalis posset voluntas viatoris mediante
dictamine possibili haberi de Deo in via libere in se causare dilectionem Dei super omnia."

and final acceptation those who do their best (*facientibus quod in se est, Deus non denegat gratiam*).

Holcot appears to have been more optimistic than Wodeham on the scope of man's abilities *in* a state of grace. At various points in his *Sentences* commentary and in his fourth *Determinatio* Holcot affirmed that a *viator* in a state of grace could avoid all sin, both venial and mortal.[125] From the standpoint of theology, individuals must be able to fulfill God's commandment not to sin; otherwise required expectations would not be in keeping with human ability, which would be unjust and irrational.[126] From the standpoint of mathematics, equal units of a temporal continuum have equal characteristics, such that what applies to any part applies to any other part and any series of them. Thus, if someone is able to avoid all sin for a brief unit of time, e.g., an hour, as everyone would admit, he can do so for any other such unit of time; and what can be done for each and every part can be done for the entire temporal continuum.[127] Wodeham rejected that position and sided with what Holcot called the "via communis antiquorum doctorum," namely that a *viator*, unless he has special help from God, such as Mary received, cannot remain sinless throughout life.[128] Similarly, again in contrast to

[125] Holcot, *In quatuor libros sententiarum quaestiones* (Lyon, 1518; reprint 1967), 1, q. 3; *Determinatio* 4. For the texts see Courtenay, *Adam Wodeham*, 101–3.

[126] Holcot, *Determinatio* 4 (Lyon, 1518), A: "Arguitur primo sic: Deus praecipit homini; ergo consulit quod vitet omne peccatum; ergo homo potest hoc facere cum adiutorio gratiae. Consequentia videtur esse nota, quia irrationabile esset quod Deus praeciperet aliquid homini quin illud sibi consuleret. Antecedens patet, quia si Deus non praeciperet aliquid huiusmodi vitare vel sub poena aeterna vel sub poena temporali, illud nollum peccatum foret, nec veniale nec mortale, sicut nullum peccatum est levare festucam. Unde non plus foret peccatum dicere verbum otiosum, nisi esset a Deo prohibitum. Sed omne prohibitum a Deo homini potest ab homine vitari. Ergo homo potest vitare omne peccatum."

[127] Ibid.: "Secundo sic: Creet Deus hominem perfectum in naturalibus. Iste statim potest incipere mereri si habeat gratiam. Et pono quod Deus conservet vitam illius per unum diem tantum. Tunc arguo sic: Per primam huius diei horam potest vitare omne peccatum, manifestum est etiam secundum eos. Dicunt enim quod homo per aliquid tempus potest esse sine quocumque peccato. Sed eadem ratione potest vitare peccatum secunda; sub eadem ratione et tertia; et sic per totum diem; ergo per totam vitam suam. Est similis ratio de quocumque adulto."

[128] Wodeham, *Lectura Oxon.*, prol., q. 2 (Vat. lat. 955, fol. 15^r; Paris, Univ. 193, fol. 12ra; Paris, Maz. 915, fol. 9va), cited and attacked this opinion: " 'Praeterea, dixi quod homo potest ultra omnem gratiam habitam proficere ultra ad maiorem vel meliorem; ergo cum aliqua gratia viae, ut videtur possit tanta esse quod illa habita potest homo ex tunc vivere sine

Wodeham's position described above, Holcot affirmed the infinite natural capacity of the soul for grace and fruition.[129]

The most heated discussion of these issues came in the period from 1328 to 1338 as found in the *Sentences* commentaries of Fitzralph, Holcot, Wodeham, Halifax, Buckingham, and, most of all, in Bradwardine's *Summa de causa Dei*, completed in 1344. Questions on free will, grace, and predestination led naturally to the larger topic of divine omnivolence, which in turn had implications for the problem of future contingents as well as God's responsibility for human sin. But one must remember that questions about the role of divine action *within* human cognition and volition formed only part of the exploration of knowing, willing, and believing.

In addition to the standard problems of grace and justification, however, there were a group of questions that centered on potentially conflicting demands placed on man by God. Some of these were biblically grounded, such as the conflict between God's commandment not to kill, assumed to be part of divine law even before the Mosaic covenant, and God's command to Abraham to sacrifice Isaac. Others hinged on whether opposed cognitions or volitions were self-contradictory and therefore could not, even *de potentia absoluta*, exist simultaneously within the same psychology, human or divine.

Among the latter were a number of questions that came to be viewed as theological *insolubilia* derived from the unrestricted lawgiving power of God. Was it possible for man to fulfill or even for God to command such hypothetical situations as "God commands that he be hated," or "God commands that he not be obeyed." In both situations it would appear that the commands could not be fulfilled without disobedience.

---

hoc, quod peccet mortaliter vel venialiter. Igitur aliquis viator ex gratia viatoribus communiter possibili et puris naturalibus cavere posset omne peccatum tam mortale quam veiale.' Sed consequens est falsum apud me, ut probabo." Wodeham, *Lectura Oxon.* 2, q. 6, a. 2 (Paris, Univ. 193, fol. 163rb; Paris, Maz. 915, fol. 156va): "An viator existens in gratia potest producere vitam suam totalem sine privilegio speciali sine hoc quod peccet venialiter. Et videtur quod sic per argumenta quibus probat hoc et tenet socius quidam [the Dominican bachelor] cuius conclusionem improbavi in lectione mea prima. Tenuit enim nuper replicans contra me quod homo existens in gratia potest vitare omne peccatum imputabile ad culpam." For the longer texts, see Courtenay, *Adam Wodeham*, 102–3.

[129] Holcot, *Determinatio* 2, a. 1 (Cambridge, Pembroke College, MS. 236, fols. 162ra–162rb; Oxford, Balliol College, MS. 246, fols. 221rb–221va).

From the standpoint of human psychology, the problem was whether one could love (i.e., wish to obey) and hate the same object at the same time; from the standpoint of the divine nature, the problem was whether God could ever command such, even *de potentia absoluta*.[130]

It needs to be kept in mind that these questions were not pursued on the level of the way God actually operates *ad extra*, but on the theoretical level, *de potentia absoluta*. The question was whether there was an inherent contradiction between these conflicting cognitions or volitions such that, even *de potentia absoluta*, they could not occur simultaneously. At the same time, these questions allowed the exploration of the nature of volition and obedience, apart from the issue of logical contradiction.

Ockham initially approached the question of hating God (*de odio Dei*) as a test case for God's freedom as lawgiver, based on his perception that loving and hating were separate qualities not necessarily or inextricably tied to goodness or evil. Under the present arrangement, *de potentia ordinata*, fulfilling the divine command to love God above all else is meritorious because God has equated *bonitas* with *diligere Deum* and *malitia* with *odire Deum*. Consequently, God could have, *de potentia absoluta*, commanded hate rather than love, and fulfilling that commandment would be just as meritorious within that system as loving God is within the present system.[131] Conflicting cognitions or volitions would only occur if the commands to love and hate existed simultaneously, which

---

[130] The question of the hatred of God is complicated by the fact that one can take *odium Dei* as an act of the will that leads toward but is not identical with damnation, or as a juridical or soteriological category identical with being an enemy of God and outside grace.

[131] Ockham, *Sent.* 2, q. 15 (5: 352): "Ad aliud dico quod licet odium, furari, adulterari et similia habeant malam circumstantiam annexam de communi lege, quatenus fiunt ab aliquo qui ex praecepto divino obligatur ad contrarium, tamen quantum ad omne absolutum in illis actibus possunt fieri a Deo sine omni circumstantia mala annexa. Et etiam meritorie possunt fieri a viatore si caderent sub praecepto divino, sicut nunc de facto eorum opposita cadunt sub praecepto." In saying this Ockham was moving beyond Scotus's division between the first two commandments of the Decalogue, which were a direct expression of eternal and natural law, and the second tablet of the Decalogue, which God could have ordained differently or could temporarily suspend. If one understands the first commandment to mean that one should only love and enjoy God, then that commandment for Ockham, like murder, adultery, or theft, could have been ordained differently in another system. The biblical examples of the hardening of Pharaoh's heart, or the Israelites despoiling Egypt, or Abraham conceiving a child by Hagar, Sarah's maid, show that there is not here an inherent contradiction.

would be impossible for God as well.[132] In his *Quodlibeta*, however, Ockham modified his earlier position. Although the ability to have decreed
otherwise would present no problem for God, the human ability to fulfill such a negative command would be blocked by conflicting volitions
inasmuch as the act of hating would be motivated by a desire to conform
to the will of God, which is an act of love.[133]

Ockham's earlier formulation on the meritorious value of fulfilling a
command to hate was later rejected at Paris by Gregory of Rimini on
grounds not too dissimilar from those Ockham eventually adopted.[134]
Without mentioning Ockham, however, subsequent discussion among
English theologians likewise centered on the conflicts in human psychology and less on God's ability or inability to command such an act.
As a free, voluntary act of a created will, Wodeham affirmed that one
could both know and reject God, just as Judas recognized God in Christ
and rejected him.[135] But one cannot desire to fulfill a divine command
and simultaneously hate God. One of the longest discussions of the issue was developed by Rosetus, who saw it as a theological *insolubilium*
which, like the liar paradox, involved self-reference and was therefore
invalid.[136] Just as the proposition "God commands that none of his com-

---

[132] Ockham, *Sent.* 2, q. 15 (5: 353): "Voluntas creata obligatur ex praecepto Dei ad dili-
gendum Deum, et ideo stante illo praecepto non potest bene odire Deum nec causare actum odiendi, sed necessario male causat malitia moris. Et hoc quia obligatur ex praecepto
Dei ad actum oppositum. Nec stante primo praecepto potest sibi Deus oppositum praecipere."

[133] Ockham, *Quodl.* 3, q. 14 (9: 256): Respondeo: si Deus posset hoc praecipere [pro aliquo tempore non diligatur ipse], sicut videtur quod potest sine contradictione, dico tunc
quod voluntas non potest pro tunc talem actum elicere . . . ; et ex hoc ipso quod sic diligeret, non faceret praeceptum divinum per casum; et per consequens sic diligendo, Deum
diligeret et non diligeret, faceret praeceptum Dei et non faceret."

[134] Rimini, *Lectura super primum et secundum Sententiarum* 1 dist. 42–44, q. 1, a. 2 (165 E–F),
ed. D. Trapp and V. Marcolino, vol. 3 (Berlin, 1984), 385–86.

[135] Wodeham, *Lectura Oxon.* 1, q. 10, B (Paris, Univ. 193, fol. 48vb); *Lectura Oxon.* 3, q. 5,
dub. 2, D: "Dices quod hac ratione posset quis licite ad praeceptum Dei Deum odire. Dicendum quod non sequitur, quia nullus potest implere praeceptum Dei sicut tenetur et obligatur nisi ex amore et fervore reverentiali exequatur quid praecipitur. Sed odium Dei per
se maxime repugnaret tali amori."

[136] Rosetus, *Sent.* 1, q. 1: "Et ideo de potentia Dei absoluta potest Deus praecipere alicui
quod odiat Deum." At several points, however, Rosetus acknowledged that one could not
fulfill such a command *ad formam verborum*. Ibid.: "Unde potest concedi quod aliquod est
praeceptum divinum rationabile, de potentia Dei absoluta, cui non potest homo confor-

mandments, including this one, be obeyed" is invalid because it is self-contradictory, so the *casus* on hating God can be reformulated to read "God commands (that is, requires loving conformity to the proposition) that he be hated." So if one understands "conformity" as *willing* obedience, then it is possible *de potentia absoluta* for God to command something that cannot be fulfilled because of contradictory volitions. But if "conformity" means only *doing* what is required, then one could fulfill such a command, although it would not be meritorious, which depends on intentionally willing, not just accidentally doing something.

The question of *odire Deum* was closely related to two other questions: the ability of God to reveal someone's damnation, and the ability of God to deceive. The first of these was almost a variation on the *de odio Dei* question. If God revealed to someone his own damnation, the general commandment to conform oneself to the will of God would come into direct conflict with the commanded and natural end of man, namely, to desire and enjoy God. Not being among the elect automatically implied that one was outside grace, an enemy of God, which was equated with *odium Dei*. Interestingly, Thomas Aquinas considered the question of revealed damnation in his disputed questions on Truth.[137] Although such could not occur *de potentia ordinata*, Thomas acknowledged the possibility *de potentia absoluta*, since it did not appear to involve an inherent contradiction. But in such a theoretical case, for Thomas, the individual would not be conforming to the will of God, since it would be a

mare se ... nisi transgrediatur illud praeceptum, saltem secundum formam verborum...." The question of Rosetus, which circulated separately as a treatise *de maximo et minimo*, was erroneously included as *Determinatio* 1 in the printed edition of Holcot's work. Wyclif also treated the question of revealed damnation and *odium Dei* under *insolubilia; Logica, Tractatus tertius*, ch. 8, ed. M. H. Dziewicki, vol. 2 (London, 1896), 212, 223–24.

[137] Thomas Aquinas, *De veritate*, q. 23, a. 8, ad 2: "Quamvis de potentia absoluta Deus possit revelare suam damnationem alicui, non tamen hoc potest fieri de potentia ordinaria, quia talis revelatio cogeret eum desperare. Et si alicui talis revelatio fieret, deberet intelligi non secundum modum prophetiae praedestinationis vel praescientiae, sed per modum prophetiae comminationis, quae intelligitur supposita conditione meritorum. Sed dato quod esset intelligenda secundum praescientiae prophetiam, adhuc non teneretur ille cui talis revelatio fieret, velle suam damnationem absolute, sed secundum ordinem iustitiae, quo Deus vult persistentes in peccato damnare. Non enim vult Deus ex parte sua aliquem damnare, sed secundum id quod ex nobis est. ... Unde velle suam damnationem absolute, non esset conformare voluntatem suam divinae, sed voluntati peccati." Scotus, *Sent.* 1, dist. 43, qq. 1–2, held that although the hatred of God was the gravest of all sins, it was impossible for the human will, whose nature and end it is to love God.

prophecy of threat, not of predestination, and since God does not directly will the damnation of anyone, which is rather a result of human
sin.

The approach of Holcot was similar yet different.[138] As in so many
areas, Holcot understood the problem in terms of mental, spoken, or
written propositions. The *casus* he constructs is one in which God reveals to Socrates that the proposition "Socrates shall be damned" is true.
Would that not create an impossible situation in which Socrates would
despair (sin mortally) and merit (conform himself to the will of God) simultaneously? If one understands the *casus* as including or allowing the
suspension of the divine requirement that one have hope, then it is possible for man to merit by despair just as by hope, since there is no absolute connection between despair and sin, only a connection established
by God. But if one understands the *casus* in the context of present law
(*de potentia ordinata*), then Holcot rejects it, since one cannot hope and
despair simultaneously. Whether Holcot is drawing upon Ockham or
not, the hypothesis of meriting through a negative action, the rejection
of an absolutely necessary connection between despair and sin, hope
and merit, and the hypothesis of a different order, *de potentia absoluta*,
are compatible with Ockham's approach to the question.

Holcot's approach to the issue of whether God could deceive or lie
(one of the oldest of scholastic questions) was similarly propositional.
This question, as Jean-François Genest has noted, was hotly debated at
Oxford in the 1320s and 1330s and was derived from the principle of
divine omnipotence (God's ability to cause directly what he causes
through other agents, who are able to lie) and from the revelation of a
foreknown event, which, since it is future and therefore contingent, can
possibly not be, thus making God a liar.[139] It was grounded as well in the
relation of the two natures of Christ. If Christ was fully human, he had
to have the ability to lie or deceive. As with Fitzralph and Wodeham,
Holcot set this problem in the context of divine revelations of future
events.[140] If future events are actually contingent on our actions, as Holcot believed, then we are in a position to alter by our actions the truth

[138] Holcot, *Sent.* 1, q. 1, a. 1 and a. 7.

[139] T. Gregory, "La tromperie divine," in *PRUP*, 187–95; J.-F. Genest, "Pierre de Ceffons
et l'hypothèse du Dieu trompeur," in *PRUP*, 197–214.

[140] Fitzralph, *Sent.* 1, q. 14 and his *Quaestio biblica*, ed. by J.-F. Genest, *Le 'De futuris conting.'* (thèse), 137–88; Wodeham, *Lectura Oxon.* 3, q. 5; Holcot, *Sent.* 1, q. 1, a. 7.

value of propositions about the immediate future, thus changing what God knows, and in the case of a revealed future contingent, possibly making divine revelations false.

These questions, like that of whether God's omnivolence made God responsible for sin, provided opportunities for exploring the relation of God and creation, as well as testing the necessity and interrelation of the structural elements in the system God had ordained. As theological *sophismata*, they were excellent devices for honing the analytical and dialectical skills of theological students. No matter how irreverent or disturbing some statements may appear, we must remind ourselves that the assertions ultimately have far less to do with the nature of God and far more with the necessity or contingency of things and relationships in the created world.

The Eucharist and Sacramental Theology

The last group of theological problems to be examined are those concerned with the sacraments, the appropriate material for commentaries on the fourth book of the *Sentences*. The balance of issues, however, was far different than what one found in Lombard's work or even in the sacramental portion of thirteenth-century theological works. For example, little or no attention was given to confirmation, marriage, ordination, or extreme unction, and only slightly more to baptism. The issues that dominated discussion were sacramental causality, transubstantiation, and penance. Those were also the sacramental concerns that dominated the daily life of the priest, particularly the educated priests for whom most scholastic theology was ultimately written.

Sacramental causality and transubstantiation were appropriate topics within which to explore physical change and the causal nexus, problems of instantaneous change and *incipit/desinit* in the moment of consecration and transubstantiation, and to examine and often reject the idea that there could be a "least part" of a consecrated host in which the whole body and blood of Christ exists. At the same time, these issues were of primary concern because they entailed some of the most innovative or controversial theories in theology. At the heart of the problem of sacramental causality lay the controversy between the concept of inherent virtue and direct, physical causality on the one side, with its broad support within the Aristotelian-influenced theology of the late thirteenth century, and, on the other side, the concept of ascribed value and indirect (but no less efficacious) causality, an idea that originated within thirteenth-century English Dominican theology but which gained its strongest support within Scotistic and Ockhamist theology.[141] Thus much of the battle between supporters of inherent virtue or power and supporters of a covenantal view of God's relationship with creation and the operation of many causal relationships within it took place over the contested ground of sacramental causality.[142] And behind it, of course, stood the implications, uncomfortable for many, of Ockham's attack on the whole notion of inherent forces or powers in natural things and on inherent common natures, issues that have been examined in an earlier chapter.[143]

Similarly, discussions over the Eucharist were enlivened by Ockham's explanation of transubstantiation in terms of succession (the substance of the body of Christ replacing the substance of bread and wine) rather than production (the substance of Christ's body made from the bread and wine), and his rejection of quantity as an entity, separate from substance and quality, in which the accidents of bread and wine could inhere after consecration.[144] The succession theory was hardly original, since it had wide support among canon lawyers and Franciscan theologians, while the production theory was maintained by Thomas and several other Dominican theologians. The second issue, however, as we have seen, was one of the points of Ockham's thought that had implications both for physics and theology, and it was one of those that was of particular concern to the investigating commission at Avignon. Without Ockham's reaffirmation and reformulation of this element of Olivi's thought and Ockham's forceful linking of the physical and theological problems, the Eucharist might well have not gotten quite as much attention in fourteenth-century English theology as, in fact, it did. At

[141] Courtenay, *Covenant and Causality*, chs. 2, 6, and 9.

[142] Ibid., ch. 6.

[143] The common element underlying Ockham's attack on common natures, inherent forces in nature, and inherent virtues in the sacraments has been examined above, ch. 7, 199–200, 205, 210–15.

[144] G. Buescher, *The Eucharistic Teaching of William Ockham* (Washington, 1950); E. Iserloh, *Gnade und Eucharistie in der philosophischen Theologie des Wilhelm von Ockham* (Wiesbaden, 1956); Courtenay, *The Eucharistic Theology of Gabriel Biel*, Ph.D. diss., Harvard University, 1967; *Covenant and Causality*, chap. 10.

the same time, the late Middle Ages witnessed a growth in Eucharistic piety, perhaps because it was that point in the potentially daily experience of the devout Christian where the divine met the human and through which grace was transmitted to the soul.

The reinterpretation of the category of quantity and the corresponding adjustment in the understanding of transubstantiation was one of several points on which Ockham and Wodeham made a common front against Chatton and others.[145] Moreover, on the related issue of the infinite divisibility of continua, Ockham and Wodeham developed or refined their views together, rather than Wodeham simply following a position already developed by Ockham.[146] In fact, in the decade or more between the Oxford careers of Ockham and Wodeham these issues received considerable attention, as can be seen in the *Sentences* commentaries of Chatton, Graystanes, Rodington, and Fitzralph.[147] Where other English theologians stood on these ideas of succession and quantity is not as clear, since they were rarely dealt with directly after 1332. Already in 1330 Holcot touched on the issues of succession and quantity only indirectly, although his position appears closer to Ockham than to Thomas.[148] Moreover, these issues are not examined in what has remained of the commentaries of Halifax, Rosetus, Kilvington, Buckingham, Stuckley, and Langeley. Whether a result of concentration on the first two books of the *Sentences* in these shortened commentaries or a preference for other topics, Eucharistic theology was all but phased out in English schools during the decades between Wodeham and Wyclif.[149]

---

[145] Wodeham, *Lectura Oxon.* 4, qq. 4–5; Chatton, *Reportatio*, 4, qq. 3–6, esp. q. 5. See also Wodeham, *Tractatus de indivisibilibus* (Florence, Bibl. Naz., MS. conv. soppr. A.III.508, fols. 135ʳ–147ʳ; Florence, Bibl. Naz., MS. conv. soppr. B.VII.1249, fols. 133ʳ–143ʳ); J. Murdoch and E. Synan, "Two Questions on the Continuum: Walter Chatton (?), O.F.M. and Adam Wodeham, O.F.M.," *FcS* 26 (1966): 212–88.

[146] Wodeham, *Tractatus de indivisibilibus* (Florence, Bibl. Naz. conv. soppr. A.III.508, fol. 140ʳᵃ): "Quaere prosecutionem in illo tractatu. Et haec argumenta fere omnia fuerant tua antequam Ockham aliquid scriberet de indivisibilibus."

[147] See forthcoming list of English *quaestiones*.

[148] Holcot, *Sent.* 4, q. 3.

[149] Eucharistic questions do not appear in the *Sentences* commentaries of Halifax, Rosetus, Kilvington, Buckingham, Went, Monachus Niger, Langeley, Stuckley, or Aston, although Pickingham included one (q. 7).

*   *   *

Finally, the doctrine of penance allowed theologians to pursue issues of sin, grace, and human volition in a sacramental context and, under the guise of a topic appropriate to the fourth book of the *Sentences*, return to one of their major preoccupations, which we have already examined in some detail. Similarly, the issue of final beatitude was often used to return to the question of fruition and the question of the capacity of the soul for grace, as was true for both Holcot and Wodeham. But penance was hardly a pretext for a discussion of other, more philosophical issues. It was that door through which one reentered a state of grace and again became a "friend of God." The topics of divine acceptation, the augmentation of grace, fruition, and volition that form the core of fourteenth-century English theology had such importance because of an overriding theological concern for salvation. The concern for problems that employed the measure languages was not simply a means to a theological end, but neither was it the dominant interest that redirected theology into mathematical and physical approaches. It was for them the fortunate circumstance in which their interests in time, motion, change, limits, and measure coincided with the most pressing theological questions of that age.

TEN

THE AUGUSTINIAN REVIVAL

✧

AMONG THE various currents of thought that have been attributed to the fourteenth century, one of the most frequently discussed has been Augustinianism.[1] Unlike Thomism and Scotism, whose origins lay in the thirteenth century, fourteenth-century Augustinianism has been viewed as a fresh, new current, generally opposed to the other major intellectual movement of northern Europe in that age, nominalism, so long the *bête noire* of late medieval studies. And yet, Augustinianism may be, like nominalism, one of the most ill-defined and confusing of labels.

There is a sense in which much of the Western intellectual tradition throughout the Middle Ages and beyond can be called Augustinian. The writings of St. Augustine were the foundation block for Latin theology, a principal source for canon law, a framework for important forms of political thinking, and one of the principal avenues through which Neoplatonism influenced philosophical thought until (and in part after) the recovery of Aristotle in the twelfth and thirteenth centuries. The Christianization of Aristotle in the thirteenth century was a modification in light of church doctrines that bore the features of Au-

---

[1] The literature on this topic is large and controversial. Among the more important contributions are: K. Werner, *Die Scholastik des späteren Mittelalters*, vol. 3: *Der Augustinismus in der Scholastik des späteren Mittelalters* (Vienna, 1883); C. Stange, "Augustinischer Nominalismus," in Stange, *Studien zu Theologie Luthers*, vol. 1 (Gütersloh, 1928), 1–19; E. Stakemeier, *Der Kampf um Augustin auf dem Tridentinum* (Paderborn, 1937); Damasus Trapp, "Augustinian Theology of the 14th Century," *Augustiniana* 6 (1956): 146–274; A. Zumkeller, "Die Augustinerschule des Mittelalters: Vertreter und philosophische-theologische Lehre," *Analecta Augustiniana* 27 (1964): 167–262; L. Grane, "Gregory von Rimini und Luthers Leipziger Disputation," *Studia Theologica* 22 (1968): 31; H. A. Oberman, "Headwaters of the Reformation: Initia Lutheri—Initia Reformationis," in *Luther and the Dawn of the Modern Era*, ed. Oberman (Leiden, 1974), 40–88; D. C. Steinmetz, "Luther and the Late Medieval Augustinians: Another Look," *Concordia Theological Monthly* 44 (1973): 245–60; Oberman, *Werden und Wertung der Reformation* (Tübingen, 1977) 82–140.

gustine's formulation. Even philosophy and science—the two areas most strongly influenced by the recovery of Aristotle—never completely lost certain Augustinian characteristics in the high and late Middle Ages.

When one speaks of an Augustinian revival in fourteenth-century thought, however, one is using the term "Augustinian" in a far more restrictive and specific sense. One is referring to aspects of thought that go beyond even the Augustinian elements in Bonaventure or Henry of Ghent, often seen as two representatives of thirteenth-century Augustinianism. What were the principal characteristics of this newer, fourteenth-century Augustinianism?

At the foundation lay a more precise, source-critical approach to the writings of Augustine. Thirteenth-century theologians knew their Augustine primarily through a few standard works (*Confessions, City of God, On Christian Doctrine*) and through the abundant quotations that circulated under Augustine's name in anthologies (*florilegia*), Gratian's *Decretum*, and Lombard's *Sentences*. Moreover, the source of a "saying" of Augustine was seldom acknowledged beyond his name and occasionally a title of a work. By the second quarter of the fourteenth century that form of citation was changing. One finds a wider variety of Augustinian works being cited, longer quotations that were not part of the previous collection of "memorable sayings," a concern that the texts quoted should be accurate, based on a reliable textual tradition, of sufficient length to reveal Augustine's thought, and referenced precisely to the work, chapter (a division which had only been recently added in the thirteenth century), and often section of chapter, so that the reader could check the quotation for himself. Much of this rigorous, scholarly attitude toward the sources may only be the application to Augustine of a humanist trait that one finds elsewhere in the fourteenth century. But it also betrays a far wider, firsthand reading of the Augustinian corpus, especially of works that had not received much attention in the thirteenth century.

This broader reading may have facilitated a shift in Augustinianism toward the mature or late Augustine as revealed in the works written after 410. This is suggested by the fact that a second and more prominent feature of the newer Augustinianism was a strong, anti-Pelagian position on the issue of grace and justification. Fourteenth-century Augustinians in this narrow sense disallowed any ability on the part of an individual to prepare oneself for the gift of grace and emphasized divine action and auxiliary grace, often at the expense of human effort and human merit. This reaffirmation of God's role in salvation, with its emphasis on grace (*sola gratia*), predestination before foreseen merits (*praedestinatio ante praevisa merita*) based on God's decree rather than God's foreknowledge, double predestination (that the final condition of the damned represents a conscious decision on God's part just as much as the beatitude of the elect), and the perseverance of the saints, went hand in hand with a stronger view of divine omnipotence that sometimes bordered on divine omnivolence. In some versions the contingency of the future (and with it the freedom of man) was reduced under the belief that the future cannot take place in any way other than as God foreknows it, while in other versions the necessity of the past was questioned under the assumption that God's omnipotence over his creation should not be limited by the passage of time.

These theological features of a newer Augustinianism were sometimes joined to elements of "Augustinian" political thought. At the opening of the fourteenth century there developed a political concept that had important ramifications for relations of church and state throughout the century. This was the idea of the lordship (*dominium*) of grace, by which was meant that only one in a state of grace had the right to exercise authority over persons and property. The idea was ostensibly derived from Augustine's *City of God* and had some of its roots in earlier papal hierocratic theory, but it owed much more to the psychology of fourteenth-century politics and a narrower and more refined exegesis of Exodus 12, 35–36: Israel despoiling Egypt. This feature of the new Augustinianism derived from Giles of Rome, who also contributed a stronger doctrine of grace in his later writings.[2] But the political dimension, although part of an Augustinian revival in the fourteenth century, was not always found in combination with a strongly anti-Pelagian view of grace and justification. And the latter view, along with a newer, critical attitude toward the sources, still remains a feature of Gregory of Rimini that separates him from Aegidian Augustinianism, as Damasus Trapp has rightly observed.[3]

No single fourteenth-century author who would be considered Au-

[2] See below, n. 7.
[3] Trapp, "Augustinian Theology."

gustinian affirmed all of the above positions. Usually, two or more of these elements are sufficient for inclusion. Nor should we expect that those we call Augustinian agreed with one another. Yet Gregory of Rimini's criticisms of Thomas Bradwardine should not prevent us from seeing certain common, Augustinian elements in their thought.

One should not confuse this newer Augustinianism with what Etienne Gilson has called "The Second Augustinian School."[4] Under that label Gilson placed together Henry of Ghent, John Duns Scotus, and the fourteenth-century tradition of Scotism, thus differentiating their "Augustinianism" from that of Bonaventure and his disciples. But in Scotus one does not find Henry's Augustinian epistemology, and in Henry one does not find Scotus's view of divine omnipotence, predestination, or the characteristic idea of *acceptatio divina*. Indeed, Henry and Scotus drew different elements from a common Augustinian soil, and Scotus attacked the ideas of Henry more often than those of any other writer. Each may be considered to represent a type of Augustinianism, but the different assumptions and approaches of the secular Henry and the Franciscan Scotus prevent our placing them together in one school. Moreover, only Scotus anticipates elements of the newer Augustinianism in his views on divine omnipotence and predestination. But the source-critical attitude and the anti-Pelagian soteriology are not yet there.

It would also be helpful if we did not use the term "Augustinianism" to describe the thought of theologians who belonged to the mendicant order known as the Augustinian Hermits or Austin Friars, as Adolar Zumkeller, Damasus Trapp, and others have done.[5] Many Austin Friars did hold positions that can be called Augustinian in the narrow sense used above and many also contributed to the source-critical attitude toward the works of Augustine. Yet not every fourteenth-century Austin affirmed the newer Augustinianism, and it is possible to find several important fourteenth-century theologians outside that order who were Augustinian in the newer sense. Augustinianism as a theological movement has too often been confused with Augustinianism as a religious order. To say it is both is to ignore the problem. In our desire to see one Augustinian revival that embraces all the evidence, we have

[4] E. Gilson, *HCP*, 446–71.

[5] Trapp, "Augustinian Theology"; Zumkeller, "Augustinerschule."

failed to develop precise terminology, a failure that may be a way of avoiding some hard but important questions. Even if we should see the Austin Friars as the main force or catalyst within the Augustinian revival, was Bradwardine's or Wyclif's Augustinianism derived from that source, and to what degree was the Augustinianism of Gregory of Rimini and Hugolino of Orvieto indebted to Bradwardine? Perhaps the greatest disadvantage in the assumption of one unified Augustinian revival, built up on evidence drawn from inside and outside the Austin Friars, from Oxford and Paris, from Italy and Germany, is that we have not adequately examined what Augustinianism meant in various places at various times. This approach has glossed over the problem that Augustinianism at Oxford appears to have little to do with the Austin Friars, and that Augustinianism at Paris is almost exclusively concerned with the Austin Friars. How are those two worlds related?

In what follows the term "Augustinianism" will be limited to the current of thought described above, regardless of the affiliation of the authors involved. Secondly, the phrase "Augustinian School" will be used for theologians of the Austin Friars, no matter what their individual intellectual orientation. There may have been a common or core teaching among the Austin Friars, as Zumkeller and others have insisted, but it would be less confusing to students of the period if we relabeled that *Lehrrichtung* as the "common teaching *within* the Augustinian School." When John Hiltalingen of Basel, teaching at Paris in the third quarter of the century, referred to "our school" (*schola nostra*), he was, as has been noted earlier, referring to all theologians of the Augustinian Hermits, particularly those who taught in the lecture halls of the house of studies at Paris. Hiltalingen's "school" meant *Ordensbrüder*, not *Lehrrichtung*.

THE NEW AUGUSTINIANISM ON THE CONTINENT

The broad outlines of the history of both Augustinianism and the Augustinian School in the fourteenth century, of which the English development forms an important chapter, are now fairly clear. One of the sources of Augustinianism lies with the conservative, anti-Averroistic movement that sponsored the condemnations of 1270 and 1277 and set the theological mood of the late thirteenth century, with its emphases on divine omnipotence and the contingency of the created order. Although many individual features of the thought of Duns Scotus can be found in earlier thirteenth-century figures, it would be hard, as Gilson once remarked, to imagine Scotus writing as he did before the Parisian Articles of 1277.[6] 1277 did not create a new Augustinianism; it was more likely the stepchild of a more conservative and traditional theology that was gaining strength in the 1270s. But the judicial victory of that tradition at Paris and Oxford facilitated the growth of Augustinianism in the late thirteenth and early fourteenth centuries.

A second and more direct source of the new Augustinianism lies in the personal intellectual development of the first theological master of the Austin Friars at Paris, Giles of Rome.[7] Beginning as a student of Thomas Aquinas, Giles moved from Christian Aristotelianism in the direction of Augustinianism across the last decades of the thirteenth century, urged on by his debates with Henry of Ghent and Godfrey of Fontaines and by the ecclesiastical polity issues raised by the conflict between Boniface VIII and Philip the Fair. After a long spiritual journey, the elements of Aristotelian metaphysics and political thought faded into the background, to be replaced by an affective theology with a strong doctrine of grace and justification alongside which Giles created his own "Augustinian" doctrine of the lordship of grace, initially useful in defense of the papal position. Giles's version of Augustinianism dominated the theology and political writings of the Austin Friars until a new force entered around 1340.

This third source was the simultaneous publication in 1344 of Thomas Bradwardine's extensive and somewhat excessive Augustinian attack on the so-called Pelagians of his day, and Gregory of Rimini's Parisian lectures on the *Sentences*.[8] Bradwardine's views, as expressed in

---

[6] Gilson, *HCP*, 408–10, 465.

[7] On the development of the thought of Giles of Rome see E. Hocedez, "Gilles de Rome et S. Thomas," in *Mélanges Mandonnet*, vol. 1 (Paris, 1930), 358–409, who noticed a number of significant differences between Thomas and Giles. Since then the list has grown. See P. W. Nash, "Giles of Rome, auditor and critic of St. Thomas," *The Modern Schoolman* 28 (1950/51): 1–20; "Giles of Rome and the Subject of Theology," *MedStud* 18 (1956): 61–92; "Giles of Rome: a pupil but not a disciple of Thomas Aquinas," in *Readings in Ancient and Medieval Philosophy*, ed. J. Collins (Westminster, Maryland, 1960), 251–57.

[8] Bradwardine's *Summa de causa Dei* circulates in the Saville edition of 1618, but for Rimini's *Lectura* there is a new critical edition edited by D. Trapp. For studies of Bradwardine see G. Leff, *Bradwardine and the Pelagians* (Cambridge, 1957); H. A. Oberman, *Archbishop Thomas Bradwardine. A Fourteenth Century Augustinian* (Utrecht, 1958); J.-F. Genest, *Le 'De*

his monumental *Summa de causa Dei*, have usually been considered unique in England, and although his position on divine will and human freedom was controversial albeit frequently cited, he is not generally credited with stimulating any Augustinian, anti-Pelagian current in English or continental thought.

Rimini, on the other hand, is often credited with ushering in a new and more thoroughgoing phase of Augustinianism at Paris. The difference between Giles of Rome and Gregory of Rimini is more than a difference between Augustinianism couched in the language of thirteenth-century metaphysics and an Augustinianism couched in the language of the fourteenth-century *moderni*. Gregory's Augustinianism is based on a more critical and extensive reading of the Augustinian corpus than was available to Giles, and with Gregory the issue of justification and related theological problems played a far more important role. Moreover, Gregory became the touchstone for Augustinianism on the Continent from the late fourteenth century into the early sixteenth.[9]

Within the history of late medieval Augustinianism, the English contribution has received little attention beyond the prominent figures of Thomas Bradwardine and John Wyclif. Surprisingly works on Bradwardine have sought to identify his opponents, those he attacked or who attacked him, not his sources. Both he and Wyclif have to a large degree been seen as self-made theologians. But is that the whole picture? Several areas bear further investigation, only some of which can be dealt with here. Is there a background at Oxford to Bradwardine's challenge, and what is the relationship, if any, between Bradwardine and Rimini or between Bradwardine and Wyclif? Moreover, to what degree was Augustinianism an influential current of thought at Oxford or in England in the fourteenth century? Finally, what did England contribute to the Augustinian revival on the Continent and through what channels was it communicated?

---

futuris contingentibus' de Thomas Bradwardine, thèse Ecole Pratique des Hautes Etudes, Paris, 1975, portions of which were published under the same title in *Recherches Augustiniennes* 14 (1979): 249–336. For studies of Rimini's Augustinianism, in addition to Trapp and Zumkeller, cited earlier, see *Gregor von Rimini. Werk und Wirkung bis zur Reformation*, ed. H. A. Oberman (Berlin, 1981).

[9] M. Schulze, " 'Via Gregorii' in Forschung und Quellen," in *Gregor von Rimini. Werk und Wirkung*, 1–126.

THE AUGUSTINIAN SCHOOL AT OXFORD

If the history of Augustinianism on the Continent in the fourteenth century is any indication, one would expect to find the early emergence of a new Augustinianism in England within the convents of the Augustinian Hermits and, in particular, in the Augustinian School at Oxford. This, however, is not the case. As we saw in chapter 6, those few Austin Friars from the early fourteenth century, some of whose questions have survived, show adherence to the teaching of Giles of Rome but no elements of the newer Augustinianism. We may take for example William Heckham, the first Austin doctor at Oxford. An abbreviated version of five theological questions are contained in Worcester Q.99, one of which was edited by Little: whether essence is indifferent to existence or nonexistence.[10] This issue was debated in thirteenth-century metaphysics, but rarely after the second decade of the fourteenth century. The question of Heckham edited by Little shows the influence of Augustine and Giles of Rome. Its abbreviated nature, however, makes it difficult to assess the degree of dependence. A more precise answer may be possible. Some of the most interesting questions of Heckham have yet to be edited, for example, questions on epistemology (whether the intellect understands through species), on contingency of the created order (whether it is repugnant to the creature to exist from all eternity; whether it is repugnant to the creature to exist necessarily), and on God's knowledge of things *ad extra*. Some of these questions are ones that might lend themselves to strong Augustinian positions, but this cannot be determined until further work is done. Whatever Heckham's own intellectual stance may have been, there is little evidence that it had much effect on subsequent generations. Outside contemporary references to Hecham, I have not found him cited in works composed after 1315, even within the Augustinian School.

The first indications of the newer Augustinianism among the English Austins occurs in the 1350s, when the thought of Gregory of Rimini is introduced from the Continent by John Klenkok.[11] Klenkok went to Oxford from Prague and read the *Sentences* in 1354–55. From Klenkok we have the only full *Sentences* commentary of an Oxford Austin, and

---

[10] A. G. Little and F. Pelster, *Oxford Theology and Theologians* (Oxford, 1934), 335–37.

[11] D. Trapp, "Augustinian Theology," 223–39; "Notes on John Klenkok O.S.A. (d. 1374)," *Augustinianum* 4 (1964): 358–404.

although it is essentially an *Expositio litteralis*, i.e., a commentary that explicates the actual text of Lombard and adds very little of the author's own thought, Klenkok does allow contemporary opinion and his own views to enter in the second and third redactions of his work. Among the older theologians he cites Richard of St. Victor, William of Auvergne, Aquinas, Kilwardby, Giles of Rome, and Duns Scotus. He is also familiar with the thought of Aureoli, Thomas of Strasbourg, Ockham, and later Oxfordians, such as Fitzralph, Wodeham, Bradwardine "et sequentes," Thomas Buckingham, and Osbert Pickingham. Where his own views come through, we find a strong Augustinian in the tradition of Gregory of Rimini, whom Klenkok admires greatly and cites frequently. He is also fond of Hugolino of Orvieto. In fact, Klenkok may have been instrumental in bringing Gregory and Hugolino to the attention of Oxford theologians.

One of Klenkok's major opponents was Uthred of Boldon, whom he attacked for being Pelagian in his attitude toward what man can do about his own salvation, *ex puris naturalibus*. While Uthred acknowledges the necessity of the auxiliary help of God, he does believe man can prepare himself sufficiently for the gift of grace, that he can turn to God of his own free will. This Klenkok rejected totally.

Two features emerge from the Oxford *Sentences* commentary of Klenkok. One of these is a strong interest in logic and a metalinguistic approach to problems in philosophy and theology, the type of concerns that came to the fore at Oxford in the period from 1330 to 1350. It tells us that these issues were not dead at Oxford in the years immediately after the Black Death but lived on at least for a short while longer. The second feature is the Augustinian doctrine of grace and justification adopted from Rimini and Hugolino.

It would appear, then, that elements of the newer Augustinianism cannot be found among the Austin Friars until the 1350s. Far from originating in the Austin convent, its major manifestation, the doctrine of grace and justification as taught by Gregory of Rimini, was introduced from the Continent. Even so, its impact was slow and mixed. The only extensive Austin scholastic text we have from this period apart from Klenkok, namely the anonymous *Sentences* commentary of an Oxford Austin Friar (*c.* 1355), shows closer affiliation to Nicholas of Aston than to Gregory of Rimini, as was true of another Oxford Austin of this period, Geoffrey Herdeby.[12] Not until we come to the anonymous Oxford commentary of *c.* 1380 (not necessarily by an Austin Friar) do we find the newer Augustinianism, specifically derived from Rimini.[13]

What we have of scholastic work surviving from the Oxford Augustinian School is admittedly scanty, delivered in a voice that is barely audible. One can detect the presence of Aegidian thought in the opening decades of the fourteenth century and a stronger, Gregorian tradition entering at mid-century. But there is no evidence for Lang's assertion that the Augustinian School was Thomistic or that it was specifically directed "against the extreme rationalism of Robert Holcot and against Nominalism."[14] There does not seem much to suggest that either Aegidian Augustinianism or Gregorian Augustinianism was especially vigorous at Oxford, and absolutely no evidence that the theologians of the Austin friary at Oxford had any effect on theologians at Oxford outside their own order.

One possible contribution made by the Oxford Austins, albeit indirect, was through the expansion of their library. Only at the end of the thirteenth century did the order launch a program to improve the library holdings at the teaching convents. A significant portion of their financial resources went to that end, and the most rapid growth was probably in the early fourteenth century. Money was put into books, not the construction of library buildings, which came later. The library at the Paris convent, the leading theological *studium* of the order, held less than 50 volumes in 1290, although it was subsequently known as one of the richer collections in Paris and almost 200 manuscripts belonging to the convent before 1400 have survived.[15] In 1372 the library

---

[12] The name of Aston is linked with the Oxford Austin Friars of the 1350s in Etienne Chaumont and John Hiltalingen of Basel. See John of Basel, *Lectura super libros sententiarum*, Munich, Staatsbibl. MS. clm 26711, fols. 162rb, 212^v; Z. Kaluza, Thomas de Cracovie (Wroclaw, 1978); Kaluza, "Le Problème du 'Deum non esse' chez Etienne de Chaumont, Nicolas Aston et Thomas Bradwardine," *Mediaevalia Philosophica Polonorum* 24 (1979): 3–19; D. Trapp, "Augustinian Theology," 229–31, 242–50; Trapp, "Hiltalinger's Augustinian Quotations," *Augustiniana* 4 (1954): 412–49.

[13] Trapp, "Clm 27034. Unchristened Nominalism and Wycliffite Realism at Prague in 1381," *RTAM* 24 (1957): 343.

[14] A. Lang, *Die Entfaltung des apologetischen Problems in der Scholastik des Mittelalters* (Freiburg i.B., 1962), 168 ff.; Lang, *Die Wege der Glaubensbegründung bei den Scholastikern des 14. Jahrhunderts* (Münster i.W., 1930), 190–210.

[15] Zumkeller, "Augustinerschule," 171; Roth, *EAF*, 1: 369.

of the Austin Friars in York, which probably numbered less than its equivalent in London or at Oxford, contained 656 volumes.[16]

Unfortunately, we do not have details on the Oxford library, and we can only conjecture about the holdings from Austin libraries in other teaching convents. Volumes that certainly would have been acquired by the Oxford convent in the early fourteenth century (if they were not present earlier) would have been most of the works of Augustine, also those of Thomas Aquinas, and probably a complete collection of the works of Giles of Rome. For our purposes the presence of good copies of almost the entire corpus of Augustine, particularly the later, anti-Pelagian writings, is important. Although the library was housed at the end of the dormitory and was for the use of Austin Friars, we must remember that the convent was the center of the School of Theology, and it is possible that others had access to the collection and that a broader, more extensive knowledge of Augustine may have been influenced by the Austin library. Those coming and going from the refectory and chapel (which included the young Wyclif as an arts student at the very time Klenkok was lecturing there in theology) could not have failed to notice the lay scribes in the west range of the cloister, who were hired to copy and expand the holdings of the Augustinian collection.

AUGUSTINIANISM AT OXFORD

Apart from the presence of the Austin Friars, Oxford had a strong tradition of Augustinianism that went back to the thirteenth century. Despite Robert Grosseteste's acknowledged interest in Aristotelian thought, his theology remained conservative.[17] It was Christocentric, showed little interest in natural theology, understood theology as exegesis of Scripture rather than as a science in the strict sense, and was af-

---

[16] Roth, *English Austin Friars*, 1: 375–76; N. R. Ker, ed., *Medieval Libraries of Great Britain* (London, 1964), 218.

[17] L. Baur, *Die Philosophie des Robert Grosseteste* (Münster i.W., 1917); G. B. Phelan, "An Unedited Text of Robert Grosseteste on the Subject-Matter of Theology," *Revue Néo-Scolastique de philosophie* 36 (1934): 172–79; L. E. Lynch, "The Doctrine of Divine Ideas and Illumination in Robert Grosseteste," *MedStud* 3 (1941): 161–73; D. A. Callus, "The Summa theologiae of Robert Grosseteste," in *Studies . . . presented to F. M. Powicke* (Oxford, 1948), 180–208; Callus, "Robert Grosseteste's Place in the History of Philosophy," in *Actes du XIe Congrès internat. de philosophie* (Bruxelles, 1953), 161–65; Gilson, *HCP*, 259–65.

fective in nature. Grosseteste was among those who fought against the tendency for theology to become more scientific and Aristotelian. Even in his philosophy and science the conservative and, indeed, Augustinian nature of his thought can be seen. Grosseteste continued to maintain an epistemology based on divine illumination (one of the hallmarks of the Augustinian tradition) and to explore the visual experience of light, associated with the nature and revelation of God. Many of these same characteristics can be seen in the thought of Roger Bacon and others at Oxford.[18] In fact, the theology taught at Oxford in the thirteenth century, whether one is looking at Grosseteste, Bacon, Kilwardby, Fishacre, or Pecham, was both conservative and Augustinian, far less influenced by Aristotle in structure and content than the Parisian theology of the same period.

Many of those Oxfordian elements were continued in the thought of John Duns Scotus, whom we have examined in connection with the Franciscan School. Scotus's stress on divine omnipotence, on the *acceptatio divina* before which human merit has no absolute standing or claim, and predestination *ante praevisa merita* all appear to be marks of a strongly Augustinian approach. These elements are mitigated in Scotus (and even more in Ockham) through his belief that God is, in a relative sense, a debtor, that God has committed himself to always reward with eternal life those who do their best to fulfill his commandments. Because of the semi-Pelagian overtones to aspects of Scotus's theology, and even more Ockham's, it would be inappropriate to place either Scotus or Ockham as major figures within an English Augustinian movement—and this despite some pronounced Augustinian characteristics. As late as 1328, when Richard Fitzralph was lecturing on the *Sentences*, one finds no evidence of the newer elements. The Augustinianism of the young Fitzralph is, as Gordon Leff has shown, almost identical with that of Henry of Ghent.[19]

When one looks into the Oxford contemporary with Bradwardine, however, one finds not only that he was not as unique as we once thought but that it was precisely in his generation at Oxford, 1330–40, that a new Augustinianism was born, the type that influenced Rimini,

[18] R. Carton, *La synthèse doctrinale de Roger Bacon* (Paris, 1924); Gilson, *HCP*, 294–312; and D. C. Lindberg, *Roger Bacon's Philosophy of Nature* (Oxford, 1983).

[19] G. Leff, *Richard Fitzralph* (Manchester, 1963), 13 and passim.

Hugolino, and others in subsequent generations. Several factors came together in that decade to produce this newer current of thought.

One factor in which English writers played the principal role was in the growth of commentaries on the works of Augustine. Augustine's works were probably never school texts and thus, unlike the Bible, Aristotle's writings, the *corpus iuris civilis*, the *Decretum* and *Decretales*, or Lombard's *Sentences*, never received extensive analytical treatment. However, to the fourteenth-century reader, Augustine's style and his classical allusions were sufficiently difficult to make an introduction useful. The growth in commentaries attests, therefore, to a growing interest in Augustine on the part of the commentators and a growth in the reading public that made the commentaries desirable or necessary.

This portion of the expansion of apparatus for understanding Augustine seems to have been a predominantly if not exclusively English effort. Already in the thirteenth century Kilwardby divided the books of *De civitate Dei* into chapters with subject titles, and the first Franciscan master at Oxford, Adam Marsh, achieved a similar division for Augustine's *De Trinitate*. In the early fourteenth century Nicholas Trevet, O.P., wrote the first commentary on *De civitate Dei*.[20] After about 1325 there was a flurry of commentaries on Augustine. John Baconthorp wrote a commentary on *De civitate Dei*, a commentary on the *De Trinitate*, and a short work of conclusions extracted from the *De Trinitate*.[21] Around 1328 Fitzralph composed his *Glosulae super De Trinitate*, which was cited by Wodeham, although copies are not known to exist.[22] The Dominican, Thomas Waleys, wrote a commentary at Avignon around 1332 on the first ten books of *De civitate Dei*, which came to replace those of his fellow religious, Trevet.[23] Finally, John Ridevall, a Franciscan theologian at Oxford, wrote a critique of Trevet's commentary (*c.* 1331), a commentary of his own on *De civitate Dei* (*c.* 1333), and a commentary on the *Confessions*.[24]

Although not all these commentaries were done at Oxford or even in England (for example, Baconthorp may have written his at Paris), they were all composed by English theologians, all of whom were connected

[20] Smalley, *EFA*, 58–65; Zumkeller, "Augustinerschule," 172.

[21] Xiberta, *SOC*, 189–90.

[22] Courtenay, *Adam Wodeham* (Leiden, 1978), 79.

[23] Smalley, *EFA*, 88–100.

[24] Smalley, *EFA*, 121–32.

with Oxford at some point. Their efforts were not to my knowledge paralleled by any similar activity among continental theologians. Moreover, although we do not know the dates of Baconthorp's commentaries on Augustine, it would seem probable that they, like all the others save Trevet's, were composed in the decade 1325–35. The fact that several of these commentaries are referred to as lectures suggests that Augustine may briefly have become a minor text in the faculty of theology or the religious schools. When one surveys these commentaries together one is struck by the surprising absence of any contribution from the Austin Friars, who contributed so much in other areas of Augustinian studies in the fourteenth century. They appear to be the only mendicant order not to have produced a commentary on a work of St. Augustine.

In light of the low profile the Austin Friars had at Oxford in the early fourteenth century and their seeming failure to contribute commentaries on Augustine, it is not surprising that when a newer, purer, more rigorous type of Augustinianism appears at Oxford we do not find its center at the Augustinian convent. What is perhaps surprising is that we also do not find it emanating from the Franciscans, where we might otherwise expect it. It comes from among the secular theologians.

Richard Fitzralph, whose *Sentences* commentary can now be dated with probability to the years 1328–29, has been called an Augustinian, though of a very traditional, even thirteenth-century type.[25] The propositions on grace, justification, and predestination that became the hallmarks of the new Augustinianism cannot be found in his lectures given before 1330. Fitzralph, however, was not untouched by the newer current of Augustinianism in the years after 1330. His interest in Augustine, beyond the positions adopted in his *Sentences* commentary, possibly began as early as his commentary on the *De trinitate*, although the loss of that work does not permit us to examine the possibility. By 1340, however, the elements of Augustinian thought are much stronger. Aubrey Gwynn and W. A. Pantin have already called our attention to Fitzralph's description of his "conversion" during his six years at the papal court in Avignon (*c.* 1337–43), couched in language taken from Augustine's Confessions:[26]

[25] Leff, *Richard Fitzralph*; Walsh, *RF*.
[26] Pantin, *ECFC*, 132–33.

Nor were You, the Solid Truth, absent from me those six years [at the Court of Rome], but, in Your Holy Scriptures you shone upon me as in a certain radiant mirror; whereas in my former years, in the trifles of the philosophers, you had been hidden from me as in a certain dark cloud. For previously, I used to think that through the teachings of Aristotle and certain argumentations that were profound only to men profound in vanity,—I used to think that I had penetrated to the depths of Your Truth, with the citizens of Your Heaven; until You, the Solid Truth, shone upon me in Your Scriptures, scattering the cloud of my error, and showing me how I was croaking in the marshes with the toads and frogs. For until I had You the Truth to lead me, I had heard, but did not understand, the tumult of the philosophers chattering against You, the pertinacious Jews, the proud Greeks, the carnal Saracens, and the unlearned Armenians. . . . At last, O Solid Truth, You so shone upon me from above, that I burned to seize and to hold You, the Truth, Jesus promised to us in the Law and Prophets. And when in the turmoil of lawsuits a certain spell of serenity had smiled upon me, I sought You in Your sacred Scriptures, intimately and importunatly, not only by reading, but also with prayer, until You came to meet me joyously in Your ways.

The importance that Scripture played in this religious conversion has long been noted. In light of what we now know of the place Scripture continued to hold in the theological curriculum of Oxford in the fourteenth century, it was not the reading of Scripture that was new to Fitzralph but a *way* of reading, or better, the purpose of reading. But not enough attention has been paid to the Augustinianism of the passage. Its style is a conscious imitation of Augustine's *Confessions*.

At a latter point in Fitzralph's career (1350–60) he came into conflict with the mendicant orders and in that controversy adopted another Augustinian position. This was the thesis of *dominium gratiae*, or lordship of grace, which Aubrey Gwynn traced from Giles of Rome, through the writers of the Augustinian Hermits, into Fitzralph and, subsequently, into Wyclif.[27] It is in Fitzralph for the first time that this idea, with its roots in Augustinian thought, is turned against a religious group or institution.

The second and more prominent secular theologian associated with this newer Augustinianism was the Mertonian mathematician and theologian, Thomas Bradwardine, whose theological positions are best represented in his *Summa de causa Dei*. Although elements of that work may have derived from his lectures on the *Sentences*, the structure of *De*

[27] A. Gwynn, *The English Austin Friars in the Time of Wyclif* (Oxford, 1940).

causa Dei owes more to the structure of Euclid's *Geometry* and thus to Bradwardine's mathematical interest than it does to the structure of Lombard's *Sentences*. In Bradwardine we meet features of Augustinianism that have the intensity and one-sidedness that we associate with Gregory and Hugolino. The foundation block is an anti-Pelagian view of grace and justification that reduces human initiative in favor of divine action. That strong view of divine omnipotence with regard to salvation is carried over into a belief in double predestination (i.e., that in addition to electing his saints God actively predestines others to hell) based solely on God's decree, not foreseen merits, and to a view of divine volition that appeared to contemporaries to remove human freedom and make God responsible for sin and evil as well as good—a position that has been called theological determinism or divine omnivolence.

Bradwardine's thesis quickly became a cause célèbre at Oxford and, later, at Paris. Few theologians did not take up the challenge and attempt to protect the freedom of man from what looked to them like a thoroughgoing, predestinarian, even predetermined view of the divine plan. It made Bradwardine a household name among the educated, inside and outside the university, and put forward a particular interpretation of Augustine that had its own long and interesting history.

Bradwardine's views on grace and justification certainly owed much to his personal understanding of the relation of human action to the divine will, an understanding that came upon him through his study of Paul and Augustine. As such it has been viewed as an intellectual conversion, parallel in some respects to that of Fitzralph. On closer examination, however, one finds that the groundwork for Bradwardine's thesis was already laid in the type of theological problems that were being addressed at Oxford in the late 1320s and the metalinguistic analyses and solutions that were being applied. The discussion of God's freedom over time and his ability to change the past is nothing new in Bradwardine. It had a much older history and was part of the scholastic debates at Oxford during the period of his education. More importantly, the position that God's foreknowledge, once revealed, implied that the future was not contingent but could only happen as God foreknew it—a position that most historians have seen as Bradwardinian and central to his view of future contingents—was already put forward at Oxford shortly before 1330 by a master of theology known only as Master Walter.[28] It caused a controversy in 1330–32 because it potentially denied human freedom and made the future determined.

Bradwardine's own contribution to that debate first appeared around 1335, possibly in his commentary on the *Sentences* but certainly in the extant treatise on future contingents.[29] Although the position taken by Bradwardine in that treatise was milder than that proposed by Master Walter, there was an immediate and widespread reaction to Bradwardine's views. Well before the publication of the completed version of his *De causa Dei* in 1344, Bradwardine's opinions were being cited by Robert of Halifax, Thomas Buckingham, and Alexander Langeley.[30] Rimini knew Bradwardine's opinions either through Halifax and Buckingham or directly through Bradwardine's treatise or an early version of *De causa Dei*, which he cited correctly. Although Rimini did not always agree with Bradwardine, he was influenced by Bradwardine's views on grace, justification, and predestination. Moreover, it was probably through Bradwardine that Rimini adopted for a time the opinion that there was no necessary contradiction in the idea of God's being able to alter the past.[31]

Bradwardine found few supporters in the Oxford of his day, but the long-range effects of Bradwardine's influence was considerable. Despite the points of disagreement between Bradwardine and Rimini recorded in the text and margins of Rimini's *Lectura*, the influence of the *Doctor Profundus* can be felt in Gregory's thought, as in that of Hugolino. At Oxford, although he continued to be attacked by Nicholas Aston, Osbert Pickingham and numerous other theologians writing after 1350, he did persuade others. The most prominent heir to at least some aspects of his thought at Oxford or in England was John Wyclif. Unfortunately, Wyclif rarely names his allies or identifies his enemies, but among those he cites, a pattern is apparent. His occasional censures of Ockham are counterbalanced by favorable citations of Bradwardine and frequent reliance on Fitzralph. Those two figures form the most

---

[28] Adam Wodeham, *Lect. Oxon.* 3, q. 4 (Paris, Univ., MS. 193, fol. 186ʳᵇ): "Opinio Galteri quod facta revelatione absoluta oppositum non potest evenire." See also Holcot, *Quaest. Quodl.*, Oxford, Balliol College, MS. 246, fol. 246ᵛᵃ; Cambridge, Pembroke College, MS. 236, fol. 185ʳᵇ.

[29] Genest, "De futuris contingentibus."

[30] Genest, "De futuris contingentibus."

[31] Courtenay, *Covenant and Causality in Medieval Thought* (London, 1984), ch. 8.

important intellectual heritage for Wyclif. We find in Wyclif a strong doctrine of grace and justification, of predestination *ante praevisa merita*, of the invisible, inward, or essential church, and the idea of the lordship of grace.

When the pieces are put together, it appears that England's contribution to the Augustinian revival in fourteenth-century Europe was considerable. Much of the source-critical work on the Augustinian texts was done by English theologians. The revival in biblical studies was particularly strong at Oxford and Cambridge.[32] The elements of the debate over future contingents that stressed the certitude of divine foreknowledge and power at the expense of contingency were put forward in the writings of Master Walter and Bradwardine. The campaign against the apparent Pelagianism of Ockham was initiated by an English theologian, John Lutterell, and pressed against Ockham and Wodeham by Halifax and, eventually, by Bradwardine. In many respects, therefore, Bradwardine was the culmination of an Augustinian revival at Oxford that reached back to 1325. Yet the real heirs to the new Augustinianism, as the mention of Wyclif suggests, are to be found in the second half of the fourteenth century, and some of the atmosphere of the post-1350 period, the emphases on penance and salvation, biblical faith, preaching, and the preference for a less scholastic style in the numerous defenses of the faith, may owe something to the position of Augustine in English thought.

[32] Smalley, *EFA*.

III

OXFORD AFTER THE BLACK DEATH

ELEVEN

THE TRANSFORMATION OF ENGLISH

SCHOLASTICISM

∽❦∾

BEYOND THE frontier of 1350 the intellectual landscape of England appears quite different. In contrast to the long list of well-known English scholastics from the first half of the fourteenth century, the only familiar name in the second half of the century is that of John Wyclif. Oxford seemingly entered an intellectual limbo in which philosophy and theology of the type associated with the university in the 1330s all but ceased and from which Oxford did not fully emerge until the arrival of humanism in the late fifteenth century. Moreover, Wyclif has been remembered as a church reformer, a biblical scholar, a political theorist, and even as heretic, but not particularly as a philosopher or scholastic theologian. In fact, Wyclif's sharp attack against the "doctors of signs," which has normally been viewed as an attack on the nominalists of his day, could as well be seen as an attack on the type of logic, physics, and theology that developed at Oxford in the previous two generations. Thus the sole prominent figure at Oxford or Cambridge in the second half of the fourteenth century displays interests and attitudes that contrast sharply with those of the previous half century.

What, then, was going on in the schools and universities in England in the age of Wyclif and Chaucer? Is the paucity of known names of late-fourteenth-century scholastics a true reflection of that era, a result of insufficient research, or a result of under-reporting? And if the type of scholastic thought developed at Oxford and elsewhere in England in the first half of the fourteenth century—the type of philosophy, theology, and science that made Oxford famous on the Continent as well as in England—died out in the second half of the century, what produced this dramatic change? Should it be viewed as decline or regeneration? And when did the change begin to take place?

Oxford's apparent loss of national and international academic prominence in the period between the middle of the fourteenth century and the age of humanism and reform in the sixteenth century has been frequently noted and almost universally deplored. As one historian has described it, "England in the fifteenth century was culturally dull, flat, and unenterprising."[1] Many would carry that evaluation back a full half century. Robson saw the paucity of English scholastic works in the generation between the publication of Bradwardine's *Summa de causa Dei* and the emergence of Wyclif to reflect "a real decline in the intellectual vigour of Oxford."[2] Whether Wyclif, whose "rise can only be understood in this context,"[3] is further evidence of that decline or a temporary respite from it, depends on the value judgment of historians. The most frequent explanation for the fifteenth-century "decline," however, has been Wyclif himself, whose heresy made Oxford suspect within England (a dangerous place to send talented but susceptible youths)[4] and a pariah abroad. Yet Wyclif can hardly be blamed for a deep intellectual ennui that set in several decades earlier, if such was the case. Consequently, among those who date the beginnings of decline at mid-century, the two most popular theories attribute that process to the cultural separation of Oxford and Paris during the Hundred Years' War and the devastating impact of the Black Death, whose combined debilitating effects were not offset by Wyclif or any of his contemporaries.[5]

---

[1] George Holmes, *The Later Middle Ages, 1272–1485* (London, 1962), 139.

[2] J. A. Robson, *Wyclif and the Oxford Schools* (Cambridge, 1961), 97. Gedeon Gál and Rega Wood date the decline among the Franciscans slightly earlier, "Richard Brinkley and his *Summa logicae*," *FcS* 40 (1980): 59: "In comparison to this imposing array of authors [from 1236–1336], the second century (1337–1437) presents a rather bleak and depressing picture. Scholars become scarcer and scarcer . . . and they are not towering figures." If the dividing line were moved to 1340, so as to include Rosetus, Halifax, Langeley, Went, and Adam of Ely with the earlier group, I would find the statement quite acceptable.

[3] Robson, *Wyclif and the Oxford Schools*, 97.

[4] The association of Oxford and heresy has been given as one of the reasons for the expansion and greater prominence of Cambridge in the fifteenth century.

[5] For example, David Knowles, *The Historian and Character* (Cambridge, 1963), 132: "Until the age of Ockham there had remained a solidarity in European intellectual life; persons, ideas, and doctrinal pronouncements circulated freely throughout north-western Europe, and in particular there was constant interchange of men and ideas between Oxford and Paris. From about the middle of the century, however, a great change began to take place. . . . the Hundred Years War and later the Great Schism isolated English thought and the two English universities both from Paris and from what may be called the theological climate of continental Europe." Robson, *Wyclif and the Oxford Schools*, 97: "How far was the Black Death responsible for this? We know that it killed Bradwardine and Hol-

To put the issue in its simplest and most direct form, was the age of Wyclif and Chaucer also the age that witnessed the collapse of English higher education and with it the loss of the medieval intellectual heritage? Were the delayed and somewhat different forms that Renaissance and Reformation took in England conditioned by the absence of intellectually vigorous academic institutions? Before those questions can be answered, we must examine the extent and quality of scholastic thought present in England during the period 1340–70 and thereby assess the degree of decline or change that may have taken place.

ON THE EVE OF THE BLACK DEATH (1340–49)

As one surveys England in the early 1340s, one initially has a sense of continuity. Many from the generation that had come to maturity in the late 1320s and early 1330s were still active in English intellectual life. Fitzralph was a highly visible prelate, and his *Summa de quaestionibus Armenorum* appeared in the 1340s. Bradwardine was chancellor at St. Paul's in London when he completed his *Summa de causa Dei* in 1344. Buckingham, while chancellor at Exeter, produced his *Quaestiones theologicae*, probably between 1346 and 1350. The picture at Oxford, however, seems far less brilliant. It now appears that the works of Kilvington, Rosetus, Halifax, Went, Langeley, Roger Swineshead, Adam Junior, and the Monachus Niger should probably all be placed before 1340. Secular masters such as Heytesbury and Dumbleton no doubt remained at Oxford after 1340, but their writings belong to the previous decade. The only arts master actively writing at Oxford in the 1340s is Richard Swineshead, whose *Calculationes* is usually dated in or shortly after 1350. And the only theologian whose work has survived and who was probably lecturing and disputing at Oxford in this period is John Stuckley, whose *Sentences* commentary was written in or shortly after 1340. If there were other fresh young minds at Merton College or in the religious convents of Oxford at that time, they did not achieve much visibility.

At the very least this represents a staggering drop in the preservation of works and known authors from the years 1340–50. It probably re-

---

cot; we can only guess at the number of young students, yet to make their names, whom it carried off."

flects a drop in production as well, since neither in England nor on the Continent in subsequent generations are any authors from this decade cited beyond those already mentioned. Yet the lack of identifiable authors and works during the 1340s should not be seen as an immediate or fundamental shift in scholastic interests or methods. The numerous figures active in philosophy and theology at Oxford in the 1350s, albeit most or all of secondary rank, reveal that the traditional disciplinary structure and values had not radically changed. The most that can be said of the 1340s is that whatever works may have been produced were for the most part not of sufficient merit in the eyes of their authors and/ or contemporaries to warrant circulation or even preservation. The work of the two authors mentioned, Stuckley at the beginning of the decade and Richard Swineshead at the end, reveal, however, that the themes and interests of the previous generation were retained and to some degree advanced. Stuckley concentrated some of his attention on the issue of whether God could deceive or command someone to hate him—a question that was evoking increasing interest in the 1330s.[6] Swineshead brought to fruition much of the mathematical physics of Bradwardine, Kilvington, and Dumbleton.[7]

It might be imagined that the quantitative decline in known authors and scholastic works after 1340 might in some way be a result of the Black Death at mid-century, on the assumption that many authors of that decade may simply not have lived long enough to circulate their works and become known. This cannot have been the case. The period of 1340–50 at Paris, which also experienced the Plague, was one of the most intellectually active decades of the century. Moreover, within the intellectual world of southern England and particularly within the walls of Oxford, works began to be cited with a year of their creation, and authors, once introduced into the body of known names, had their reputations assured. In the late medieval world of contemporary *auctoritates*, as the biography of Scotus amply attests, longevity has little to do with fame.

[6] Courtenay, "The 'Sentences' Commentary of Stukle: A New Source for Oxford Theology in the Fourteenth Century," *Traditio* 34 (1978): 435–38; J.-F. Genest, "Le *De futuris contingentibus* de Thomas Bradwardine," *Recherches Augustiniennes* 14 (1979): 249–336.

[7] A. Maier, *Die Vorläufer Galileis in 14. Jahrhundert*, 2nd ed. (Rome, 1966); Maier, *An der Grenze zwischen Scholastik und Naturwissenschaft*, 2nd ed. (Rome, 1952); J. Weisheipl, "Ockham and Some Mertonians," *MedStud* 30 (1968): 207–13.

A far more probable factor in the decline of Oxford authors in the 1340s was the condition of Greyfriars and recruitment among the Franciscans. The intellectual vitality of Oxford's "golden years" was largely a result of Franciscan and Mertonian scholars, and to a somewhat lesser degree, the Dominicans. The impressive run of Franciscan authors, however, appears to cease around 1340, and there was only a moderate recovery in subsequent generations. This may have been a delayed result of recruitment problems the Franciscans experienced in the 1320s and 1330s in the wake of the crisis over apostolic poverty, the effects of which would not have been evident at the university level for a decade or more. Recruitment problems do not, of course, explain the declining performance of the secular masters at Merton, or that of the Dominicans. But perhaps the reduced level of intellectual excitement and exchange produced by the eclipse of the Franciscans altered the atmosphere and made scholastic debate and publication less important. Without a sufficient number of challenging minds among colleagues, providing models, peer stimulation, and expectations of performance, and without the presence of a sizable and eager audience, much of the social and psychological support of the scholastic enterprise may have been removed—at least below the level of a necessary critical mass. Whatever the reason, it is clear that the intellectual life that does continue at Oxford after 1350 was not carried forward by the group that had most sustained its reputation in the first half-century, namely the Franciscans.

What effect did the Plague of 1348–49 have upon Oxford and, by extention, upon the cultural life of England? Far less than is usually imagined. What can be determined about the death rate among Oxford students and masters suggests that it was far closer to the aristocratic average of 25 percent than to the 40 percent average for the clergy and lower urban and rural population. A number of major scholastic figures died in those years, whether victims of plague or not: Baconthorp, Holcot, Bradwardine, perhaps Dumbleton, to name a few. Yet many others survived: Fitzralph, Wodeham, Buckingham, Heytesbury, and both Roger and Richard Swineshead. Heytesbury and Richard Swineshead even remained active at Oxford. As has been discussed in detail elsewhere,[8] the famous names that disappear in 1349 were, for the most

[8] Courtenay, "The Effect of the Black Death on English Higher Education," *Speculum* 55 (1980): 696–714.

part, past their academic careers and were no longer actively writing. And those who continued or who soon appear at Oxford in the 1350s received their basic education and much of their university study before the Black Death.

Where we would expect the Plague to have had a serious effect on education (because of the paucity of qualified teachers) would be at the elementary and secondary levels, the results of which would not have begun to appear at the university level before around 1360. The universities, which required far fewer teachers and retained through the Plague years most of those it had, could and apparently did continue to attract qualified students to replace any immediate drop in numbers.

The mendicant and monastic orders, however, were more severely affected by the Plague. Unlike the university as a whole, which attracted students from a wide social and geographical spectrum, the religious orders selected and sent to the universities only those from their own group, a pool that was suddenly reduced in 1349 by some 30 to 40 percent. In combination with the recruitment problems of the Franciscans, referred to above, the total effect was probably crippling among the religious houses of study.

LOGIC AND THEOLOGY (1350–65)

If one were to judge on the basis of the number of known scholastic figures active and the quantity of production, Oxford in the period between the Black Death and the beginning of Wyclif's writing career hardly qualifies as an intellectual wasteland.[9] Among those contributing to logic and natural philosophy were Richard Swineshead, Richard Billingham,[10] Richard Brinkley, a Franciscan,[11] Richard Feribrigge,[12]

[9] The few detailed studies that have been made of this period of English thought, however, share a negative judgment. The pioneering work remains unpublished: Stephen L. Forte, *A Study of Some Oxford Schoolmen of the Middle of the Fourteenth Century with Special Reference to Worcester Cathedral MS. F.65*, (B. Litt. thesis, Oxford, 1947), to which Robson's *Wyclif and the Oxford Schools* is heavily indebted. See also David Knowles, "The Centured Opinions of Uthred of Boldon," *The Proceedings of the British Academy* 37 (1951): 305–42, repr. in *Historian and Character*, 129–70; Joel Bender, *Nicholas Aston: A Study in Oxford Thought after the Black Death*, Ph.D. diss., University of Wisconsin, Madison, 1979.

[10] Billingham's tenure at Oxford was at least from 1344 to 1361, during which time he completed his degree in arts (by 1349) and most of his theological training. All of his extant

Ralph Strode,[13] William Rede,[14] Henry Hopton,[15] and possibly Robert Fland.[16] The scholastic theologians of this period include Nicholas Aston,[17] Osbert Pickingham,[18] Uthred of Boldon,[19] Richard Brinkley,[20] William Trevelles,[21] several anonymous commentaries on the *Sentences*,[22] and the foreign scholars John Klenkok and Peter of Candia.[23]

---

writings are in the area of logic: *Speculum iuvenum*, sometimes referred to as *De probationibus propositionum; De sensu composito et diviso; Conclusiones*; a *Sophisma*; and *De significato propositionis*. Only the first of these, his *Speculum* is more than a short treatise or circulated widely. He was already known on the Continent by 1360 and is cited in the first (anonymous) commentary in MS. Vat. lat. 986, and by Nicole Oresme and John Hiltalingen of Basel. He is frequently mentioned in later English works in logic, and his *Speculum* was commented on by later logicians, including Edward Upton. On Billingham see: Emden, *BRUO* 1: 188–89; James Weisheipl, "Repertorium Mertonense," *MedStud* 31 (1969): 176–77; C. Michalski, "La Physique nouvelle et les differents courants philosophiques au XIVᵉ siècle," *Bulletin internat. de l'Acad. Polonaise des Sciences et des Lettres*, classe d'hist. et de phil. (Cracow, 1928), 112–13, 137–40; Alfonso Maierù, "Lo *Speculum puerorum sive Terminus est in quem* di Riccardo Billingham," in *A Giuseppe Ermini* [also *Studi medievali* 10,3] (Spoleto, 1970), 297–397; L. M. De Rijk, "The Place of Billingham's *Speculum puerorum* in 14th and 15th Century Logical Tradition with the Edition of Some Alternative Tracts," *Studia Mediewistyczne* 16 (1975): 99–153; "Another *Speculum puerorum* attributed to Richard Billingham. Introduction and Text," *Medioevo* 1 (1975): 203–35; "Richard Billingham's Works on Logic," *Vivarium* 14 (1976): 121–38; "Semantics in Richard Billingham and Johannes Venator," in *ELI*, 167–83. Billingham's reputation as a nominalist was created by Franz Ehrle, *Der Sentenzenkommentar Peters von Candia* (Münster, 1925), because Billingham's name was often cited in the company of Heytesbury and others. Yet there is nothing particularly nominalist nor Ockhamist about Billingham's *Speculum*. The belief that Billingham studied theology and wrote a *Sentences* commentary was circulated by Michalski on the grounds that Billingham is cited in the first *Sentences* commentary in MS. Vat. lat. 986 on issues of natural theology.

[11] Brinkley has only recently begun to receive attention. His *Sentences* commentary probably dates from the 1350s, while his *Logica* shows signs of having been written later, after 1360. In contrast to Billingham, Brinkley's *Logica* is a long work, running to over 100 folios in the two manuscripts of the complete work. Portions of that work have been edited by Gedeon Gál and Rega Wood, "Richard Brinkley and his *Summa logicae*," *FcS* 40 (1980): 59–101. An abbreviation or summary of the *Quaestiones in Sententias* of Brinkley was compiled by Etienne Gaudet at Paris around 1362. It has been edited by Zenon Kaluza and will soon be published.

[12] Two of Feribrigge's works have survived, both in logic: *Logica seu de veritate et falsitate propositionum* and *Consequentiae*. Neither work is very long, and they probably date to the 1350s. The opening two chapters of part one of the longer work have been edited by Francesco del Punta, "La *Logica* di R. Feribrigge nella tradizione manoscritta italiana," in *ELI*, 53–85. Del Punta is planning a full edition.

[13] The complete text of Strode's *Logica* survives in only one manuscript, Oxford, Bodl. MS. Canon. Misc. 219, copied at the end of the fourteenth century by an arts student from

In addition, others were known and cited as authors but their scholastic works have not survived, for example William Folville, O.F.M. and regent master at Cambridge around 1354, and William of Bermingham, D.Th. by 1362 but known for his opinions in logic.[24] Those in religious orders were more numerous within the theological group: Pickingham

---

Italy. Sections of it, however, are found in many manuscripts. It is of medium length and is divided into six short treatises: introduction, logical principles, supposition, consequences, obligations, and insolubles. See Paul Spade, *The Mediaeval Liar: A Catalogue of the 'Insolubilia'-Literature* (Toronto, 1975), 87–91; A. Maierù, "Le Ms. Oxford, Canonici Misc. 219 et la *Logica* de Strode," in *ELI*, 87–110, which contains an edition of the treatise on insolubles; W. K. Seaton, "An Edition and Translation of the *Tractatus de consequentiis* by Ralph Strode, Fourteenth-Century Logician and Friend of Geoffrey Chaucer," Ph.D. diss., University of California, Berkeley, 1973.

[14] On Rede see Emden, *BRUO* 3: 1556–60; Weisheipl, "Repertorium Mertonense," 218. His only extant work is on astronomy: *Tabulae astronomicae*, or *Canones tabularum*.

[15] Hopton was sequentially a fellow of University College (1357–61) and Queen's College (1361–67). He had already begun the study of theology by 1362, and his treatises in logic (his *Tractatus de insolubilibus*) and natural philosophy (*Disputationes*) probably date from the late 1350s or early 1360s. See Emden, *BRUO* 2: 960; Spade, *The Mediaeval Liar*, 56–57.

[16] Paul Spade has dated Fland's *Insolubilia* between 1335 and 1370. In addition, his *Consequentiae* and *Obligationes* have survived, all of which have now been edited by Spade. See Spade, *The Mediaeval Liar*, 95–97; "Robert Fland's *Consequentiae*: An Edition," *MedStud* 38 (1976): 54–84; "Robert Fland's *Insolubilia*: An Edition, with Comments on the Dating of Fland's Works," *MedStud* 40 (1978): 56–80; "Robert Fland's *Obligationes*: An Edition," *MedStud* 42 (1980): 41–60.

[17] The basic details of Aston's career are given in Emden, *BRUO* 1: 68. Subsequent information can be found in Zenon Kaluza, "L'Oeuvre théologique de Nicolas Aston," *AHDL* 45 (1978): 45–82; "Le problème du 'Deum non esse' chez Etienne de Chaumont, Nicolas Aston et Thomas Bradwardine," *Mediaevalia Philosophica Polonorum* 24 (1979): 3–19; and Bender, *Nicholas Aston*.

Confusion over the date of his *Sentences* commentary has been caused by a failure to pay sufficient attention to the documentary evidence and by the linking of "Aston" (in the form "Astensis") with the name/label "Achilles." The term "Achilles" had several meanings in the fourteenth century. One meaning was the mathematical argument on motion entailed in Zeno's paradox of Achilles and the tortoise, recounted in Aristotle's *Physics* 6: 9. "Achilles" could also mean an invincible argument, and so it was used by Nicholas of Autrecourt in his *Exigit ordo* (*c.* 1340). It was also the name or nickname of a near contemporary of Hugolino of Orvieto; A. Zumkeller, *Hugolin von Orvieto und seine theologische Erkenntnislehre* (Würzburg, 1941), 289; Hugolinus de urbe veteri, *Commentarius in quattuor libros sententiarum*, vol. 1, ed. W. Eckermann (Würzburg, 1980), 68. The "opinio" of this particular "Achilles" was that the object of knowledge was the proposition itself (*vera et formata*), a position akin to that of Ockham.

When in his *Sentences* commentary Aston labeled his preferred argument for the exist-

(Carmelite); Boldon (Benedictine); Brinkley and Candia (Franciscan); and Klenkok (Augustinian).

But what of the character and quality of the work of these authors? Apart from Swineshead, the quality of whose work is well recognized, the philosophical works of this period are largely on an introductory

---

ence of God "Achilles," he meant only that it was for him an invincible argument, and in subsequent discussions it became known as the "Achilles argument of Aston"; e.g., John of Basel, *Lectura in Sententias* (MS. Clm 26711, fol. 154va): "arguo ratione Haston, articulo primo, ratione quam vocat Achilles"; Angelus Dobelin, *Lectura in Sententias* (Jena, Bibl. Univ., MS. Elect. 47, fol. 32vb): "Aston . . . fecit argumentum quod est Achilles"; Dionysius de Montina, *In quatuor libros Sententiarum* (Paris, 1511), fol. 14vb: "Achilles astensis." Achilles was never part of Aston's name (mistakenly construing "Achilles astensis" to mean [Nicholas] Achilles de Aston), and Hugolino in 1348 was referring to an entirely different person.

Aston was still referred to as *Magister* [*artium*] in 1350, not bachelor of the *Sentences* as Robson maintained, *Wyclif and the Oxford Schools*, 106. Consequently, he must have read the *Sentences* after 1350.

[18] Xiberta, *SOC*, 241–77 still remains the best account of the life, writings, and thought of Pickingham. The dating of Osbert's *Lectura* is determined by the fact that he cites Aston and John Trevaur, and in turn is cited by Klenkok and the anonymous Augustinian bachelor.

[19] Knowles, "Uthred of Boldon."

[20] See above, n. 11. Kaluza has established that the *Sentences* commentary of Brinkley was known in Paris by 1362 or 1363, when it is cited by Etienne Gaudet, and then subsequently by John Hiltalingen of Basel, James of Eltville, Etienne Chaumont, Dionysius of Montina, Angelus Dobelin, Henry Totting of Oyta, and Peter of Candia. Allowing time for it to cross the Channel, its *terminus ante quem* would be around 1360. Its *terminus post quem* is more difficult to determine. It would appear that Brinkley was familiar with arguments contained in the *Sentences* commentary of Aston, thus placing Brinkley's *Lectura* in or after 1352. A date closer to 1360, however, seems more appropriate. If Gál and Wood are correct in dating Brinkley's *Summa logicae* between 1360 and 1373, then the latter was probably written or revised after (but not too long after) his *Sentences* commentary—a not unusual practice among the Franciscans, as the biography of Ockham illustrates. But Brinkley's use of Billingham, Bermingham, and Feribrigge (whose opinions in logic can best be dated to the early 1350s) need not push the date of his *Logica* much past the late 1350s. In light of the conjectured date of Brinkley's *Sentences* commentary (between 1352 and 1360), a date between 1355 and 1365 for the *Logica* would seem more appropriate.

[21] Trevelles was M.A. by 1354, B.Th. by 1361, when he was a fellow of Queen's College, still B.Th. in Febr. 1363, and D.Th. by 1368. See Forte; Emden, *BRUO* 3: 1899–1900.

[22] A commentary of an Augustinian bachelor of the early 1350s is contained in Paris, Bibl. Nat. MS. lat. 16 535, fols. 75^r–110^r, and another anonymous commentary is contained in Oxford, Merton College MS. O.I.9 (Coxe 284), fols. 66^r–96^v.

[23] On Klenkok, a German Augustinian Hermit, see D. Trapp, "Augustinian Theology of

level. It is a commonplace in Oxford logical treatises even before 1350 (one thinks of the introduction to Heytesbury's *Regula solvendi sophismata*) for authors to describe their works as written for beginning students in logic, as indeed most of them were.[25] This description, however, seems particularly appropriate for the logical works of Billingham, Strode, Brinkley, and Feribrigge. Their circulation in Italy in the late fourteenth and throughout the fifteenth centuries may have been precisely because they served that introductory need.

Secondly, these works are all dependent upon and fall within the category of the new logic as it was developed at Oxford in the first half of the fourteenth century. These authors did not write commentaries on Aristotle's logic but wrote treatises on terms, propositions, consequences, insolubles, and other types of treatises on the properties of terms. In that sense they belong to the tradition of "modern" or terminist logic, a tradition that includes Peter of Spain and Burley as well as Ockham and Heytesbury. They do not show any particular inclination toward the speculative grammar of the Modist logicians.

At this point, however, some important differences between these logicians and Ockham have to be recognized. To the degree that their writings reveal their position, these logicians of the 1350s were realists

---

the 14th Century," *Augustiniana* 6 (1956): 203, 223–39; "Notes on John Klenkok, o.s.a. (d. 1374)," *Augustinianum* 4 (1964): 358–404. On Candia, a Greek Franciscan, see Franz Ehrle, *Der Sentenzenkommentar Peters von Candia, des Pisaner Papstes Alexanders V* (Münster, 1925); Stephen F. Brown, "Peter of Candia's Sermons in Praise of Peter Lombard," in *Studies Honoring Ignatius Charles Brady, Friar Minor* (St. Bonaventure, 1976), 141–76.

[24] On Folville see Emden, *BRUC*, 236; on Bermingham, Emden, *BRUO* 1: 177.

[25] Cf. Ockham, *SL*, 6: "Et quia plerumque contingit ante magnam experientiam logicae subtilitatibus theologiae aliarumque Facultatum iuniores impendere studium, ac per hoc in difficultates eis inexplicabiles incidunt, quae tamen aliis parvae sunt aut nullae, et in multiplices prolabuntur errores, veras demonstrationes tamquam sophismata respuentes et sophisticationes pro demonstrationibus recipientes, tractatum hunc duxi scribendum. . . ." Kilvington, *Sophismata*, unpublished transl. by N. and B. E. Kretzmann: "I am led to do this by the requests of certain young men who have been pressing their case very hard." Heytesbury, *Regula solvendi sophismata*, transl. Paul Spade, *William Heytesbury on "Insoluble" Sentences* (Toronto, 1979): "You young men in your first year of logical studies, I would deliver into your care, to the extent that the barrenness of my ability would manage, a brief compendium (*summa*) of the rules for solving sophisms." Both secular students and those in religious orders studied logic between the ages of fourteen and twenty. That group would always seem "young" to those *writing* treatises in logic, who were between the ages of twenty-five and thirty-five.

on the question of universals; they understood simple supposition to stand for common natures in things; and they affirmed the real existence (*res extra*) of the categories, not limiting their ontology simply to substance and quality.[26] Brinkley's *Summa logicae*, which was composed at the request of his superiors, may have been intended as a substitute text within Franciscan circles for Ockham's popular *Summa logicae*, since one of the fundamental differences between those two works is Brinkley's objections to the points on which Ockham's work was controversial. Realist attitudes, however much they were challenged by Ockham, Wodeham, Heytesbury, or Dumbleton, had remained viable at Oxford throughout the first half of the century and seem to have reigned unopposed after 1350. If Wyclif seriously felt himself to be surrounded by "doctors of signs" and by that phrase meant nominalists, it is impossible to identify anyone among his contempories or recent predecessors who can be so described, unless it be the aging Heytesbury.

Brinkley was opposed to another approach in logic which has nothing to do with Ockham and may be a clue to what Wyclif meant by "doctors of signs." Brinkley criticized the practice of certain contemporary logicians to consider spoken and written terms and propositions to be more important than mental terms (concepts) and mental propositions. For them logic is *in vocibus*. The truth or falsity of propositions is determined not by the mental proposition or by the actual state of affairs *ad extra*, but by the verbal meaning of the expressions used *(proprietas vocis), de virtute sermonis.*[27]

[26] Brinkley best illustrates these positions; see Gál and Wood, "Richard Brinkley." On Strode's realism, see unpublished paper of Spade, International Medieval Conference, Kalamazoo, Michigan, 1984. Unfortunately, the type of writings extant from Billingham, Feribrigge, Hopton, and Fland—practical works on rules and techniques for proving propositions or solving sophisms and insolubles—do not discuss these issues.

While these three issues (universals, supposition, and the categories) were closely linked in Ockham's logic, it needs to be remembered that the third issue is not derived from or necessarily related to the first two. As Paul Spade has already noted, *Peter of Ailly: Concepts and Insolubles* (Dordrecht, 1980), 96, one can be a realist and have a reduced ontology, or be a nominalist on universal concepts and yet affirm the real existence of the ten categories.

[27] Gál and Wood, "Richard Brinkley," 67: "Admittit tamen usus modernorum huiusmodi propositiones vocales, credentes eas esse veras, sive intellectus consideret de suppositis subiecti in talibus propositionibus sive non; credentes logicam esse in vocibus, non subordinatam conceptibus in anima. Sed nitentes subordinare conceptus in anima ipsis vocibus, omnem propositionem concedunt vel negant secundum proprietatem vocis. Ideo ad virtutem sermonis respiciunt tanquam ad causam primam in propositionibus admitten-

This approach to logic bears little resemblance to Ockham, who affirmed the priority of mental language and attacked the restriction of the truth value of propositions to the literal meaning of words, since it ignored the intention of the author and the use of figures of speech.[28] The position described by Brinkley does, however, resemble to some degree Holcot's approach to logic.[29]

Evidence for the nature of theological teaching at Oxford in this period is not as meager as has often been suggested. The commentaries of Aston, Pickingham, and Klenkok have survived, and for Boldon we have his reply to his critics (probably Klenkok and the Dominican William Jordan) who compiled a list of propositions taken from his commentary that was subsequently condemned.[30] We also have a summary of a *Sen-*

---

dis vel negandis a logico. Alii ponunt primam radicem logicae esse in conceptibus animae et in compositione et divisione illorum conceptuum et non in voce nisi dum et quatenus subordinantur conceptibus. Et tales concedunt et negant propositiones in voce secundum veritatem et falsitatem in illis propositionibus in anima quibus tales propositiones subordinantur." For the context of the controversy over *de virtute sermonis* see my "Force of Words and Figures of Speech. The Crisis over *Virtus Sermonis* in the Fourteenth Century," *FcS* 44 (1984).

[28] See Ockham on relation of mental, spoken, and written language, *SL*, 11–14; and on validity of propositions containing terms that are not intended literally, *de virtute sermonis*, *SL*, 236–38.

[29] For example, in Holcot's quodlibetal question edited by E. A. Moody, "A Quodlibetal Question of Robert Holkot, O.P. on the Problem of the Objects of Knowledge and of Belief," *Speculum* 39 (1964): 53–74.

[30] The lectures on the *Sentences* for Aston, Pickingham, and Boldon can be placed between 1350 and 1354, probably in that sequence. Klenkok, who read the *Sentences* at Oxford in 1354–55 and who incepted in theology on Aug. 5, 1359 (see above, n. 3), cited Uthred as *socius*, Osbert as *doctor*, and Osbert, in turn, cited Aston. Klenkok was referring to the theological opinions of Osbert, whom he cites as a "doctor (i.e., master of theology) of our university." Osbert's academic rank may correspond to the time at which Klenkok revised his commentary (1355–59), but there is no doubt that Osbert had read the *Sentences* by or at the time Klenkok read, i.e., 1354. Aston was not yet a bachelor of theology in 1350, when he first appears in the rolls of Queen's College. The opinions to which Osbert refers are found in Aston's commentary, but they are issues that might also have been discussed in his earlier work on insolubles. While it is possible that Aston, Pickingham, and Klenkok all read in the same year, it is more likely that the commentaries of the first two should be placed within the previous four years. With the exception of Aston, the "contemporaries" against whom Osbert fashions his own positions date from the late 1330s and early 1340s: Buckingham, Bradwardine, Heytesbury, and John Trevaur (B.Th. by 1343). The dates

tences commentary from another Augustinian, otherwise anonymous, that dates to the middle of the 1350s.[31] Finally, we have a summary of the *Sentences* commentary of Brinkley, probably dating to the late 1350s, some *determinationes* of Trevelles, and at least one other anonymous *Sentences* commentary.[32]

Looking at this material as a whole, several observations can be made. When compared with the high productivity of authors from the 1330s and the survival rate of their works, the number of *Sentences* commentaries declines slightly, but not drastically. Far more has survived from the 1350s than from the previous decade, and the number of known authors with surviving works is greater than for the decade of the 1320s.

If the number of extant *Sentences* commentaries remained relatively high during the 1350s, the number of manuscript copies does not. With the exception of Osbert, whose commentary survives in twelve manuscripts, copies of works surviving from this decade are few: five manuscripts for Klenkok; three manuscripts and a summary for Aston; one summary each for the commentaries of the Augustinian anonymous and Brinkley. That small amount of preservation or survival is already

---

given in my *Adam Wodeham* for Aston and Pickingham were based on the erroneous statement in Robson, *Wyclif and the Oxford Schools*, 106, that Aston was already a bachelor of theology in 1350. For Uthred see: M. E. Marcett, *Uthred de Boldon, Friar William Jordan, and Piers Plowman* (New York, 1938); C. H. Thompson, *Uthred of Boldon, a study in fourteenth-century political theory*, Ph.D. diss., University of Manchester, 1936; Knowles, "Censured Opinions of Uthred of Boldon."

[31] Paris, Bibl. Nat., MS. lat. 16 535, fols. 75^r–110^r, 116^r–17^v. On this author, see Z. Kaluza, *Thomas de Cracovie. Contribution à l'histoire du Collège de la Sorbonne* (Wroclaw, 1978), 72, n. 29; "Le problème du 'Deum non esse,' " 3–19.

[32] Brinkley's commentary and disputed questions occur in abbreviated form in Paris, Bibl. Nat., MS. lat. 16 535, fols. 123–29; Paris, Bibl. Nat., MS. lat. 16 408, fols. 40–42; Paris, Bibl. Nat., MS. lat. 16 409, fols. 73–76. On Brinkley's theological work see Kaluza, *Thomas de Cracovie*, 134–36; and "Le problème du 'Deum non esse.' " Kaluza is preparing an edition of the Brinkley abbreviation as well as the entire text of his *Summa logicae*. Trevelles, a fellow of Queen's College, read the *Sentences* at Oxford between 1354 and 1361. His *Determinationes* are contained in Worcester Cathedral, MS. F .65, fols. 5^r, 25^v. Other works are the anonymous *Quaestiones in Sententias* in Oxford, Merton College, MS. O.1.9, fols. 66^r–96^v, and briefly discussed in Robson, *Wyclif and the Oxford Schools*, 104–6. The anonymous English *Sentences* commentary (perhaps by a Frater Petrus) found in MS. Vat. lat. 13002, fols. 46^r–73^v, 79^v–90^r, 2^r–44^v, may date to this period, but considering the other works in the manuscript, Oxford in the late 1330s is a more likely location.

a feature of most English scholastic theological works written after the mid-1330s. Even allowing for the possibility that manuscripts of lesser known authors might be more subject to discarding or neglect, the paucity of manuscripts suggests a smaller audience for these later authors. They were, however, reasonably well known at Paris within a few years of their writing, and were remembered and discussed in the works of Parisian theologians from 1360 to 1380.

When we consider their structure, the theological works of the 1350s are of small to medium length, usually consisting of some eight to twelve questions that pose issues of contemporary theological interest arranged roughly according to the outline of Lombard's *Sentences*. But that was nothing new in 1350. Shorter commentaries with fewer but longer questions was a practice already established at Oxford by 1335. In that sense, as in some others, the commentaries of Aston, Pickingham, and Brinkley are the natural successors to those of Kilvington, Rosetus, Halifax, and Buckingham. The textual content of the commentaries of the 1350s, however, is less polished and professional. Whether a result of imperfect revision, poor scribes, or simply the style and reasoning of the authors, the arguments of this period sometimes appear incomplete, chaotic, or rambling.

With the exception of the Dominicans, whose intellectual contribution had already diminished by the mid-1330s, the religious orders are fairly evenly represented among these authors. Moreover, the small amount of theological work published by secular scholars is not unusual. Most of the seculars who contributed to logic and natural philosophy at Oxford in the fourteenth century left no *Sentences* commentaries and, despite the overwhelming predominance of theological degrees among them, often no theological works at all. One thinks in particular of Burley, Heytesbury, Dumbleton, and Swineshead. Campsall was known as a theologian, but his theological work has not survived. Bradwardine wrote his *De futuris contingentibus* and his highly influential *Summa de causa Dei*, but no *Sentences* commentary survived. Harclay, Fitzralph, and Buckingham, by contrast, were known almost exclusively as theologians. Only Bradwardine and Kilvington adequately bridge the worlds of arts and theology. To see the 1350s in proper perspective, therefore, we should not expect surviving theological work from most of the secular scholars who made reputations in logic. The proportion of arts to theological work among the seculars seems consistent with earlier decades.

There is one new element here that should be noted. Secular scholars who made reputations in logic and natural philosophy in the first half of the fourteenth century either became theologians or, in a very few cases, remained simply arts masters before going on to a post-university career. By contrast, Ralph Strode, one of the most prominent logicians of the 1350s, chose a career in law. The significance of that shift will be viewed in a larger context in the final chapter.

When we consider the content of Oxford theological works in the 1350s we find, as with those in logic, that the interests and approaches of the previous two decades were continued. The earlier misimpression that such was not the case was formed by comparing the English authors of the 1350s and 1360s with Parisian authors from the second half of the thirteenth century, such as Thomas Aquinas. But that is not a valid comparison for English scholasticism, and it obscures the striking continuity in themes and approaches that runs from the 1330s to the 1360s.

The principal feature of that continuity is the use of linguistic analysis in theology as well as in logic, and the penetration of the techniques, language, and problems of logic and natural philosophy into the realm of theology. Arguments are built on the "*sit casus*" structure. There is frequent use of the algebraic-like practice of assigning letter values to parts (often indefinite places or quantities) of a proposition or *casus*, thus reducing the length of arguments while increasing applicability. There is the continued concern with problems of place, time, distance, velocity, the instant, beginning and ceasing, and the latitude of forms. Aston's *Sentences* commentary, for example, is extensively devoted to problems in logic, much of it a disquisition on the character of negative propositions and the analysis of words implying privation and negation. Some of his arguments on these issues stem directly from his earlier treatise on insolubles in which he argued that no negative proposition signifies "just as it is."[33] The occasional manuscript attribution of some

---

[33] In the third question of his *Sentences* commentary (Worcester Cath. MS. F. 65, fol. 49[va]) Aston remarked: "Ideo notandum est quod nulla negativa propositio significat sicut est, ut alias probavi in tractatu de insolubilibus. . . ." In his opening question, however, a similar passage uses the future tense (Worc. Cath. MS. F. 65, fol. 44[va]): "Ex isto sequitur quod nulla

of Osbert's questions to Heytesbury, or Kilvington's work to Osbert, suggests a close relation in the minds of scribes.[34] Xiberta's study, which presents a picture of Osbert as a more traditional theologian (i.e., pre-1320), does not adequately reflect the main structure, arguments, and conclusions of Osbert.[35]

Several topics central to English scholastic thought in the 1330s and 1340s continued in discussion into the early 1360s: the problem of divine determinism that was touched off by Bradwardine's treatise on future contingents and by his subsequent *De causa Dei*; the problem of future contingents itself; problems concerning human free will, merit, and justification; and questions related to the Beatific Vision.

As with the crisis over Bradwardine's view of divine will and power, so echoes of the debate over the ontological status of the Aristotelian categories continued in the 1350s. We have already noted Brinkley's realism and his rejection of several fundamental positions of Ockham. Similarly, Aston maintained that relation was a real entity apart from things related, and that quantity was also a *res extra*.[36] We do find, however, that an unidentified *socius* of Aston, with whom he debates in his opening question, rejected the "real" status of relation and quantity, siding with Ockham that only substance and quality are real things.[37]

---

propositio negativa significat sicut est. Et per hoc principium necessarium faciliter posset homo solvere propositiones quae dicuntur insolubilia non negando casum. Sed tanseo, quia alias tradam solutionem insolubilium in quodam tactatu ad hoc specialiter deputato." Both the Worcester and Oriel College (MS. 15, fol. 211ᵛᵃ) have "tradam," but in light of the frequent scribal errors in both manuscripts, the ease of reading the minims for 'vi' as 'm', and the structure of the rest of the sentence, I would conjecture that the intended word was "tractavi."

[34] Both in Madrid, Univ., MS. 118.z.16, fol. 132ᵛᵇ, and Troyes, Bibl. de la Ville, MS. 505, fol. 79ʳ, Osbert's opening question *ad bibliam* is attributed to Heytesbury; and Osbert's *replicatio* 4 appears to be little more than a republication of the opening question of Kilvington's *Lectura*. There are also links with Buckingham. At the end of his commentary (q. 8) Osbert refers his reader to Buckingham's *Lectura*.

[35] Xiberta, *SOC*, 253–77.

[36] Worcester, MS. F.65, fol. 44ʳᵃ; Oxford, Oriel MS. 15, fol. 211ʳᵃ; Bender, "Nicholas Aston," 219: "Probo quod opinio ponens relationes non distingui ab absolutis, et ex hoc sequi quod propositio falsa significat praecise sicut est, decipitur per fallaciam figurae dictionis." See also Bender, *Nicholas Aston*, 238. For additional material on Aston's view of quantity, see Kaluza, "L'Oeuvre théologique de Nicolas Aston," 81.

[37] Bender, *Nicholas Aston*, 219: "In ista materia dicit quidam magister reverendus quod unio non est res distincta ab unitis, nec aliqua relatio distinguitur ab absolutis realiter.

The combination of a strong belief in the freedom and power of the human will and a pastoral concern to promote good and meritorious actions on the part of the faithful kept alive the controversy over Pelagianism in the face of the Augustinian revival. Uthred of Boldon stands out as a strong proponent of the power of the unaided human will to conquer sin and achieve good and meritorius deeds *de potentia ordinata*. His position goes beyond Holcot's belief that the efforts of a virtuous pagan might not only be good but would be rewarded by God with the gift of wisdom and, in certain circumstances, with grace and acceptation.[38]

In contrast to the first half of the fourteenth century, one seldom encounters discussions in which the dialectic of divine power is used as a problem-solving technique or a way of formulating a conclusion. The distinction occurs only a few times in Aston and Pickingham. Uthred often used the phrase *"de communi lege"* but seldom its companion *"de potentia absoluta."* Counterfactual possibilities, *de potentia Dei absoluta*, did not, therefore, preoccupy English authors of the second half of the century. Issues of relative and absolute necessity in the orders of nature and grace appear to have lost their appeal or the burning immediacy that they held for English authors before 1340.

Perhaps the most interesting theological development of the period—an issue born in the 1330s but which comes into greater prominence in the 1350s—was the way in which the new logic provided a ground for the revival of Anselm's ontological argument, which defines God as that being a greater than which cannot be conceived, and attempts to prove existence on the basis of that definition. Despite the overwhelmingly negative treatment Anselm's argument received in the thirteenth and early fourteenth centuries, it occasionally had its defenders. Henry of Ghent in particular put forward a metaphysical ar-

---

Immo dicit quod omnis res est substantia vel qualitas, et ex hoc sequitur quod propositio falsa significat praecise sicut est." "Magister reverendus" is a honorific expression, as is obvious from Bender, *Nicholas Aston*, 210: "per magistrum reverendum qui tertio loco intravit ad Sententias isto anno. . . ."

[38] See Uthred's propositions in Knowles. For Holcot's views on the virtuous pagan, see *In quatuor libros Sententiarum quaestiones* (Lyons, 1518), 3, q. 1 TT; H. A. Oberman, "Facientibus quod in se est Deus non denegat gratiam. Robert Holcot, O.P., and the Beginning of Luther's Theology," *Harvard Theological Review* 55 (1962): 317–42; *The Harvest of Medieval Theology* (Cambridge, Mass., 1963), 235–48.

gument for the existence of God based on the nature of being.[39] The essence of true being (being *qua* being) is necessary and identical with its existence. Therefore the existence of God is entailed in the definition of God as first or true being. That approach, however, was not particularly convincing to later writers, most of whom continued to take the position that only *a posteriori* proofs had any ultimate value, even as probable arguments for the existence of God.[40]

Anselm's argument reappeared at Oxford in the late 1330s, not in a metaphysical form but through the logical analysis of propositions. As far as can be presently determined, Monachus Niger, about 1336, was the first to reaffirm Anselm's argument on the basis of propositional analysis.[41] According to Monachus, anyone who understands the phrase "a greater than God cannot exist" must understand the subject-phrase "a greater than God." Thus "a greater than God" can be thought even though a greater than God cannot be thought (since for every instance presented, God is greater). The resulting proposition "a greater can be thought than that than which no greater can be thought" is self-contradictory, as is the proposition "a greater can exist than that than which no greater can exist." Thus the second part of the disjunctive

---

[39] Henry of Ghent, *Summae quaestionum ordinariarum*, art. 21, q. 4; art. 22, qq. 1–5; art. 24, q. 6; Gilson, *HCP*, 448–49.

[40] It is well recognized that Scotus favored *a posteriori* arguments for God's existence; *Opus Oxon.*, prol., q. 2; *Opus Oxon.* 1, dist. 2, pt. 1, qq. 1–2; 1, dist. 3, q. 2; 2, q. 2; *De primo principio* 3 and 4. Yet he felt (*Opus Oxoniensis* 1, 2, 2) that Anselm's argument had merit, especially with a few friendly improvements, principally the addition of the words "without contradiction" to the first premise. Some have felt that since Scotus thought Anselm's argument needed "touching up" (*potest colorari*), it was not very convincing but constituted only *persuasiones probabiles*, as he said in his *Reportata Parisiensis* 1: 2, 3. Yet "probable arguments" carry far more weight in the language of late scholasticism than is generally realized, and the term *color* (meaning "beauty," "value," "well formed") was a positive phrase; e.g., Osbert, *Sent.*, q. 8 (Prague, Bibl. cap. metro., MS. c.105, fol. 64ᵛ): "Sed audeo dicere quod argumentum apparentem habet colorem"; Wyclif, *De tempore* (Cambr., Trinity College, MS. B.16. 2, fol. 41ʳᵃ): "tunc opinio Platonis haberet magnum colorem"; Wyclif, *De scientia Dei* (Cambr., Trinity B.16.2, fol. 55ᵛᵃ): "Sed hoc non habet colorem"; Ibid., fol. 66ᵛᵇ: "habent manifestum colorem." Scotus's argument anticipates Aston, or more correctly, Aston probably derived certain elements from Scotus. For Ockham's treatment see *Sent.* 1, d. 2, q. 10; d. 3, q. 2; d. 3, q. 4; *Quodl.* 1, q. 1; *Quaestiones in lib. I Physicorum*, qq. 132–36.

[41] Julius Weinberg appears to have been the first to notice this discussion, although he mistakenly assumed that "monachus" referred to the white monk, John of Mirecourt. See J. Weinberg, *Ockham, Descartes, and Hume* (Madison, 1977), 15–21.

"God exists or a greater than God exists" is false, and thus the first part is true: God exists.

Gregory of Rimini, writing around 1343, took Monachus's argument seriously but rejected it.[42] In the sentence "a greater than God cannot exist," the phrase "a greater than God" does not supposit for anything, because the statement is negative, just as in the tautological expression "what cannot be thought cannot be thought." Rimini's critique, therefore, is based on the principle that every substantive part of a meaningful and true statement does not have to have a referent.

Bradwardine proceeded from another direction.[43] For him, the proposition "God exists" (*Deum esse*) precedes all other things and truths in the ontological order. It is the first true proposition, just as "God does not exist" (*Deum non esse*) is the first false proposition. Through an analysis of the interaction of the possible and impossible, Bradwardine moved from logical possibility to real necessity. The possible is the non-contradictory. On the basis of what we mean by God, the true proposition "God can exist" becomes the true proposition "God does exist," which in turn becomes the true proposition "God exists necessarily."

Aston, who discarded Bradwardine's argument as too theological and insufficiently logical, developed what he felt was a far more convincing argument.[44] Changes in states of affairs, according to Aston, affect the truth or falsity of propositions about those states of affairs, but self-contradictory propositions remain such regardless of states of affairs. If God exists, then the proposition "God does not exist" is not only false but contradictory, just as is the compound proposition "the king sits and no king sits." Because of the formal nature of contradictory compound or disjunctive propositions, or because necessary existence is somehow entailed in the term "God," Aston maintained that the proposition "God does not exist" is a contradiction, and therefore God exists.

This was the argument that Aston called his "Achilles" and which made his reputation in subsequent decades. It was shared by the anonymous Augustinian at Oxford and also adopted by John of Ripa at Paris

---

[42] Rimini, *In primum Sententiarum*, d. 42–44, q. 3, a. 3; Weinberg, *Ockham, Descartes, and Hume*, 15–21.

[43] Bradwardine's position is discussed by Zenon Kaluza, "Le problème du 'Deum non esse.'"

[44] Bender, *Nicholas Aston*, 291–96.

around 1358.[45] It was rejected as invalid by Brinkley and, around 1370, by Etienne Chaumont at Paris.[46] Its attractiveness lived on, however, as can be seen in Aston's argument being adopted by a theological bachelor at Prague in the 1380s.[47]

The decade of the 1350s was not, in retrospect, a period of sudden and dramatic change. Logicians and theologians were still active in significant numbers, debating and writing in a university context and, for the most part, applying familiar "modern" techniques to questions similar to those of the previous generation. Yet in the larger context of 1340 to 1365 changes are apparent. There was a quantitative decline in scholastic production from which the 1350s were only a temporary respite. Moreover, the quality of thought among the majority of this group does not appear to be up to the level of the earlier "golden age." Judgments of quality are, of course, difficult, and far more study needs to be given to the authors of this period before their contributions can be fully or adequately assessed. But on the basis of present knowledge, a weakening of intellectual resources had already taken place by 1340.

The early stages of that decline (if such is the appropriate label) had nothing to do with the Plague at mid-century. It started almost a decade earlier, and it would appear that the Black Death did not substantially reduce the number of active English scholars nor seriously handicap the production of scholastic philosophy and theology, at least not before 1360 or 1365. Whether the Plague ultimately affected the quality of work in the period from 1350 to 1365 by reducing the size of the total group from which good scholars emerged is another matter. The recurrence of plague in 1360 may have been as serious for Oxford as the original outbreak in 1348. The number of fellows at Queen's College, which had begun to take its place alongside Merton as an active center of philosophy and theology, was reduced to three. The hurried election of three new fellows in 1361 (far below the founder's original intention of twelve fellows in addition to the provost), lest the scholarly community die out, reflects the concern over the effects of high mortality as

---

[45] Kaluza, "Le problème du 'Deum non esse.' "

[46] Ibid.

[47] D. Trapp, "Clm 27034. Unchristened Nominalism and Wycliffite Realism at Prague in 1381," *RTAM* 24 (1957): 347.

well as the difficulty of finding qualified candidates among younger Oxford scholars in 1361.[48]

The evidence is strong that ties between England and the Continent did not decline in this period. Almost everything that we know to have been circulated in England (apart from the single copy, student notebook manuscripts at Worcester Cathedral or Merton College) was also known on the Continent—and apparently, if we are to judge by the surviving manuscript evidence, far better known and circulated there than in England. Heytesbury's *Regula solvendi sophismata* (1335) was in Germany within two years of its appearance.[49] Authors of the mid- to late 1330s, such as Rosetus, Halifax, Buckingham, and Langeley were known in Paris by the early 1340s.[50] Bradwardine's *Summa de causa Dei* was being cited at Paris within a year or two of its completion in 1344.[51] Stuckley, from the early 1340s, was known in Paris by 1348.[52] And the writings of Billingham, Aston, Pickingham, Brinkley, and others from the 1350s were known at Paris within five to eight years of composition.[53] Clearly, the early phases of the Hundred Years' War represented no insurmountable barrier for the transmission of learning. If, as was shown in chapter 5, contact with the Continent remained throughout the fourteenth century, if direct or indirect contact with Paris itself was such that Paris could and did import large amounts of English thought from 1340 to 1380, if the failure in England to keep up awareness of or interest in Parisian thought came *before* not *after* the "golden age" of the

[48] J. Magrath, *The Queen's College*, vol. 1 (Oxford, 1921), 102–4, esp. 103, n. 1. There may well have been other factors in reducing the number of fellows. The high price of agricultural labor after 1350 may have reduced college income, which in turn would have limited the number of fellowships below the level originally set by the founder.

Among those associated with Queen's in this period are Aston, Hopton, and Trevelles, followed in the next generation by Wyclif, Scharpe, Alyngton, Upton, and others.

[49] Erfurt, MS. Amplon. F.135, fols. 1–17, dated 1337.

[50] For citations of English authors by Parisian authors, see Trapp, "Augustinian Theology of the Fourteenth Century."

[51] Parisian citations of Bradwardine's opinions, originally based on his *De futuris contingentibus* and early versions of his *Summa*, rapidly change to book and chapter references to the latter.

[52] Stuckley is cited both by Pierre Ceffons and Hugolino of Orvieto. See Courtenay, "The *Sentences*-Commentary of Stukle: A New Source for Oxford Theology in the Fourteenth Century," *Traditio* 34 (1978): 435–38.

[53] See Z. Kaluza, "Thomas de Cracovie."

1330s, then any change in the quality or character of Oxford thought in the second half of the fourteenth century had nothing to do with separation or isolation from Paris.

The fact that contemporaries on the Continent thought that the views of English authors after 1340 were of sufficient merit to accord those authors a place in scholastic discussion alongside the "giants" of the previous generation does not by itself alter the qualitative judgment of their thought. The high reputation English thought achieved at Paris and elsewhere during the 1340s probably created a demand for the latest Oxford authors and works whether or not they were up to the level of Ockham, Wodeham, Bradwardine, or Kilvington. At home in England, most post-1340 authors were rarely cited in scholastic treatises, and the loss of the great mendicant libraries of Oxford, London, and York also probably meant the loss of the two or three copies ever extant of many late-fourteenth-century works. Had it not been for the vigor and dedication of scholars and scribes among the Benedictines and Carmelites, whose role in the second half of the century will be discussed in the last chapter, English manuscripts of these post-1340 authors would be almost nonexistent.

WYCLIF AT OXFORD

The basic outline of John Wyclif's academic career is well established.[54] Born in the early 1330s, he probably came to Oxford as a beginning arts student about 1350. He first appears in the documents as a bachelor of arts and probationary fellow of Merton College in the late spring of 1356. If his career followed the normal pattern, he would have incepted as master of arts a year or two later—and so he is designated in 1360 when he was holding the office of Master of Balliol. From 1361 to 1363 he was rector at Fillingham in Lincolnshire, a living in the gift of Balliol College. In the autumn of 1363 he returned to Oxford to take rooms at Queen's College and begin his study of theology. He almost certainly read the *Sentences* in 1369–70 and incepted as regent master of theology, probably in 1372.

The academic writings from this period of Wyclif's life were probably

---

[54] Robson, *Wyclif and the Oxford Schools*; W. R. Thomson, *The Latin Writings of John Wyclyf* (Toronto, 1983); A. Kenny, *Wyclif* (Oxford, 1985).

written across fewer years than is sometimes thought. If the writing pattern of earlier secular scholars is any guide, the philosophical treatises would have been written before the theological treatises, but all would have been written after Wyclif became master of arts around 1358. Considering the expressed application to theology that even his earliest treatises in logic have, it is likely that all of his writings, including the treatises in logic and metaphysics, took their final form after he became a student in theology in 1363. The theological portion of what came to be known as his *Summa de ente*, in turn, dates to the period 1369–74, and the years 1372–74 marked the beginning of his magisterial scriptural commentaries.

Wyclif's philosophical writings cover most areas of logic, physics, and metaphysics. The treatises in logic were, as was normal, written for beginning students in logic, "pro iuvenum eruditione," as he stated in his *De propositionibus insolubilibus*.[55] They were also written for the use of those who would some day be applying logic to Scripture.[56] The content of these treatises was not new, yet there seemed to be a student demand for fresh versions, and, as Wyclif remarked, the "shelf life" of these works was about twenty years.[57]

Wyclif undertook the *type* of work in logic that had become characteristic of Oxford in the early fourteenth century: analysis of terms and propositions, supposition, the operation of verbs of knowing, doubting and believing, beginning and ceasing, consequences, rules of obligations, and insolubles. There is no radical return to the structure and techniques of the nonterminist current of thirteenth-century logic. Wyclif tried to equip his students to survive in the world of fourteenth-century English logic, to distinguish and defend their way out of obliga-

[55] A similar phrase occurs in his *Logicae continuatio* in *Tractatus de logica*, ed. M. H. Dziewicki, vol. 1 (London, 1893), 75: "Iuvenum rogatibus quibus afficior superatus. . . ."

[56] The opening words of Wyclif's first work in logic reflect this; *Tractatus de logica*, ed. M. H. Dziewicki, vol. 1 (London, 1893), 1: "Motus sum per quosdam legis Dei amicos certum tractatum ad declarandam logicam sacrae scripturae compilare. Nam videns multos ad logicam transeuntes, qui per illam proposuerant legem Dei melius cognovisse, et propter insipidam terminorum mixtionem gentilium in omni probatione propositionum propter vacuitatem operis eam deserentes, propono ad acuendum mentes fidelium ponere probationes propositionum que debent elici ex scripturis."

[57] *De veritate sacrae scripturae* 1: 54: "Aliae logicae sunt periodice et nimis multiplices; periodice quia, ut patet in Oxonia, vix durat una aliena logica per viginti annos sed saepissime variantur."

tion-settings, *casus* by *casus*, *sophisma* by *sophisma*. Only occasionally did he find some of these settings to be pointless, sophistical quibbles.[58] Wyclif was never opposed to the restructuring of the study of logic around the "properties of terms" and the various genre that made up the *logica modernorum* which had come to maturity in the early decades of the fourteenth century and which were standard in the Oxford of his day. In that broad and stylistic sense Wyclif was as much a "terminist" as any of his contemporaries or predecessors.

There is also no discernible drop in the level of sophistication that would suggest any significant decline in the quality of his own training. Here as elsewhere, Wyclif was not always careful in correctly describing the positions of earlier writers,[59] and some of his argumentation is not convincingly structured or carefully thought through and worded. Yet he understood English logic as well as most in the fourteenth century, and what differences exist between his own work and that of previous generations is not really a qualitative issue or a function of failed education.

Two differences, however, emerge that set Wyclif off from a significant portion of fourteenth-century English logic. One of these was his realism, which he shared with many in his own immediate educational environment but which separated him from some of the major names in English logic, most notably Ockham, Holcot, and Heytesbury. Increasingly, Wyclif's logical treatises focused on issues where his realist viewpoint could attack the nominalistic presuppositions of some of his contemporaries and earlier writers. Between his *De Logica* (*c.* 1360) and his *De universalibus* (*c.* 1368/69) there is a gradual surfacing of Wyclif's antagonism to "Ockham and the other doctors of signs."[60] And much of

---

[58] Wyclif, *Logicae continuatio*, ch. 5, *Tractatus de logica*, vol. 1, ed. M. H. Dziewicki (London, 1893), 104–5; *Tractatus tertius*, ch. 1; *Tractatus de logica*, vol. 2, ed. M. H. Dziewicki (London, 1896), 14.

[59] In these early writings Wyclif never cites fourteenth-century authors but refers only to *moderni*, which in his time could mean any recent or contemporary author. He does, however, refer by name to a small group of earlier authorities from Aristotle to Grosseteste.

[60] Wyclif, *De universalibus*, ed. I. Müller, P. Spade, and A. Kenny (Oxford, 1984), defends realism specifically against "Ockham et multos alios doctores signorum." *Tractatus tertius de logica*, 2: 33: "Nec dubito quin . . . concedendum est communiter illa universalia esse. . . . Et propter ignorantiam talium universalium lapsi sunt moderni in multos errores. . . .";

his *Tractatus tertius* was written to combat a nominalistic interpretation of universals, simple supposition, and the categories of quantity, relation, motion, and time.

A second difference was Wyclif's antagonism toward one of the most important aspects of the logic of tensed propositions: the recognition of their changing truth value. Many English logicians, far from ignoring the existing physical realities that lay beyond terms and propositions, assumed that the truth value of particular propositions depended on the actual state of affairs at a given moment in time, and the truth value of universal propositions (to the degree that they were simply the compilation of all similar particular propositions), would also depend on the actual state of affairs remaining true. From Holcot to Pickingham there were numerous treatments of how propositions can change from true to false and from false to true solely through the passage of time and the changing pattern of events, thus seemingly changing what God knows or wills from moment to moment. In fact, the freedom of the human will with regard to alternative courses of action potentially made God's knowledge (assuming God knows propositions) change, increase, or decrease.[61] The truth or falsity of universal propositions for Wyclif, however, was based on the eternal reality of intelligible being and the "real" status of universals. The *res* behind the terms of propositions were ultimately not physical objects in time but eternal universals in God and beyond time, an element that comes out strongly in the meta-

---

Ibid., 3: 94: "Ratio autem difficultatis ad assentiendum istae sententiae est fluctuatio in rebus communibus, et [doctrina] illorum qui verbis negant communia praeter signa."

Wyclif was not entirely negative toward Ockham and attributed some "erroneous" ideas to followers who mixed Ockham's views with those of other theologians; Wyclif, *De universalibus*, ch. 15 (Cambr. Trinity College, MS. B.16. 2, fol. 35ra): "sed non credo ista fuisse verba vel sententia venerabilis inceptor Ocham sed alicuius qui partem coepit ab eo et partem ab aliis sanctis doctoribus." Ibid., fol. 34vb: "Tertio vere venerabilis inceptor Ocham posuit in ultimis diebus suis quod res singularis ut intellecta a Deo est idea, nec videtur ratio quin per idem sit genus vel species secundum modum intelligendi Dei vel hominis." Wyclif's attack on the *doctores signorum* was famous in his day, as can be seen from the *determinatio* of John Kenningham in *Fasciculi Zizaniorum*, ed. W. W. Shirley, Rolls Series (London, 1858), 64.

[61] For the position of Holcot on the ability of men to change God's propositional knowledge see E. A. Moody, "A Quodlibetal Question of Robert Holkot, O.P. on the Problem of the Objects of Knowledge and of Belief," *Speculum* 39 (1964): 53–74. A similar statement by Pickingham is quoted at length in Xiberta, *SOC*, 263.

physical portion of his *Summa de ente*.[62] It was precisely the procedure of subjecting the truth of particular propositions to changed conditions during an *obligatio* that Wyclif saw as sophistical quibbles, sleight-of-hand games, such as those played at Christmas.[63]

As we have seen, Wyclif was not in fact surrounded by nominalists who judged the truth of propositions by the operation of terms rather than real, existing individuals and universals. All that has survived from the years 1345 to 1365 shows it to be an age of realism. What was already in the writings of Burley and Sutton was expanded upon in Aston, Brinkley, Strode, and Feribrigge. But whether Wyclif perceived nominalists among his contemporaries, or had in mind authors two generations earlier (as the phrase "Ockham and the other doctors of signs" might suggest), or so characterized less thoroughgoing realists, his was the most compelling and extensive realism that had been presented at Oxford for many generations, perhaps (or so Wyclif felt) since Grosseteste.[64]

Realism was not the only element Wyclif had picked up from his early Oxford education. Wyclif's attitude toward *dominium* and ecclesiastical possessions as well as his eventual antipathy toward the religious orders owed much to the later writings of Fitzralph.[65] Similarly, Wyclif's attack on the modern Pelagians, his strong sense of grace and predestination, and his ideas on divine omnipotence, omniscience, and omnivolence that tended in the direction of divine determinism had their roots in Bradwardine's *De causa Dei*.[66] And Wyclif's indivisibilism was part of a

[62] Robson, *Wyclif and the Oxford Schools*, 141–70.

[63] *Tractatus tertius*, ch. 1; *Tractatus de logica*, vol. 2, 14: "Inter alias alterationes sunt huiusmodi disputationes de signis; et huiusmodi demonstrationes singularium mihi odibiles, quia indoctuales. Conformiter dicitur ad talem syllogismum: 'Tu es asinus, vel manus mea clauditur; sed nulla manus mea clauditur; ergo tu es asinus.' Concedenda enim est consequentia, et antecedens est negandum. Et si verificetur maior pro tempore suae prolationis, claudendo manum, more ioculantium in Natali, et pro tempore prolationis minoris verificetur illa, aperiendo ambas manus, illud nec probat antecedens esse verum nec fuisse verum; quia pro nullo instanti foret actus principalis totius antecedentis verus: quod tamen requiretur."

[64] Wyclif's respect for Grosseteste and his assumption that they shared the same position on universals and divine ideas appears both in his treatises on logic and in his *Summa de ente*.

[65] Robson, *Wyclif and the Oxford Schools*, 70–96; Walsh, *RF*, 59, 377–82.

[66] H. A. Oberman, *Archbishop Thomas Bradwardine. A Fourteenth-Century Augustinian* (Utrecht, 1958), 198–204; Robson, *Wyclif and the Oxford Schools*, 36–69, 176–83, 196–214.

minor but nevertheless long Oxford tradition that included Harclay and Chatton.[67]

Two of the most interesting sources within Wyclif's immediate Oxford background were Aston and Uthred. Aston and Wyclif were both realists, and it was probably Aston's argumentation he had in mind when Wyclif affirmed that the existence of God could be proven infallibly by an argument from pure philosophy.[68] And although Wyclif opposed the semi-Pelagian view of grace and justification found in Uthred as well as Uthred's defense of monastic possession against Fitzralph, Wyclif's total rejection of annihilation, grounded as it was in his view of the eternity and indestructibility of intelligible being, was probably in part derived from Uthred's opposition to annihilation, developed in the mid-1350s, which was in turn derived from positions developed by Fitzralph.[69] Moreover, Wyclif's statement in his 1379 reply to Ralph

[67] J. E. Murdoch and E. A. Synan, "Two Questions on the Continuum: Walter Chatton (?), O.F.M. and Adam Wodeham, O.F.M.," *FcS* 26 (1966): 212–25; *CHLMP*, 576.

[68] Kaluza, "Le problème du 'Deum non esse' "; Bender, *Nicholas Aston*, 99–104. The first proposition of a *determinatio* of Wyclif as copied down by a monk of Worcester (Worcester Cath. MS. F.65, fol. 33ʳ) ran: "Deum esse probari potest per infallibilem demonstrationem a puro philosopho." Text cited from Robson, *Wyclif and the Oxford Schools*, 142.

[69] Uthred was *socius* of Klenkok in 1354, D.Th. in October, 1357, and regent at Oxford as well as prior/warden of Durham College from 1357 to 1367, when he retired to Finchale. Klenkok remained regent at Oxford from his inception in 1359 until 1363, after which he became provincial in Saxony (1363–68) and regent at Prague (1369–70). The fact that some of the opinions that ended up in the "friar's list" and in Uthred's *Contra querelas fratrum* appear in Klenkok's *Lectura Oxoniensis* suggests that: (1) The friars extracted some (perhaps most) of these statements or opinions from the *Sentences* commentary, disputations, and determinations of Uthred from the period 1354–59. (2) The "friar's list" was probably compiled during the years 1359–66. The letter of a monk of St. Mary's, York, to Uthred in December, 1366, reveals the opposition that was already formed between Uthred and William Jordan, Prior of the Dominicans at York from the late 1350s, noted theologian, and frequent visitor to Avignon. (3) Klenkok was probably responsible for calling attention to (and perhaps disseminating in Augustinian circles) a significant number of Uthred's "questionable" opinions. The importance of the Augustinian convent at York and its close association with Oxford would have formed the natural link between Klenkok's attack of 1354–63 and Jordan's attack before 1366. (4) York was probably the location for the compilation of the "friar's list." This would fit in with Uthred's statement that it was not drawn up "in scolis nec in locis aptis pro veritate discutienda sed a tergo resistunt veritati scolasticae." (5) Uthred's reply can be dated 1367–68, and the list of propositions condemned by Simon Langham, Archbishop of Canterbury, occurred in November, 1368.

Thus the views of Uthred on annihilation and other topics date to the period 1354–60. The earliest evidence for Wyclif's similar teaching is in the last section of the first part of

Strode that there has to be at least an instant between baptism and death for a child, foreknown not to be predestined (*parvulus praescitus*), to sin in order for God to condemn justly, is remarkably close to Uthred's position.[70] Finally, both Uthred and Wyclif rejected the view of created grace as an absolutely distinct entity that is simply infused into a believer.[71]

In what sense, then, does Wyclif or his generation mark a change in the intellectual and academic life of England? It was not a change in the size and content of scholastic treatises before 1370. The shrinking of *Sentences* commentaries had already occurred in the 1330s. If there was to some degree a thinning in quality and quantity within scholastic production, there was also a unity of style and approach that extends from the 1330s into the 1360s. The presence of realism is more pronounced, but that begins to appear in the 1350s, not in the writings of Wyclif.

---

his *Summa de ente*, dated 1371–72, after the period of Uthred's writing as well as his condemnation.

[70] For Wyclif's reply to Strode, see *Responsiones ad argumenta Radulfi Strode*, ed. J. Loserth, in Johannis Wyclif, *Opera minora* (London, 1913), 176–77. Uthred's statement is given in Knowles, *The Historian and Character*, 164: " 'Quod impossibile est de lege communi aliquem dampnari, sine peccato actuali ab ipso commisso.' Hunc tenui sicut proximum precedentem."

[71] For Uthred see Knowles, *The Historian and Character*, 165: " 'Quod gratia iuxta communiter ponentes est truffa.' Hunc dixi, eo quod iuxta communiter ponentes gratia ponitur aliquid esse absolutum, creaturae superinfusum, et ab ipsa creatura absolute distinctum, quod videtur esse in natura superfluum et sic truffa." Wyclif, although he affirmed the traditional distinction between created and uncreated grace, (1) saw grace as an interior change, parallel to how the same substance is bread before consecration and, without change or annihilation, is the body of Christ after consecration; and (2) opposed conceiving the habit of grace as a "quiddity." *De scientia Dei* (Camb., Trinity Col., MS. B.16. 2, fol. 61[vb]): "Putavit enim Pelagius, quod gratia qua homo est gratus Deo formaliter sit una res quae potest per se esse." And if, Wyclif continued, one defines grace as an absolute, self-sufficient quality, then one is able to talk about its being necessary *de potentia ordinata* while not necessary *de potentia absoluta*, as do the "moderns" (contemporary theologians). In *De volutione Dei* (also written around 1370) he drew upon Bradwardine to make the following point, *De Ente*, ed. M. H. Dziewicki (London, 1909), 195: "Et super hoc ponunt [i.e., *pelagianos illos modernos* of the previous paragraph] quod gratia Dei sit qualitas absoluta, potens per se esse, sic quod de Dei potentia absoluta, sed non de lege, homo posset mereri sine tali." But Wyclif did not share the view of these *fantasiantes*. As he said in the previous treatise (Robson, *Wyclif and the Oxford Schools*, 210), "Sed, si non fallor, in toto corpore Scripture non potest fundari talem gratiam esse dandam."

Certainly Wyclif represented a vast increase in writing activity of an arts or theological master at Oxford—far more than immediate contemporaries or those from the 1340s and 1350s. That in itself may have impressed contemporaries and built his reputation as the most learned man of the university. Moreover, in Wyclif, in contrast to the previous generation, there is a noticeable shift in the group of topics considered important. One still finds the problem of grace and justification, the interaction of human and divine volition, divine omnipotence, the problem of divine foreknowledge and future contingents (perhaps now less central than before), and Eucharistic theology. The fascination, however, with modal logic and the logic of tensed propositions, the application of the dialectic of absolute and ordained power, the exploration of the impact of time and tense on divine commandments, knowledge, and will, the psychology of conflicting demands, particularly as expressed in the question *de odio Dei*, while they make their appearance occasionally in the pages of Wyclif's works, do not receive the same attention they did in the first half century. For most questions there was a considerable shift in *how* they were treated and what conclusions were arrived at.

The themes that came to dominate Wyclif's writings after 1374, namely Scripture, Eucharistic theology, ecclesiastical power and possession, as well as the increased polemical edge to his style, are all elements that strike a new note. There was never much of the traditional scholastic structure in Wyclif's writings, such as the *quaestio* method of analysis and exposition or the straight commentary (other than the Bible). The movement away from traditional scholastic forms of presentation became more marked after 1370. There we find less concern with past authority, even with Augustine and Grosseteste; a movement away from Bradwardinian formulations; a greater reliance on Scripture; a more direct, apodictic, at times evangelical style of writing; a greater concern with the practical and devotional.[72] Despite the eventual negative reaction to many aspects of Wyclif's theological and ecclesiastical doctrine, it is exactly these features that we find dominating the last decades of the fourteenth century in England. In that respect, if in no others, Wyclif was a man of his age and a formative influence.

[72] This shift in tone has been noted both by Robson, *Wyclif and the Oxford Schools*, 163, and Thomson, *Latin Writings*, 34–35.

TWELVE

PIETY AND LEARNING IN THE
AGE OF CHAUCER

༄

THE HALF DECADE of 1375–80 marked an important transition period in the lives of the two most prominent men of learning and letters
in late fourteenth-century England: Wyclif and Chaucer. These were
the years in which Wyclif's views on the Eucharist and church property
crystallized opposition against him and led to his removal from the lecture halls of Oxford—the end of the public academic career of the most
distinguished and productive scholastic theologian of the age in England and the beginning of his popular influence that lasted well into the
next century. Yet these were also the years in which Chaucer was rapidly moving up in royal favor, becoming eventually Clerk of the Works
and achieving a literary reputation that reached abroad and touched a
wider audience in England than any poet before the second half of the
sixteenth century. The intellectual and literary life of England before
1370 was still very much the life of the schools—perhaps not as vigorous
as once (with the notable exception of Wyclif himself), but still dominant. For the period after 1370 cultural historians have been concerned
with a different social setting and literary product: the work of the Pearl
Poet, Gower's *Confessio amantis*, the redactions or versions of *Piers Plowman*, and most prominently the writings of Geoffrey Chaucer.

Is that apparent shift from the theology of the schools to the literature of courts based on the survival of certain works, on the impression
formed by the declining star of Wyclif's career occurring as Chaucer's
rose, or were the changes that had gradually been appearing in English
studia since 1340 coming to a final and dramatic conclusion? Before we
can determine what the last three or four decades of the fourteenth
century were like from a cultural perspective, we first need to examine
the degree of continuity and change in education and learning.

LOGIC AND THEOLOGY, 1370–1400

One of the most prominent features of English learning in the first half of the fourteenth century had been its contributions in logic, and it would appear that this changed little, quantitatively speaking, in succeeding generations. The production of texts and treatises in logic, and more particularly the fusion of logical and physical perspectives in these treatises that had been a hallmark of the English approach, continued into the late fourteenth century and beyond. The activity of the 1350s, which we surveyed in the previous chapter, was continued in the writings of the Carmelite Richard Lavenham[1] and the secular masters John Hunter,[2] Robert Alyngton,[3] John Scharpe,[4] Edward Upton,[5] John

[1] A. B. Emden, *BRUO* 2: 1109–10; C. L. Kingsford, "Lavenham, Richard," in *DNB* 11: 652–53; C. H. Lohr, "Medieval Latin Aristotle Commentaries, Authors: Narcissus—Richardus," *Traditio* 28 (1972): 393–94. Several of Lavenham's treatises are now published: P. V. Spade, "The Treatises *On Modal Propositions* and *On Hypothetical Propositions* by Richard Lavenham," *MedStud* 35 (1973): 49–59; "Five Logical Tracts by Richard Lavenham," in J. Reginald O'Donnell, ed., *Essays in Honour of Anton Charles Pegis* (Toronto, 1974), 70–124; "Notes on Some Manuscripts of Logical and Physical Works by Richard Lavenham," *Manuscripta* 19 (1975): 139–46; "Richard Lavenham's Obligationes: Edition and Comments," *RCSF* 33 (1978): 224–41; "Richard Lavenham and the Cambridge Logic," *Historiographia Linguistica* 7 (1980): 241–47; "Notes on Richard Lavenham's So-Called *Summulae logicales*, with a Partial Edition of the Text," *FcS* 40 (1980): 370–407.

[2] On Hunter or Huntman (Venator) see P. V. Spade, *The Mediaeval Liar: A Catalogue of the "Insolubilia"-Literature* (Toronto, 1975), 68–69; L. M. De Rijk, "Semantics in Richard Billingham and Johannes Venator," in *ELI*, 167–83. It seems likely that the Hunter who authored the extensive *Logica* (MS. Vat. lat. 2130, fols. 49^r–141^r) and the *Insolubilia* (MSS. in Oxford, Erfurt, and the Vatican) is the same as John Huntman described in Emden, *BRUO* 2: 987–88. Huntman became B.Th. between 1387 and 1390; D.Th. by 1394, and chancellor at Lincoln from 1390 to 1410.

[3] Emden, *BRUO* 1: 30–31.

[4] Scharpe (often spelled Sharp) was a German student from Münster in Westphalia and completed his work in arts at Prague, where he was regent master in the early 1380s. He attended Oxford in the 1390s, becoming fellow of Queen's College in 1391, B.Th. in 1396, and incepted as regent master not long after. He remained at Oxford at least until 1404. In addition to his philosophical works (*Universalia, Quaestiones de passionibus entis, Quaestiones super libros Physicorum*, and *Quaestio de anima*), he wrote treatises against Wyclif. See Emden, *BRUO* 3: 1680; L. A. Kennedy, "The *De anima* of John Sharpe," *FcS* 29 (1969): 249–70; C. H. Lohr, "Medieval Latin Aristotle Commentaries, Authors: Johannes de Kanthi—Myngodus," *Traditio* 27 (1971): 279–80.

[5] Upton was principal of St. Edmund's Hall in 1384. His *Conclusiones proportionum* is found in Oxford, Bodl. MS. 676, fols. 38^r–49^v; Emden, *BRUO* 3: 1932.

Chilmark,[6] William Mylverley,[7] and others,[8] some of them connected with Queen's College. Lavenham was particularly prolific, writing over sixty treatises and commentaries in logic, physics, moral philosophy, and theology (anti-Wycliffite tracts, for the most part).

If production of works in logic remained high throughout the second half of the century, the issue of quality is more open to debate.[9] Many of these treatises and books were written for beginners, young students between the ages of fourteen and eighteen, although some (as in the case of Wyclif's treatises) were written either for theological students or for those in arts preparing for theology. Consequently the level of sophistication is not high, nor is the degree of innovation. Their authors were attempting to teach the characteristics of certain types of terms and the behavior of the various categories or types of propositions. Beyond this instruction in basic knowledge, the emphasis was on how to handle certain problems or situations that would normally occur in disputations: teaching the student how to "respond."

These features were not new in post-1350 England. Heytesbury's *Regula solvendi sophismata* was written with precisely the same goals in mind, and its popularity among succeeding generations probably had more to do with that practical function than with the innovative qualities of the work. And in the later period Aston was consciously trying to be innovative in his *De insolubilibus* when he argued that negative propositions do not signify *praecise sicut est*. Yet on balance, and apart from the intentions of individual authors, there does seem to have been more innovation and a higher level of sophistication in many of the logico-

[6] Some of the treatises of Chilmark are included in Oxford, Bodl. 676, fols. 11ʳ–38ʳ (*Tractatus de motu*), fols. 52ᵛ–69ʳ (*De proportione*), fols. 69ᵛ–75ᵛ (*De qualitate et quantitate et veritate propositionis*), fols. 76ʳ–101ʳ (*De alteratione*); Emden, *BRUO* 1: 416.

[7] Emden, *BRUO* 2: 1284; Lohr, "Medieval Latin Aristotle Commentaries," *Traditio* 24 (1968): 203; Robson, *Wyclif and the Oxford Schools* (Cambridge, 1961), 100.

[8] For example: H. Bricmore, whose *Notulae* on Burley and others is found in Oxford, Corpus Christi, MS. 230, fol. 33; five other treatises in Oxford, Bodl., Rawlinson MS. A. 428; commentaries on Boethius's *De divisione, Topica*, and Aristotle's *Posterior Analytics* in Vat. MS. Ottob. lat. 1276, fols. 141–55, 155–60, 161–220 respectively; cited in Bodl. MS. 676, fol. 213ʳ. Master Grene, who refers to Alyngton, and whose *De quantitate* is found in Bodl. MS. 676, fols. 178ʳ–227ᵛ. Roger Consel, whose *De proportione* appears in Bodl. MS. 676, fols. 149ʳ–62ʳ.

[9] On the quality of late fourteenth-century English logic see the forthcoming essay by Paul Spade in *HUO* 2.

physical treatises written between 1310 and 1350 than in those written after 1350. That change, however, was probably not so much a result of a decline in scholarly ability as it was of a different set of priorities and goals. The strong market among continental schools (especially in Italy, Germany, and central Europe) for the works of Heytesbury, Strode, Feribrigge, Brinkley, and Hunter was based primarily on their usefulness, their having been recently written and therefore supposedly "up-to-date," and because many of them coincided with a realist approach in logic and metaphysics that was gaining ground all across Europe in the late fourteenth and early fifteenth centuries.[10]

When we turn our attention from logic to scholastic theology, we encounter not only a loss of innovation within the traditional forms but a quantitative decline as well, particularly in the most distinctive vehicle for late scholasticism: the *Sentences* commentary. The shift to a commentary structured around fewer but longer questions had already occurred in the early 1330s, and in the decade from 1350 to 1360, as we have seen, the number of *Sentences* commentaries and their content almost regained the level of the late 1330s. That situation changed markedly after 1360. Wyclif left no *Sentences* commentary (a fact that should not be obscured by claiming that the second half of his *Summa de ente* and his *De incarnatione verbi* were derived from it), and his theological writings after 1372 have a considerably less scholastic, more evangelical style. The best-known theologians from the last part of the century: William Jordan, O.P., John Kenningham, O. Carm., William Woodford, O.F.M., Thomas Netter, O. Carm., John Waldeby, O.E.S.A., and so many others left no *Sentences* commentaries and no scholastic work for the other traditional genre. The only *Sentences* commentaries and re-

---

[10] Unfortunately, the work on late fourteenth-century English logic, particularly at Oxford, begun by Julian Deal and Paul Spade is still at a beginning stage. For the continuation of English fourteenth-century logic see L. M. De Rijk, "Logica Cantabrigiensis—A Fifteenth-Century Cambridge Manual of Logic," *Revue internationale de philosophie* 29 (1975): 297–315; "Logica Oxoniensis," *Medioevo* 3 (1977): 121–64; Spade, "Richard Lavenham and the Cambridge Logic"; E. J. Ashworth, "The 'Libelli Sophistarum' and the Use of Medieval Logic Texts at Oxford and Cambridge in the Early Sixteenth Century," *Vivarium* 17 (1979): 134–58; "A Note on Paul of Venice and the Oxford Logica of 1483," *Medioevo* 4 (1978): 93–99 [revised and published after the previous one, despite the dates of publication]; "A Note on an Early Printed Logic Text in Edinburgh University Library," *The Innes Review* 30 (1979): 77–79.

lated works that can with any certainty be placed in the period 1360 to 1420 are the *Repertorium argumentorum* of the Yorkshire Carmelite Stephen Patrington, compiled during the years before 1389; an anonymous *Lectura Oxoniensis* dating around 1380; and the *Sentences* commentary of the Dominican Thomas Claxton in the opening years of the fifteenth century. Moreover, in contrast to writers of the period before 1340, the works of most English scholastic authors after that date survive in very few manuscripts—often these are single copies and/or *quaestiones* in unfinished form collected by students.

The small number of extant *Sentences* commentaries and the small number of manuscript copies of most scholastic work of late fourteenth-century English theologians may be to some degree an adverse result of having appeared in the wrong place at the wrong time. Some writings may have fallen victim to the destruction of works tainted with Wycliffite heresy, but the absence of *Sentences* commentaries among the leaders of "orthodoxy" in that age suggests that heresy cannot have been a prominent factor in the decline of that form of scholasticism. More realistically, fifteenth-century neglect coupled with the devastating effects of the dispersement of religious libraries at the Dissolution and the eventual abandonment and destruction of "unneeded" manuscripts was particularly hard on scholastic texts that did not have antiquarian or humanist value. Far less survives in England from England's scholastic heritage than almost anywhere else in Europe. And the works of lesser-known authors would presumably have been even more easily discarded than those of eminent status. England was not entirely even-handed in the destruction of its scholastic heritage. Moreover, if political and cultural conditions slowed the exportation of English texts to the Continent after 1360 (with the exception of high-demand areas such as Paris in the 1360s and Padua in the 1390s), then we would not expect those texts in sufficient number to have reached the libraries where they would have been preserved and further copied.

But such a drastic decline cannot be solely a result of the vagaries of preservation. It is telling in this regard to realize how few commentaries from this period known to have once existed are not extant in some form.[11] Even more telling is the fact that the names of post-1340 Eng-

---

[11] All bachelors of theology lectured on the *Sentences*, but only a small number of those were ever circulated in written form. In the "known-to-have-existed" (and still-hoped-for)

lish authors do not abound in the margins of those English scholastic texts that have survived from the late fourteenth century, indicating that attention even in England was focused on the heritage of the early fourteenth century, not on their own age, apart from the controversies that surrounded Wyclif.[12] This situation must be evaluated over against events on the Continent, where traditional forms of academic theological activity, most prominently the *Sentences* commentary, remained popular, and where each generation added its group of quotable names and opinions to the scholastic heritage.

Some insight into this question may be gained by looking at the non-

---

category are the commentaries of Burley, Folville, Trevaur, Lavenham, Scharpe, and the full text of Brinkley.

[12] Those writing after 1340, despite the fact that they were known and read both in England and on the Continent, did not become "major" names in the scholastic literature in the same way as did Ockham, Fitzralph, Wodeham, Bradwardine, Buckingham, and Halifax. Fourteenth-century theologians were remembered by having their names attached to positions on certain questions. Occasionally there are signs of fresh reading in the later period, but it is more often the case that on certain issues there are a group of names and positions that are expected to appear. Either because the first half of the fourteenth century provided later writers with enough names and positions on certain questions such that more were not needed, or because, with very few exceptions, it was rare that these later writers added anything particularly significant to individual questions, one does find a sharp break between those frequently cited and those occasionally cited that corresponds to those active before or after 1340. That feature does not change in the last part of the century. The frequently cited names in a scholastic text of 1370 or 1390 are from the first half of the fourteenth century. As one searches the manuscripts of works written in the second half of the fourteenth century, either in England or on the Continent, one finds very few citations to authors writing later than 1340.

Late fourteenth-century writers were not less cited because their work was less available and less well known. There was less demand for copies of their work because they were rarely cited. This is not the vicious circle it appears to be. Knowledge of contemporary authorities was usually derived from their being cited in other works, not from their being read. Generally, one writer borrowed his list of quotable opinions from the margins of earlier *Sentences* commentaries; in many cases he may never have seen the cited work nor even have been able to find a copy, should he have been interested. The small amount of manuscript evidence is to a large degree a function of reputation.

Another factor, however, is that since English authors after 1340 are cited less frequently on the Continent than those before 1340 (with a few exceptions, such as *De causa Dei*), there may have been less interest on the Continent in obtaining copies of these works and perhaps some serious problems in locating copies and thus obtaining exemplars. Even so, the post-1340 authors are better preserved on the Continent than in England, something that is true for almost any fourteenth-century scholastic author.

polemical scholastic works in theology that were produced after 1360. Patrington's work is a highly condensed collection of arguments in which individual sections rarely occupy more than a portion of a column of manuscript text.[13] They were compiled by Patrington at Oxford and elsewhere, either from oral presentation in lectures and disputations or, more likely, from codices and *quaterni* available to him.[14] The source of individual arguments is not indicated (truth in the form of persuasive reasoning belongs to everyone), but positions of "authorities" on specific questions are sometimes indicated. Thus one encounters the names of Scotus, Ockham, Fitzralph (usually his *De pauperie Salvatoris*), Holcot, Heytesbury, Botiler,[15] and Wyclif (on time and eternity, verification of propositions, annihilation, and the Incarnation). Properly speaking, it is not a *reportatio* or an *abbreviatio* (all compiled during or after the lectures) but an outline, notebook, or sourcebook which Patrington mined for purposes of his own lectures and which no doubt proved useful to others for much the same reason. It is similar in function to the collections by Etienne Gaudet and Etienne Chaumont at Paris. The content of the work—the range of topics and approaches— is almost identical with that of the first half of the century. Problems and techniques had apparently altered little in the classrooms of the 1380s.

The same holds true for the *Lectura Oxoniensis*, which is a working (albeit truncated) copy of actual lectures, similar in structure to the shorter English commentaries that became so prevalent after 1335.[16] The en-

[13] Three manuscripts of Patrington's *Repertorium argumentorum* have survived: Cambridge, St. John's College, MS. D.28 (James 103), fols. 1–109; Florence, Bibl. Laurenziana, MS. Plut.17, sin. cod. x, fols. 1ʳ–113ᵛ; Venice, San Marco MS. z. lat. 280, fols. 21ʳ–131ʳ. On Patrington see Emden, *BRUO* 3: 1435–36; C. L. Kingsford, "Patrington, Stephen," in *DNB* 15, 492–93; B. Xiberta, "Etienne de Patrington," in *Dictionnaire de Spiritualité*, vol. 4 (Paris, 1961), col. 1517; L. A. Kennedy, "Late-Fourteenth-Century Philosophical Scepticism at Oxford," *Vivarium* 23, 2 (1985): 124–51; "A Carmelite Fourteenth-Century Theological Notebook," *Carmelus* 33 (1986): 70–102; and the forthcoming paper by L. Eldridge, "*Pearl* and the Equality of Reward in Heaven."

[14] Cambridge, St. John's College, MS. D.28 (James 103), fol. 109: "Explicit reportorium magistri Stephani de Patrington quod collegit Oxonie et alibi antequam ad gradum assumptus fuerat doctoralem."

[15] The most likely candidate is Almaricus (Aymer) le Botiler, who was arts master and senior proctor for Oxford in 1330. See Emden, *BRUO* 2: 1116–17.

[16] Munich, Staatsbibl. MS. Clm 27034, fols. 178ʳ–233ᵛ. For a description see D. Trapp, "Clm 27034. Unchristened Nominalism and Wycliffite Realism at Prague in 1381," *RTAM* 24 (1957): 320–60, esp. 325–27, 338–49.

tire commentary purports to be on one question, which is divided into four subquestions called articles that correspond to the subject matter of the four books of the *Sentences*. These, in turn, are divided into subarticles. Among the fourteenth-century authors cited are Ockham (known as the Inceptor), Fitzralph, Halifax, Rimini, and Wyclif. The author sides with Ockham and Rimini in maintaining that time, motion, and successive change ought not to be distinguished *realiter* from individual, permanent things.[17] This fragmentary commentary is also of interest in that it puts Wyclif's opinions in the context of university scholastic debate instead of the political diatribes that stylistically are removed from the classroom and the scholastic tradition.

Claxton's commentary is by far the longest and resembles in structure the traditional *Sentences* commentaries of the pre-1335 era.[18] In form it strikes the reader as a product of another age. Unlike the scholastic works of English Dominicans after 1315, it is strongly committed to the thought of the Angelic Doctor. The revival of Thomism in the opening years of the fifteenth century was primarily an Italian phenomenon that had its first flowering in the person of John Capreolus at Paris but also owed something to German Dominicans in the mid-fourteenth century. England made its own contribution at the end of the fourteenth century. The polemical writings of William Jordan reveal elements of Thomism. The index of Thomas owed a great deal to the work of the English Benedictine William Sudbury in the closing years of the fourteenth century. The culmination of the revival of Thomas in England, however, was Claxton, whose Thomism helped set the direction of some of English theology in the fifteenth century.

---

[17] MS. Clm 27034, fols. 192^v–94^v: "Utrum tempus et motus et mutationes ceterae, quae successivae appellantur, a singulis permanentibus realiter distinguantur. . . . Praemissis opinionibus omissis, teneo partem negativam quaestionis sicut tenere videntur Gregorius et Inceptor super secundum; et pro parte ista sufficiunt mihi argumenta eorum."

[18] Claxton was regent master for the Oxford Dominicans in 1413. His commentary has survived two manuscripts: Cambridge, Gonville and Caius, MS. 370 (592), fols. 1–216 (book 1), apparently Claxton's own copy; and Florence, Bibl. Naz., MS. conv. soppr. B.VI.340, which in addition to his full *Sentences* commentary contains his *Quodlibeta*, two of which have been edited by Grabmann. On Claxton see: Emden, *BRUO* 1: 426; M. Grabmann, "Thomas de Claxton, O.P. (*c.* 1400). Quaestiones de distinctione inter esse et essentiam reali atque de analogia entis," *Acta Pontificiae Academiae Romanae* 8 (1941–42): 92–153; *Mittelalterliches Geistesleben*, vol. 3 (Munich, 1956), 372–73.

nated in the thirteenth and early fourteenth centuries. By the fifteenth century civil law equalled, then surpassed theology in student enrollment at Oxford and Cambridge, and the faculties of canon and civil law together far outweighed theology.

Throughout the high and late Middle Ages one encounters, particularly on the lips of theologians, the *topos* of the money-hungry lawyers who were displacing theologians at universities and corrupting church and society. But by the second half of the fourteenth century that shift in discipline was well established, and higher studies at Oxford and Cambridge usually meant law. That statement does not include those arts masters who, like Ralph Strode, pursued advanced study in common law outside the university. The shift from theology to law can also be seen when one surveys the English episcopate in the late fourteenth century. Of those with university training (and this was by far the dominant group) the majority had their highest degree in law, and the percentage among the most active and well rewarded within that group was even higher.

It is hard to know whether the pattern of choosing law graduates for high position in church and state was a simple result of an excess of talented and well-connected graduates in law, or whether the move to law careers while in school responded to a pattern of post-graduate appointment already visible in English society. Whatever the connection, the shift took place in the second half of the fourteenth century and by the fifteenth century, in the words of one historian, both church and university had become "immoderately legalistic."[21]

The shift from theology to law has to be combined with another factor: the growing influence of the aristocracy, both as students and as patrons. There had throughout the fourteenth century been sons of noble families attending Oxford and Cambridge, but that practice became more common in the second half of the century. By and large, those of the highest social class chose law as the preferred course of study, which gave added prestige and influence to that faculty. Moreover, the aristocracy gradually gained an influence on university life that it did not possess in the earlier period. We begin to find those of aristocratic back-

[21] Cobban, "Theology and Law," 72. Distaste over the importance of legal education in England was even voiced by Erasmus: "The study of English law is as far removed as can be from true learning, but in England those who succeed in it are highly thought of"; cited from R. W. Chamber, *Thomas More* (London, 1938), 85.

ground or from well-connected families obtaining high office within the university. The first of these was Robert of Stratford, appointed chancellor of Oxford from outside the university during the Stamford schism in 1335–38. The chancellorships of John Northwode (1345–48), Humphrey de Charlton (1355–57), and William Courtenay (1367–69) point in the same direction. And enhanced prominence at the university level paralleled appointments in church and state. Increasingly, high office was being awarded to those from noble, wealthy, or well-connected families, or to those who were within the patronage network of those families—connections that were often forged at the university.

It is to be expected that this shift in popularity among the higher faculties would send into law some talented and energetic young minds who might have chosen theology in an earlier generation. The declining percentage of theological students also explains some of the quantitative drop in written scholastic activity among theologians. A more important element in that quantitative drop, however, was the degree to which visibility and reputation through academic achievement and publication ceased to be an effective or worthwhile means of attracting a patron and thus ensuring a successful career. As was argued earlier, attracting a patron was never the sole or perhaps even primary factor in producing the type and quantity of work that was done at Oxford in the early fourteenth century. But among motives it was never wholly absent. In this respect, internal university expectations paralleled or blended with expectations outside the universities. In the second half of the century a higher percentage of church positions went to nongraduates, and of university men a higher percentage went to those in law, often on the basis of patron-client relationships. High achievement in arts and theology, considering all the time and effort it took, did not significantly improve one's chances of a successful post-university career. This did not preclude a modest continuation of the type of technical work in logic, physics, and theology that had built the reputation of Oxford, but it did reduce the flow of young men trying to make their careers in this way and goes far to explain the drop in scholastic production that we have noted in the second half of the century.

No doubt the numerical reduction had its own negative effect. People tend to be attracted into an enterprise that is occupying the efforts of the most respected within the same group. The excitement of learning is contagious. And many who might otherwise not have attempted dis-

tinguished academic careers were probably pulled into the effort
through the challenge of the intense intellectual atmosphere generated
at Greyfriars or Merton. But when the number of those so engaged
dropped below a certain critical level, as suggested earlier, it probably
ceased to have the same appeal for the younger generation.

CHANGING INTERESTS—NEW AUDIENCES

Fears about the effect on church life and spirituality of the preponder-
ance of law among university students were not unknown, and at Cambridge in particular, college foundations in the fifteenth century attempt to instill some strength into the theological faculty by reserving a
higher number of fellowships for theologians.[22] It is questionable, however, whether the theological program at Oxford or Cambridge, as it
developed in the early fourteenth century, encouraged much spirituality or religious zeal. The application of a logic *de proprietatibus terminorum* to theological *sophismata* expanded the frontier of speculative
theology immensely and reinforced and aided the developments in
logic and physics. On the other hand, it gave a one-sided approach to
biblical exegesis. It did little or nothing to train one in preaching. In fact
the only areas in which the theology of the schools touched the religion
of the parish was in the not inconsequential areas of eucharistic doctrine and penitential practice. Encouraging theological study at a university as a way of saving the church from the lawyers did not address
the more fundamental question of whether the existing theological curriculum helped develop faith or spiritual insight.

The inappropriateness of some, perhaps much, of university theological training for the pastoral ministry was noted at various times
within the fourteenth century, and a serious attempt at curricular reform was attempted in the 1340s. The contrast Fitzralph drew between
his eventual biblical faith and his earlier "croaking in the marsh" of university philosophy and theology was not a unique perception.[23] Some of
this attitude lay behind Benedict XII's attempts at educational reform
in the late 1330s and his investigations into orthodoxy at Paris in the

[22] Cobban, "Theology and Law."
[23] Pantin, *ECFC*, 132–33; see above, ch. 10, p. 321.

early 1340s.[24] Clement VI's call for abandoning a philosophizing form of theological study (specifically the English method that had caught on at Paris in the 1340s) and for a return to biblical study mirrored the curricular reform that Fitzralph and, to some degree, Conrad of Megenberg had in mind.[25]

Despite these efforts, the system of university theological training did not change much, and the content of university-produced theological works both at Paris and Oxford in the second half of the fourteenth century, as we have seen, remained much the same. Yet in England, theologians took less interest in this aspect of their training. More important for them (to judge by their career and writings) were preaching, biblical study, devotional literature, and the defense of the faith against heresy.

The new areas of scholarly activity that resulted in publication and made reputations lay along the boundary area between university and society where learning could be brought to bear on issues of greater moment and popular appeal than those of the classroom. The model was already established by Holcot's *Sapientia*, Bradwardine's *Summa de causa Dei*, and Fitzralph's *Summa de quaestionibus Armenorum* and *De pauperie Salvatoris*—all of which were aimed at and were highly successful among a growing literate population, much of it university-connected and church-employed, but some of it not. The theological "market" in the second half of the fourteenth century lay in the areas of sermon literature, biblical studies, and religious, doctrinal, or political controversies that had extra- or supra-university significance and appeal.

The suddenness of these changing interests and perspectives emerges when we look closely at the religious orders upon whom so much of Oxford's and Cambridge's prominence depended in the earlier part of the century. In comparison to their intellectual stature in the thirteenth and early fourteenth centuries, the Franciscans and Dominicans barely make a ripple on the surface of academic life in late fourteenth-century England, and not terribly much more on church affairs. The Dominicans do not figure prominently at Oxford after 1335. Franciscan scholastic work virtually disappears after 1340, leaving the field

[24] W. J. Courtenay and K. H. Tachau, "Ockham, Ockhamists, and the English-German Nation at Paris, 1339–1341," *History of Universities* 2 (1982): 53–96.

[25] *CUP* 2: 587–90; W. J. Courtenay, "The Reception of Ockham's Thought at the University of Paris," in *PRUP*, 54.

to the seculars. Thus the personnel of English academic theology was strikingly different by mid-century. This probably had its effect on the type and amount of scholastic theology produced. College-affiliated seculars had never been as productive in theology as they were in philosophy. The brilliant work of the Mertonians had largely been in the latter area throughout the fourteenth century, and it is unfair and ahistorical to regret the absence of Mertonian "theology" in this later period when, apart from Bradwardine and Buckingham, this had never been the strong suit of Mertonian scholars.

The prominent Dominicans and Franciscans in the last half of the century concentrated their efforts in areas that were only marginally university-connected. Both William Jordan, O.P. and William Woodford, O.F.M. wrote several scriptural commentaries, some of which have survived and some of which may have been composed during their regencies in theology.[26] Both are primarily remembered, however, for their anti-Wycliffite treatises: Woodford's written at Oxford and Jordan's at York.[27] The same is true for the Dominican Roger Dymock, who wrote against the Lollards at century's end.[28] Even William Folville, once regent master for the Franciscans at Cambridge and cited in his day on the margins of *Sentences* commentaries, is remembered today for his presence at the Blackfriars Council in 1382 and his defense of the right of mendicants to recruit boys within the university community below the age of eighteen.[29] Most of these polemical tracts were written because the issues concerned were institutional and doctrinal. They affected church and society, not simply the university.

The same holds true for the writings of the Austin Friars Thomas Winterton, John Bankyn, and Thomas Ashbourne.[30] Once friendly and sympathetic toward Wyclif (as Woodford seems originally to have

[26] Jordan's commentary on Romans has not survived, but for Woodford see *RepBib* 2: 438–39. The Augustinian John Klenkok wrote a commentary on Acts (Eichstätt MS. 204, fols. 117–192) and perhaps one on Matthew; *RepBib* 3: 370–71.

[27] For example, Woodford's *De sacramento eucharistiae, Determinationes,* and *De causis condemnationis.* On Woodford see Emden, *BRUO* 3: 2081–82, J. I. Catto, *William Woodford, OFM, c. 1330–1397,* Doc. diss., University of Oxford, 1969; and for Jordan Emden, *BRUO* 2: 1022.

[28] *Liber contra xii errores et hereses Lollardorum,* ed. H. S. Cronin (London, 1922).

[29] Emden, *BRUC,* 230.

[30] On Winterton see Emden, *BRUO* 3: 2062; Roth, *EAF* 1: 80–86, 392–93, 593–94; on Ashbourne and Bankyn Emden, *BRUO* 1: 54 and 104; Roth, *EAF,* 395–96, 508–9, 511–12.

been), united as they were in the traditions of Oxford theology and their attitudes toward the taxation of monastic properties, they formed the vocal opposition by 1381.

Other Augustinians, however, reveal a different dimension to mendicant interests. Both William Flete and John Waldeby (the latter an Oxford graduate) wrote numerous devotional treatises, and Flete became for a time the spiritual director of Catherine of Siena.[31] In addition to his guides to the spiritual life, Waldeby, a noted preacher, left behind several volumes of sermons.

The two most active and prominent groups in both church and university in the second half of the century were the Benedictines and the Carmelites—two groups that have not been credited with any significant role in late medieval intellectual life (thanks largely to the neglect of historians) but whose changing patterns of interest and writing best reflect some of the larger cultural changes going on in the late fourteenth century.

Benedictines, for example, came late to university education, later in England than on the Continent. Yet by the second decade of the fourteenth century they were promoting their own masters and producing a series of theologians, some of whom made significant reputations in the universities of late medieval Europe: Richard Bromwich,[32] Robert Graystanes, the anonymous Monachus Niger, John Bode,[33] and Uthred

---

[31] On Flete see Emden, *BRUC*, 234, 676; Roth, *EAF*, 69–70, 183–89, 404–7, 538–40; on Waldeby see Emden, *BRUO* 3: 1957–58; Roth, *EAF*, 400–404, 581–90.

[32] Bromwich's *Sentences* commentary, read at Oxford between 1307 and 1311 (he was not yet B.Th. in 1307 and was D.Th. by 1313), survives in only one copy: Worcester Cath. Lib., MS. F.139.

[33] The belief that the Benedictine John Bode (or Bodi), regent master in theology in 1357, is identical with John Body, fellow of Merton College in 1338 (and possibly as early as 1334) rests on the similarity of their names and Bode's having authored a collection of *sophismata* more typical of secular masters than of those in religious orders. But the Mertonian John Body would have had to have been B.A. at the time of admission to Merton, and his degree in a higher faculty would have been obtained in the next decade. While it is possible that the Mertonian could have become a Benedictine, the practice of short regencies among the religious and the separation in dates suggests that these were two different individuals, as Emden realized; and the balance of evidence suggests that the author of 'A' *est unum calidum* is to be identified with the Benedictine master. See Emden, *BRUO* 1: 209; P. Duhem, *Etudes sur Leonard de Vinci*, vol. 3 (Paris, 1913), 474–77; *Le système du monde*, vol. 7 (Paris, 1956), 648–50; A. Maier, *An der Grenze von Scholastik und Naturwissenschaft*, 2nd ed.

of Boldon. The Benedictines were also able to attract prominent Oxford scholars into their midst: Roger Swineshead (not the Calculator, Richard Swineshead) and Reginald Lambourne.[34] The number of scholastic manuscripts of Benedictine provenance attests to a keen interest in the intellectual life of the universities.[35] Yet the prominent Benedictines of the last generation of the century were of an entirely different nature: Bishop Thomas Brinton,[36] a noted preacher following in the tradition of John Shepeye; the preacher and cardinal, Adam Easton,[37] and the poet John Lydgate.[38] Their reputations were not based on scholastic activity while at the university but rather on their roles as preacher or poet.

A similar picture emerges from the Carmelites. Only slightly less prominent than the Benedictines in the earlier part of the century, they produced a modest string of theologians: Robert Walsingham and John Baconthorp in the opening years of the century, and Osbert Pickingham at mid-century. Apart from Lavenham and Patrington, whose contributions to logic and theology have already been examined, the leading Carmelite scholars of the last few decades, John Kenningham and Thomas Netter, were principally known for their writings against Wyclif, and to a lesser extent their scriptural commentaries.[39] Their post-university careers outshone their earlier academic achievements. The same holds true for Lavenham, who was for a time Richard II's confessor, and for Patrington, whose post-university career included a

---

(Rome, 1952), 267, 355; H.L.L. Busard, "Unendliche Reihen in *A est unum calidum*," *Archive for History of Exact Sciences* 2 (1965): 387–97; *CHLMP*, 540, 865.

[34] Emden, *BRUO* 2: 1086–87; Robson, *Wyclif and the Oxford Schools*, 101.

[35] Beyond the wealth of scholastic materials in the library of the Cathedral of Worcester, two of the richest English manuscripts for Oxford authors of the first half of the century are of Benedictine provenance: London, Brit. Lib., MS. Royal 10.c.6 and Oxford, Oriel College, MS. 15.

[36] *DNB* 2: 1258, and Emden, *BRUO* 1: 268–69.

[37] *DNB* 6: 333–34, and Emden, *BRUO* 1: 620–21.

[38] Emden, *BRUO* 2: 1185–86.

[39] On Kenningham see Emden, *BRUO* 2: 1077; on Netter, Emden, *BRUO* 2: 1343–44, *DNB* 14: 231–34. Netter's *Doctrinale fidei* is of fundamental importance, but neither Kenningham's nor Netter's commentaries have survived; *RepBib* 3: 370; 5: 369–70. The same is true for the scriptural commentaries of Lavingham and Patrington; *RepBib* 5: 87; 303; although Richard Maidstone's commentary on the Song of Songs has survived (Paris, Bibl. Nat., MS. lat. 13198; *RepBib* 5: 87).

term as preacher and theological master at Lincoln Cathedral, confessor for Henry V, and eventually bishop of Chichester.

Several common concerns stand out among late fourteenth-century theologians from religious orders. First, a deeper commitment to biblical study, initially rooted perhaps in the obligation of regent masters to lecture on the Bible, but now encouraged by the papacy, by prominent ecclesiastics and university scholars as disparate as Fitzralph and Wyclif, and by a growing demand among literate laity, particularly in the area of vernacular translation. The more biblical and evangelical tone of Wyclif's writings and interests after 1372 is further evidence of this trend. A second and closely connected concern was in preaching. The importance of preaching may have had its roots in the evangelical awakening of the twelfth century and the rise of the mendicant orders, especially the Dominicans, but fourteenth-century England had a large number of scholar-prelate-preachers: Shepeye, Fitzralph, Brinton, Easton, to name only a few. A third concern was the production of spiritual, devotional treatises, many of them written for those in religious life, many of them for pious lay people. A final concern were the ecclesiastical and doctrinal controversies that raged around Wyclif.

Beneath all these concerns is the presence of new audiences whose interests and needs engaged the attention of scholars, audiences primarily found outside universities and composed of clerics, lawyers, civil servants, merchants, and, among the latter groups, their wives and older children. Paramount were the religious faithful, a portion of which had acquired Latin literacy, toward whom much of the scriptural, homiletical, and devotional writings were directed. One factor no doubt present in all this but difficult to assess accurately is the issue of scholarly activity as a vehicle for visibility and as a response to contemporary expectations. Before 1350 achievement in the schools brought visibility, which in turn helped attract a patron. There was, in fact, very little market outside universities, church, law careers, and political life for the skills of logical reasoning, debate oratory, and writing. The audience for the work of the scholar was mostly confined to the schools, to those who had attended them, and to the Latin language. After 1350 the growth of lay literacy provided a new audience and a new market (both for Latin as well as the vernacular)—and with that new market an increased influence of their tastes and needs on scholars. To some degree—perhaps to a large degree—the importance of biblical study, sermons, devotional treatises, and vernacular literature for the last decades of the fourteenth century was in response to the interests of an ever widening literate populace.[40] All these factors combined in the second half of the century to curtail the amount of traditional scholarly activity that had been the most distinguishing feature of Oxford academic life before 1360. And the new scholarly and religious interests—the Bible, preaching, devotional literature, and ecclesiastical and doctrinal controversies—were to remain the areas of concern, particularly in England, well into the sixteenth century.

FROM SCHOOLS TO COURT CIRCLES: SCHOLASTICISM AND MIDDLE ENGLISH LITERATURE

The reign of Richard II (1377–99) coincided with the flowering of English vernacular literature, some of it produced by university-trained scholars, almost all of it written by men familiar to some degree with the language and topics of the schools. It is not surprising, therefore, that late scholasticism should have had some influence on Middle English literature. More remarkable is the small extent of that influence and the fact that English culture in the Riccardian period is no longer university-based but centered in the courtly society of greater London.

The significance and indeed the very existence of "a court culture" in late fourteenth-century England has become a controversial issue.[41] Outside of tastes in fashion, architectural and artistic displays of divinely-ordained kingship, and the occasional commissioning of literary works, Richard did not dictate or even orchestrate the *forms* and *substance* of art and literature during his reign.[42] On the other hand, it is

---

[40] Perhaps the prognostication literature of John Ashenden (in astrology) and Reginald Lambourne (Mertonian, O.F.M., and O.S.B.) is also reflective of broadening interests. For recent literature on lay literacy see above, ch. 1, n. 25.

[41] The principal book expounding the court-culture setting of Middle English literature is Gervase Mathew, *The Court of Richard II* (London, 1968). See also Richard Green, *Poets and Princepleasers. Literature and the English Court in the Late Middle Ages* (Toronto, 1980). An opposing view is taken by many of the contributors to *English Court Culture in the Later Middle Ages*, ed. V. J. Scattergood and J. W. Sherborne (London, 1983).

[42] In his prologue to *Confessio amantis* John Gower portrays the work as a response to the king's request "to do some new thing" that the king might read, and Chaucer's *Legend of Good Women* seems to be closely connected with Richard's patronage. On the latter see Mar-

unwise to dismiss the role of patronage or a courtly audience from the setting of Middle English literature. There was never one court culture, taste, or style, dictated from above. There were, however, certain tastes in art and literature that were shared within a social class, partly aristo-cratic, partly bourgeois, partly administrative, that was inter-connected through ties of blood, marriage, or patronage. The danger has been to define courtly society too closely around "The Royal Court" and to de-fine patronage as a monetary dependency in which the work of the client is a direct result of the desires of the patron. There were many courts and many degrees of affiliation, from physical presence or em-ployment within a household to occasional favors for those serving or living elsewhere. There were many forms of patronage, which was al-most invariably sought from multiple sources. And the paucity of "com-missioned" literary work does not mean that authors were not writing for particular audiences, nor that authors did not seek advancement or favors by dedicating specific works to one or more potential patrons, often in succession.

The degree to which vernacular poets were clients and court authors is not our concern here. Nor should it be argued that the kind of tal-ented young minds so enamored with scholastic philosophy and theol-ogy in the first half of the century were being attracted into literary ca-reers in the second half. The rise of vernacular literature did not displace scholasticism, whose reduced profile in the late fourteenth cen-tury was, as we have seen, a result of the declining role of the Francis-cans, institutional and career changes within universities, and broader social forces. Moreover, the audiences for late scholasticism and vernac-ular literature continued to differ, although both genre touched the growing body of literate laity, especially those in law and administrative service.

Our primary concern is with the degree to which late scholasticism in-fluenced the themes or approaches of vernacular literature. The intel-lectual and educational background of Middle English literature has become something of a growth industry in the last two decades, partic-ularly after the appearance of Heiko Oberman's *Harvest of Medieval Theology* provided a mine of information on late medieval nominalism

---

garet Galway, "Geoffrey Chaucer, J. P. and M. P.," *Modern Language Review* 36 (1941): 3–36. I am grateful to Russell Peck for calling my attention to these references.

readily accessible in English.[43] If, as Charles Muscatine and others asserted,[44] it was time to move away from discussions of form, style, and structuralism and return to an exploration of the historical context of Middle English literature, then nominalism and the schools—the other face of late medieval learning—provided a ready source of meaningful parallels and an occasional academic context for poetic perceptions, language, and allusions. Familiarity with Oxford, as passages in Chaucer and Langland reveal, raises the possibility that English poets were influenced by its personalities and ideas far more than has been recognized.

Some literary critics have adopted the approach of looking for structural and perceptual similarities between nominalism (sometimes misinterpreted as atomism, individualism, or skepticism) and fourteenth-century poetry.[45] Others have pursued Chaucer's or Langland's contacts with Oxford or Oxford scholars,[46] while others have sought ties in the commonality or direct influence of certain philosophical and theological themes, such as differing approaches to the interrelation of

[43] H. A. Oberman, *The Harvest of Medieval Theology* (Cambridge, Mass., 1963). The only book that has explored the frontier between literature and late scholasticism is Janet Coleman's *Piers Plowman and the "Moderni"* (Rome, 1981). Also see Coleman, *Medieval Readers and Writers, 1350–1400* (London, 1981), P. Boitani and A. Torti, eds., *Intellectuals and Writers in Fourteenth-Century Europe* (Tübingen and Cambridge, 1986), and Russell Peck's forthcoming *The Philosophical Chaucer*.

[44] Charles Muscatine, *Poetry and Crisis in the Age of Chaucer* (Notre Dame, 1972).

[45] Such was the approach taken at the session on "Nominalist Aesthetics in the 14th Century" at the 1977 meeting of the International Congress on Medieval Studies at Kalamazoo, Michigan. A different set of compatible approaches between literature and certain English "nominalists" was earlier suggested by Judson Allen, "The Library of a Classicizer: The Sources of Robert Holkot's Mythographic Learning," *Arts libéraux et philosophie au moyen âge* (Paris and Montréal, 1969), 721–29; Allen, *The Friar as Critic* (Nashville, 1971).

[46] Mathew, *The Court of Richard II*, 86; D. C. Fowler, "Poetry and the Liberal Arts: The Oxford Background of Piers Plowman," in *Arts libéraux et philosophie*, 715–19; J.A.W. Bennett, *Chaucer at Oxford and at Cambridge* (Oxford, 1974). The nonscholastic view of Middle English literature was forcefully expressed by D. W. Robertson, Jr., *Preface to Chaucer* (Princeton, 1962), 315: "It may be true that allegory did not flourish in scholastic debate, but nothing else of any literary importance flourished there either." Some fascinating information on elementary and secondary schooling derived from Middle English literature can be found in Nicholas Orme, "Chaucer and Education," *The Chaucer Review* 16 (1981): 38–59; Orme, "Langland and Education," *History of Education* 11 (1982): 251–66.

grammar and reality,[47] the epistemology of intuitive cognition,[48] the interest in mathematics and physics,[49] the dialectic of absolute and ordained power,[50] or the problem of the virtuous pagan.[51] Most, however, have concentrated on the mutually central problem of salvation, of Augustinian and semi-Pelagian versions of grace and justification to which the dialectic of divine power and salvation outside the church are directly related.[52] A detailed re-examination of scholastic elements and

[47] Paula Carlson, *The Grammar of God: Grammatical Metaphor in 'Piers Plowman' and 'Pearl,'* Ph.D. diss., Columbia, 1983.

[48] B. J. Harwood, "Piers Plowman: Fourteenth-Century Skepticism and the Theology of Suffering," *Bucknell Review* 19 (1971): 119–36; L. Eldredge, "Boethian Epistemology and Chaucer's *Troilus* in the Light of Fourteenth-Century Thought," *Mediaevalia* 2 (1976): 49–75.

[49] L. Eldredge, "Late Medieval Discussions of the Continuum and the Point of the Middle English *Patience*," *Vivarium* 17 (1979): 90–115; Eldredge, "Sheltering Space and Cosmic Space in the Middle English *Patience*," *Annuale Medievale* 21 (1981): 121–33.

[50] J. F. McNamara, *Responses to Ockhamist Theology in the Poetry of the Pearl-poet, Langland, and Chaucer*, Ph.D. diss., Louisiana State, 1968; L. Eldredge, "The Concept of God's Absolute Power at Oxford in the Later Fourteenth Century," in *By Things Seen: Reference and Recognition in Medieval Thought*, ed. D. L. Jeffrey (Ottawa and Grand Rapids, 1979), 211–26; Kathleen M. Ashley, "Divine Power in Chester Cycle and Late Medieval Thought," *Journal of the History of Ideas* 39 (1978): 387–404; James R. Royse, "Nominalism and Divine Power in the Chester Cycle," *Journal of the History of Ideas* 40 (1979): 475–76, and Ashley's reply, "Chester Cycle and Nominalist Thought," ibid., 477; Coleman, *Piers Plowman and the "Moderni."* The absolute/ordained distinction and related themes have recently been used to enlighten Milton: J. P. Rumrich, "Milton, Duns Scotus, and the Fall of Satan," *Journal of the History of Ideas* 46 (1985): 33–49.

[51] A. J. Minnis, *Chaucer and Pagan Antiquity* (Cambridge, 1982; A. C. Spearing, *Medieval to Renaissance in English Poetry* (Cambridge 1985), esp. 43–58; Coleman, *Piers Plowman and the "Moderni,"* 108–46; L. Eldredge, "Pearl and the Equality of Reward in Heaven," forthcoming.

[52] R. W. Frank, Jr., *Piers Plowman and the Scheme of Salvation* (New Haven, 1957); McNamara, "Responses to Ockhamist Theology"; E. Kirk, *The Dream Thought of Piers Plowman* (New Haven, 1972); Coleman, *Piers Plowman and the "Moderni"*; M. Carruthers, *The Search for Truth* (Evanston, 1973); B. J. Harwood, "*Liberum-Arbitrium* in the C-Text of *Piers Plowman*," *Philological Quarterly*, 52 (1973), 680–95; R. Peck, "Chaucer and the Nominalist Questions," *Speculum*, 53 (1978), 745–60; D. Baker, "From Plowing to Penitence: *Piers Plowman* and Fourteenth-Century Theology," *Speculum*, 55 (1980), 715–25; M.-L. Zanoni, *Divine Order and Human Freedom in Chaucer's Poetry and Philosophical Tradition*, Ph.D. diss., Cornell, 1982; R. Adams, "Piers's Pardon and Langland's Semi-Pelagianism," *Traditio* 39 (1983), 367–418.

parallels in the works of the Middle English poets will not be attempted here, since it deserves separate and extensive treatment. The foregoing study, however, does expose the need to modify some of the assumptions and conclusions of past research in this important area, and it suggests certain limits within which meaningful results might be obtained.

First, the widespread number of grammar schools and schools of higher learning throughout the fourteenth century means that the tonsured clerk was a common sight in the streets of larger English towns, and that it would have been unlikely for anyone from a family of some means not to have received an elementary education, nor for any observant person not to have brushed the edges of scholastic debate, logical or theological. Considering the common denominators of scholastic content and life style that the schools possessed, one does not need to hypothesize intimate association with "Oxenford" or "Cambrigge" beyond what is documented by direct reference to those university towns. Although Lydgate attended Oxford and other writers betray familiarity with that university,[53] the major point and place of contact between scholars and poets was London, with its own scholastic institutions, with its inner-locking network of social and professional groups. As academic achievement became less crucial as a means of career advancement in late medieval England, the cultivation of extra-university contacts and attachment to households of *familiares* became even more important. It was in such settings that university scholars met poets, musicians, artists and architects. And it was as secretaries and envoys abroad or in the halls and chambers of London that both scholars and literary figures came into contact with Italian humanism.[54]

Second, if the immediate educational contact of Middle English poets would have been the schools and universities of the second half of the century, then there is no reason to suppose that nominalism (in the philosophical sense) was a major element shaping their language and perceptions. The only scholars who shared Ockham's position on universals, the categories, or simple supposition are the anonymous *socius* of

---

[53] Emden, *BRUO* 2: 1185–86; *DNB* 12: 306–16.

[54] On humanism in England see R. Weiss, *Humanism in England during the 15th Century* (Oxford, 1967); B. Boyd, "Whatever Happened to Chaucer's Renaissance," *Fifteenth-Century Studies* 1 (1978): 15–21; Boyd, "Geoffrey Chaucer of England and the Italian *Trecento*," in *Ecumenismo della cultura*, vol. 2 (Florence, 1981), 43–48.

Aston in the early 1350s and the anonymous author of the *Lectura Oxoniensis* writing around 1380. The spirit of the age in England was clearly in the direction of realism. If there are any *contemporary* philosophical or theological influences, therefore, of the late fourteenth-century schools on the language and content of English literature, they should probably be sought in realism, simplified logic, and practical theology, not in the direction of Ockham or nominalism.

Third, even if one were to define nominalism as the application of the dialectic of divine power, particularly to problems of grace, justification, and the sacraments (the themes of covenant and a self-binding God), the distinction of absolute and ordained power did not operate as a major analytic tool in the scholastic writings of late medieval England as it had before 1340.[55] All aspects of the events and means relating to salvation remained central (Incarnation, redemption, justification, penance, the Eucharist), but the cutting edge of discussion in England after mid-century was no longer the *absoluta/ordinata* distinction.

Fourth, the issues and scholars that are occasionally mentioned in literary works are principally those of the first half of the century, with the important exceptions of Chaucer's mention of the "philosophical" Strode and Chaucer's interest in astronomy and astrology, which continued to be studied at Oxford throughout the century.[56] These references bear the same association of name and topic/position that had become common in the margins of late medieval theological texts, where many of the issues and personalities of early fourteenth-century thought continued to be cited in the schools despite internal changes and the reduced evidence of academic activity worth preserving. If those at Oxford after 1370 took less interest in circulating or continuing the scholarship of the classroom, with the exception of treatises in logic and astronomy, it is not surprising that we find so little echo of *late* fourteenth-century scholasticism in the literature of that age. What late fourteenth-century Oxford exported was not its current logic, epistemology, or scholastic theology but its practical, eucharistic, and penitential theology, both Wycliffite and anti-Wycliffite. It may well be that

---

[55] This point has also been noted by Eldredge, "The Concept of God's Absolute Power," 216–17. In contrast to Eldredge, I find Woodford's use of the distinction directly within the tradition of Scotus and Ockham, in no sense representing a later misinterpretation.

[56] See Chaucer's dedication to Strode in his *Troilus and Criseyde*, and Chaucer's *Treatise on the Astrolabe* and *Equatorie of the Planetis*.

major personalities and issues of the "golden age" of English scholasticism found some place in the vernacular literature of later generations because they had become commonplace, part of the academic folklore of a broader and more popular level of society, disseminated by scholars (even lawyers) as they carried their university learning into a wider, nonacademic world.

Finally, the theological themes we do find in Middle English literature are precisely those that were of concern to scholars and poets alike in the second half of the century, derived in part from the impressive discussions of the psychology of the human will that were so important for English theologians during the 1320s and 1330s. These common interests were biblical themes and imagery, and the penitential themes of vices and virtues, grace and justification, moral choice, sin and repentance, predestination and human liberty, and the conflicts and ambiguities that life presents to the average Christian.[57]

---

[57] These are themes that Morton Bloomfield highlighted decades ago and which have been the most durable aspects of the common frontier between late scholasticism and Middle English literature.

EPILOGUE

SCHOLARS are just now beginning to appreciate the enormous influence exercised by the content and methodology of English thought upon the cultural life of northern and southern Europe during the century or more between 1340 and 1450. When one looks at the degree to which the topics, language, methods of analysis, and argumentation that were developed in England in the early fourteenth century, particularly at Oxford, were adopted in the universities and lesser schools throughout continental Europe in the second half of the fourteenth century, this English achievement ranks alongside Italian humanism as one of the two foremost intellectual developments of late medieval and early Renaissance society. Whether one is looking at changes in the arts and theological faculties of Paris, Erfurt, Prague, or Bologna, or at the introduction of English logic and science into Italy, or at the influence of the political treatises of Ockham or Fitzralph, or at the impact of Wyclif's thought on Jan Hus and Bohemia, it would be difficult to overemphasize the dimensions of the legacy of English thought on the Continent.

The foregoing work has concentrated on the method and content of the English achievement itself, exploring its origins, the range of its influence within and outside the schools, and its fate on English soil in the decades after the Black Death. The approach taken has been founded on two presuppositions. First, medieval thought (or that of almost any period) cannot be understood apart from the educational institutions that shaped it, provided its audience or consumers, its means of production, and its contextual purpose. And in late medieval Europe educational setting meant not just universities but the lesser *studia* and houses of study, which, more often than we have realized, were important places for the development and exchange of ideas. Second, one must be equally aware of the social uses of learning. Intellectual life for the participants was one part of their larger, multi-faceted careers, for which learning and scholastic treatises were often means as well as ends, and where some of the ideas developed in the schools were carried over into political, religious, and social life.

It is one of the ironies of late medieval history that in the decades after 1340, as English thought began to revolutionize the curriculum of continental schools, the quality and quantity of English logic and theology became only a pale reflection of what they had been in the previous half century. The change was not immediate. There was considerable activity in logic and physics in the 1350s; Wyclif initially showed an interest in some of the topics of earlier English thought; and one finds *Sentences* commentaries at century's end showing features that go back more than fifty years. In general, however, a significant drop or change had taken place by 1365, fed perhaps by a temporary decline in elementary and secondary education, but largely due to changing interests in English society that moved the universities more in the directions of law and practical theology, and moved those outside the schools more in the direction of the visual and poetic achievements of courtly society.

When looked at from this perspective, the flourishing of Middle English literature took place in a different setting, a different world—one just as vital and energetic as the early fourteenth century. One has only to look at the achievements in architecture and painting, in the luxurious detail of ecclesiastical and domestic furnishings, or developments in secular music. If the theological side of university learning did not appear equally rich in the late fourteenth century, it was because interests had shifted away from rigorous scholastic speculation and analysis to a more biblical and devotional type of religious interest that centered attention on the themes of salvation, penance, and eucharistic piety. In content and style, the theological works produced by the educated elite of the late fourteenth century only barely betray their scholastic parentage from the world of medieval universities. With them we have already entered a world that would typify English educated society well into the sixteenth century.

SELECTED BIBLIOGRAPHY

MANUSCRIPTS

Assisi, Biblioteca comunale, MS. 133

Basel, Universitätsbibliothek, MS. B.V.30

Bruxelles, Bibliothèque Royale, MSS. 1551, 1552.

Cambridge: Gonville and Caius College, MSS. 281, 370 (592); Pembroke College, MS. 236; St. John's College, MS. D.28 (James 103); Trinity College, MS. B.16.2

Eichstätt, Staats- und Seminarbibliothek, MS. 204

Erfurt, Wissenschaftliche Bibliothek der Stadt, CA F.135, CA Q.255, 288, 395

Florence, Biblioteca Nazionale, MSS. conv. soppr. A.III. 508, B.VI.340, B.VII.1249, C.V.357, J.VI.20

Heiligenkreutz, Stiftsbibliothek, MS. 185

Jena, Universitätsbibliothek, MS. Elect. 47

London: British Library, MS. Royal 10.VI; Westminster Abbey, MS. 13

Madrid, Biblioteca de la Universidad, MS. 118.Z.16

Melk, Stiftsbibliothek, MS. 1941

Munich, Staatsbibliothek, Clm 26711, 27034

Oxford: Balliol College, MSS. 63, 71, 246; Bodleian Library, MS. Bodl. 676, MS. Canon Misc. 177, MS. Rawlinson A.428; Corpus Christi College, MS. 138; Magdalen College, MS. 217; Merton College, MS. 113, 143, 284 (O.1.9); New College, MS. 134; Oriel College, MS. 15.

Paris: Bibliothèque Mazarine, MS. 915; Bibliothèque Nationale, MSS. lat. 14576, 15800, 15853, 15884, 15887, 16408, 16409, 16535; Bibliothèque de l'Université, MS. 193

Prague, Knihovna Metropolitni Kapituli, MS. C.105

Troyes, Bibliothèque de la Ville, MSS. 62, 634, 505

Vatican City: Archivo Segreto Vaticano, Reg. Vat. 129, no. 332; Biblioteca Apostolica, MS. Chigi B.V.66, MSS. Vat lat. 955, 986, 1087, 2130, 3088, 13002, MS. Vat. Ottob. lat. 1276

Venice, Bibl. San Marco, MS. Z lat. 280

Vienna, Österreichische Nationalbibliothek, MS. lat. 1512, MS. Pal. lat. 5460

Worcester, Cathedral Library, MSS. F.65, 139; MS. Q.99

REFERENCE WORKS

Bliss, W. H., ed. *Calendar of Entries in the Papal Registers Relating to Great Britain and Ireland. Petitions to the Pope.* London, 1896.

Doucet, V. *Commentaires sur les Sentences.* Quaracchi, 1954.

Emden, A. B. *A Biographical Register of the University of Cambridge to 1500.* Cambridge, 1963.

—— *A Biographical Register of the University of Oxford to 1500.* 3 vols. Oxford, 1957–59.

Glorieux, P. *La Littérature quodlibétique.* 2 vols. Kain and Paris, 1925–35.

—— *Répertoire des maîtres en théologie de Paris au XIIIe siècle.* Paris, 1933.

Heynck, V. "Ockham-Literatur 1919–1949," *Franziskanische Studien* 32 (1950): 165–83.

Ker, N. R. *Medieval Libraries of Great Britain.* 2nd ed. London, 1964.

Le Neve, John. *Fasti Ecclesiae Anglicanae, 1300–1541.* Compiled and revised by J. M. Horn and B. Jones. Rev. ed., 11 vols. London, 1962–65.

Lohr, C. H. "Medieval Latin Aristotle Commentaries," *Traditio* 23 (1967): 313–413; 24 (1968): 149–245; 26 (1970): 135–216; 27 (1971): 251–351; 28 (1972): 281–396; 29 (1973): 93–197; 30 (1974): 119–44.

Mynors, A. B. *Catalogue of the Manuscripts of Balliol College Oxford.* Oxford, 1963.

Powicke, F. M. *The Medieval Books of Merton College.* Oxford, 1931.

Reilly, J. P. "Ockham Bibliography: 1950–1967," *FcS* 28 (1968): 197–214.

Schmitt, C. B. *A Critical Survey and Bibliography of Studies on Renaissance Aristotelianism, 1958–1969.* Padua, 1971.

Stegmüller, F. *Repertorium Biblicum Medii Aevi.* 11 vols. Madrid, 1949–1980.

—— *Repertorium Commentariorum in Sententias Petri Lombardi.* 2 vols. Würzburg, 1947.

PRINTED SOURCES

Individual questions of fourteenth-century scholastic authors have occasionally been edited and published along with interpretive discussion. These have been included in the section on secondary literature. In particular see: Boehner, Brown, Courtenay, De Rijk, Etzkorn, Fitzpatrick, Gál, Gelber, Genest, Henninger, Hoffmann, Lee, Lindberg, Maierù, Maurer, Moody, Murdoch, O'Callighan, O'Donnell, Reina, Tachau, Tweedale, Wood, and Zumkeller.

Adam Wodeham. *Super quatuor libros Sententiarum.* Abbrev. Henry Totting of Oyta. Paris, 1512.

Alain de Lille. *Regulae theologiae. PL* 210, 621–84.

Alexander of Hales. *Glossa in quatuor libros sententiarum Petri Lombardi.* 4 vols. Quaracchi, 1951–57.

Anstey, H., ed. *Munimenta Academica or Documents Illustrative of Academical Life and Studies at Oxford.* 2 vols. Rolls Series. London, 1868.

Auctarium Chartularii Universitatis Parisiensis. Edited by H. Denifle and E. Chatelain; A. Gabriel. 6 vols. Paris, 1894–1964.

Bonaventure. *Opera Omnia.* 11 vols. Quaracchi, 1882–1902.

Chartularium Universitatis Parisiensis. Edited by H. Denifle and E. Chatelain. 4 vols. Paris, 1889–97.

Du Boulay, C. E. *Historia Universitatis Parisiensis.* 6 vols. Paris, 1665–73.

Ehrle, F. *I più antichi statuti della Facultà theologica dell'università di Bologna.* Bologna, 1932.

Fournier, M. *Les statuts et privilèges des universités françaises.* 4 vols. Paris, 1890–94.

Germain, A., ed. *Cartulaire de l'Université de Montpellier.* 2 vols. Montpellier, 1890; 1912.

Gibson, S. *Statuta Antiqua Universitatis Oxoniensis.* Oxford, 1931.

Gregory of Rimini. *Lectura super primum et secundum Sententiarum.* Edited by D. Trapp and V. Marcolino. 6 vols. Berlin, 1978–84.

Hackett, M. B. *The Original Statutes of Cambridge University.* Cambridge, 1970.

Henry of Ghent. *Quodlibeta.* 2 vols. Paris, 1518; Louvain, 1961.

Hugolino Malabranca of Orvieto. *Commentarius in quattuor libros sententiarum,* vol. 1. Edited by W. Eckermann. Würzburg, 1980.

John Buridan. *Sophisms on Meaning and Truth.* Edited and transl. by T. K. Scott. New York, 1966.

John Duns Scotus. *Opera Omnia.* Edited by C. Balić. Vatican, 1959–.

John Wyclif. *De universalibus.* Edited by I. Müller, Paul Spade, and A. Kenny. Oxford, 1984.

—— *Opera minora.* Edited by J. Loserth. London, 1913.

—— *Tractatus de logica.* Edited by M. H. Dziewicki. 3 vols. London, 1893–99; repr. New York, London, and Frankfurt, 1966.

Malagola, Carlo. *Statuti delle università e dei collegi dello studio Bolognese.* Bologna, 1888.

Paul of Venice. *Logica magna,* pt. 1, fasc. 1. Edited and transl. by N. Kretzmann. Oxford, 1979.

—— *Logica magna,* pt. 2, fasc. 6. Edited and transl. by F. del Punta and M. M. Adams. Oxford, 1978.

—— *Logica magna (Tractatus de Suppositionibus).* Edited and transl. by Alan R. Perreiah. St. Bonaventure, N.Y., 1971.

Peter Abelard. *Dialectica.* Edited by L. M. De Rijk. Assen, 1956.

Peter Aureoli. *Scriptum super primum Sententiarum.* Edited by E. M. Buytaert. 2 vols. St. Bonaventure, N.Y., 1953; 1956.

Peter Lombard. *Sententiae in IV libris distinctae.* 2 vols. Grottaferrata, 1971; 1981.

Peter of Spain. *Summulae Logicales.* Edited by I. M. Bocheński. Turin, 1947.

—— *Tractatus syncategorematum.* Transl. by J. P. Mullally. Milwaukee, 1964.

Richard de Bury. *Philobiblion.* Edited by E. C. Thomas. London, 1888.

Richard of Campsall. *The Works of Richard of Campsall.* Edited with introduction by E. A. Synan. 2 vols. Toronto, 1968; 1982.

Robert Holcot. *In quatuor libros Sententiarum quaestiones.* Lyon, 1518; Frankfurt, 1967.

Roger Dymock. *Liber contra xii errores et hereses Lollardorum.* Edited by H. S. Cronin. London, 1922.

Salter, H. E., W. A. Pantin, and H. G. Richardson, eds. *Formularies which bear on the History of Oxford, c. 1204–1420.* Oxford, 1942.

Salter, H. E., ed. *Snappe's Formulary and Other Records.* Oxford, 1924.

Thomas Aquinas. *Opera Omnia.* Stuttgart, 1980.

Thomas Bradwardine. *Summa de causa Dei.* Edited by H. Saville. London, 1618.

Thorndike, Lynn., ed. *University Records and Life in the Middle Ages.* New York, 1944.

Walter Burley. *De puritate artis logicae tractatus longior.* Edited by Ph. Boehner. Franciscan Institute Publications, 9. St. Bonaventure, N.Y., 1955.

William of Ockham. *Philosophical Writings: A Selection.* Edited by Ph. Boehner. New York, 1964.

—— *Ockham's Theory of Terms.* Transl. by Michael J. Loux. Notre Dame, 1974.

—— *Ockham's Theory of Propositions.* Transl. by A. J. Freddoso and H. Schuur-man. Notre Dame, 1980.

—— *Opera Philosophica et Theologica.* Edited by Gedeon Gál et al. St. Bonaven-ture, N.Y., 1964–85.

—— *Tractatus de praedestinatione et de praescientia Dei et de futuris contingentibus of William of Ockham.* Edited by Ph. Boehner. St. Bonaventure, N.Y., 1945.

William of Sherwood. *Introductio in logicam.* Edited by M. Grabmann. *Sitzungs-berichte der Bayerischen Akademie der Wissenschaften.* Phil.-hist. Abteil. 10. Mu-nich, 1937.

—— *Syncategoremata.* Edited by J. R. O'Donnell. *MedStud* 3 (1941): 46–93.

—— *William of Sherwood's Introduction to Logic.* Transl. by N. Kretzmann. Min-neapolis, 1966.

—— *William of Sherwood's Treatise on Syncategorematic Words.* Transl. by N. Kretz-mann. Minneapolis, 1968.

SECONDARY LITERATURE

Adams, Marilyn M. "Intuitive Cognition, Certainty, and Skepticism in William of Ockham," *Traditio* 26 (1970): 389–98.

Adams, R. "Piers's Pardon and Langland's Semi-Pelagianism," *Traditio* 39 (1983): 367–418.

Allen, Judson B. *The Friar as Critic; Literary Attitudes in the Later Middle Ages.* Nashville, 1971.

—— "The Library of a Classiciser: The Sources of Robert Holkot's Mythographic Learning," in *Arts libéraux et philosophie au moyen âge.* Actes du IVe congrès internationale de philosophie médiévale. (Paris and Montréal, 1969): 721–29.

Arbesmann, Rudolf. *Der Augustiner-Eremitenorden und der Beginn der humanistischen Bewegung.* Würzburg, 1965.

Arnold, E. "Für Geschichte der Suppositionstheorie," *Symposion; Jahrbuch für Philosophie* 3 (1952): 1–134.

Arnold, I.D.O. "Thomas Sampson and the 'Orthographia Gallica,' " *Medium Aevum* 6 (1937): 193–209.

Ashley, K. M. "Chester Cycle and Nominalist Thought," *Journal of the History of Ideas* 40 (1979): 477.

—— "Divine Power in Chester Cycle and late Medieval Thought," *Journal of the History of Ideas* 39 (1978): 387–404.

Ashworth, E. J. "The 'Libelli Sophistarum' and the Use of Medieval Logic Texts at Oxford and Cambridge in the Early Sixteenth Century," *Vivarium* 17 (1979): 134–58.

—— "A Note on an Early Printed Logic Text in Edinburgh University Library," *The Innes Review* 30 (1979): 77–79.

—— "A Note on Paul of Venice and the Oxford Logica of 1483," *Medioevo* 4 (1978): 93–99.

Aston, M. "Lollardy and Literacy," *History* 62 (1977): 347–71.

Aston, T. H. "Oxford's Medieval Alumni," *Past and Present* 74 (1977): 3–40.

—— G. D. Duncan, and T.A.R. Evans. "The Medieval Alumni of the University of Cambridge," *Past and Present* 86 (1980): 9–86.

Asztalos, Monika, ed. *The Editing of Theological and Philosophical Texts from the Middle Ages.* Stockholm, 1986.

Auer, J. "Die 'skotistische' Lehre von der Heilsgewissheit Walter von Chatton, der erste 'Skotist,' " *Wissenschaft und Weisheit* 15 (1952): 1–19.

Baker, D. "From Plowing to Penitence: *Piers Plowman* and Fourteenth-Century Theology," *Speculum* 55 (1980): 715–25.

Baker, Timothy. *Medieval London.* London, 1970.

Balić, C. *Les commentaires de Jean Duns Scot sur les quatre livres de sentences.* Louvain, 1927.

—— "Henricus de Harclay et Ioannes Duns Scotus," *Mélanges offerts à Etienne Gilson* (Toronto, 1959): 93–121.

Barbet, J. "Le commentaire des Sentences de Jean de Rodington, O.F.M. (1348) d'après les mss. Reims 503 et Toulouse 192," *Bulletin d'information de l'Institut de recherche et d'histoire des textes* 3 (1954): 55–63.

Barraclough, G. *Papal Provisions*. Oxford, 1935.

Baudry, L. "Gauthier de Chatton et son commentaire des sentences," *AHDL* 14 (1943–45): 337–69.

—— *Guillaume d'Occam. Sa vie, ses oeuvres, ses idées sociales et politiques*. Vol. 1. Paris, 1950.

Baur, L. *Die Philosophie des Robert Grosseteste*. Münster i.W., 1917.

Baylor, Michael G. *Action and Person: Conscience in Late Scholasticism and the Young Luther*. Leiden, 1977.

Bennett, J.A.W. *Chaucer at Oxford and at Cambridge*. Oxford, 1974.

Bennett, M. J. *Community, Class, and Careerism: Cheshire and Lancashire Society in the Age of 'Sir Gawain and the Green Knight.'* Cambridge, 1983.

Biard, J. "La redéfinition Ockhamiste de la signification," in *Sprache und Erkenntnis im Mittelalter*, Miscellanea Mediaevalia 13.1 (Berlin, 1981): 451–58.

Bocheński, I. M. *A History of Formal Logic*. Notre Dame, 1961.

Boehner, Ph. *Collected Articles on Ockham*, E. M. Buytaert, ed. St. Bonaventure, N.Y., 1958.

Boitani, Piero and Anna Torti, eds. *Intellectuals and Writers in Fourteenth-Century Europe*. Tübingen and Cambridge, 1986.

—— *Literature in Fourteenth-Century England*. Tübingen and Cambridge, 1983.

Bond, J. D. "Richard Wallingford," *Isis* 4 (1922): 459–65.

Booth, Alan D. "The Schooling of Slaves in First Century Rome," *American Philological Society* 109 (1979): 11–19.

Bosl, Karl. *Regularkanoniker (Augustinerchorherren) und Seelsorge in Kirche und Gesellschaft des europäischen 12. Jahrhunderts*. Bayerische Akademie der Wissenschaften, phil.-hist. Klasse, n.F. 86. Munich, 1979.

Bottin, F. "Analisi linguistica e fisica Aristotelica nei 'Sophysmata' de Richard Kilmington," *Filosofia e Politica, e altri saggi* (Padua, 1973): 125–45.

—— "L'*Opinio de Insolubilibus* di Richard Kilmyngton," *RCSF* 28 (1973): 408–21.

—— "Un testo fondamentale nell'ambito della 'Nuova Fisica' di Oxford: I *Sophismata* di Richard Kilmington," in *AM*, 201–5.

Boyd, B. "Geoffrey Chaucer of England and the Italian *Trecento*," in *Ecumenismo della cultura*. Vol. 2. (Florence, 1980): 43–48.

—— "Whatever happened to Chaucer's Renaissance," *Fifteenth Century Studies* 1 (1978): 15–21.

Boyle, Leonard. "Aspects of Clerical Education in Fourteenth-Century England," *Fourteenth Century*, Acta 4. Center for Medieval and Early Renaissance Studies, SUNY (Binghamton, N.Y., 1977): 19–32.

—— "The Constitution 'Cum ex eo' of Boniface VIII," *MedStud* 24 (1962): 263–302.

—— "The Curriculum of the Faculty of Canon Law at Oxford in the First Half of the Fourteenth Century," in *Oxford Studies presented to Daniel Callus* (Oxford, 1964): 135–62.

—— "Notes on the Education of the *Fratres communes* in the Dominican Order in the Thirteenth Century," in *Xenia Medii Aevi Historiam Illustrantia oblata Thomae Kaeppeli O.P.* (Rome, 1978): 249–67.

—— *Pastoral Care, Clerical Education and Canon Law, 1200–1400*. London, 1981.

Braakhuis, H.A.G. *De 13de eeuwse tractaten over syncategormatische termen*. Doctoral thesis, University of Leiden, 1979.

—— et al., eds. *English Logic and Semantics from the End of the Twelfth Century to the Time of Ockham and Burleigh*. 4th European Symposium on Medieval Logic and Semantics. Nijmegen, 1981.

Brampton, C. K. "Gauthier de Chatton et la provenance des mss. lat. Paris Bibl. Nat. 15886 et 15887," *Etudes Franciscaines* 14 (1964): 200–5.

—— "Guillaume d'Ockham fut-il maître en Theologie?" *Etudes Franciscaines* 13 (1963): 53–59.

—— "Personalities at the Process against Ockham at Avignon, 1324–26," *FcS* 26 (1966): 4–25.

—— "The Probable Order of Ockham's non-polemical Works," *Traditio* 19 (1963): 469–83.

—— "Traditions Relating to the Death of William of Ockham," *AFH* 53 (1960): 442–49.

Breen, Q. "Giovanni Pico della Mirandola on the Conflict of Philosophy and Rhetoric," *Journal of the History of Ideas* 13 (1952): 384–426.

Brlek, M. *De Evolutione Iuridica Studiorum in Ordine Minorum*. Dubrovnik, 1942.

Brown, Stephen, "A Modern Prologue to Ockham's Natural Philosophy," in *Sprache und Erkenntnis im Mittelalters*. A. Zimmerman, ed. Miscellanea Mediaevalia 13.1 (Berlin, 1981): 107–29.

—— "Peter of Candia's Sermons in Praise of Peter Lombard," *Studies Honoring Ignatius Charles Brady, Friar Minor*. Romano Stephen Almagno and Conrad L. Harkins, eds. (St. Bonaventure, N.Y., 1976): 141–76.

—— "Sources for Ockham's Prologue to the *Sentences*," *FcS* 26 (1966): 36–65; 27 (1967): 39–107.

—— "Walter Burleigh's Treatise *De suppositionibus* and its Influence on William of Ockham," *FcS* 32 (1972): 15–64.

—— "Walter Chatton's *Lectura* and William of Ockham's *Quaestiones in Libros Physicorum Aristotelis*," in *Essays Honoring Alan B. Wolter*. W. A. Frank and G. J. Etzkorn, eds. Franciscan Institute Publications, Theol. ser. 10 (St. Bonaventure, 1985): 81–115.

Buescher, G. N. *The Eucharistic Teaching of William of Ockham*. Washington, 1950.

Bullet, G. *Vertus morales infuses et vertus morales acquises selon Saint Thomas d'Aquin.* Fribourg, 1958.

Bullough, V. L. "Medical Study at Mediaeval Oxford," *Speculum* 36 (1961): 600–12.

——— "The Medieval Medical School at Cambridge," *MedStud* 24 (1962): 161–68.

Burr, David. *The Persecution of Peter Olivi.* Transactions of the American Philosophical Society, N.S. 66.5 (1976).

——— "Petrus Ioannis Olivi and the Philosophers," *FcS* 31 (1971): 41–71.

——— "Quantity and Eucharistic Presence: The Debate from Olivi through Ockham," *Collectanea Franciscana* 44 (1974): 5–44.

Bursill-Hall, G. L. *Speculative Grammars of the Middle Ages.* The Hague, 1971.

Busard, H.L.L. "Unendliche Reihen in *A est unum calidum*," *Archive for History of Exact Sciences* 2 (1965): 387–97.

Carlson, Paula. *The Grammar of God: Grammatical Metaphor in 'Piers Plowman' and 'Pearl'.* Ph.D. diss., Columbia, 1983.

Carruthers, M. *The Search for Truth.* Evanston, 1973.

Catto, J. I., ed. *The History of the University of Oxford.* Vol. 1, *The Early Oxford Schools.* Oxford, 1984.

——— *William Woodford, O.F.M., c. 1330–1397.* Doc. diss., Oxford University, 1969.

Cavanaugh, Susan Hagen. *A Study of Books privately owned in England, 1300–1450.* Ph.D. diss., University of Pennsylvania, 1980.

Chenu, M. D. "Les Quaestiones de Thomas Buckingham," in *Studia medievalia in honorem admodum Reverendi Patris Raymundi Josephi Martin, Ordinis Praedicatorum.* (Bruges, 1949): 229–41.

——— *La théologie comme science au XIIIe siècle.* Paris, 1957.

Christianson, Paul. "Books and their Makers in Medieval London," *Wooster* 96 (Spring, 1982): 10–15.

Clagett, M. *The Science of Mechanics in the Middle Ages.* Madison, 1959.

Clancy, M. T. *From Memory to Written Record, England, 1066–1307.* Cambridge, Mass. and London, 1979.

Clark, D. "Voluntarism and Rationalism in the Ethics of Ockham," *FcS* 31 (1971): 72–87.

Clark, J. W. "The Libraries at Lincoln, Westminster and St. Paul's," *Cambridge Antiquarian Society, Proceedings* 9 (1896–98): 37–60.

Classen, P. *Studium und Gesellschaft im Mittelalter*, J. Fried, ed. Stuttgart, 1983.

Clough, C. H., ed. *Profession, Vocation, and Culture in Later Medieval England.* Liverpool, 1982.

Cobban, Alan B. *The King's Hall within the University of Cambridge in the Later Middle Ages.* Cambridge, 1969.

—— "The Medieval Cambridge Colleges: A Quantitative Study of Higher Degrees to *c*. 1500," *History of Education* 9 (1980): 1–12.

—— *The Medieval Universities*. London, 1975.

—— "Theology and Law in the Medieval Colleges of Oxford and Cambridge," *BJRL* 65 (1982): 57–77.

Coleman, J. "Jean de Ripa O.F.M. and the Oxford Calculators," *MedStud* 37 (1975): 130–89.

—— *Medieval Readers and Writers, 1350–1400*. New York, 1981.

—— *Piers Plowman and the Moderni*. Rome, 1981.

Coleman, T. *Modistic Grammar*. Ph.D. diss., University of Toronto, 1976.

Cosman, M. P. and B. Chandler, eds. *Machaut's World. Science and Arts in the Fourteenth Century*. Annals of the New York Academy of Sciences, 314. New York, 1978.

Courtenay, William J. *Adam Wodeham*. Leiden, 1978.

—— "Alexander Langeley, O.F.M.," *Manuscripta* 18 (1974): 96–104.

—— *"Antiqui* and *Moderni* in Late Medieval Thought," *Journal of the History of Ideas* 48 (1987): 1–8.

—— "Augustinianism at Oxford in the Fourteenth Century," *Augustiniana* 30 (1980): 58–70.

—— "The Bible in the Fourteenth Century: Some Observations," *Church History* 54 (1985): 176–87.

—— *Covenant and Causality in Medieval Thought*. London, 1984.

—— "The Dialectic of Omnipotence in the High and Late Middle Ages," in *Divine Omniscience and Omnipotence in Medieval Philosophy*, T. Rudavsky, ed. (Dordrecht, 1985): 243–69.

—— "The Early Stages in the Introduction of Oxford Logic into Italy," in *ELI*, 12–32.

—— "The Effect of the Black Death on English Higher Education," *Speculum* 55 (1980): 696–714.

—— *The Eucharistic Theology of Gabriel Biel*. Ph.D. diss., Harvard University, 1967.

—— "Force of Words and Figures of Speech: The Crisis over *Virtus sermonis* in the Fourteenth Century," *FcS* 44 (1984).

—— "John of Mirecourt and Gregory of Rimini on Whether God Can Undo the Past," *RTAM* 39 (1972): 224–56; 40 (1973): 147–74.

—— "The London *Studia* in the Fourteenth Century," *Medievalia et Humanistica*, ser. 2, 13 (1984): 127–41.

—— "The Lost Matthew Commentary of Robert Holcot, O.P.," *AFP* 50 (1980): 103–12.

—— "Necessity and Freedom in Anselm's Conception of God," *Analecta Anselmiana* 4.2 (1975): 39–64.

Courtenay, William J. "Nicholas of Assisi and Vatican MS. Chigi B V 66," *Scriptorium* 36 (1982): 260–63.

—— "Nominalism and Late Medieval Religion," in *The Pursuit of Holiness*, C. Trinkaus and H. A. Oberman, eds. (Leiden, 1974): 26–59.

—— and K. Tachau. "Ockham, Ockhamists, and the English-German Nation at Paris, 1339–1341," *History of Universities* 2 (1982): 53–96.

—— "Ockhamism among the Augustinians: The Case of Adam Wodeham," in *Scientia Augustiniana*. C. P. Mayer and W. Eckermann, eds. (Würzburg, 1975): 267–75.

—— "Recent Work on Fourteenth-Century Oxford Thought," *History of Education Quarterly*, 25 (1985): 227–32.

—— "The Reception of Ockham's Thought at the University of Paris," in *PRUP*, 43–64.

—— "The Reception of Ockham's Thought in Fourteenth-Century England," in *From Ockham to Wyclif*. A. Hudson and M. Wilks, eds. (Oxford, 1987): 89–107.

—— "A Revised Text of Robert Holcot's Quodlibetal Dispute on Whether God is Able to Know More than He Knows," *Archiv für Geschichte der Philosophie* 53 (1971): 1–21

—— "The Role of English Thought in the Transformation of University Education in the Late Middle Ages," in *Rebirth, Reform, and Resilience in the Late Middle Ages 1300–1700*. J. A. Kittelson, ed. (Columbus, Ohio, 1984): 103–62.

—— "The *Sentences*-Commentary of Stukle: A New Source for Oxford Theology in the Fourteenth Century," *Traditio* 34 (1978): 435–38.

—— "Some Notes on Robert of Halifax, O.F.M.," *FcS* 33 (1973): 135–42.

Cova, L. "Francesco di Meyronnes e Walter Catton nella controversia scolastica sulla 'notitia intuitiva de re non existente,' " *Medioevo* 2 (1976): 227–51.

Cowie, L. W., "The London Austin Friars," *History Today* 29 (1979): 38–45.

Coxito, A. A. *Lógica, Semântica, et Conhecimento na Escolástica Peninsula Pré-Renascentista*. Coimbra, 1981.

Crump, C. G. and E. F. Jacob, eds. *The Legacy of the Middle Ages*. Oxford, 1926; 1932; 1969.

Daiches, D. and A. Thorlby, eds. *Literature and Western Civilization: The Medieval World*. London, 1973.

Dales, Richard C. "Henry of Harclay on the Infinite," *Journal of the History of Ideas* 45 (1984): 295–301.

—— *The Scientific Achievement of the Middle Ages*. Philadelphia, 1973.

Dal Pra, M. "La teoria del 'significato totale' delle proposizione nel pensiero di Gregorio da Rimini," *RCSF* 11 (1956): 287–311.

Davis, L. Donald. "The Intuitive Knowledge of Non-Existents and the Problem of Late Medieval Skepticism," *NS* 49 (1975): 410–30.

Day, Sebastian. *Intuitive Cognition. A Key to the Significance of the Later Scholastics*. St. Bonaventure, N.Y., 1947.

Deeley, A. "Papal Provisions and Rights of Royal Patronage in the Early Fourteenth Century," *EHR* 43 (1928): 497–527.

De la Torre, B. R. *Thomas Buckingham's 'Ostensio meriti liberae actionis,' Conclusiones 1 to 15: 'De contingentia futurorum et arbitrii libertate': An Edition and Study*. Ph.D. diss., University of Toronto, 1979.

Del Punta, Francesco. "La *Logica* di R. Feribrigge nella tradizione manoscritta italiana," in *ELI*, 53–85.

De Rijk, L. M. "Another *Speculum puerorum* attributed to Richard Billingham. Introduction and Text," *Medioevo* 1 (1975): 203–35.

—— "Logica Cantabrigiensis—A Fifteenth-Century Cambridge Manual of Logic," *Revue internationale de philosophie* 29 (1975): 297–315.

—— *Logica Modernorum*. 2 vols. Assen, 1962; 1967.

—— "Logica Oxoniensis," *Medioevo* 3 (1977): 121–64.

—— "The Place of Billingham's 'Speculum puerorum' in 14th and 15th Century Logical Tradition with the Edition of Some Alternative Tracts," *Studia Mediewistyczne* 16·(1975): 99–153.

—— "Richard Billingham's Works on Logic," *Vivarium* 14 (1976): 121–38.

—— "Semantics in Richard Billingham and Johannes Venator," *ELI*, 167–83.

—— "Some Thirteenth Century Tracts on the Game of Obligations," *Vivarium* 14 (1976): 26–61.

Dettloff, W. *Die Entwicklung der Akzeptations- und Verdienstlehre von Duns Scotus bis Luther*. Münster i.W., 1963.

—— *Die Lehre von der Acceptatio divina bei Johannes Duns Scotus*. Werl i.W., 1954.

De Vooght, P. *Les sources de la doctrine chrétienne*. Bruges, 1954.

Dickinson, J. C. *The Origins of the Austin Canons and their Introduction into England*. London, 1950.

Dinneen, F. P. "Distinguo. Modi Significandi and Covert Case Roles," *Historiographia Linguistica* 7 (1980): 39–52.

Dobson, Barrie. "The Late Middle Ages, 1215–1500," in *A History of York Minster*. G. E. Aylmer and Reginald Cant, eds. (Oxford, 1977): 44–109.

—— "Oxford Graduates and the So-Called Patronage Crisis of the Late Middle Ages," in *The Church in a Changing Society* (Uppsala, 1978): 211–16.

Doucet, V. "Le Studium Franciscain de Norwich en 1337 d'après le MS. Chigi B v 66 de la Bibliothèque Vaticane," *AFH* 46 (1953): 85–98.

Eckermann, W. *Wort und Wirklichkeit*. Würzburg, 1978.

Edwards, Kathleen. "Bishops and Learning in the Reign of Edward II," *Church Quarterly Review* 138 (1944): 57–86.

—— *The English Secular Cathedrals in the Middle Ages*. 2nd ed. Manchester, 1967.

Ehrle, F. *Der Sentenzenkommetar Peters von Candia*. Franziskanische Studien, 9. Münster i.W., 1925.

Eldredge, L. "Boethian Epistemology and Chaucer's *Troilus* in the Light of Fourteenth-Century Thought," *Mediaevalia* 2 (1976): 49–75.

—— "The Concept of God's Absolute Power at Oxford in the Later Fourteenth Century," in *By Things Seen: Reference and Recognition in Medieval Thought*. D. L. Jeffreys, ed. (Ottawa, 1979): 211–26.

—— "Late Medieval Discussions of The Continuum and the Point of the Middle English Patience," *Vivarium* 17 (1979): 90–115.

—— "Sheltering Space and Cosmic Space in the Middle English *Patience*," *Annuale Medievale* 21 (1981): 121–33.

Elie, H. *Le complexe significabile*. Paris, 1936.

Emden, A. B. "Northerners and Southerners in the Organisation of the University to 1509," in *Oxford Studies Presented to Daniel Callus* (Oxford, 1964): 1–30.

Etzkorn, G. J. "John Reading on the Existence and Unicity of God, Efficient and Final Causality," *FcS* 41 (1981): 110–221.

—— "Walter Chatton and the Controversy on the Absolute Necessity of Grace," *FcS* 37 (1977): 32–65.

Favier, J. *Nouvelle Histoire de Paris. Paris au XV^c siècle, 1380–1500*. Paris, 1974.

Fitzpatrick, N. A. "Walter Chatton on the Univocity of Being: A Reaction to Peter Aureoli and William Ockham," *FcS* 31 (1971): 88–177.

Forte, Stephen L. *A Study of Some Oxford Schoolmen of the Middle of the Fourteenth Century with Special Reference to Worcester Cathedral MS.F65*. Oxford B.Litt., 1947.

Fowler, D. C. "Poetry and the Liberal Arts: The Oxford Background of Piers Plowman," in *Arts libéraux et philosophie au moyen âge* (Paris, Montréal, 1969): 715–19.

Fowler, R. C. "Cistercian Scholars at Oxford," *EHR* 23 (1908): 84–85.

Frank, Jr., R. W. *Piers Plowman and the Scheme of Salvation*. New Haven, 1957.

Gabriel, Astrik. "Les étudiants étrangers à l'Université de Paris au xv^c siècle," *Annales de l'Université de Paris* 29 (1959): 377–400.

—— *Garlandia. Studies in the History of the Medieval University*. Frankfurt, 1969.

Gál, Gedeon, "Adam Wodeham's Question on the 'Complexe Significabile' as the Immediate Object of Scientific Knowledge," *FcS* 37 (1977): 66–102.

—— "Gualteri de Chatton et Guillelmi de Ockham Controversia de Natura Conceptus Universalis," *FcS* 27 (1967): 191–212.

—— "Henricus de Harclay: Quaestio de significato conceptus universalis," *FcS* 31 (1971): 178–234.

—— "Quaestio Ioannis de Reading De necessitate specierum intelligibilium. Defensio doctrinae Scoti," *FcS* 29 (1969): 66–156.

—— and Rega Wood, "Richard Brinkley and his 'Summa logicae,' " *FcS* 40 (1980): 59–101.

—— "William of Ockham died 'impenitent' in April 1347," *FcS* 42 (1982): 90–95.

Gardner, John. *The Life and Times of Chaucer*. New York, 1977.

Garin, Eugenio, "La cultura fiorentina nella seconda metà del '300 e i 'barbari Britanni,' " *La Rassegna della letteratura italiana* 64 (1960): 181–95, and in *L'età nuova* (Naples, 1969): 139–66.

—— *La disputa delle arti nel Quattrocento*. Florence, 1947.

—— *Prosatori latini del Quattrocento*. Milan, 1952.

Gelber, Hester. *Exploring the Boundaries of Reason: Three Questions on the Nature of God by Robert Holcot, O.P.* Toronto, 1983.

—— *Logic and the Trinity: A Clash of Values in Scholastic Thought, 1300–1335*. Ph.D. diss., University of Wisconsin, Madison, 1974.

Genest, J.-F. "Le *De futuris contingentibus* de Thomas Bradwardine," *Recherches Augustiniennes* 14 (1979): 249–336.

—— Le *'De futuris contingentibus' de Thomas Bradwardine*. Mémoire pour le Diplôme de l'Ecole Pratique des Hautes Etudes, 5e section, Paris, 1975.

Ghellinck, J. de. "Une bibliophile au xiv siècle: Richard d'Aungerville," *RHE* 18 (1920): 271–312, 482–502; 19 (1923): 157–200.

Gieben, Servus. "Thomas Gascoigne and Robert Grosseteste: Historical and Critical Notes," *Vivarium* 8 (1970): 56–67.

Gilbert, Neal W. "The Early Italian Humanists and Disputation," in *Renaissance Studies in Honor of Hans Baron*. A. Molho and J. Tedeschi, eds. (Florence and DeKalb, Ill., 1971): 203–26.

—— "Ockham Wyclif, and the 'Via Moderna,' " in *AM*, 85–125.

—— "Richard de Bury and the 'Quires of Yesterday's Sophisms,' " in *Philosophy and Humanism. Renaissance Essays in Honor of Paul Oskar Kristeller*. E. P. Mahony, ed. (New York, 1976): 229–57.

Gillon, L.-B. *La théorie des oppositions et la théologie du péché au XIIIᵉ siècle*. Paris, 1937.

Gilson, Etienne. *History of Christian Philosophy in the Middle Ages*. New York, 1955.

—— *The Unity of Philosophical Experience*. New York, 1937.

Glorieux, P. "Duns Scotus et les 'Notabilia Cancellarii,' " *AFH* 24 (1931): 3–14.

—— "Sentences," *Dictionnaire de théologie catholique* 14 (1941): 1860–84.

Goddu, A. *The Physics of William of Ockham*. Leiden, 1984.

Grabmann, Martin. "Bearbeitungen und Auslegungen der aristotelischen Logik aus der Zeit von Peter Abaelard bis Petrus Hispanus," *Abhandlungen der Preussischen Akademie der Wissenschaften*. Phil.-hist. Klasse, 5. Berlin, 1937.

Grabmann, Martin. *Mittelalterliches Geistesleben; Abhandlungen zur Geschichte der Scholastik und Mystik.* 3 vols. Munich, 1926–56.

—— "Thomas de Claxton, O.P. (ca. 1400). Quaestiones de distinctione inter esse et essentiam reali atque de analogia entis," *Acta Pontificae Academiae Romanae* 8 (1941–42): 92–153.

Grane, L. "Gregory von Rimini und Luthers Leipziger Disputation," *Studia Theologica* 22 (1968): 29–49.

Grant, Edward. *Physical Science in the Middle Ages.* New York, 1971.

Green, Richard F. *Poets and Princepleasers. Literature and the English Court in the Late Middle Ages.* Toronto, 1980.

Greive, H. "Zur Relationslehre Wilhelms von Ockham," *FzS* 49 (1967): 248–58.

Gründel, J. *Die Lhre von den Umständen der menschlichen Handlung im Mittelalter.* Münster i.W., 1963.

Guillemain, Bernard. *La cour pontificale d'Avignon (1309–1376): Etude d'une société.* Paris, 1962.

Gwynn, A. *The English Austin Friars in the Time of Wyclif.* Oxford, 1940.

Haines, R. M. "Education in English Ecclesiastical Legislation of the Later Middle Ages," in *Councils and Assemblies,* Studies in Church History 7. G. J. Cuming and D. Baker, eds. (Cambridge, 1978): 161–75.

—— "The Education of the English Clergy during the Later Middle Ages: Some Observations on the Operation of Pope Boniface VIII's Constitution Cum Ex Eo (1298)," *Canadian Journal of History* 4–5 (1969–70): 1–22.

Hamm, B. *Promissio, Pactum, Ordinatio. Freiheit und Selbstbindung Gottes in der scholastischen Gnadenlehre.* Tübingen, 1977.

Harwood, B. J. "*Liberum-Arbitrum* in the C-Text of *Piers Plowman,*" *Philological Quarterly* 52 (1972): 680–95.

—— "Piers Plowman: Fourteenth-Century Skepticism and the Theology of Suffering," *Bucknell Review* 19 (1971): 119–36.

Hay, Denys. *Europe in the Fourteenth and Fifteenth Centuries.* New York, 1966.

Henisch, B. A. *Fast and Feast.* University Park, Pa., 1976.

Henninger, M. "Henry of Harclay on the Formal Distinction in the Trinity," *FcS* 41 (1981): 250–335.

—— "Henry of Harclay's Questions on Divine Prescience and Predestination," *FcS* 40 (1980): 167–223.

Henry, D. P. *Medieval Logic and Metaphysics.* London, 1972.

—— "Ockham and the Formal Distinction," *FcS* 25 (1965): 285–92.

Hinnebusch, William A. *The History of the Dominican Order.* New York, 2 vols., 1966, 1973.

Hissette, Roland. *Enquête sur les 219 articles condamnés à Paris de 7 mars 1277.* Louvain, 1977.

Hochstetter, E. *Studien zur Metaphysik und Erkenntnislehre Wilhelms von Ockham.* Berlin, 1927.

Hoffmann, F. "Robert Holcot: Die Logik in der Theologie," in *Die Metaphysik im Mittelalter.* 2nd International Congress of Medieval Philosophy (Berlin, 1963): 624–39.

—— "Der Satz als Zeichen der theologischen Aussage bei Holcot, Crathorn, und Gregor von Rimini," *Der Begriff der Repraesentatio im Mittelalter.* Miscellanea Mediaevalia 8 (Berlin, 1971): 296–313.

—— *Die Schriften des Oxforder Kanzlers Johannes Lutterell.* Erfurter Theologische Studien 6. Leipzig, 1959.

—— *Die Theologische Methode des Oxforder Dominikanerlehrers Robert Holcot.* Münster i.W., 1972.

Hudson, A. and M. Wilks, eds. *From Ockham to Wyclif.* Studies in Church History, Subsidia 5. Oxford, 1987.

Humphreys, K. W. *The Book Provisions of the Medieval Friars, 1215–1400.* Amsterdam, 1964.

Hunt, R. W. *The History of Grammar in the Middle Ages.* G. L. Bursill-Hall, ed. Amsterdam, 1980.

—— "Oxford Grammar Masters in the Middle Ages," in *Oxford Studies presented to Daniel Callus* (Oxford, 1964): 163–93.

Hyde, J. K., "Some Uses of Literacy in Venice and Florence in the 13th and 14th Centuries," *TRHS* ser. 5, 29 (1979): 109–28.

Ijsewijn, J. and J. Paquet, eds. *The Universities in the Late Middle Ages.* Louvain, 1978.

Irwin, Raymond. *The English Library: Sources and History.* London, 1966.

Iserloh, E. *Gnade und Eucharistie in der philosophischen Theologie des Wilhelm von Ockham.* Wiesbaden, 1956.

Issac, J. *Le Peri hermeneias en occident de Boèce à Saint Thomas.* Bibl. thomiste, 29. Paris, 1953.

Jacob, E. F. "English University Clerks in the later Middle Ages: The Problem of Maintenance," *BJRL* 29 (1945–46): 304–25.

—— *Essays in Later Medieval History.* Manchester, 1968.

—— "Petitions for Benefices from English Universities during the Great Schism," *TRHS* 4th ser., 27 (1945): 41–59.

—— "On the Promotion of English University Clerks during the Later Middle Ages," *JEH* 1 (1950): 172–86.

James, M. R. "The Catalogue of the Library of the Augustinian Friars at York," *Fasciculus Ioanni Willis Clark dicatus* (Cambridge, 1909): 2–96.

Jarrett, Bede. *The English Dominicans.* London, 1921.

Kaeppeli, Th. *Le procès contre Thomas Waleys O.P.* Rome, 1936.

Kaluza, Z. "L'Oeuvre théologique de Nicolas Aston," *AHDL* 45 (1978): 45–82.

Kaluza, Z. "La prétendue discussion parisienne de Thomas Bradwardine avec Thomas de Buckingham: Témoignage de Thomas de Cracovie," *RTAM* 43 (1976): 219–36.

—— and P. Vignaux, eds. *Preuve et raisons à l'Université de Paris: Logique, ontologie, et théologie au XIVe siècle*. Paris, 1984.

——"Le problème du 'Deum non esse' chez Etienne de Chaumont, Nicolas Aston et Thomas Bradwardine," *Mediaevalia Philosophica Polonorum* 24 (1979): 3–19.

——"Quelques traces du commentaire des sentences de Thomas Felthorp," *Freiburger Zeitschrift für Philosophie und Theologie* 30 (1983): 189–99.

—— *Thomas de Cracovie*. Wroclaw, 1978.

Kennedy, L. A. "The *De anima* of John Sharpe," *FcS* 29 (1969): 249–70.

—— "A Carmelite Fourteenth-Century Theological Notebook," *Carmelus* 33 (1986): 70–102.

—— "Late-Fourteenth-Century Philosophical Scepticism at Oxford," *Vivarium* 23.2 (1985): 124–51.

—— "Philosophical Scepticism in England in the Mid-Fourteenth Century," *Vivarium* 21 (1983): 35–57.

—— "Theology the Handmaiden of Logic: A *Sentences* Commentary used by Gregory of Rimini and John Hiltalingen," *Augustiniana* 33 (1983): 142–64.

Kenny, A. *Wyclif*. Oxford, 1985.

Ker, N. "The Books of Philosophy Distributed at Merton College in 1372 and 1375," *Medieval Studies for J.A.W. Bennett*. P. L. Heyworth, ed. (Oxford, 1981): 347–94.

—— "Oxford College Libraries before 1500," in *Universities in the Late Middle Ages*, J. Ijsewijn and J. Paquet, eds. (Louvain, 1978): 293–311.

Kibre, Pearl. *The Nations of the Medieval Universities*. Cambridge, Mass., 1948.

—— *Scholarly Privileges in the Middle Ages*. Cambridge, Mass., 1962.

Kingsford, C. L. *The Grey Friars of London*. Aberdeen, 1915.

Kirk, E. *The Dream Thought of Piers Plowman*. New Haven, 1972.

Kittelson, J. M. and P. J. Transue, eds. *Rebirth, Reform, and Resilience: Universities in Transition, 1300–1700*. Columbus, Ohio, 1984.

Kneale, W. and M. *The Development of Logic*. Oxford, 1962.

Knowles, David. "The Censured Opinions of Uthred of Boldon," *The Proceedings of the British Academy* 37 (1951): 305–42. Repr. in *The Historian and Character* (Cambridge, 1963): 129–70.

Knudsen, C. *Walter Chattons Kritik an Wilhelm von Ockhams Wissenschaftslehre*. Bonn, 1976.

Koch, J. *Durandus de S. Porciano O.P.*. Beiträge zur Geschichte der Philosophie des Mittelalters, 26. Münster i.W., 1927.

—— *Kleine Schriften*. Rome, 1973.

Kölmel, W. "Das Naturrecht bei Wilhelm von Ockham," *FzS* 35 (1953): 39–85.

Kraus, J. *Quaestiones de universalibus magistrorum Crathorn, O.P., annonymi O.F.M., Ioannis Canonici, O.F.M.* Münster i.W., 1937.

—— "Die Stellung des Oxforder Dominikanerlehrers Crathorn zu Thomas von Aquin," *Zeitshrift für katholische Theologie* 57 (1933): 66–88.

—— "Die Universalien lehre des Oxforder Kanzlers Heinrich von Harclay in ihrer Mittelstellung zwischen skotistischem Realismus und ockhamistischem Nominalismus," *Divus Thomas* (Fribourg) 10 (1932): 36–58, 475–508; 11 (1933): 76–96, 288–314.

Kretzmann, Norman, A. Kenny, Jan Pinborg, eds. *Cambridge History of Later Medieval Philosophy*. Cambridge, 1982.

Kretzmann, Norman, ed. *Infinity and Continuity in Ancient and Medieval Thought*. Cornell, 1982.

—— et al. "L.M. De Rijk on Peter of Spain," *Journal of the History of Philosophy* 16 (1978): 325–33.

—— "Medieval Logicians on the Meaning of the *Propositio*," *Journal of Philosophy* 67 (1970): 767–87.

—— "Richard Kilvington and the Logic of Instantaneous Speed," in *Studi sul XIV secolo in memoria di Anneliese Maier*. A. Maierù and A. Paravicini Bagliani, eds. (Rome, 1981): 143–78.

—— "Semantics, History of," *The Encyclopedia of Philosophy* 7 (New York, 1967): 358–406.

—— "Sensus Compositus, Sensus Divisus, and Propositional Attitudes," *Medioevo* 7 (1981): 195–229.

—— "Socrates is Whiter than Plato begins to be White," *Nous* 11 (1977): 3–15.

Kristeller, Paul Oskar. "Florentine Platonism and Its Relation with Humanism and Scholasticism," *Church History* 8 (1939): 201–11.

—— *Medieval Aspects of Renaissance Learning*. Durham, N.C., 1974.

—— *Renaissance Thought*. 2 vols. New York, 1961; 1965.

Lang, A. *Die Entfaltung des apologetischen Problems in der Scholastik des Mittelalters*. Freiburg, i.B., 1962.

—— *Die Wege der Glaubensbegrundung bei den Scholastikern des 14. Jahrhunderts*. Münster i.W., 1930.

Leader, D. R. "Grammar in Late-Medieval Oxford and Cambridge," *History of Education* 12 (1983): 9–14.

Lechner, J. *Johannes von Rodington, OFM und sein Quodlibet de conscientia*. Beiträge zur Geschichte der Philosophie der Mittelalters, supp. 3.2 (1935): 1112–68.

—— "Kleine Beiträge zur Geschichte des Englischen Franziskaner-Schrifttums im Mittelalter," *PhilJahr* 53 (1940): 374–85.

—— "Die Quästionen des Sentenzkommentars des Johannes von Rodington O.F.M.," *FzS* 22 (1935): 232–48.

Leclercq, J. "La théologie comme science d'après la littérature quodlibétique," *RTAM* 11 (1939): 351–74.

Lee, A. R. *Thomas Buckingham. A Critical edition with commentary of the first question of the 'Quaestiones super Sentences.'* B.Litt. thesis, Oxford, 1975.

Leff, Gordon. *Bradwardine and the Pelagians.* Cambridge, 1957.

—— *Paris and Oxford Universities in the Thirteenth and Fourteenth Centuries.* New York, 1968.

—— *Richard Fitzralph.* Manchester, 1963.

—— *William of Ockham.* Manchester, 1975.

Leibold, G. "Zu Interpretationsfragen der Universalienlehre Ockhams," in *Sprache und Erkenntnis im Mittelalter,* Miscellanea Mediaevalia 13.1 (Berlin, 1981): 459–64.

Lewry, O. "The Oxford Condemnations of 1277 in Grammar and Logic," in *English Logic and Semantics from the End of the Twelfth Century to the Time of Ockham and Burleigh.* Braakhuis, H.A.G. et al., eds. 4th European Symposium on Medieval Logic and Semantics (Nijmegen, 1981): 235–78.

Lickteig, Franz-Bernard. *The German Carmelites at the Medieval Universities.* Ph.D. diss., Catholic University of America, Washington, D.C., 1977.

Lindberg, David C. *Roger Bacon's Philosophy of Nature.* Oxford, 1983.

—— ed. *Science in the Middle Ages.* Chicago, 1978.

Little, A. G. "Cistercian Students at Oxford in the Thirteenth Century," *EHR* 8 (1893): 83–85.

—— "Educational Organisation of the Mendicant Friars in England (Dominicans and Franciscans)," *TRHS,* n.s. 8 (1894): 49–70.

—— *Franciscan Papers, Lists, and Documents.* Manchester, 1943.

—— "The Franciscan School at Oxford in the Thirteenth Century," *AFH* 19 (1926): 803–74.

—— *The Grey Friars in Oxford.* Oxford, 1892.

—— "Theological Schools in Medieval England," *EHR* 55 (1940): 624–30.

—— and F. Pelster, *Oxford Theology and Theologians.* Oxford, 1934.

Longpré, E. "Jean de Reading et le Bx. Jean Duns Scot," *La France Franciscaine* 7 (1924): 99–109.

Loux, M. J. "*Significatio* and *Suppositio*: Reflections on Ockham's Semantics," *NS* 53 (1979): 407–27.

Luttrell, A. "Giovanni Contarini, A Venetian at Oxford: 1392–1399," *Journal of the Warburg and Courtauld Institutes* 29 (1966): 424–36.

Lytle, Guy Fitch. "The Careers of Oxford Students in the Later Middle Ages," in *Rebirth, Reform, and Resilience: Universities in Transition, 1300–1700.* J. M. Kittelson and P. J. Transue, eds. (Columbus, Ohio, 1984): 213–53.

—— *Oxford Students and English Society: c. 1300–1510.* Ph.D. diss., Princeton University, 1976.

—— "Patronage and the Election of Winchester Scholars during the late Middle Ages and Renaissance," in *Winchester College*. R. Custance, ed. (Oxford, 1982): 167–88.

—— "Patronage Patterns and Oxford Colleges, *c.* 1300–*c.* 1510," in *The University in Society*. L. Stone, ed. Vol. 1 (Princeton, 1974): 111–49.

—— "The Social Origins of Oxford Students in the Late Middle Ages: New College, *c.* 1380–*c.* 1510," in *The Universities in the Late Middle Ages*. J. Ijsewijn and J. Paquet, eds. (Louvain, 1978): 426–54.

—— "A University Mentality in the Later Middle Ages: The Pragmatism, Humanism, and Orthodoxy of New College, Oxford," in *Genèse et débuts du grand schism d'occident* (Paris, 1980): 201–30.

—— " 'Wykehamist Culture' in pre-Reformation England," in *Winchester College*. R. Custance, ed. (Oxford, 1982): 129–66.

Mahoney, E. P., ed. *Philosophy and Humanism. Renaissance Essays in Honor of Paul Oskar Kristeller*. New York, 1976.

Maier, Anneliese. *An der Grenze von Scholastik und naturwissenschaft.* 2nd ed. Rome, 1952.

—— *Ausgehendes Mittelalter; Gesammelte Aufsätze zur Geistesgeschichte des 14. Jahrhunderts.* 3 vols. Rome, 1964–67.

—— *On the Threshold of Exact Science: Selected Writings of Anneliese Maier on Late Medieval Natural Philosophy.* ed. and transl. S. D. Sargent. Philadelphia, 1982.

—— *Die Vorläufer Galileis im 14. Jahrhundert.* 2nd ed. Rome, 1966.

—— *Zwei Grundproblemen der scholastischen Naturphilosophie.* 3rd ed. Rome, 1968.

—— *Zwischen Philosophie und Mechanik.* Rome, 1958.

Maierù, A., ed. *English Logic in Italy in the 14th and 15th Centuries.* Naples, 1982.

—— "Logica aristotelica e teologia trinitaria. Enrico Totting da Oyta," in *Studi sul XIV secolo in memoria di Annaliese Maier*. A. Maierù and A. Paravicini Bagliani, eds. (Rome, 1981): 281–512.

—— "Logique et théologie trinitaire dans le moyen âge tardif: deux solutions en présence," in *The Editing of Theological and Philosophical Texts*, M. Asztalos, ed. (Stockholm, 1986): 185–201.

—— "Logique et théologie trinitaire: Pierre d'Ailly," in *PRUP*, 253–68.

—— "Lo *Speculum puerorum sive Terminus est in quem* di Riccardo Billingham," in *A Giuseppe Ermini*, vol. 3, *Studi Medievali* 10.3 (1969) (Spoleto, 1970): 297–397.

—— and A. Paravicini Bagliani, eds. *Studi sul XIV secolo in memoria di Anneliese Maier*. Storia e Letteratura, 151. Rome, 1981.

—— "Tecniche di insegnamento," in *Le scuole degli ordini mendicanti*. (Todi, 1978): 307–52.

—— *Terminologia logica della tarda scholastica.* Rome, 1972.

Marcett, M. E. *Uthred de Bolden, Friar William Jordan and Piers Plowman*. New York, 1938.

Martin, G. "Ist Ockhams Relationstheorie Nominalismus?", *FzS* 32 (1950): 31–49.

Mathew, Gervase. *The Court of Richard II*. London, 1968.

Maurer, A. "Henry of Harclay: disciple or critic of Duns Scotus?" in *Die Metaphysik im Mittelalter*. Miscellanea Mediaevalia 2 (Berlin, 1963): 563–71.

—— "Henry of Harclay's Disputed Question on the Plurality of Forms," *Essays in Honour of Anton Charles Pegis*. J. Reginald O'Donnell, ed. (Toronto, 1974): 125–59.

—— "Henry of Harclay's Question on the Univocity of Being," *MedStud* 16 (1954): 1–18.

—— "Henry of Harclay's Questions on Immortality," *MedStud* 19 (1957): 79–107.

—— "Henry of Harclay's Questions on the Divine Ideas," *MedStud* 23 (1961): 163–93.

—— "St. Thomas and Henry of Harclay on Created Nature," in *III Congresso internazionale di filosofia medioevale* (Milan, 1966): 542–49.

—— "William of Ockham on the Language of Reality," in *Sprache und Erkenntnis im Mittelalter*, Miscellanea Mediaevalia 13, 2 (Berlin, 1981): 795–802.

McGrade, A. Stephen "Ockham and the Birth of Individual Rights," in *Authority and Power: Studies on Medieval Law and Government*. B. Tierney and P. Linehan, eds. (Cambridge, 1980): 149–65.

—— "Ockham on Enjoyment—Towards an Understanding of Fourteenth-Century Philosophy and Psychology," *Review of Metaphysics* 34 (1981): 706–28.

—— *Political Thought of William of Ockham*. Cambridge, 1974.

McNamara, J. F. *Responses to Ockhamist Theology in the Poetry of the Pearl-poet, Langland, and Chaucer*. Ph.D. diss., Louisiana State University, 1968.

Michalski, C. "Les courants critiques et sceptiques dans la philosophie du XIVe siècle," *Bulletin internationale de l'Académie Polonaise des Sciences et des Lettres*. Classe hist./phil. (Cracow, 1927): 192–242.

—— "Les courants philosophiques à Oxford et à Paris pendant le XIVe siècle," *Bulletin internationale de l'Académie Polonaise des Sciences et des Lettres*. Classe hist./phil. (Cracow, 1922): 59–88.

—— "Le criticisme et le scepticisme dans la philosophie du XIVe siècle," *Bulletin internationale de l'Académie Polonaise des Sciences et des Lettres*. Classe hist./phil. (Cracow, 1927): 41–122.

—— "La physique nouvelle et les différent courants philosophiques au XIVe siècle," *Bulletin internationale de l'Académie, Polonaise des Sciences et des Lettres*. Classe hist./phil. (Cracow, 1928): 93–164.

—— "Le problème de la volonté à Oxford et à Paris au XIVe siècle," *Studia Philosophica: Commentarii Societatis Philosophicae Polonorum* 2 (Lvov, 1937): 233–367.

—— "Les sources du criticisme et du scepticisme dans la philosophie du xive siècle," *Fifth International Congress of Historical Sciences.* (Bruxelles, 1923–24): 241–68.

—— "Die vielfachen Redaktionen einiger Kommentare zu Petrus Lombardus," *Miscellanea Fr. Ehrle.* Vol. 1 (Rome, 1924): 219–64.

Miethke, Jürgen. "Die Kirche und die Universitäten im 13. Jahrhundert," in *Schulen und Studium im sozialen Wandel des Hohen und späteren Mittelalters,* J. Fried, ed. Vortäge und Forschungen, 30 (Sigmaringen, 1986): 285–320.

—— "Marsilius und Ockham. Publikum und Leser ihrer politischen Schriften im späteren Mittelalter," *Medioevo* 6 (1980): 543–67.

—— *Ockhams Weg zur Sozialphilosophie.* Berlin, 1969.

—— "Wilhelm von Ockham," in *Gestalten der Kirchengeschichte.* Greschat, M., ed. Vol. 4 (Stuttgart, 1983): 155–75.

—— "Zur Bedeutung der Ekklesiologie für die politische Theorie im späteren Mittelalter," in *Soziale Ordnungen im Selbstverständnis des Mittelalters.* Miscellanea Mediaevalia 12/2 (Berlin, 1980): 369–88.

Miner, J. N. "Schools and Literacy in Later Medieval England," *British Journal of Educational Studies* 11 (1962–63): 16–27.

—— "The Teaching of Latin in Later Medieval England," *MedStud* 23 (1961): 1–20.

Minnis, Alastair J. *Chaucer and Pagan Antiquity.* Cambridge, 1982.

—— "Chaucer's Pardoner and the 'Office of the Preacher,' " in *Intellectuals and Writers in Fourteenth-Century Europe.* P. Boitani and A. Torti, eds. (Tübingen and Cambridge, 1986): 88–119.

—— *Medieval Theory of Authorship. Scholastic Literary Attitudes in the Later Middle Ages.* London, 1984.

Mohan, G. E. "The Prologue to Ockham's Exposition of the Physics of Aristotle," *FcS* 5 (1945): 235–46.

Mollat, G. *La Collation des bénéfices ecclésiastiques sous les Papes d'Avignon, 1305–78.* Paris, 1921.

—— *The Popes at Avignon.* 9th edition. London, 1963.

Monahan, E. J. "Human Liberty and Free Will According to John Buridan," *MedStud* 16 (1954): 72–86.

Moody, E. A. "Empiricism and Metaphysics in Medieval Philosophy," *The Philosophical Review* 67 (1958): 145–63; repr. in *Studies,* 287–304.

—— *The Logic of William of Ockham.* New York, 1935.

—— "Ockham and Aegidius of Rome," *FcS* 9 (1949): 417–42; repr. in *Studies,* 161–88.

—— "A Quodlibetal Question of Robert Holkot, O.P. on the Problem of the Objects of Knowledge and of Belief," *Speculum* 39 (1964): 53–74.

—— *Studies in Medieval Philosophy, Science, and Logic.* Berkeley, 1975.

O'Dwyer, B. W. "The Problem of Education in the Cistercian Order," *Journal of Religious History* 3 (1965): 238–45.

Orme, Nicholas. "Chaucer and Education," *The Chaucer Review* 16 (1981): 38–59.

—— "Education and Learning at a Medieval English Cathedral: Exeter, 1380–1548," *JEH* 32 (1981): 265–83.

—— *Education in the West of England, 1066–1548*. Exeter, 1976.

—— *English Schools in the Middle Ages*. London, 1973.

—— "Langland and Education," *History of Education* 11 (1982): 251–66.

—— "Schoolmasters, 1307–1509," in *Profession, Vocation, and Culture in Later Medieval England*. C. H. Clough, ed. (Liverpool, 1982): 218–41.

Ouy, G. *Un commentateur des "Sentences" au XIVe siècle, Jean de Mirecourt*. Doc. thesis, Ecole de Chartes, Paris, 1946.

Oxford Studies Presented to Daniel Callus. Oxford, 1964.

Ozment, Steven. *The Age of Reform, 1250–1550*. New Haven, 1980.

Panaccio, C. "Guillaume d'Occam et les pronoms demonstratifs," in *Sprache und Erkenntnis im Mittelalter*, Miscellanea Mediaevalia 13.1 (Berlin, 1981): 465–70.

Pannenberg, W. *Die Prädestinationslehre des Duns Skotus*. Göttingen, 1954.

Pantin, W. A. *Canterbury College, Oxford*. Oxford, 1947.

—— *The English Church in the Fourteenth Century*. Cambridge, 1955; Notre Dame, 1963.

Paqué, R. *Das Pariser Nominalistenstatut*. Berlin, 1970.

Parkes, M. B. "The Literacy and the Laity," in *Literature and Western Civilization: The Medieval World*. D. Daiches and A. Thorlby, eds. (London, 1973): 555–77.

Peck, R. "Chaucer and the Nominalist Questions," *Speculum* 53 (1978): 745–60.

Pelster, Fr. "Heinrich von Harclay, Kanzler von Oxford, und seine Quästionen," in *Miscellanea Fr. Ehrle*. 1 (Rome, 1924): 307–56.

—— "Das Leben und die Schriften des Oxforder Dominikanerlehrers Richard Fishacre," *Zeitschrift für katholische Theologie* 54 (1930): 515–53.

—— "Nominales und reales in 13. Jahrhundert," *Sophia* (1946): 154–61.

—— "Zur Scotus-Forschung," *Theologische Revue* 28 (1929): 145–52.

Perreiah, Alan R. *Paul of Venice. A Bibliographical Guide*. Bowling Green, Ohio, 1986.

Pinborg, Jan "The English Contribution to Logic before Ockham," *Synthese* 40 (1979): 19–42.

Pinborg, Jan et al. "The Commentary on 'Priscianus Maior' Ascribed to Robert Kilwardby," *CIMGL* 15 (1975).

—— *Die Entwicklung der Sprachtheorie im Mittelalter*. Beiträge zur Geschichte der Philosophie und Theologie des Mittelalters, 42.2. Münster, i.W., 1967.

—— ed. *The Logic of John Buridan*. Copenhagen, 1976.

—— "Die Logik der Modiste," *Studia Mediewistyczne* 16 (1975): 39–97.

—— *Logik und Semantik im Mittelalter*. Stuttgart, 1972.

—— "Magister abstractionum," *CIMGL* 18 (1976): 1–4.

—— "A Note on Some Theoretical Concepts of Logic and Grammar," *Revue Internationale de Philosophie* 29 (1975): 286–96.

—— and S. Ebbesen "Thirteenth Century Notes on William of Sherwood's Treatise on Properties of Terms," *CIMGL* 47 (1984): 103–41.

Pollard, G. "The University and the Book Trade in Medieval Oxford," *Beiträge zum Berufsbewusstsein des mittelalterlichen Menschen. Miscellanea Mediaevalia* 3 (Berlin, 1964): 336–44.

Poskitt, Margaret E. "The English Carmelite Province: 15th Century," *The Aylesford Review* 1 (1956): 98–102.

—— "The English Carmelites: Houses of Study and Educational Methods," *The Aylesford Review* 5 (1963): 226–37.

Price, R. "William of Ockham and *Suppositio Personalis*," *FcS* 30 (1970): 131–40.

Randall, J. H. "Paduan Aristotelianism: an Appraisal," *Aristotelismo padovano e filosofia aristotelica*. Atti del XII Congresso internazionale di filosofia, 9 (Florence, 1960): 199–206.

—— "Paduan Aristotelianism Reconsidered," in *Philosophy and Humanism. Renaissance Essays in Honor of Paul Oskar Kristeller*. E. P. Mahoney, ed. (New York, 1976): 275–82.

—— *The School of Padua and the Emergence of Modern Science*. Padua, 1961.

Rashdall, Hastings. *The Universities of Europe in the Middle Ages*. ed. F. M. Powicke and A. B. Emden. 3 vols. Oxford, 1936.

Reina, Maria Elena. "La prima questione del prologo del 'commento alle sentenze' di Walter Chatton," *RCSF* 25 (1970): 48–74, 290–314.

Richards, R. C. "Ockham and Skepticism," *NS* 42 (1968): 345–63.

Richardson, H. G. "Business Training in Medieval Oxford," *American Historical Review* 46 (1940–41): 259–80.

Richter, V. "Ockham und Moderni in der Universalienfrage," in *Sprache und Erkenntnis im Mittelalter*, Miscellanea Mediaevalia 13.1 (Berlin, 1981): 471–75.

—— "Zum incipit des Physikkommentars von Ockham," *PhilJahr* 81 (1974): 197–201.

Rickert, Edith. *Chaucer's World*. New York, 1948.

Robertson, D. W. *Preface to Chaucer*. Princeton, 1962.

Robson, J. A. *Wyclif and the Oxford Schools*. Cambridge, 1961.

Rodes, Robert E. *Ecclesiastical Administration in Medieval England: The Anglo-Saxons to the Reformation*. Notre Dame, 1977.

Roensch, F. J. *Early Thomist School*. Dubuque, 1964.

Rosenthal, J. T. "Aristocratic Cultural Patronage and Book Bequests, 1350–1500," *BJRL* 64 (1982): 522–48.

Rosenthal, J. T. "English Medieval Education Since 1970—So Near and Yet So Far," *History of Education Quarterly* 22, (1982): 499–511.

—— *The Training of an Elite Group: English Bishops in the Fifteenth Century.* Transactions of the American Philosophical Society, n.s. 60, pt. 5 (1970).

Roth, F. *The English Austin Friars, 1249–1538.* New York, 1966.

Royse, James S. "Nominalism and Divine Power in the Chester Cycle," *Journal of the History of Ideas* 40 (1979): 475–76.

Rudavsky, T., ed. *Divine Omniscience and Omnipotence in Medieval Philosophy.* Dordrecht, 1985.

Rumrich, J. P. "Milton, Duns Scotus, and the Fall of Satan," *Journal of the History of Ideas* 46 (1985): 33–49.

Ryan, J. J. *The Nature, Structure and Function of the Church in William of Ockham.* Missoula, 1979.

Salamucha, J. "Die Aussagenlogik bei Wilhelm Ockham," *FzS* 32 (1950): 97–134.

Salter, H. E. *Medieval Oxford.* Oxford, 1936.

Scattergood, V. J., and J. W. Sherborne, ed. *English Court Culture in the Later Middle Ages.* London, 1983.

Schepers, H. "Holkot contra dicta Crathorn," *PhilJahr* 77 (1970): 320–54; 79 (1972): 106–36.

Schwamm, H. *Das göttliche Vorherwissen bei Duns Scotus und seinen ersten Anhängern.* Innsbruck, 1934.

Scott, T. K. "Nicholas of Autrecourt, Buridan, and Ockhamism," *Journal of the History of Philosophy* 9 (1971): 15–41.

—— "Ockham on Evidence, Necessity, and Intuition," *Journal of the History of Philosophy* 7 (1969): 27–49.

Seaton, W. K. *An Edition and Translation of the "Tractatus de consequentiis" by Ralph Strode, Fourteenth-Century Logician and Friend of Geoffrey Chaucer.* Ph.D. diss., University of California, Berkeley, 1973.

Shapiro, H. *Motion, Time and Place according to William of Ockham.* St. Bonaventure, N.Y., 1957.

Siclari, A. "La 'Dialectica' di Giovanni di Damasco e la 'Summa logicae' di Guglielmo di Occam," in *Sprache und Erkenntnis im Mittelalter*, Miscellanea Mediaevalia 13.1 (Berlin, 1981): 476–87.

Smalley, B. *English Friars and Antiquity in the Early Fourteenth Century.* Oxford, 1960.

—— "Robert Holcot, O.P.," *AFP* 26 (1956): 5–97.

—— "Thomas Waleys, O.P.," *AFP* 24 (1954): 50–107.

Spade, Paul V. "An Anonymous Tract on *Insolubilia* from Ms Vat. lat. 674: An Edition and Analysis of the Text," *Vivarium* 9 (1971): 1–18.

—— "Five Logical Tracts by Richard Lavenham," in *Essays in Honor of Anton Charles Pegis.* J. Reginald O'Donnell, ed. (Toronto, 1974): 70–124.

—— *The Mediaeval Liar: a Catalogue of the 'Insolubilia'-Literature.* Toronto, 1975.

—— "Notes on Richard Lavenham's So-Called *Summulae logicales* with a Partial Edition of the Text," *FcS* 40 (1980): 370–407.

—— "Notes on Some Manuscripts of Logical and Physical Works by Richard Lavenham," *Manuscripta* 19 (1975): 139–46.

—— "Ockham on Self-reference," *Notre Dame Journal of Formal Logic* 15 (1974): 298–300.

—— "Ockham's Distinctions between Absolute and Connotative Terms," *Vivarium* 13 (1975): 55–76.

—— "The Origins of the Medieval *Insolubilia*-Literature," *FcS* 33 (1973): 292–309.

—— *Peter of Ailly: Concepts and Insolubles: An Annotated Translation.* Dordrecht, 1980.

—— "Richard Lavenham and the Cambridge Logic," *Historiographica Linguistica* 7 (1980): 241–47.

—— "Richard Lavenham's *Obligationes*: Edition and Comments," *RCSF* 33 (1978): 224–41.

—— "Robert Fland's *Consequentiae*: An Edition," *MedStud* 78 (1976): 54–84.

—— "Robert Fland's *Insolubilia*: An Edition, with Comments on the Dating of Fland's Works," *MedStud* 39 (1978): 56–80.

—— "Robert Fland's *Obligationes*: An Edition," *MedStud* 42 (1980): 41–60.

—— "Roger Swyneshead's *Insolubilia*: Edition and Comments," *AHDL* 46 (1979): 177–220.

—— "Roger Swyneshead's *Obligationes*: Edition and Comments," *AHDL* 44 (1977): 243–85.

—— "Some Epistemological Implications of the Burley-Ockham Dispute," *FcS* 35 (1975): 212–22.

—— "The Treatises *On Modal Propositions* and *On Hypothetical Propositions* by Richard Lavenham," *MedStud* 35 (1973): 49–59.

—— *William Heytesbury on "Insoluble" Sentences.* Toronto, 1979.

—— "William Heytesbury's Position on 'Insolubles': One Possible Source," *Vivarium* 14 (1976): 114–20.

Sprengard, K. A. *Systematisch-Historische Untersuchungen zur Philosophie des XIV. Jahrhunderts.* 2 vols. Bonn, 1967–68.

Steinmetz, D. C. "Luther and the Late Medieval Augustinians: Another Look," *Concordia Theological Monthly* 44 (1973): 245–60.

Stock, Brian. *The Implications of Literacy: Written Language and Models of Interpretation in the Eleventh and Twelfth Centuries.* Princeton, 1983.

Stone, L., ed. *The University in Society.* 2 vols. Princeton, 1974.

Streveler, P. "Gregory of Rimini and the Black Monk on Sense and Reference. An Example of Fourteenth Century Philosophical Analysis," *Vivarium* 18 (1980): 67–78.

—— "Ockham and his Critics on: Intuitive Cognition," *FcS* 35 (1975): 223–36.

Sullivan, T. *Benedictines at the University of Paris in the Late Middle Ages.* Ph.D. diss., University of Wisconsin, Madison, 1982.

Swanson, R. N. *Universities, Academics, and the Great Schism.* Cambridge, 1979.

—— "Universities, Graduates, and Benefices in Later Medieval England," *Past and Present* no. 106 (Feb. 1985): 28–61.

Swiniarski, J. "A New Presentation of Ockham's Theory of Supposition with an Evaluation of some Contemporary Criticisms," *FcS* 30 (1970): 181–217.

Sylla, E. *The Oxford Calculators and the Mathematics of Motion, 1320–50: Physics and Measurement by Latitudes.* Ph.D. diss., Harvard University, 1970.

—— "Medieval Concepts of the Latitude of Forms: The Oxford Calculators," *AHDL* 40 (1973): 223–83.

—— "Medieval Quantifications of Qualities: the 'Merton School,' " *Archive for History of Exact Sciences* 8 (1971): 9–39.

Synan, E. A. "Richard of Campsall, an English Theologian of the 14th Century," *MedStud* 14 (1952): 1–8.

Tachau, K. "Adam Wodeham on First and Second Intentions," *CIMGL* 35 (1980): 29–55.

—— "French Theology in the mid-Fourteenth Century," *AHDL* 51 (1984): 41–80.

—— and William Courtenay. "Ockham, Ockhamists, and the English-German Nation at Paris, 1339–1341," *History of Universities* 2 (1982): 53–96.

—— "Peter Aureol on Intentions and the Intuitive Cognition of Non-Existents," *CIMGL* 44 (1983): 122–50.

—— "The Problem of the *Species in medio* at Oxford in the Generation after Ockham," *MedStud* 44 (1982): 394–443.

—— "The Response to Ockham's and Aureol's Epistemology (1320–1340)," in *ELI*, 186–217.

—— *Vision and Certitude in the Age of Ockham.* Ph.D. diss., University of Wisconsin, Madison, 1981.

Talbot, C. H. "The English Cistercians and the Universities," *Los Monjes y los Estudios.* IV Semana de Estudios Monasticos (Poblet, 1963): 209–34.

—— "Medicine," in *Sciences in the Middle Ages.* David Lindberg, ed. (Chicago, 1978): 391–428.

—— *Medicine in Medieval England.* London, 1967.

—— "Simon Bredon (*c.* 1300–1372), Physician, Mathematician and Astronomer," *British Journal for the History of Science* 1 (1962–63): 19–30.

Theissing, H. *Glaube und Theologie bei Robert Cowton OFM.* Münster i.W., 1969.

Thompson, A. Hamilton. *The English Clergy and their Organization in the Later Middle Ages.* Oxford, 1947.

Thompson, C. H. *Uthred of Boldon, A Study in Fourteenth-Century Political Theory.* Ph.D. diss., University of Manchester, 1936.

Thomson, W. R. *The Latin Writings of John Wyclif.* Toronto, 1983.

Thorndike, Lynn. "Elementary and Secondary Education in the Middle Ages," *Speculum* 15 (1940): 400–408.

—— *A History of Magic and Experimental Science.* 8 vols. New York, 1923–1958.

—— *The "Sphere" of Sacrobosco and Its Commentators.* Chicago, 1949.

Tierney, Brian and P. Linehan, eds. *Authority and Power: Studies on Medieval Law and Government.* Cambridge, 1980.

—— *Foundations of the Conciliar Theory.* Cambridge, 1955.

—— "Ockham, the Conciliar Theory and the Canonists," *Journal of the History of Ideas* 15 (1954): 40–70.

Tillotson, J. H. "Pensions, Corrodies and Religious Houses: An Aspect of the Relations of Crown and Church in Early Fourteenth-Century England," *The Journal of Religious History* 8 (1974): 127–43.

Trapp, Damasus. "Augustinian Theology of the 14th Century," *Augustiniana* 6 (1956): 146–274.

—— "Clm 27034. Unchristened Nominalism and Wycliffite Realism at Prague in 1381," *RTAM* 24 (1957): 320–60.

—— "Dreistufiger Editionsprozess und dreiartige Zitationsweise bei den Augustinertheologen des 14. Jahrhunderts?" *Augustiniana* 25 (1975): 283–92.

—— "Hilktalinger's Augustinian Quotations," *Augustiniana* 4 (1954): 412–49.

—— "'Moderns' and 'Modernists' in MS Fribourg Cordeliers 26," *Augustinianum* 5 (1965): 241–70.

—— "Notes on John Klenkok, OSA, (d. 1374)," *Augustinianum* 4 (1964): 358–404.

Turner, Ralph V., "The *Miles Literatus* in Twelfth- and Thirteenth-Century England: How Rare a Phenomenon?" *American Historical Review* 83 (1978): 928–45.

Tweedale, Martin M. *Abailard on Universals.* Amsterdam, 1976.

—— *John of Rodyngton on Knowledge, Science, and Theology.* Ph.D. diss., U.C.L.A., 1965.

Uña Juarez, A. *La filosofía del siglo XIV. Contexto cultural de Walter Burley.* El Escorial, 1978.

Urban, Linwood. "William of Ockham's Theological Ethics," *FcS* 33 (1973): 310–50.

Vale, M.G.A. *Piety, Charity and Literacy among the Yorkshire Gentry, 1370–1480.* York, 1976.

Vasoli, Cesare. "Polemiche occamiste," *Rinascimento* 3 (1952), 119–41.

Verger, Jacques. *Les universités au moyen âge*. Paris, 1973.

Vignaux, Paul. *Justification et prédestination au XIVᵉ siècle*. Paris, 1934.

Vignaux, Paul. "Nominalisme," *Dictionnaire de théologie catholique*. Vol. 11.1 (Paris, 1930): 717–84.

Walsh, Katherine. *A Fourteenth-Century Scholar and Primate, Richard Fitzralph in Oxford, Avignon, and Armagh*. Oxford, 1981.

Webering, D. *Theory of Demonstration according to William Ockham*. St. Bonaventure, N.Y., 1953.

Weinberg, J. *Ockham, Descartes, and Hume*. Madison, 1977.

Weisheipl, James A. "Curriculum of the Faculty of Arts at Oxford in the early Fourteenth Century," *MedStud* 26 (1964): 143–85.

—— "Developments in the Arts Curriculum at Oxford in the Early Fourteenth Century," *MedStud* 28 (1966): 151–75.

—— *Friar Thomas d'Aquino*. New York, 1974.

—— "The Nature, Scope, and Classification of the Sciences," *Studia Mediewistyczne* 18 (1977): 85–101.

—— "Ockham and some Mertonians," *MedStud* 30 (1968): 163–213.

—— "Reportorium Mertonense," *MedStud* 31 (1969): 174–224.

Weiss, Roberto. *Humanism in England during the Fifteenth Century*. Oxford, 1941.

Wilpert, P., ed. *Antike und Orient im Mittelalter*, Miscellanea Mediaevalia 1 (Berlin, 1962).

Wilson, C. *William Heytesbury. Medieval Logic and the Rise of Mathematical Physics*. Madison, 1956.

Wippel, John F. "The Quodlibetal Question as a Distinctive Literary Genre," *Les genres littéraires dans les sources théologiques et philosophiques médiévales*. Publications de l'Institut d'études médiévales, ser. 2, vol. 5 (Louvain-la-neuve, 1982): 67–84.

Wolter, A. "Native Freedom of the Will as a Key to the Ethics of Scotus," *Deus et Homo ad mentem I. Duns Scoti*. Acta Tertii Congr. Scotistici Internat. (Rome, 1972): 359–70.

Wood, Rega. "Adam Wodeham on Sensory Illusions with an Edition of 'Lectura Secunda,' Prologus, Quaestio 3," *Traditio* 38 (1982): 213–52.

Wood-Legh, K. *Church Life in England under Edward III*. Cambridge, 1934.

Wright, J. R. *The Church and the English Crown, 1305–1334: A Study Based on the Register of Archbishop Walter Reynolds*. Toronto, 1980.

Xiberta, B. M. *De scriptoribus scholasticis saeculi XIV ex ordine Carmelitarum*. Louvain, 1931.

Young, N. Denholm. "Richard de Bury (1287–1345)," *TRHS*, 4th ser., 20 (1937): 135–68.

Ympa, Eelcko. "Les 'Cursores" chez les Augustins," *RTAM* 26 (1956): 137–44.

—— *La formation des professeurs chez les Ermites de Saint-Augustine de 1256 à 1354.* Paris, 1956.

—— "La promotion au lectorat chez les Augustins et le 'De lectorie gradu' d'Ambroise de Cora," *Augustiniana* 13 (1963): 391–417.

Zanoni, M.-L. *Divine Order and Human Freedom in Chaucer's Poetry and Philosophical Tradition.* Ph.D. diss., Cornell, 1982.

Zimmermann, A., ed. *Antiqui und Moderni.* Miscellanea Mediaevalia 9. Berlin, 1974.

—— ed. *Sprache und Erkenntnis im Mittelalter.* Miscellanea Mediaevalia 13. Berlin, 1981.

Zumkeller, A. "Die Augustinerschule des Mittelalters: Vertreter und philosophisch-theologische Lehre," *Analecta Augustiniana* 27 (1964): 167–262.

—— *Hugolin von Orvieto und seine theologische Erkenntnislehre.* Würzburg, 1941.

INDEX

P

Library of Congress Cataloging-in-Publication Data

COURTENAY, WILLIAM J.
SCHOOLS & SCHOLARS IN FOURTEENTH-CENTURY ENGLAND
WILLIAM J. COURTENAY.

P.   CM.
BIBLIOGRAPHY: P.
INCLUDES INDEX.
ISBN 0-691-05500-9
1. EDUCATION—ENGLAND—HISTORY. 2. EDUCATION,
MEDIEVAL—ENGLAND.
I. TITLE. II. TITLE: SCHOOLS AND SCHOLARS IN
FOURTEENTH-CENTURY ENGLAND.
LA631.3.C68 1987   370'.942—dc19
87-14808 CIP

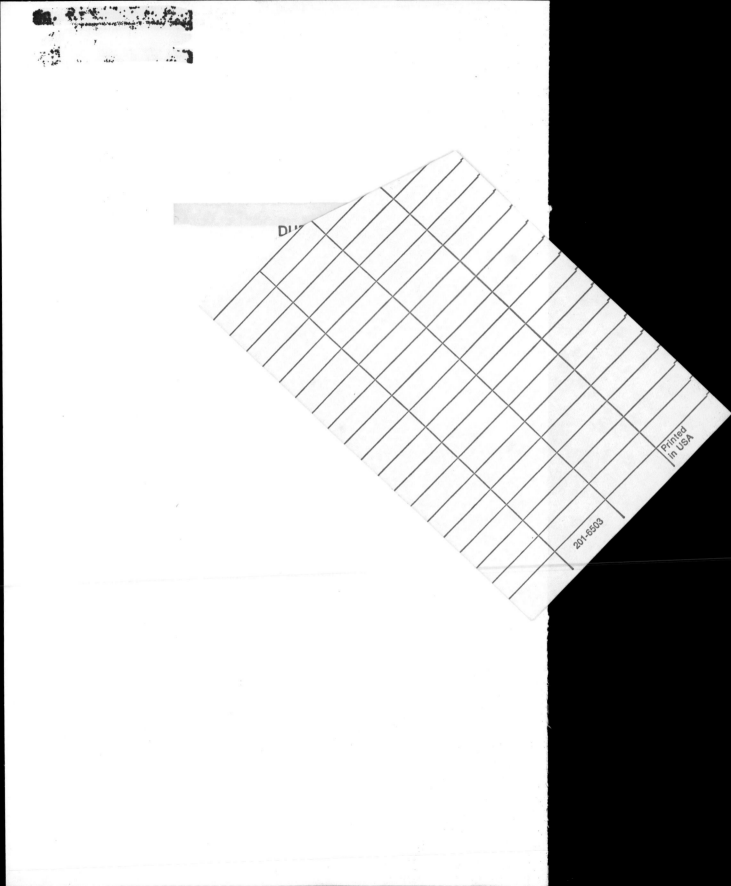

201-6503

Printed
in USA